Principles of Macroeconomics

Principles of Macroeconomics

Dirk Mateer
Pennsylvania State University

Lee Coppock
University of Virginia

W. W. NORTON & COMPANY
NEW YORK • LONDON

W. W. Norton & Company has been independent since its founding in 1923, when William Warder Norton and Mary D. Herter Norton first published lectures delivered at the People's Institute, the adult education division of New York City's Cooper Union. The firm soon expanded its program beyond the Institute, publishing books by celebrated academics from America and abroad. By midcentury, the two major pillars of Norton's publishing program—trade books and college texts—were firmly established. In the 1950s, the Norton family transferred control of the company to its employees, and today—with a staff of four hundred and a comparable number of trade, college, and professional titles published each year—W. W. Norton & Company stands as the largest and oldest publishing house owned wholly by its employees.

ISBN 978-0-393-92373-5

W. W. Norton & Company, Inc., 500 Fifth Avenue, New York, NY 10110-0017
wwnorton.com

W. W. Norton & Company Ltd., Castle House, 75/76 Wells Street, London W1T 3QT

2 3 4 5 6 7 8 9 0

CONTENTS

Principles of Macroeconomics

Photo to come

Introductory
MATERIAL

The Five Foundations of Economics

Economics is the dismal science.

Perhaps you have heard of the "dismal science"? This derogatory term was first used by historian and essayist Thomas Carlyle in the nineteenth

century. He called economics the dismal science after he read a prediction from economist Thomas Malthus stating that because our planet had limited resources, continued population growth would ultimately lead to widespread starvation.

Malthus was a respected thinker, but he was unduly pessimistic. The world population was one billion in 1800, and it is seven billion today. One of the things that Malthus did not take into account was increases in technology and productivity. Today, the efficiency of agricultural production enables seven billion people to live on this planet. Economists, like meteorologists, often get a bad rap; when we are right, no one notices, but when we are wrong, people demand answers. This textbook will provide the tools you need to be able to make your own assessments about the economy. What other discipline helps you discover how the world works, how to be an informed citizen, and how to live your life to the fullest? Economics can improve your understanding of the stock market and help you make better personal finance decisions. If you are concerned about Social Security, this textbook explains how it works. If you are interested in learning more about health care, the answers are here. Economics provides answers to all of these questions and much more.

In this chapter, you will learn about the five foundations of economics—incentives, trade-offs, opportunity cost, marginal thinking, and the principle that trade creates value. You will find that many of the more

Predicting the future is a tough business.

CQ: New caption spec TK next pass

complex problems presented later in the text are derived from one of these foundations. Once you have mastered these five concepts, the most involved processes can be reduced to combinations of these foundations. Think of this chapter as a road map that provides a broad overview of your journey into economics. Let's get started!

BIG QUESTIONS

* **What is economics?**
* **What are the five foundations of economics?**

Scarcity
refers to the limited nature of society's resources.

Economics
is the study of how people allocate their limited resources to satisfy their nearly unlimited wants.

Microeconomics
is the study of the individual units that make up the economy.

Macroeconomics
is the study of the overall aspects and workings of an economy.

What Is Economics?

Economists study how decisions are made. Examples of economic decisions include whether or not you should buy or lease a car, sublet your apartment, and buy that Gibson guitar you've been eyeing. And, just as individuals must choose what to buy within the limits of the income they possess, society as a whole must determine what to produce from its limited set of resources.

Of course, life would be a lot easier if we could have whatever we wanted whenever we wanted it. Unfortunately, life does not work that way. Our wants and needs are nearly unlimited, but the resources available to satisfy these wants and needs are, always limited. The term used to describe the limited nature of society's resources is **scarcity**. Even the most abundant resources, like the water we drink and the air we breathe, are not always abundant enough everywhere to meet the wants and needs of every person. So, how do individuals and societies make decisions about scarce resources? This is the basic question economists seek to answer. **Economics** is the study of how people allocate their limited resources to satisfy their nearly unlimited wants.

Microeconomics and Macroeconomics

The study of economics is divided into two subfields: *microeconomics* and *macroeconomics*. **Microeconomics** is the study of the individual units that make up the economy. **Macroeconomics** is the study of the overall aspects and workings of an economy, such as inflation, growth, employment, such as inflation,

Water is scarce . . .

growth, employment, interest rates, and the productivity of the economy as a whole. To see if you understand the difference, consider a worker who gets laid off and becomes unemployed. Is this an issue that would be addressed in microeconomics or macroeconomics? The question seems to fit parts of both definitions. The worker is an individual, which is micro, but employment is one of the broad areas of concern for economists, which is macro. Don't let this confuse you. Since only one worker is laid off, this is a micro issue. If many workers had been laid off and this led to a higher unemployment rate across the entire economy, it would be an issue broad enough to be studied by macroeconomists.

. . . and so are diamonds!

PRACTICE WHAT YOU KNOW

Microeconomics and Macroeconomics: The Big Picture

Identify whether each of the following statements identifies a microeconomic or a macroeconomic issue.

This mosaic of the flag illustrates the difference between micro and macro.

The national savings rate is less than 2% of disposable income.

Answer: The national savings rate is a statistic based on the average amount each household saves as a percentage of income. As such, this is a broad measure of savings and something that describes a macroeconomic issue.

Jim was laid off from his last job and is currently unemployed.

Answer: Jim's personal financial circumstances constitute a microeconomic issue.

Apple decides to open up 100 new stores.

Answer: Even though Apple is a very large corporation and 100 new stores will create many new jobs, Apple's decision is a microeconomic issue because the basis for its decision is best understood as part of the firm's competitive strategy.

The government passes a jobs bill designed to stabilize the economy during a recession.

Answer: You might be tempted to ask how many jobs are created before deciding, but that is not relevant to this question. The key part of the statement refers to "stabiliz[ing] the economy during a recession." This is an example of a *fiscal policy*, in which the government takes an active role in managing the economy. Therefore, it is a macroeconomic issue.

What Are the Five Foundations of Economics?

The study of economics can be complicated, but we can make it very accessible by breaking down the specific economic process that you are exploring into a set of component parts. The five foundations that are presented here are the key component parts of economics. They are a bit like the natural laws of physics or chemistry. Almost every economic subjects can be analyzed through the prism of one of those foundations. By mastering the five foundations, you will be on your way to succeeding in this course and thinking like an economist

Incentives

Incentives

Incentives
are factors that motivate a person to act or exert effort.

When you are faced with making a decision, you usually make the choice that you think will most improve your situation. In making your decision, you respond to **incentives**—factors that motivate you to act or to exert effort. For example, the choice to study for an exam you have tomorrow instead of spending the evening with your friends is based on the belief that doing well on the exam will provide a greater benefit. You are incentivized to study because you know that an A in the course will raise your grade-point average and make you a more attractive candidate on the job market when you are finished with school. We can further divide incentives into two paired categories: *positive and negative*, and *direct and indirect*.

Positive and Negative Incentives

Positive incentives are those that encourage action. For example, end-of-the year bonuses motivate employees to work hard throughout the year, higher oil prices cause suppliers to extract more oil, and tax rebates encourage citizens to spend more money. Negative incentives also encourage action. For instance, the fear of receiving a speeding ticket keeps motorists from driving too fast, and the dread of a trip to the dentist motivates people to brush their teeth regularly. In each case, a potential negative consequence spurs individuals to action.

Conventional wisdom tells us that "learning is its own reward," but try telling that to most students. Teachers are aware that incentives, both positive and negative, create additional interest among their students to learn the course material. Positive incentives include bonus points, gold stars, public praise, and extra credit. Many students respond to these encouragements by studying more. However, positive incentives are not enough. Suppose that your instructor never gave any grade lower than an A. Your incentive to participate actively in the course, do assignments, or earn bonus points would be small. For positive incentives to work, they generally need to be coupled with negative incentives. This is why instructors require students to complete assignments, take exams, and write papers. Students know that if they do not complete these requirements they will get a lower grade, perhaps even fail the class.

Direct and Indirect Incentives

In addition to being positive and negative, incentives can also be direct and indirect. For instance, if one gas station lowers its prices, it most likely will get business from customers who would not usually stop there. This is a direct incentive. Lower gasoline prices also work as an indirect incentive, since lower prices might encourage consumers to use more gas.

Direct incentives are easy to recognize. "Cut my grass and I'll pay you $30" is an example of a direct incentive. Indirect incentives are much harder to recognize. But learning to recognize them is one of the keys to mastering economics. For instance, consider the indirect incentives at work in welfare programs. Almost everyone agrees that societies should provide a safety net for those without employment or whose income isn't enough to meet basic needs.

Thus, a society has a direct incentive to alleviate suffering caused by poverty. But how does a society provide this safety net without taking away the incentive to work? In other words, if the amount of welfare a person receives is higher than the amount that person can hope to make from a job, the welfare recipient might decide to stay on welfare rather than go to work. The indirect incentive to stay on welfare creates an *unintended consequence*—people who were supposed to use government assistance as a safety net until they can find a job use it instead as a permanent source of income.

Policymakers have the tough task of deciding how to balance such conflicting incentives. To decrease the likelihood that a person will stay on welfare, policymakers could cut benefits. But this might leave some people without enough to live on. For this reason, many government programs specify limits on the amount of time people can receive benefits. Ideally, this allows the welfare programs to

Public assistance: a hand in time of need or an incentive not to work?

continue to meet basic needs while creating incentives that encourage recipients to search for jobs and acquire skills that will enable them to do better in the workforce. We'll learn more about the issues of welfare in Chapter 15.

ECONOMICS IN THE REAL WORLD

How Incentives Create Unintended Consequences

Let's look at an example of how incentives operate in the real world and how they can lead to consequences no one envisioned when implementing them. Two Australian researchers noted a large spike in births on July 1, 2004.[1] The sudden spike was not an accident. Australia, like many other developed countries, has seen the fertility rate fall below replacement levels, which is the birthrate necessary to keep the population from declining. In response to falling birthrates, the Australian government decided to enact a "baby bonus" of $3,000 for all babies born on or after July 1, 2004. (One Australian dollar equals one U.S. dollar.)

The policy was designed to provide a direct incentive for couples to have children and, in part, to compensate them for lost pay and the added costs of raising a newborn. However, this direct incentive had an indirect incentive attached to it, too—the couples found a way to delay the birth of their children until after July 1, perhaps jeopardizing the health of both the infants and the mothers. This was clearly an unintended consequence. Despite reassurances from the government that would-be parents would not put financial gain over

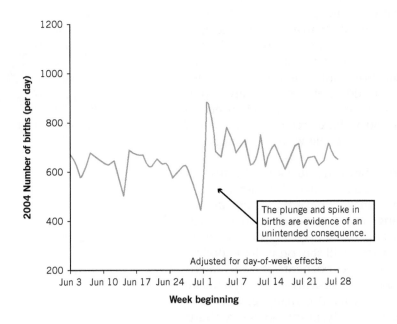

---

1. See Joshua S. Gans and Andrew Leigh, "Born on the First of July: An (un)natural experiment in birth timing," *Journal of Public Economics* 93 (2009): 246–263.

the welfare of their newborns, over 1,000 births were switched from late June to early July through a combination of additional bed rest and pushing scheduled caesarian sections back a few days. This behavior is testament to the power of incentives.

On a much smaller scale, the same dynamic exists in the United States around January 1 each year. Parents can claim a tax credit for the entire year, whether the child is born in January or in December. This gives parents an incentive to ask for labor to be induced or for a caesarian section to be performed late in December so they can have their child before January 1 and thereby capitalize on the tax advantages. Ironically, hospitals and newspapers often celebrate the arrival of the first baby of the new year even though his or her parents might actually be financially worse off because of the infant's January 1 birthday. ✳

Incentives and Innovation

Incentives also play a vital role in innovation, the engine of economic growth. There is no better example than Steve Jobs and Apple: between them, he and the company he founded held over 300 patents at the time of his death in 2011.

In the United States, the patent system and copyright laws guarantee inventors a specific period of time in which they can exclusively sell their work. This system encourages innovation by creating a powerful financial reward for creativity. Without patents and copyright laws, inventors would bear all the costs, and almost none of the rewards, for their efforts. Why would firms invest in research and development or artists create new music if others could immediately copy and sell their work? To reward the perspiration and inspiration required for innovation, society needs patents and copyrights to create the right incentives for economic growth.

In recent years, new forms of technology have made the illegal sharing of copyrighted material quite easy. As a result, illegal downloads of music and movies are widespread. When musicians, actors, and studios cannot effectively protect what they have created, they earn less. So illegal downloads reduce the incentive to produce new content. Will the next John Lennon or Jay-Z work so hard? Will the next Dan Brown or J. K. Rowling hone the writing craft so diligently if there is so much less financial reward for success? Is the "I want it for free" culture causing the truly gifted to be less committed to their craft, thus depriving society of excellence? Maintaining the right rewards, or incentives, for hard work and innovation is essential for advancing our society.

Incentives Are Everywhere

There are many sides to incentives. However, financial gain almost always plays a prominent role. In the film *All the President's Men*, the story of the Watergate scandal that led to the unraveling of the Nixon administration in the early 1970s, a secret source called "Deep Throat" tells Bob Woodward, an investigative reporter at the *Washington Post*, to "follow the money." Woodward responds, "What do you mean? Where?" Deep Throat responds, "Just . . . follow the money." That is exactly what Woodward did. He eventually pieced everything together and followed the "money" trail all the way to President Nixon.

Incentives

Ferris Bueller's Day Off

Many people believe that the study of economics is boring. In *Ferris Bueller's Day Off* (1986), Ben Stein plays a high school economics teacher who sedates his class with a monotone voice while referring to many abstract economic theories and uttering the unforgettable "Anyone, anyone?" while trying to engage his students. The scene is iconic because it is a boring economics lecture that inspires Ferris and his friends to skip school, which leads to his wild adventures. In fact, the movie is really about incentives and trade-offs.

Was this your first impression of economics?

Understanding the incentives that caused the participants in the Watergate scandal to do what they did led Bob Woodward to the truth. Economists use the same process to explain how people make decisions, how firms operate, and how the economy functions. In fact, understanding incentives, from positive to negative and direct to indirect, is the key to understanding economics. If you remember only one concept from this course, it should be that incentives matter!

Trade-offs

Trade-offs

In a world of scarcity, each and every decision incurs a cost. Even time is a scarce resource; after all, there are only 24 hours in a day. So deciding to read one of the Harry Potter books now means that you won't be able to read one of the Twilight books until later. More generally, doing one thing often means that you will not have the time, resources, or energy to do something else. Casting a ballot in an election is another good example, since you can only vote for one person at a time. Similarly, paying for a college education can require spending tens of thousands of dollars that might be used elsewhere instead.

Trade-offs are an important part of policy decisions. For instance, one decision that some modern governments face is the trade-off between a clean environment and a higher level of income for its citizens. Transportation and industry cause air pollution. Developed nations can afford expensive technology that reduces pollution-causing emissions. But developing nations, like China, generally have to focus their resources elsewhere. In the months leading up to the 2008 Olympics, China temporarily shut down many factories and discouraged the use of automobiles in order to reduce smog in Beijing. The air improved, and the Olympics showcased China's remarkable growth into a global economic powerhouse. However, the cost of keeping the air clean—shutting down factories and restricting transportation—is not a trade-off China is willing to make for longer than a few weeks. The Chinese people, like the rest of us, want clean air *and* a high standard of living, but for the time being most Chinese seem willing to accept increased pollution if it means the potential for a higher level of income. In more developed countries, higher standards of living already exist and the cost of pollution control will not cause the economy's growth to slow down to unacceptable levels. People in these countries are much less likely to accept more pollution in order to raise the level of income even further.

Opportunity Cost

The existence of trade-offs requires making hard decisions. Choosing one thing means giving up something else. Suppose that you receive two invitations—the first to spend the day hiking, and the second to go to a concert—and both events occur at the same time. No matter which event you choose, you will have to sacrifice the other option. In this example, you can think of the cost of going to the concert as the lost

Would you choose clean air or economic prosperity?

opportunity to be on the hike. Likewise, the cost of going hiking is the lost opportunity to go to the concert. No matter what choice you make, there is an *opportunity cost*, or next-best alternative, that must be sacrificed. **Opportunity cost** is the highest-valued alternative that must be sacrificed in order to get something else.

Opportunity cost

Every time we make a choice, we experience an opportunity cost. The key to making the best possible decision is to minimize your opportunity cost by selecting the option that gives you the largest benefit. If you prefer going to a concert, you should go to the concert. What you give up, the hike, has less value to you than the concert; so it has a lower opportunity cost.

The hiking/concert choice is a simple and clear example of opportunity cost. Usually, it takes deliberate effort to see the world through the opportunity-cost prism. But it is a worthwhile practice because it will help you make better decisions. For example, imagine you are a small-business owner. Your financial officer informs you that you have had a successful year and made a sizable profit. So everything is good, right? Not so fast. An economist will tell you to ask yourself, "Could I have made *more* profit doing something differently?" Good economic thinkers ask this question of themselves all the time. "Could I be using my time, talents, or energy on another activity that would be even more profitable for me?"

Opportunity cost is the highest-valued alternative that must be sacrificed in order to get something else.

Do you have the moves like Jagger?

Profits on a balance sheet are only part of the story, because they only measure how well a business does relative to the bottom line. Accountants cannot measure what *might* have been better. For example, suppose that your business had decided against an opportunity to open a new store. A few months later, a rival opened a very successful store in the same location you had considered. Your profits were good for the year, but if you had made the investment in the new store, your profits could have been even better. So when economists mention opportunity cost, they are assessing whether the alternatives are better than what you are currently doing, which considers a larger set of possible outcomes.

Mick Jagger did just that. Before joining the Rolling Stones, he had been attending the London School of Economics. For Mick, the opportunity cost of becoming a musician was forgoing a degree in economics. Given the success of the Rolling Stones, it is hard to fault his decision!

ECONOMICS IN THE REAL WORLD

Breaking the Curse of the Bambino: How Opportunity Cost Causes a Drop in Hospital Visits While the Red Sox Play

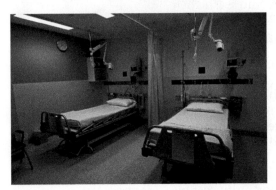

Emergency room beds are empty. Are the Sox playing?

If you are injured or severely ill, you head straight to the emergency room, right? Not so fast! A study published in the *Annals of Emergency Medicine* found that visits to the ER in the Boston area fell by as much as 80% when the Red Sox were playing games in the 2004 playoffs.[2] Part of the decline is attributable to more people sitting inside at home—presumably watching the ballgame—instead of engaging in activities that might get them hurt. But the study was able to determine that this did not explain the entire decline in emergency room visits. It turns out that a surprising number of people are willing to put off seeking medical attention for a few hours. Apparently, for some people the opportunity cost of seeking medical attention is high enough to postpone care until after the Red Sox game. ✳

Marginal thinking

Economic thinking requires a purposeful evaluation of the available opportunities to make the best decision possible.

Marginal Thinking

The process of systematically evaluating a course of action is referred to as *economic thinking*. **Economic thinking** involves a purposeful evaluation of the available opportunities to make the best decision possible. In this con-

2. Ben Y. Reis, John S. Brownstein, and Kenneth D. Mandl, "Running Outside the Baseline: Impact of the 2004 Major League Baseball Postseason on Emergency Department Use," *Annals of Emergency Medicine* 46, no. 4 (2005): 386–387.

text, economic thinkers use a process called *marginal analysis* to break down decisions into smaller parts. Often, the choice is not between doing and not doing something, but between doing more or less of something. For instance, if you take on a part-time job while in school, you probably wrestle with the question of how many hours to work. If you work a little more, you can earn additional income. If you work a little less, you have more time to study. Working more has a tangible benefit (more money), and a tangible cost (poor grades). All of this should sound familiar from our earlier discussion about trade-offs. The work-study trade-off affects how much money you have and what kind of grades you make. An economist would say that your

Economics helps us understand why dust bunnies are safe from the vacuum when they are hidden from view.

decision—weighing how much money you want against the grades you want—is a decision at the *margin*. What exactly does the word "margin" mean? There are many different definitions. To a reader, the margin is the blank space bordering a page. "Margin" can also be thought of as the size of a victory. In economics, **marginal thinking** requires decision-makers to evaluate whether the benefit of one more unit of something is greater than its cost. This can be quite challenging, but understanding how to analyze decisions at the margin is essential to becoming a good economist.

Marginal thinking requires decision-makers to evaluate whether the benefit of one more unit of something is greater than its cost.

For example, have you ever wondered why people straighten their places, vacuum, dust, scrub the bathrooms, clean out their garages, and wash their windows, but leave the dust bunnies under the refrigerator? The answer lies in thinking at the margin. Moving the refrigerator out from the wall to clean requires a significant effort for a small benefit. Guests who enter the kitchen can't see under the refrigerator. So most of us ignore the dust bunnies and just clean the visible areas of our homes. In other words, when economists say that you should think at the margin, what they really mean is that people weigh the costs and benefits of their actions and choose to do the things with the greatest payoff. For most of us, that means being willing to live with dust bunnies. The *marginal cost* of cleaning under the refrigerator, or on top of the cabinets, or even behind the sofa cushions, is too high and the added value of making the effort, or the *marginal benefit*, is too low to justify the additional cleaning.

ECONOMICS IN THE REAL WORLD

Why Buying and Selling your Textbooks Benefits You at the Margin

New textbooks are expensive. The typical textbook purchasing pattern works as follows: you buy a textbook at the start of the term, often at full price, and sell it back at the end of the term for half the price you paid. Ouch. Nobody likes to make a bad investment, and textbooks depreciate the moment that students buy them. Even non-economists know not to buy high and sell low—but that is the textbook cycle for most students.

Why do students buy and sell textbooks?

One solution would be to avoid buying textbooks in the first place. But that is not practical, nor is it a good decision. To understand why, let's use marginal analysis to break the decision into two separate components: the decision to buy and the decision to resell.

Let's start with the decision to buy. A rational buyer will only purchase a textbook if the expected value of the information included in the book is greater than the cost. For instance, say the book contains mandatory assignments or information that is useful for your major and you decide that it is worth $200 to you. If you are able to purchase the book for $100, the gain from buying the textbook would be $100. But what if the book is supplemental reading and you think it is worth only $50? If you value the book at $50 and it costs $100, purchasing the book would entail a $50 loss. If students only buy the books from which they receive gains, every textbook bought will increase the welfare of someone.

A similar logic applies to the resale of textbooks. At the end of the course, once you have learned the information inside the book, the value of hanging on to it is low. You might think it is worth $20 to keep the textbook for future reference, but if you can sell it for $50, the difference represents a gain of $30. In this case, you would decide to sell.

We have seen that buying and selling are two separate decisions made at the margin. If you combine these two decisions and argue that the purchase price ($100) and resale price ($50) are related, as most students typically think they are, you will arrive at a faulty conclusion that you have made a poor decision. That is simply not true.

Textbooks may not be cheap, but they create value twice—once when bought and again when sold. This is a win-win outcome. Since we assume that decision-makers will not make choices that leave them worse off, the only way to explain why students buy textbooks and sell them again later is because the students benefit at the margin from both sides of the transaction. ✳

Trade creates value

Trade

Imagine trying to find food in a world without grocery stores. The task of getting what you need to eat each day would require visiting many separate locations. Traditionally, this need to bring buyers and sellers together was met by weekly markets, or bazaars, in central locations like town squares.

Markets bring buyers and sellers together to exchange goods and services. As commerce spread throughout the ancient world, trade routes developed. Markets grew from infrequent gatherings, where exchange involved trading goods and services for other goods and services, into more sophisticated systems that use cash, credit, and other financial instruments. Today, when we think of markets we often think of eBay or craigslist, where goods can be transferred from one person to another with the click of a mouse. For instance, if you want to find a rare DVD of season 1 of *Entourage*, there is no better place to look than eBay, which allows users to search for just about any product, bid on it, and then have it sent directly to their homes.

Markets
bring buyers and sellers together to exchange goods and services.

Trade is the voluntary exchange of goods and services between two or more parties. Voluntary trade among rational individuals creates value for everyone involved. Imagine you are on your way home from class and you want to pick up a gallon of milk. You know that milk will be more expensive at a convenience store than it will be at the grocery store five miles away, but you are in a hurry to study for your economics exam and are willing to pay up to $5.00 for the convenience of getting it quickly. At the store, you find that the price is $4.00 and you happily purchase the milk. This ability to buy for less than the price you are willing to pay provides a positive incentive to make the purchase. But what about the seller? If the store owner paid $3.00 to buy the milk from a supplier, and you are willing to pay the $4.00 price that he has set in order to make a profit, the store owner has an incentive to sell. This simple voluntary transaction has made both sides better off.

Trade
is the voluntary exchange of goods and services between two or more parties.

By fostering the exchange of goods, trade helps to create additional growth through specialization. **Comparative advantage** refers to the situation in which an individual, business, or country can produce at a lower opportunity cost than a competitor can. Comparative advantage harnesses the power of specialization. As a result, it is possible to be a physician, teacher, or plumber and not worry about how to do everything yourself. The physician becomes proficient at dispensing medical advice, the teacher at helping students, and the plumber at fixing leaks. The physician and the teacher call the plumber when they need work on their plumbing. The teacher and the plumber see the doctor when they are sick. The physician and the plumber send their children to school to learn from the teacher. On a broader scale, this type of trading of services increases the welfare of everyone in society. Trade creates gains for everyone involved.

Comparative advantage
refers to the situation where an individual, business, or country can produce at a lower opportunity cost than a competitor can.

The same process is at work among businesses. For instance, Starbucks specializes in making coffee and Honda makes automobiles. You would not want

Our economy depends on specialization.

to get your morning cup of joe at Honda any more than you would want to buy a car from Starbucks!

Specialization exists at the country level as well. Some countries have highly developed workforces capable of managing and solving complex processes. Other countries have large pools of relatively unskilled labor. As a result, businesses that need skilled labor gravitate to countries where they can easily find the workers they need. Likewise, firms with production processes that rely on unskilled labor look for employees in less-developed countries. By harnessing the power of increased specialization, global companies and economies create value through increased production and growth.

However, globalized trade is not without controversy. When goods and jobs are free to move across borders, not everyone benefits equally. Consider the case of an American worker who loses her job when her position is outsourced to a call center in India. The jobless worker now has to find new employment—a process that will require significant time and energy. In contrast, the new position in the call center in India provides a job and an income that improve the life of another worker. Also, the American firm enjoys the advantage of being able to hire lower-cost labor elsewhere. The firm's lower costs often translate into lower prices for domestic consumers. None of those advantages make the outsourcing of jobs any less painful for affected workers, but it is an important component of economic growth in the long run.

The Benefits of Trade

ECONOMICS IN THE MEDIA

Trade Makes Us Better Off

What would happen if you could trade something you had and get something better in return? Find out what happens in one case in this short classroom demonstration filmed in one of your textbook author's classes.

Check out this video on YouTube: http://www.youtube.com/watch?v=BdI6UamG6BI. It shows the incentives behind trade.

This simple demonstration illustrades the gains from trade.

PRACTICE WHAT YOU KNOW

The Opportunity Cost of Attending College

Question: What is the opportunity cost of attending college?

Answer: When people think about the cost of attending college, they usually think of tuition, room and board, textbooks, and travel-related expenses. While those expenses are indeed a part of going to college, they are not the full opportunity cost of attending college. The opportunity cost is the next-best alternative that is sacrificed. This means that the opportunity cost—or what you potentially could have done if you were not in college—includes the lost income you could have earned working a full-time job. If you take the cost of attending college plus the forgone income lost while in college, it is a very expensive proposition. Setting aside the question of how much more you might have to pay for room and board at college rather than elsewhere, consider the costs of tuition and books. Those fees can be $40,000 or more at many of the nation's most expensive colleges. Add those out-of-pocket expenses to the forgone income from a full-time job that might pay $40,000, and your four years in college can easily cost over a quarter of a million dollars.

Spending thousands on college expenses? You could be working instead!

Conclusion

Is economics the dismal science?

We began this chapter by discussing this misconception. Now that you have begun your exploration of economics, you know that this is not true. Economists ask, and answer, big questions about life. This is what makes the study of economics so fascinating. Understanding how an entire economy operates and functions may seem like a daunting task, but it is not nearly as hard as it sounds. If you remember the first time you drove a car, the process is similar. When you are learning to drive, everything seems difficult and unfamiliar. Learning economics is the same way. However, once you learn a few key principles, and practice them, you can become a good driver quite quickly. In the next chapter, we will use the ideas developed here to explore the issue of trade in greater depth.

ECONOMICS FOR LIFE

Midcareer Earnings by Selected Majors

A 2008 study by PayScale surveyed 1.2 million full-time employees across the United States who possessed a bachelor's degree but no advanced degree. Twenty popular subjects are listed in the graph below.

   Not all majors are created equal. However, the majors that produce more income initially do not necessarily keep their advantage a decade or two later. That means that today's newly minted economics majors, with a median starting salary of $48,000, will likely surpass those who majored in computer science in earnings by the time they reach midcareer. The same holds true for political science majors, who have a lower starting salary than accounting majors but eventually surpass them. In the long run, pay growth matters to income level as much as, if not more than, starting salary. In terms of salary, any decision about what to major in that only looks at starting pay is misleading. How much you make over your whole career is what matters!

Will you make more by majoring in economics or finance?

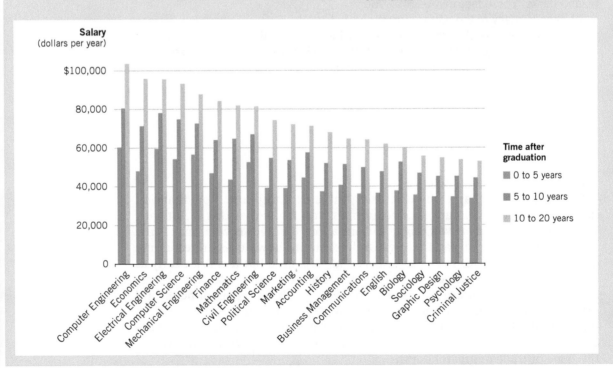

Salary (dollars per year)

Time after graduation
- 0 to 5 years
- 5 to 10 years
- 10 to 20 years

Computer Engineering, Economics, Electrical Engineering, Computer Science, Mechanical Engineering, Finance, Mathematics, Civil Engineering, Political Science, Marketing, Accounting, History, Business Management, Communications, English, Biology, Sociology, Graphic Design, Psychology, Criminal Justice

ANSWERING THE BIG QUESTIONS

1. What is economics?

 ✳ Economics is the study of how people allocate their limited resources to satisfy their nearly unlimited wants. Because of the limited nature of society's resources, even the most abundant resources are not always abundant enough everywhere to meet the wants and needs of every person. So how do individuals and societies make decisions about how to use the scarce resources at our disposal? This is the basic question economists seek to answer.

2. What are the five foundations of economics?

The five foundations of economics are: incentives; trade-offs; opportunity cost; marginal thinking; and the principle that trade creates value.

 ✳ Incentives matter because they help economists explain how decisions are made.
 ✳ Trade-offs exist when a decision-maker has to choose a course of action.
 ✳ Each time we make a choice, we experience an opportunity cost, or a lost chance to do something else.
 ✳ Marginal thinking requires a decision-maker to weigh the extra benefits against the extra costs.
 ✳ Trade creates value because participants in markets are able to specialize in the production of goods and services that they have a comparative advantage in making.

Each of the five foundation concepts developed in this chapter will reappear throughout the book and enable you to solve complex problems.

 Every time we encounter one of the five concepts, you will see an icon of a house to remind you of what you have learned. As you become more adept at economic analysis, it will not be uncommon to use two or more of these foundational ideas to explain the economic world around us.

Incentives
Trade-offs
Opportunity cost
Marginal thinking
Trade creates value

CONCEPTS YOU SHOULD KNOW

comparative advantage (p. 00)   macroeconomics (p. 00)   opportunity cost (p. 00)
economics (p. 00)   marginal thinking (p. 00) scarcity (p. 00)
economic thinking (p. 00)   markets (p. 00)   trade (p. 00)
incentives (p. 00)   microeconomics (p. 00)

QUESTIONS FOR REVIEW

1. How would you respond if your instructor gave daily quizzes on the course readings? Is this a positive or a negative incentive?

2. Explain why many seniors often earn lower grades in their last semester before graduation. Hint: this is an incentive problem.

3. What is the opportunity cost of reading this textbook?

4. Comment on the following statement: "Trade is like football: one team wins and the other loses."

5. Give a personal example of how pursuing your self-interest has made society better off.

STUDY PROBLEMS (* *denotes a solved problem at the end of the section*)

* 1. What role do incentives play in each of the following situations?
     a. You learn that you can resell a ticket to next week's homecoming game for twice what you paid.
     b. A state government announces a "sales tax holiday" for back-to-school shopping during one week each August.

2. Compare your standard of living with that of your parents when they were the same age as you are now. Ask them or somebody you know around their age to recall where they were living and what they owned. What has happened to the average standard of living over the last 25 years? Explain your answer.

3. By referencing events in the news or something from your personal experiences, describe one example of each of the five foundations of economics.

* 4. Suppose that Colombia is good at growing coffee but not very good at making computer software, and that Canada is good at making computer software but not very good at growing coffee. If Colombia decided to grow only coffee and Canada only made computer software, would both countries be better or worse off? Can you think of a similar example from your life?

5. After some consideration, you decide to hire someone to help you move. Wouldn't it be cheaper to move yourself? Do you think this is a rational choice? Explain your response.

* 6. The website www.ultrinsic.com has developed an "**ult**erior motive that causes the person to have an int**rinsic** love of knowledge." At Ultrinsic, students pay a small entry fee to compete in grades-based contests for cash prizes. Suppose that 20 students from your economics class each pay $20 to enter a grades-based contest. This would create a $400 prize pool. An equal share of the $400 pot is awarded at the end of the term to each contestant who earns an A in the course. If four students earn A's, they each receive $100. If only one student earns an A, that person gets the entire $400 pot. What economic concept is Ultrinsic harnessing in order to encourage participants to learn more?

SOLVED PROBLEMS

1.a. Since your tickets are worth more than you paid for them, you have a direct positive incentive to resell them.

b. The "sales tax holiday" is a direct positive incentive to buy more clothes during the back-to-school period. An unintended consequence of this policy is that fewer purchases are likely to be made both before and after the tax holiday.

4. If Colombia decided to specialize in the production of coffee, it could trade coffee to Canada in exchange for computer software. This process illustrates gains from specialization and trade. Both countries have a comparative advantage in producing one particular good. Colombia has ideal coffee-growing conditions, and Canada has a workforce that is more adept at writing software. Since each country specializes in what it does best, they are able to produce more value than what they could produce by trying to make both products on their own.

6. Ultrinsic is using the power of incentives to motivate learning. Earning a letter grade is a positive motivation to do well, or a penalty—or negative incentive—when you do poorly. Ultrinsic takes this one step further, as the student who earns an A also receives a small cash payment—a positive incentive. This provides extra motivation to study hard and achieve an A, since it pays, as opposed to earning a B or lower.

Model Building and Gains from Trade

Trade always results in winners and losers.

When most people think of trade, they think of it as a zero-sum game. For instance, suppose that you and your friends are playing Magic. Players

collect cards with special powers in order to assemble decks to play the game. Magic players love to trade their cards, and it is often the case that novice players do not know which cards are the most powerful or rare. When someone swaps one of the desirable cards, the other player is probably getting a much better deal. In other words, there is a winner and a loser. Now think of international trade. Many people believe that rich countries exploit the natural resources of poor countries and even steal their most talented workers. In this view, the rich countries are winners and the poor countries are losers. Still others think of trade as the redistribution of goods. If you trade your kayak for a friend's bicycle, no new goods are created; so how can this possibly create value? After all, someone must have come out ahead in the trade.

In this chapter, we will see that trade is not an imbalanced equation of winners and losers. To help us understand trade, the discussion will make a number of simplifying assumptions. We will also consider how economists use the scientific method to help explain the world we live in. These foundations will serve as the tools we need to explore the more nuanced reasons why trade creates value.

Photo to come

Q: "New
ption spec
next pass"

BIG QUESTIONS

* **How do economists study the economy?**
* **What is a production possibilities frontier?**
* **What are the benefits of specialization and trade?**
* **What is the trade-off between having more now or having more later?**

How Do Economists Study the Economy?

Economics is a social science that uses the scientific method. This is accomplished by the use of economic models that focus on specific relationships in the economy. In order to create these models, economists make many simplifying assumptions. This approach helps identify the key relationships that drive the economic decisions that we are interested in exploring. In this section, you will begin to learn about how economists approach their discipline and the tools they use.

The Scientific Method in Economics

On the television show *MythBusters*, popular myths are put to the test by Jamie Hyneman and Adam Savage. In Savage's words, "We replicate the circumstances, then duplicate the results." The entire show is dedicated to scientifically testing the myths. At the end of each episode, the myth is confirmed, labeled plausible, or busted. For instance, during a memorable episode Hyneman and Savage explored the reasons behind the *Hindenburg* disaster. The *Hindenburg* was a German passenger airship, or zeppelin, that caught fire and was destroyed as it attempted to dock in New Jersey on May 6, 1937. Thirty-six people died during the disaster.

Some people have hypothesized that the painted fabric used to wrap the zeppelin sparked the fire. Others have claimed that the hydrogen used to give the airship lift was the primary cause of the disaster. To test the hypothesis that the potentially incendiary paint used on the fabric was to blame, Hyneman and Savage built two small-scale models. The first model was filled with hydrogen and had a nonflammable skin; the second model used a replica of the original fabric for the skin but did not contain any hydrogen. Hyneman and Savage then compared the burn times of their models with the original footage of the disaster.

After examining the results, they determined that the myth of the incendiary paint was "busted"; the model containing the hydrogen burned twice as fast as the one with just the painted fabric skin.

Economists work in much the same way: they use the scientific method to answer questions about observable phenomena and to explain how the world works. The scientific method consists of several steps. First, researchers observe a phenomenon that interests them. Based on these observations, they develop a hypothesis, which is an explanation for the phenomenon. Then, they construct a model to test the hypothesis. Finally, they design experiments to test how well the model (which is based on the hypothesis) works. After collecting the data from the experiments, they can verify, revise, or refute the hypothesis. After many tests, they may agree that the hypothesis is well supported enough to qualify as a theory.

The scientific method was used to discover why the *Hindenburg* caught fire.

The economist's laboratory is the world around us, and it ranges from the economy as a whole to the decisions made by firms and individuals. As a result, economists cannot always design experiments to test their hypotheses. Often, they must gather historical data or wait for real-world events to take place—for example, the Great Recession of 2008–2009—in order to better understand the economy.

Positive and Normative Analysis

As scientists, economists strive to approach their subject with objectivity. This means that they rigorously avoid letting personal beliefs and values influence the outcome of their analysis. In order to be as objective as possible, economists deploy positive analysis. A **positive statement** can be tested and validated. Each positive statement can be thought of as a description of "what is." For instance, the statement "the unemployment rate is 7.0%" is a positive statement because it can be tested by gathering data. In contrast, a **normative statement** cannot be tested or validated; it is about "what ought to be." For instance, the statement "an unemployed worker should receive financial assistance to help make ends meet" is a matter of opinion. One can reasonably argue that financial assistance to the unemployed is beneficial for society as a whole because it helps eliminate poverty. However, many would argue that financial assistance to the unemployed provides the wrong incentives. If the financial assistance provides enough to meet basic needs, workers may end up spending more time remaining unemployed than they otherwise would. Neither opinion is right or wrong; they are differing viewpoints based on values, beliefs, and opinions.

Economists are concerned with positive analysis. In contrast, normative statements are the realm of policy-makers, voters, and philosophers. For example, if the unemployment rate rises, economists try to understand the

A **positive statement** can be tested and validated; it describes "what is."

A **normative statement** is an opinion that cannot be tested or validated; it describes "what ought to be."

conditions that created the situation. Economics does not attempt to determine who should receive unemployment assistance, which involves normative analysis. Economics, done properly, is confined to positive analysis.

Economic Models

Thinking like an economist means learning how to analyze complex issues and problems. Many economic topics, such as international trade, Social Security, job loss, and inflation, are complicated. To analyze these phenomena and to determine the effect of various policy options related to them, economists use models, or simplified versions of reality. Models help us analyze the component parts of the economy.

A good model should be simple to understand, flexible in design, and able to make powerful predictions. Let's consider one of the most famous models in history, designed by Wilbur and Orville Wright. Before the Wright brothers made their famous first flight in 1903, they built a small wind tunnel out of a six-foot-long wooden box. Inside the box they placed an aerodynamic measuring device, and at one end they attached a small fan to supply the wind. The brothers then tested over 200 different wing configurations to determine the lifting properties of each design. Using the data on aerodynamics they collected, the Wright brothers were able to determine the best type of wing to use on their aircraft.

Similarly, economic models provide frameworks that enable us to predict the effect that changes in prices, production processes, and government policies have on real-life behavior.

Ceteris Paribus

Ceteris paribus
is the concept under which economists examine a change in one variable while holding everything else constant.

Using a controlled setting that held many other variables constant enabled the Wright brothers to experiment with different wing designs. By altering only a single element—for example, the angle of the wing—they could test whether the change in design was advantageous. The process of examining a change in one variable while holding everything else constant involves a concept known as **ceteris paribus**, from the Latin meaning "other things being equal." This idea is central to model building. If the Wright brothers had changed many variables simultaneously and found that the wing worked better, they would have had no way of knowing which change was responsible for the improved performance. For this reason, engineers generally modify only one element at a time and test only that one element before moving on to test additional elements.

Like the Wright brothers, economists start with a simplified version of reality. Economists build models, change one variable at a time, and ask whether the change in the variable had a positive or negative impact on performance. Perhaps the best-known economic model is supply and demand, which economists use to explain how markets function. We'll get to supply and demand in Chapter 3.

Endogenous versus Exogenous Factors

Endogenous factors
are the variables that can be controlled for in a model.

Models must account for factors that we can control and factors that we can't. The Wright brothers' wind tunnel was critical to their success because it enabled them to control for as many *endogenous factors* as possible before attempting to fly. Factors that we know about and can control are **endogenous factors**. For example, the wind tunnel enabled the Wright brothers to see how well each wing design—an important part of the model—performed under controlled conditions.

Once the Wright brothers had determined the best wing design, they built the full-scale airplane that took flight at Kitty Hawk, North Carolina. At that point the plane, known as the "Flyer," was no longer in a controlled environment. It was subject to the gusting wind and other *exogenous factors* that made the first flight so challenging. Factors beyond our control—outside the model—are known as **exogenous factors**.

Building an economic model is very similar to the process Wilbur and Orville used. We need to be mindful of three factors: (1) what we include in the model, (2) the assumptions we make when choosing what to include in the model, and (3) the outside conditions that can affect our model's

The Wright brothers' wind tunnel

Exogenous factors are the variables that are cannot be controlled for in a model.

performance. In the case of the first airplane, the design was an endogenous factor because it was within the Wright brothers' control. In contrast, the weather (wind, air pressure, and other atmospheric conditions) was an exogenous factor because it was something that the Wright brothers could not control. Because the world is a complex place, an airplane model that flies perfectly in a wind tunnel may not fly reliably once it is exposed to the elements. Therefore, if we add more exogenous variables, or factors we cannot control—for example, wind and rain—to test our model's performance, the test becomes more realistic.

The Danger of Faulty Assumptions

In every model, we make certain choices about which variables to include and how to model them. Ideally, we would like to include all the important variables inside the model and exclude all the variables that should be ignored.

However, no matter what we include, using a model that contains faulty assumptions can lead to spectacular policy failures. There is no better example than the financial crisis and Great Recession that began in 2008. We will go into this in much greater detail in later chapters.

In the years leading up to the crisis, banks sold and repackaged mortgage-backed securities under the faulty assumption that real estate prices would always rise. (These types of securities are investments that are backed by the underlying value of a bundle of mortgages.) In fact, the computer models used by many of the banks did not even have a variable for declining real estate prices. Investors around the globe bought these securities because they thought they were safe. This sounded perfectly reasonable in a world where real estate prices were rising on an annual basis. Unfortunately, that assumption turned out to be false. From 2006 to 2008, real estate prices fell. Because of one faulty assumption, the entire financial market teetered on the edge of collapse. This vividly illustrates the danger of poor modeling.

Models can be useful, but as the current financial crisis shows, they are also potentially dangerous. Models necessarily simplify the world by using a set of assumptions. It is critical that the assumptions be correct. But because a model is always a simplification, decision-makers must be careful about assuming that a model can present a solution for complex problems.

In the late 1990s and early 2000s, some investors believed that real estate prices could only rise.

PRACTICE WHAT YOU KNOW

Positive versus Normative Statements

Question: Which of the following statements are positive and which ones are normative?

1. Winters in Arkansas are too cold.
2. Everyone should work at a bank to see the true value of money.
3. The current exchange rate is 0.7 British pounds per U.S. dollar.
4. On average, people save 15% when they switch to Geico.
5. Everyone ought to have a life insurance policy.
6. University of Virginia graduates earn more than Duke University graduates.
7. Harvard University is the top education institution in the country.
8. The average temperature in Fargo, North Dakota, in January is 56 degrees Fahrenheit.

You should eat five servings of fruit or vegetables each day. Is that a positive or a normative statement?

Answers

1. The word "too" is a matter of opinion. This is a normative statement.
2. While working at a bank might give someone an appreciation for the value of money, the word "should" is an opinion. This is a normative statement.
3. You can look up the current exchange rate and verify if this statement is true or false. This is a positive statement.
4. This was a claim made by the insurance company Geico in one of its commercials. Don't let that fool you. It is still a testable claim. If you had the data from Geico, you could see if the statement is correct or not. This is a positive statement.
5. It sounds like a true statement, or at least a very sensible one. However, the word "ought" makes it an opinion. This is a normative statement.
6. You can look up the data and see which university's graduates earn more. This is a positive statement.
7. Many national rankings indicate that this is true, but others do not. Since different rankings are based on different assumptions, it is not possible to identify a definitive "top" school. This is a normative statement.
8. The statement is wrong. North Dakota is much colder than that in January. However, the statement can be verified by looking at climatological data. This is a positive statement.

What Is a Production Possibilities Frontier?

Now it's time for our first economic model. However, before you go on, you might want to review the appendix on graphing at the end of this chapter. It covers graph-reading skills that are used in this section. Graphs are one of the key tools in economics because they provide a visual display of the relationship between two variables over time. Your ability to read a graph and understand the model it represents is crucial to learning economics.

Trade-offs

In Chapter 1, we learned that economics is about the trade-offs individuals and societies face every day. For instance, you may frequently have to decide between spending more time studying to get better grades or going to a party with your friends. The more time you study, the less time you have for your friends. Similarly, a society has to determine how to allocate its resources. The decision to build new roads will mean there is less money available for new schools, and vice versa.

A **production possibilities frontier** is a model that illustrates the combinations of outputs that a society can produce if all of its resources are being used efficiently. In order to preserve *ceteris paribus*, we assume that the technology available for production and the quantity of resources remain constant. These assumptions allow us to model trade-offs more clearly.

A **production possibilities frontier** is a model that illustrates the combinations of outputs that a society can produce if all of its resources are being used efficiently.

Let's begin by imagining a society that produces only two goods—pizzas and chicken wings. This may not seem very realistic, since a real economy comprises millions of different goods and services, but the benefit of this approach is that it enables us to understand the trade-offs in the production process without making the analysis too complicated.

Figure 2.1 shows the production possibilities frontier for our two-product society. Remember that the number of people and the total resources in this two-product society are fixed. Later, we will relax these assumptions and make our model more realistic. If the economy uses all of its resources to produce pizzas, it can produce 100 pizzas and 0 wings. If it uses all of its resources to produce wings, it can make 300 wings and 0 pizzas. These outcomes are represented by points A and B on the production possibilities frontier. It is unlikely that the society will choose either of these extreme outcomes because it is human nature to enjoy variety.

If our theoretical society decides to spend some of its resources producing pizzas and some of its resources making wings, its economy will end up with a combination of pizzas and wings that can be placed somewhere along the production possibilities frontier (PPF) between points A and B. At point C, for example, the society would deploy its resources to produce 70 pizzas and 90 wings. At point D, the combination would be 50 pizzas and 150 wings. Each point along the production possibilities frontier represents a possible set of outcomes that the society can choose if it uses all of its resources efficiently.

Notice that some combinations of pizza and wings cannot be produced. This is because resources within the society are scarce. Our theoretical society would enjoy point E, but given the available resources, it cannot produce at that output level. Points beyond the production possibilities frontier are desirable but not feasible, given the resources and technology that the society has available.

FIGURE 2.1

The Production Possibilities Frontier for Pizza and Wings

The production possibilities frontier shows the trade-off between producing pizzas and producing wings. Any combination of pizzas and wings is possible along, or inside, the line. Combinations of pizza and wings beyond the production possibilities frontier—for example, at point E—are not possible with the current set of resources. Point F and any other points located in the blue-shaded region are inefficient.

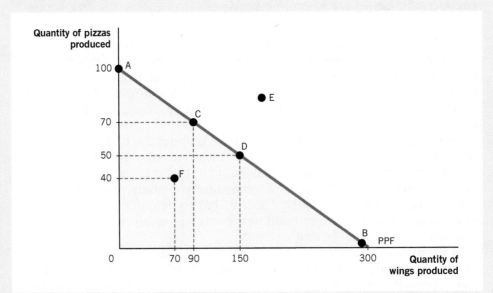

At any combination of wings and pizzas along the production possibilities frontier, the society is using all of its resources in the most productive way possible. But what about point F and any other points that might be located in the blue-shaded region? These points represent outcomes inside the production possibilities frontier, which indicate an inefficient use of the society's resources. Consider, for example, the resource of labor. If employees spend many hours at work surfing the Web instead of doing their jobs, the output of pizzas and wings will drop and will no longer be efficient. As long as the workers use all of their time efficiently, they will produce the maximum amount of pizza and wings.

Whenever society is producing on the production possibilities frontier, the only way to get more of one good is to accept less of another. Since an economy operating along the frontier will be efficient at any point, economists do not favor one point over another. But a society may favor one particular point over another because it prefers that combination of goods. For example, in our theoretical two-good society, if wings suddenly become more popular, the movement from point C to point D will represent a desirable trade-off. The society will have 20 fewer pizzas (from 70 to 50) but 60 additional wings (from 90 to 150).

The Production Possibilities Frontier and Opportunity Cost

Trade-offs

Since our two-good society produces only pizzas and wings, the trade-offs that occur along the production possibilities frontier represent the opportunity cost of producing one good instead of the other. As we noted in Chapter 1, an opportunity cost is the highest-valued alternative given up to pursue another course of action. As Figure 2.1 shows, when society moves from point C to point D, it gives up 20 pizzas; this is the opportunity cost of producing more wings. The movement from D to C has an opportunity cost of 60 wings.

Until now, we have assumed that there would be a constant trade-off between the number of pizzas and the number of wings produced. However, that is not typically the case. Not all resources in our theoretical society are perfectly adaptable for use in making pizzas and wings. Some workers are good at making pizzas, and others are not so good. When the society tries to make as many pizzas as possible, it will be using both types of workers. That is, to get more pizzas, the society will have to use workers who are increasingly less skilled at making them. This means that pizza production will not expand at a constant rate. You can see this in the new production possibilities frontier in Figure 2.2; it is bowed outward rather than a straight line.

Since resources are not perfectly adaptable, production does not expand at a constant rate. For example, in order to produce 20 extra pizzas, the society can move from point E (30 pizzas) to point D (50 pizzas). But moving from

Opportunity
cost

FIGURE 2.2

The Law of Increasing Relative Cost

To make more pizzas, the society will have to use workers who are increasingly less skilled at making them. As a result, as we move up along the PPF, the opportunity cost of producing an extra 20 pizzas rises from 30 wings between points E and D to 80 wings between points C and B.

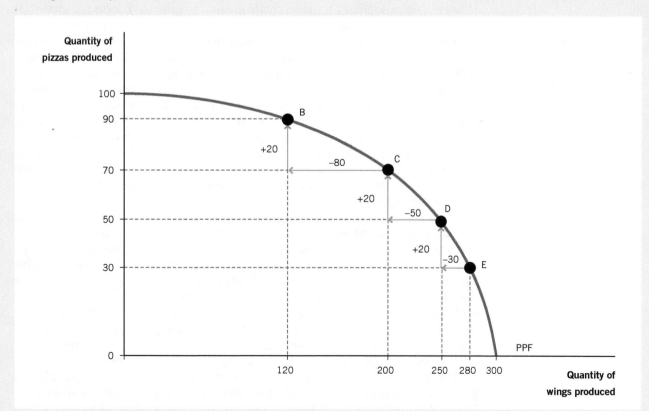

point E (280 wings) to point D (250 wings) means giving up 30 wings. So moving from E to D has an opportunity cost of 30 wings. Suppose that the society decides it wants more pizza and moves from point D (50 pizzas) to point C (70 pizzas). Now the opportunity cost of more pizza is 50 wings, since wing production declines from 250 to 200. If the society decides that 70 pizzas are not enough, it can expand pizza production from point C (70 pizzas) to point B (90 pizzas). Now the society gives up 80 wings. Notice that as we move up along the PPF, the opportunity cost of producing an extra 20 pizzas rises from 30 wings to 80 wings. This reflects the increased trade-off necessary to produce more pizzas.

The **law of increasing relative cost** states that the opportunity cost of producing a good rises as a society produces more of it.

A bowed-out production possibilities frontier reflects the increasing opportunity cost of production. This is described by the **law of increasing relative cost**, which states that the opportunity cost of producing a good rises as a society produces more of it. Changes in relative cost mean that a society faces a significant trade-off if it tries to produce an extremely large amount of a single good.

The Production Possibilities Frontier and Economic Growth

So far, we have modeled the location of the production possibilities frontier as a function of the resources available to society at a particular moment in time. However, most societies hope to create economic growth. Economic growth is the process that enables a society to produce more output in the future.

We can use the production possibilities frontier to explore economic growth. For example, we can ask what would happen to the PPF if our theoretical two-good society developed a new technology that increases efficiency and, therefore, productivity. Suppose that a new pizza assembly line improves the pizza production process and that the development of the new assembly line does not require the use of more of the society's resources—it is simply a redeployment of the resources that already exist. This development would allow the society to make more pizza with the same number of workers. Or it would allow the same amount of pizza to be made with fewer workers than previously. Either way, the society has expanded its resource base. The change is shown in Figure 2.3.

With the new technology, it becomes possible to produce 120 pizzas using the same number of workers and in the same amount of time that it previously took to produce 100 pizzas. Although the ability to produce wings has not changed, the new pizza-making technology causes the production possibilities frontier to expand outward from PPF_1 to PPF_2. It is now possible for the society to move from point C to point G, where it can produce more of both (80 pizzas and 210 wings). Why can the society produce more of both? Because the improvement in pizza-making technology—the assembly line—allows deployment of the labor force in a way that also increases the production of wings. Improvements in technology make point G possible.

The production possibilities frontier will also expand if the population grows. A larger population means more workers to help make pizza and wings. Figure 2.4 illustrates what happens when the society adds a worker to help

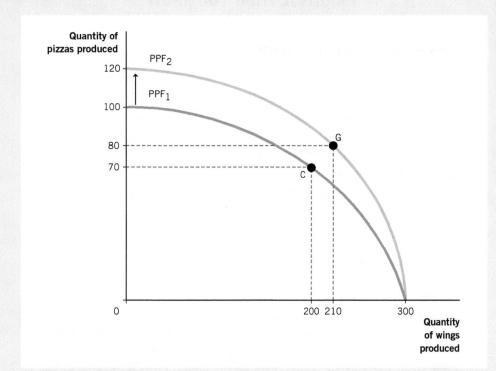

FIGURE 2.3

A Shift in the Production Possibilities Frontier

A new pizza assembly line that improves the productive capacity of pizza-makers shifts the PPF upward from PPF_1 to PPF_2. Not surprisingly, more pizzas can be produced. Comparing points C and G, you can see that the enhanced pizza-making capacity also makes it possible to produce more wings at the same time.

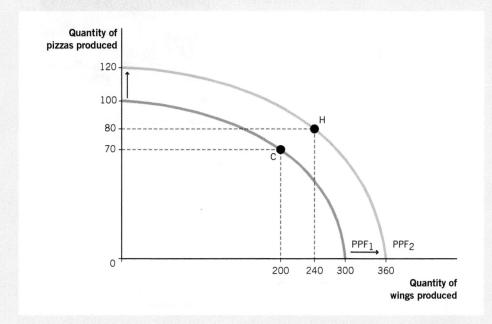

FIGURE 2.4

More Resources and the Production Possibilities Frontier

When more resources are available for the production of either pizza or wings, the entire PPF shifts upward and outward. This makes a point like H, along PPF_2, possible.

PRACTICE WHAT YOU KNOW

The Production Possibilities Frontier

Question: Are the following statements true or false? Base your answers on the PPF shown below.

1. Point A represents the amount of cars and bicycles that will be sold.
2. The movement along the curve from point C to point A shows the opportunity cost of producing more bicycles.
3. If we have high unemployment, the PPF shifts inward.
4. If an improved process for manufacturing cars is introduced, the *entire* PPF will shift outward.

Answers

1. False. Point A represents the number of cars and bicycles produced, not sold.
2. False. Moving from point C to point A shows the opportunity cost of producing more cars, not more bicycles.
3. False. Unemployment does not shift the curve inward, since the PPF is the maximum that can be produced when all resources are being used. More unemployment would locate society at a point inside the PPF, since some people who could help produce more cars or bicycles would not be working.
4. False. The PPF will shift outward along the car axis, but it will not shift upward along the bicycle axis.

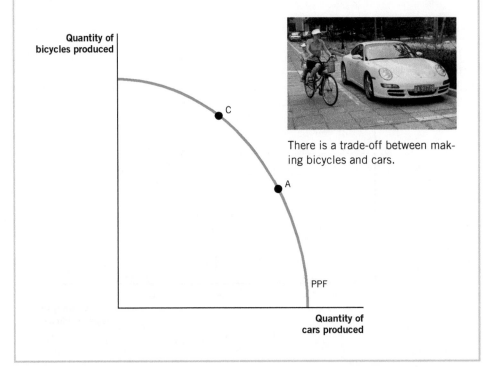

There is a trade-off between making bicycles and cars.

produce pizza and wings. With more workers, the society is able to produce more pizzas and wings than before. This causes the curve to shift from PPF_1 to PPF_2, expanding up along the y axis and out along the x axis. Like improvements in technology, additional resources expand the frontier and enable the society to reach a point—in this case, H—that was not possible before. The extra workers have pushed the entire frontier out, not just one end, as the pizza assembly line did.

What Are the Benefits of Specialization and Trade?

We have seen that improving technology and adding resources make an economy more productive. A third way to create gains for society is through specialization and trade. Determining what to specialize in is an important part of this process. Every worker, business, or country is relatively good at producing certain products or services. Suppose that you decide to learn about information technology. You earn a certificate or degree and find an employer who hires you for your specialized skills. Your information technology skills determine your salary. As a result, you can use your salary to purchase other goods and services that you desire and that you are not so skilled at making yourself.

In the next section, we will explore why specializing and exchanging your skilled expertise with others makes gains from trade possible.

Gains from Trade

Let's return to our two-good economy. Now we'll make the further assumption that this economy has only two people. One person is better at making pizzas, and the other is better at making wings. When this is the case, the potential gains from trade are clear. Each person will specialize in what he or she is better at producing and then will trade in order to acquire some of the good that the other person produces.

Figure 2.5 shows the production potential of the two people in our economy, Debra Winger and Mike Piazza. From the table, we see that if Debra Winger devotes all of her work time to making pizzas, she can produce 60 pizzas. If she does not spend any time on pizzas, she can make 120 wings. In contrast, Mike Piazza can spend all his time on pizzas and produce 24 pizzas, or all his time on wings and produce 72 wings.

The graphs show a side-by-side illustration of the amount of pizza and wings that each person produces daily. Wing production is plotted on the x axis, and pizza production is on the y axis. Each of the production possibilities frontiers is drawn from data in the table at the top of the figure.

Debra and Mike each face a constant trade-off between producing pizza and producing wings. Debra produces 60 pizzas for every 120 wings; this means her trade-off between producing pizza and wings is fixed at 1:2. Mike produces 24 pizzas for every 72 wings. His trade-off between producing pizzas

FIGURE 2.5

The Production Possibilities Frontier with No Trade

Debra Winger (a) can produce more pizza and more wings than Mike Piazza (b). Since Debra is more productive in general, she produces more of each food. When Debra and Mike both produce each item, Debra makes 40 units of each and Mike makes 18 units of each.

	Daily production	
Person	Pizzas	Wings
Debra Winger	60	120
Mike Piazza	24	72

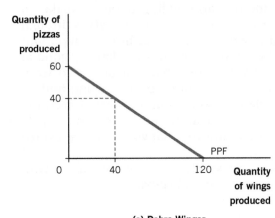

(a) Debra Winger

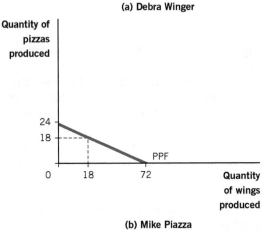

(b) Mike Piazza

and wings is fixed at 1:3. Since Debra and Mike can choose to produce at any point along their production possibilities frontiers, let's assume that they each want to produce an equal number of pizzas and wings. When this is the case, Debra produces 40 pizzas and 40 wings, while Mike produces 18 pizzas and 18 wings. Since Debra is more productive in general, she produces more of each food. We say that Debra has an **absolute advantage**, meaning that she has the ability to produce more with the same quantity of resources than Mike can produce.

Absolute advantage refers to the ability of one producer to make more than another producer with the same quantity of resources.

At first glance, it would appear that Debra should continue to work alone. But consider what happens if they each specialize and then trade. Table 2.1 compares production with and without specialization and trade. Without trade, Debra and Mike have a combined production of 58 units of pizza and wings (Debra's 40 + Mike's 18). But when Debra specializes and produces only pizza, her production is 60 units. In this case, her individual pizza output is greater than the combined output of 58 pizzas (Debra's 40 + Mike's 18). Similarly, if Mike specializes in wings, he is able to make 72 units. His individual wing output is greater than their combined output of 58 wings (Debra's 40 + Mike's 18). Specialization has resulted in the production of 2 additional pizzas and 14 additional wings.

Trade creates value

Specialization leads to greater productivity. But Debra and Mike would like to eat both pizza and wings. So if they specialize and then trade with each other, they will benefit. If Debra gives Mike 19 pizzas in exchange for 47 wings, they are each better off by 1 pizza and 7 wings. This result is evident in the final column of Table 2.1 and in Figure 2.6.

In Figure 2.6a, we see that at point A Debra produces 60 pizzas and 0 wings. If she does not specialize, she produces 40 pizzas and 40 wings, represented at B. If she specializes and then trades with Mike, she can have 41 pizzas and 47 wings, shown at C. Her value gained from trade is 1 pizza and 7 wings. In Figure 2.6b, we see a similar benefit for Mike. If he produces only wings, he will have 72 wings, shown at A. If he does not specialize, he produces 18 pizzas and 18 wings. If he specializes and trades with Debra, he can have 19 pizzas and 25 wings, shown at C. His value gained from trade is 1 pizza and 7 wings. In spite of Debra's absolute advantage in making both pizzas and wings, she is still better off trading with Mike. This amazing result occurs because of specialization. When they spend their time on what they do best, they are able to produce more collectively and then divide the gain.

TABLE 2.1

The Gains from Trade

| Person | Good | Without trade | | With specialization and trade | | Gains from trade |
		Production	Consumption	Production	Consumption	
Debra	Pizza	40	40	60	41 (keeps)	+ 1
	Wings	40	40	0	47 (from Mike)	+ 7
Mike	Pizza	18	18	0	19 (from Debra)	+ 1
	Wings	18	18	72	25 (keeps)	+ 7

FIGURE 2.6

The Production Possibilities Frontier with Trade

(a) If Debra produces only pizza, she will have 60 pizzas, shown at point A. If she does not specialize, she will produce 40 pizzas and 40 wings (B). If she specializes and trades with Mike, she will have 41 pizzas and 47 wings (C). (b) If Mike produces only wings, he will have 72 wings (A). If he does not specialize, he will produce 18 pizzas and 18 wings (B). If he specializes and trades with Debra, he can have 19 pizzas and 25 wings (C).

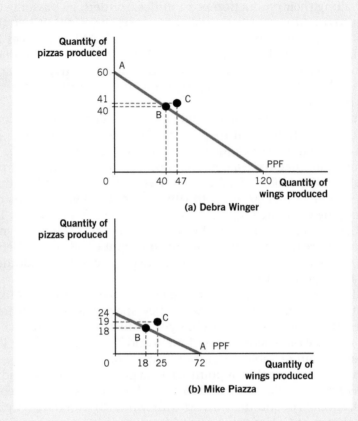

Comparative Advantage

We have seen that specialization enables workers to enjoy gains from trade. The concept of opportunity cost provides us with a second way of validating the principle that trade creates value. Recall that opportunity cost is the highest-valued alternative that is sacrificed to pursue something else. Looking at Table 2.2, you can see that in order to produce 1 more pizza Debra must give up producing 2 wings. We can say that the opportunity cost of 1 pizza is 2 wings. We can also reverse the observation and say that the opportunity cost of one wing is 1/2 a pizza. In Mike's case, each pizza he produces means giving up the production of 3 wings. In other words, the opportunity cost for him to produce 1 pizza is 3 wings. In reverse, we can say that when he produces 1 wing, he gives up 1/3 of a pizza.

Recall from Chapter 1 that comparative advantage is the ability to make a good at a lower cost than another producer. Looking at Table 2.2, you can see that Debra has a lower opportunity cost of producing pizzas than Mike—she gives up 2 wings for each pizza she produces, while he gives up 3 wings for each pizza he produces. In other words, Debra has a comparative advantage in producing pizzas. However, Debra does not have a comparative advantage in producing wings. For Debra to produce 1 wing, she would have to give up production of 1/2 a pizza. Mike, in contrast, gives up 1/3 of a pizza each time he produces 1 wing. So Debra's opportunity cost for producing wings

TABLE 2.2		
The Opportunity Cost of Pizza and Wings		
	Opportunity cost	
Person	**1 Pizza**	**1 Wing**
Debra Winger	2 wings	1/2 of a pizza
Mike Piazza	3 wings	1/3 of a pizza

is higher than Mike's. Because Mike is the low-opportunity-cost producer of wings, he has a comparative advantage in producing them. Recall that Debra has an absolute advantage in the production of both pizzas and wings; she is better at making both. However, from this example we see that she cannot have a comparative advantage in making both goods.

Applying the concept of opportunity cost helps us to see why specialization enables people to produce more. Debra's opportunity cost of producing pizzas (she gives up making 2 wings for every pizza) is less than Mike's opportunity cost of producing pizzas (he gives up 3 wings for every pizza). Therefore, Debra should specialize in producing pizzas. If you want to double-check this result, consider who should produce wings. Debra's opportunity cost of producing wings (she gives up 1/2 a pizza for every wing she makes) is more than Mike's opportunity cost of producing wings (he gives up 1/3 of a pizza for every wing he makes). Therefore, Mike should specialize in producing wings. When Debra produces only pizzas and Mike produces only wings, their combined output is 60 pizzas and 72 wings.

Finding the Right Price to Facilitate Trade

We have seen that Debra and Mike will do better if they specialize and then trade. But how many wings should it cost to buy a pizza? How many pizzas for a wing? In other words, what trading price will benefit both parties? To answer this question, we need to return to opportunity cost. This process is similar to the trading of lunch food that you might recall from grade school. Perhaps you wanted a friend's apple and he wanted a few of your Oreos. If you agreed to trade three Oreos for the apple, the exchange benefited both parties because you valued your three cookies less than your friend's apple and your friend valued your three cookies more than his apple.

In our example, Debra and Mike will benefit from exchanging a good at a price that is lower than the opportunity cost of producing it. Recall that Debra's opportunity cost is 1 pizza per 2 wings. We can express this as a ratio of 1:2. This means that any exchange with a value lower than 1:2 (0.50) will be beneficial to her since she ends up with more pizza and wings than she had without trade. Mike's opportunity cost is 1 pizza per 3 wings, or a ratio of 1:3 (0.33). For trade to be mutually beneficial, the ratio of the amount exchanged must fall between the ratio of Debra's opportunity cost of 1:2 and the ratio of Mike's opportunity cost of 1:3. If the ratio falls outside of that range, Debra and Mike will be better off without trade, since the price of trading, which is the ratio in this case, will not be attractive to both parties. In the

Opportunity
cost

TABLE 2.3		
Gaining from Trade		
Person	Opportunity cost	Ratio
Debra Winger	1 pizza equals 2 wings	1:2 = 0.50
Terms of trade	19 pizzas for 47 wings	19:47 = 0.40
Mike Piazza	1 pizza equals 3 wings	1:3 = 0.33

Trade creates value

example, shown in Table 2.3, Debra trades 19 pizzas for 47 wings. The ratio of 19:47 (0.40) falls between Debra's and Mike's opportunity costs.

As long as the terms of trade fall between the opportunity costs of the trading partners, the trade benefits both sides. But if Mike insists on a trading ratio of 1 wing for 1 pizza, which would be a good deal for him, Debra will refuse to trade because she will be better off producing both goods on her own. Likewise, if Debra insists on receiving 4 wings for every pizza she gives to Mike, he will refuse to trade with her because he will be better off producing both goods on his own.

ECONOMICS IN THE MEDIA

Opportunity Cost

Saving Private Ryan

In most war movies, the calculus of battle is quite apparent. One side wins if it loses fewer airplanes, tanks, or soldiers during the course of the conflict or attains a strategic objective worth the cost. These casualties of war are the trade-off that is necessary to achieve victory. The movie *Saving Private Ryan* (1998) is different because in its plot the calculus of war does not add up; the mission is to save a single man. Private Ryan is one of four brothers who are all fighting on D-Day—June 6, 1944—the day the Allies landed in Normandy, France, to liberate Europe from Nazi occupation. In a twist of fate, all three of Ryan's brothers are killed. As a result, the general in charge believes that the family has sacrificed enough and sends orders to find Ryan and return him home.

The catch is that in order to save Private Ryan the army needs to send a small group of soldiers to find him. A patrol led by Captain Miller loses many good men in the process, and those who remain begin to doubt the mission. Captain Miller says to the sergeant, "This Ryan better be worth it. He better go home and cure a disease, or invent a longer-lasting

Saving one life means sacrificing another.

light bulb." Now another catch is that there is no way of knowing what will happen in the future. Captain Miller hopes that saving Private Ryan will be worth the sacrifices they are making. That is how he rationalizes the decision to try to save him.

The opportunity cost of saving Private Ryan ends up being the lives that the patrol loses—lives that otherwise could have been pursuing a strategic military objective. In that sense, the entire film is about opportunity cost.

ECONOMICS IN THE REAL WORLD

Why Shaquille O'Neal Has Someone Else Help Him Move

Shaquille O'Neal is a mountain of a man—7'1" tall and over 300 pounds. At times during his Hall of Fame basketball career, he was traded from one team to another. Whenever he was traded, he had to relocate to a new city. Given his size and strength, you might think that Shaquille would have moved his household himself. But despite the fact that he could replace two or more ordinary movers, he kept playing basketball and hired movers. Let's examine the situation to see if this was a wise decision.

During his career, Shaquille had an absolute advantage in both playing basketball and moving furniture. But, as we have seen, an absolute advantage doesn't mean that Shaquille should do both tasks himself. When he was traded to a new team, he could have asked for a few days to pack up and move, but each day spent moving would have been one less day he was able to work with his new team. When you are paid millions of dollars to play a game, the time spent moving is time lost practicing or playing basketball, which incurs a substantial opportunity cost.

Experienced movers can make about $50 an hour. If Shaquille was able to replace two movers, his value as a mover would have been only $100 an hour. If he put in a ten-hour day, he could have saved the cost of two movers, or $1,000 a day. In this situation, many people might have chosen to do their own moving. But $1,000 is not a lot of money to Shaquille. He could have been making more by playing basketball or filming a commercial. However, since Shaquille is now retired, the value of his time is lower. If the opportunity cost of his time becomes low enough, it is conceivable that next time he will move himself rather than pay movers. ✳

Shaq would be a big help when moving.

PRACTICE WHAT YOU KNOW

Opportunity Cost

Question: Imagine that you are traveling to visit your family in Chicago. You can take a train or a plane. The plane ticket costs $300, and it takes 2 hours each way. The train ticket costs $200, and it takes 12 hours each way. Which form of transportation should you choose?

Answer: The key to answering the question is learning to value time. The simplest way to do this is to calculate the financial cost savings of taking the train and compare that to the value of the time you would save if you took the plane.

Will you travel by plane or train?

Cost savings with train	Round-trip time saved with plane
$300 − $200 = $100	24 hours − 4 hours = 20 hours
(plane) − (train)	(train) − (plane)

A person who takes the train can save $100, but it will cost 20 hours to do so. At an hourly rate, the savings would be $100/20 hours = $5/hour. If you value your time at exactly $5 an hour, you will be indifferent between plane and train travel. If your time is worth more than $5 an hour, you should take the plane, and if your time is worth less than $5 an hour, you should take the train.

It is important to note that this approach gives us a more realistic answer than simply observing ticket prices. The train has a lower ticket price, but very few people ride the train instead of flying because the opportunity cost of their time is worth more to them than the difference in the ticket prices. This is why most business travelers fly—it saves valuable time. Good economists learn to examine the full opportunity cost of their decisions, which must include both the financials and the cost of time.

We have examined this question by holding everything else constant, or applying *ceteris paribus*. At no point did we discuss possible side issues such as the fear of flying, sleeping arrangements on the train, or anything else that might be relevant to someone making the decision.

Opportunity cost

What Is the Trade-off between Having More Now or Having More Later?

So far, we have examined short-run trade-offs. In looking at our wings-pizza trade-off, we were essentially living in the moment. But both individuals and society as a whole must weigh the benefits available today with those available tomorrow.

Study now . . .   . . . enjoy life later.

Many of life's important decisions are about the long run. We must decide where to live, whether and whom to marry, whether and where to go to college, and what type of career to pursue. Getting these decisions right is far more important than simply deciding how many wings and pizzas to produce. For instance, the decision to save money requires giving up something you want to buy today for the benefit of having more money available in the future. Similarly, if you decide to go to a party tonight, you benefit today, while staying home to study creates a larger benefit at exam time. We are constantly making decisions that reflect this tension between today and tomorrow—eating a large piece of cake or a healthy snack, taking a nap or exercising at the gym, buying a jet ski or investing in the stock market. Each of these decisions is a trade-off between the present and the future.

Trade-offs

Consumer Goods, Capital Goods, and Investment

We have seen that the trade-off between the present and the future is evident in the tension between what we consume now and what we plan to consume later. Any good that is produced for present consumption is a **consumer good**. These goods help to satisfy our wants now. Food, entertainment, and clothing are all examples of consumer goods. **Capital goods** help in the production of other valuable goods and services in the future. Capital goods are everywhere. Roads, factories, trucks, and computers are all capital goods.

For households, education is also a form of capital. The time you spend earning a college degree makes you more attractive to future employers. Even though education is not a durable good, like a house, it can be utilized in the future to earn more income. When you decide to go to college instead of working, you are making an *investment* in your human capital. **Investment** is the process of using resources to create or buy new capital.

Since we live in a world with scarce resources, every investment in capital goods has an opportunity cost of forgone consumer goods. For example, if you decide to buy a new laptop to take notes in class, you cannot use the money you spent to travel over spring break. Similarly, a firm that decides to invest in a new factory to expand future production is unable to use that money to hire more workers now.

The decision between whether to consume or to invest has a significant impact on economic growth in the future, or the long run. What happens when society makes a choice to produce many more consumer goods than capital goods? Figure 2.7a shows the result. When relatively few resources are invested in producing capital goods in the short run, not very much new capital is created. Since new capital is a necessary ingredient for economic growth in the future, the long-run production possibilities curve only expands a small amount.

What happens when society makes a choice to plan for the future by producing more capital goods than consumer goods? Figure 2.7b shows the result. With investment in new capital, the long-run production possibilities curve expands outward much more.

All societies face the trade-off between spending today and investing for tomorrow. Emerging global economic powers like China and India are good examples of the benefit of investing in the future. Over the last 20 years, the

Consumer goods
are produced for present consumption.

Capital goods
help produce other valuable goods and services in the future.

Investment
is the process of using resources to create or buy new capital.

FIGURE 2.7

Investing in Capital Goods and Promoting Growth

(a) When a society chooses point A in the short run, very few capital goods are created. Since capital goods are needed to enhance future growth, the long-run PPF expands, but only slightly.
(b) When a society chooses point B in the short run, many capital goods are created, and the long-run PPF expands significantly.

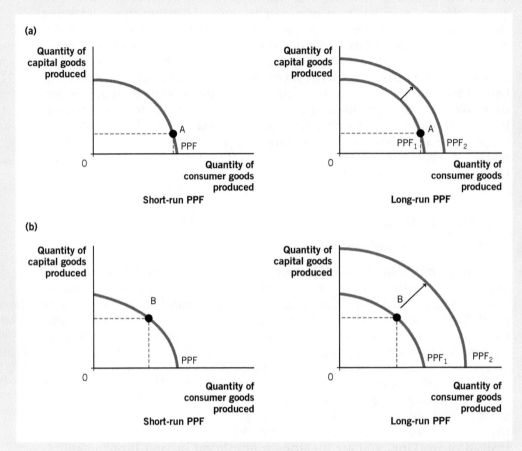

citizens of these countries have invested significantly more on the formation of capital goods than have the citizens in wealthier nations in North America and Europe. Not surprisingly, economic growth rates in China and India are much higher than in more developed countries. Part of the difference in investment rates can be explained by the fact that the United States and Europe already have larger capital stocks per capita and have less to gain than developing countries from operating at point B in Figure 2.7b. The Chinese government clearly prefers point B at this stage of its economic development, but point B is not necessarily better than point A. Developing nations, like China, are sacrificing the present for a better future, while many developed countries, like the United States, take a more balanced approached to weighing current needs against future growth. For Chinese workers, this trade-off typically means longer work hours and higher savings rates than their American counterparts can claim, despite far lower average salaries. In contrast, American workers have much more leisure time and more disposable income, a combination that leads to far greater rates of consumption.

The Trade-off between the Present and the Future

A Knight's Tale

Before the late Heath Ledger starred in *Brokeback Mountain*, or played the Joker in *The Dark Knight*, he played an entrepreneurial peasant in *A Knight's Tale* (2001).

In the movie, three peasants unexpectedly win a jousting tournament and earn 15 silver coins. Then they face a choice about what to do next. Two of the three want to return to England and live the high life for a while, but the third (played by Ledger) suggests that they take 13 of the coins and reinvest them in training for the next tournament. He offers to put in all 5 of his coins and asks the other two for 4 coins each. His partners are skeptical about the plan because Ledger's character is good with the sword and not very good with the lance. For them to win additional tournaments, they will have to invest considerable resources in training and preparation.

The movie illustrates the trade-off between enjoying consumer goods in the short run and investing in capital goods in the long run. The peasants' choice to forgo spending their winnings

Learning to joust is a long-term skill.

to enjoy themselves now in order to prepare for the next tournament is not easy. None of the three has ever had any money. Five silver coins represent an opportunity, at least for a few days, to live the good life. However, the plan will elevate the three out of poverty in the long term if they can learn to compete at the highest level. Therefore, investing the 13 coins is like choosing point B in Figure 2.8b. Investing now will allow their production possibilities frontier to grow over time, affording each of them a better life in the long run.

PRACTICE WHAT YOU KNOW

Trade-offs

Question: Your friend is fond of saying he will study later. He eventually does study, but he often doesn't get quite the grades he had hoped for because he doesn't study enough. Every time this happens, he says, "It's only one exam." What advice would you give?

No pain, no gain.

Answer: Your friend doesn't understand long-term trade-offs. You could start by reminding him that each decision has a consequence at the margin and also later in life. The marginal cost of not studying enough is a lower exam grade. To some extent, your friend's reasoning is correct. How well he does on one exam over four years of college is almost irrelevant. The problem is that many poor exam scores have a cumulative effect over the semesters. If your friend graduates with a 2.5 GPA instead of a 3.5 GPA because he did not study enough, his employment prospects will be significantly diminished.

Marginal thinking

ECONOMICS FOR LIFE

Failing to Account for Exogenous Factors When Making Predictions

Predictions are often based on past experiences and current observations. Many of the least accurate predictions fail to take into account how much technological change influences the economy. Here, we repeat a few predictions as a cautionary reminder that technology doesn't remain constant.

PREDICTION: "There is no reason anyone would want a computer in their home." Said in 1977 by Ken Olson, founder of Digital Equipment Corp. (DEC), a maker of mainframe computers.

FAIL: Over 80% of all American households have a computer today.

PREDICTION: "There will never be a bigger plane built." Said in 1933 by a Boeing engineer referring to the 247, a twin-engine plane that holds 10 people.

FAIL: Today, the Airbus A380 can hold more than 800 people.

PREDICTION: "The wireless music box has no imaginable commercial value. Who would pay for a message sent to no one in particular?" Said by people in the communications industry when David Sarnoff (founder of NBC) wanted to invest in the radio.

FAIL: Radio programs quickly captured the public's imagination.

PREDICTION: "The world potential market for copying machines is five thousand at most." Said in 1959 by executives of IBM to the people who founded Xerox.

FAIL: Today, a combination printer, fax machine, and copier costs less than $100. There are tens of millions of copiers in use throughout the United States.

PREDICTION: "The Americans have need of the telephone, but we do not. We have plenty of messenger boys." Said in 1878 by Sir William Preece, chief engineer, British Post Office.

FAIL: Today, almost everyone in Britain has a telephone.

These predictions may seem funny to us today, but note the common feature: they did not account for how the new technology would affect consumer demand and behavior. Nor do these predictions anticipate how improvements in technology through time make future versions of new products substantially better. The lesson: don't count on the status quo. Adapt with the times to take advantage of opportunities.

Epic fail: planes have continued to get larger despite predictions to the contrary.

Source: Listverse, http://listverse.com/2007/10/28/top-30-failed-technology-predictions

Conclusion

Does trade create winners and losers? After reading this chapter, you should know the answer: trade creates value. We have dispelled the misconception that many first-time learners of economics begin with—that every trade results in a winner and a loser. The simple, yet powerful, idea that trade creates value has far-reaching consequences for how we should organize our society. Voluntary trades will maximize society's wealth by redistributing goods and services to people who value them the most.

We have also developed our first model, the production possibilities frontier. This model illustrates the benefits of trade and also enables us to describe ways to grow the economy. Trade and growth rest on a more fundamental idea—specialization. When producers specialize, they focus their efforts on those goods and services for which they have the lowest opportunity cost and trade with others who are good at making something else. In order to have something valuable to trade, each producer, in effect, must find its comparative advantage. As a result, trade creates value and contributes to an improved standard of living in society.

In the next chapter, we examine the supply-and-demand model to illustrate how markets work. While the model is different, the fundamental result we learned here—that trade creates value—still holds.

Trade
creates
value

ANSWERING THE BIG QUESTIONS

1. How do economists study the economy?

* Economists design theories and then test them by collecting real data. The economist's laboratory is the world around us; it ranges from the economy as a whole to the decisions that firms and individuals make. A good model should be simple to understand, flexible in design, and able to make powerful predictions. A model is both more realistic and harder to understand when it involves many variables. Maintaining a positive framework is crucial for economic analysis because it allows decision-makers to observe the facts objectively.

2. What is a production possibilities frontier?

* A production possibilities frontier is a model that illustrates the combinations of outputs that a society can produce if all of its resources are being used efficiently. Economists use this model to illustrate trade-offs and to explain opportunity costs and the role of additional resources and technology in creating economic growth.

3. What are the benefits of specialization and trade?

* Society is better off if individuals and firms specialize and trade on the basis of the principle of comparative advantage.
* Parties that are better at producing goods and services than their potential trading partners, or hold an absolute advantage, still benefit from trade because this allows them to specialize and trade what they produce for other goods and services that they are not as skilled at making.
* As long as the terms of trade fall between the opportunity costs of the trading partners, the trade benefits both sides.

4. What is the trade-off between having more now or having more later?

* All societies face a critical trade-off between consumption in the short run and greater productivity in the long run. Investments in capital goods today help to spur economic growth in the future. However, since capital goods are not consumed in the short run, this means that society must be willing to sacrifice how well it lives today in order to have more later.

CONCEPTS YOU SHOULD KNOW

absolute advantage (p. 00)
capital goods (p. 00)
ceteris paribus (p. 00)
consumer goods (p. 00)
endogenous factors (p. 00)

exogenous factors (p. 00)
investment (p. 00)
law of increasing relative
   cost (p. 00)
normative statement (p. 00)

positive statement (p. 00)
production possibilities
   frontier (p. 00)

QUESTIONS FOR REVIEW

1. What is a positive economic statement? What is a normative economic statement? Provide an example of each.

2. Is it important to build completely realistic economic models? Explain your response.

3. Draw a production possibilities frontier curve. Illustrate the set of points that is not possible, the set of points that is efficient, and the set of points that is not feasible.

4. Why does the production possibilities frontier bow out? Give an example of two goods for which this would be the case.

5. Does having an absolute advantage mean that you should undertake everything on your own? Why or why not?

6. What criteria would you use to determine which of two workers has a comparative advantage in performing a task?

7. Why does comparative advantage matter more than absolute advantage for trade?

8. What factors are most important for economic growth?

STUDY PROBLEMS

* 1. Michael and Angelo live in a small town in Italy. They work as artists. Michael is the more productive artist. He can produce 10 small sculptures each day but only 5 paintings. Angelo can produce 6 sculptures each day but only 2 paintings.

	Output per day	
	Sculptures	Paintings
Michael	10	5
Angelo	6	2

   a. What is the opportunity cost of a painting for each artist?
   b. Based on your answer in part a, who has a comparative advantage in producing paintings?
   c. If the two men decide to specialize, who should produce the sculptures and who should produce the paintings?

* 2. The following table shows scores that a student can earn on two upcoming exams according to the amount of time devoted to study:

Hours spent studying for economics	Economics score	Hours spent studying for history	History score
10	100	0	40
8	96	2	60
6	88	4	76
4	76	6	88
2	60	8	96
0	40	10	100

   a. Plot the production possibilities frontier.
   b. Does the production possibilities frontier exhibit the law of increasing relative cost?
   c. If the student wishes to move from a grade of 60 to a grade of 88 in economics, what is the opportunity cost?

3. Think about comparative advantage when answering this question: Should your professor, who has highly specialized training in economics, take time out of his teaching schedule to mow his lawn? Defend your answer.

＊ 4. Are the following statements positive or normative?
   a. My dog weighs 75 pounds.
   b. Dogs are required by law to have rabies shots.
   c. You should take your dog to the veterinarian once a year for a check-up.
   d. Chihuahuas are cuter than bulldogs.
   e. Leash laws for dogs are a good idea because they reduce injuries.

5. How does your decision to invest in a college degree add to your capital stock? Show this on your projected production possibilities frontier for 10 years from now compared to your production possibilities frontier without a college degree.

＊ 6. Suppose that an amazing new fertilizer doubles the production of potatoes. How would this discovery affect the production possibilities frontier between potatoes and carrots? Would it now be possible to produce more potatoes *and* more carrots, or only more potatoes?

7. Suppose that a politician tells you about a plan to create two expensive but necessary programs to build more production facilities for solar power and wind power. At the same time, the politician is unwilling to cut any other programs. Use the production possibilities frontier graph below to explain if this is possible.

＊ 8. Two friends, Rachel and Joey, enjoy baking bread and making apple pies. Rachel takes 2 hours to bake a loaf of bread and 1 hour to

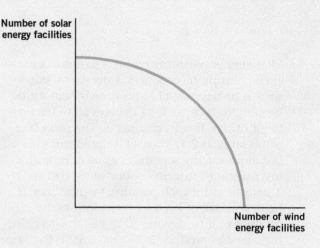

make a pie. Joey takes 4 hours to bake a loaf and 4 hours to make a pie.
   a. What are Joey's and Rachel's opportunity costs of baking bread?
   b. Who has the absolute advantage in making bread?
   c. Who has a comparative advantage in making bread?
   d. If Joey and Rachel each decides to specialize in order to increase their joint production, what should Joey produce? What should Rachel produce?
   e. The price of a loaf of bread can be expressed in terms of an apple pie. If Joey and Rachel are specializing in production and decide to trade with each other, what range of ratios of bread and apple pie would allow both parties to benefit from trade?

9. Where would you plot unemployment on a production possibilities frontier? Where would you plot full employment on a production possibilities frontier? Now suppose that in a time of crisis everyone pitches in and works much harder than usual. What happens to the production possibilities frontier?

SOLVED PROBLEMS

1.a. Michael's opportunity cost is 2 sculptures for each painting he produces. How do we know this? If he devotes all of his time to sculptures, he can produce 10. If he devotes all of his time to paintings, he can produce 5. The ratio 10:5 is the same as 2:1. Michael is therefore twice as fast at producing sculptures as he is at producing paintings. Angelo's opportunity cost is 3 sculptures for each painting he produces. If he devotes all of his time to sculptures, he can produce 6. If he devotes all of his time to paintings, he can produce 2. The ratio 6:2 is the same as 3:1.

b. For this question, we need to compare Michael's and Angelo's relative strengths. Michael produces 2 sculptures for every painting, and Angelo produces 3 sculptures for every painting, Since Michael is only twice as good at producing sculptures, his opportunity cost of producing each painting is 2 sculptures instead 3. Therefore, Michael is the low-opportunity-cost producer of paintings.

c. If they specialize, Michael should paint and Angelo should do the sculptures. You might be tempted to argue that Michael should just work alone, but if Angelo does the sculptures, it frees up Michael to concentrate on the paintings. This is what comparative advantage is all about.

2.a.

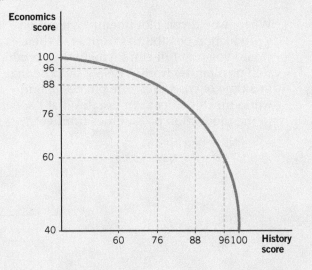

b. Yes, since it is not a straight line.

c. The opportunity cost is that the student's grade falls from 96 to 76 in history.

4.a. Positive.
b. Positive.
c. Normative.
d. Normative.
e. Normative.

6. A new fertilizer that doubles potato production will shift the entire PPF out along the potato axis but not along the carrot axis. Nevertheless, the added ability to produce more potatoes means that less acreage will have to be planted in potatoes and more land can be used to produce carrots. This makes it possible to produce more potatoes and carrots at many points along the production possibilities frontier. Figure 2.3 has a nice illustration if you are unsure how this works.

8.a. Rachel gives up 2 pies for every loaf she makes. Joey gives up 1 pie for every loaf he makes.
b. Rachel.
c. Joey.
d. Joey should make the bread and Rachel the pies.
e. Rachel makes 2 pies per loaf and Joey makes 1 pie per loaf. So any trade between 2:1 and 1:1 would benefit them both.

Graphs in Economics

Many beginning students try to understand economics without taking the time to learn the meaning and importance of graphs. This is shortsighted. You can "think" your way to a correct answer in a few cases, but the models we build and illustrate with graphs are designed to help analyze the tough questions, where your intuition can lead you astray.

Economics is fundamentally a quantitative science. That is, in many cases economists solve problems by finding a numerical answer. For instance, economists determine the unemployment rate, the rate of inflation, the growth rate of the economy, prices, costs, and much more. Economists also like to compare present-day numbers to numbers from the immediate past and historical data. Throughout your study of economics, you will find that many data-driven topics—for example, financial trends, transactions, the stock market, and other business-related variables—naturally lend themselves to graphic display. You will also find that many theoretical concepts are easier to understand when depicted visually in graphs and charts.

Economists also find that graphing can be a powerful tool when attempting to find relationships between different sets of observations. For example, the production possibilities frontier model we presented earlier in this chapter involved the relationship between the production of pizzas and wings. The graphical presentations made this relationship, the trade-off between pizzas and wings, much more vivid.

In this appendix, we begin with simple graphs, or visuals, involving a single variable and then move to graphs that consist of two variables. Taking a few moments to read this material will help you learn economics with less effort and with greater understanding.

Graphs That Consist of One Variable

There are two common ways to display data with one variable: bar graphs and pie charts. A **variable** is a quantity that can take on more than one value. Let's look at the market share of the largest carbonated beverage companies. Figure 2A.1 shows the data in a bar graph. On the vertical axis is the market share held by each firm. On the horizontal axis are the three largest firms (Coca-Cola, Pepsi, and Dr. Pepper Snapple) and the separate category for the remaining firms, called "Others." Coca-Cola Co. has the largest market share at 42%, followed by PepsiCo Inc. at 30% and Dr. Pepper Snapple at 16%. The

A **variable** is a quantity that can take on more than one value.

height of each firm's bar represents its market share percentage. The combined market share of the other firms in the market is 12%.

We illustrate the same data from the beverage industry on a pie chart in Figure 2A.2. Now the market share is expressed as the size of the pie slice for each firm.

FIGURE 2A.1

Bar Graphs

Each firm's market share in the beverage industry is represented by the height of the bar.

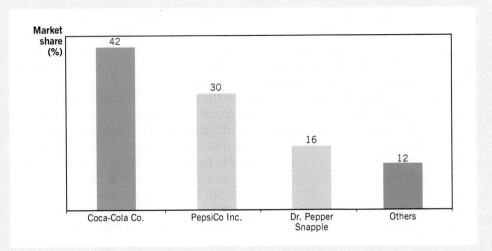

FIGURE 2A.2

Pie Chart

Each firm's market share in the beverage industry is represented by the size of the pie slice.

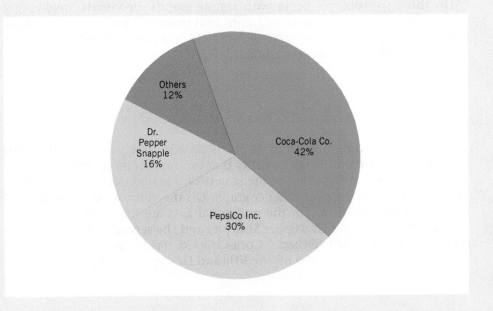

Advice on When to Use a Bar Graph or a Pie Chart

The information in a bar graph and a pie chart is the same, so does it matter which visualization you use? Bar graphs are particularly good for comparing sizes or quantities, while pie charts are generally better for illustrating proportions. However, there is an episode from *How I Met Your Mother* where Marshall says, "Here's a pie chart that shows the bars I like to go to, and here's a bar chart that shows my favorite pies." His point is that it doesn't really matter which visualization you use; what matters is how the audience sees your graph or chart.

Time-Series Graphs

A time-series graph displays information about a single variable across time. For instance, if you want to show how the rate of inflation has varied over a certain period of time, you could list the annual inflation rates in a lengthy table, or you could illustrate each point as part of a time series in a graph. Graphing the points makes it possible to quickly determine when inflation was at its highest and lowest without having to scan through the entire table. Figure 2A.3 illustrates this point.

Graphs That Consist of Two Variables

Sometimes, understanding graphs requires you to visualize relationships between two economic variables. Each variable is plotted on a coordinate system, or two-dimensional grid. The coordinate system allows us to map a

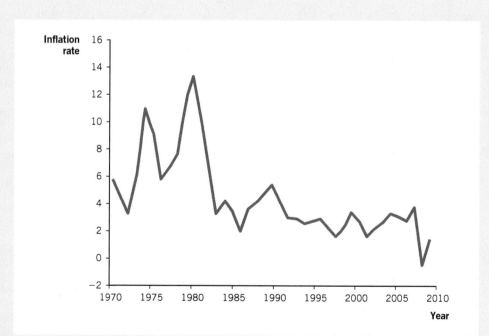

FIGURE 2A.3

Time-Series Graph

In a time-series graph, you immediately get a sense of when the inflation rate was highest and lowest, the trend through time, and the amount of volatility in the data.

series of ordered pairs that show how the two variables relate to each other. For instance, suppose that we examine the relationship between the amount of lemonade sold and the air temperature, as shown in Figure 2A.4.

The air temperature is graphed on the *x* axis (horizontal) and cups of lemonade sold on the *y* axis (vertical). Within each ordered pair (*x,y*), the first value, *x*, represents the value along the *x* axis and the second value, *y*, represents the value along the *y* axis. For example, at point A, the value of *x*, or the temperature, is 0 and the value of *y*, or the amount of lemonade sold, is also 0. No one would want to buy lemonade when the temperature is that low. At point B, the value of *x*, the air temperature, is 50 degrees and *y*, the number of cups of lemonade sold, is 10. By the time we reach point C, the temperature is 70 degrees and the amount of lemonade sold is 30 cups. Finally, at point D, the temperature has reached 90 degrees and 60 cups of lemonade are sold.

The type of graph you see in Figure 2A.4 is known as a **scatterplot**; it shows the individual (*x,y*) points in a coordinate system. Note that in this example the amount of lemonade sold rises as the temperature increases. When the two variables move together in the same direction, we say that there is a **positive correlation** between them. Conversely, if we graph the relationship between hot chocolate sales and temperature, we find that they move in opposite directions; as the temperature goes down, hot chocolate consumption goes up (see Figure 2A.5). This data reveals a **negative correlation**; it occurs when two variables, such as hot chocolate and temperature, move in opposite directions. Since economists are ultimately interested in using models and graphs to make predictions and test theories, the coordinate system makes both positive and negative correlations easy to observe.

Figure 2A.5 illustrates the difference between a positive correlation and a negative correlation. Figure 2A.5a uses the same information as Figure 2A.4. When the temperature increases, the quantity of lemonade sold increases as

A scatterplot
is a graph that shows individual (x,y) points.

Positive correlation
occurs when two variables move in the same direction.

Negative correlation
occurs when two variables move in the opposite direction.

FIGURE 2A.4

Plotting Points in a Coordinate System

Within each ordered pair (*x,y*), the first value, *x*, represents the value along the *x* axis and the second value, *y*, represents the value along the *y* axis. The combination of all the (*x,y*) pairs is known as a scatterplot.

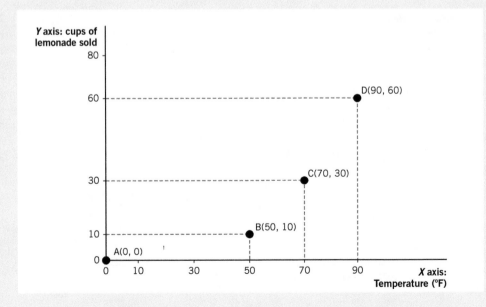

well. However, in 2A.5b we have a very different set of ordered pairs. Now, as the temperature increases, the quantity of hot chocolate sold falls. This can be seen by starting with point E, where the temperature is 32 degrees and hot chocolate consumption is 60 cups. At point F, the temperature rises to 50 degrees, but hot chocolate consumption falls to 30 cups. Finally, at point G the temperature is 70 degrees and hot chocolate consumption is down to 10 cups. The green line connecting points E–G illustrates the negative correlation between hot chocolate consumption and temperature, since the line is downward sloping. This contrasts with the positive correlation in Figure 2A.5a, where lemonade consumption rises from point B to point D and the line is upward sloping.

The Slope of a Curve

A key element in any graph is the **slope**, or the rise along the y axis (vertical) divided by the run along the x axis (horizontal). The *rise* is the amount that the vertical distance changes. The *run* is the amount that the horizontal distance changes.

$$\text{slope} = \frac{\text{change in } y}{\text{change in } x}$$

Slope

refers to the change in the rise along the y axis (vertical) divided by the change in the run along the x axis (horizontal).

FIGURE 2A.5

Positive and Negative Correlations

Panel (a) displays the positive relationship, or correlation, between lemonade consumption and higher temperatures. Panel (b) displays the negative relationship, or correlation, between hot chocolate consumption and higher temperatures.

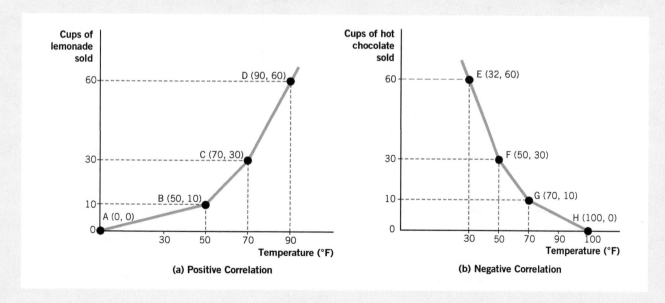

A slope can take on a positive, negative, or zero value. A slope of zero—a straight line—indicates that there is no change in *y* for a given change in *x*. However, that result is not very interesting. The slope can be positive, as it is in Figure 2A.5a, or negative, as it is in 2A.5b. Figure 2A.6 highlights the changes in *x* and *y* between the points on Figure 2A.5. (The change in a variable is often notated with a Greek delta symbol, Δ.)

In Figure 2A.6a, the slope from point B to point C is

$$\text{slope} = \frac{\text{change in } y}{\text{change in } x} = \frac{(30 - 10) \text{ or } 20}{(70 - 50) \text{ or } 20} = 1$$

All of the slopes in Figure 2A.6 are tabulated in Table 2A.1.

Each of the slopes in Figure 2A.6a is positive, and the values slowly increase from 0.2 to 1.5 as you move along the curve from point A to point D—see Table 2.A1a. However, in Figure 2A.6b, the slopes are negative as you move along the curve from E to H—see Table 2.A1b. An upward, or positive, slope indicates a positive correlation, while a downward, or negative, slope indicates a negative correlation.

FIGURE 2A.6

Positive and Negative Slopes

Notice that in both panels the slope changes values from point to point. Because of this we say that the relationships are nonlinear. In (a), as you move along the curve from point A to point D, the slopes are positive. However, in (b) the slopes are negative as you move along the curve from E to H. An upward, or positive, slope indicates a positive correlation, while a negative slope indicates a negative correlation.

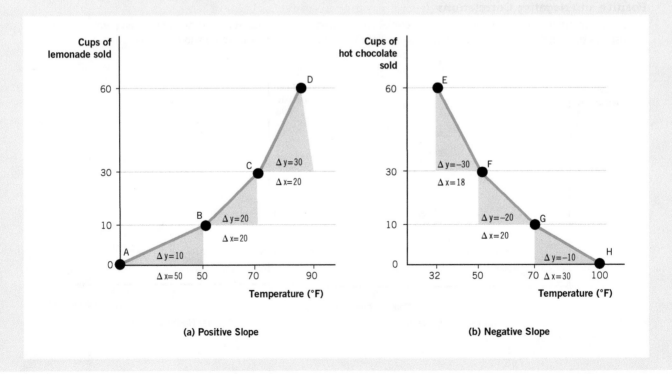

(a) Positive Slope

(b) Negative Slope

TABLE 2A.1

Positive and Negative Slopes

(a)		(b)	
Points	Slope	Points	Slope
A to B	0.2	E to F	−1.7
B to C	1.0	F to G	−1.0
C to D	1.5	G to H	−0.3

Notice that in both panels of Figure 2A.6 the slope changes values from point to point. Because of this, we say that the relationships are *nonlinear*. The slope tells us something about how responsive consumers are to changes in temperature. Consider the movement from point A to point B in Figure 2A.6a. The change in *y* is 10, while the change in *x* is 50 and the slope (10/50) is 0.2. Since zero indicates no change and 0.2 is close to zero, we can say that lemonade customers are not very responsive as the temperature rises from 0 to 50 degrees. However, they are much more responsive from point C to point D, when the temperature rises from 70 to 90 degrees. At this point, lemonade consumption—the change in *y*—rises from 30 to 60 cups and the slope is now 1.5. The strength of the positive relationship is much stronger, and as a result the curve is much steeper, or more vertical. This contrasts with the movement from point A to point B, where the curve is flatter, or more horizontal.

The same analysis can be applied to Figure 2A.6b. Consider the movement from point E to point F. The change in *y* is −30, the change in *x* is 18, and the slope is −1.7. This value represents a strong negative relationship, so we would say that hot chocolate customers were quite responsive; as the temperature rose from 32 to 50 degrees, they cut their consumption of hot chocolate by 30 cups. However, hot chocolate customers are not very responsive from point G to point H, where the temperature rises from 70 to 100 degrees. In this case, consumption falls from 10 to 0 cups and the slope is −0.3. The strength of the negative relationship is much weaker (closer to zero) and, as a result, the line is much flatter, or more horizontal. This contrasts with the movement from point E to point F, where the curve was steeper, or more vertical.

Formulas for the Area of a Rectangle and a Triangle

Sometimes, economists interpret graphs by examining the area of different sections below a curve. Consider the demand for Bruegger's bagels shown in Figure 2A.7. The demand curve has a downward slope, which tells us that when the price of bagels falls, consumers will buy more bagels. But this curve also can tell us about the revenue the seller receives, shown by the green rectangle. One of the most important considerations for the firm is how much money it receives from sales of its product. In this case, the sale price of each bagel is $0.60 and Bruegger's sells 4,000 bagels each week. We can illustrate the total amount Bruegger's takes in by shading the area bounded by the number of sales and the price. In addition, we can identify the benefit consumers receive from purchasing bagels. This is shown by the blue triangle. Since many buyers are willing to pay more than $0.60 per bagel, we can visualize the "surplus" that consumers get from Bruegger's Bagels by highlighting the blue triangular area under the blue line and above $0.60.

To calculate the area of a rectangle, we use the formula:

$$\text{Area of a rectangle} = \text{height} \times \text{base}$$

In Figure 2A.7, the green rectangle is the amount of revenue that Bruegger's Bagels receives when it charges $0.60. The total revenue is $0.60 × 4,000, or $2,400.

To calculate the area of a triangle, we use the formula:

$$\text{Area of a triangle} = 1/2 \times \text{height} \times \text{base}$$

In Figure 2A.7, the blue triangle represents the amount of surplus consumers get from buying bagels. The amount of consumer surplus is 1/2 × $0.60 × $4,000, or $1,200.

Cautions in Interpreting Numerical Graphs

In Chapter 2, we utilized *ceteris paribus*, or the condition of holding everything else around us constant while analyzing a specific relationship. Suppose that you omitted an important part of the relationship. What effect would this have on your ability to use graphs as an illustrative tool? Consider the

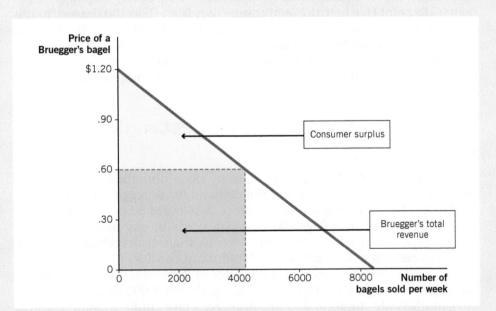

FIGURE 2A.7

Working with Rectangles and Triangles

We can determine the area of the green rectangle by multiplying the height by the base. This gives us $0.60 × 4,000, or $2,400 for the total revenue earned by Bruegger's Bagels. We can determine the area of a triangle by using the formula 1/2 × height × base. This gives us 1/2 × $0.60 × 4,000, or $1,200 for the area of consumer surplus.

relationship between lemonade consumption and bottles of suntan lotion. The graph of the two variables would look something like Figure 2A.8.

Looking at Figure 2A.8, you would not necessarily know that something is wrong. However, when you stop to think about the relationship, you quickly recognize that the result is deceptive. Since the slope is positive, the graph

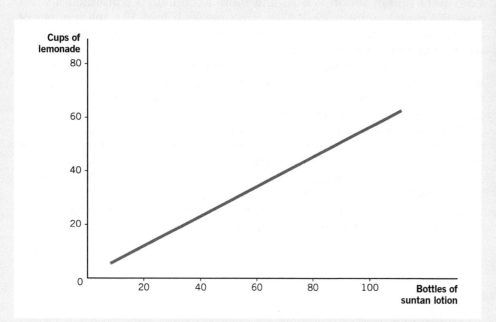

FIGURE 2A.8

Graph with an Omitted Variable

What looks like a strongly positive correlation is misleading. The demand for lemonade and suntan lotion rises because the temperature rises, so the correlation between lemonade and suntan lotion use is deceptive, not informative.

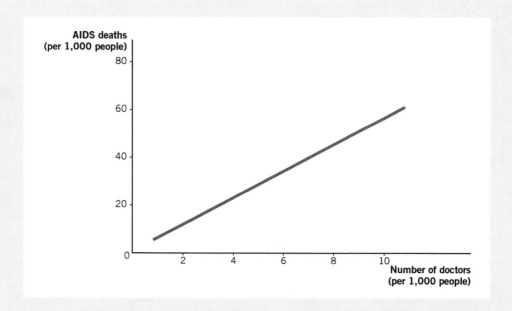

FIGURE 2A.9

Reverse Causality and an Omitted Variable

At a quick glance, this figure should strike you as odd. AIDS deaths are associated with having more doctors in the area. But the doctors are there to help and treat people, not harm them. This is an example of reverse causation.

Causality
occurs when one variable influences the other.

Reverse causation
occurs when causation is incorrectly assigned among associated events.

indicates that there is a positive correlation between the number of bottles of suntan lotion used and the amount of lemonade people drink. At first glance this seems reasonable, since we associate suntan lotion and lemonade with summer activities. But the association is not **causal**, occurring when one variable influences the other. Using more suntan lotion does not cause people to drink more lemonade. It just so happens that when it is hot outside, more suntan lotion is used and more lemonade is consumed. In this case, the causal factor is heat! The graph makes it look like the number of people using suntan lotion affects the amount of lemonade being consumed, when in fact they are not directly related.

Another possible mistake is known as **reverse causation**, which occurs when causation is incorrectly assigned among associated events. Suppose that in an effort to fight the AIDS epidemic in Africa, a research organization notes the correlation shown in Figure 2A.9.

After looking at the data, it is clear that as the number of doctors per 1,000 people goes up, so do rates of death from AIDS. The research organization puts out a press release claiming that doctors are responsible for increasing AIDS deaths, and the media hypes the discovery. But hold on! Maybe there happen to be more doctors in areas with high incidences of AIDS because that's where they are most needed. Coming to the correct conclusion about the data requires that we do more than simply look at the correlation.

CONCEPTS YOU SHOULD KNOW

causality (p. 00)   reverse causation (p. 00)   variable (p. 00)
negative correlation (p. 00)   scatterplot (p. 00)
positive correlation (p. 00)   slope (p. 00)

STUDY PROBLEMS

1. The following table provides the price and the quantity demanded of apples (per week).

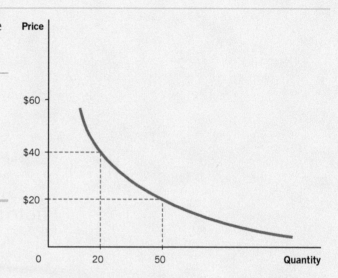

Price per Apple	Quantity Demanded
$0.25	10
0.50	7
0.75	4
1.00	2
1.25	1
1.50	0

   a. Plot the data provided in the table into a graph.
   b. Is the relationship between the price of apples and the quantity demanded negative or positive?

* 2. In the following graph, calculate the value of the slope if the price rises from $20 to $40.

3. Explain the logical error in the following sentence: "As ice cream sales increase, the number of people who drown increases sharply. Therefore, ice cream causes drowning."

SOLVED PROBLEMS

2. The slope is calculated by using the formula:

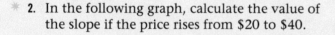

$$\text{slope} = \frac{\text{change in } y}{\text{change in } x} = 20/-30 = -0.6667$$

Photo to come

The Role of
MARKETS

CHAPTER

3 | The Market at Work: Supply and Demand

Demand matters more than supply.

What do Starbucks, Nordstrom, and Microsoft have in common? If you guessed that they all have headquarters in Seattle, that's true. But even

MIS CONCEPTION

more interesting is that each company supplies a product much in demand by consumers. Starbucks supplies coffee from coast to coast and seems to be everywhere someone

wants a cup of coffee. Nordstrom, a giant retailer with hundreds of department stores, supplies fashion apparel to meet a broad spectrum of individual demand, from the basics to designer collections. Microsoft supplies software for customers all over the world. Demand for Microsoft products has made large fortunes for founder Bill Gates and the other investors in the company.

Notice the two recurring words in the previous paragraph: "supply" and "demand". These words are consistently used by economists when describing how an economy like ours functions. Students often think that demand matters more than supply. Since we have much more experience as buyers than as sellers, our first instinct is to wonder how much something costs to buy rather than how much it costs to produce. This one-sided impression of the market undermines our ability to fully appreciate how prices are determined. To help correct this misconception, this chapter describes how markets work and the nature of competition. To shed light on the process, we will introduce the formal model of demand and supply. We will begin by looking at demand and supply separately. Then we will combine them to see how they interact to establish the market price and determine how much is produced.

Black Friday crush at Target.

BIG QUESTIONS

* ✳ **What are the fundamentals of markets?**
* ✳ **How is demand determined?**
* ✳ **What determines supply?**
* ✳ **What happens when both supply and demand shift?**

What Are the Fundamentals of Markets?

In a market economy, resources are allocated among households and firms with little or no government interference.

Markets bring trading partners together to create order out of chaos. Companies supply goods and services, and customers want to obtain the goods and services that companies supply. In a **market economy**, resources are allocated among households and firms with little or no government interference. Adam Smith, the founder of modern economics, described the dynamic best: "It is not from the benevolence of the butcher, the brewer, or the baker, that we expect our dinner, but from their regard to their own interest." In other words, producers earn a living by selling the products that consumers want. Consumers are also motivated by self-interest; they must decide how to use their money to select the goods that they need or want the most. This process, which Adam Smith called the *invisible hand*, guides resources to their highest-valued use.

The exchange of goods and services in a market economy happens through prices that are established in markets. Those prices change according to the level of demand for a product and how much is supplied. For instance, hotel rates near Disney World are reduced in the fall when demand is low, and they peak in March near the week of Easter when spring break occurs. If spring break takes you to a ski resort, instead, you will find lots of company and high prices. But if you are looking for an outdoor adventure during the summer, ski resorts have plenty of lodging available at great rates.

Similarly, many parents know how hard it is to find a reasonably priced

Peak season is expensive . . .

hotel room in a college town on graduation weekend. Likewise, a pipeline break or unsettled political conditions in the Middle East can disrupt the supply of oil and cause the price of gasoline to spike overnight. When higher gas prices continue over a period of time, consumers respond by changing their driving habits or buying more fuel-efficient cars.

Why does all of this happen? Supply and demand tell the story. We will begin our exploration of supply and demand by looking at where they interact—in markets. The degree of control over the market price is the distinguishing feature between *competitive markets* and *imperfect markets*.

Competitive Markets

Buyers and sellers of a specific good or service come together to form a market. Formally, a market is a collection of buyers and sellers of a particular product or service. The buyers create the demand for the product, while the sellers produce the supply. It is the interaction of

. . . but off-season is a bargain.

the buyers and sellers in a market that establishes the price and the quantity produced of a particular good or the amount of a service offered.

Markets exist whenever goods and services are exchanged. Some markets are online, and others operate in traditional "brick and mortar" stores. Pike Place Market in Seattle is a collection of markets spread across nine acres. For over a hundred years, it has brought together buyers and sellers of fresh, organic, and specialty foods. Since there are a number of buyers and sellers for each type of product, we say that the markets at Pike Place are *competitive*. A **competitive market** is one in which there are so many buyers and sellers that each has only a small impact on the market price and output. In fact, the impact is so small that it is negligible.

At Pike Place Market, like other local produce markets, the goods sold are similar from vendor to vendor. Because each buyer and seller is small relative to the whole market, no one individual has any influence over the market price. These two characteristics—similar goods and many participants—create a highly competitive market in which the price and quantity sold are determined by the market rather than by any one person or business.

A **competitive market** exists when there are so many buyers and sellers that each has only a small impact on the market price and output.

To understand how this works, let's take a look at sales of salmon at Pike Place Market. On any given day, dozens of vendors sell salmon at this market. So, if a single vendor is absent or runs out of salmon, the quantity supplied that day will not be significantly altered—the remaining sellers will have no trouble filling the void. The same is true for those buying salmon—customers will have no trouble finding

One of many vendors at Pike Place Market

salmon at the remaining vendors. Whether a particular salmon buyer decides to show up on a given day makes little difference when hundreds of buyers visit the market each day. No single buyer or seller has any appreciable influence over the price that prevails in the salmon market. As a result, the market for salmon at Pike Place Market is a competitive one.

Imperfect Markets

An **imperfect market**
is one in which either
the buyer or the seller has an
influence on the market price.

A **monopoly**
exists when a single com-
pany supplies the entire
market for a particular good
or service.

Markets are not always competitive, though. An **imperfect market** is one in which either the buyer or the seller has an influence on the market price. For example, the Empire State Building affords a unique view of Manhattan. Not surprisingly, the cost of taking the elevator to the top of the building is not cheap. But many customers buy the tickets anyway because they have decided that the view is worth the price. The managers of the Empire State Building can set a high price for tickets because there is no other place in New York City with such a great view. From this, we see that when sellers produce goods and services that are different from their competitors', they gain some control, or leverage, over the price that they charge. The more unusual the product being sold, the more control the seller has over the price. When a seller has some control over the price, we say that the market is imperfect. Specialized products, such as popular video games, front-row concert tickets, or dinner reservations at a trendy restaurant, give the seller substantial pricing power.

In between the highly competitive environment at the Pike Place Market and markets characterized by a lack of competition, such as the Empire State Building with its unique view, there are many other varieties of markets. Some, like the market for fast-food restaurants, are highly competitive but sell products that are not identical. Other businesses—for example, Microsoft—function like *monopolies*. A **monopoly** exists when a single company supplies the entire market for a particular good or service. We'll talk a lot more about different market structures such as monopoly in later chapters. But even in imperfect markets, the forces of supply and demand have a significant influence on producer and consumer behavior. For the time being, we'll keep our analysis focused on supply and demand in competitive markets.

How Is Demand Determined?

Demand exists when an individual or a group wants something badly enough to pay or a trade for it. How much an individual or a group actually

The Empire State Building has the best view in New York City.

PRACTICE WHAT YOU KNOW

Markets and the Nature of Competition

Question: Which of the following are competitive markets?

1. Gas stations at a busy interstate exit
2. A furniture store in an isolated small town
3. A fresh produce stand at a farmer's market

Answers

Is this a competitive market?

1. Because each gas station sells the same product and competes for the same customers, they often charge the same price. This is a competitive market. However, gas stations also differentiate themselves by offering many conveniences such as fast food, clean restrooms, ATM machines, and so forth. The result is that individual stations have some market power.

2. Residents would have to travel a significant distance to find another store. This allows the small-town store to charge more than other furniture stores. The furniture store has some monopoly power. This is not a competitive market.

3. Since consumers can buy fresh produce in season from many stands at a farmer's market, individual vendors have very little market pricing power. They must charge the same price as other vendors in order to attract customers. This is a competitive market.

---

buys will depend on the price. In economics, the amount of a good or service purchased at the current price is known as the **quantity demanded**.

When the price of a good increases, consumers often respond by purchasing less of the good or buying something else. For instance, many consumers who would buy salmon at $5.00 per pound would likely buy something else if the price rose to $20.00 per pound. Therefore, as price goes up, quantity demanded goes down. Similarly, as price goes down, quantity demanded goes up. This inverse relationship between the price and the quantity demanded is referred to as the *law of demand*. The **law of demand** states that, *all other things being equal, the quantity demanded falls when the price rises, and the quantity demanded rises when the price falls*. This holds true over a wide range of goods and settings.

The quantity demanded is the amount of a good or service that buyers are willing and able to purchase at the current price.

The law of demand states that, all other things being equal, quantity demanded falls when prices rise, and rises when prices fall.

The Demand Curve

A **demand schedule** is a table that shows the relationship between the price of a good and the quantity demanded.

A **demand curve** is a graph of the relationship between the prices in the demand schedule and the quantity demanded at those prices.

We can create a table that lists various prices of a good and the number of people willing to purchase that good at any given price. A table that shows the relationship between the price of a good and the quantity demanded is known as a **demand schedule**. Table 3.1 shows Meredith Grey's hypothetical demand schedule for salmon. When the price is $20.00 or more per pound, Meredith will not purchase any salmon. However, below $20.00 the amount that Meredith purchases is inversely related to the price. For instance, at a price of $10.00, Meredith's quantity demanded is 4 pounds per month. If the price rises to $12.50 per pound, she demands 3 pounds. Every time the price increases, Meredith buys less salmon. In contrast, every time the price falls, she buys more. If the price falls to zero, Meredith would demand 8 pounds. That is, even if the salmon is free, there is a limit to her demand because she would grow tired of eating the same thing.

The numbers in Meredith's demand schedule from Table 3.1 are plotted on a graph in Figure 3.1, known as a *demand curve*. A **demand curve** is a graph of the relationship between the prices in the demand schedule and the quantity demanded at those prices. For simplicity, the demand "curve" is often drawn as a straight line. Economists always place the independent variable, which is the price, on the y axis, and the dependent variable, which is the quantity demanded, on the x axis. The relationship between the price and the quantity demanded produces a downward-sloping curve. In Figure 3.1, we see that as the price rises from $0.00 to $20.00 along the y axis, the quantity demanded decreases from 8 to 0 pounds along the x axis.

Market Demand

So far, we have studied individual demand, but markets comprise many different buyers. In this section, we will examine the collective demand of all of the buyers in a given market.

TABLE 3.1

Meredith's Demand Schedule for Salmon

Price of salmon (per pound)	Pounds of salmon demanded (per month)
$20.00	0
17.50	1
15.00	2
12.50	3
10.00	4
7.50	5
5.00	6
2.50	7
0.00	8

FIGURE 3.1

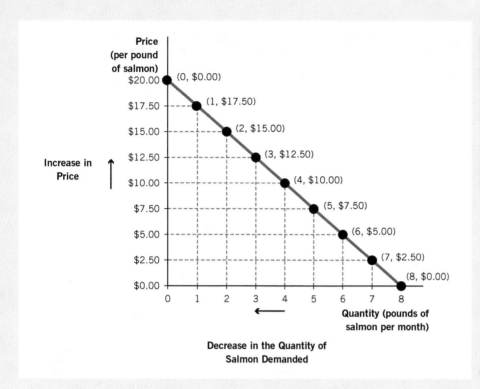

Meredith's Demand Curve for Salmon

Meredith's demand curve for salmon plots the data from Table 3.1. When the price of salmon is $10.00 per pound, she buys 4 pounds. If the price rises to $12.50 per pound, Meredith reduces the quantity that she buys to 3 pounds. The figure illustrates the law of demand by showing a negative relationship between price and the quantity demanded.

The **market demand** is the sum of all the individual quantities demanded by each buyer in a market at each price. During a typical day at Pike Place Market, over 100 individuals buy salmon. However, to make our analysis simpler, let's assume that our market consists of only two buyers, Derek and Meredith, each of whom enjoys eating salmon. Figure 3.2 shows individual demand schedules for the two people in this market, a combined market demand schedule, and the corresponding graphs. At a price of $10.00 per pound, Derek buys 2 a month, while Meredith buys 4 pounds. To determine the market demand curve, we add Derek's 2 pounds to Meredith's 4 for a total of 6. As you can see in the table within Figure 3.2, by adding Derek and Meredith's demand we arrive at the total (that is, combined) market demand. The law of demand is shown on any demand curve with movements up or down the curve that reflect the effect of a change in price on the quantity demanded for the good or service. Only a change in price can cause a movement along a demand curve.

Market demand is the sum of all the individual quantities demanded by each buyer in the market at each price.

Shifts in the Demand Curve

We have examined the relationship between price and quantity demanded. This relationship, described by the law of demand, shows us that when price changes, consumers respond by altering the amount they purchase. But in addition to price, many other variables influence how much of a good or service is purchased. For instance, news about the possible risks or benefits associated with the consumption of a good or service can change overall demand.

FIGURE 3.2

Calculating Market Demand

To calculate the market demand for salmon, we add Derek's demand and Meredith's demand.

Price of salmon (per pound)	Derek's demand (per month)	Meredith's demand (per month)	Combined market demand
$20.00	0	0	0
$17.50	0	1	1
$15.00	1	2	3
$12.50	1	3	4
$10.00	2	4	6
$7.50	2	5	7
$5.00	3	6	9
$2.50	3	7	10
$0.00	4	8	12

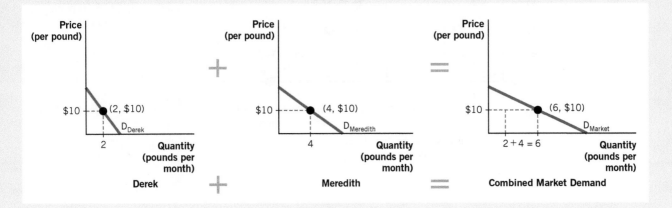

Suppose that the government issues a nationwide safety warning that cautions against eating cantaloupe because of a recent discovery of the bacteria *Listeria* bacteria in some melons. The government warning would cause consumers to buy fewer cantaloupes at any given price, and overall demand would decline. Looking at Figure 3.3, we see that an overall decline in demand will cause the entire demand curve to shift to the left of the original curve (which represents 6 cantaloupes), from D_1 to D_2. Note that though the price remains at $5 per cantaloupe, demand has moved from 6 melons to 3. Figure 3.3 also shows what does *not* cause a shift in demand curve: the price. The orange arrow along D_1 indicates that the quantity demanded will rise or fall in response to a price change. *A price change causes a movement along a given demand curve, but it cannot cause a shift in the demand curve.*

A decrease in overall demand causes the demand curve to shift to the left. What about when a variable causes overall demand to increase? Suppose that the press has just announced the results of a medical study indicating that cantaloupe contains a natural substance that lowers cholesterol. Because of the newly discovered health benefits of cantaloupe, overall demand for it would increase. This increase in demand would shift the demand curve to the right, from D_1 to D_3, as Figure 3.3 shows.

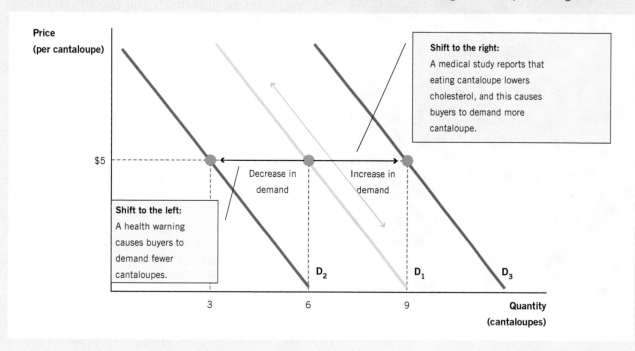

FIGURE 3.3

A Shift in the Demand Curve

When the price changes, the quantity demanded changes along the existing demand curve in the direction of the orange arrow. A shift in the demand curve, indicated by the black arrows, occurs when something other than price changes.

In the example above, we saw that demand shifted because of changes in consumers' tastes and preferences. However, there are many different variables that can shift demand. These include changes in buyers' income, the price of related goods, changes in taste and preferences, buyers,' expectations regarding the future price, and the number of buyers.

Figure 3.4 provides an overview of the variables or factors that can shift demand. The easiest way to keep all of these elements straight is to ask yourself a simple question: *Would this change cause me to buy more or less of the good?* If the change lowers your demand for the good, you shift the demand curve to the left. If the change increases your demand for the good, you shift the curve to the right.

If a new medical study indicates that eating more cantaloupe lowers cholesterol, would this finding cause a shift in demand or a slide along the demand curve?

Bill Gates does not have to worry about the relationship between income and demand. Do you?

An **Inferior good** is purchased out of necessity rather than choice.

Changes in Income

When your income goes up, you have more to spend. Assuming that prices don't change, individuals with higher incomes are able to buy more of what they want. Similarly, when your income declines, your purchasing power, or how much you can afford, falls. In either case, the amount of income you make affects your overall demand.

When economists look at how consumers spend, they often differentiate between two types of goods: *normal* and *inferior*. A consumer will buy more of a **normal good** as his or her income goes up (assuming all other factors remain constant). An example of a normal good is a meal at a restaurant. When income goes up and the demand for restaurant meals increases, the demand curve shifts to the right. Similarly, if income falls and the demand for restaurant meals goes down, the demand curve shifts to the left.

While a consumer with an increase in income may purchase more of some things, the additional purchasing power will mean that here the purchases less of other things, such as *inferior goods*. An **inferior good** is purchased out of necessity rather than choice. Examples include used cars as opposed to new cars, rooms in boarding houses as opposed to one's own apartment or house, and hamburger as opposed to filet mignon. As income goes up, consumers buy less of an inferior good because they can afford something better. Within a specific product market, you can often find examples of inferior and normal goods in the form of different brands.

The Price of Related Goods

Complements are two goods that are used together. When the price of a complementary good rises, the demand for the related good goes down.

Substitutes are two goods that are used in place of each other. When the price of a substitute good rises, the quantity demanded falls and the demand for the related good goes up.

Another factor that can shift the demand curve is the price of related goods. Certain goods directly influence the demand for other goods. These goods are known as *complements* and *substitutes*. **Complements** are two goods that are used together. **Substitutes** are two goods that are used in place of each other.

Consider this pair of complements: color ink cartridges and photo paper. You need both to print a photo in color. What happens when the price of one— say, color ink cartridges—rises? As you would expect, the quantity demanded of ink cartridges goes down. But demand for its complement, photo paper, also goes down. This is because people are not likely to use one without the other.

Substitute goods work the opposite way. When the price of a substitute good increases, the quantity demanded declines and the demand for the alternative good increases. For example, if the price of the Nintendo Wii goes up and the price of Microsoft's Xbox remains unchanged, the demand for Xbox will increase while the quantity demanded of the Wii will decline.

Changes in Tastes and Preferences

In fashion, types of apparel go in and out of style quickly. Walk into Nordstrom or another clothing retailer, and you will see that fashion changes from season to season and year to year. For instance, what do you think of Madras shorts? They were popular 20 years ago and they may be popular again now, but it is safe to assume that in a few years Madras shorts will once again go out of style. While something is popular, demand increases. As soon as it falls out of favor, you can expect demand for it to return to its former level. Tastes and preferences can change quickly, and this fluctuation alters the demand for a particular good.

Fashion faux pas, or *c'est magnifique*?

Though changes in fashion trends are usually purely subjective, other changes in preferences are often the result of new information about the goods and services that we buy. Recall our example of shifting demand for cantaloupe as the result of either the *listeria* infection or new positive medical findings. This is one example of how information can influence consumers' preferences. Contamination would cause a decrease in demand because people would no longer care to eat cantaloupe. In contrast, if people learn that eating cantaloupe lowers cholesterol, their preference for the melon will go up.

Expectations Regarding the Future Price

Have you ever waited to purchase a sweater because warm weather was right around the corner and you expected the price to come down? Conversely, have you ever purchased an airline ticket well in advance because you figured that the price would rise as the flight filled up? In both cases, expectations about the future influenced your current demand. If we expect a price to be higher tomorrow, we are likely to buy more today to beat the price increase. This leads to an increase in current demand. Likewise, if you expect a price to decline soon, you might delay your purchases to try to capitalize on a lower price in the future. An expectation of a lower price in the future will therefore decrease current demand.

The Number of Buyers

Recall that the market demand curve is the sum of all individual demand curves. Therefore, another way for the market demand to increase is for more individual buyers to enter the market. In the United States, we add 3 million people each year to our population through immigration and births. All those new people have needs and wants like the 300 million rest of us who are already here. Collectively, they add about 1% to the overall size of many existing markets on an annual basis.

The number of buyers also varies by age. Consider two markets—one for baby equipment, such as diapers, high chairs, and strollers, and the other for health care, including medicine, cancer treatments, hip replacement surgery, and nursing facilities. In countries with aging populations—for example, in Italy, where the birthrate has plummeted over several generations—the demand for baby equipment will decline and the demand for health care will expand. Therefore, demographic changes in society are another source of shifts in demand. In many markets, ranging from movie theater attendance to home ownership, population trends play an important role in determining whether the market is expanding or contracting.

What Determines Supply?

Even though we have learned a great deal about demand, our understanding of markets is incomplete without also analyzing supply. Let's start by focusing on the behavior of producers interested in selling fresh salmon at Pike Place Market.

We have seen that with demand, price and output are negatively related. With supply, however, the price level and quantity supplied are positively related. For instance, few producers would sell salmon if the market price was $2.50 per pound, but many would sell it if the price was $20.00. (At $20.00, producers earn more profit than when the price they receive is $2.50). The **quantity supplied** is the amount of a good or service that producers are willing and able to sell at the current price. Higher prices cause the quantity supplied to increase. Conversely, lower prices cause the quantity supplied to decrease.

When price increases, producers often respond by offering more for sale. As price goes down, quantity supplied also goes down. This direct relationship

The **quantity supplied** is the amount of a good or service that producers are willing and able to sell at the current price.

Factors That Shift the Demand Curve

The demand curve shifts to the left when a factor adversely affects demand. The demand curve shifts to the right when a factor positively influences demand. (*Note*: a change in price does not cause a shift. Price changes cause slides along the demand curve.)

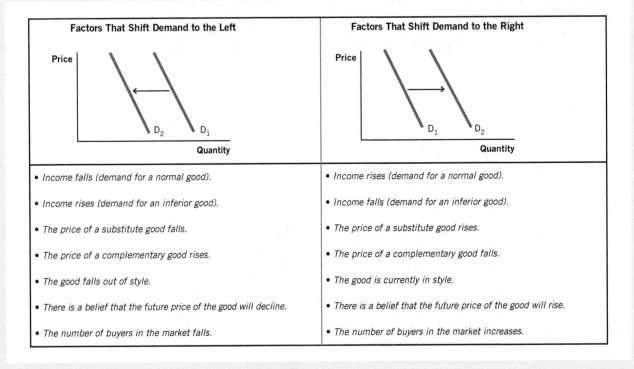

Shifting the Demand Curve

The Hudsucker Proxy

This 1994 film chronicles the introduction of the hula hoop, a toy that set off one of the greatest fads in U.S. history. According to Wham-O, the manufacturer of the hoop, when the toy was first introduced in the late 1950s over 25 million were sold in four months.

One scene from the movie clearly illustrates the difference between movements along the demand curve and a shift of the entire demand curve.

The Hudsucker Corporation has decided to sell the hula hoop for $1.79. We see the toy-store owner leaning next to the front door waiting for customers to enter. But business is slow. The movie cuts to the president of the company, played by Tim Robbins, sitting behind a big desk waiting to hear about sales of the new toy. It is not doing well. So the store lowers the price, first to $1.59, then to $1.49, and so on, until finally the hula hoop is "free with any purchase." But even this is not enough to attract consumers, so the toy-store owner throws the hula hoops into the alley behind the store.

One of the unwanted toys rolls across the street and around the block before landing at the foot of a boy who is skipping school. He picks up the hula hoop and tries it out. He is a natural. When school lets out, a throng of students rounds the corner and sees him playing with the hula hoop. Suddenly, everyone wants a hula hoop and there is a run on the toy store. Now preferences have changed, and the overall demand has increased. The hula hoop craze is born. In economic terms, we can say that the increased demand has shifted the entire demand curve to the right. The toy store responds by ordering new hula hoops and raising the price to $3.99—the new market price after the increase, or shift, in demand.

This scene reminds us that changes in price cannot shift the demand curve. Shifts in demand

How did the hula hoop craze start?

can only happen when an outside event influences human behavior. The graph below uses demand curves to show us the effect.

First part of the scene: The price drops from $1.79 to "free with any purchase." Demand does not change—we only slide downward along the demand curve (D_1), resulting in a negligible increase in the quantity demanded.

Second part of the scene: The hula hoop craze begins and kids run to the toy store. The sudden change in behavior is evidence of a change in tastes, which shifts the demand curve to the right (D_2).

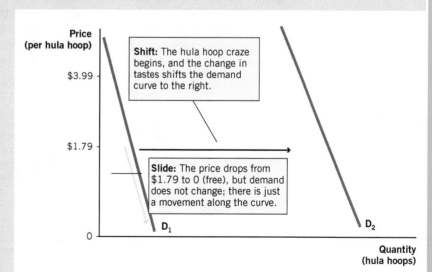

Price (per hula hoop)

$3.99

$1.79

Shift: The hula hoop craze begins, and the change in tastes shifts the demand curve to the right.

Slide: The price drops from $1.79 to 0 (free), but demand does not change; there is just a movement along the curve.

D_1 D_2

0

Quantity (hula hoops)

PRACTICE WHAT YOU KNOW

Shift or Slide?

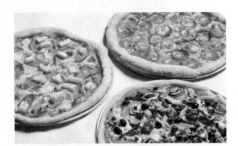 

Cheap pizza or . . .   . . . cheap drinks?

Suppose that a local pizza place likes to run a "late-night special" after 11 p.m. The owners have contacted you for some advice. One of the owners tells you, "We want to increase the demand for our pizza." He proposes two marketing ideas to accomplish this:

1. Reduce the price of large pizzas.
2. Reduce the price of a complementary good—for example, offer two half-priced bottles or cans of soda with every large pizza ordered.

Question: What will you recommend?

Answer: First, consider why "late-night specials" exist in the first place. Since most people prefer to eat dinner early in the evening, the store has to encourage late-night patrons to buy pizzas by stimulating demand. "Specials" of all sorts are used during periods of low demand when regular prices would leave the establishment largely empty.

Next, look at what the question asks. The owners want to know which option would "increase demand" more. The question is very specific; it is looking for something that will increase (or shift) demand.

Consider the first option, a reduction in the price of pizzas. Let's look at this graphically (see below). A reduction in the price of a large pizza causes a movement along the demand curve, or a change in the quantity demanded.

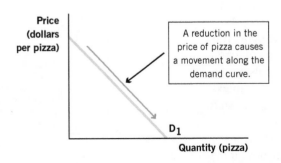

Now consider the second option, a reduction in the price of a complementary good. Let's look at this graphically (see below).

A reduction in the price of a complementary good (like soda) causes the entire demand curve to shift. This is the correct answer, since the question asks which marketing idea would increase (or shift) demand more.

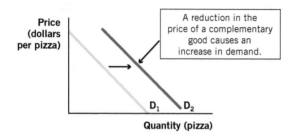

Recall that a reduction in the price of a complementary good shifts the demand curve to the right. This is the correct answer by definition! The other answer, cutting the price of pizzas, will cause an increase in the quantity demanded, or a movement along the existing demand curve.

If you move along a curve instead of shifting it, you will analyze the problem incorrectly.

between price and quantity supplied is referred to as the *law of supply*. The **law of supply** states that, all other things being equal, the quantity supplied increases when the price rises, and the quantity supplied falls when the price falls. This law holds true over a wide range of goods and settings.

The Supply Curve

A **supply schedule** is a table that shows the relationship between the price of a good and the quantity supplied. The supply schedule for salmon in Table 3.2 shows how many pounds of salmon Sol Amon, owner of Pure Food Fish, would sell each month at different prices (Pure Food Fish is a fish stand that sells all kinds of freshly caught seafood). When the market price is $20.00 per pound, Sol is willing to sell 800 pounds. At $12.50, Sol's quantity offered is 500 pounds. If the price falls to $10.00, he offers 100 fewer pounds, or 400. Every time the price falls, Sol offers less salmon. This means he is constantly adjusting the amount he offers. As the price of salmon falls, so does Sol's profit from selling it. Since Sol's livelihood depends on selling seafood, he has to find a way to compensate for the lost income. So he might offer more cod instead.

Sol and the other seafood vendors must respond to price changes by adjusting what they offer for sale in the market. This is why Sol offers more salmon when the price rises, and less salmon when the price declines.

When we plot the supply schedule in Table 3.2, we get the *supply curve* shown in Figure 3.5. A **supply curve** is a graph of the relationship between the prices in the supply schedule and the quantity supplied at those prices. As you can see in Figure 3.5, this relationship produces an upward-sloping curve.

The **law of supply** states that, all other things being equal, the quantity supplied of a good rises when the price of the good rises, and falls when the price of the good falls.

A **supply schedule** is a table that shows the relationship between the price of a good and the quantity supplied.

A **supply curve** is a graph of the relationship between the prices in the supply schedule and the quantity supplied at those prices.

TABLE 3.2	
Pure Food Fish's Supply Schedule for Salmon	
Price of salmon (per pound)	**Pounds of salmon supplied (per month)**
$20.00	800
$17.50	700
$15.00	600
$12.50	500
$10.00	400
$ 7.50	300
$ 5.00	200
$ 2.50	100
$ 0.00	0

Sellers are more willing to supply the market when prices are high, since this generates more profits for the business. The upward-sloping curve means that the slope of the supply curve is positive, which illustrates a direct, or positive, relationship. For instance, when the price of salmon increases from $10.00 to $12.50 per pound, Pure Food Fish will increase the quantity it supplies to the market from 400 to 500 pounds.

FIGURE 3.5

Pure Food Fish's Supply Curve for Salmon

Pure Food Fish's supply curve for salmon plots the data from Table 3.3. When the price of salmon is $10.00 per pound, Pure Food Fish supplies 400 pounds. If the price rises to $12.50 per pound, Pure Food Fish increases the quantity that it supplies to 500 pounds. The figure illustrates the law of supply by showing a positive relationship between price and the quantity supplied.

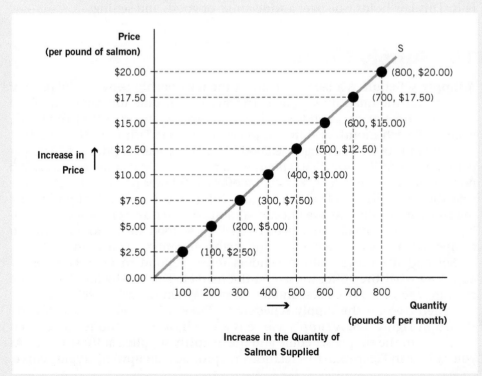

Market Supply

Sol Amon is not the only vendor selling fish at the Pike Place Market. The **market supply** is the sum of the quantities supplied by each seller in the market at each price. However, to make our analysis simpler, let's assume that our market consists of just two sellers, City Fish and Pure Food Fish, each of which sells salmon. Figure 3.6 shows supply schedules for those two fish sellers and the combined, total-market supply schedule and the corresponding graphs.

Looking at the supply schedule (the table within the figure), you can see that at a price of $10.00 per pound, City Fish supplies 100 pounds of salmon, while Pure Food Fish supplies 400. To determine the total market supply, we add City Fish's 100 pounds to Pure Food Fish's 400 for a total market supply of 500.

Market supply
is the sum of the quantities supplied by each seller in the market at each price.

Shifts in the Supply Curve

We have seen that the relationship between price and quantity supplied follows the law of supply: whenever the price changes, producers respond by altering the amount they supply. Yet in reality many variables influence how much is

FIGURE 3.6

Calculating Market Supply
Market supply is calculated by adding together the amount supplied by individual vendors. Each vendor's supply, listed in the second and third columns of the table, is illustrated graphically below. The total supply, shown in the last column of the table, is illustrated in the Combined Market Supply graph below.

Price of salmon (per pound)	City Fish's supply (pounds of salmon)	Pure Food Fish's supply (pounds of salmon)	Combined Market supply (pounds of salmon)
$20.00	200	800	1000
$17.50	175	700	875
$15.00	150	600	750
$12.50	125	500	625
$10.00	100	400	500
$7.50	75	300	375
$5.00	50	200	250
$2.50	25	100	125
$0.00	0	0	0

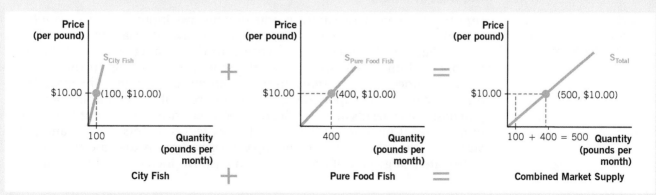

The first Starbucks opened in 1971 in Pike Place Market.

supplied. When a variable other than the price changes, the entire supply curve shifts. For instance, suppose that food scientists at Starbucks discover a new way to brew a richer coffee at half the cost. The new process would increase the company's profits because its costs of supplying a cup of coffee would go down. The increased profits as a result of lower costs motivate Starbucks to sell more coffee and open new stores. Therefore, overall supply increases. Looking at Figure 3.7, we see that the supply curve shifts to the right of the original curve, from S_1 to S_2. Note that the retail price of coffee ($3 per cup) has not changed. When we shift the curve, we assume that price is constant and that something else has changed. In this case, the new brewing process, which has reduced the cost of producing coffee, has stimulated additional supply.

We have just seen that an increase in supply causes the supply curve to shift to the right. But what happens when a variable causes supply to decrease? Suppose that a hurricane devastates the coffee crop in Colombia and reduces world supply by 10% for that year. There is no way to make up for the destroyed coffee crop, and for the rest of the year at least, the quantity of coffee supplied will be less than the previous year. This decrease in supply shifts the supply curve in Figure 3.7 to the left, from S_1 to S_3.

Many variables can shift supply, but Figure 3.7 also reminds us of what does *not* cause a shift in supply: the price. Recall that price is the variable that causes the supply curve to slope upward. The orange arrow along S_1 indicates that the quantity supplied will rise or fall in response to a price change. *A price change causes a movement along the supply curve, not a shift in the curve.*

Factors that shift the supply curve include the cost of inputs, changes in technology and the production process, taxes and subsidies, the number of firms in the industry, and price expectations. Figure 3.8 provides an overview of these variables that shift the supply curve. The easiest way to keep them all straight is to ask yourself a simple question: *Would the change cause a business to produce more or less of the good?* If the change would lower the business's willingness to supply the good or service, the supply curve shifts to the left. If the change would increase the business's willingness to supply the good or service, the supply curve shifts to the right.

The Cost of Inputs

Inputs
are resources used in the production process.

Inputs are resources used in the production process. Inputs can take a number of forms and may include workers, equipment, raw materials, buildings, and capital. Each of these resources is critical to the production process. When the prices of inputs change, so does the seller's profit margin. If the cost of inputs declines, profit margins improve. Improved profit margins make the firm more willing to supply the good. So, for example, if Starbucks is able to purchase coffee beans at a significantly reduced price, it will want to supply more coffee. Conversely, higher input costs reduce profits. For instance, at Starbucks, the salaries of store employees, or baristas as they are commonly called, are a large part of the production cost. An increase in the minimum

FIGURE 3.7

A Shift in the Supply Curve

When price changes, the quantity supplied changes along the existing supply curve, illustrated here by the orange arrow. A shift in supply occurs when something other than price changes, illustrated by the black arrows.

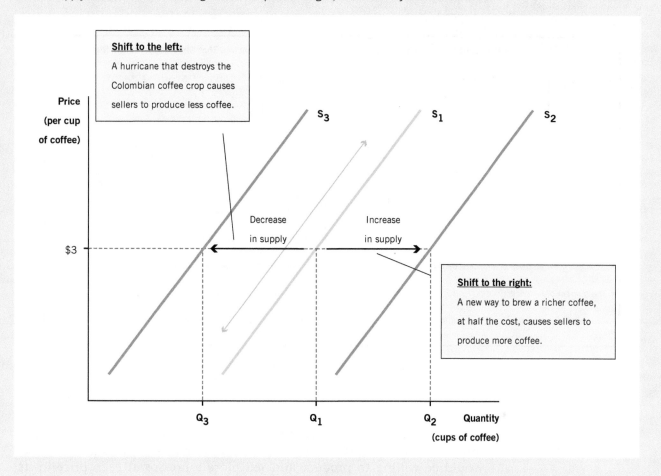

wage would require Starbucks to pay its workers more. This would raise the cost of making coffee, cut into Starbucks' profits, and make Starbucks less willing to supply coffee at the same price.

Changes in Technology or the Production Process

Technology encompasses knowledge that producers use to make their products. An improvement in technology enables a producer to increase output with the same resources or to produce a given level of output with fewer resources. For example, if a new espresso machine works twice as fast as the

FIGURE 3.8

Factors That Shift the Supply Curve

The supply curve shifts to the left when a factor negatively affects supply. The supply curve shifts to the right when a factor positively influences supply. (*Note*: a change in price does not cause a shift. Price changes cause slides along the supply curve.)

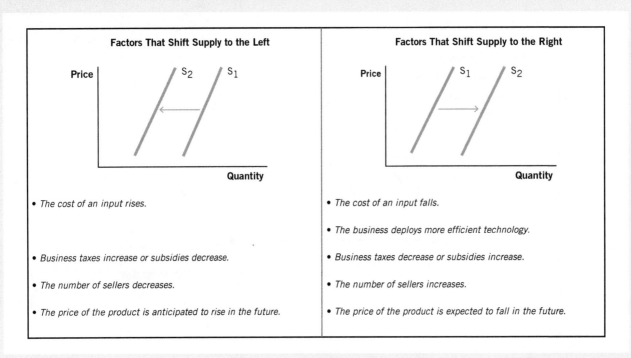

Factors That Shift Supply to the Left

- *The cost of an input rises.*
- *Business taxes increase or subsidies decrease.*
- *The number of sellers decreases.*
- *The price of the product is anticipated to rise in the future.*

Factors That Shift Supply to the Right

- *The cost of an input falls.*
- *The business deploys more efficient technology.*
- *Business taxes decrease or subsidies increase.*
- *The number of sellers increases.*
- *The price of the product is expected to fall in the future.*

old technology, Starbucks could serve its customers more quickly, reduce long lines, and increase the number of sales it makes. As a result, Starbucks would be willing to produce and sell more espressos at each price in its established menu. In other words, if the producers of a good discover a new and improved technology or a better production process, there will be an increase in supply; the supply curve for the good will shift to the right.

Taxes and Subsidies

Taxes placed on suppliers are an added cost of doing business. For example, if property taxes are increased, this raises the cost of doing business. A firm may attempt to pass along the tax to consumers through higher prices, but this will discourage sales. In other cases, the firm will simply have to accept the taxes as an added cost of doing business. Either way, a tax makes the firm less profitable. Lower profits make the firm less willing to supply the product and, thus, shift the supply curve to the left. As a result, the overall supply declines.

The reverse is true for a subsidy, which is a payment made by the government to encourage the consumption or production of a good or service. For example, a large portion of the cost of flu shots is subsidized. The subsidized price causes an increase in the quantity demanded and increases the immunization rates, exactly as desired.

The Number of Firms in the Industry

We saw that when there were more total buyers, the demand curve shifted to the right. A similar dynamic happens with an increase in supply. Each additional firm (or seller) that enters the market increases the available supply of a good. In graphic form, the supply curve shifts to the right to reflect the increased production. By the same reasoning, if the number of firms in the industry decreases, the supply curve will shift to the left. Changes in the number of firms in a market are a regular part of business. For example, if a new pizza joint opens up nearby, more pizzas can be produced and supply expands. Conversely, if a pizza shop closes, the number of pizzas produced falls and supply contracts.

Price Expectations

A seller who expects a higher price for a product in the future may wish to delay sales until a time when it will bring a higher price. For instance, florists know that the

Baristas' wages make up a large share of the cost of selling coffee.

demand for roses spikes on Valentine's Day and Mother's Day. Because of higher demand, they can charge higher prices. In order to be able to sell more flowers during the times of peak demand, many florists work longer hours and hire temporary employees. This allows them to make more deliveries and therefore increase their ability to supply flowers while the price is high.

Likewise, the expectation of lower prices in the future will cause sellers to offer more while prices are still relatively high. This is particularly noticeable in the electronics sector where newer—and much better—products are constantly being developed and released. Sellers know that their current offerings will soon be replaced by something better and that then consumer demand for the existing technology will plummet. This means that prices typically fall when a product has been on the market for a time. Since producers know that the price will fall, they supply as many of the new models as possible before the next wave of innovation cuts the price that they can charge.

We have seen that a number of variables or factors can influence supply. Each of these variables can shift the entire supply curve to the right or left. A shift to the right will occur when the change in the variable results in an additional supply of the good or service. A shift to the left will occur when a change in the variable results in a smaller supply of the good or service.

ECONOMICS IN THE REAL WORLD

Why Do the Prices of New Electronics Always Drop?

The first personal computers released in the 1980s cost as much as $10,000. Today, a laptop computer can be purchased for less than $500. When a new technology emerges, prices are initially very high and then tend to fall rapidly. The first PCs created a profound change in the way people could work with information. Prior to the advent of the PC, complex programming could be done only on

Why did consumers pay $5,000 for this?

large mainframe computers that often took up as much space as a whole room. But at first only a few people could afford a PC. What makes emerging technology so expensive when it is first introduced and so inexpensive later in its life cycle? Supply and demand tell the story.

In the case of PCs and other recent technologies, both demand and supply increase through time. Demand increases as consumers find more uses for the new technology. An increase in demand, by itself, would ordinarily drive the price up. However, producers are eager to supply this new market and ramp up production quickly. Since the supply expands more rapidly than the demand, there is both an increase in the quantity sold and a lower price.

Differences in expectations account for some of the difference between the increase in supply and demand. Both parties expect the price to fall, and they react accordingly. Suppliers try to get their new products to market as quickly as possible—before the price starts to fall appreciably. Therefore, the willingness to supply the product expands quickly. Consumer demand is slower to pick up because consumers expect the price to fall. This expectation tempers their desire to buy the new technology immediately. The longer they wait, the lower the price will be. Therefore, demand does not increase as fast as the supply. ✳

What Happens When Both Supply and Demand Shift?

We have examined supply and demand separately. Now it is time to see how the two interact. The real power and potential of supply and demand analysis is in how well it predicts prices and output in the entire market.

PRACTICE WHAT YOU KNOW

The Supply and Demand of Ice Cream

I scream, you scream, we all scream for ice cream.

Question: Which of the following will increase the demand for ice cream?

a. A decrease in the price of the butterfat used to make ice cream

b. A decrease in the price of ice cream

c. An increase in the price of the milk used to make ice cream

d. An increase in the price of frozen yogurt, a substitute for ice cream

Answer: If you answered b, you made a common mistake. A change in the price of a good cannot change overall market demand; it can only cause a movement along an existing curve. So, as important as price changes are, they are not the right answer. First, you need to look for an event that shifts the entire curve.

Answers a and c refer to the prices of butterfat and milk. Since these are the inputs of production for ice cream, a change in prices will shift the supply curve. That leaves answer d as the only possibility. Answer d is correct since the increase in the price of frozen yogurt will cause the consumer to look elsewhere. Consumers will substitute away from frozen yogurt and toward ice cream. This shift in consumer behavior will result in an increase in the demand for ice cream even though its price remains the same.

Question: Which of the following will decrease the supply of chocolate ice cream?

a. A medical report finding that consuming chocolate prevents cancer

b. A decrease in the price of chocolate ice cream

c. An increase in the price of chocolate, an ingredient used to make ice cream

d. An increase in the price of whipped cream, a complementary good

Answer: We have already seen that b cannot be the answer because a change in the price of the good cannot change supply; it can only cause a movement along an existing curve. Answers a and d would both cause a change in demand without affecting the supply curve. That leaves answer c as the only possibility. Chocolate is a necessary ingredient used in the production process. Whenever the price of an input rises, it squeezes profit margins, and this results in a decrease in supply at the existing price.

Supply, Demand, and Equilibrium

Let's consider the market for salmon again. This example meets the conditions for a competitive market because the salmon sold by one vendor is essentially the same as the salmon sold by another.

In Figure 3.9, we see that when the price of salmon fillets is $10 per pound, consumers demand 500 pounds and producers supply 500. This is represented graphically at point E, known as the point of **equilibrium**, where the demand curve and the supply curve intersect. At this point, the two opposing forces of supply and demand are perfectly balanced.

Notice that at $10.00 per fillet, the quantity demanded equals the quantity supplied. At this price, and only this price, the entire supply of salmon in the market is sold. Moreover, every buyer who wants salmon is able to find some and every producer is able to sell his or her entire stock. We say that $10.00 is the **equilibrium price** because the quantity supplied equals the quantity demanded. The equilibrium price is also called the *market-clearing price,* since this is the only price at which no surplus or shortage of the good exists. Similarly, there is also an **equilibrium quantity**, of 500 pounds, at which the quantity supplied equals the quantity demanded. When the market is in equilibrium, we sometimes say that *the market clears* or that *the price clears the market.* The equilibrium point has a special place in economics because movements away from that point throw the market out of balance. The equilibrium process is so powerful that it is often referred to as the *law of supply and demand.* According to the **law of supply and demand**, *market prices adjust to bring the quantity supplied and the quantity demanded into balance.*

Equilibrium
occurs at the point where the demand curve and the supply curve intersect.

The **equilibrium price**
is the price at which the quantity supplied is equal to the quantity demanded. This is also known as the *market-clearing price.*

The **equilibrium quantity**
is the amount at which the quantity supplied is equal to the quantity demanded.

The **law of supply and demand**
states that the market price of any good will adjust to bring the quantity supplied and the quantity demanded into balance.

FIGURE 3.9

The Salmon Market

At the equilibrium point, E, supply and demand are perfectly balanced. At prices above the equilibrium price, a surplus of goods exists, while at prices below the equilibrium price, a shortage of goods exists.

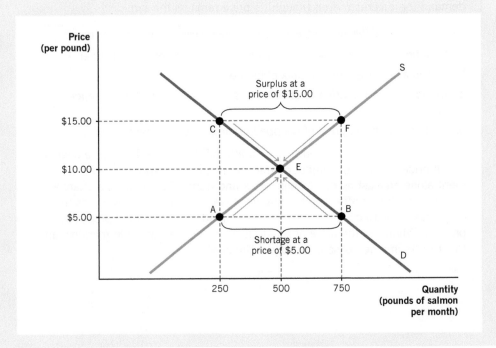

Shortages and Surpluses

How does the market respond when it is not in equilibrium? Let's look at two other prices for salmon shown on the *y* axis in Figure 3.9: $5.00 and $15.00 per pound.

At a price of $5.00 per pound, salmon is quite attractive to buyers but not very profitable to sellers—the quantity demanded is 750 pounds, represented by point B on the demand curve (D). However, the quantity supplied, which is represented by point A on the supply curve (S), is only 250. So at $5.00 per pound there is an excess quantity of 500 pounds demanded. This excess demand creates disequilibrium in the market.

When there is more demand for a product than sellers are willing or able to age supply, we say there is a *shortage*. A **shortage** occurs whenever the quantity supplied is less than the quantity demanded. In our case, at a price of $5.00 there are three buyers for each pound of salmon. New shipments of salmon fly out the door. This is a strong signal for sellers to raise the price. As the market price increases in response to the shortage, sellers continue to increase the quantity that they offer. You can see this on the graph in Figure 3.9 by following the upward-sloping arrow from point A to point E. At the same time, as the price rises, buyers will demand an increasingly smaller quantity, represented by the upward-sloping arrow from point B to point E along the demand curve. Eventually, when the price reaches $10.00, will be the quantity supplied and the quantity demanded will be equal. The market will be in equilibrium.

> **A shortage**
> occurs whenever the quantity supplied is less than the quantity demanded.

What happens when the price is set above the equilibrium point—say, at $15.00 per pound? At this price salmon is quite profitable for sellers but not very attractive to buyers. The quantity demanded, represented by point C on the demand curve, is 250 pounds. However, the quantity supplied, represented by point F on the supply curve, is 750. In other words, sellers provide 500 pounds more than buyers wish to purchase. This excess supply creates disequilibrium in the market. Any buyer who is willing to pay $15.00 for a pound of salmon can find some since there are three pounds available for every customer. This situation is known as a *surplus*. A **surplus**, or excess supply, occurs whenever the quantity supplied is greater than the quantity demanded.

> **A surplus**
> occurs whenever the quantity supplied is greater than the quantity demanded.

When there is a surplus, sellers realize that salmon has been oversupplied. This is a strong signal to lower the price. As the market price decreases in response to the surplus, more buyers enter the market and purchase salmon. This is represented on the graph in Figure 3.9 by the downward-sloping arrow

moving from point C to point E along the demand curve. At the same time, sellers reduce output, represented by the downward-sloping arrow moving from point F to point E on the supply curve. As long as the surplus persists, the price will continue to fall. Eventually, the price will reach $10.00 per pound. At this point, the quantity supplied and the quantity demanded will be equal and the market will be in equilibrium again.

In competitive markets, surpluses and shortages are resolved through the process of price adjustment. Buyers who are unable to find enough salmon at $5.00 per pound compete to find the available stocks; this drives the price up. Likewise, businesses that cannot sell their product at $15.00 per pound must lower their prices to reduce inventories; this drives the price down.

Every seller and buyer has a vital role to play in the market. Venues like the Pike Place Market bring buyers and sellers together. Amazingly, all of this happens spontaneously, without the need for government planning to ensure an adequate supply of the goods that consumers need. You might think that a decentralized system would create chaos, but nothing could be further from the truth. Markets work because buyers and sellers can rapidly adjust to changes in prices. These adjustments bring balance. When markets were suppressed in communist command economies during the twentieth century, shortages were commonplace, in part because there was no market price system to signal that additional production was needed. (A command economy is one in which supply and price are regulated by the government rather than by market forces). This led to the creation of many black markets (see Chapter 5).

How do markets respond to additional demand? In the case of the bowling cartoon shown above, the increase in demand comes from an unseen customer who wants to use a bowling lane already favored by another patron. An increase in the number of buyers causes an increase in demand. The lane is valued by two buyers, instead of just one, so the owner is contemplating a price increase! This is how markets work. Price is a mechanism to determine which buyer wants the good or service the most.

In summary, Figure 3.10 provides four examples of what happens when either the supply or the demand curve shifts. As you study these, you should develop a sense for how price and quantity are affected by changes in supply and demand. When one curve shifts, we can make a definitive statement about how price and quantity will change. In the chapter appendix that follows, we consider what happens when supply and demand change at the same time. There you will discover the challenges in simultaneously determining price and quantity when more than one variable changes.

Conclusion

Does demand matter more than supply? As you have learned in this chapter, the answer is no. Demand and supply contribute equally to the functioning of markets. Five years from now, if someone asks you what you remember about your first course in economics, you will probably respond with two words, "supply" and "demand." These two opposing forces enable economists to model market behavior through prices. Prices help establish the market equilibrium, or the price at which supply and demand are in balance. At the equilibrium point, every good and service produced has a

FIGURE 3.10

**Price and Quantity
When Either Supply or
Demand Changes**

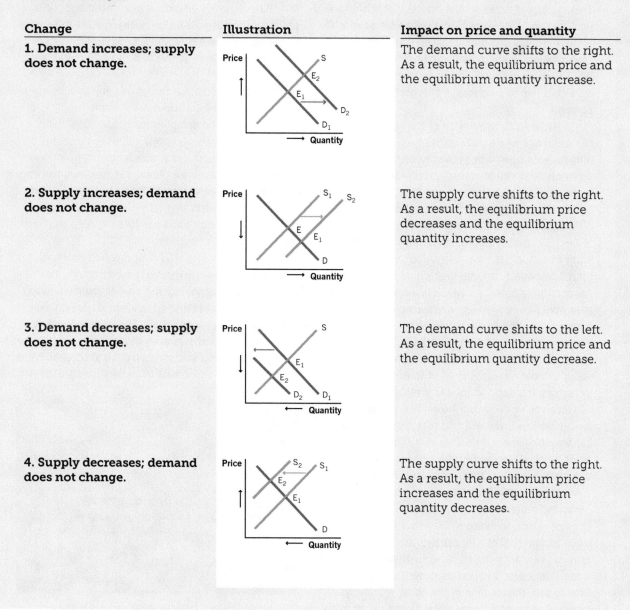

Change	Illustration	Impact on price and quantity
1. Demand increases; supply does not change.		The demand curve shifts to the right. As a result, the equilibrium price and the equilibrium quantity increase.
2. Supply increases; demand does not change.		The supply curve shifts to the right. As a result, the equilibrium price decreases and the equilibrium quantity increases.
3. Demand decreases; supply does not change.		The demand curve shifts to the left. As a result, the equilibrium price and the equilibrium quantity decrease.
4. Supply decreases; demand does not change.		The supply curve shifts to the right. As a result, the equilibrium price increases and the equilibrium quantity decreases.

corresponding buyer who wants to purchase it. When the market is out of equilibrium, it causes a shortage or surplus. These conditions persist until buyers and sellers have a chance to adjust the quantity they demand and the quantity they supply, respectively. This refutes the misconception we noted at the beginning of the chapter.

ECONOMICS FOR LIFE

Bringing Supply and Demand Together: Advice for Buying Your First Place

There is an old adage in real estate, "location, location, location." Why does location matter so much? Simple. Supply and demand. There are only so many places to live in any given location—that is the supply. The most desirable locations have many buyers who'd like to purchase in that area—that is the demand.

Consider for a moment all of the variables that can influence where you want to live. As you're shopping for your new home, you may want to consider proximity to where you work, your favorite restaurants, public transportation, and the best schools. You'll also want to pay attention to the crime rate, differences in local tax rates, traffic concerns, noise issues, and nearby zoning restrictions. In addition, many communities have restrictive covenants that limit how owners can use their property. Smart buyers determine how the covenants work and whether they would be happy to give up some freedom in order to maintain an attractive neighborhood. Finally, it is always a good idea to visit the neighborhood in the evening or on the weekend to meet your future neighbors before you buy. All of these variables determine the demand for any given property.

Once you've done your homework and settled on a neighborhood, you will find that property values can vary tremendously across very short distances. A home along a busy street may sell for half the price of a similar property that backs up to a quiet park a few blocks away. Properties near a subway line command a premium, as do properties with views or close access to major employers and amenities (such as parks, shopping centers, and places to eat). Here is the main point to remember, even if some of these things aren't important to you: when it comes time to sell, the location of the home will always matter. The number of potential buyers depends on the characteristics of your neighborhood and the size and condition of your property. If you want to be able to sell your place easily, you'll have to consider not only where you want to live now but who might want to live there later.

All of this discussion brings us back to supply and demand. The best locations are in short supply and high demand. The combination of low supply and high demand causes property values in those areas to rise. Likewise, less desirable locations have lower property values because demand is relatively low and the supply is relatively high. Since first-time buyers often have wish lists that far exceed their budgets, considering the costs and benefits will help you find the best available property.

There is a popular HGTV show called *Property Virgins* that follows first-time buyers through the process of buying their first home. If you have never seen the show, watching an episode is one of the best lessons in economics you'll ever get. Check it out, and remember that even though you may be new to buying property, you still can get a good deal if you use some basic economics to guide your decision.

Where you buy is more important than what you buy.

In the next chapter, we will extend our understanding of supply and demand by examining how sensitive, or responsive, consumers and producers are to price changes. This will allow us to determine whether price changes have a big effect on behavior or not.

ANSWERING THE BIG QUESTIONS

1. What are the fundamentals of markets?

* A market consists of a group of buyers and sellers for a particular product or service.
* When competition is present, markets produce low prices.
* Not all markets are competitive. When suppliers have market power, markets are imperfect and prices are higher.

2. How is demand determined?

* The law of demand states that there is an inverse relationship between the price and the amount that the consumer wishes to purchase.
* As a result of the law of demand, the demand curve is downward sloping.
* A price change causes a movement along the demand curve, not a shift in the curve.
* Changes other than price cause the demand curve to shift.

3. What determines supply?

* The law of supply states that there is a direct relationship between the price and the amount that is offered for sale.
* The supply curve is upward sloping.
* A price change causes a movement along the supply curve, not a shift in the curve.
* Changes in the prices of inputs, new technologies, taxes, subsidies, the number of sellers, and expectations about the future price all influence the location of the new supply curve and cause the original supply curve to shift.

4. What happens when supply and demand shift?

* Supply and demand interact through the process of market coordination.
* Together, supply and demand create a process that leads to equilibrium, the balancing point between the two opposing forces. The market-clearing price and output are determined at the equilibrium point.
* When the price is above the equilibrium point, a surplus exists and inventories build up. This will cause suppliers to lower their price in an effort to sell the unwanted goods. The process continues until the equilibrium price is reached.
* When the price is below the equilibrium point, a shortage exists and inventories are depleted. This will cause suppliers to raise their price in order to ration the good. The price rises until the equilibrium point is reached.

CONCEPTS YOU SHOULD KNOW

competitive market (p. 00)
complement (p. 00)
demand curve (p. 00)
demand schedule (p. 00)
equilibrium (p. 00)
equilibrium price (p. 00)
equilibrium quantity (p. 00)
imperfect market (p. 00)
inferior good (p. 00)

inputs (p. 00)
law of demand (p. 00)
law of supply (p. 00)
law of supply and demand (p. 00)
market demand (p. 00)
market economy (p. 00)
market supply (p. 00)
monopoly (p. 00)
normal good (p. 00)

quantity demanded (p. 00)
quantity supplied (p. 00)
shortage (p. 00)
substitutes (p. 00)
supply curve (p. 00)
supply schedule (p. 00)
surplus (p. 00)

QUESTIONS FOR REVIEW

1. What is a competitive market it, and how does A depend on the existence of many buyers and sellers?

2. Why does the demand curve slope downward?

3. Does a price change cause a movement along a demand curve or a shift of the entire curve? What factors cause the entire demand curve to shift?

4. Describe the difference between inferior and normal goods.

5. Why does the supply curve slope upward?

6. Does a price change cause a movement along a supply curve or a shift of the entire curve? What factors cause the entire supply curve to shift?

7. Describe the process that leads the market toward equilibrium.

8. What happens in a competitive market when the price is above or below the equilibrium price?

9. What roles do shortages and surpluses play in the market?

STUDY PROBLEMS

1. In the song "Money, Money, Money" by ABBA, the lead singer, Anni-Frid Lyngstad, is tired of the hard work life requires and plans to marry a wealthy man. If she is successful, how would this marriage change the artist's demand for goods? How would it change her supply of labor? Illustrate both changes with supply and demand curves. Be sure to explain what is happening in the diagrams. (Note: the full lyrics for the song can be found by Googling the song title and ABBA. For inspiration, try listening to the song while you solve the problem!)

2. For each of the following, scenarios, determine if there is an increase or a decrease in demand for the good a in *italics*.
   a. The price of *oranges* increases.
   b. The cost of producing *tires* increases.

   c. Samantha Brown, who is crazy about *air travel*, gets fired from her job.
   d. A local community has a mosquito problem because of an unusually wet spring. What happens to the demand for *citronella*, a mosquito deterrent?
   e. Many motorcycle enthusiasts enjoy riding without a helmet (in states where this is permitted by law). The price of new motorcycles rises. What happens to the demand for *helmets*?

3. For each of the following, scenarios, determine if there is an increase or a decrease in supply for the good in *italics*.
   a. The price of *silver* increases.
   b. Growers of *tomatoes* experience an unusually good growing season.

c. New medical evidence reports that consumption of *organic products* reduces the incidence of cancer.

d. The wages of low-skill workers, a resource used to help produce *clothing*, increase.

e. The price of movie tickets, a substitute for *video rentals*, goes up.

4. Are laser pointers and cats complements or substitutes? (Not sure? Search for videos of cats and laser pointers online.) Discuss.

* 5. The market for ice cream has the following demand and supply schedules:

Price (per quart)	Quantity demanded (quarts)	Quantity supplied (quarts)
$2	100	30
$3	80	45
$4	60	60
$5	40	75
$6	20	90

a. What are the equilibrium price and equilibrium quantity in the ice cream market? Confirm your answer by graphing the demand and supply curves.

b. If the actual price was $3 per quart, what would drive the market toward equilibrium?

6. Starbucks Entertainment announced in a 2007 news release that Dave Matthews Band's *Live Trax* CD was available only at the company's coffee shops in the United States and Canada. The compilation features recordings of the band's performances dating back to 1995. Why would Starbucks and Dave Matthews have agreed to partner in this way? To come up with an answer, think about the nature of complementary goods and how both sides can benefit from this arrangement.

7. The Seattle Mariners wish to determine the equilibrium price for seats for each of the next two seasons. The supply of seats at the ballpark is fixed at 45,000.

Price (per seat)	Quantity demanded in year 1	Quantity demanded in year 2	Quantity supplied
$25	75,000	60,000	45,000
$30	60,000	55,000	45,000
$35	45,000	50,000	45,000
$40	30,000	45,000	45,000
$45	15,000	40,000	45,000

Draw the supply curve and each of the demand curves for years 1 and 2.

* 8. Demand and supply curves can also be represented with equations. Suppose that the quantity demanded, Q_D, is represented by the following equation:

$$Q_D = 90 - 2P$$

The quantity supplied, Q_S, is represented by the equation:

$$Q_S = P$$

a. Find the equilibrium price and quantity. **Hint:** Set $Q_D = Q_S$ and solve for the price, P, and then plug your result back into either of the original equations to find Q.

b. Suppose that the price is $20. Determine Q_D and Q_S.

c. At a price of $20, is there is a surplus or a shortage in the market?

d. Given your answer in part c, will the price rise or fall in order to find the equilibrium point?

SOLVED PROBLEMS

5.

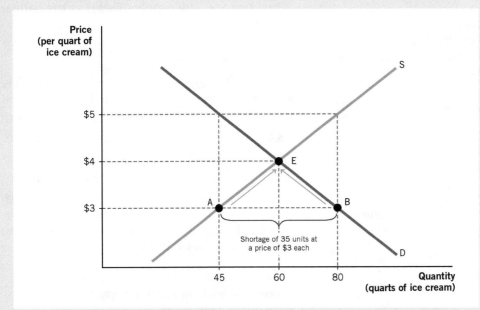

a. The equilibrium price and quantity are 60 units (quarts) at $4, which is the price at which supply and demand are equal. The next step is to graph the curves. This is done above.

b. A shortage of 35 units of ice cream exists at $3; therefore, there is excess demand. Ice cream sellers will raise their price as long as excess demand exists. That is, as long as the price is below $4, the shortage continues. It is not until $4 that the equilibrium point is reached and the shortage is resolved.

8.a. The first step is to set $Q_d = Q_s$. Doing so gives us $90 - 2P = P$. Solving for price, we find that $90 = 3P$, or $P = 30$. Once we know that $P = 30$, we can plug this value back into either of the original equations, $Q_d = 90 - 2P$ or $Q_s = P$. Beginning with Q_d, we get

$90 - (30) = 90 - 60 = 30$, or we can plug it into $Q_s = P$, so $Q_s = 30$. Since we get a quantity of 30 for both Q_d and Q_s, we know that the price of $30 is correct.

b. In this part, we plug $20 into Q_d. This yields $90 - 2(20) = 50$. Now we plug $20 into Q_s. This yields 20.

c. Since $Q_d = 50$ and $Q_s = 20$, there is a shortage of 30 units.

d. Whenever there is a shortage of a good, the price will rise in order to find the equilibrium point.

Changes in Both Demand and Supply

We have considered what would happen if supply *or* demand changed. But life is often more complex than that. To provide a more realistic analysis, we need to be able to shift supply and demand at the same time. Doing this adds considerable uncertainty to the analysis.

Suppose that a major drought hits the United States. The water shortage reduces both the amount of farmed salmon and the ability of wild salmon to spawn in streams and rivers. Figure 3A.1a shows the ensuing decline in the salmon supply, from point S progressively leftward, represented by the dotted supply curves. At the same time, a medical journal reports that people who consume at least four pounds of salmon a month live five years longer than those who consume an equal amount of cod. Figure 3A.1b shows the ensuing rise in the demand for salmon, from point D progressively rightward, represented by the dotted demand curves. This scenario leads to a twofold change. Because of the water shortage, the supply of salmon shrinks. At the same time, new information about the health benefits of eating salmon causes demand for salmon to increase. There is less salmon available, yet more people want it. When something is in high demand and suppliers cannot provide enough of it, the market-clearing price must rise.

However, the effect on the equilibrium quantity is not certain. In this situation, we have a simultaneous decrease in supply and increase in demand. Since we do not know the size of the supply reduction or the demand increase, the overall effect on the equilibrium quantity cannot be determined. This result is evident in Figure 3A.1c, where the shaded areas overlap in the purple region. The points where supply and demand cross within this area represent the set of possible new market equilibriums. Since each of the possible points of intersection in the purple region occurs at prices greater than $10.00 per pound, we know that the price must rise. However, the left half of the purple region produces equilibrium quantities less than 500 pounds of salmon, while the right half of the purple region results in equilibrium quantities greater than 500. Therefore, the equilibrium quantity may rise or fall.

When supply and demand both change, it is only possible to determine the price *or* the quantity, not both. The world we live in is complex, and often more than one variable will change simultaneously. When this occurs, it is not possible to be as definitive as when only one variable—supply or demand—changes. The new equilibrium, E_1, is no longer a single point but a range of outcomes represented by the shaded purple area in Figure 3A.1c. Therefore, we cannot be exactly sure where the new price *and* quantity will settle. For a closer look at four uncertain outcomes, see Figure 3A.2.

A Shift in Supply and Demand

When supply and demand both shift, the resulting equilibrium can no longer be identified as an exact point. This is seen in (c), which combines the supply shift in (a) with the demand shift in (b). When supply decreases and demand increases, the result is that the price must rise, but the equilibrium quantity is unknown.

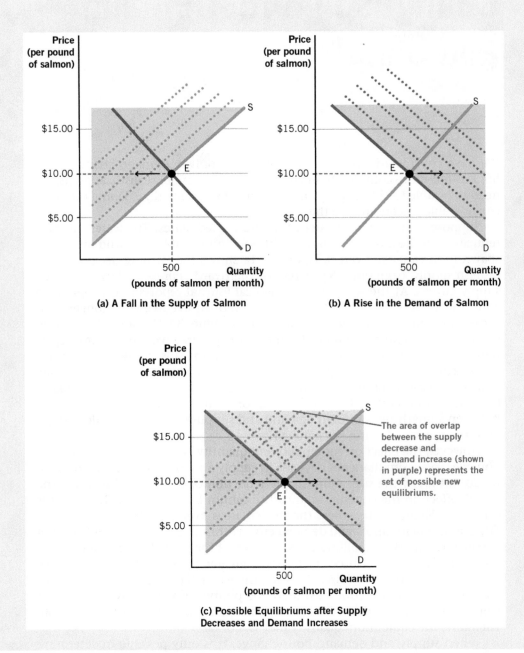

(a) A Fall in the Supply of Salmon

(b) A Rise in the Demand of Salmon

The area of overlap between the supply decrease and demand increase (shown in purple) represents the set of possible new equilibriums.

(c) Possible Equilibriums after Supply Decreases and Demand Increases

FIGURE 3.2A

Price and Quantity
When Demand and
Supply Both Change

Change	Illustration	Impact on price and quantity
1. Demand and supply both increase.	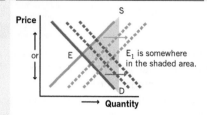	The demand and supply curves shift to the right. The shifts reinforce each other with respect to quantity, but they act as countervailing forces along the Price axis. Price will be indeterminate.
2. Demand and supply both decrease.	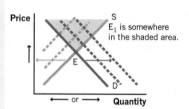	The demand and supply curves shift to the left. The shifts reinforce each other with respect to quantity, but they act as countervailing forces along the Price axis. Price will be indeterminate.
3. Demand increases and supply decreases.	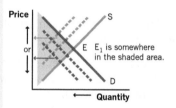	The demand curve shifts to the right and the supply curve shifts to the left. The shifts reinforce each other with respect to price, but they act as countervailing forces along the Quantity axis. Quantity will be indeterminate.
4. Demand decreases and supply increases.	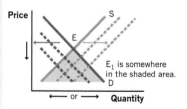	The demand curve shifts to the left and the supply curve shifts to the right. The shifts reinforce each other with respect to price, but they act as countervailing forces along the Quantity axis. Quantity will be indeterminate.

PRACTICE WHAT YOU KNOW

When Supply and Demand Both Change: Hybrid Cars

Hybrid cars are becoming increasingly common.

Question: At lunch, two friends are engaged in a heated argument. Their exchange goes like this:

The first friend begins, "The supply of hybrid cars and the demand for hybrid cars will both increase, I'm sure of it. I'm also sure the price of hybrids will go down."

The second friend interrupts, "I agree with the first part of your statement, but I'm not sure about the price. In fact, I'm pretty sure that hybrid prices will rise."

They go back and forth endlessly, each unable to convince the other, so they turn to you for advice. What do you say to them?

Answer: Your friends could both be correct. When supply and demand both shift at the same time, we can be sure about how price or quantity will respond, but not both. In this case, supply and demand both shift out to the right, so we know the quantity bought and sold will increase. However, since an increase in supply would normally lower the price and an increase in demand would typically raise the price, we can't be sure whether the price will rise or fall. The overall price will rise if the increase in demand is larger than the increase in supply. However, if the increase in supply is larger than the increase in demand, prices will fall.

QUESTIONS FOR REVIEW

A1. What happens to price and quantity when supply and demand change at the same time?

A2. Is there more than one potential equilibrium point when supply and demand change at the same time?

STUDY PROBLEM

1. Check out this short video from www.forbes.com on the oil market: http://video.forbes.com/fvn/business/pm_non022208?partner=truveo. Using your understanding of the market forces of supply and demand, explain how the market works. In your explanation, be sure to illustrate how increasing global demand for oil has impacted the equilibrium price.

Elasticity

Sellers charge the highest price possible.

Many students believe that sellers charge the highest price possible for their product or service—that if they can get one more penny from

a customer, they will, even if it makes the customer angry. It turns out that this belief is wrong. What *is* accurate is that producers charge the highest price they can while maintaining the goodwill of most of their customers.

In the previous chapter, we learned that demand and supply help regulate economic activity by balancing the interests of buyers and sellers. We also observed how that balance is achieved through prices. Higher prices cause the quantity supplied to rise and the quantity demanded to fall. In contrast, lower prices cause the quantity supplied to fall and the quantity demanded to rise. In this chapter, we will examine how decision-makers respond to differences in price and also to changes in income.

The concept of *elasticity*, or responsiveness to a change in market conditions, is a tool that we need to master in order to fully understand supply and demand. By utilizing elasticity in our analysis, our understanding will become much more precise. This will enable us to determine the impact of policy measures on the economy, to vote more intelligently, and even to make wiser day-to-day decisions, like whether or not to eat out. Elasticity will also help us to understand the faulty logic behind the common misconception that sellers charge the highest possible price.

BIG QUESTIONS

* What is the price elasticity of demand, and what are its determinants?
* How do changes in income and the prices of other goods affect elasticity?
* What is the price elasticity of supply?
* How do the price elasticity of demand and supply relate to one another?

What Is the Price Elasticity of Demand, and What Are Its Determinants?

Many things in life are replaceable, or have substitutes: boyfriends come and go, people rent DVDs instead of going out to a movie, and students ride their bikes to class instead of taking the bus. Pasta fans may prefer linguini to spaghetti or angel hair, but all three taste about the same and can be substituted for one another in a pinch. In cases such as pasta, where consumers can easily purchase a substitute, we think of demand as being *responsive*. That is, a small change in price will likely cause many people to switch from one good to another.

Trade-offs

In contrast, many things in life are irreplaceable or have few good substitutes. Examples include electricity, a hospital emergency room visit, or water for a shower. A significant rise in price for any of these items would probably not cause you to consume a smaller quantity. If the price of electricity goes up, you might try to cut your usage somewhat, but you would probably not start generating your own power. Likewise, you could try to treat a serious medical crisis without a visit to the ER—but the consequences of making a mistake would be enormous. Even something as simple as taking a shower has few good alternatives. In cases such as these, we say that consumers are *unresponsive*, or unwilling to change their behavior, even when the price of the good or service changes.

The responsiveness of buyers and sellers to changes in price or income is known as **elasticity**. Elasticity is a useful concept because it allows us to measure how much consumers and producers change their behavior when prices or income changes. In the next section, we look at the factors that determine the elasticity of demand.

Your "average"-looking boyfriend is replaceable.

Elasticity is a measure of the responsiveness of buyers and sellers to changes in price or income.

Determinants of the Price Elasticity of Demand

The law of demand tells us that as price goes up, quantity demanded goes down, and as price goes down, quantity demanded goes up. In other words, there is an inverse relationship between the price of a good and the quantity demanded. Elasticity allows us to measure how much the quantity demanded changes in response to a change in price. If the quantity demanded changes significantly as a result of a price change, then demand is *elastic*. If the quantity demanded changes a small amount as a result of a price change, then demand is *inelastic*. For instance, if the price of a sweatshirt with a college logo rises by $10 and the quantity demanded falls by half, we'd say that the price elasticity of demand for those sweatshirts is elastic. But if the $10 rise in price results in very little or no change in the quantity demanded, the price elasticity of demand for the sweatshirts is inelastic. The **price elasticity of demand** measures the responsiveness of quantity demanded to a change in price.

The **price elasticity of demand** is a measure of the responsiveness of quantity demanded to a change in price.

Four determinants play a crucial role in influencing whether demand will be elastic or inelastic. These are the existence of substitutes, the share of the budget spent on a good, whether the good is a necessity or a luxury good, and time and the adjustment process.

The Existence of Substitutes

The most important determinant of price elasticity is the number of substitutes available. When substitutes are plentiful, market forces tilt in favor of the consumer. For example, imagine that an unexpected freeze in Florida reduces the supply of oranges. As a result, the supply of orange juice shifts to the left (picture the supply curves we discussed in Chapter 3), and since demand remains unchanged, the price of orange juice rises. However, the consumer of orange juice can find many good substitutes. Since cranberries, grapes, and apple crops are unaffected by the Florida freeze, prices for juices made with those fruits remain constant. This leads to a choice: a consumer could continue to buy orange juice at a higher price or choose to pay a lower price for a fruit juice that may not be his first choice but is nonetheless acceptable. Faced with higher orange juice prices, some consumers will switch. How quickly this switch takes place, and to what extent consumers are willing to replace one product

Beyoncé is irreplaceable.

with another, determines whether demand is elastic or inelastic. Since many substitutes for orange juice exist, the price elasticity of demand for orange juice is elastic, or responsive to price changes.

What if there are no good substitutes? Let's return to the Empire State Building example from the previous chapter. Where else in New York City can you get such an amazing view? Nowhere! Since the view is unbeatable, the number of close substitutes is small; this makes demand more inelastic, or less responsive to price changes.

To some degree, the price elasticity of demand depends on consumer preferences. For instance, sports fans are often willing to shell out big bucks to follow their passions. Amateur golfers can play the same courses that professional golfers do. But the opportunity to golf where the professionals play does not come cheaply. A round of golf at the Tournament Players Club at Sawgrass, a famous course in Florida, costs close to $300. Why are some golfers willing to pay that much? For an avid golfer with the financial means, the

Would you pay $300 to play this golf course?

experience of living out the same shots seen on television tournaments is worth $300. In this case, demand is inelastic—the avid golfer does not view other golf courses as good substitutes. However, less enthusiastic golfers, or those without the financial resources, are happy to golf on a less expensive course even if the pros don't play it on TV. When less expensive courses serve as good substitutes, the price tag makes demand elastic. Ultimately, whether demand is inelastic or elastic depends on the buyer's preferences and resources.

The Share of the Budget Spent on the Good

Despite the example above of an avid and affluent golfer willing to pay a premium fee to play at a famous golf course, in most cases fee is a critical element in determining what we can afford and what we will choose to buy. If you plan to purchase a 70-inch-screen TV, which can cost as much as $3,000, you will probably be willing to take the time to find the best deal. Because of the high cost, even a small-percentage discount in the price can cause a relatively large change in consumer demand. A "10% off sale" may not sound like much, but when purchasing a big-ticket item like a TV, it can mean hundreds of dollars in savings. In this case, the willingness to shop for the best deal indicates that the price matters, so demand is elastic.

Incentives

The price elasticity of demand is much more inelastic for inexpensive items on sale. For example, if a candy bar is discounted 10%, the price falls by pennies. The savings from switching candy bars is not enough to make a difference in what you can afford elsewhere. Therefore, the incentive to switch is small. Most consumers still buy their favorite candy since the price difference is so insignificant. In this case, demand is inelastic because the amount of money in the consumer's budget is large compared to the savings gained by purchasing a less desirable candy bar.

Necessities versus Luxury Goods

A big-screen TV and a candy bar are both luxury goods. You don't need to have either one. But some goods are necessities. For example, you have to pay your rent and water bill, purchase gasoline for your car, and eat. When a consumer purchases a necessity, he or she is generally thinking about the need, not the price. When the need trumps the price, we expect demand to be relatively inelastic. Therefore, the demand for things like soap, toothpaste, and heating oil all tend to have inelastic demand.

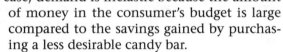

Saving 10% on this purchase adds up to hundreds of dollars.

Time and the Adjustment Process

When the market price changes, consumers and sellers respond. But that sellers does not remain the same over time. As time passes, both consumers and sellers are able to find substitutes. To understand these different market responses, economists consider time in three distinct periods: the *immediate run*, the *short run*, and the *long run*.

Saving 10% on this purchase amounts to a few pennies.

In the **immediate run**, there is no time for consumers to adjust their behavior. Consider the demand for gasoline. When the gas tank is empty, you have to stop at the nearest gas station and pay the posted price. Filling up as soon as possible is more important than driving around searching for the lowest price. Inelastic demand exists whenever price is secondary to the desire to attain a certain amount of the good. So in the case of an empty tank, the demand for gasoline is inelastic.

But what if your tank is not empty? The **short run** is a period of time when consumers can partially adjust their behavior (and, in this case, can search for a good deal on gas). When consumers have some time to make a purchase, they gain flexibility. This allows them to shop for lower prices at the pump, carpool to save gas, or even change how often they drive. In the short run, flexibility reduces the demand for expensive gasoline and makes consumer demand more elastic.

This is NOT the time to try and find cheap gas.

Finally, if we relax the time constraint completely, it is possible to use even less gasoline. The **long run** is a period of time when consumers have time to fully adjust to market conditions. If gasoline prices are high in the long run, consumers can relocate closer to work and purchase fuel-efficient cars. These changes further reduce the demand for gasoline. As a result of the flexibility that additional time gives the consumer, the demand for gasoline becomes more elastic.

We have looked at four determinants of elasticity—substitutes, the share of the budget spent on the good, necessities versus luxury goods, and time. Each is significant, but the number of substitutes tends to be the most influential factor and dominates the others. Table 4.1 will help you develop your intuition about how different market situations influence the overall elasticity of demand.

In the immediate run, there is no time for consumers to adjust their behavior.

The short run is a period of time when consumers can partially adjust their behavior.

The long run is a period of time when consumers have time to fully adjust to market conditions.

Computing the Price Elasticity of Demand

Until this point, our discussion of elasticity has been descriptive. However, to apply the concept of elasticity in decision-making, we need to be able to view it in a more quantitative way. For example, if the owner of a business is trying to decide whether to put a good on sale, he or she needs to be able to estimate how many new customers would purchase it at the sale price. Or if a government is considering a new tax, it needs to know how much revenue that tax would generate. These are questions about elasticity that we can evaluate by using a mathematical formula.

The Price Elasticity of Demand Formula

Let's begin with an example of a pizza shop. Consider an owner who is trying to attract more customers. For one month, he lowers the price by 10% and is pleased to find that sales jump by 30%.

TABLE 4.1

Developing Intuition for the Price Elasticity of Demand

Example	Discussion	Overall elasticity
Football tickets for a true fan	Being able to watch a game live and go to pre- and post-game tailgates is a unique experience. For many fans, the experience of going to the game has few close substitutes; therefore, the demand is relatively inelastic.	Tends to be relatively inelastic
Assigned textbooks for a class	The information inside a textbook is valuable. Substitutes such as older editions and free online resources are not exactly the same. As a result, most students buy the required course materials. Acquiring the textbook is more important than the price paid; therefore, the demand is inelastic. The fact that a textbook is needed in the short run (for a few months while taking a class) also tends to make the demand inelastic.	Tends to be inelastic
A slice of pizza from Domino's	In most locations, many pizza competitors exist, so there are many close substitutes. This tends to make the demand for a particular brand of pizza elastic.	Tends to be elastic
A red Pontiac Torrent	There are many styles, makes, and colors of cars to choose from. With large purchases, consumers are sensitive to smaller percentages of savings. Moreover, people typically plan their car purchases many months or years in advance. The combination of all these factors makes the demand for any particular model and color relatively elastic.	Tends to be relatively elastic

Here is the formula for the price elasticity of demand (E_D):

(Equation 4.1) $$\text{Price Elasticity of Demand} = E_D = \frac{\text{percentage change in the quantity demanded}}{\text{percentage change in price}}$$

Using the data from the example, we can calculate the price elasticity of demand as follows:

$$\text{Price Elasticity of Demand} = E_D = \frac{30\%}{-10\%} = -3$$

What does that mean? The price elasticity of demand, −3 in this case, is expressed as a coefficient (3) with a specific sign (it has a minus in front of it). The coefficient, 3, tells us how much the quantity demanded changed (30%) compared to the price change (10%). In this case, the percentage change in the quantity demanded is three times the percentage change in the price. Whenever the percentage change in the quantity demanded is larger than the percentage change in price, we say that demand was elastic. In other words, the price drop made a big difference in how much pizza consumers purchased from the pizza shop. If the opposite occurs and a price

Price Elasticity of Demand

Jingle All the Way

This amusing comedy from 1996 features two fathers who procrastinate until Christmas Eve to try to buy a Turbo Man action figure for their children for Christmas morning. It's the only present that their kids truly want from Santa. The problem is that almost every child in America feels the same way—demand has been so unexpectedly strong that the stock of toys has almost completely sold out, creating a short-term shortage. However, related items, like Turbo Man's pet, Booster, are readily available.

The two dads wind up at the Mall of America, where a toy store has received a last-minute shipment of Turbo Man, attracting a crowd of desperate shoppers. The store manager announces that the list price has doubled and institutes a lottery system to determine which customers will be able to buy the toy. The bedlam that this creates is evidence that the higher price did not decrease the demand for Turbo Man.

Based on this description, what can we say about the price elasticity of demand for Turbo Man and Booster?

Turbo Man: The toy is needed immediately, and because kids are clamoring for it specifically, no good substitutes exist. Also, because the cost of the toy is relatively small (as a share of a shopper's budget), people are not as concerned about getting a good deal. Demand is, therefore, relatively inelastic.

Is the demand for Turbo Man elastic or inelastic?

Booster: Without Turbo Man, Booster is just another toy. Therefore, the demand for Booster is much more elastic than for Turbo Man, since there are many good substitutes. We see this in the movie when the toy store manager informs the crowd that the store has plenty of Boosters available, and the throng yells back, "We don't want it!"

drop makes a small difference in the quantity that consumers purchase, we say that demand was inelastic.

The negative (minus) sign in front of the coefficient is equally important. Recall that the law of demand describes an inverse relationship between the price of a good and the quantity demanded; when prices rise, the quantity demanded falls. The E_D coefficient reflects this inverse relationship with a negative sign. In other words, the pizza shop drops its price and consumers buy more pizza. Since pizza prices and consumer purchases of pizza generally move in opposite directions, the sign of the price elasticity of demand is almost always negative.

The Midpoint Method

The calculation above was simple because we looked at the change in price and the change in the quantity demanded from only one direction—that is, from a high price to a lower price. However, the complete—and proper—way to calculate elasticity is from both directions. Consider the following demand schedule (it doesn't matter what the product is):

Price	Quantity demanded
$12	20
$ 6	30

Let's calculate the elasticity of demand. If the price drops from $12 to $6—a drop of 50%—the quantity demanded increases from 20 to 30—a rise of 50%. Plugging the percentage changes into E_D yields

$$\text{Price Elasticity of Demand} = E_D = \frac{50\%}{-50\%} = -1.0$$

But if the price rises from $6 to $12—an increase of 100%—the quantity demanded falls from 30 to 20, or decreases by 33%. Plugging the percentage changes into E_D yields

$$\text{Price Elasticity of Demand} = E_D = \frac{-33 \text{ percent}}{100 \text{ percent}} = -0.33$$

This result occurs because percentage changes are usually calculated by using the initial value as the base, or reference point. In this example, we worked the problem two ways: by using $12 as the starting point and dropping the price to $6, and by using $6 as the starting point and increasing the price to $12. Even though we are measuring elasticity over the same range of values, the percentage changes are different.

To avoid this problem, economists use the *midpoint method*, which gives the same answer for the elasticity no matter what point you begin with. Equation 4.2 uses the midpoint method to express the price elasticity of demand. While this equation looks more complicated than Equation 4.1, it is not. The midpoint method merely specifies how to plug in the initial and ending values for price and the quantity to determine the percentage changes. Q_1 and P_1 are the initial values, and Q_2 and P_2 are the ending values.

(Equation 4.2)

$$E_D = \frac{\text{change in Q} \div \text{average value of Q}}{\text{change in P} \div \text{average value of P}}$$

$$= \frac{(Q_2 - Q_1) \div [(Q_1 + Q_2) \div 2]}{(P_2 - P_1) \div [(P_1 + P_2) \div 2]}$$

The change in the quantity demanded, $(Q_2 - Q_1)$, and the change in price, $P_2 - P_1$, are each divided by the average of the initial and ending values, or $[(Q_1 + Q_2) \div 2]$ and $[(P_1 + P_2) \div 2]$, to provide a way of calculating elasticity.

The midpoint method is the preferred method for solving elasticity problems. To see why this is the case, let's return to our pizza demand example.

If the price rises from \$6 to \$12, the quantity demanded falls from 30 to 20. Here the initial values are $P_1 = 6 and $Q_1 = 30$. The ending values are $P_2 = 12 and $Q_2 = 20$. Using the midpoint method:

$$E_D = \frac{(20 - 30) \div [(30 + 20) \div 2]}{($12 - $6) \div [($12 + $6) \div 2]} = \frac{-10 \div 25}{$6 \div $9} = -0.58$$

If the price falls from \$12 to \$6, quantity rises from 20 to 30. This time, the initial values are $P_1 = 12 and $Q_1 = 20$. The ending values are $P_2 = 6 and $Q_2 = 30$. Using the midpoint method:

$$E_D = \frac{(30 - 20) \div [(20 + 30) \div 2]}{($6 - $12) \div [($6 + $12) \div 2]} = \frac{10 \div 25}{-$6 \div $9} = -0.58$$

When we calculated the price elasticity of demand from \$6 to \$12 using \$6 as the initial point, $E_D = -0.33$. Moving in the opposite direction, from \$12 to \$6, made \$12 the initial reference point and $E_D = -1.0$. The midpoint method shown above splits the difference and uses \$9 and 25 pizzas as the midpoints. This approach makes the calculation of the elasticity coefficient the same, -0.58, no matter what direction the price moves. Therefore, economists use the midpoint method to standardize the results. So, using the midpoint method, we arrived at an elasticity coefficient of -0.58, which is between 0 and -1. What does that mean? In this case, the percentage change in the quantity demanded is less than the percentage change in the price. Whenever the percentage change in the quantity demanded is smaller than the percentage change in price, we say that demand is inelastic. In other words, the price drop does not make a big difference in how much pizza consumers purchased from the pizza shop. When the elasticity coefficient is less than -1, the opposite is true, and we say that demand is elastic.

Graphing the Price Elasticity of Demand

Visualizing elasticity graphically helps us understand the relationship between elastic and inelastic demand. Figure 4.1 shows elasticity graphically. As demand becomes increasingly elastic, or responsive to price changes, the demand curve flattens.

Figure 4.1a depicts the price elasticity for pet care. Many pet owners report that they would pay any amount of money to help their sick or injured pet get better. (Of course, pet care is not perfectly inelastic, because there is certainly a price beyond which some pet owners would not or could not pay; but for illustrative purposes, let's say that pet care *is* perfectly elastic.) For these pet owners, the demand curve is a vertical line. If you look along the Quantity axis, you will see that the quantity of pet care demanded (Q_D) remains constant no matter what it costs. At

For many pet owners, the demand for veterinary care is perfectly inelastic.

FIGURE 4.1

Elasticity and the Demand Curve

For any given price change across two demand curves, demand will be more elastic on the flatter demand curve than on the steeper demand curve. In (a), the demand is perfectly inelastic, so the price does not matter. In (b), the demand is relatively inelastic, so the price is less important than the quantity purchased. In (c), the demand is relatively elastic, so the price matters more than quantity. In (d), the demand is perfectly elastic, so price is all that matters.

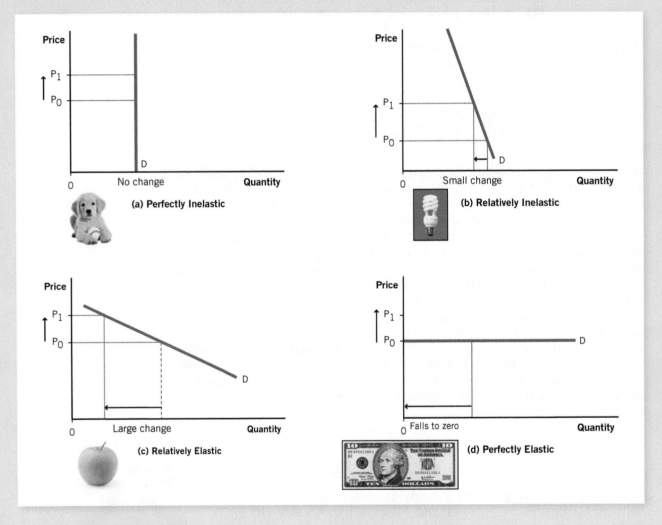

(a) Perfectly Inelastic

(b) Relatively Inelastic

(c) Relatively Elastic

(d) Perfectly Elastic

the same time, the price increases from P_0 to P_1. We can calculate the price elasticity coefficient as follows:

$$E_{\text{pet care}} = \frac{\text{percentage change in } Q_D}{\text{percentage change in P}} = \frac{0}{\text{percentage change in P}} = 0$$

When zero is in the numerator, we know that the answer will be zero no matter what we find in the denominator. This makes sense. Many pet owners will try to help their pet feel better no matter what the cost, so we can say that their demand is *perfectly inelastic*. This means that value of E_d will always be zero.

Moving on to Figure 4.1b, we consider the demand for electricity. Whereas many pet owners will not change their consumption of health care for their pet no matter what the cost, consumers of electricity will modify their use of electricity in response to price changes. When the price of electricity goes up, they will use less, and when it goes down, they will use more. But since living without electricity is not practical, using less is a matter of making relatively small lifestyle adjustments—buying energy-efficient light bulbs or turning down the thermostat a few degrees. As a result, the demand curve in 4.1b is relatively steep, but not completely vertical as it was in 4.1a.

When the variation on the Quantity axis is small compared to the variation on the Price axis, the price elasticity is *relatively inelastic*. Plugging these changes into the elasticity formula, we get

$$E_{electricity} = \frac{\text{percentage change in } Q_D}{\text{percentage change in P}} = \frac{\text{small change}}{\text{large change}}$$

The demand for electricity is relatively inelastic.

Recall that the law of demand describes an inverse relationship between price and output. Therefore, the changes along the Price and Quantity axes will always be in the opposite direction. A price elasticity of zero tells us there is no change in the quantity demanded when price changes. So when demand is relatively inelastic, the price elasticity of demand must be relatively close to zero. The easiest way to think about this is to consider how a 10% increase in electric rates works for most households. How much less electricity would you use? The answer for most people would be a little less, but not 10% less. You can adjust your thermostat, but you still need electricity to run your appliances and lights. When the price changes more than quantity changes, there is a larger change in the denominator. Therefore, the price elasticity of demand is between 0 and −1.

In Figure 4.1c, we consider an apple. Since there are many good substitutes for an apple, the demand for an apple is *relatively elastic*. The flexibility of consumer demand for apples is illustrated by the degree of responsiveness we see along the Quantity axis relative to the change exhibited along the Price axis. We can observe this by noting that a relatively elastic demand curve is flatter than an inelastic demand curve. So, whereas perfectly inelastic demand shows no change in demand with an increase in price, and relatively inelastic demand shows a small change in demand with an increase in price, relatively elastic demand shows a large change. Placing this information into the elasticity formula gives us

The demand for an apple is relatively elastic.

$$E_{apples} = \frac{\text{percentage change in } Q_D}{\text{percentage change in P}} = \frac{\text{large change}}{\text{small change}}$$

Now the numerator—the percentage change in Q_D—is large, and the denominator—the percentage change in P—is small. E_D is less than −1. Recall that the sign must be negative, since there is an inverse relationship between price and the quantity demanded. As the price elasticity of demand moves farther away from zero, the consumer becomes more responsive to price change. Since many other fruits are good substitutes for apples, a small change

The demand for a $10 bill is perfectly elastic.

in the price of apples will have a large change in the quantity demanded.

Figure 4.1d provides an interesting example: the demand for a $10 bill. Would you pay $11.00 to get a $10 bill? No. Would you pay $10.01 for a $10 bill? Still no. However, when the price drops to $10.00, you will probably become indifferent. Most of us would exchange $10 bills with someone else. The real magic here occurs when the price drops to $9.99. How many $10 bills would you buy if you could buy them for $9.99 or less? The answer: as many as possible! This is exactly what happens in currency markets, where small differences among currency prices around the globe motivate traders to buy and sell large quantities of currency and clear a small profit on the difference in exchange rates. This extreme form of price sensitivity is illustrated by a perfectly horizontal demand curve, which means that demand is *perfectly elastic*. Solving for the elasticity yields

$$E_{\$10 \text{ bill}} = \frac{\text{percentage change in } Q_D}{\text{percentage change in P}} = \frac{\text{nearly infinite change}}{\text{very small (\$0.01) change}}$$

We can think of this very small price change, from $10.00 to $9.99, as having essentially an unlimited effect on the quantity of $10 bills demanded. Traders go from being uninterested in trading at $10.00 to seeking to buy as many $10 bills as possible when the price drops to $9.99. As a result, the price elasticity of demand approaches infinity (∞).

There is a fifth type of elasticity, not depicted in Figure 4.1. *Unitary elasticity* is the special name that describes the situation in which elasticity is neither elastic nor inelastic. This occurs when the E_D is exactly -1, and it happens when the percentage change in price is exactly equal to the percentage change in quantity demanded. This characteristic of unitary elasticity will be important when we discuss the connection between elasticity and total revenue later in this chapter. You're probably wondering what an example of a unitary good would be. Relax. It is impossible to find a good that has a price elasticity of exactly -1 at all price points. It is enough to know that unitary demand represents the crossover from elastic to inelastic demand.

Now that you have had a chance to look at all four panels in Figure 4.1, here is a handy mnemonic that you can use to keep the difference between inelastic and elastic demand straight.

$$\mathbf{I} = \text{inelastic and} \quad \mathbf{E} = \text{elastic}$$

The "I" in the word "inelastic" is vertical, just like the inelastic relationships we examined in Figure 4.1. Likewise, the letter "E" has three horizontal lines to remind us that elastic demand is flat.

Finally, it is possible to pair the elasticity coefficients with an interpretation of how much price matters. You can see this in Table 4.2. When price does not matter, demand is perfectly inelastic (denoted by the coefficient of zero). Conversely, when price is the only thing that matters, demand becomes

TABLE 4.2			
The Relationship between Price Elasticity of Demand and Price			
Elasticity	E_d coefficient	Interpretation	Example in Figure 4.1
Perfectly inelastic	$E_D = 0$	Price does not matter.	Saving your pet
Relatively inelastic	$0 > E_D > -1$	Price is less important than the quantity purchased.	Electricity
Unitary	$E_D = -1$	Price and quantity are equally important.	
Relatively elastic	$-1 > E_D > -\infty$	Price is more important than the quantity purchased.	An apple
Perfectly elastic	$E_D \rightarrow -\infty$	Price is everything.	A $10 bill

perfectly elastic (denoted by $-\infty$). In between these two extremes, the extent to which price matters determines whether demand is relatively inelastic, unitary, or relatively elastic.

Time, Elasticity, and the Demand Curve

We have already seen that increased time makes demand more elastic. Figure 4.2 shows this graphically. When the price rises from P_1 to P_2, consumers cannot immediately avoid the price increase. For example, if your gas tank is almost empty, you must purchase gas at the new price. Over a slightly longer time horizon—the short run—consumers are more flexible and are able drive less in order to avoid higher-priced gasoline. This means that in the short run, consumption declines to Q_2. In the long run, when consumers have time to purchase a more fuel-efficient vehicle or move closer to work, purchases fall even further. As a result, the demand curve continues to flatten and the quantity demanded falls to Q_3.

Slope and Elasticity

In this section, we pause to make sure that you understand what you are observing in the figures. The demand curves shown in Figures 4.1 and 4.2 are straight lines, and therefore they have a constant slope, or steepness. (A refresher on slope is part of the appendix to Chapter 2.) So, looking at Figures 4.1 and 4.2, you might think that slope is the same as the price elasticity. But slope does not equal elasticity.

Consider, for example, a trip to Starbucks. Would you buy a tall skinny latte if it cost $10? How about $7? What about $5? Say you decide to buy the skinny latte because the price drops from $5 to $4. In this case, a small price change, a drop from $5 to $4, causes you to make the purchase. You can say the demand for skinny lattes is relatively elastic. Now look at Figure 4.3, which shows a demand curve for skinny lattes. At $5 the consumer purchases 0 lattes, at $4 she purchases 1 latte, at $3 she purchases 2, and she continues to buy one additional latte with each $1 drop in price. As you progress downward along the demand curve, price becomes less of an inhibiting factor and, as a result, the price elasticity of demand slowly becomes more inelastic. Notice that the slope of a linear demand curve is constant. However, when we calculate the price elasticity of demand between the various points in Figure 4.3, it becomes clear that demand is increasingly inelastic as we move down the demand curve. You can see this in the change in E_d from -9.1 to -0.1.

Perfectly inelastic demand would exist if the elasticity coefficient reached zero. Recall that a value of zero means that there is no change in the quantity demanded as a result of a price change. Therefore, values close to zero reflect inelastic demand, while those farther away reflect more elastic demand.

FIGURE 4.2

Elasticity and the Demand Curve over Time

Increased time acts to make demand more elastic. When the price rises from P_1 to P_2, consumers are unable to avoid the price increase in the immediate run. In the short run (D_2), consumers become more flexible and consumption declines to Q_2. Eventually, in the long run (D_3), there is time to make lifestyle changes that further reduce consumption. As a result, the demand curve continues to flatten and the quantity demanded falls to Q_3 in response to higher prices.

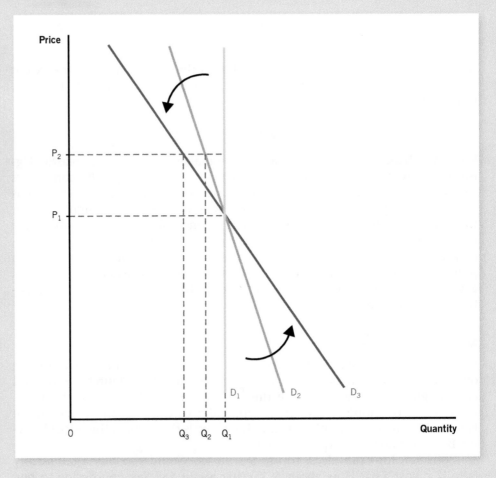

Price Elasticity of Demand and Total Revenue

Understanding the price elasticity of demand for the product you sell is important when running a business. The responsiveness of consumers to price changes determines whether a firm would be better off raising or lowering its price for a given product. In this section, we explore the relationship between the price elasticity of demand and a firm's total revenue.

But first we need to understand the concept of *total revenue*. **Total revenue** is the amount that consumers pay and sellers receive for a good. It is calculated by multiplying the price of the good by the quantity of the good that is sold. Table 4.3 reproduces the table from Figure 4.3 and adds a column for the total revenue. We find the total revenue by multiplying the price of a tall skinny latte by the quantity purchased.

After calculating total revenue at each price, we can look at the column of elasticity coefficients for a possible relationship. When we link revenues

Total revenue is the amount that consumers pay and sellers receive for a good.

FIGURE 4.3

The Difference between Slope and Elasticity

Along any straight demand curve, the price elasticity of demand (E_D) is not constant. You can see this by noting how the price elasticity of demand changes from highly elastic near the top of the demand curve to highly inelastic near the bottom of the curve.

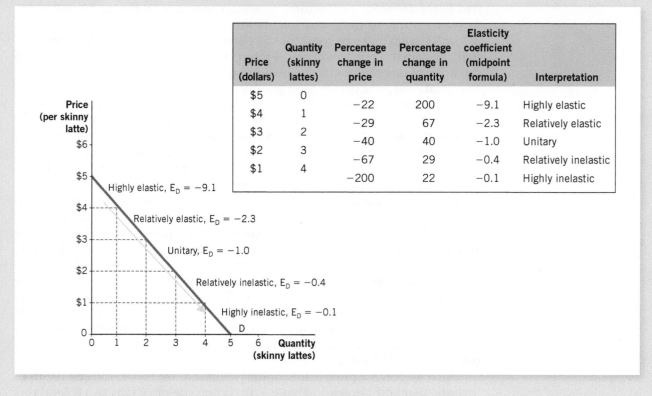

Price (dollars)	Quantity (skinny lattes)	Percentage change in price	Percentage change in quantity	Elasticity coefficient (midpoint formula)	Interpretation
$5	0				
$4	1	−22	200	−9.1	Highly elastic
$3	2	−29	67	−2.3	Relatively elastic
$2	3	−40	40	−1.0	Unitary
$1	4	−67	29	−0.4	Relatively inelastic
		−200	22	−0.1	Highly inelastic

Highly elastic, $E_D = -9.1$
Relatively elastic, $E_D = -2.3$
Unitary, $E_D = -1.0$
Relatively inelastic, $E_D = -0.4$
Highly inelastic, $E_D = -0.1$

TABLE 4.3

The Price Elasticity of Demand and Total Revenue

Price (P) (per skinny latte)	Quantity (Q) (skinny lattes)	Total revenue P × Q	Percentage change in price	Percentage change in quantity	Elasticity coefficient	Interpretation
$5	0	$0				
			−22	200	−9.1	Highly elastic
$4	1	$4				
			−29	67	−2.3	Relatively elastic
$3	2	$6				
			−40	40	−1.0	Unitary
$2	3	$6				
			−67	29	−0.4	Relatively inelastic
$1	4	$4				
			−200	22	−0.1	Highly inelastic
$0	5	$0				

Trade-offs

with the price elasticity of demand, a trade-off emerges. (This occurs because total revenue and elasticity relate to price differently. Total revenue involves multiplying the price times the quantity, while elasticity involves dividing the change in quantity demanded by the price.) Total revenue is zero when the price is too high ($5 or more) and when the price is $0. Between these two extremes, prices from $1 to $4 generate positive total revenue. Consider what happens when the price drops from $5 to $4. At $4, the first latte is purchased. Total revenue is $4 × 1 = $4. This is also the range at which the price elasticity of demand is highly elastic. As a result, lowering the price increases revenue. This continues when the price drops from $4 to $3. Now two lattes are sold, so the total revenue continues to rise to $3 × 2 = $6. As we continue to make our calculations, we see that until the price drops below $3, total revenue continues to climb. At the same time, the price elasticity of demand remains elastic. From this we conclude that when the price elasticity of demand is elastic, lowering the price will increase total revenue. This relationship is shown seen graphically in Figure 4.4a.

At a price of $4, one unit is sold and total revenue is $4. When the price drops to $3, two units are sold, so the total revenue is now $3 × 2 = $6. So, by lowering the price from $4 to $3 the business has generated $2 more in revenue. But to generate this extra revenue, the business has lowered the price from $4 to $3 and therefore has given up $1 for each unit it sells. This is represented by the pink-shaded area under the demand curve in Figure 4.4a.

When the price drops from $3 to $2, the total revenue stays at $6. This result occurs because demand is unitary, as shown in Figure 4.4b. This special condition exists when the percentage price change is exactly offset by an equal percentage change in the quantity demanded. In this situation, revenue remains constant. At $2, three lattes are purchased, so the total is $2 × 3, which is the same as it was when $3 was the purchase price. As a result, we can see that total revenues have reached a maximum. Between $3 and $2, the price elasticity of demand is unitary. This finding does not necessarily mean that the firm will operate at the unitary point. Maximizing profit, not revenue, is the ultimate goal of a business, and we have not yet accounted for costs in our calculation of profits.

Once we reach a price below unitary demand, we move into the realm of inelastic demand, shown in Figure 4.4c. When the price falls to $1, total revenue declines to $4. This result occurs because the price elasiticity of demand

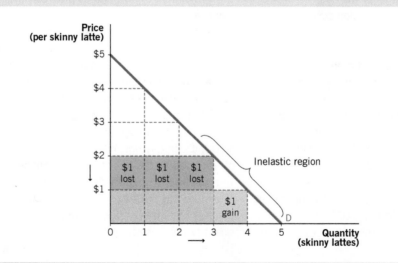

FIGURE 4.4

(a) The Total Revenue Trade-off When Demand Is Elastic

In the elastic region of the demand curve, lowering the price will increase total revenue. The gains from increased purchases, shown in the blue-shaded area, are greater than the losses from a lower pur-chase price, shown in the pink-shaded area.

(b) . . . When Demand Is Unitary

When demand is unitary, lowering the price will no longer increase total revenue. The gains from increased purchases, shown in the blue-shaded area, are equal to the losses from a lower pur-chase price, shown in the pink-shaded area.

(c) . . . When Demand Is Inelastic

In the inelastic region of the demand curve, lower-ing the price will decrease total revenue. The gains from increased purchases, shown in the blue-shaded area, are smaller than the losses from a lower pur-chase price, shown in the pink-shaded area.

is now relatively inelastic, or price insensitive. In other words, latte consumers adding a fourth drink will not gain as much benefit as they did when they purchased the first. Even though the price is declining by $1, price is increasingly unimportant; as you can see by the blue squares, it does not spur a large increase in consumption.

As we see in Figure 4.4c, at a price of $2, three units are sold and total revenue is $2 × 3 = $6. When the price falls to $1, four units are sold, so the total revenue is now $4 × 1 = $4. By lowering the price from $2 to $1, the business has lost $2 in extra revenue. This occurs because the business does not generate enough extra revenue from the lower price. Lowering the price from $2 to $1 causes a loss of $3 in existing sales revenue (the pink boxes). At the same time, it generates only $1 in new sales (the blue box).

In this analysis, we see that once the demand curve enters the inelastic area, lowering the price decreases total revenue. This is an unambiguously bad

ECONOMICS IN THE MEDIA

Elasticity and Total Revenue

D'oh! The Simpsons and Total Revenue

In the episode "Bart Gets an Elephant," the Simpsons find that their pet elephant, Stampy, is eating them out of house and home. So Bart devises a plan to charge admission for people to see the elephant. He begins by charging $1. However, the revenue collected is not enough to cover Stampy's food bill. When Homer discovers that they are not covering their costs, he raises the cost to see the elephant to $100. However, Homer is not the smartest businessman in the world, and all of the customers who would have paid Bart's $1 admission stay away. We can use our understanding of elasticity to explain why Homer's plan backfires.

Homer's plan is to increase the price. This would work if the demand to see the elephant were inelastic, but it is not. For $100 you could see a concert, attend a major sporting event, or eat out at a very nice restaurant! You'd have to really want to see the elephant to be willing to pay $100. It doesn't help that you can also go to any of the best zoos in the country, and see hundreds of other animals as well, for much less money. Homer's plan is doomed to fail because no one is willing to pay $100. Remember that total revenue = price × quantity purchased. If

The Simpsons cannot afford Stampy. What should they do?

the quantity demanded falls to zero, zero times anything is still zero. So Homer's plan does not generate any revenue.

In contrast, Bart's admission price of $1 brings in $58 in revenue. This is a good start, but not enough to cover Stampy's $300 food bill. Homer actually had the right idea here. Raising the price above $1 would generate more revenue up to a point. Would most of the customers pay $2 to see the elephant? Most likely. $5? Possibly. $10? Maybe. $100? Definitely not. Why not? There is a trade-off dictated by the law of demand. Higher prices will reduce the quantity demanded and vice versa. Therefore, the trick to maximizing total revenue is to balance increases in price against decreases in the quantity purchased.

outcome for a business. The lower price brings in less revenue and requires the business to produce more goods. Since making goods is costly, it does not make sense to lower prices into the region where revenues decline. We can be sure that no business will intentionally operate in the inelastic region of the demand curve.

How Do Changes in Income and the Prices of Other Goods Affect Elasticity?

We have seen how consumer demand responds to changes in the price of a single good. In this section, we will examine how responsive demand is to changes in income and to price changes in other goods.

Income Elasticity

Changes in personal income can have a large effect on consumer spending. After all, the money in your pocket influences not only how much you buy, but also the types of purchases you make. A consumer who is low on money may opt to buy a cheap generic product, while someone with a little extra cash can afford to upgrade. The grocery store aisle reflects this. Store brands and name products compete for shelf space. Lower-income shoppers can choose the store brand to save money, while more affluent shoppers can choose their favorite brand-name product without worrying about the purchase price. The **income elasticity of demand** (E_I) measures how a change in income affects spending. It is calculated by dividing the change in the quantity demanded by the change in personal income:

The income elasticity of demand measures how a change in income affects spending.

$$E_I = \frac{\text{percentage change in the quantity demanded}}{\text{percentage change in income}}$$

(Equation 4.3)

Unlike the price elasticity of demand, which is negative, the income elasticity of demand can be either positive or negative. When higher levels of income enable the consumer to purchase more, the goods that are purchased are *normal goods*, a term we learned about in Chapter 3. Since the demand for normal goods goes up with income, they have a positive income elasticity—a rise in income will cause a rise in the quantity purchased. For instance, if you receive a 20% pay raise and you decide to pay an extra 10% on your cable TV bill to add HBO, the resulting income elasticity is positive, since 10% divided by 20% is 0.5. Whenever the good is normal, the result is a positive income elasticity of demand, and purchases of the good rise as income expands.

Normal goods fall into two categories: *necessities* and *luxuries*. Goods that people consider to be necessities generally

Clothing purchases expand with income.

PRACTICE WHAT YOU KNOW

The Price Elasticity of Demand

In this section, there are two questions to give you practice computing the price elasticity of demand. Before we do the math, ask yourself whether you think the price elasticity of demand for either subs or the antibiotic amoxicillin is elastic.

Question: A store manager decides to lower the price of a featured sandwich from $3 to $2, and she finds that sales during the week increase from 240 to 480 units. Is demand elastic?

Answer: Consumers were flexible and bought significantly more sandwiches in response to the price drop. Let's calculate the price elasticity of demand (E_D) using Equation 4.2. Recall that

$$E_D = \frac{(Q_2 - Q_1) \div [(Q_1 + Q_2) \div 2]}{(P_2 - P_1) \div [(P_1 + P_2) \div 2]}$$

Plugging in the values from above yields

$$E_D = \frac{(480 - 240) \div [(240 + 480) \div 2]}{(\$2 - \$3) \div [(\$2 + \$3) \div 2]} = \frac{240 \div 360}{-\$1 \div \$2.50}$$

Therefore, $E_D = -1.67$.

Whenever the price elasticity of demand is less than -1, demand is considered elastic: the percentage change in the quantity demanded is greater than the percentage change in price. This outcome is exactly what the store manager expected. But subs are one just option for a meal; there are many other choices, such as salads, burgers, and chicken—all of which cost more than the now-reduced sandwich. Therefore, we should not be surprised that there is a relatively large percentage increase in sub purchases by price-conscious customers.

Is the demand for a sub or amoxicillin more elastic?

Question: A local pharmacy manager decides to raise the price of a 50-pill prescription of amoxicillin from $8 to $10. The pharmacy tracks the sales of amoxicillin over the next month and finds that sales decline from 1,500 to 1,480 boxes. Is the price elasticity of demand elastic?

Answer: First, let's consider the potential substitutes for amoxicillin. To be sure, it's possible to substitute other drugs, but they might not be as effective. Therefore, most patients prefer to use the drug prescribed by their doctor. Also, in this case the cost of the drug is relatively small. Finally, patients' need for amoxicillin is a short-run consideration. They want the medicine now so they will get better! All three factors would lead us to believe that the demand for amoxicillin is relatively inelastic. Let's find out if that intuition is confirmed in the data.

(CONTINUED)

(CONTINUED)

The price elasticity of demand using the midpoint method is

$$E_D = \frac{(Q_2 - Q_1) \div [(Q_1 + Q_2) \div 2]}{(P_2 - P_1) \div [(P_1 + P_2) \div 2]}$$

Plugging in the values from the example yields

$$E_D = \frac{(1480 - 1500) \div [(1480 + 1500) \div 2]}{(\$10 - \$8) \div [(\$8 + \$10) \div 2]}$$

Simplifying produces this:

$$E_D = \frac{-20 \div 1490}{\$2 \div \$9}$$

Therefore, $E_D = -0.06$. Recall that an E_D near zero indicates that the price elasticity of demand is highly inelastic, which is what we suspected. The price increase does not cause consumption to fall very much. If the store manager had been hoping to bring in a little extra revenue from the sales of amoxicillin, his plan was successful. Before the price increase, the business sold 1,500 units at $8, so revenues were $12,000. After the price increase, sales decreased to 1,480 units, but the new price is $10, so revenues now are $14,800. Raising the price of amoxicillin helped the pharmacy make an additional $2,800 in revenue.

have income elasticities between 0 and 1. For example, expenditures on items such as milk, clothing, electricity, and gasoline are unavoidable, and consumers at any income level must buy them no matter what. Although purchases of necessities will increase as income rises, they do not rise as fast as the increase in income does. Therefore, as income increases, spending on necessities will expand at a slower rate than the increase in income.

Air travel is a luxury good.

Rising income enables consumers to enjoy significantly more luxuries. This produces an income elasticity of demand greater than 1. For instance, a family of modest means may travel almost exclusively by car. However, as the family's income rises, they can afford air travel. A relatively small jump in income can cause the family to fly instead of drive.

In Chapter 3, we saw that *inferior goods* are those that people will choose not to purchase when their income goes up. Inferior goods have a negative income elasticity, because as income expands, the demand for the good declines. We see this in Table 4.4 with the example of macaroni and cheese, an inexpensive meal. As a household's income rises, it is able to afford healthier food and more variety in the meals it enjoys. Consequently, the number of times that mac and cheese is served declines. The decline in consumption indicates that mac and cheese is an inferior good, and this is reflected in the negative sign of the income elasticity.

TABLE 4.4			
Income Elasticity			
Type of good	**Subcategory**	**E_I coefficient**	**Example**
Inferior		$E_I < 0$	Macaroni and cheese
Normal	Necessity	$0 < E_I > 1$	Milk
Normal	Luxury	$E_I > 1$	Diamond ring

Cross-Price Elasticity

The **cross-price elasticity of demand** measures the responsiveness of the quantity demanded of one good to a change in the price of a related good.

Now we will look at how a price change in one good can affect the demand for a related good. For instance, if you enjoy pizza, the choice between ordering from Domino's or Pizza Hut is influenced by the price of both goods. The **cross-price elasticity of demand** (E_C) measures the responsiveness of the quantity demanded of one good to a change in the price of a related good.

(Equation 4.4)

$$E_C = \frac{\text{percentage change in the quantity demanded of one good}}{\text{percentage change in the price of a related good}}$$

Consider how two goods are related to each other. If the goods are substitutes, a price rise in one good will cause the quantity demanded of that good to decline. At the same time, since consumers can purchase the substitute good for the same price as before, demand for the substitute good will increase. When the price of Domino's pizza rises, consumers will buy more pizza from Pizza Hut.

The opposite is true if the goods are complements. When goods are related to each other, a price increase in one good will make the joint consumption of both goods more expensive. Therefore, the consumption of both goods will decline. For example, a price increase for turkeys will cause the quantity demanded of both turkey and gravy to decline. This means that the cross-price elasticity of demand is negative.

What if there is no relationship? For example, if the price of basketballs goes up, that probably will not affect the quantity demanded of bedroom slippers. In this case, the cross-price elasticity is neither positive nor negative; it is zero. Table 4.5 lists cross-price elasticity values according to type of good.

To learn how to calculate cross-price elasticity, let's consider an example from the skit "Lazy Sunday" on *Saturday Night Live*. The skit features Chris Parnell and Andy Samberg rapping about going to see *The Chronicles of Narnia* and eating cupcakes. In one inspired scene, they describe enjoying the soft drink Mr. Pibb with Red Vines candy and call the combination "crazy

TABLE 4.5

Cross-Price Elasticity

Type of good	E_I coefficient	Example
Substitutes	$E_C > 0$	Pizza Hut and Domino's
No relationship	$E_C = 0$	A basketball and bedroom slippers
Complements	$E_C < 0$	Turkey and gravy

delicious." From this, we can construct a cross-price elasticity example. Suppose that the price of a two-liter bottle of Mr. Pibb falls from $1.49 to $1.29. In the week immediately preceding the price drop, a local store sells 60 boxes of Red Vines. After the price drop, sales of Red Vines increase to 80 boxes. Let's calculate the cross-price elasticity of demand for Red Vines when the price of Mr. Pibb falls from $1.49 to $1.29.

The cross-price elasticity of demand using the midpoint method is

Have you tried Mr. Pibb and Red Vines together?

$$E_C = \frac{(Q_{RV2} - Q_{RV1}) \div [(Q_{RV1} + Q_{RV2}) \div 2]}{(P_{MP2} - P_{MP1}) \div [(P_{MP1} + P_{MP2}) \div 2]}$$

Notice that there are now additional subscripts to denote that we are measuring the percentage change in the quantity demanded of good RV (Red Vines) in response to the percentage change in the price of good MP (Mr. Pibb).

Plugging in the values from the example yields

$$E_C = \frac{(20) \div [(60 + 80) \div 2]}{(-\$0.20) \div [(\$1.49 + \$1.29) \div 2]}$$

Simplifying produces

$$E_C = \frac{20 \div 70}{-\$0.20 \div \$1.39}$$

Solving for E_C gives us a value of -1.01. Because the result is a negative value, this confirms our intuition that two goods that go well together ("crazy delicious") are complements, since the decrease in the price of Mr. Pibb causes consumers to buy more Red Vines.

ECONOMICS IN THE REAL WORLD

The Wii Rollout and Changes in the Video Game Industry

The Wii rollout generated long waiting lines.

When Nintendo launched the Wii console in late 2006, it fundamentally changed the gaming industry. The Wii uses motion-sensing technology. Despite relatively poor graphics, it provided a completely different gaming experience from its competitors, Playstation 3 (PS3) and the Xbox 360. Yet the PS3 and Xbox 360 had larger storage capacities and better graphics, in theory making them more attractive to gamers than the Wii.

During the 2006 holiday shopping season, the three systems had three distinct price points:

Wii = $249
Xbox = $399
Playstation 3 = $599

Wii and Xbox sales were very strong. As a result, both units were in short supply in stores. However, PS3 sales did not fare as well as its manufacturer, Sony, had hoped. The Wii outsold the PS3 by a more than 4:1 ratio, and the Xbox 360 outsold the PS3 by more than 2:1 during the first half of 2007. More telling, a monthly breakdown of sales figures across the three platforms shows the deterioration in the PS3 and Xbox 360 sales.

Units Sold in January 2007:

Wii: 460,000
Xbox 360: 249,000
PS3: 244,000

Units Sold in April 2007:

Wii: 360,000 (−22%)
Xbox 360: 174,000 (−30%)
PS3: 82,000 (−66%)

Faced with quickly falling sales, Sony lowered the price of the PS3 console. The company understood that consumer demand was quite elastic and that lowering the price was the only way to retain customers. Indeed, the lower price stimulated additional interest in the PS3 and helped to increase the number of units sold in the second half of the year. Without a firm grasp of the price elasticity of demand, Sony would not have made this move.

Meanwhile, interest in the Wii continued to be strong. For Nintendo, the market demand was relatively inelastic. Nintendo could have raised the price of its console but chose not to do so. One reason is that Nintendo also makes money by selling peripherals and games. These are strong complements to the console, and a higher console price would discourage customers from purchasing the Wii. Since the cross-price elasticity of demand for peripherals and games is highly negative, this strategy makes economic sense. Nintendo had chosen not to do this, in part, because the company wanted to maximize not only the console price, but also the prices of all of the related components. Nintendo's strategy worked. The four top-selling games during 2007 were all associated with the Wii rollout. ✳

PRACTICE WHAT YOU KNOW

Income Elasticity

Question: A college student eats ramen noodles twice a week and earns $300/week working part-time. After graduating, the student earns $1,000/week and eats ramen noodles every other week. What is the student's income elasticity?

Yummy, or all you can afford?

Answer: The income elasticity of demand using the midpoint method is

$$E_I = \frac{(Q_2 - Q_1) \div [(Q_1 + Q_2) \div 2]}{(I_2 - I_1) \div [(I_1 + I_2) \div 2]}$$

Plugging in yields

$$E_I = \frac{(0.5 - 2.0) \div [(2.0 + 0.5) \div 2]}{(\$1000 - \$300) \div [(\$300 + \$1000) \div 2]}$$

Simplifying yields

$$E_I = \frac{-1.5 \div 1.25}{\$700 \div \$650}$$

Therefore, $E_I = -1.1$.

The income elasticity of demand is positive for normal goods and negative for inferior goods. Therefore, the negative coefficient indicates that ramen noodles are an inferior good over the range of income—between $300 and $1,000, in this example. This result should confirm your intuition. The higher post-graduation income enables the student to substitute away from ramen noodles and toward other meals that provide more nourishment and enjoyment.

What Is the Price Elasticity of Supply?

Sellers, like consumers, are sensitive to price changes. However, the determinants of the *price elasticity of supply* are substantially different from the determinants of the price elasticity of demand. The **price elasticity of supply** is a measure of the responsiveness of the quantity supplied to a change in price.

In this section, we examine how much sellers respond to price changes. For instance, if the market price of gasoline increases, how will oil companies respond? The answer depends on the elasticity of supply. Oil must be refined into gasoline. If it is difficult for oil companies to increase their output of gasoline significantly, even if the price increases a lot, the quantity of gasoline supplied will not increase much. In this case, we say that the price elasticity

The **price elasticity of supply** is a measure of the responsiveness of the quantity supplied to a change in price.

What would it take to own a slice of paradise?

of supply is inelastic, or unresponsive. However, if the price increase is small and suppliers respond by offering significantly more gasoline for sale, the price elasticity of supply is elastic. We would expect to observe this outcome if it were easy to refine oil into gasoline.

When supply is not able to respond to a change in price, we say it is inelastic. Think of an oceanfront lot. The amount of land next to the ocean is fixed. If the price of oceanfront property rises, the supply of land cannot adjust to the price increase. In this case, the supply is perfectly inelastic and the elasticity is zero. Recall that a price elasticity coefficient of zero means that supply does not change as price changes.

When the ability of the supplier to make quick adjustments is limited, the elasticity of supply is less than 1. For instance, when a cellular network becomes congested, it takes suppliers a long time to provide additional capacity. They have to build new cell towers, which requires the purchase of land and additional construction costs. In contrast, a local hot dog vendor can easily add another cart in relatively short order. As a result, for the hot dog vendor, supply elasticity is elastic with an elasticity coefficient that is greater than 1. Table 4.6 examines the price elasticity of supply. Recall that the law of supply states that there is a direct relationship between the price of a good and the quantity that a firm supplies. As a result, the percentage change in the quantity supplied and the percentage change in price move in the same direction. The E_S coefficient reflects this direct relationship with a positive sign.

Determinants of the Price Elasticity of Supply

When we examined the determinants of the price elasticity of demand, we saw that consumers had to consider the number of substitutes, how expensive the item was compared to their overall budget, and the amount of time they had

TABLE 4.6

A Closer Look at the Price Elasticity of Supply

Elasticity	E_S coefficient	Example	
Perfectly inelastic	$E_S = 0$	Oceanfront land	
Relatively inelastic	$0 < E_S < 1$	Cellphone tower	
Relatively elastic	$E_S > 1$	Hot dog vendor	

to make a decision. Time and the adjustment process are also key elements in determining the price elasticity of supply. However, there is a critical difference: the degree of flexibility that producers have in bringing their product to the market quickly.

The Flexibility of Producers

When a producer can quickly ramp up output, supply tends to be elastic. One way to maintain flexibility is to have spare production capacity. Extra capacity enables producers to quickly meet changing price conditions, so supply is more responsive, or elastic. The ability to store the good is another way to stay flexible. Producers who have stockpiles of their products can respond more quickly to changes in market conditions. For example, De Beers, the international diamond conglomerate, stores millions of uncut diamonds. As the price of diamonds fluctuates, De Beers can quickly change the supply of diamonds it offers to the market. Likewise, hot dog vendors can relocate quickly from one street corner to another or add carts if demand is strong. However, many businesses cannot adapt to changing market conditions quickly. For instance, a golf course cannot easily build nine new holes to meet additional demand. This limits the golf course owner's ability to adjust quickly and increase the supply of golfing opportunities as soon as the fee changes.

Time and the Adjustment Process

In the immediate run, businesses, just like consumers, are stuck with what they have on hand. For example, a pastry shop that runs out of chocolate glazed donuts cannot bake more instantly. As we move from the immediate run to the short run and a price change persists through time, supply—just like demand—becomes more elastic. For instance, a golf resort may be able to squeeze extra production out of its current facility by staying open longer hours or moving tee times closer together, but those short-run efforts will not match the production potential of adding another course in the long run.

Figure 4.5 shows how the two determinants of supply elasticity are mapped onto the supply curve. In the immediate run, the supply curve is vertical (S_1). A vertical curve tells us that there is no responsiveness when the price changes. As producers gain additional time to make adjustments, the supply curve rotates from S_1, the immediate run, to S_2, the short run, to S_3, the long run. Like the demand curve, the supply curve becomes flatter through time. The only difference is that the supply curve rotates clockwise, whereas, as we saw in Figure 4.2, the demand curve rotates counterclockwise. With both supply and demand, the most important thing to remember is that more time allows for greater adjustment, so the long run is always more elastic.

Calculating the Price Elasticity of Supply

Like the price elasticity of demand, we can calculate the price elasticity of supply. This is useful when a business owner must decide how much to produce at various prices. The elasticity of supply measures how quickly the producer is able to change production in response to changes in price. When the price elasticity of supply is elastic, producers are able to quickly adjust production. If the price elasticity of supply is inelastic, production tends to remain roughly constant, despite large swings in price.

Here is the formula for the price elasticity of supply (E_S):

(Equation 4.5)

$$E_S = \frac{\text{percentage change in the quantity supplied}}{\text{percentage change in the price}}$$

Have you ever shopped for Solo cups?

This equation is almost exactly the same as that of the price elasticity of demand. The only difference is that we are measuring the percentage change in the quantity supplied in the numerator.

Consider how the manufacturer of Solo cups might respond to an increase in demand that causes the cups' market price to rise. The company's ability to change the amount it produces depends on the flexibility of the manufacturing process and the length of time needed to ramp up production. Suppose that the price of the cups rises by 10%. The company can increase its production by 5% immediately, but it will take many months to expand production by 20%. What can we say about the price elasticity of supply in this case? Using Equation 4.5, we can take the percentage change in the quantity supplied immediately (5%) and divide that by

FIGURE 4.5

Elasticity and the Supply Curve

Increased flexibility and more time make supply more elastic. When price rises from P_1 to P_2, producers are unable to expand output immediately and the supply curve remains at Q_1. In the short run (S_2), the firm becomes more flexible and output expands to Q_2. Eventually, in the long run (S_3), the firm is able produce even more, and it moves to Q_3 in response to higher prices.

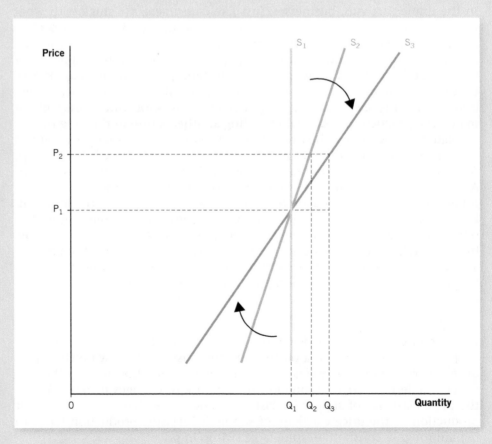

PRACTICE WHAT YOU KNOW

The Price Elasticity of Supply

Question: Suppose that the price of a barrel of oil increases from $60 to $100. The new output is 2 million barrels a day, and the old output is 1.8 million barrels. What is the price elasticity of supply?

Answer: The price elasticity of supply using the midpoint method is

$$E_D = \frac{(Q_2 - Q_1) \div [(Q_1 + Q_2) \div 2]}{(P_2 - P_1) \div [(P_1 + P_2) \div 2]}$$

Plugging in the values from the example yields

$$E_S = \frac{(0.2M) \div [(1.8M + 2.0M) \div 2]}{(\$40) \div [(\$60 + \$100) \div 2]}$$

Oil companies have us over a barrel.

Simplifying yields

$$E_S = \frac{0.2M \div 1.9M}{\$40 \div \$80}$$

Therefore, $E_S = 0.20$.

Recall from our discussion of the law of supply that there is a direct relationship between the price and the quantity supplied. Since E_S in this case is positive, we see that output rises as price rises. However, the magnitude of the output increase is quite small—this is reflected in the coefficient 0.20. Because oil companies cannot easily change their production process, they have a limited ability to respond quickly to rising prices. That inability is reflected in a coefficient that is relatively close to zero. A zero coefficient would mean that suppliers could not change their output at all. Here suppliers are able to respond, but only in a limited capacity.

the percentage change in price (10%). This gives us an $E_S = 0.5$, which signals that the elasticity of supply is relatively inelastic. However, with time the firm is able to increase the quantity supplied by 20%. If we divide 20% by the percentage change in the price (10%), we get $E_S = 2.0$, which indicates that the price elasticity of supply is relatively elastic in the long run.

How Do the Price Elasticity of Demand and Supply Relate to Each Other?

The interplay between the price elasticity of supply and the price elasticity of demand allows us to explain more fully how the economy operates. With an understanding of elasticity at our disposal, we can make a much richer and deeper analysis of the world around us. For instance, suppose that we are concerned about what will happen to the price of oil as economic development spurs additional demand in China and India. An examination of the determinants of the price elasticity of supply quickly confirms that oil producers have a limited ability to adjust production in response to rising prices. Oil wells can be uncapped to meet rising demand, but it takes years to bring the new capacity online. Moreover, storing oil reserves, while possible, is expensive. Therefore, the short-run supply of oil is quite inelastic. Figure 4.6 shows the combination of inelastic supply-side production constraints in the short run and the inelastic short-run demand for oil.

An increase in global demand from D_1 to D_2 will create significantly higher prices (from $60 to $90) in the short run. This occurs because increasing oil production is difficult in the short run. Therefore, the short-run supply curve (S_{SR}) is relatively inelastic. In the long run, though, oil producers are able to bring more oil to the market when prices are higher, so the supply curve rotates clockwise (S_{LR}), becoming more elastic, and the market price falls to $80.

What does this example tell us? It reminds us that the interplay between the price elasticity of demand and the price elasticity of supply determines the magnitude of the resulting price change. We cannot observe demand in isolation without also considering how supply responds. Similarly, we

FIGURE 4.6

A Demand Shift and the Consequences for Short- and Long-Run Supply

When an increase in demand causes the price of oil to rise from $60 to $90 per barrel, initially producers are unable to expand output very much—production expands from Q_1 to Q_2. However, in the long run, as producers expand production, the price will fall back to $80.

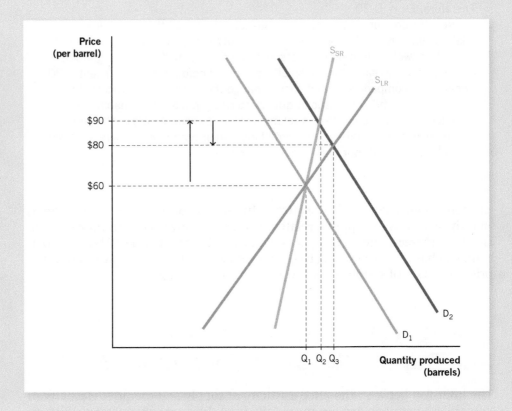

PRACTICE WHAT YOU KNOW

Elasticity: Trick or Treat Edition

How much would you spend on a Halloween pumpkin?

Question: An unusually bad growing season leads to a small pumpkin crop. What will happen to the price of pumpkins as Halloween approaches?

Answer: The demand for pumpkins peaks in October and rapidly falls after Halloween. Purchasing a pumpkin is a short-run decision to buy a unique product that takes up a relatively small share of the consumer's budget. As a result, the price elasticity of demand for pumpkins leading up to Halloween tends to be quite inelastic. At the same time, a small crop causes the entire supply curve to shift left. This causes the market price of pumpkins to rise. Since the demand is relatively inelastic in the short run and the supply of pumpkins is fixed, we expect the price to rise significantly. After Halloween, the price of any remaining pumpkins falls, since demand declines dramatically.

cannot simply think about the short-run consequences of demand and supply shifts; we also must consider how prices and quantity will vary in the long run. Armed with this knowledge, you can begin to see the power of the supply and demand model to explain the world around us.

Conclusion

Do sellers charge the highest price possible? We can now answer this misconception definitively: no. Sellers like higher prices in the same way consumers like lower prices, but that does not mean that they will charge the highest price possible. At very high prices, we learned that consumer demand is quite elastic. Therefore, a seller who charges too high a price will not sell much. As a result, firms learn that they must lower their price in order to attract more customers.

The ability to determine whether demand and supply are elastic or inelastic also enables economists to calculate the effects of personal, business, and policy decisions. When you combine the concept of elasticity with the supply and demand model from Chapter 3, you get a very powerful tool. As a result, we can now say much more about how the world works than we could before. In subsequent chapters, we will employ the understanding of elasticity to refine our models of economic behavior and make our results more realistic.

Price Elasticity of Supply and Demand: Buying Your First Car

When you buy a car, your knowledge of price elasticity can help you negotiate the best possible deal.

Recall that the three determinants of price elasticity of demand are (1) the share of the budget, (2) the number of available substitutes, and (3) the time you have to make a decision.

Let's start with your budget. You should have one in mind, but don't tell the salesperson what you are willing to spend; that is a vital piece of personal information you want to keep to yourself. If the salesperson suggests that you look at a model that is too expensive, just say that you are not interested. You might reply, "Buying a car is a stretch for me; I've got to stay within my budget." If the salesperson asks indirectly about your budget by inquiring whether you have a particular monthly payment in mind, reply that you want to negotiate over the invoice price once you decide on a vehicle. Never negotiate on the sticker price, which is the price you see in the car window, because it includes thousands of dollars in markup. You want to make it clear to the salesperson that the price you pay matters to you—that is, your demand is elastic.

Next, make it clear that you are gathering information and visiting other dealers. That is, reinforce that you have many available substitutes. Even if you really want a Honda, do not voice that desire to the Honda salesperson. Perhaps mention that you are also visiting the Toyota, Hyundai, and Ford showrooms. Compare what you've seen on one lot versus another. Each salesperson you meet should hear that you are seriously considering other options. This indicates to each dealership that your demand is elastic and that getting your business will require that they offer you a better price.

Taking your time to decide is also important. Never buy a car the first time you walk onto a lot. If you convey the message that you want a car immediately, you are saying that your demand is inelastic. If the dealership thinks that you have no flexibility, the staff will not give you their best offer. Instead, tell the salesperson that you appreciate their help and that you will be deciding over the next few weeks.

A good salesperson will know you are serious and will ask for your phone number or email address and contact you. The salesperson will sweeten the deal if you indicate you are narrowing down your choices and they are in the running. You wait. You win.

Also know that salespeople and dealerships have times when they want to move inventory. August is an especially good month to purchase. In other words, the price elasticity of supply is at work here as well. A good time to buy is when the dealer is trying to move inventory to make room for new models, because prices fall for end-of-the-model-year closeouts. Likewise, many sales promotions and sales bonuses are tied to the end of the month, so salespeople will be more eager to sell at that time.

Watch out for shady negotiation practices!

ANSWERING THE BIG QUESTIONS

1. What is the price elasticity of demand, and what are its determinants?

* The price elasticity of demand is a measure of the responsiveness of quantity demanded to a change in price.

* Demand will generally be more elastic if there are many substitutes available, if the item accounts for a large share of the consumer's budget, or if the consumer has plenty of time to make a decision.

* Economists categorize time in three distinct periods: the immediate run, where there is no time for consumers to adjust their behavior; the short run, where consumers can adjust, but only partially; and the long run, where consumers have time to fully adjust to market conditions.

* The price elasticity of demand can be calculated by taking the percentage change in the quantity demanded and dividing it by the percentage change in price. A value of zero indicates that the quantity demanded does not respond to a price change; if the price elasticity is zero, demand is said to be perfectly inelastic. When the price elasticity of demand is between 0 and −1, demand is inelastic. If the price elasticity of demand is less than −1, demand is elastic.

2. How do changes in income and the prices of other goods affect elasticity?

* The income elasticity of demand measures how a change in income affects spending. Normal goods have a positive income elasticity. Inferior goods have a negative income elasticity.

* The cross-price elasticity of demand measures the responsiveness of the quantity demanded of one good to a change in the price of a related good. Positive values for the cross-price elasticity mean that the two goods are substitutes, while negative values indicate that the two goods are complements. If the cross-price elasticity is zero, then the two goods are not correlated with each other.

3. What is the price elasticity of supply?

* The price elasticity of supply is a measure of the responsiveness of the quantity supplied to a change in price. Supply will generally be more elastic if producers have flexibility in the production process and ample time to adjust production.

* The price elasticity of supply is calculated by dividing the percentage change in the quantity supplied by the percentage change in price. A value of zero indicates that the quantity supplied does not respond to a price change; if the price elasticity is zero, supply is said to be perfectly inelastic. When the price elasticity of supply is between 0 and 1, demand is relatively inelastic. If the price elasticity of supply is greater than 1, supply is elastic.

4. How do the price elasticity of demand and supply relate to each other?

* The interplay between the price elasticity of demand and the price elasticity of supply determines the magnitude of the resulting price change.

CONCEPTS YOU SHOULD KNOW

cross-price elasticity of demand (p. 000)

elasticity (p. 000)

immediate run (p. 000)

income elasticity of demand (p. 000)

long run (p. 000)

price elasticity of demand (p. 000)

price elasticity of supply (p. 000)

short run (p. 000)

total revenue (p. 000)

QUESTIONS FOR REVIEW

1. Define the price elasticity of demand.

2. What are the three determinants of the price elasticity of demand?

3. Give an example of a good that has elastic demand. What is the value of the price elasticity if demand is elastic? Give an example of a good that has inelastic demand. What is the value of the price elasticity if demand is inelastic?

4. What is the connection between total revenue and the price elasticity of demand? Illustrate this relationship along a demand curve.

5. Explain why slope is different from elasticity.

6. Define the price elasticity of supply.

7. What are the two determinants of the price elasticity of supply?

8. Give an example of a good that has elastic supply. What is the value of the price elasticity if supply is elastic? Give an example of a good that has an inelastic supply. What is the value of the price elasticity if supply is inelastic?

9. Give an example of a normal good. What is the income elasticity of a normal good? Give an example of a luxury good. What is the income elasticity of a luxury good? Give an example of a necessity. What is the income elasticity of a necessity? Give an example of an inferior good. What is the income elasticity of an inferior good?

10. Define the cross-price elasticity of demand. Give an example with negative cross-price elasticity, another with zero cross-price elasticity, and a third with positive cross-price elasticity.

STUDY PROBLEMS

*1. If the government decided to impose a 50% tax on grey T-shirts, would this move generate a large or small increase in revenues? Use elasticity to explain your answer.

2. College logo T-shirts priced at $15 sell at a rate of 25 per week, but when the bookstore marks them down to $10, it finds that it can sell 50 T-shirts per week. What is the price elasticity of demand for the logo T-shirts?

3. Check out the following video: http://www .youtube.com/watch?v=ncZkrO06le8. Do the early shoppers appear to have elastic or inelastic demand on Black Friday? Explain your response.

4. If a 20% increase in price causes a 10% drop in the quantity demanded, is the price elastic-

ity of demand for this good elastic, unitary, or inelastic?

5. Characterize each of the following goods as perfectly elastic, relatively elastic, relatively inelastic, or perfectly inelastic.
   a. a life-saving medication
   b. a photocopy that costs 11 cents at one copy store, when all of the store's competitors charge 10 cents per copy
   c. a fast-food restaurant located in the food court of a shopping mall
   d. the water bill you pay

6. A local paintball business receives total revenue of $8,000 a month when it charges $10 per person, and $10,000 in total revenue when it charges $6 per person. Over that range of

prices, does the business face elastic, unitary, or inelastic demand?

7. At a price of $200, a cellphone company manufactures 300,000 units. At a price of $150, the company produces 200,000 phones. What is the price elasticity of supply?

8. Do customers who visit convenience stores at 3 a.m. have a price elasticity of demand that is more or less elastic than those who visit at 3 p.m.?

9. A worker gets a 25% raise. As a result, he decides to eat out twice as much as before and cut back on the number of frozen lasagna dinners from once a week to once every other week. Determine the income elasticity of demand for eating out and for having frozen lasagna dinners.

10. The cross-price elasticity of demand between American Eagle and Hollister is 2.0. What does that tell us about the relationship between these two stores?

11. A local golf course is considering lowering its fees in order to increase the revenue coming in. Under what conditions is the fee reduction a good idea?

12. A private university notices that in-state and out-of-state students seem to respond differently to tuition changes.

Tuition	Quantity demanded (in-state applicants)	Quantity demanded (out-of-state applicants)
$10,000	6,000	12,000
$15,000	5,000	9,000
$20,000	4,000	6,000
$30,000	3,000	3,000

As the price of tuition rises from $15,000 to $20,000, what is the price elasticity of demand for in-state applicants and also for out-of-state applicants?

SOLVED PROBLEMS

1. To answer this question, we need to consider the price elasticity of demand. The tax is only on grey T-shirts. This means that T-shirt customers who buy other colors can avoid the tax entirely—which means that the demand for grey T-shirts is relatively elastic. Since not many grey T-shirts will be sold, the government will generate a small increase in revenues from the tax.

9. In this question a worker gets a 25% raise, so we can use this information in the denominator when determining the income elasticity of demand. We are not given the percentage change for the meals out, so we need to plug in how often the worker ate out before (once a week) and the amount he eats out after the raise (twice a week).
Plugging into E_I gives us
$$E_I = \frac{(2-1) \div [(1+2) \div 2]}{25\%}$$
Simplifying yields
$$E_I = \frac{1 \div 1.5}{25\%}$$

Therefore, $E_I = 2.67$.

The income elasticity of demand for eating out is positive for normal goods. Therefore, eating out is a normal good. This result should confirm your intuition.

Let's see what happens with frozen lasagna once the worker gets the 25% raise. Now he cuts back on the number of lasagna dinners from once a week to once every other week.

Plugging into E_I gives us
$$E_I = \frac{(0.5-1) \div [(1+0.5) \div 2]}{25\%}$$
Simplifying yields
$$E_I = \frac{-0.5 \div 0.75}{25\%}$$

Therefore, $E_I = -2.67$. The income elasticity of demand for having frozen lasagna is negative. Therefore, frozen lasagna is an inferior good. This result should confirm your intuition.

Price Controls

The minimum wage helps everyone earn a living wage.

You are probably familiar with the minimum wage, which is an example of a *price control*. If you have ever worked for the minimum wage, you

MIS CONCEPTION

probably think that raising it sounds like a great idea. You may support minimum wage legislation because you believe it will help struggling workers to make ends meet. After all,

it seems reasonable that firms should pay workers at least enough to cover the necessities of life, or what is referred to as a living wage.

Price controls are not a new idea. The first recorded attempt to control prices was four thousand years ago in ancient Babylon, when King Hammurabi decreed how much corn a farmer could pay for a cow. Similar attempts to control prices occurred in ancient Egypt, Greece, and Rome. Each attempt ended badly. In Egypt, farmers revolted against tight price controls and intrusive inspections, eventually causing the economy to collapse. In Greece, the Athenian government set the price of grain at a very low level. Predictably, the supply of grain dried up. In 301 CE, the Roman government under Emperor Diocletian prescribed the maximum price of beef, grains, clothing, and many other articles. Almost immediately, markets for these goods disappeared.

History has shown us that price controls generally do not work. Why? Because they disrupt the normal functioning of the market. By the end of this chapter, we hope that you will understand why price controls such as minimum wage laws are rarely the win-win propositions that legislators often claim. To help you understand why price controls lead to disequilibrium in markets, this chapter focuses on the two most common types of price controls: *price ceilings* and *price floors*.

The code of Hammurabi established the first known price controls.

BIG QUESTIONS

* When do price ceilings matter?
* What effects do price ceilings have on economic activity?
* When do price floors matter?
* What effects do price floors have on economic activity?

When Do Price Ceilings Matter?

Price controls
are an attempt to set
prices through government
involvement in the market.

Price ceilings
are legally established
maximum prices for goods
or services.

Price controls are an attempt to set prices through government involvement in the market. In most cases, and certainly in the United States, price controls are enacted to ease perceived burdens on the population. A **price ceiling** creates a legally established maximum price for a good or service. In the next section, we will consider what happens when a price ceiling is in place. Price ceilings create many unintended effects that policymakers rarely acknowledge.

Understanding Price Ceilings

To understand how price ceilings work, let's try a simple thought experiment. Suppose that prices are rising because of inflation. The government is concerned that people with low incomes will not be able to afford enough to eat. To help the disadvantaged, legislators pass a law stating that no one can charge more than $0.50 for a loaf of bread. (Note that this price ceiling is about one-third the typical price of generic white bread.) Does the new law accomplish its goal? What happens?

The law of supply and demand tells us that if the price drops, consumer demand will increase. At the same time, the quantity supplied will fall because producers will be receiving lower profits for their efforts. This twin dynamic of increased consumer demand and reduced quantity will cause a shortage of bread.

On the demand side, consumers will want more bread than is available at the legal price. There will be long lines for bread, and many people will not be able to get the bread they want. On the supply side, producers will look for ways to maintain their profits. They can reduce the size of each loaf they produce. They can also use cheaper ingredients, thereby lowering

Empty shelves signal a shortage of products.

the quality of their product, and they can stop making fancier varieties. In addition, *black markets* will develop to help supply meet demand.

Black markets are illegal markets that arise when price controls are in place. For instance, in the former Soviet Union price controls on bread and other essentials led to very long lines. In our bread example, many people who do not want to wait in line for bread, or who do not obtain it despite waiting in line, will resort to illegal means to obtain it. This means that sellers will go underground and charge higher prices to deliver customers the bread they want.

Table 5.1 summarizes the likely outcome of price controls on bread.

Black markets are illegal markets that arise when price controls are in place.

Incentives

TABLE 5.1

A Price Ceiling on Bread

Question	Answer / Explanation	Result
Will there be more or less bread for sale?	Consumers will want to buy more since the price is lower, but producers will manufacture less. The net result will be a shortage of bread.	Empty shelves.
Will the size of a typical loaf change?	Since the price is capped at $0.50 per loaf, manufacturers will try to maintain profits by reducing the size of each loaf.	No more giant loaves.
Will the quality change?	Since the price is capped, producers will use cheaper ingredients, and many expensive brands and varieties will no longer be profitable to produce. Thus the quality of available bread will decline.	Focaccia bread will disappear.
Will the opportunity cost of finding bread change?	The opportunity cost of finding bread will rise. This means that consumers will spend significant resources going from store to store to see if a bread shipment has arrived and waiting in line for a chance to get some.	Bread lines will become the norm.
Will people have to break the law to buy bread?	Since bread will be hard to find and people will still need it, a black market will develop. Those selling and buying on the black market will be breaking the law.	Black-market bread dealers will help reduce the shortage.

If you can touch the ceiling, you can't go any higher. A binding price ceiling stops prices from "rising."

The Effect of Price Ceilings

Now that we have some understanding of how a price ceiling works, we can transfer that knowledge into the supply and demand model for a deeper analysis of how price ceilings affect the market. To explain when price ceilings matter in the short run, we will examine the outcomes of two types of price ceilings: nonbinding and binding.

Nonbinding Price Ceilings

The effect of a price ceiling depends on the level at which it is set. When a price ceiling is above the equilibrium price, we say it is *nonbinding*. Figure 5.1 shows a price ceiling of $2.00 per loaf in a market where $2.00 is above the equilibrium price (P_E). All prices at or below $2.00 (the green area) are legal. Prices above the price ceiling (the red area) are illegal. But since the market equilibrium (E) occurs in the green area, the price ceiling does not influence the market; it is nonbinding. As long as the equilibrium price remains below the price ceiling, price will continue to be regulated by supply and demand. Since there is rarely a compelling political reason to set a price ceiling above the equilibrium price, nonbinding price ceilings are unusual.

Binding Price Ceilings

When a price ceiling is below the market price, it creates a binding constraint that prevents supply and demand from clearing the market. In Figure 5.2,

FIGURE 5.1

A Nonbinding Price Ceiling

The price ceiling ($2.00) is set above the equilibrium price ($1.00). Since market prices are set by the intersection of supply (S) and demand (D), as long as the equilibrium price is below the price ceiling, the price ceiling is nonbinding and has no effect.

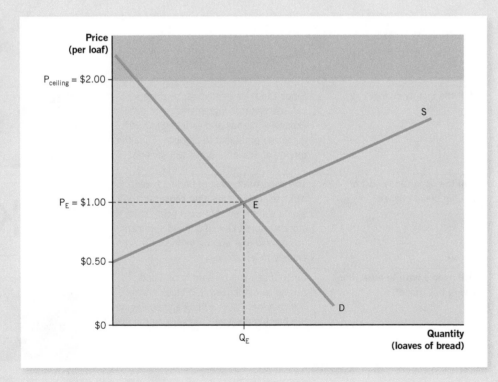

the price ceiling for bread is set at $0.50 per loaf. Since $0.50 is well below the equilibrium price of $1.00, this creates a binding price ceiling. Notice that at a price of $0.50, the quantity demanded (Q_D) is greater than the quantity supplied (Q_S)—in other words, a shortage exists. Shortages typically cause prices to rise, but the imposed price ceiling prevents that from happening. A price ceiling of $0.50 allows only the prices in the green area. The market cannot reach the equilibrium point E at $1.00 per loaf because it is located above the price ceiling, in the red area.

The black-market price is also set by supply and demand. Since prices above $0.50 are illegal, sellers are unwilling to produce more than Q_S. Once the price ceiling is in place, sellers cannot legally charge prices above the ceiling, so the incentive to produce along the original supply curve vanishes. Since a shortage still exists, an illegal market will form to resolve the shortage. At that point, purchasers can illegally resell what they have just bought at $0.50 for far more than what they just paid. Since the supply of legally produced bread is Q_S, the intersection of the vertical dashed line that reflects Q_S and the demand curve at point $E_{black\ market}$ establishes the black-market price $P_{black\ market}$, at $2.00 per loaf for illegally sold bread. Since the black-market price is substantially more than the market equilibrium price (P_E) of $1.00, illegal suppliers (underground bakers) will also enter the market in order to satisfy demand. As a result, the black-market price eliminates the shortage caused by the price ceiling. However, the price ceiling has created two unintended consequences: a smaller supply of bread (Q_S is less than Q_E), and a higher price for those who are forced to purchase it on the black market.

Incentives

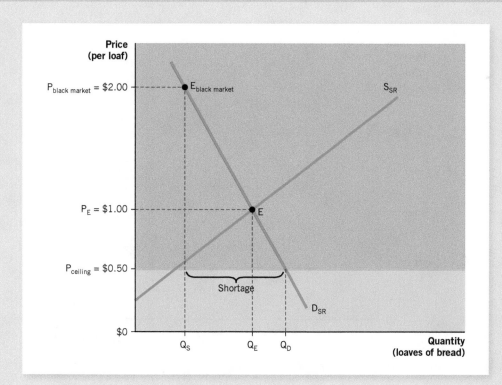

FIGURE 5.2

A Binding Price Ceiling

A binding price ceiling prevents sellers from increasing the price and causes them to reduce the quantity they offer for sale. As a consequence, prices no longer signal relative scarcity. Consumers desire to purchase the product at the price-controlled level, and this creates a shortage in the short run; many will be unable to obtain the good. As a result, those who are shut out of the market will turn to other means to acquire the good. This establishes a black market for the good at a price of the black market.

Price Ceilings in the Long Run

In the long run, supply and demand become more elastic, or flatter. Recall from Chapter 4 that when consumers have additional time to make choices, they find more ways to avoid high-priced goods and more ways to take advantage of low prices. Additional time also gives producers the opportunity to produce more when prices are high and less when prices are low. In this section, we consider what will happen if a binding price ceiling on bread remains in effect for a long time. We have already observed that when binding price ceilings are in effect in the short run, shortages and black markets develop. Are the long-run implications of price ceilings more or less problematic than the short-run implications? Let's find out by looking at what happens to both supply and demand.

Figure 5.3 shows the result of a price ceiling that remains in place for a long time. Here the supply curve is more elastic than its short-run counterpart in Figure 5.2. The supply curve is flatter because in the long run producers respond by producing less bread and converting their facilities to make similar products that are not subject to price controls—for example, bagels and rolls—that will bring them a reasonable return on their investments. Therefore, in the long run the quantity supplied (Q_S) grows even smaller.

The demand curve is also more elastic in the long run. In the long run, more people will attempt to take advantage of the low price ceiling by changing their eating habits to consume more bread. Even though consumers will

FIGURE 5.3

The Effect of a Binding Price Ceiling in the Long Run

In the long run, increased elasticity on the part of both producers and consumers makes the shortage larger than it was in the short run. Consumers adjust their demand to the lower price and want more bread. Producers adjust their supply and make less of the unprofitable product. As a result, products become progressively harder to find.

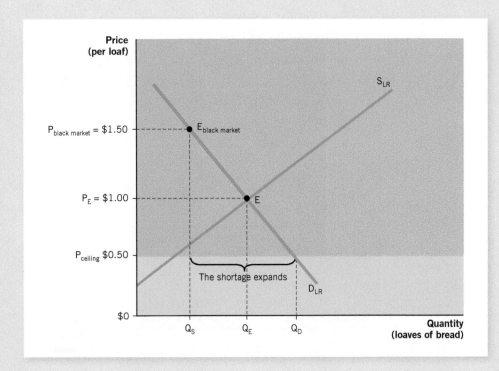

Price Ceilings

Moscow on the Hudson

This 1984 film starring Robin Williams chronicles the differences between living in the United States and the former Soviet Union. In Moscow, we see hundreds of people waiting in line to receive essentials like bread, milk, and shoes. In the Soviet Union, production was controlled and prices were not allowed to equalize supply and demand. As a result, shortages were common. Waiting in line served as a rationing mechanism in the absence of price adjustments.

This film is memorable because of the reactions that Robin Williams's character has once he immi-

Soviet-era food-rationing coupon

Soviet-era bread line

grates to the United States. In one inspired scene, he walks into a supermarket to buy coffee. He asks the manager where the coffee aisle is located, and when he sees that the aisle is not crowded, he asks the manager where the coffee line is located. The manager responds that there is no coffee line, so Williams walks down the coffee aisle slowly, naming each variety. We see his joy at being able to buy coffee without waiting and at having so many options to choose from. This scene nicely showcases the differences between the market system of the United States and the controlled economy of the former Soviet Union.

often find empty shelves in the long run, their demand for cheap bread will increase. At this point, a flatter demand curve means that consumers are more flexible. As a result, the quantity demanded (Q_D) expands and bread is hard to find at $0.50 per loaf. The shortage will become so acute that consumers will turn to bread substitutes, like bagels and rolls, that are more plentiful because they are not price controlled.

Increased elasticity on the part of both producers and consumers magnifies the unintended consequences we observed in the short run. Therefore, products subject to a price ceiling become progressively harder to find in the long run. A black market will develop. However, in the long run our bread consumers will choose substitutes for expensive black-market bread, and then demand will go down. In the long run, this will cause somewhat lower black-market prices.

PRACTICE WHAT YOU KNOW

Price Ceilings: Concert Tickets

Question: Suppose that fans of Avicii persuade Congress to impose a price ceiling of $25 for every Avicii concert ticket. Would this policy affect the number of people who attend his concerts?

You've got "a good feeling" about this concert.

Answer: The price ceiling prevents supply and demand from reaching the equilibrium price. As a result, at $25 there is a shortage of tickets. Since Avicii controls when and where he tours, he will choose to tour less in the United States and more in countries that do not regulate the ticket prices he can charge. This will make it more difficult for his U.S. fans to see him perform live, so the answer to the question is yes: the policy will influence the number of people who attend Avicii concerts (fewer in the United States, and more abroad).

What Effects Do Price Ceilings Have on Economic Activity?

We have seen the logical repercussions of a hypothetical price ceiling on bread and the incentives it creates. Now let's use supply and demand analysis to examine two real-world price ceilings: *rent control* and *price gouging laws*.

Rent Control

Rent control
is a price ceiling that applies to the housing market.

Under **rent control**, a local government caps the price of apartment rentals to keep housing affordable. While this may be a laudable goal, rent control doesn't work. In fact, it doesn't help poor residents of a city to find affordable housing or gain access to housing at all. In addition, these policies contribute to dangerous living conditions.

Mumbai, India, provides a chilling example of what can happen when rent controls are applied over an extended period. In Mumbai, many rent-controlled buildings have become dilapidated. Every monsoon season, several of these buildings fall—often with tragic consequences. Since the rent that property owners are permitted to charge is so low, they have less income to use for maintenance. Therefore, they cannot afford to maintain the buildings properly and make a reasonable profit. As a result, rent-control policies have led to the decay of many apartment buildings not just in Mumbai but also worldwide.

To understand how a policy can backfire so greatly, let's look at the history of rent control in New York City. In 1943, in the midst of World War II, the federal government established the Emergency Price Control Act. The act was designed to keep inflation in check during the war, when many essential commodities were scarce. After the war, the federal government ended price controls, but the state of New York continued rent control. Today, there are approximately one million rent-controlled units in New York City. Rent controls limit the price a landlord can charge a tenant for rent. They also require that the landlord provide certain basic services; but not surprisingly, landlords keep maintenance to a minimum.

Many apartment buildings in Mumbai, India, are dilapidated as a result of rent-control laws.

Does the presence of so many rent-controlled apartments mean that less affluent households can easily find a cheap place to rent? Hardly. When a rent-controlled unit is vacated, the property is generally no longer subject to rent control. Since most rent-controlled apartments are passed by tenants from generation to generation to remain in the program, rent control no longer even remotely serves its original purpose of helping low-income households. Clearly, the law was never intended to subsidize fancy vacation homes, but that's what it does! This has happened, in part, because some tenants who can afford to live elsewhere choose not to. Their subsidized rent enables them to save enough money to have a second or third home in places such as upstate New York, Florida, or Europe.

Incentives

The attempt to make housing more affordable in New York City has, ironically, made housing harder to obtain. It has encouraged the building of upscale properties rather than low-income units, and it has created a set of behaviors among landlords that is inconsistent with the ideals of justice and affordability that rent control was designed to address. Figure 5.4 shows why rent control fails. As with any price ceiling, rent control causes a shortage since the demand in the short run (D_{SR}) is greater than the supply in the short run (S_{SR}). Because rent-controlled apartments are vacated slowly, the supply of rent-controlled units contracts in the long run, which causes the supply curve to become more elastic (S_{LR}). Demand also becomes more elastic in the long run (D_{LR}), which causes the quantity demanded for rent-controlled units to rise ($Q_{D_{LR}}$). The combination of fewer available units and more consumers looking for rent-controlled units leads to a larger shortage in the long run.

Price Gouging

Another kind of price control, **price gouging laws**, places a temporary ceiling on the prices that sellers can charge during times of national emergency until markets function normally again. Over 30 states in the United States have laws against price gouging. Like all price controls, price gouging laws have

Price gouging laws place a temporary ceiling on the prices that sellers can charge during times of emergency.

Large generator: $900 after Hurricane Wilma hit.

unintended consequences. This became very apparent in the southern United States in 2005.

The hurricane season of 2005 was arguably the worst in U.S. history. Katrina and Rita plowed through the Gulf of Mexico with devastating effects, especially in Louisiana and Texas. Later that year, Wilma grew into the most powerful hurricane ever recorded in the Atlantic basin. When Wilma hit Fort Myers, Florida, in November, it ended a season for the record books. Florida has one of the strictest price gouging laws in the country. The statute makes it illegal to charge an "excessive" price immediately following a natural disaster. The law is designed to prevent the victims of natural disasters from being exploited in a time of need. But does it work?

Consider David Medina of Miami Beach. Immediately after Wilma hit, he drove to North Carolina, purchased 35 gas-powered generators, and returned to Florida, where he sold them from the back of his truck. He charged $900 for large generators, which he had purchased for $529.99, and $600 for small generators, which had cost him $279.99. After selling most of the units, Medina was arrested for price gouging. Under Florida law, his remaining generators were confiscated, and he was fined $1,000 for each sale. In addition, he was charged with selling without a business license. While there is no doubt that Medina intended to capitalize on the misfortune of others, it is hard to prove that he did any harm. The people who bought from

FIGURE 5.4

Rent Control in the Short Run and Long Run

Because rent-controlled apartments are vacated slowly, the supply of units contracts in the long run and the supply curve becomes more elastic. Demand also becomes more elastic in the long run, causing the quantity demanded to rise. The combination of fewer units available to rent and more consumers looking to find rent-controlled units leads to a larger shortage in the long run.

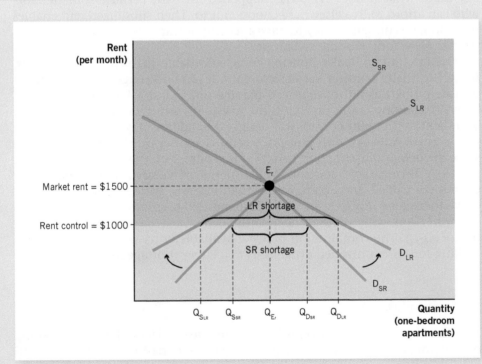

him did so voluntarily, each believing that the value of the generator was greater than the price Medina was charging.

Prices act to ration scarce resources. When the demand for generators or other necessities is high, the price rises to ensure that the available units are distributed to those who value them the most. More important, the ability to charge a higher price provides sellers with an incentive to make more units available. If there is limited ability for the price to change when demand increases, there will be a shortage. Therefore, price gouging legislation means that devastated communities must rely exclusively on the goodwill of others and the slow-moving machinery of government relief efforts. This closes off a third avenue, entrepreneurial activity, as a means to alleviate poor conditions.

Incentives

Figure 5.5 shows how price gouging laws work and the shortage they create. If the demand for gas generators increases immediately after a disaster (D_{after}), the market price rises from $530 to $900. But since $900 is considered excessive, sales at that price are illegal. This creates a binding price ceiling for as long as a state of emergency is in effect. Whenever a price ceiling is binding, it creates a shortage. You can see this in the figure in the difference between quantity demanded and quantity supplied at the price ceiling level mandated by the law. In this case, the normal ability of supply and demand to ration the available generators is short-circuited. Since more people demand generators after the disaster than before it, those who do not get to the store soon enough are out of luck. When the emergency is lifted and the market returns to normal, the temporary shortage created by legislation against price gouging is eliminated.

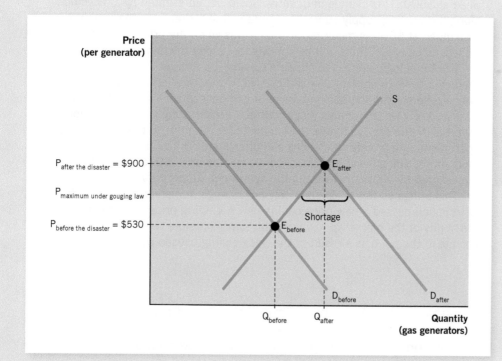

FIGURE 5.5

Price Gouging

Price gouging laws serve as a nonbinding price ceiling during normal times. However, when a natural disaster strikes, price gouging laws go into effect. In our example, this shifts the demand curve for generators to the right and causes the new equilibrium price (E_{after}) to rise above the legal limit. This creates a shortage. When the emergency is lifted, the market demand returns to normal, and the temporary shortage created by price gouging legislation is eliminated.

PRACTICE WHAT YOU KNOW

Price Ceilings: Student Rental Apartments

Here is a question that often confuses students.

Question: Imagine that a city council decides that the market price for renting student apartments is too high and passes a law that establishes a rental price ceiling of $600 per month. The result of the price ceiling is a shortage. Which of the following caused the shortage of apartments?

a. Both suppliers and demanders. Landlords will cut the supply of apartments, and the demand from renters will increase.

b. A spike in demand from many students who want to rent cheap apartments

c. The drop in supply caused by apartment owners pulling their units off the rental market and converting them into condos for sale

d. The price ceiling set by the city council

Answer: Many students think that markets are to blame when shortages (or surpluses) exist. The first reaction is to find the culpable party—either the supplier or the demander, or both.

Answer (a) is a typical response. But be careful. Supply and demand have not changed—they are exactly the same as they were before the price ceiling was implemented. What *has* changed is the quantity of apartments supplied at $600. This change in quantity would be represented by a movement along the existing supply curve. The same is true for renters. The quantity demanded at $600 is much larger than it was when the price was not controlled. Once again, there will be a movement along the demand curve.

The same logic applies to answers (b) and (c). Answer (b) argues that there is a spike in student demand caused by the lower price. But price cannot cause a shift in the demand curve; it can only cause a movement along a curve. Likewise, (c) argues that apartment owners supply fewer units for rent. Landlords cannot charge more than $600 per unit, so they convert some apartments into private residences and offer them for sale in order to make more profit. Since fewer apartments are available at $600, this would be represented by a movement along the apartment supply curve.

Shabby chic. Would a price ceiling make apartments more affordable for college students?

This brings us to (d). There is only one change in market conditions: the city council passed a new price ceiling law. A binding price ceiling disrupts the ability of the market to reach equilibrium. Therefore, we can say that the change in the price as a result of the price ceiling caused the shortage.

When Do Price Floors Matter?

In this section, we examine price floors. Like price ceilings, price floors create many unintended effects that policymakers rarely acknowledge. However, unlike price ceilings, price floors result from the political pressure of suppliers to keep prices high. Most consumers prefer lower prices when they shop, so the idea of a law that keeps prices high may sound like a bad one to you. However, if you are selling a product or service, you might think that legislation to keep prices high is a very good idea. For instance, many states establish minimum prices for milk. As a result, milk prices are higher than they would be if supply and demand set the price. **Price floors** create legally established minimum prices for goods or services. The minimum wage law is another example of a price floor. In this section, we will follow the same progression that we did with price ceilings. We begin with a simple thought experiment. Once we understand how price floors work, we will use supply and demand analysis to examine the short- and long-term implications for economic activity.

Understanding Price Floors

To understand how price floors affect the market, let's try a thought experiment. Suppose that a politician suggests we should encourage dairy farmers to produce more milk so that supplies will be plentiful and everyone will get enough calcium. In order to accomplish this, a price floor of $6 per gallon—about twice the price of a typical gallon of fat-free milk—is enacted to make production more attractive to producers. What repercussions should we expect?

First, more milk will be available for sale. We know this because the higher price will cause dairies to increase the quantity that they supply. At the same time, because consumers must pay more, the quantity demanded will fall. The result will be a surplus of milk. Since every gallon of milk that is produced but not sold hurts the dairies' bottom line, sellers will want to lower their prices enough to get as many sales as possible before the milk goes bad. But the price floor will not not allow the market to respond, and sellers will be stuck with milk that goes to waste. They will be tempted to offer illegal discounts in order to recoup some of their costs.

What happens next? Since the surplus cannot be resolved through lower prices, the government will try to help equalize supply and demand through other means. This can be accomplished in one of two ways: by restricting the supply of the good or by stimulating additional demand. Both solutions are problematic. If production is restricted, dairy farmers will not be able to generate a profitable amount of milk. Likewise, stimulating additional demand is not as simple as it sounds. Let's consider how this works with other crops.

In many cases, the government purchases surplus agricultural production. This occurs most notably with corn, soybeans, cotton, and rice. Once the government buys the surplus production, it often sells the surplus below cost to developing countries to avoid having the crop go to waste. This strategy has the unintended consequence of making it cheaper for consumers in these developing nations to buy excess agricultural output from developed nations like the United States than to have local farmers grow the crop. International treaties ban the practice of dumping surplus production, but it continues under the guise of humanitarian aid. This practice makes little economic sense. Table 5.2 summarizes the result of our price-floor thought experiment using milk.

The Effect of Price Floors

We have seen that price floors create unintended consequences. Now we will use the supply and demand model to analyze how price floors affect the market. We'll take a look at the short run first.

If you're doing a handstand, you need the floor for support. A binding price floor keeps prices from "falling."

Price floors
are legally established minimum prices for goods or services.

Got milk? Controlled milk prices prevent many customers from saying yes to that question.

TABLE 5.2

A Price Floor on Milk

Question	Answer / Explanation		Result
Will the quantity of milk for sale change?	Consumers will purchase less since the price is higher, but producers will manufacture more. The net result will be a surplus of milk.		There will be a surplus of milk.
Would producers sell below the price floor?	Yes. A surplus of milk would give sellers a strong incentive to undercut the price floor in order to avoid having to discard leftover milk.	TK	Illegal discounts will help to reduce the milk surplus.
Will dairy farmers be better off?	Not if they have trouble selling what they produce.		There might be a lot of spoiled milk.

Nonbinding Price Floors

Like price ceilings, price floors can be binding or nonbinding. Figure 5.6 illustrates a nonbinding price floor of $2 per gallon on milk. As you can see, at $2 the price floor is below the equilibrium price (P_E), so the price floor is nonbinding. Since the actual market price is above the legally established minimum price (P_{floor}), the price floor does not prevent the market from reaching equilibrium at point E. Consequently, the price floor has no impact on the market. As long as the equilibrium price remains above the price floor, price is regulated by supply and demand.

Full shelves signal a market at equilibrium.

Binding Price Floors

For a price floor to have an impact on the market, it must be set above the market equilibrium price. In that case, it is known as a binding price floor. And with a binding price floor, the quantity supplied will exceed the quantity demanded. Figure 5.7 illustrates a binding price floor in the short run. Continuing our example of milk prices, at $6 per gallon the price floor is above the equilibrium price of $3. Market forces always attempt to restore the equilibrium between supply and demand at point E. So we know that there is downward pressure on the price. At a price floor

FIGURE 5.6

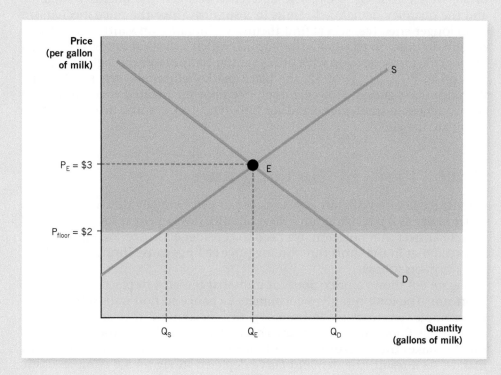

A Nonbinding Price Floor

Under a nonbinding price floor, price is regulated by supply and demand. Since the price floor ($2) is below the equilibrium price ($3), the market will voluntary charge more than the legal minimum. Therefore, this price floor will have no effect on sales and purchases of milk.

FIGURE 5.7

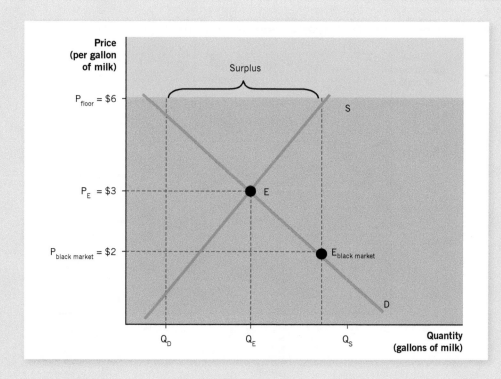

A Binding Price Floor in the Short Run

A binding price floor creates a surplus. This has two unintended consequences: a smaller demand than the equilibrium quantity ($Q_D < Q_E$), and a lower black-market price to eliminate the glut of the product.

of $6, we see that $Q_S > Q_D$. The difference between the quantity supplied and the quantity demanded results in a surplus. Since the price mechanism is no longer effective, sellers find themselves holding unwanted inventories of milk. In order to eliminate the surplus, which will spoil unless it is sold, a black market may develop with prices substantially below the legislated price. At a price ($P_{black\ market}$) of $2, the black market eliminates the surplus that the price floor caused. However, the price floor has created two unintended consequences: a smaller demand for milk ($Q_D < Q_E$), and a black market to eliminate the glut.

Incentives

Price Floors in the Long Run

Once price-floor legislation is passed, it can be politically difficult to repeal. What happens if a binding price floor on milk stays in effect for a long time? To help answer that question, we need to consider elasticity. We have already observed that in the short run binding price ceilings cause shortages and that black markets follow.

Figure 5.8 shows a price floor for milk that remains in place well past the short run. The long run gives consumers a chance to find milk substitutes—for example, products made from soy, rice, or almond that are not subject to the price floor—at lower prices. This added flexibility on the part of consumers makes the long-run demand for milk more elastic in an unregulated market. As a result, the demand curve depicted in Figure 5.8 is more elastic

FIGURE 5.8

The Effect of a Binding Price Floor in the Long Run

When a price floor is left in place over time, supply and demand each become more elastic. This leads to a larger surplus ($Q_S > Q_D$) in the long run. Since sellers are unable to sell all that they produce at $6 per gallon, a black market develops in order to eliminate the glut of milk.

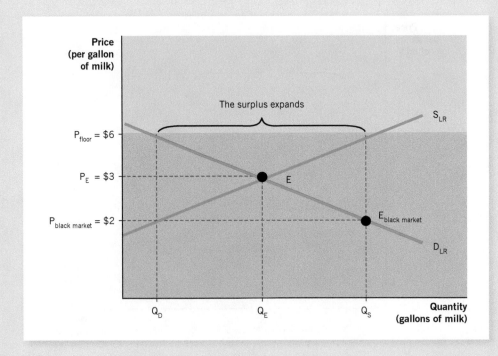

than its short-run counterpart in Figure 5.7. The supply curve also becomes flatter since firms (dairy farms) are able to produce more milk by acquiring additional land and production facilities. Therefore, a price floor ($6) that remains in place over time causes the supply and demand curves to become more elastic. This magnifies the shortage.

What happens to supply? In the long run, producers are more flexible and therefore supply is more elastic. The pool of potential milk producers rises as other closely related businesses retool their operations to supply more milk. The flatter supply curve in Figure 5.8 reflects this flexibility. As a result, Q_S expands and becomes much larger than it was in Figure 5.7. The increased elasticity on the part of both producers and consumers (1) makes the surplus larger in the long run and (2) magnifies the unintended consequences we observed in the short run.

PRACTICE WHAT YOU KNOW

Price Floors: Fair-Trade Coffee

Fair-trade coffee is sold through organizations that purchase directly from growers. The coffee is usually sold for a higher price than standard coffee. The goal is to promote more humane working conditions for the coffee pickers and growers. Fair-trade coffee has become more popular but still accounts for a small portion of all coffee sales, in large part because it is substantially more expensive to produce.

Question: Suppose that proponents of fair-trade coffee successfully lobby Congress to impose a price floor of $15 for every pound of coffee that is sold. Will this policy cause more or fewer people to buy fair-trade coffee?

Answer: Fair-trade producers typically sell their product at a higher price than mass-produced coffee brands. Therefore, a $15 price floor is binding for inexpensive brands like Folgers but nonbinding for premium coffees, which include fair-trade sellers. The price floor will reduce the price disparity between fair-trade coffee and mass-produced coffee.

To see how this works, consider a fair-trade coffee producer who charges $20 per pound and a mass-produced brand that sells for $10 per pound. A price floor of $15 reduces the difference between the price of fair-trade coffee and the inexpensive coffee brands, which now must sell for $15 instead of $10. This lowers the consumer's opportunity cost of choosing fair-trade coffee. Therefore, sales of Folgers and other inexpensive brands will decline. As a result, fair-trade producers will benefit indirectly from the price floor. Thus the answer to the question at the top is that *more* people will buy fair-trade coffee as a result of this price-floor policy.

Would fair-trade coffee producers benefit from a price floor?

What Effects Do Price Floors Have on Economic Activity?

We have seen the logical repercussions of a hypothetical price floor on milk and the incentives it creates. Now let's use supply and demand analysis to examine two real-world price floors: *minimum wage laws* and *agricultural price supports*.

The Minimum Wage

The minimum wage is the lowest hourly wage rate that firms may legally pay their workers.

The **minimum wage** is the lowest hourly wage rate that firms may legally pay their workers. Minimum wage workers can be skilled or unskilled and experienced or inexperienced. The common thread is that these workers, for a variety of reasons, lack better prospects. A minimum wage functions as a price floor. Figure 5.9 shows the effect of a binding minimum wage. Note that the wage, or the cost of labor, on the y axis ($10 per hour) is the price that must be paid. However, the market equilibrium wage ($7), or W_E, is below the minimum wage. The minimum wage prevents the market from reaching W_E at E (the equilibrium point) because only the wages in the green shaded area are legal. Since the demand for labor depends on how much it costs, the minimum wage raises the cost of hiring workers. Therefore, a higher

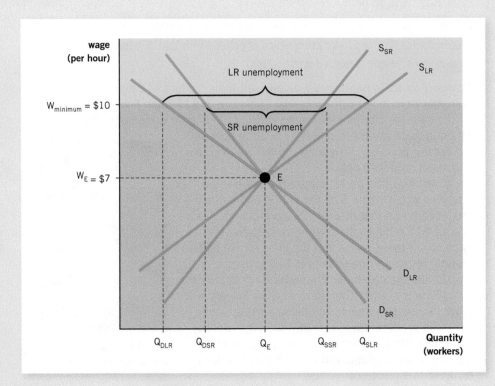

minimum wage will lower the quantity of labor demanded. However, since businesses still need to serve their customers, this means that labor expenses for the firm ordinarily rise in the short run. At the same time, firms will look for ways to substitute additional capital for workers. As a result, a binding minimum wage results in unemployment in the short run since $Q_{S_{SR}} > Q_{D_{SR}}$.

Businesses generally want to keep costs down, so in the long run they will try to reduce the amount they spend on labor. They might replace workers with machinery, shorten work hours, offer reduced customer service, or even relocate to countries that do not have minimum wage laws. As we move past the short run, more people will attempt to take advantage of higher minimum wages. Like firms, workers will adjust to the higher minimum wage over time. Some workers who might have decided to go to school full-time or remain retired, or who simply want some extra income, will enter the labor market because the minimum wage is now higher. As a result, minimum wage jobs will become progressively harder to find and unemployment will be magnified. The irony is that in the long run the minimum wage, just like any other price floor, has created two unintended consequences: a smaller demand for workers willing to take low-paying jobs ($Q_{D_{LR}}$ is significantly less than Q_E), and a larger supply of workers, ($Q_{S_{LR}}$) looking for those jobs.

Proponents of minimum wage legislation are aware that it often creates unemployment. To address this problem, they support investment in training, education, and the creation of government jobs programs to provide more work opportunities. While jobs programs increase minimum wage jobs, training and additional education enable workers to acquire skills needed for jobs that pay more than the minimum wage. Economists generally believe that education and training programs have longer-lasting benefits to society as whole since they enable workers to obtain better-paying jobs on a permanent basis.

ECONOMICS IN THE REAL WORLD

Wage Laws Squeeze South Africa's Poor

Consider this story that appeared in the *New York Times* in 2010.

NEWCASTLE, South Africa—The sheriff arrived at the factory here to shut it down, part of a national enforcement drive against clothing manufacturers who violate the minimum wage. But women working on the factory floor— the supposed beneficiaries of the crackdown—clambered atop cutting tables and ironing boards to raise anguished cries against it. Thoko Zwane, 43, who has worked in factories since she was 15, lost her job in Newcastle when a Chinese-run factory closed in 2004. More than a third of South Africans are jobless. "Why? Why?" shouted Nokuthula Masango, 25, after the authorities carted away bolts of gaily colored fabric. She made just $36 a week, $21 less than the minimum wage, but needed the meager pay to help support a large extended family that includes her five unemployed siblings and their children.

The women's spontaneous protest is just one sign of how acute South Africa's long-running unemployment crisis has become. With their own economy saddled with very high unemployment rates, the women feared being out of work more than getting stuck in poorly paid jobs.

Trade-offs

In the years since the end of apartheid, the South African economy has grown, but not nearly fast enough to end an intractable unemployment crisis.

Would you work for less than the minimum wage?

For over a decade, the jobless rate has been among the highest in the world, fueling crime, inequality, and social unrest in the continent's richest nation. The global economic downturn has made the problem much worse, wiping out more than a million jobs. Over a third of South Africa's workforce is now idle. And 16 years after Nelson Mandela led the country to black majority rule, more than half of blacks ages 15 to 34 are without work—triple the level for whites.

"The numbers are mind-boggling," said James Levinsohn, a Yale University economist.[1] ✳

The Minimum Wage Is Often Nonbinding

Most people believe that raising the minimum wage is a simple step that the government can take to improve the standard of living of the working poor. However, in most places the minimum wage is often nonbinding and therefore has no impact on the market. Adjusting for inflation, the federal minimum wage was highest in 1968, so in real terms minimum wage workers are earning less today than they did almost half a century ago. Why would we have a minimum wage if it is largely nonbinding?

To help us answer this question, consider the two nonbinding minimum wage rates ($7 and $9) shown in Figure 5.10. The rate of $7 per hour is far below the equilibrium wage of $10 ($W_E$), so at that point supply and demand will determine the wage. Suppose that politicians decide to raise the minimum wage to $9. This new minimum wage of $9 would remain below the market wage, so there would be no impact on the labor market for workers who are willing to accept the minimum wage. Therefore, an increase in the minimum wage from $7 to $9 an hour will not create unemployment. Unemployment will occur only when the minimum wage rises above $10.

Politicians know that most voters have a poor understanding of basic economics. As a result, a politician can seek to raise the minimum wage with great fanfare. Voters would support the new rate because they do not know that it is likely to be nonbinding; they expect wages to rise. In reality, nothing will change, but the perception of a benevolent action will remain. In fact, since its inception in 1938, increases in the minimum wage in the United States have generally trailed the market wage and therefore have avoided creating unemployment. Actually, the minimum wage adjusts sporadically upward every few years but rarely rises enough to cause the market wage to fall below it. This creates the illusion that the minimum wage is lifting wages. However, it does not cause any of the adverse consequences of a binding minimum wage.

In an effort to raise the minimum wage beyond the national rate, a number of states have enacted higher minimum wage laws. Not surprisingly, some of the states with the highest minimum wage rates, like Washington, Oregon,

1. Celia W. Dugger, "Wage Laws Squeeze South Africa's Poor," *New York Times*, September 27, 2010, A1.

and California, also have unemployment rates that are among the highest in the country—evidence that binding minimum wage rates can have serious consequences.

ECONOMICS IN THE REAL WORLD

A Sweet Deal, If You Can Get It

Sugar is one of life's small pleasures. It can be extracted and refined from sugar cane and sugar beets, two crops that can be grown in a variety of climates around the world. Sugar is both plentiful and cheap. As a result, Americans enjoy a lot of it—an average of over 60 pounds of refined sugar per person each year!

We would consume a lot more sugar if it was not subject to price controls. After the War of 1812, struggling sugar cane producers asked the government to pass a tariff that would protect domestic production. Over the years, price supports of all kinds have served to keep domestic sugar production high. The result is an industry that depends on a high price to survive. Under the current price-support system, the price of U.S.-produced sugar is roughly two to three times the world price. This has led to a bizarre set of incentives whereby U.S. farmers grow more sugar than they should and use land that is not well suited to the crop. For instance, sugar cane requires a subtropical climate, but most of the U.S. crop is grown in Louisiana, a region that is prone to hurricanes in the summer and killing freezes in the late fall. As a result, many sugar cane crops there are completely lost.

Incentives

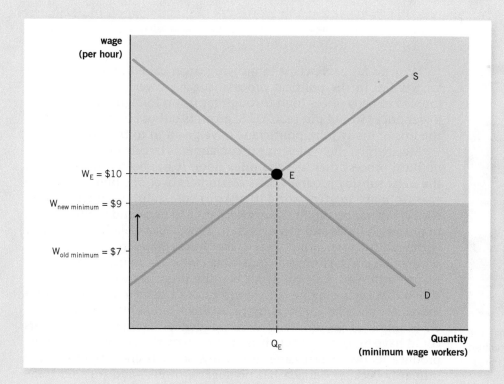

FIGURE 5.10

A Nonbinding Minimum Wage

An increase in the minimum wage from $7 to $9 remains nonbinding. Therefore, it will not change the demand for labor or the unemployment rate. If the minimum wage rises above the market wage, additional unemployment will occur.

The Minimum Wage

30 Days

The (2005) pilot episode of this reality series focused on the minimum wage. Morgan Spurlock and his fiancée spend 30 days in a poor neighborhood of Columbus, Ohio. The couple attempt to survive by earning minimum wage (at that time, $5.15 an hour) in order to make ends meet. In addition, they are required to start off with only one week's minimum wage (about $300) in reserve. Also, they cannot use credit cards to pay their bills. They experience firsthand the struggles that many minimum wage households face when living paycheck to paycheck. *30 Days* makes it painfully clear how difficult it is for anyone to live on the minimum wage for a month, let alone for years.

A quote from Morgan Spurlock sums up what the episode tries to convey: "We don't see the people that surround us. We don't see the people who are struggling to get by that are right next to us. And I have seen how hard the struggle is. I have been here.

Could you make ends meet earning the minimum wage?

And I only did it for a month, and there's people who do this their whole lives."

After watching this episode of *30 Days*, it is hard not to think that raising the minimum wage is a good idea. Unfortunately, the economic reality is that raising the minimum wage does not guarantee that minimum wage earners will make more and also be able keep their jobs.

Which of these is the *real* thing? The Coke on the right, with high-fructose corn syrup, was made in the United States; the other, with sugar, was made in Mexico.

Why do farmers persist in growing sugar cane in Louisiana? The answer lies in the political process: sugar growers have effectively lobbied to keep prices high through tariffs on foreign imports. Since lower prices would put many U.S. growers out of business and cause the loss of many jobs, politicians have given in to their demands.

Meanwhile, the typical sugar consumer is largely oblivious to the political process that sets the price floor. It has been estimated that the sugar subsidy program costs consumers over one billion dollars a year. To make matters worse, thanks to corn subsidies high-fructose corn syrup has become a cheap alternative to sugar and is often added to processed foods and soft drinks. In 1980, Coca-Cola replaced sugar with high-fructose corn extract in the United States in order to reduce production costs. However, Coca-Cola continues to use sugar cane in many Latin American countries because it is cheaper. New research shows that high-fructose corn syrup causes a metabolic reaction that makes people who ingest it more inclined to obesity. Ouch! This is an example of an unintended consequence that few policymakers could have imagined. There is no reason why the United States must produce its own sugar cane. Ironically, sugar is cheaper in Canada primarily because Canada has no sugar growers—and thus no trade restrictions or government support programs. ✳

PRACTICE WHAT YOU KNOW

Price Ceilings and Price Floors: Would a Price Control on Internet Access Be Effective?

A recent study found the following demand and supply schedule for high-speed Internet access:

Price of Internet	Connections demanded (millions of units)	Connections supplied (millions of units)
$60	10.0	62.5
$50	20.0	55.0
$40	30.0	47.5
$30	40.0	40.0
$20	50.0	32.5
$10	60.0	25.0

In today's Internet age, four degrees of separation are all that stand between you and the rest of the world.

Question: What are the equilibrium price and equilibrium quantity of Internet service?

Answer: First, look at the table to see where supply and demand are equal. At a price of $30, consumers purchase 40 million units and producers supply 40 million units. Therefore, the equilibrium price is $30 and the equilibrium quantity is 40 million. At any price above $30, the quantity supplied exceeds the quantity demanded, so there is a surplus. The surplus gives sellers an incentive to cut the price until it reaches the equilibrium point, E. At any price below $30, the quantity demanded exceeds the quantity supplied, so there is a shortage. The shortage gives sellers an incentive to raise the price until it reaches the equilibrium point, E.

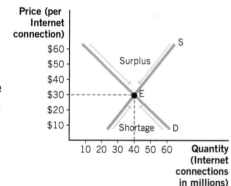

Question: Suppose that providers convince the government that maintaining high-speed access to the Internet is an important element of technology infrastructure. As a result, Congress approves a price floor at $10 above the equilibrium price to help companies provide Internet service. How many people are able to connect to the Internet?

Answer: Adding $10 to the market price of $30 gives us a price floor of $40. At $40, consumers demand 30 million connections. Producers provide 47.5 million connections. This is a surplus of 17.5 million units (shown). A price floor means that producers cannot cut the price below that point to increase the quantity that consumers demand. As a result, only 30 million units are sold. So only 30 million people connect to the Internet.

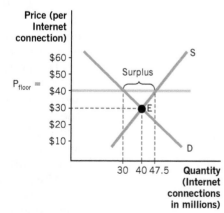

Question: When teachers realize that fewer people are purchasing Internet access, they demand that the price floor be repealed and a price ceiling be put in its place. Congress

(CONTINUED)

(CONTINUED)

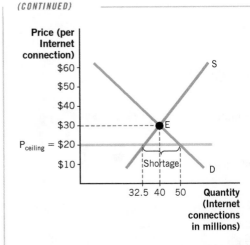

acts immediately to remedy the problem, and a new price ceiling is set at $10 below the market price. Now how many people are able to connect to the Internet?

Answer: Subtracting $10 from the market price of $30 gives us a price ceiling of $20. At $20 per connection, consumers demand 50 million connections. However, producers provide only 32.5 million connections. This is a shortage of 17.5 million units (shown). A price ceiling means that producers cannot raise the price, which will cause an increase in the quantity supplied. As a result, only 32.5 million units are sold, so only 32.5 million people connect to the Internet.

Question: Which provides the greatest access to the Internet: free markets, price floors, or price ceilings?

Answer: With no government intervention, 40 million connections are sold. Once the price floor is established, there are 30 million connections. Under the price ceiling, 32.5 million connections exist. Despite legislative efforts to satisfy both producers and consumers of Internet service, the best solution is to allow free markets to regulate access to the good.

Conclusion

Does the minimum wage help everyone earn a living wage? We learned that it is possible to set the minimum wage high enough to guarantee that each worker will earn a living wage. However, the trade-off in setting the minimum wage substantially higher is that it becomes binding and many workers will no longer have jobs. In other words, setting the minimum wage high enough to earn a living wage won't raise every worker out of poverty because many of those workers will no longer have jobs.

The policies presented in this chapter—rent control, price gouging laws, the minimum wage, and agricultural price controls—create unintended consequences. Attempts to control prices should be viewed cautiously. When the price signal is suppressed through a binding price floor or a binding price ceiling, the market's ability to maintain order is diminished, surpluses and shortages develop and expand through time, and obtaining goods and services becomes difficult.

The role of markets in society has many layers, and we've only just begun our analysis. In the next chapter, we will develop a technique to measure the gains that consumers and producers enjoy in unregulated markets, and we will consider the distortions created by tax policy. Then, in Chapter 7, we will consider two cases—externalities and public goods—in which the unregulated market produces an output that is not socially desirable.

Price Gouging: Disaster Preparedness

Disasters, whether natural or human-made, usually strike quickly and without warning. You and your family may have little or no time to decide what to do. That's why it is important to plan for the possibility of disaster and not wait until it happens. Failing to plan is planning to fail. In this box, we consider a few simple things you can do now to lessen the impact of a disaster on your personal and financial well-being.

During a disaster, shortages of essential goods and services become widespread. In the 30 states where price gouging laws are on the books, they prevent merchants from charging unusually high prices. If you live in one of these states, cash alone can't save you. You will have to survive on your own for a time before help arrives and communication channels are restored.

Taking measures to prepare for a disaster reduces the likelihood of injury, loss of life, and property damage far more than anything you can do after a disaster strikes. An essential part of disaster planning should include financial planning. Let's begin with the basics. Get adequate insurance to protect your family's health, lives, and property; plan for the possibility of job loss or disability by building a cash reserve; and safeguard your financial and legal records. It is also important to set aside extra money in a long-term emergency fund. Nearly all financial experts advise saving enough money to cover your expenses for six months. Most households never

come close to reaching this goal, but don't let that stop you from trying.

Preparing a simple disaster supply kit is also a must. Keep enough water, nonperishable food, sanitation supplies, batteries, medications, and cash on hand for three days. Often, the power is out after a disaster, so you cannot count on ATMs or banks to be open. These measures will help you to weather the immediate impact of a disaster.

Finally, many documents are difficult to replace. Consider investing in a home safe or safe deposit box to ensure that your important records survive. Place your passports, Social Security cards, copies of drivers' licenses, mortgage and property deeds, car titles, wills, insurance records, and birth and marriage certificates out of harm's way.

Will you be ready if disaster strikes?

ANSWERING THE BIG QUESTIONS

1. When do price ceilings matter?

* A price ceiling is a legally imposed maximum price. When the price is set below the equilibrium price, the quantity demanded will exceed the quantity supplied. This will result in a shortage. Price ceilings matter when they are set below the equilibrium price.

2. What effects do price ceilings have on economic activity?

*Price ceilings create two unintended consequences: a smaller supply of the good (Q_S) and a higher price for consumers who turn to the black market.

3. When do price floors matter?

*A price floor is a legally imposed minimum price. The minimum wage is an example of a price floor. If the minimum wage is set above the equilibrium wage, a surplus of labor will develop. However, if the minimum wage is nonbinding, it will have no effect on the market wage. Thus price floors matter when they are set above the equilibrium price.

4. What effects do price floors have on economic activity?

*Price floors lead to many unintended consequences, including surpluses, the creation of black markets, and artificial attempts to bring the market back into balance. For example, proponents of a higher minimum wage are concerned about finding ways to alleviate the resulting surplus of labor, or unemployment.

CONCEPTS YOU SHOULD KNOW

black market (p. 000)
minimum wage (p. 000)
price ceiling (p. 000)

price control (p. 000)
price floor (p. 000)

price gouging laws (p. 000)
rent control (p. 000)

QUESTIONS FOR REVIEW

1. Does a price ceiling cause a shortage or a surplus? Provide an example to support your answer.

2. Does a price floor cause a shortage or a surplus? Provide an example to support your answer.

3. Will a surplus or a shortage caused by a price control become smaller or larger over time?

4. Are price gouging laws an example of a price floor or a price ceiling?

5. What will happen to the market price when a price control is nonbinding?

6. Why do most economists oppose attempts to control prices? Why does the government attempt to control prices anyway, in a number of markets?

STUDY PROBLEMS

1. In the song "Minimum Wage," the punk band Fenix TX comments on the inadequacy of the minimum wage to make ends meet. Using the poverty thresholds provided by the Census Bureau,[1] determine whether the federal minimum wage of $7.25 an hour provides enough income for a single full-time worker to escape poverty.

* 2. Imagine that the community you live in decides to enact a rent control of $700 per month on every one-bedroom apartment. Using the following table, determine the market price and equilibrium quantity without rent control. How many one-bedroom apartments will be rented after the rent-control law is passed?

Monthly rent	Quantity demanded	Quantity supplied
$600	700	240
$700	550	320
$800	400	400
$900	250	480
$1,000	100	560

3. Suppose that the federal government places a binding price floor on chocolate. To help support the price floor, the government purchases all of the leftover chocolate that consumers do not buy. If the price floor remains in place for a number of years, what do you expect to happen to each of the following?

a. quantity of chocolate demanded by consumers
b. quantity of chocolate supplied by producers
c. quantity of chocolate purchased by the government

4. Suppose that a group of die-hard sports fans is upset about the high price of tickets to many games. As a result of their lobbying efforts, a new law caps the maximum ticket price to any sporting event at $50. Will more people be able to attend the games? Explain your answer. Will certain teams and events be affected more than others? Provide examples.

5. Many local governments use parking meters on crowded downtown streets. However, the parking spaces along the street are typically hard to find because the metered price is often set below the market price. Explain what happens when local governments set the meter price too low. Why do you think the price is set below the market-clearing price?

1. www.census.gov/hhes/www/poverty/data/threshld/index.html

6. Imagine that local suburban leaders decide to enact a minimum wage. Will the community lose more jobs if the nearby city votes to increase the minimum wage to the same rate? Discuss your answer.

✳ 7. Examine the following graph.

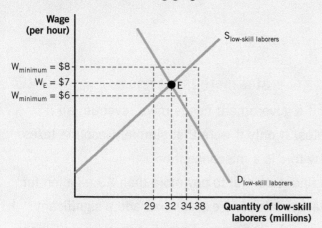

How many low-skill laborers will be unemployed when the minimum wage is $8 an hour? How many low-skill workers will be unemployed when the minimum wage is $6 an hour?

8. The demand and supply curves that we use can also be represented with equations. Suppose that the demand for low-skill labor, Q_D, is represented by the following equation, where W is the wage rate:

$$Q_D = 53,000,000 - 3,000,000\,W$$

The supply of low-skill labor, Q_S, is represented by the equation

$$Q_S = -10,000,000 + 6,000,000\,W$$

a. Find the equilibrium wage. (**Hint**: Set $Q_D = Q_S$ and solve for the wage, W. Then plug the result back into either of the original equations to find Q_E.)
b. Find the equilibrium quantity. (**Hint**: Now plug the value you got in part (a) back into Q_D or Q_S. You can double-check your answer by plugging the answer from part (a) into both Q_D and Q_S to see that you get the same result.)
c. What happens if the minimum wage is $8? (**Hint**: Plug W = 10 into both Q_D and Q_S.) Does this cause a surplus or a shortage?
d. What happens if the minimum wage is $6? (**Hint**: Plug W = 10 into both Q_D and Q_S.) Does this cause a surplus or a shortage?

SOLVED PROBLEMS

2. The equilibrium price occurs where the quantity demanded is equal to the quantity supplied. This occurs when $Q_D = Q_S = 800$. When the quantity is 800, the monthly rent is $800. Next the question asks how many one-bedroom apartments will be rented after a rent-control law limits the rent to $700 a month. When the rent is $700, the quantity supplied is 320 apartments. It is also worth noting that the quantity demanded when the rent is $700 is 550 units, so there is a shortage of $550 - 320 = 230$ apartments once the rent-control law goes into effect.

7. How many low-skill laborers will be unemployed when the minimum wage is $8 an hour? The quantity demanded is 29M, and the quantity supplied is 38M. This results is $38M - 29M = 9M$ unemployed low-skill workers.

How many low-skill workers will be unemployed when the minimum wage is $6 an hour? Since $6 an hour is below the market-equilibrium wage of $7, it has no effect. In other words, a $6 minimum wage is nonbinding, and therefore no unemployment is caused.

CHAPTER 6 | The Efficiency of Markets and the Costs of Taxation

Raising tax rates always generates more tax revenue.

Many people believe that if a government needs more revenue, all it needs to do is raise tax rates. If only it were that simple. Gasoline taxes demonstrate why this is a misconception.

MISCONCEPTION

Most people find it painful to pay more than $3 a gallon for gas. In many places, sales and excise taxes add a significant amount to the price. For example, the price of gasoline throughout Europe is often more than double that in the United States, largely because of much higher gasoline taxes. Other countries, like Venezuela, Saudi Arabia, and Mexico, subsidize gasoline so that their citizens pay less than the market price. In countries where gasoline is subsidized, consumers drive their cars everywhere, mass transportation is largely unavailable, and there is little concern for fuel efficiency. In contrast, as you might imagine, in countries with high gasoline taxes consumers drive less, use public transportation more, and tend to purchase fuel-efficient vehicles.

How high do gasoline taxes have to rise before large numbers of people significantly cut back on their gasoline consumption? The answer to that question will help us understand the misconception that raising tax rates always generates more tax revenue.

In the previous chapter, we learned about the market distortions caused by price controls. We observed that efforts to manipulate market prices not only cause surpluses and shortages, but also lead to black markets. In this chapter, we will quantify how markets enhance the welfare of society. We begin with consumer surplus and producer surplus, two concepts that illustrate how taxation, like price controls, creates distortions in economic behavior by altering the incentives that people face when consuming and producing goods that are taxed.

Photo to come

How much do taxes cost the economy?

BIG QUESTIONS

* What are consumer surplus and producer surplus?
* When is a market efficient?
* Why do taxes create deadweight loss?

What Are Consumer Surplus and Producer Surplus?

Welfare economics
is the branch of economics that studies how the allocation of resources affects economic well-being.

Markets create value by bringing together buyers and sellers so that consumers and producers can mutually benefit from trade. **Welfare economics** is the branch of economics that studies how the allocation of resources affects economic well-being. In this section, we develop two concepts that will help us measure the value that markets create: *consumer surplus* and *producer surplus*. In competitive markets, the equilibrium price is simultaneously low enough to attract consumers and high enough to encourage producers. This balance between demand and supply enhances the welfare of society. That is not to say that society's welfare depends solely on markets. People also find satisfaction in many nonmarket settings, including spending time with their families and friends, and doing hobbies and charity work. We will incorporate aspects of personal happiness into our economic model in Chapter 16. For now, let's focus on how markets enhance human welfare.

Consumer Surplus

Willingness to pay
is the maximum price a consumer will pay for a good.

Consider three students: Frank, Beanie, and Mitch. Like students everywhere, each one has a maximum price he is willing to pay for a new economics textbook. Beanie owns a successful business, so for him the cost of a new textbook does not present a financial hardship. Mitch is a business major who really wants to do well in economics. Frank is not serious about his studies. Table 6.1 shows the maximum value that each student places on the textbook. This value, called the **willingness to pay**, is the maximum price a consumer will pay for a good. The willingness to pay is also known as the reservation price. In an auction or a negotiation, the willingness to pay, or reservation price, is the price beyond which the consumer decides to walk away from the transaction.

Consider what happens when the price of the book is $151. If Beanie purchases the book at $151, he pays $49 less than the $200

How much will they pay for an economics textbook?

TABLE 6.1

Willingness to Pay for a New Economics Textbook

Buyer	Willingness to pay
Beanie	$200
Mitch	150
Frank	100

maximum he was willing to pay. He values the textbook at $49 more than the purchase price, so buying the book will make him better off.

Consumer surplus is the difference between the willingness to pay for a good and the price that is paid to get it. While Beanie gains $49 in consumer surplus, a price of $151 is more than either Mitch or Frank is willing to pay. Since Mitch is willing to pay only $150, if he purchases the book he will experience a consumer loss of $1. Frank's willingness to pay is $100, so if he buys the book for $151 he will experience at a consumer loss of $51. Whenever the price is greater than the willingness to pay, a rational consumer will decide not to buy.

Consumer surplus
is the difference between the willingness to pay for a good and the price that is paid to get it.

Using Demand Curves to Illustrate Consumer Surplus

In the previous section, we discussed consumer surplus as an amount. We can also illustrate it graphically with a demand curve. Figure 6.1 shows the demand curve drawn from the data in Table 6.1. Notice that the curve looks

FIGURE 6.1

Demand Curve for an Economics Textbook

The demand curve has a step for each additional textbook purchase. As the price goes down, more students buy the textbook.

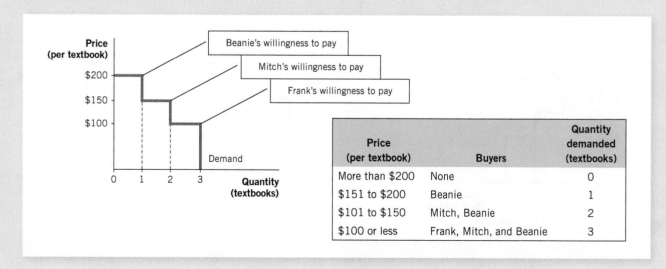

Price (per textbook)	Buyers	Quantity demanded (textbooks)
More than $200	None	0
$151 to $200	Beanie	1
$101 to $150	Mitch, Beanie	2
$100 or less	Frank, Mitch, and Beanie	3

like a staircase with three steps—one for each additional textbook purchase. Each point on a market demand curve corresponds to one unit sold, so if we added more consumers into our example, the "steps" would become narrower and the demand curve would become smoother.

At any price above $200, none of the students wants to purchase a textbook. This relationship is evident on the *x* axis where the quantity demanded is 0. At any price between $150 and $200, Beanie is the only buyer, so the quantity demanded is 1. At prices between $100 and $150, Beanie and Mitch are each willing to buy the textbook, so the quantity demanded is 2. Finally, if the price is $100 or less, all three students are willing to buy the textbook, so the quantity demanded is 3. As the price falls, the quantity demanded increases.

We can measure the total extent of consumer surplus by examining the area under the demand curve for each of our three consumers, as shown in Figure 6.2. In Figure 6.2a the price is $175, and only Beanie decides to buy. Since his willingness to pay is $200, he is better off by $25; this is his consumer surplus. The green-shaded area under the demand curve and above the price represents the benefit Beanie receives from purchasing a textbook at a price of $175. When the price drops to $125, as shown in Figure 6.2b, Mitch also decides to buy a textbook. Now the total quantity demanded is 2 textbooks. Mitch's willingness to pay is $150, so his consumer surplus, represented by the pink-shaded area, is $25. However, since Beanie's willingness to pay is $200, his consumer surplus rises from $25 to $75. So a textbook price of $125 raises the total consumer surplus to $100. In other words, lower prices create more consumer surplus in this market—and in any other.

FIGURE 6.2

Determining Consumer Surplus from a Demand Curve

(a) At a price of $175, Beanie is the only buyer, so the quantity demanded is 1. (b) At a price of $125, Beanie and Mitch are each willing to buy the textbook, so the quantity demanded is 2.

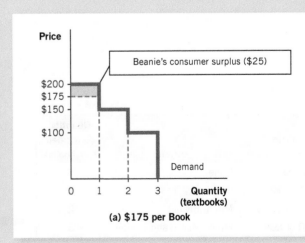

(a) $175 per Book

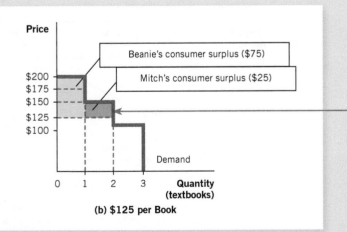

(b) $125 per Book

We were asked to use a pink shade instead of orange. There is no pink shade in the color palette, so we used created one using the settings of C3 M77 Y9 K0. Is this okay as set?

TABLE 6.2	
Willingness to Sell Tutoring Services	
Seller	**Willingness to sell**
Beanie	$30/hr
Mitch	20/hr
Frank	10/hr

Producer Surplus

Sellers also benefit from market transactions. In this section, our three students discover that they are good at economics and decide to go into the tutoring business. They do not want to provide this service for free, but each has a different minimum price, or *willingness to sell*. The **willingness to sell** is the minimum price a seller will accept to sell a good or service. Table 6.2 shows each tutor's willingness to sell his services.

Consider what happens at a tutoring price of $25 per hour. Since Frank is willing to tutor for $10 per hour, every hour that he tutors at $25 per hour earns him $15 more than his willingness to sell. This extra $15 per hour is his *producer surplus*. **Producer surplus** is the difference between the willingness to sell a good and the price that the seller receives. Mitch is willing to tutor for $20 per hour and earns a $5 producer surplus for every hour he tutors. Finally, Beanie's willingness to tutor, at $30 per hour, is more than the market price of $25. If he tutors, he will have a producer loss of $5 per hour.

How do producers determine their willingness to sell? They must consider two factors: the direct costs of producing the good and the indirect costs, or opportunity costs. Students who are new to economics often mistakenly assume that the cost of producing an item is the only cost to consider in making the decision to produce. But producers also have opportunity costs. Beanie, Mitch, and Frank each has a unique willingness to sell because each has a different opportunity cost. Beanie owns his own business, so for him the time spent tutoring is time that he could have spent making money elsewhere. Mitch is a business student who might otherwise be studying to get better grades. Frank is neither a businessman nor a serious student, so the $10 he can earn in an hour of tutoring is not taking the place of other earning opportunities or studying more to get better grades.

Using Supply Curves to Illustrate Producer Surplus

Continuing our example, the supply curve in Figure 6.3 shows the relationship between the price for an hour of tutoring and the quantity of tutors who are willing to work. As you can see on the supply schedule (the table within the figure), at any price less than $10 per hour no one wants to tutor. At prices between $10 and $19 per hour, Frank is the only tutor, so the

Willingness to sell is the minimum price a seller will accept to sell a good or service.

Producer surplus is the difference between the willingness to sell a good and the price that the seller receives.

Opportunity cost

FIGURE 6.3

Supply Curve for Economics Tutoring

The supply curve has three steps, one for each additional student who is willing to tutor. Progressively higher prices will induce more students to become tutors.

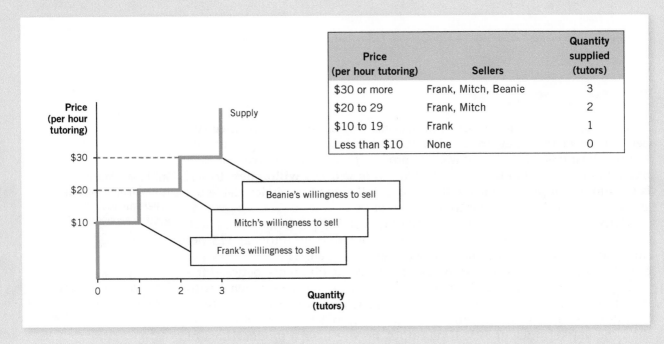

Price (per hour tutoring)	Sellers	Quantity supplied (tutors)
$30 or more	Frank, Mitch, Beanie	3
$20 to 29	Frank, Mitch	2
$10 to 19	Frank	1
Less than $10	None	0

quantity supplied is 1. Between $20 and $29 per hour, Frank and Mitch are willing to tutor, so the quantity supplied rises to 2. Finally, if the price is $30 or more, all three friends are willing to tutor, so the quantity supplied is 3. As the price they receive for tutoring rises, the number of tutors increases from 1 to 3.

What do these relationships between price and supply tell us about producer surplus? Let's turn to Figure 6.4. By examining the area above the supply curve, we can measure the extent of producer surplus. In Figure 6.4a, the price of an hour of tutoring is $15. At that price, only Frank decides to tutor. Since he would be willing to tutor even if the price were as low as $10 per hour, he is $5 better off tutoring. Frank's producer surplus is represented by the pink-shaded area between the supply curve and the price of $15. Since Beanie and Mitch do not tutor when the price is $15, they do not receive any producer surplus. In Figure 6.4b, the price for tutoring is $25 per hour. At this price, Mitch also decides to tutor. His willingness to tutor is $20, so when the price is $25 per hour his producer surplus is $5, represented by the blue-shaded area. Since Frank's willingness to tutor is $10, at $25 per hour his producer surplus rises to $15. By looking at the shaded boxes in Figure 6.4b, we see that an increase in the rates for tutoring raises the combined producer surplus of Frank and Mitch to $20.

FIGURE 6.4

Determining Producer Surplus from a Supply Curve

(a) The price of an hour of tutoring is $15. At this price, only Frank decides to tutor. (b) The price for tutoring is $25 per hour. At this price, Mitch also decides to tutor.

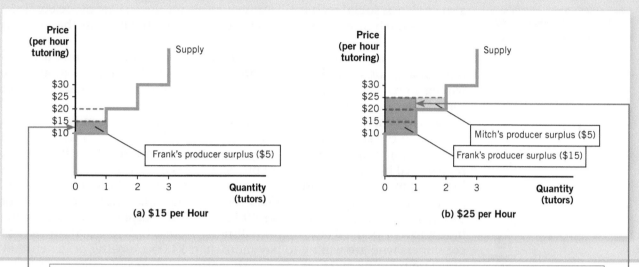

(a) $15 per Hour

(b) $25 per Hour

We were asked to use a pink shade instead of orange. There is no pink shade in the color palette, so we used created one using the settings of C3 M77 Y9 K0. Is this okay as set?

PRACTICE WHAT YOU KNOW

Consumer and Producer Surplus: Trendy Fashion

Leah decides to buy a new jacket from D&G for $80. She was willing to pay $100. When her friend Becky sees the jacket, she loves it and thinks it is worth $150. So she offers Leah $125 for the jacket, and Leah accepts. Leah and Becky are both thrilled with the exchange.

Question: Determine the total surplus from the original purchase and the additional surplus generated by the resale of the jacket.

Rachel Bilson wearing a D&G jacket

Answer: Leah was willing to pay $100 and the jacket cost $80, so she keeps the difference, or $20, as consumer surplus. When Leah resells the jacket to Becky for $125, she earns $25 in producer surplus. At the same time, Becky receives $25 in consumer surplus, since she was willing to pay Leah up to $150 for the jacket but Leah sells it to her for $125. The resale generates an additional $50 in surplus.

When Is a Market Efficient?

Total surplus,
also known as social welfare,
is the sum of consumer surplus and producer surplus.

We have seen how consumers benefit from lower prices and how producers benefit from higher prices. When we combine the concepts of consumer and producer surplus, we can build a complete picture of the welfare of buyers and sellers. Adding consumer and producer surplus gives us **total surplus**, also known as **social welfare**, because it measures the welfare of society. Total surplus is the best way economists have to measure the benefits that markets create.

Figure 6.5 illustrates the relationship between consumer and producer surplus for a gallon of milk. The demand curve shows that some customers are willing to pay more for a gallon of milk than others. Likewise, some sellers (producers) are willing to sell milk for less than others.

Let's say that Alice is willing to pay $7.00 per gallon for milk, but when she gets to the store she finds it for $4.00. The difference between the price she is willing to pay, represented by point A, and the price she actually pays, represented by E (the equilibrium price), is $3.00 in consumer surplus. This is indicated by the blue arrow showing the distance from $4.00 to $7.00. Alice's friend Betty is willing to pay $5.00 for milk, but, like Alice, she finds it for $4.00. Therefore, she receives $1.00 in consumer surplus, indicated by the blue arrow at point B showing the distance from $4.00 to $5.00. In fact, all consumers who are willing to pay more than $4.00 are better off when they purchase the milk at $4.00. We can show this total area of consumer surplus

Trade
creates
value

Consumer and Producer Surplus for a Gallon of Milk

Consumer surplus is the difference between the willingness to pay along the demand curve and the equilibrium price, P_E. It is illustrated by the blue-shaded triangle. Producer surplus is the difference between the willingness to produce along the supply curve and the equilibrium price. It is illustrated by the pink-shaded triangle.

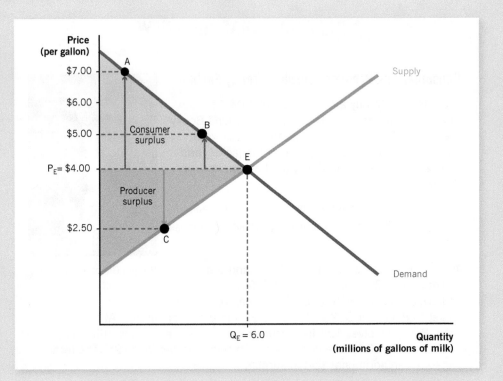

Efficiency

Old School

In the 2003 movie *Old School*, Frank tries to give away a bread maker he received as a wedding present. First he offers it to a friend as a housewarming gift, but it turns out that this is the friend who originally gave him the bread maker. Ouch! Later in the movie, we see Frank giving the bread maker to a small boy at a birthday party. Both efforts at re-gifting fail miserably.

From an economic perspective, giving the wrong gift makes society poorer. If you spend $50 on a gift and give it to someone who thinks it is only worth $30, you've lost $20 in value. Whenever you receive a shirt that is the wrong size or style, a fruitcake you won't eat, or something that is worth less to you than what the gift-giver spent on it, an economic inefficiency has occurred. Until now, we have thought of the market as enhancing efficiency by increasing the total surplus in society. But we can also think of the billions of dollars spent on mismatched gifts as a failure to maximize the total surplus involved in exchange. In other words, we can think of the efficiency of the gift-giving process as less than 100 percent.

Given what we have learned so far about economics, you might be tempted to argue that cash is the best gift you can give. When you give cash, it is never the wrong size or color, and the recipients can use it to buy whatever they want. However, very few people actually give cash (unless it is requested). Considering the advantages of cash, why don't more people give it instead of gifts? One reason is that cash seems impersonal. A second reason is that cash communicates exactly how much the giver spent. To avoid both problems, most people rarely give cash. Instead, they buy personalized gifts to communicate how much they care, while making it hard for the recipient to determine exactly how much they spent.

One way that society overcomes inefficiency in gifting is through the dissemination of information. For instance, wedding registries provide a convenient way for people who may not know the newlyweds very well to give them what they want. Similarly, prior to holidays many people tell each other what they would

like to receive. By purchasing gifts that others want, givers can exactly match what the recipients would have purchased if they had received a cash transfer. This eliminates any potential inefficiency. At the same time, the giver conveys affection—an essential part of giving. To further reduce the potential inefficiencies associated with giving, many large families practice holiday gift exchanges. And another interesting mechanism for eliciting information involves Santa Claus. Children throughout the world send Santa Claus wish lists for Christmas, never realizing that the parents who help to write and send the lists are the primary beneficiaries.

To the economist, the strategies of providing better information, having gift exchanges, and sending wish lists to Santa Claus are just a few examples of how society tries to get the most out of the giving process—and that is something to be joyful about!

Frank re-gifts a bread maker.

The buyer and seller each benefit from this exchange.

An outcome reflects efficiency when an allocation of resources maximizes total surplus.

on the graph as the blue-shaded triangle bordered by the demand curve, the y axis, and the equilibrium price (P_E). At every point in this area, the consumers who are willing to pay more than the equilibrium price for milk will be better off.

Continuing with Figure 6.5, producer surplus follows a similar process. Suppose that the Contented Cow dairy is willing to sell milk for $2.50 per gallon, represented by point C. Since the equilibrium price is $4.00, the business makes $1.50 in producer surplus. This is indicated by the red arrow at point C showing the distance from $4.00 to $2.50. If we think of the supply curve as representing the costs of many different sellers, we can calculate the total producer surplus as the pink-shaded triangle bordered by the supply curve, the y axis, and the equilibrium price. The shaded blue triangle (consumer surplus) and the shaded red triangle (producer surplus) describe the increase in total surplus, or social welfare, created by the production and exchange of the good at the equilibrium price. At the equilibrium quantity of 6 million gallons of milk, output and consumption reach the largest possible combination of producer and consumer surplus. In the region of the graph beyond 6 million units, buyers and sellers will experience a loss.

When an allocation of resources maximizes total surplus, the result is said to reflect **efficiency**. Efficiency occurs at point E when the market is in equilibrium. To think about why the market creates the largest possible total surplus, or social welfare, it is important to recall how the market allocates resources. Consumers who are willing to pay more than the equilibrium price will buy the good because they will enjoy the consumer surplus. Producers who are willing to sell the good for less than the market-equilibrium price will enjoy the producer surplus. In addition, consumers with a low willingness to buy (less than $4.00) and producers with a high willingness to sell (more than $4.00) do not participate in the market since they would be worse off. Therefore, the equilibrium output at point E maximizes the total surplus and is also an efficient allocation of resources.

The Efficiency-Equity Debate

When economists model behavior, we assume that participants in a market are rational decision-makers. We assume that producers will always operate in the region of the triangle that represents producer surplus and that consumers will always operate in the region of the triangle that represents consumer surplus. We do not, for example, expect Alice to pay more than $7.00 for a gallon of milk or the Contented Cow dairy to sell a gallon of milk for less than $2.50 per gallon. In other words, for the market to work efficiently, voluntary

Efficiency only requires that the pie gets eaten. Equity is a question of who gets the biggest share.

PRACTICE WHAT YOU KNOW

Total Surplus: How Would Lower Income Affect Urban Outfitters?

Question: If a drop in consumer income occurs, what will happen to the consumer surplus that customers enjoy at Urban Outfitters? What will happen to the amount of producer surplus that Urban Outfitters receives? Illustrate your answer by shifting the demand curve appropriately and labeling the new and old areas of consumer and producer surplus.

Answer: Since the items sold at Urban Outfitters are normal goods, a drop in income causes the demand curve (D) to shift to the left. The black arrow shows the leftward shift in graph (b) below. When you compare the area of consumer surplus (in blue) before and after the drop in income,—that is, graphs (a) and (b)—you can see that it shrinks. The same is true when comparing the area of producer surplus (in pink) before and after.

   Your intuition might already confirm what the graphs tell us. Since consumers have less income, they buy fewer clothes at Urban Outfitters— so consumer surplus falls. Likewise, since fewer customers buy the store's clothes, Urban Outfitters sells less—so producer surplus falls. This is also evident in graph (b), since $Q_2 < Q_1$.

Does less income affect total surplus?

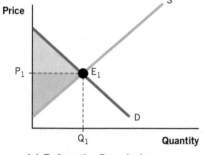

(a) Before the Drop in Income

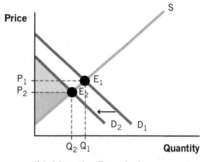

(b) After the Drop in Income

instances of consumer loss must be rare. We assume that self-interest helps to ensure that all participants will benefit from an exchange.

   However, the fact that both parties benefit from an exchange does not mean that each benefits equally. Economists are also interested in the distribution of the gains. **Equity** refers to the fairness of the distribution of benefits among the members of a society. In a world where no one cared about equity, only efficiency would matter and no particular division would be preferred. Another way of thinking about fairness versus efficiency is to consider a pie. If our only concern is efficiency, we will simply want to make sure that that none of the pie goes to waste. However, if we care about equity, we will also want to make sure that the pie is divided equally among those present and that no one gets a larger piece than any other.

Equity
refers to the fairness of the distribution of benefits within the society.

In our first look at consumer and producer surplus, we have assumed that markets produce efficient outcomes. But in the real world, this is not always the case. Markets also fail; their efficiency can be compromised in a number of ways. We will discuss market failure in much greater detail in subsequent chapters. For now, all you need to know is that failure can occur.

Why Do Taxes Create Deadweight Loss?

Taxes provide many benefits. They also remind us that "there is no free lunch"; for example, we don't pay the police dispatcher before dialing 911, but society has to collect taxes in order for the emergency service to exist. Taxes help to pay for many of modern society's needs—public transportation, schools, police, the court system, and the military, to name just a few. Most of us take these services for granted, but without taxes it would be hard to pay for them. How much does all of this cost? When you add all the federal, state, and local government budgets in the United States, you get five trillion dollars a year! (See www.usdebtclock.org.)

Opportunity cost

These taxes incur opportunity costs, since the money could have been used in other ways. In this section, we will use the concepts of consumer and producer surplus to explain the effect of taxation on social welfare and market efficiency. Taxes come in many sizes and shapes. Considering there are taxes on personal income, payroll, property, corporate profits, sales, and inheritances, the complexity makes it difficult to analyze the broad impact of taxation on social welfare and market efficiency. Fortunately, we do not have to examine the entire tax code all at once. In this chapter, we will explore the impact of taxes on social welfare by looking at one of the simplest taxes, the *excise tax*.

Excise taxes
are taxes levied on a particular good or service.

Incidence
refers to the burden of taxation on the party who pays the tax through higher prices, regardless of whom the tax is actually levied on.

Tax Incidence

Economists want to know how taxes affect the choices that consumers and producers make. When a tax is imposed on an item, do buyers switch to alternative goods that are not taxed? How do producers respond when the products they sell are taxed? Since taxes cause prices to rise, they can affect how much of a good or service is bought and sold. This is especially evident with **excise taxes**, or taxes levied on one particular good or service. For example, all fifty states levy excise taxes on cigarettes, but the amount assessed varies tremendously. In New York, cigarette taxes are over $4.00 per pack, while in a handful of tobacco-producing states such as Virginia and North Carolina, the excise tax is less than $0.50. Overall, excise taxes, such as those on cigarettes, alcohol, and gasoline, account for less than 4% of all tax revenues. But because we can isolate changes in consumer behavior that result from taxes on one item, they help us understand the overall effect of a tax.

In looking at the effect of a tax, economists are also interested in the **incidence** of taxation, which refers to the burden of taxation on the party who pays the tax through

Why do we place excise taxes on cigarettes . . .   . . . and gasoline?

higher prices. To understand this idea, consider a $1.00 tax on milk purchases. Each time a consumer buys a gallon of milk, the cash register adds $1.00 in tax. This means that to purchase the milk, the consumer's willingness to pay must be greater than the price of the milk plus the $1.00 tax.

The result of the $1.00 tax on milk is shown in Figure 6.6. Because of the tax, the price of milk goes up and the demand curve shifts down (from D_1 to D_2). Why does the demand curve shift? Since consumers must pay the purchase price as well as the tax, the extra cost makes them less likely to buy milk at every price, which causes the entire demand curve to shift down. The intersection of the new demand curve (D_2) with the existing supply curve (S) creates a new equilibrium price of $3.50 ($E_2$), which is $0.50 lower than the original price of $4.00. But even though the price is lower, consumers are still worse off. Since they must also pay part of the $1.00 tax, the total price to them rises to $4.50 per gallon.

At the same time, because the new equilibrium price after the tax is $0.50 lower than it was before the tax, the producer splits the tax incidence with the buyer. The producer receives $0.50 less, and the buyer pays $0.50 more.

The tax on milk purchases also affects the amount sold in the market, which we also see in Figure 6.6. Since the after-tax equilibrium price (E_2) is lower, producers of milk reduce the quantity they sell to 750 gallons. Therefore, the market for milk becomes smaller than it was before the good was taxed.

Excise taxes paid by consumers are relatively rare because they are highly visible. If every time you bought milk you were reminded that you had to pay a $1.00 tax, it would be hard to ignore. As a result, politicians often prefer to place the tax on the seller. The seller will then include the tax in the sale price, and buyers will likely forget that the sale price is higher than it would be without the tax.

Let's return to the $1.00 tax on milk. This time, the tax is placed on the seller. Figure 6.7 shows the result. First, look at the shift in the supply curve.

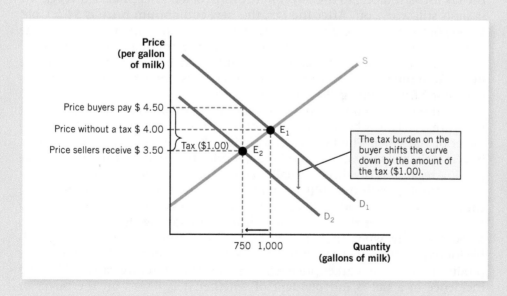

FIGURE 6.6

A Tax on Buyers
After the tax, the new equilibrium price (E_2) is $3.50, but the buyer must also pay $1.00 in tax. Therefore, despite the drop in price, the buyer still owes $4.50. A similar logic applies to the producer. Since the new equilibrium price after the tax is $0.50 lower, the producer shares the tax incidence equally with the seller in this example. The consumer pays $0.50 more, and the seller nets $0.50 less.

FIGURE 6.7

A Tax on Sellers

After the tax, the new equilibrium price (E_2) is $4.50, but $1.00 must be paid in tax to the government. Therefore, despite the rise in price, the seller nets only $3.50. A similar logic applies to the consumer. Since the new equilibrium price after the tax is $0.50 higher, the consumer shares the $1.00/gallon tax incidence equally with the seller. The consumer pays $0.50 more, and the seller nets $0.50 less.

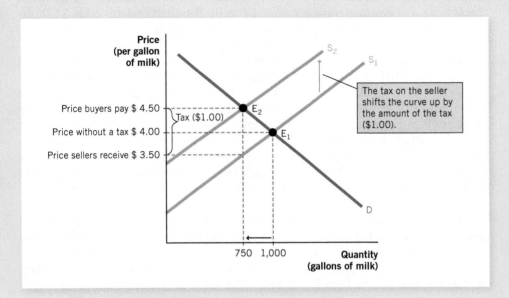

Why does it shift? The $1.00 per gallon tax on milk lowers the profits that milk producers expect to make, which causes them to produce less milk at every price level. As a result, the entire supply curve shifts to the left in response to the tax that milk producers owe the government. The intersection of the new supply curve (S_2) with the existing demand curve creates a new equilibrium price (E_2) of $4.50—which is $0.50 higher than the original equilibrium price of $4.00 ($E_1$). This occurs because the seller passes part of the tax increase along to the buyer in the form of a higher price. However, the seller is still worse off. After the tax, the new equilibrium price is $4.50, but $1.00 goes as tax to the government. Therefore, despite the rise in price, the seller nets only $3.50, which is $0.50 less than the original equilibrium price.

The tax also affects the amount of milk sold in the market. Since the new equilibrium price after the tax is higher, consumers reduce the quantity demanded from 1,000 gallons to 750 gallons.

It's important to notice that the result in Figure 6.7 looks much like that in Figure 6.6. This is because it does not matter whether a tax is levied on the buyer or the seller. The tax places a wedge of $1.00 between the price that buyers ultimately pay ($4.50) and the net price that sellers ultimately receive ($3.50), regardless of who is actually responsible for paying the tax.

Continuing with our milk example, when the tax was levied on sellers, they were responsible for collecting the entire tax ($1.00 per gallon), but they transferred $0.50 of the tax to the consumer by raising the market price to $4.50. Similarly, when the tax was levied on consumers, they were responsible for paying the entire tax, but they essentially transferred $0.50 of it to the producer, since the market price fell to $3.50. Therefore, we can say that the incidence of a tax is independent of whether it is levied on the buyer or the seller. However, depending on the price elasticity of supply and demand, the tax incidence need not be shared equally, as we will see later. All of this means that the government doesn't get to determine whether consumers or producers bear the tax incidence—the market does!

Deadweight Loss

Recall that economists measure economic efficiency by looking at total consumer and producer surplus. We have seen that a tax raises the total price consumers pay and lowers the net price producers receive. For this reason, taxes reduce the amount of economic activity. The decrease in economic activity caused by market distortions, such as taxes, is known as **deadweight loss**.

In the previous section, we observed that the tax on milk caused the amount purchased to decline from 1,000 to 750 gallons—a reduction of 250 gallons sold in the market. In Figure 6.8, the yellow triangle represents the deadweight loss caused by the tax. When the price rises, consumers who would have paid between $4.00 and $4.49 will no longer purchase milk. Likewise, the reduction in the price the seller can charge means that producers who formerly sold a gallon of milk for between $3.51 and $4.00 will no longer be willing to do so. The combined reductions in consumer and producer surplus equal the deadweight loss produced by a $1.00 tax on milk.

In the next sections, we will examine how differences in the price elasticity of demand lead to varying amounts of deadweight loss. We will evaluate what happens when the demand curve is perfectly inelastic, somewhat elastic, and perfectly elastic.

Deadweight loss
is the decrease in economic activity caused by market distortions.

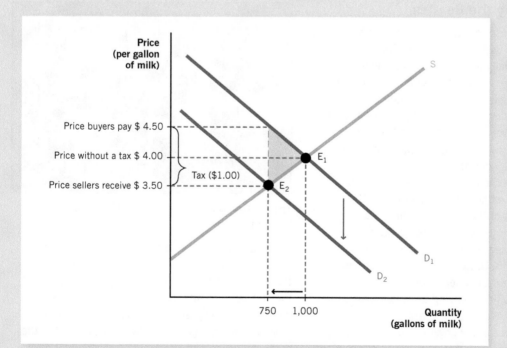

FIGURE 6.8

The Deadweight Loss from a Tax

The yellow triangle represents the deadweight loss caused by the tax. When the price rises, all consumers who would have paid between $4.00 and $4.49 no longer purchase milk. Likewise, the reduction in revenue the seller receives means that producers who formerly sold a gallon of milk for between $3.51 and $4.00 will no longer be willing to do so.

How do phone companies get away with all the added fees per month?
Answer: inelastic demand.

Tax Revenue and Deadweight Loss When Demand Is Inelastic

In Chapter 4, we saw that necessary goods and services—for example, water, electricity, and phone service—have highly inelastic demand. These goods and services are often taxed. For example, consider all the taxes associated with your cell phone bill: sales tax, city tax, county tax, federal excise tax, and annual regulatory fees. In addition, many companies add surcharges, including activation fees, local number portability fees, telephone number pooling charges, emergency 911 service, directory assistance, telecommunications relay service surcharges, and cancellation fees. Of course, there is a way to avoid all these fees: don't use a cell phone! However, many people today feel that cell phones are a necessity. Cell phone providers and government agencies take advantage of the consumer's strongly inelastic demand by tacking on these extra charges.

Figure 6.9 shows the result of a tax on products with almost perfectly inelastic demand, such as phone service—something people feel they need to have no matter what the price. The demand for access to a phone (either a landline or a cell phone) is perfectly inelastic. Recall that whenever demand is perfectly inelastic, the demand curve is vertical. Figure 6.9a shows the market for phone service before the tax. The blue rectangle represents consumer surplus (C.S.), and the red triangle represents producer surplus (P.S.). Now

ECONOMICS IN THE MEDIA

Taxing Inelastic Goals

"Taxman" by the Beatles

"Taxman" was inspired by the theme song from the popular 1960s television series *Batman*. The Beatles—especially George Harrison, who wrote the song—had grown quite bitter about how much they were paying in taxes. In the beginning of the song, Harrison sings, "Let me tell you how it will be. There's one for you, nineteen for me." This refers to the fact that the British government taxed high-wage earners £19 out of every £20 they earned. Since the Beatles' considerable earnings placed them in the top income tax bracket in the United Kingdom, a part of the group's earnings was subject to the 95% tax introduced by the government in 1965. As a consequence, the Beatles became tax exiles living in the United States and other parts of Europe, where tax rates were lower.

The inevitability of paying taxes is a theme that runs throughout the song. The lyrics mention that when you drive a car, the government can tax the "street"; if you try to sit, the government can tax "your seat"; if you are cold, the government can tax "the

The Beatles avoided high taxes by living outside the United Kingdom.

heat"; and if you decide to take a walk, it can tax your "feet"! The only way to avoid doing and using these things is to leave the country—precisely what the Beatles did. All these examples (streets, seats, heat, and walking) are necessary activities, which makes demand highly inelastic. Anytime that is the case, the government can more easily collect the tax revenue it desires.

FIGURE 6.9

A Tax on Products with Almost Perfectly Inelastic Demand

(a) Before the tax, the consumer enjoys the consumer surplus (C.S.) noted in blue, and the producer enjoys the producer surplus (P.S.) noted in red. (b) After the tax, the incidence, or the burden of taxation, is borne entirely by the consumer. A tax on a good with almost perfectly inelastic demand, such as phone service, represents a transfer of welfare from consumers of the good to the government, reflected by the reduced size of the blue rectangle in (b) and the creation of the green tax-revenue rectangle between P_1 and P_2.

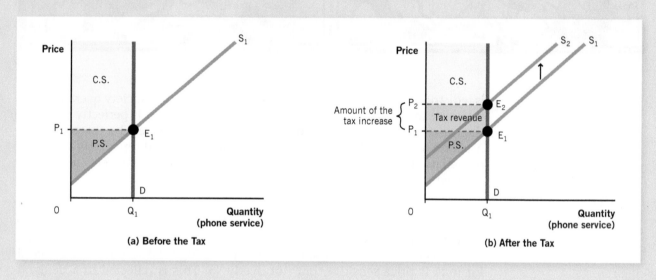

imagine that a tax is levied on the seller, as shown in Figure 6.9b. The supply curve shifts from S_1 to S_2. The shift in supply causes the equilibrium point to move from E_1 to E_2 and the price to rise from P_1 to P_2, but the quantity supplied, Q_1, remains the same. We know that when demand is perfectly inelastic, a price increase does not alter how much consumers purchase. So the quantity demanded remains constant at Q_1 even after the government collects tax revenue equal to the green-shaded area.

There are two reasons why the government may favor excise taxes on goods with almost perfectly (or highly) inelastic demand. First, because these goods do not have substitutes, the tax will not cause consumers to buy less. Thus, the revenue from the tax will remain steady. Second, since the number of transactions, or quantity demanded (Q_1), remains constant, there will be no deadweight loss. As a result, the yellow triangle we observed in Figure 6.8 disappears in Figure 6.9 because the tax does not alter the efficiency of the market. Looking at Figure 6.9, you can see that the same number of transactions exist in (a) and (b). This means that the total surplus, or social welfare, is equal in both panels. You can also see this by comparing the shaded areas in both panels. The sum of the blue-shaded area of consumer surplus and the red-shaded area of producer surplus in (a) is equal to the sum of the consumer surplus, producer surplus, and tax revenue in (b). The green area is subtracted entirely from the blue rectangle, which indicates that the surplus

is redistributed from consumers to the government. But society overall enjoys the same total surplus. Thus, we see that when demand is perfectly inelastic, the incidence, or the burden of taxation, is borne entirely by the consumer. A tax on a good with almost perfectly inelastic demand represents a transfer of welfare from consumers of the good to the government, reflected by the reduced size of the blue rectangle in (b).

Tax Revenue and Deadweight Loss When Demand Is More Elastic

Now consider a tax on a product with more elastic demand, such as milk, the subject of our earlier discussion on calculating total surplus. The demand for milk is price sensitive, but not overly so. This is reflected in a demand curve with a typical slope as shown in Figure 6.10. Let's compare the after-tax price, P_2, in Figures 6.9b and 6.10b. When demand is almost perfectly inelastic, as it is in Figure 6.9b, the price increase from P_1 to P_2 is absorbed entirely by the consumer. But in Figure 6.10b, because demand is more sensitive to price, suppliers must absorb part of the tax, from P_1 to P_3, themselves. Thus, they net P_3, which is less than what they received when the good was not taxed. In addition, the total tax revenue generated (the green-shaded area) is not as large in Figure 6.9b as in Figure 6.10b, because as the price of the good rises some consumers no longer buy it and the quantity demanded falls from Q_1 to Q_2.

Notice that both consumer surplus (C.S.), the blue triangle, and producer surplus (P.S.), the red triangle, are smaller after the tax. Since the price rises after the tax increase (from P_1 to P_2), those consumers with a relatively low willingness to pay for the good are priced out of the market. Likewise, sellers with relatively high costs of production will stop producing the good, since the price they net after paying the tax drops to P_3. The total reduction in economic activity, the change from Q_1 to Q_2, is the deadweight loss (D.W.L.) indicated by the yellow triangle.

The incidence of the tax also changes from Figure 6.9 to Figure 6.10. A tax on a good for which demand and supply are each somewhat elastic will cause a transfer of welfare from consumers and producers of the good to the government. At the same time, since the quantity bought and sold in the market declines, it also creates deadweight loss. Another way of seeing this result is to compare the red- and blue-shaded areas in Figure 6.10a with the red- and blue-shaded areas in Figure 6.10b. The sum of the consumer surplus and producer

FIGURE 6.10

A Tax on Products with More Elastic Demand

(a) Before the tax, the consumer enjoys the consumer surplus (C.S.) noted in blue, and the producer enjoys the producer surplus (P.S.) noted in red. (b) A tax on a good for which demand and supply are each somewhat elastic will cause a transfer of welfare from consumers and producers to the government. It will also create deadweight loss (D.W.L.), shown in yellow, since the quantity bought and sold in the market declines (from Q_1 to Q_2).

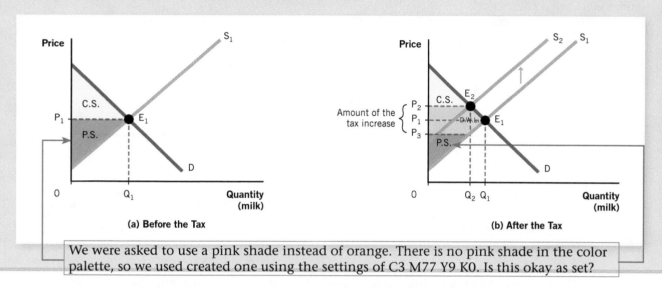

(a) Before the Tax

(b) After the Tax

> We were asked to use a pink shade instead of orange. There is no pink shade in the color palette, so we used created one using the settings of C3 M77 Y9 K0. Is this okay as set?

surplus in (a) is greater than the sum of the consumer surplus, tax revenue, and producer surplus in (b). Therefore, the total surplus, or efficiency of the market, is smaller. The tax is no longer a pure transfer from consumers to the government, as was the case in Figure 6.9.

Tax Revenue and Deadweight Loss When Demand Is Highly Elastic

We have seen the effect of taxation when demand is inelastic and somewhat elastic. What about when demand is highly elastic? For example, a customer who wants to buy fresh lettuce at a produce market will find many local growers charging the same price and many varieties to choose from. If one of the vendors decides to charge $1 per pound above the market price, consumers will stop buying from that vendor. They will be unwilling to pay more when they can get the same product from another grower at a lower price; this is the essence of elastic demand.

Figure 6.11 shows the result of a tax on lettuce, a good with highly elastic demand. After all, when lettuce is taxed consumers can switch to other greens such as spinach, cabbage, or endive and completely avoid the tax. In this market, consumers are so price sensitive that they are unwilling to accept any price increase. And because sellers are unable to raise the equilibrium price, they bear the entire incidence of the tax. This has two effects. First, producers are less willing to sell the product at all prices. This shifts the supply curve from S_1 to S_2. Since consumer demand is highly elastic, consumers

FIGURE 6.11

A Tax on Products with Highly Elastic Demand

(a) Before the tax, the producer enjoys the producer surplus (P.S.) noted in red. (b) When consumer demand is highly elastic, consumers pay the same price after the tax as before. But they are worse off because less is produced and sold; the quantity produced moves from Q_1 to Q_2. The result is deadweight loss (D.W.L.), as shown by the yellow triangle in (b). The total surplus, or efficiency of the market, is much smaller than before. The size of the tax revenue (in green) is also noticeably smaller in the market with highly elastic demand.

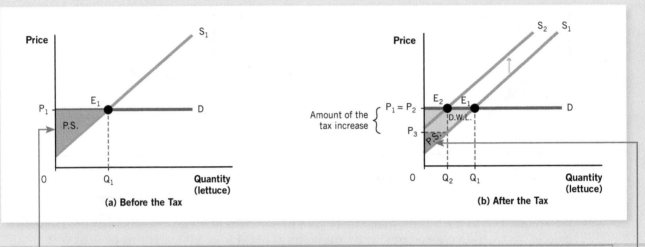

(a) Before the Tax

(b) After the Tax

We were asked to use a pink shade instead of orange. There is no pink shade in the color palette, so we used created one using the settings of C3 M77 Y9 K0. Is this okay as set?

pay the same price as before ($P_1 = P_2$). However, the tax increase causes the producer to net less, or P_3. Since P_3 is substantially lower than the price before the tax, or P_2, producers offer less for sale after the tax is implemented. This is shown in Figure 6.11b in the movement of quantity demanded from Q_1 to Q_2. Since Q_2 is smaller than Q_1, there is also more deadweight loss than we observed in Figure 6.10b. Therefore, the total surplus, or efficiency of the market, is much smaller than before. Comparing the green-shaded areas of Figures 6.10b and 6.11b, you see that the size of the tax revenue continues to shrink. There is an important lesson here for policymakers—they should tax goods with relatively inelastic demand. Not only will this lessen the deadweight loss of taxation, but it will also generate larger tax revenues for the government.

So far, we have varied the elasticity of the demand curve while holding the elasticity of the supply curve constant. What would happen if we did the reverse and varied the elasticity of the supply curve while keeping the elasticity of the demand curve constant? It turns out that there is a simple method for determining the incidence and deadweight loss in this case. The incidence of a tax is determined by the relative steepness of the demand curve compared to the supply curve. When the demand curve is steeper (more inelastic) than the supply curve, consumers bear more of the incidence of the tax. When the supply curve is steeper (more inelastic) than the demand curve, suppliers bear more of the incidence of the tax. Also, whenever the supply and/or demand curves are relatively steep, deadweight loss is minimized.

Let's explore an example in which we consider how the elasticity of demand and elasticity of supply interact. Suppose that a $3 per pound tax is placed on shiitake mushrooms, an elastic good. Given the information in Figure 6.12, we will compute the incidence, deadweight loss, and tax revenue from the tax.

Let's start with the incidence of the tax. After the tax is implemented, the market price rises from $7 to $8 per pound. But since sellers must pay $3 to the government, they keep only $5. Tax incidence measures the share of the tax paid by buyers and sellers, so we need to compare the incidence of the tax paid by each party. Since the

How much would you pay per pound for these mushrooms?

market price rises by $1 (from $7 to $8), buyers are paying $1 of the $3 tax, or 1/3. Since the amount the seller keeps falls by $2 (from $7 to $5), sellers are paying $2 of the $3 tax, or 2/3. Notice that the demand curve is more elastic (flatter) than the supply curve; therefore, sellers have a limited ability to raise price.

Now let's determine the deadweight loss caused by the tax—that is, the decrease in economic activity. This is represented by the decrease in the total surplus found in the yellow triangle in Figure 6.12. In order to compute the amount of the deadweight loss, we need to determine the area of the triangle:

$$\text{The area of a triangle} = \frac{1}{2} \times \text{base} \times \text{height}$$

(Equation 6.1)

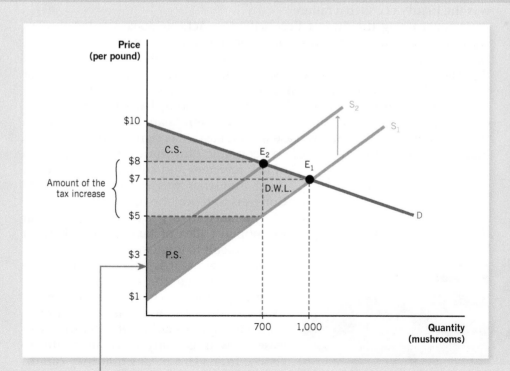

FIGURE 6.12

A Realistic Example

A $3 per pound tax is placed on mushroom suppliers. This drives the equilibrium price up from E_1 ($7) to E_2 ($8). Notice that the price only rises by $1. This means that the consumer picks up $1 of the $3 tax and the seller must pay the remaining $2. Therefore, most of the incidence is borne by the seller. Finally, neither the demand curve nor the supply curve is relatively inelastic, so the amount of deadweight loss (D.W.L.) is large.

We were asked to use a pink shade instead of orange. There is no pink shade in the color palette, so we used created one using the settings of C3 M77 Y9 K0. Is this okay as set?

The triangle in Figure 6.12 is sitting on its side, so its height is $1000 - 700 = 300$, and its base is $\$8 - \$5 = \$3$.

(Equation 6.2)
$$\text{Deadweight loss} = \frac{1}{2} \times 300 \times \$3 = \$450$$

Finally, what is the tax revenue generated by the tax? In Figure 6.12, the tax revenue is represented by the green-shaded area, which is a rectangle. We can calculate the tax revenue by determining the area of the rectangle:

(Equation 6.3)
$$\text{The area of a rectangle} = \text{base} \times \text{height}$$

The height of the tax-revenue rectangle is the amount of the tax ($\$3$), and the number of units sold after the tax is 700.

(Equation 6.4)
$$\text{Tax revenue} = \$3 \times 700 = \$2{,}100.$$

ECONOMICS IN THE REAL WORLD

The Short-Lived Luxury Tax

The Budget Reconciliation Act of 1990 established a special luxury tax on the sale of new aircraft, yachts, automobiles, furs, and jewelry. The act established a 10% surcharge on new purchases as follows: aircraft over $500,000; yachts over $100,000; automobiles over $25,000, and furs and jewelry over $10,000. The taxes were expected to generate approximately $2 billion a year. However, revenue fell far below expectations, and thousands of jobs were lost in each of the affected industries. Within three years, the tax was repealed. Why was the luxury tax such a failure?

When passing the Budget Reconciliation Act, lawmakers failed to consider basic demand elasticity. Because the purchase of a new aircraft, yacht, car, fur, or jewelry is highly discretionary, many wealthy consumers decided that they would buy substitute products that fell below the tax threshold or buy a used product and refurbish it. Therefore, the demand for these luxury goods turned out to be highly elastic. We have seen that when goods with elastic demand are taxed, the resulting tax revenues are small. Moreover, in this example the resulting decrease in purchases was significant. As a result, jobs were lost in the middle of an economic downturn. The combination of low revenues and crippling job losses in these industries was enough to convince Congress to repeal the tax in 1993.

The failed luxury tax is a reminder that the populist idea of taxing the rich is far more difficult to implement than it appears. In simple terms, it is nearly impossible to tax the toys that the rich enjoy because wealthy people can spend their money in so many different ways. In other words, they have options about whether to buy or lease, as well as many good substitutes to choose from. This means that they can, in many cases, avoid paying luxury taxes. ✳

If you were rich, would this be your luxury toy?

Balancing Deadweight Loss and Tax Revenues

Up to this point, we have kept the size of the tax increase constant. This enabled us to examine the impact of the elasticity of demand and supply on deadweight loss and tax revenues. But what happens when a tax is high enough to significantly alter consumer or producer behavior? For instance, in 2002 the Republic of Ireland instituted a tax of 15 euro cents on each plastic bag in order to curb litter and encourage recycling. As a result, consumer use of plastic bags quickly fell by over 90%. Thus, the tax was a major success because the government achieved its goal of curbing litter. In this section, we will consider how consumers respond to taxes of different sizes, and we will determine the relationship among the size of a tax, the deadweight loss, and tax revenues.

Incentives

Figure 6.13 shows the market response to a variety of tax increases. The five panels in the figure begin with a reference point, panel (a), where no tax is levied, and progress toward panel (e), where the tax rate becomes so extreme that it curtails all economic activity.

PRACTICE WHAT YOU KNOW

Deadweight Loss of Taxation: The Politics of Tax Rates

Imagine that you and two friends are discussing the politics of taxation. One friend, who is fiscally conservative, argues that tax rates are too high. The other friend, who is more progressive, argues that tax rates are too low.

What is the optimal tax rate?

Question: Is it possible that both friends could be right?

Answer: Surprisingly, the answer is yes. When tax rates become extraordinarily high, the amount of deadweight loss dwarfs the amount of tax revenue collected. We observed this in the discussion of the short-lived luxury tax above. Fiscal conservatives often note that taxes inhibit economic activity. They advocate lower tax rates and limited government involvement in the market, preferring to minimize the deadweight loss on economic activity—see panel (b) in Figure 6.13. However, progressives prefer somewhat higher tax rates than fiscal conservatives, since a moderate tax rate—see panel (c)—generates more tax revenue than a small tax does. The additional revenues that moderate tax rates generate can fund more government services. Therefore, a clear trade-off exists between the size of the public sector and market activity. Depending on how you view the value created by markets versus the value added through government provision, there is ample room for disagreement about the best tax policy.

FIGURE 6.13

Examining Deadweight Loss and Tax Revenues

The panels show that increased taxes result in higher prices. Progressively higher taxes also lead to more deadweight loss (D.W.L.), but higher taxes do not always generate more revenue, as evidenced by the reduction in revenue that occurs when tax rates become too large in panels (d) and (e).

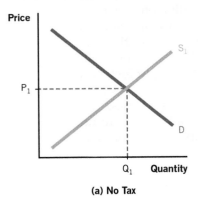

(a) No Tax

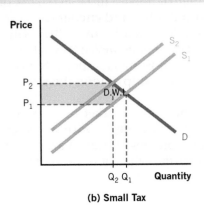

(b) Small Tax

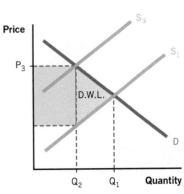

(c) Moderate Tax

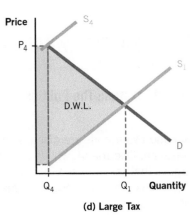

(d) Large Tax

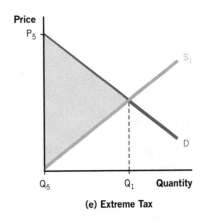

(e) Extreme Tax

Excise Taxes Are Almost Impossible to Avoid

The federal government collected $75 billion in excise taxes in 2011. Excise taxes are placed on many different products, making them almost impossible to avoid. They also have the added advantages of being easy to collect, hard for consumers to detect, and easier to enact politically than other types of taxes. You'll find excise taxes on many everyday household expenses—what you drink, the gasoline you purchase, plane tickets, and much more. Let's add them up.

1. **Gasoline.** 18.3 cents per gallon. This generates $37 billion and helps finance the interstate highway system.

2. **Cigarettes and tobacco.** $1 per pack and up to 40 cents per cigar. This generates $18 billion for the general federal budget.

3. **Air travel.** 7.5% of the base price of the ticket plus $3 per flight segment. This generates $10 billion for the Transportation Security Administration and the Federal Aviation Administration.

4. **Alcohol.** 5 cents per can of beer, 21 cents per bottle of wine, and $2.14 for spirits. This generates $9 billion for the general federal budget.

These four categories account for $74 billion in excise taxes. You could still avoid the taxman with this simple prescription: don't drink, don't travel, and don't smoke. Where does that leave you? Way

out in the country somewhere far from civilization. Since you won't be able to travel to a grocery store, you'll need to live off the land, grow your own crops, and hunt or fish.

But there is still one last federal excise tax to go.

5. **Hunting and fishing.** Taxes range from 3 cents for fishing tackle boxes to 11% for archery equipment. This generates $1 billion for fish and wildlife services.

Living off the land and avoiding taxes just got much harder, and that's the whole point. The government taxes products with relatively inelastic demand because most people will still purchase them after the tax is in place. As a result, avoiding taxes isn't practical. The best you can do is reduce your tax burden by altering your lifestyle or what you purchase.

Data from Jill Barshay, "The $240-a-Year Bill You Don't Know You're Paying," *Fiscal Times*, Sept. 7, 2011.

Excise taxes are everywhere.

As taxes rise, so do prices. You can trace this rise from (a), where there is no tax and the price is P_1, all the way to (e), where the extreme tax causes the price to rise to P_5. At the same time, deadweight loss (D.W.L.) also rises. You can see this by comparing the sizes of the yellow triangles. The trade-off is striking. Without any taxes, deadweight loss does not occur. But as soon as taxes are in place, the market-equilibrium quantity demanded begins to decline,

Trade-offs

moving from Q_1 to Q_5. As the number of transactions (quantity demanded) declines, the area of deadweight loss rapidly expands.

When taxes are small, as in Figure 6.13b, the tax revenue (green rectangle) is large relative to the deadweight loss (yellow triangle). However, as we progress through the panels, this relationship slowly reverses. In (c) the size of the tax revenue remains larger than the deadweight loss. However, in (d) the magnitude of the deadweight loss is far greater than the tax revenue. This means that the size of the tax in (d) is creating a significant cost in terms of economic efficiency. Finally, (e) shows an extreme case in which all market activity ceases as a result of the tax. Since nothing is produced and sold, there is no tax revenue.

Conclusion

Let's return to the misconception we started with: raising tax rates always generates more tax revenue. That's true up to a point. At low and moderate tax rates, increases do lead to additional revenue. However, when tax rates become too high, tax revenues decline as more consumers and producers find ways to avoid paying the tax.

In the first part of this chapter, we learned that society benefits from unregulated markets because they generate the largest possible total surplus. However, society also needs the government to provide an infrastructure for the economy. The tension between economic activity and the amount of government services needed is reflected in tax rates. The taxation of specific goods and services gives rise to a form of market failure called deadweight loss, which causes reduced economic activity. Thus, any intervention in the market requires a deep understanding of how society will respond to the incentives created by the legislation. In addition, unintended consequences can affect the most well-intentioned tax legislation and, if the process is not well thought through, can cause inefficiencies with far-reaching consequences. Of course, this does not mean that taxes are undesirable. Rather, society must balance (1) the need for tax revenues and the programs those revenues help fund, with (2) trade-offs in the market.

ANSWERING THE BIG QUESTIONS

1. What are consumer surplus and producer surplus?

 * Consumer surplus is the difference between the willingness to pay for a good and the price that is paid to get it. Producer surplus is the difference between the willingness to sell a good and the price that the seller receives.

 * Total surplus is the sum of consumer and producer surplus that exists in a market.

2. When is a market efficient?

* Markets maximize consumer and producer surplus, provide goods and services to buyers who value them most, and reward sellers who can produce goods and services at the lowest cost. As a result, markets create the largest amount of total surplus possible.

* Whenever an allocation of resources maximizes total surplus, the result is said to be efficient. However, economists are also interested in the distribution of the surplus. Equity refers to the fairness of the distribution of the benefits among the members of the society.

3. Why do taxes create deadweight loss?

* Deadweight loss occurs because taxes increase the purchase price, which causes consumers to buy less. Deadweight loss can be minimized by placing a tax on a good or service that has inelastic demand or supply.

* Economists are also concerned about the incidence of taxation. Incidence refers to the burden of taxation on the party who pays the tax through higher prices, regardless of whom the tax is actually levied on. The incidence is determined by the balance between the elasticity of supply and the elasticity of demand.

CONCEPTS YOU SHOULD KNOW

consumer surplus (p. 000)
deadweight loss (p. 000)
efficiency (p. 000)
equity (p. 000)

excise taxes (p. 000)
incidence (p. 000)
producer surplus (p. 000)
social welfare (p. 000)

total surplus (p. 000)
welfare economics (p. 000)
willingness to pay (p. 000)
willingness to sell (p. 000)

QUESTIONS FOR REVIEW

1. Explain how consumer surplus is derived from the difference between the willingness to pay and the market-equilibrium price.

2. Explain how producer surplus is derived from the difference between the willingness to sell and the market-equilibrium price.

3. Why do economists focus on consumer and producer surplus and not on the possibility of consumer and producer loss? Illustrate your answer on a supply and demand graph.

4. How do economists define efficiency?

5. What type of goods should be taxed in order to minimize deadweight loss?

6. Suppose that the government taxes a good that is very elastic. Illustrate what will happen to the consumer surplus, producer surplus, tax revenue, and deadweight loss on a supply and demand graph.

7. What happens to tax revenues as tax rates increase?

STUDY PROBLEMS

1. A college student enjoys eating pizza. Her willingness to pay for each slice is shown in the following table:

Number of pizza slices	Willingness to pay (per slice)
1	$6
2	$5
3	$4
4	$3
5	$2
6	$1
7	$0

a. If pizza slices cost $3 each, how many slices will she buy? How much consumer surplus will she enjoy?
b. If the price of slices falls to $2, how much consumer surplus will she enjoy?

2. A cash-starved town decides to impose a $6 excise tax on T-shirts sold. The following table shows the quantity demanded and the quantity supplied at various prices.

Price per T-shirt	Quantity demanded	Quantity supplied
$19	0	60
$16	10	50
$13	20	40
$10	30	30
$ 7	40	20
$ 4	50	10

a. What are the equilibrium quantity demanded and the quantity supplied before the tax is implemented? Determine the consumer and producer surplus before the tax.

b. What are the equilibrium quantity demanded and the quantity supplied after the tax is implemented? Determine the consumer and producer surplus after the tax.

c. How much tax revenue does the town generate from the tax?

d. Compute the deadweight loss created by the tax.

3. Andrew paid $30 to buy a potato cannon, a cylinder that shoots potatoes hundreds of feet. He was willing to pay $45. When Andrew's friend Nick learns that Andrew bought a potato cannon, he asks Andrew if he will sell it for $60, and Andrew agrees. Nick is thrilled, since he would have paid Andrew up to $80 for the cannon. Andrew is also delighted. Determine the total surplus from the original purchase and the additional surplus generated by the resale of the cannon.

4. If the government wants to raise tax revenue, which of the following items are good candidates for an excise tax? Why?

a. granola bars
b. cigarettes
c. toilet paper
d. automobile tires
e. bird feeders

* 5. If the government wants to minimize the deadweight loss of taxation, which of the following items are good candidates for an excise tax? Why?

a. bottled water
b. prescription drugs
c. oranges
d. batteries
e. luxury cars

6. A new medical study indicates that eating blueberries helps prevent cancer. If the demand for blueberries increases, what will happen to the size of the consumer and producer surplus? Illustrate your answer by shifting the demand curve appropriately and labeling the new and old areas of consumer and producer surplus.

7. Use the following graph to answer questions a–f.

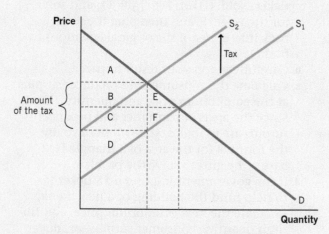

a. What area represents consumer surplus before the tax?

b. What area represents producer surplus before the tax?

c. What area represents consumer surplus after the tax?

d. What area represents producer surplus after the tax?

e. What area represents the tax revenue after the tax?

f. What area represents the deadweight loss after the tax?

8. The cost of many electronic devices has fallen appreciably since they were first introduced. For instance, computers, cell phones, microwaves, and calculators not only provide more functions but do so at a lower cost. Illustrate the impact of lower production costs on the supply curve. What happens to the size of the consumer and producer surplus? If consumer demand for cell phones is relatively elastic, who is likely to benefit the most from the lower production costs?

9. Suppose that the demand for a concert, Q_D, is represented by the following equation, where P is the price of concert tickets and Q is the number of tickets sold:

$$Q_D = 2500 - 120P$$

The supply of tickets, Q_S, is represented by the equation:

$$Q_S = 500 + 80P$$

a. Find the equilibrium price and quantity of tickets sold. (**Hint:** Set $Q_D = Q_S$ and solve for the wage, P, and then plug the result back into either of the original equations to find Q_E.)

b. Carefully graph your result in part a.

c. Calculate the consumer and producer surplus at the equilibrium price and quantity. (**Hint:** Since the areas of consumer and producer surplus are triangles, you will need to use the formula for the area of a triangle [1/2 × base × height] to solve the problem.)

d. If the government imposes a $5 ticket tax to help fund the building of a new arena, calculate the new equilibrium price, equilibrium quantity, consumer surplus, producer surplus, tax revenue, and deadweight loss created by the tax increase. (**Hint:** The new demand curve is $Q_D = 2500 - 120[P + T]$. Simplifying yields $Q_D = 2500 - 120P - 120T$, and plugging in $T = 5$ further simpli-

fies the new demand curve to $Q_D = 2500 - 120P - 600$, or $Q_D = 1900 - 120P$.)

10. In this chapter, we have focused on the effect of taxes on social welfare. However, governments also subsidize goods, or make them cheaper to buy or sell. How would a $2,000 subsidy on the purchase of a new hybrid vehicle impact the consumer surplus and producer surplus in the hybrid market? Use a supply and demand diagram to illustrate your answer. Does the subsidy create deadweight loss?

✳ 11. Suppose that a new $50 tax is placed on each cell phone. From the information in the graph below, compute the incidence, deadweight loss, and tax revenue of the tax.

a. What is the incidence of the tax?

b. What is the deadweight loss of the tax?

c. What is the amount of tax revenue generated?

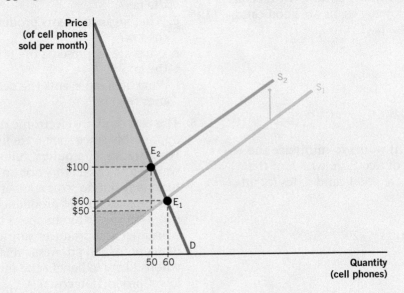

SOLVED PROBLEMS

5. a. Many good substitutes are available: consumers can drink tap water, filtered water, or other healthy beverages instead of bottled water. Therefore, bottled water is not a good candidate for an excise tax.

   b. Taxing prescription drugs will generate significant revenues without reducing sales much, if at all. There is almost

no deadweight loss because consumers have few, if any, alternatives. Thus, prescription drugs are a good candidate for an excise tax.

   c. Consumers can select many other fruits to replace oranges. The deadweight loss will be quite large. Therefore, oranges are not a good candidate for an excise tax.

d. Without batteries, many devices won't work. The lack of substitutes makes demand quite inelastic, so the deadweight loss will be small. Thus, batteries are an excellent candidate for an excise tax.

e. Wealthy consumers can spend their income in many ways. They do not have to buy luxury cars. As a result, the tax will create a large amount of deadweight loss. Therefore, luxury cars are a poor candidate for an excise tax.

11. a. After the tax is implemented, the market price rises from $60 to $100; but since sellers must pay $50 to the government, they net only $50. Tax incidence measures the share of the tax paid by buyers and sellers. Since the market price rises by $40 (from $60 to $100), buyers are paying $40 of the $50 tax, or 4/5. Since the net price falls by $10 (from $60 to $50), sellers are paying $10 of the $50 tax, or 1/5.

b. The deadweight loss is represented by the decrease in the total surplus found in the yellow triangle. In order to compute the amount of the deadweight loss, we need to determine the area inside the triangle. The area of a triangle is found by taking 1/2 × base × height. The triangle is sitting on its side, so the height of the triangle is 10 (60 − 50) and the base is $5 ($10 − $5). Hence the deadweight loss is 1/2 × 10 × $5 = $25.

c. The tax revenue is represented by the green-shaded area. You can calculate the tax revenue by multiplying the amount of the tax ($50) by the number of units sold after the tax (50). This equals $2,500.

Chapter 7

Introduction to Macroeconomics and GDP

Misconception: We have no reliable way to gauge the health of an economy.

If you read the business sections in newspapers, or watch the news on TV, you may notice that people often disagree on how the economy is doing. This might give you the impression that we aren't able to measure the performance of the economy very well. But in fact, there is a reliable and objective measure of economic performance in a country. This measure is the primary focus of this chapter.

How can you tell if you if you have a good day at work or school? The answer is often tied to your productivity – how much you got done. Or the answer may be related to how much income you earned. Productivity and income are also useful measures for evaluating the performance of an entire economy. A productive economy is a healthy economy and this is also an economy that generates income for its workers. This chapter describes how economists measure the health of an economy, using a measure of both output and income.

The Big Questions

How is macroeconomics different from microeconomics?
What does GDP tell us about the economy?
How is GDP computed?
What are some shortcomings of GDP data?

How is macroeconomics different from microeconomics?

Macroeconomics is the study of the economy of an entire nation or society. This is different from microeconomics, which studies the behavior of individual people, firms, and industries. In microeconomics you study what people buy, what jobs they take, how they distribute their income between purchases and savings; you also study the decisions of firms and how they compete with other firms. In macroeconomics, we study what happens when national output of goods and services rises and falls, when overall national employment levels rise and fall, and when the overall price level goes up and down.

For example, in microeconomics, you study the markets for salmon fillets (an example from Chapter 3). You study the behavior of people who consume salmon and firms that sell salmon – demanders and suppliers. Then you bring them together to see how the equilibrium price depends on the behavior of both demanders and suppliers.

...but widespread unemployment is a macroeconomic issue.

Macroeconomics is the study of the broader economy. It looks at the big picture created by all markets in the economy – the markets for salmon, coffee, computers, cars, haircuts, and health care, just to name a few. In macroeconomics, we examine total output in an economy, rather than just a single firm or industry. We look at total employment across the economy, rather than employment at a single firm. We look at all prices in the economy, rather than the price of just one product, such as salmon. Table 7.1 presents a selection of topics from the different perspectives of macroeconomics and macroeconomics.

Table 7.1
Microeconomics versus Macroeconomics

	Microeconomics	Macroeconomics
Income	The income of a person or the revenue of a firm.	The income of an entire nation or national economy.
Output	The production of a single worker, firm, or industry.	The production of an entire economy.
Employment	The job status and decisions of an individual or firm.	The job status of a national population, particularly the number of unemployed.
Prices	The price of a single good.	The combined prices of all goods in an economy.

What does GDP tell us about the economy?

Economists measure the total output of an economy as a gauge of its overall health. An economy that produces a large amount of valuable output is a healthy economy. If output falls for a period of time, there is something wrong in the economy. The same is true for individuals. If you have a fever for a few days, your output goes down – you don't go to the gym, you study less, and you may call in sick for work. We care about measuring our economic output because it gives us a good sense of the overall health of an economy, much like a thermometer that measures our body temperature can give us an indication of our overall health. In this section, we introduce and explain our measure of an economy's output.

Production equals income

This chapter is about the measurement of a nation's output, but it's also about the measurement of a nation's income. There's a good reason these two concepts are linked – output and income are essentially the same thing. Nations and individuals that produce large amounts of highly-valued output are relatively wealthy. Nations and individuals that don't produce much highly-valued output are relatively poor. This is no coincidence.

  Let's say you open a coffee shop in your college town. You buy or rent the equipment you need to produce coffee —everything from coffee beans and espresso machines to electricity. You hire the workers you need to keep the business running. Using these resources, you produce output like cappuccinos, espressos and draft coffee. The first day you sell 600 different coffee drinks at an average of $4 each, for a total of $2,400. This dollar figure is a measure of your firm's production or output on that day, and it is also a measure of the income received. You use the income to pay for your resources and to pay yourself. If you sell even more on the second day, the income generated increases. If you sell less, income goes down.

> **Gross domestic product (GDP)** is the market value of all final goods and services produced within a country during a specific period of time.

  The same holds true for nations. **Gross domestic product (GDP)** is the market value of all final goods and services produced in a nation within a specific period of time, typically a year. GDP is the primary measure used to gauge the output of a nation. But GDP also measures a nation's income.

  GDP is the sum of all the output from coffee shops, doctor's offices, software firms, fast-food restaurants and all the other firms that produce goods and services within a nation's borders. The sale of this output becomes income to the owners of the firms and the resource suppliers. This dual function of GDP is part of the reason we focus on GDP as a barometer of the economy. When GDP goes up, national output and income are both higher. When GDP falls, the economy is producing less than before, and total national income is falling.

Three uses of GDP data

Before analyzing the components of GDP, let's see why GDP is such an important indicator. In this section, we briefly explain the three primary uses of GDP data: to estimate living standards across time and across nations, to measure economic growth, and to determine whether an economy is experiencing recession or expansion.

Measuring living standards

Imagine two very different nations. In the first nation, people work long hours in physically taxing labor and yet their pay allows them to purchase only life's necessities – meager amounts of food, clothing, and shelter. In this nation, very few can afford a high school education or health care from a trained physician. In the second nation, virtually nobody starves, people tend to work in an air-conditioned environment, almost everyone graduates from high school, and many receive college degrees. The first nation we described is similar to life in the United States two centuries ago; the second describes life in the United States today. Everybody would agree that living standards are higher in the modern United States since most people can afford more of what they generally desire: goods, services, and leisure.

We can see these differences in living standards in GDP data. GDP in modern America is much higher than GDP was in 19th century America. Both output and income are higher, and this indicates that living standards are also higher. While not perfect, GDP offers us a way of measuring living standards across both time and place.

Let's look at the nations with highest GDP in the world. Table 7.2 lists the world's largest economies by GDP in 2010. The third column shows GDP for the top fifteen economies. This column gives us a picture of the overall output and income of each of these nations. Total world GDP in 2010 was $63 trillion, which means the United States alone produced almost 25% of all final goods and services in the world. The most significant recent movement on this list belongs to China; in 1999 China ranked seventh but by 2010, it had moved into second place.

Table 7.2
World's Largest Economies by GDP

Rank	Country	2010 GDP (Billions of Dollars)	Per Capita GDP (Dollars)
1	United States	$14,582	$47,184
2	China	5,878	4,393
3	Japan	5,497	43,137
4	Germany	3,309	40,509
5	France	2,560	39,460
6	United Kingdom	2,246	36,100
7	Brazil	2,088	10,710
8	Italy	2,051	33,917
9	India	1,729	1,477
10	Canada	1,574	46,148
11	Russian Federation	1,480	10,440
12	Spain	1,407	30,542
13	Mexico	1,038	9,166
14	South Korea	1,015	20,757
15	Australia	925	42,131

Source: World Bank. All data in 2010 U.S. Dollars.

Although total GDP is important, it is not the best indicator of living standards for a typical person. Table 7.2 reveals that in 2010, Japan and China had about the same amount of overall GDP. Yet the population of China is about ten times the population of Japan. If we divide the GDP of each nation by its population, we find that in Japan there is about $43,000 worth of GDP (or income) for every person, and $4,300 per person in China.

When we want to gauge living standards for an average person, we compute **per capita GDP**, which is GDP per person. That is, to gauge the living standards of an average person in a country, we divide the country's total GDP by its population. Per capita GDP is listed in the last column of Table 7.2.

> **Per capita GDP** is GDP per person.

Measuring economic growth

We also use GDP data to measure economic growth. Think of this as changes in living standards over time. When economies grow, living standards rise, and we can see this in the GDP data.

Figure 7.1 shows the change in per capita real GDP in the United States from 1960-2010. The rise indicates that living standards rose over the last 50 years in the United States, even though growth was not positive in every year. The data shows that income for the average person is now nearly three times what it was in 1960. So the typical person can now afford about three times as much education, food, vacation, air-conditioning, houses and cars as the average person in 1960.

Figure 7.1
U.S. Per Capita Real GDP, 1960 – 2010

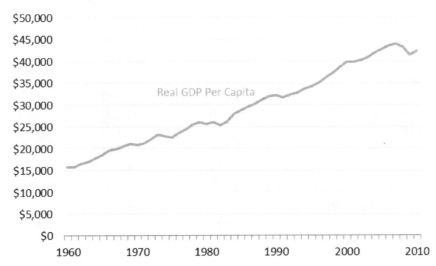

Source: BEA, Census Bureau.

The positive slope in this graph indicates increased living standards in the United States since 1960. It shows that the average person earns significantly more income today, even after adjusting for inflation. This data shows us that U.S. economic growth in this period averaged about 2%.

Now, you might notice that in this section, we have added the word *real* to our discussion of GDP. Figure 7.1 plots real per capita GDP. This is because we are now looking at data over time, and so we have to adjust our GDP data for changes in prices that occur over time. Prices of goods and services almost always rise over time, due to *inflation.* **Inflation** is the growth rate of the overall level of prices in an economy. Since GDP is calculated using market values (prices) of goods and services, inflation causes GDP to go up even if there is no change in the quantity of goods and services produced. Therefore, when we look at GDP data over time, we have to adjust it for the effects of inflation. **Real GDP** is GDP adjusted for changes in overall price levels. The way we compute real GDP is discussed later in this chapter. For now, just note that any time we evaluate GDP figures over time, we must use real GDP, which accounts for inflation.

> **Inflation** is the growth rate of the overall level of prices in an economy.

> **Real GDP** is GDP adjusted for changes in overall prices levels.

Economic growth is measured as the percent change in real per capita GDP. Notice that this measure starts with GDP data but then adjusts for both population growth and inflation. Given this definition, you should view Figure 7.1 as a picture of economic growth in the United States. But despite what you see in the U.S. GDP data, you should not presume that economic growth is automatic or even typical. Figure 7.2 shows the experience of six other nations – six distinct experiences. The per capita real GDP in Poland, Turkey and Mexico rose significantly over the period, more than doubling since 1950. India stagnated for many years and then recently began to grow. Sadly, the data for Nicaragua and Somalia indicates that citizens in these nations are poorer now than they were in 1950.

> **Economic growth** is measured as the percent change in real per capita GDP.

Figure 7.2
Real Per Capita GDP in Six Nations, 1950–2008

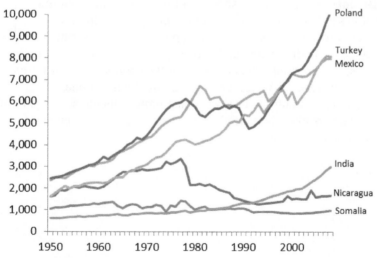

Data in 1990 international dollars.
Source: Angus Maddison Data, which is in 1990 international dollars.

Economic growth for six different nations measured by per capita real GDP, shows that growth is not guaranteed. The levels for Poland, Turkey and Mexico more than doubled since 1950. The per capita GDP of India began increasing more recently, but that of Nicaragua and Somalia declined.

Economic growth and its causes is one of the primary topics macroeconomists study. In Chapter 13, we consider the factors that lead to growth like that in the United States, Poland, Turkey, Mexico, and, more recently, India. We also consider why economies like Nicaragua and Somalia struggle to grow. Since real per capita GDP measures living standards, these issues are critical to the real people's lives around the globe.

Measuring business cycles

We have seen that GDP is used to measure living standards and economic growth. It is also used to determine whether the economy is expanding or contracting in the short run. In recent years this use of GDP had gotten a lot of media attention because of concerns about *recessions*. **Recessions** are short run economic downturns that typically last about six to eighteen months. Even the mere threat of recession strikes fear in people's hearts, because income levels fall and many people lose their jobs or cannot find work during recessions. The U.S. recession that began in 2007 and lasted into 2009 has been dubbed the "Great Recession," because of its length and depth. It lasted 19 months and real GDP fell by almost 9 percent in the last three months of 2008. In addition, the recovery from the Great Recession has been very slow.

> **A recession** is a short-run economic downturn.

Even if an economy is expanding in the long run, it is normal to go through temporary downturns. **Business cycles** are the short-run fluctuations in economic activity. Figure 7.3 illustrates a theoretical business cycle in relationship to the long-term trend in Real GDP growth. The straight line represents the long-run trend of real GDP. The slope of the trend-line is the average long run growth of real GDP. For the United States, this is about 3% per year. But the economy doesn't typically grow at exactly 3% per year. Instead of tracking exactly along the trend line, the economy experiences fluctuations in output. The wavy line represents the actual path of real GDP over time. It climbs to peaks when GDP growth is higher than usual and falls to troughs when output growth is below trend.

> **A business cycle is a** short-run fluctuation in economic activity.

Figure 7.3
The Business Cycle

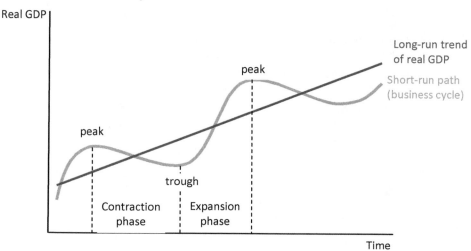

The long run trend shows consistent growth. The business cycle reflects the fluctuations that an economy typically exhibits. When the economy is growing faster than long run trend, it is in the expansionary period of the business cycle. But when growth slows to less than trend, the economy is in contraction. In real life, the cycle is not nearly as smooth and easy to spot as we picture here.

An economic expansion refers to the phase of the business cycle where the economy is growing faster than usual.

The peaks and troughs divide the business cycle into two phases: *expansions* and *contractions*. **Expansions** occur from the bottom of a trough to the next peak, when the economy is growing faster than usual. After a period of time, the economy enters a recession, or **contraction**—the period from the peak downward to the trough. During this phase, the economy is growing at a slower rate than usual. During expansions, jobs are easier to find and average income levels are climbing. But during contractions, more people lose their jobs and income levels often fall.

An economic contraction refers to the phase of the business cycle where the economy is growing slower than usual.

Figure 7.3 makes it look like business cycles are uniform and predictable. Reality is very different. Figure 7.4 plots U.S. real GDP over time, with contractionary periods—the recessions—shaded. GDP consistently declines in these recessionary periods, but they certainly don't occur in a consistent, predictable pattern. You can easily spot the Great Recession, which began in December of 2007 and lasted through June of 2009.

Figure 7.4
U.S. Real GDP and Recessions, 1960-2010

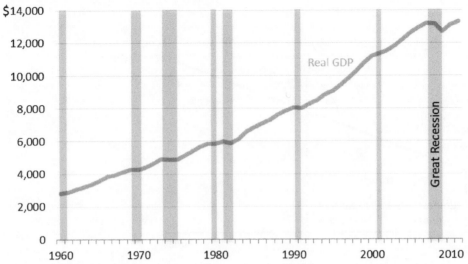

Source: Bureau of Economic Analysis.

Over time, U.S. real GDP fluctuates. The shaded areas are areas indicate periods of recession. Real GDP consistently declines during the recessions. The Great Recession, which began in December of 2007 and lasted through June of 2009, was a particularly deep and lengthy modern recession.

Practice What You Know
Three uses of GDP data

GDP as an economic barometer

Question: Determine which of the three uses of GDP is called for in each particular case.

a. In 2011, many claimed that the economy of India began slowing as GDP growth declined from 8.4% in 2010 to 6.9% in mid-2011.

Answer: This is reflects a cylical use of GDP data, indicating a potential recession. The question looks explicitly at a short-run window of data.

b. Nicaragua and Haiti are the poorest nations in the Western Hemisphere, with annual 2010 per capita GDP of only $1,132 and $671 respectively.

Answer: This uses data to show living standards. The figures indicate that average Nicarauguans and Haitians have to live on very small amounts of income each year.

c. The economy of Italy has slowed considerably over the past two decades, as evidenced by an average growth of real GDP of only 1.25% per year from 1990 to 2010.

Answer: This observation looks at growth rates over almost twenty years, which means it is using GDP data to look at long-run growth.

How is GDP computed?

We defined GDP as the market value of all final goods and services produced within a country during a specific period of time. In this section we examine the definition more carefully in order to give you a deeper understanding of what goes into GDP and what does not.

Counting market values

Nations produce a wide variety of goods and services, measured in various units. Computation of GDP literally requires addition of apples and oranges, and every other final good and service produced in a nation. How can we add everything from cars to corn to haircuts to gasoline to prescription drugs in a way that makes sense? Certainly, we can't just add quantities. For example, in 2010, the United States produced about 8 million motor vehicles and about 12 billion bushels of corn. Looking only at quantities, one might conclude that because we produced about 1,500 bushels of corn for every car, corn production is much more important to the U.S. economy. But of course this is wrong; a bushel of corn is not worth nearly as much as a car.

To add corn and cars and the other goods and services in GDP, we use market values. That is, we include not only the quantity data, but also the price of the good or service. Figure 7.5 offers an example with fairly realistic data. If corn production is 12 billion bushels and these bushels sell for $5 each, the contribution of corn to GDP is $60 billion. If car production is 8 million vehicles and they sell for $30,000 each, the contribution of cars to GDP is $240 billion. If these were the only goods produced in a given year, GDP would be $300 billion.

Figure 7.5
Using market values to compute GDP

	Quantity	x	Price	=	Market Value
Corn	12 billion bushels	x	$5	=	$60 billion
Cars	8 million vehicles	x	$30,000	=	$240 billion
					$300 billion

> GDP uses market values add together many types of goods. In this example, the contribution to GDP from corn production is $60 billion and the contribution from car production is $240 billion.

GDP uses market values, and these market values include both price and quantity information. Remember the purpose of GDP data is to evaluate the health of an economy. But the health of the economy depends on the total quantities of goods and services produced, represented in the "quantity" column of Figure 7.5. Market values allow us to add together many types of goods. At the same time, market values rely on prices, which can rise when inflation occurs. What if the prices of both cars and corn rise but quantities produced remained unchanged? The GDP figure will rise even though production stayed the same. This is why we compute real GDP by adjusting for inflation.

Including goods and services

Physical goods are easy to visualize, but less than half of U.S. GDP is goods; the majority is *services*. **Services** are output that provides benefits without production of a tangible product. Consider a service like a visit to a doctor for a physical. The doctor examines you and offers some medical advice, but you leave with no tangible output.

A service is an output that provides benefits without production of a tangible product.

The composition of U.S. GDP has evolved over time. In the past, the dominant industries in the U.S. were manufacturing goods like autos, steel, and household goods. Today, a majority of U.S. GDP is service output such as medical, financial, transportation, education, and technology services. Figure 7.6 shows services as a share of U.S. GDP since 1960. As you can see, it has grown from 50% in 1960 to about 70% in 2010.

Figure 7.6
Services as a share of U.S. GDP, 1960-2010

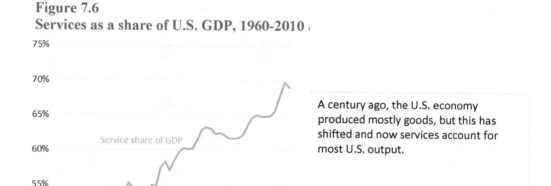

A century ago, the U.S. economy produced mostly goods, but this has shifted and now services account for most U.S. output.

Source: BEA.

Some people lament this move toward a service-dominated economy. They argue that manufacturing industries were a source of prosperity for our economy in the past, and are necessary for future growth. This is not a partisan issue; politicians from both major parties take this stand. However, this argument does not account for the nature of modern economic growth.

A century ago, the significant economic growth in the United States came from manufacturing output.   But two centuries ago, the economic growth came from agricultural output.   Economies evolve. Just because past growth was spurred by innovations in manufacturing does not mean future growth shouldn't be provided through services.

Including only final goods and services

GDP is the summation of spending on goods and services. But not all spending counts. To see why, consider the all the spending involved in building a single good, a cell phone. Table 7.3 outlines some intermediate steps required to produce a cell phone that sells for $199. In the process of producing a cell phone, the manufacturer uses many *intermediate goods*. **Intermediate goods** are goods that firms repackage or bundle with other goods for sale at a later stage. For example, the cell phone case and keyboard are intermediate goods because the phone manufacturer shop combines these with other intermediate goods, like the operating system, to produce a cell phone, the *final good*. **Final goods** are goods sold to final users. The sale of the cell phone is included as part of GDP.

> **An intermediate good** is a good that firms repackage or bundle with other goods for sale at a later stage.

> **A final good** is a good sold to final users.

What happens if we count the value of each intermediate step in making a cell phone? We start with the outer case, which costs $5 to produce. Once that case is purchased, the component hardware, which costs $10, must be installed, bringing the value of the phone to $15. The software, which costs $15, is installed, raising the value of the phone to $30. The phone is then purchased by a cell phone provider who connects it to its network; this costs another $49, raising the value to $79. Finally, the phone is sold to the consumer for $199. The final value in this string of events, the retail price, is the true value the cell phone creates in the economy. If we counted the value of each intermediate step, we would arrive at a total of $338, which overstates the value of the phone in the economy. You cannot get an accurate measure of GDP by summing up all of the sales made throughout the economy during the year since many of those sales will reflect the intermediate steps in the production process.

It is possible to get an accurate measurement of GDP by taking the sale price of the final good or by taking the value added at each step along the way, but not both; that would be double-counting.

Table 7.3
Intermediate steps in cell phone production

Steps	Value added during step	Prices of completed steps
1. Outer case and keyboard	$5	$5
2. Internal hardware	10	15
3. Install operating system	15	30
4. Connect to network	49	79
5. Retail Sale	120	199
Sum Total	$199	$338

Including only production from a particular time period

GDP only counts goods and services that are produced during a given period of time. Goods or services produced in earlier years do not count in this year's GDP. For instance, when a new car is produced, it adds to GDP in the year it is sold. However, a used car that is resold does not count in GDP since it was already counted in GDP for the year it was produced and sold the first time. If we counted the used car when it was resold we would be counting that car as part of GDP twice—also known as double-counting—even though it was produced only once.

In addition, sales of financial assets like stocks and bonds do not count toward GDP. Sales of these financial assets, which we cover in Chapter 11, do not create anything new; they just transfer ownership from one person to another. In this way, they are like used goods. Note, however, that brokerage fees count as payment for the brokerage service and are included.

Looking at GDP as different types of expenditures

In this section we look more closely at different categories of goods and services included in GDP. The Bureau of Economic Analysis (BEA) is the U.S. government agency that tallies GDP data. This task is called *national income accounting*. The BEA breaks GDP into four major categories: *consumption (C)*, *investment (I)*, *government purchases (G)*, and *net exports (NX)*. Using this framework it is possible to express GDP as:

$$GDP = C + I + G + NX \tag{7.1}$$

Table 7.4 details the composition of U.S. GDP in 2010. Total GDP was about 14.5 trillion dollars. How much is 14.5 trillion dollars? If you laid 14.5 trillion one-dollar bills side-by-side that would be enough to cover every U.S. highway, street, and county road more than twice! That is a lot of money. Keep in mind, U.S. GDP is still almost three times larger than the GDP of any other nation.

Table 7.4
The pieces of GDP in 2010, billions of dollars

Consumption (C)		**$10,245.5**	71%
Durable Goods	$1,085.5		
Nondurable Goods	2,301.5		
Services	6,858.5		
Investment (I)		**1,795.1**	12%
Business Fixed Investment	1,728.2		
Residential Construction	338.1		
Change in Business Inventories	66.9		
Government Purchases (G)		**3,002.8**	21%
Federal	1,222.8		
State and Local	1,780.0		
Net Exports (NX)		**-516.9**	-4%
Exports	1,839.8		
Imports	2,356.7		
Total GDP		**$14,526.5**	100%

Source: Bureau of Economic Analysis.

Looking at Table 7.4, you can see consumption is by far the largest component in GDP, followed by government spending and investment. Note that the value of net exports is negative. This occurs because the United States imports more foreign goods than it exports. Let's take a closer look at each of these four components of GDP.

Consumption

Consumption (C) is the purchase of final goods and services by households, with the exception of new housing. For most people, a large majority of income is spent on consumption goods and services. Consumption goods include everything from groceries to automobiles. You can see in Table 7.4 that services are a very big portion of consumption spending. These services include things such as haircuts, doctor's visits, or help from a real estate agent.

> **Consumption (C)** is the purchase of final goods and services by households, excluding new housing.

Consumption goods can be divided into two categories. *Non-durable* consumption goods are consumed over a short period of time and *durable* consumption goods are consumed over a long period of time. This distinction is important when the economy swings back and forth between good times and bad times. Sales of durable goods, for example automobiles, appliances and computers, are subject to significant cyclical fluctuations that correlate to the health of the economy. Since durable goods are generally designed to last many years, consumers tend to purchase more of these when the economy is strong. They put off purchases of durables goods, and make them last longer, when the economy is weak. For example, you can live with your old computer for another year but it might be hard to go without fresh produce. Sales of non-durables such as food, magazines, medications, or just about anything you can find in your local grocery store, tend to be relatively stable. By their very nature, non-durables don't last as long and so consumers must often purchase them regardless of economic conditions.

Investment (I)

When you hear the word "investment" you likely think of savings, or stocks and bonds. But in macroeconomics, **investment (I)** refers to private spending on tools, plant, and equipment used to produce future output. Investment can be something as simple as the purchase of a shovel, a tractor, or a personal computer to help a small business produce goods and services for its customers. Investment also includes the construction of large factories. When Pfizer builds a new factory for manufacturing a new drug, it is making an investment. Similarly, when Wal-Mart builds a new warehouse that is an investment. A newly-built house purchased by a family is also counted as an investment. That may seem odd since most of us think of a home purchase as something that is consumed, but this is the way home purchases enter the national income accounts.

> **Investment (I)** is private spending on tools, plant, and equipment used to produce future output.

Investment also includes all purchases by businesses that add to their inventories. For example, when a large printing business is confident that demand for books and magazines will be robust in the months ahead, it increases its supply of paper so it will not be caught short. Paper takes a long time to deliver, and if the printer doesn't have the paper on hand when an order comes through from a publisher, it might lose the business to a printer who does have paper. Since inventories represent a stock of goods that firms can use to produce their product in the future, an increase in inventories increases the capacity of the firm to produce more. Increases in inventories are an investment in the future.

Government purchases (G)

National, state, and local governments purchase many goods and services. Those expenditures are included in GDP as *government spending*. **Government spending (G)** includes spending by all levels of government on final goods and services. For example, every government employee receives a salary that is part of GDP. Similarly, governments spend money purchasing buildings, equipment, and supplies from private sector firms. Governments also make expenditures on a variety of public works projects, including national defense, highway construction, schools, and post offices.

> **Government spending (G)** includes spending by all levels of government on final goods and services.

However, one form of government outlay does not count in GDP. *Transfer payments* that the government makes to households, like welfare payments or unemployment insurance are not direct purchases of new goods and services. Rather, they act to increase household income. Since an increase in income does not, by itself, fit the expenditure definition of GDP, transfer payments are not included. When households subsequently spend the payments that they receive from the government on new goods and services, these expenditures enter GDP as part of C or I.

Net exports (NX)

The United States produces some goods and services that are exported to other countries and the United States also imports some goods and services that are produced elsewhere. Only exports are counted in GDP because they are produced in the United States. Imports, on the other hand, are produced elsewhere but used here. Since our goal is to measure domestic production accurately, GDP includes only **net exports (NX)**, which are exports minus imports. We can also write this in equation form as:

> **Net exports (NX)** are exports minus imports of final goods and services.

$$\text{Net exports (NX)} = \text{exports} - \text{imports} \qquad (7.2)$$

When spending on imports is larger than spending on exports, net exports are negative. Net exports are typically negative for the United States.

Notice that imports enter the GDP calculations as a negative value: GDP = C + I + G + (exports – imports). From this it would be easy to conclude that imports are harmful to an economy, because they seem to reduce GDP. However, adding the different components together (C, I, G, and NX), called *national income accounting*, really is just that – accounting. The primary goal is to keep a record of how people are buying the goods and services produced in the United States. More imports coming in means more goods and services for people in this nation. All else equal, this does not make us worse off.

Real GDP: adjusting GDP for price changes

In 2005, the United States economy produced GDP of $12.6 trillion. Just six years later, in 2011, it produced over $15 trillion. That's almost a 20% increase in just six years. Is that really possible? Think about that in long-run historical terms. Is it possible that the U.S. economy grew to $12.6 trillion over more than two centuries, but then, just six years later grew to over $15 trillion? What's more, this happened in spite of the Great Recession from 2007 to 2009. That is what the GDP data tells us. But if we look closer, we'll see that much of the recent increase in GDP is actually due to inflation

The raw GDP data, based on market values, is computed using the prices of goods and services current at the time the GDP is produced. Economists refer to these prices as the *current prices*. The GDP calculated from current prices is called **nominal GDP**. Figure 7.7 compares nominal and real GDP from 2005 to 2011. Notice that nominal GDP rises much faster than real GDP. While nominal GDP rose by about 20%, real GDP increased by just 5%. The difference between these is inflation.

> **Nominal GDP is** GDP measured in current prices.

Figure 7.7
U.S. nominal and real GDP, 2005-2011, billions of dollars

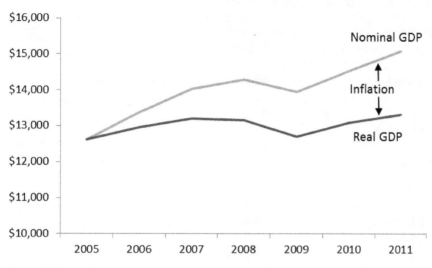

Source: BEA

Nominal GDP typically rises faster than real GDP since it rises with growth in real production and growth in prices (inflation). From 2005 to 2011, nominal GDP in the United States rose by 20%, but three-fourths of that increase was due to inflation. The increase in real GDP over the same period was just over 5%.

Computing nominal GDP is straightforward –we add the actual prices of all final goods and services. But to compute real GDP, we also need a measure of overall prices, which we call a *price level*. A **price level** is an index of the average prices of goods and services throughout the economy. It goes up when prices generally rise and falls when prices across the economy fall. Chapter 9 is devoted to prices and the calculation of price levels. For now, take the price data as given, and think of the price level as an indicator of changes in the general level of all prices across the economy.

A price level is an index of the average prices of goods and services throughout the economy.

The price level we use to adjust GDP data, known as the **GDP deflator,** includes the prices of the final goods and services counted in GDP. The GDP deflator is used to "deflate" all the price inflation out of nominal GDP so we can see real GDP. Let's look at some actual data. Table 7.5 shows U.S. nominal GDP and price level data from 2000 to 2011.   The price level is set at 100 in 2005 and rose to 103.2 in 2006. This indicates that, on average, prices across the economy rose by about 3% between 2005 and 2006.

The GDP deflator is a measure of the price level that includes prices of the final goods and services included in GDP.

Table 7.5
U.S. nominal GDP and price level, 2000 - 2010

Year	Nominal GDP (billions of dollars)	Price Level (GDP Deflator)
2000	$9,951.5	88.7
2001	10,286.2	90.7
2002	10,642.3	92.2
2003	11,142.2	94.1
2004	11,853.3	96.8
2005	12,623.0	100.0
2006	13,377.2	103.2
2007	14,028.7	106.2
2008	14,291.5	108.6
2009	13,939.0	109.7
2010	14,526.5	111.0
2011	15,094.0	113.4

Source: BEA.

To compute real GDP, we extract the current prices of goods and services and then insert prices from a common year, or *base year* that has been agreed upon. We can do this in two steps:

1. **Filter out the current prices from the nominal GDP data.**

   Do this by dividing nominal GDP by the price level for the year the GDP was produced.

2. **Put in the constant prices from the base year.**

   Now we just multiply by the price level (100) from the base year.

Putting these two steps together, we compute real GDP for any year (*t*) as:

$$Real\ GDP_t = \frac{Nominal\ GDP_t}{Price\ Level_t} \times 100$$

                                    Step 1   Step 2

(7.3)

For example, nominal GDP in 2010 was $14.5265 trillion, and the price level was 111. To convert this to real GDP, we divide by 111 and multiply by 100:

$$Real\ GDP_{2010} = \frac{\$14.5265}{111} \times 100 = \$13.0869\ trillion$$

Figure 7.8 takes you through both steps of this conversion.

Figure 7.8
Converting nominal GDP into real GDP

Data for 2010:

Nominal GDP = **$14.5265** trillion
Price Level (GDP deflator) = **111**

General Steps	Our Example
Step 1: Filter out current prices.	$14.5265 ÷ 111 = 0.130869
Step 2: Input base-year prices.	0.130869 x 100 = $13.0869

To calculate real GDP from the nominal GDP data, we filter out prices from 2010 and then multiply by the price level from the base year, 2005. This leaves us with real GDP, or GDP in 2005 prices.

The figure $13.0869 trillion is the U.S. GDP in 2010, adjusted for inflation. Economists and the financial media use other terms for real GDP; sometimes they might say "current year GDP in 2005 prices," or "GDP in constant 2005 dollars." Whenever you consider changes in GDP over time, you should look for these terms to insure your data is not biased by price changes.

Growth rates

For many macroeconomic applications it is useful to calculate growth rates. For example, let's say you read that that GDP in Mexico in 2010 was about $1 trillion. You might consider this troubling for the future of the Mexican economy, since $1 trillion is very small compared to the U.S. GDP of $14.5 trillion. But maybe you also read that Mexico's GDP grew by 18% in 2010 (it did!), you will probably get a different, and more positive impression. In general, growth rates convey additional, often more illuminating, information.

Growth rates are calculated percentage changes in a variable. For example, the growth of U.S. nominal GDP in 2010 is computed as:

$$Nominal\ GDP\ growth\ in\ 2010 = \frac{GDP_{2010} - GDP_{2009}}{GDP_{2009}} \times 100 \qquad (7.4)$$

Unless noted otherwise, the data comes from the end of the period. Therefore, the nominal GDP growth computed above tells us the percentage change in U.S. GDP from the end of 2009 to the end of 2010, or over the course of 2010. Using actual data, this is:

$$Nominal\ GDP\ growth\ in\ 2010 =$$

$$\%\ change\ in\ nominal\ GDP =$$

$$\frac{\$14.5265 - \$13.939}{\$13.939} \times 100 = \mathbf{4.2\%}$$

We can also compute the growth rate of the price level (GDP deflator) for 2010:

$$Price\ Level\ growth\ rate =$$

$$\%change\ in\ price\ level =$$

$$\frac{111 - 109.7}{109.7} \times 100 = \mathbf{1.2\%}$$

This means that throughout the U.S. economy in 2010, inflation was 1.2%.

Armed with these two computations, we can derive one more useful formula for evaluating GDP data. Recall that nominal GDP, which is the raw GDP data, includes information on both the price level and real GDP. When either of these changes, it affects nominal GDP. In fact, the growth rate of nominal GDP is approximately equal to the sum of the growth rates of these two pieces:

Growth of nominal GDP $\approx$ growth of real GDP + growth of price level   (7.5)

Since growth rates are calculated as percentage changes, we can rewrite equation 19.5 as:

% change in nominal GDP $\approx$ % change in real GDP + % change in price level   (7.6)

This equation is a simple way of dissecting the growth of GDP into its respective parts. For example, since we know nominal GDP grew by 4.2% in 2010, and the price level grew by 1.2%, the remaining nominal GDP growth of 3% is the result of growth in real GDP.

Practice What You Know
Computing real and nominal GDP growth

GDP growth in Mexico

The table below presents GDP data for Mexico. Use the data to answer the following questions.

Year	Nominal GDP Growth Rate	Price Level Growth Rate
2007	9	6
2008	6	6
2009	-19	4
2010	18	4.4

Source: World Bank

Question:

What was the rate of growth of real GDP in Mexico in 2010?

Answer:

Using equation 19.6 we know:

% change in real GDP + % change in price level = %Δ in nominal GDP

And rewriting the equation, we can solve for real GDP growth as:

% change in real GDP = %change in nominal GDP − % change in price level

For 2010, we have:

% change in real GDP = 18 − 4.4 = **13.6**.

That's impressive.

Question:

Now compute real GDP growth in Mexico in 2009.

Answer:

Using the 2009 data in the same equation, we get:

$$\% \text{ change in real GDP} = -19 - 4 = \mathbf{-23}.$$

This means 2009 was a pretty rough year for the Mexican economy.

What are some shortcomings of GDP data?

We began this chapter with a claim that GDP is the single best measure of economic activity. Along the way, we have learned that nominal GDP fails to account for changes in prices and that real GDP is a better measure of economic activity. We also talked about how real GDP per capita accounts for population differences. You will be relieved to learn that we are done introducing new variations of GDP! However, there are some problems with relying on GDP as a measure of a nation's well-being. In this section we highlight four shortcomings that limit the effectiveness of GDP as a measure of the health of an economy. At the end of this section, we will consider why we continue to rely on GDP.

Non-market goods

Many goods and services are produced but not sold. Those goods and services are not counted in GDP, even though they create value for society. For instance, washing your own dishes, mowing your own grass, or washing your car are services produced, but not counted in GDP. When the non-market segment of an economy is large, there can be a dramatic undercounting of the annual output being produced. In less-developed societies where many households live off the land and produce goods for their own consumption, GDP – or the measure of market activity – is a poor measure of the economic output.

Underground economy

The underground, or shadow, economy describes transactions that are not reported to the government, and therefore not taxed. Usually these transactions are settled in cash. Some of these transactions are legal, such as when bartenders and waitresses collect tips, contractors build additions to homes, and landscapers cut lawns. But the underground economy also includes transactions like illegal exchanges of drugs. Transactions in the underground economy are not directly measurable because the income is not reported. Therefore, they are not included in official measures of GDP.

How big is the underground economy? No one is exactly sure. The Organization for Economic Cooperation and Development (OECD) has estimated that for wealthy developed economies, it is roughly 15 percent of GDP, in transitioning economies the percentage rises to between 21 and 30 percent of GDP. However, in the world's most under-developed economies, like Nicaragua or Somalia, the underground economy can be as much as 45 percent of GDP.

The United States is widely believed to have one of the smallest shadow economies in the world with approximately 10 percent of GDP unaccounted for in the official measurement. Why is the underground economy so small in the United States? The simple answer is that in the United States, and many other developed economies, most citizens can earn more by legitimately participating in the economy than by engaging in illegal activities. In short, a strong economy that creates jobs and opportunities for advancement helps to reduce the size of the underground economy. In addition, corruption is much less common. This means participants in the economy rarely face demands for bribes or kickbacks from the authorities or organized crime. This is not the case in many developing nations. For example, Somalia, which ranks last on Transparency International's corruption index, has widespread piracy and virtually no formal economy that is not subject to bribery and thuggery.

Economics in the Real World:
America's "shadow economy" is bigger than you think – and growing.

Journalist Taylor Barnes wrote about America's underground economy in 2009. Barnes visited Malcolm X Boulevard on West 125th Street in New York city and reported several instances of underground transaction for everything from moving companies to sales of makeup, food stamps, and fake handbags.

According to Barnes:

> *Pinning down the informal economy is as tough as catching a fake Louis Vuitton vendor running from the police. But it's huge in the United States – larger than the official output of all but the upper crust of nations across the globe. And, due to the recent recession, it's growing.*

Barnes cites the estimates of economist Friedrich Schneider, which put the size of the U.S. underground economy at around $1 trillion, or 8% of measured GDP. This estimate only includes legal activity; it excludes illegal activities like drug deals.

Source: http://www.csmonitor.com/Business/2009/1112/americas-shadow-economy-is-bigger-than-you-think-and-growing

Economics in the Media
Underground economy

Traffic

Traffic looks at America's war on drugs through the lives of the people who live it. The characters range from the nation's Drug Czar, to his cocaine-using daughter, to the cops who fight the war on both sides of the U.S./Mexican border, to the drug dealers who profit from trafficking the drugs.

In one scene a suspected drug trafficker is being interrogated by two agents from the Drug Enforcement Agency. The suspect explains that the cocaine flow from Mexico into the United States cannot be stopped because there is too much demand in the United States and because Mexican dealers are willing to "throw supply at the problem." That is, the Mexican drug lords recognize that some of their shipments will be seized but enough will get through to reach their customers in the United States to make the risks worthwhile.

One of the ironies about measuring GDP is that while the drug trades are not part of GDP—because those illegal market transactions are not formally recorded—the people involved in fighting the war on drugs, and sales of drug paraphernalia are included in GDP.

The movie also traces the lives of a successful businessman who has made millions selling drugs. We see his estate, luxury cars, trophy wife, and all the accruements of success – his purchases, made from illegal sales, are counted in GDP because GDP was designed to measure the sales of final goods and services.

So while GDP cannot measure the economic activity in the underground economy, it can indirectly capture some of those transactions when the gains from selling drugs are used to purchase legal products.

Quality of the environment

Since GDP only measures the final amount of goods and services produced in a given time period it is not able to distinguish how those goods and services are produced. Imagine two economies, both with same real GDP per capita. One economy relies on clean energy for its production and the other has lax environmental standards. Citizens in both countries enjoy the same standard of living but their well-being is not the same. The lax environmental standards in the second economy create air and water pollution and lead to health problems for its citizens. Since there is more to life than the goods and services we buy, using GDP to infer that both places are equally desirable would be inaccurate.

Leisure time

Since GDP only counts market activity, it fails to capture how long laborers work to produce goods and services. For most developed nations, according to the OECD, the average workweek is a shade over 35 hours. However, there are wide variations in how hard laborers work from one country to the next. At the high end, laborers in South Korea average 46 hours per week. In contrast, laborers in the Netherlands average less than 28 hours per week. This means comparisons of GDP across countries do not account for the extra time available to workers in countries with substantially fewer-hours-worked. For example, in the United States the average work week is 36 hours. A comparison with Japan, which also averages 36 hours per work week, would be valid, but a comparison of the GDP in the United States with Sweden (31 hours) or Greece (41 hours) would be misleading.

Why don't we correct some of the deficiencies of GDP by including them in our calculations? If we did, GDP might be a better gauge of well-being. For instance, there are many other measurements that one might use to judge the success of a country. In addition to the production of goods and services, one might look at life expectancy, educational levels, access to health care, crime rates, or any of a host of other statistics to tell you whether or not a country is a good place to live.

One problem with including all the additional factors into GDP is that they are also difficult to measure. Moreover, the combined statistic that we would create would be even more challenging to understand. Therefore, we limit GDP to measuring economic production, knowing that it is not a perfect measure of well-being. In addition, GDP is actually correlated with many of the variables we care about. In Chapter 24, we present international data that shows increases in GDP are associated with increases in many measures of human welfare. A country with a higher GDP per capita can focus on economic values beyond the basic necessities. Therefore, higher levels of GDP are highly correlated with a better environment, higher quality and better access to health care, more education, more leisure time, and low crime rates.

Practice What You Know
Shortcomings of GDP data

GDP as an economic barometer

In many parts of the world a significant amount of effort is devoted to non-market production in the household. For example, Zimbabwe has a very high rate of non-market household production. On the other hand, Canada has a low rate of non-market household production.

Question:

How does the difference in non-market household production affect a comparison between Zimbabwe and Canada?

Answer:

The GDP statistics of Zimbabwe are biased downward more than the statistics of Canada, since a larger portion of its actual production goes unreported. As such, while Zimbabwe is actually poorer nation than Canada, the official statistics exaggerate the difference sightly.

Economics for Life
GDP Data releases

How to obtain and interpret the latest GDP data

At the end of each month, new GDP data is released by the United States government. The data is sometimes confusing, and often you'll read different interpretations of the same data. In addition, we've observed a pessimistic bias in almost all economic data reporting. But you can look at the data for yourself and determine just how good or bad the news actually is.

The agency that calculates GDP data is the Bureau of Economic Analysis (BEA). You can find all the latest data at their website: www.bea.gov. The data is reported for each year and also each quarter, but adjusted to an annual basis.

GDP data is not known instantaneously, so the most recent data looks at the prior quarter. For example, if you visit the BEA website in February of 2014, you will find GDP data for the last quarter of 2013 (October - December). Since GDP is so difficult to estimate, it takes almost three months to arrive at a final estimate of GDP for a particular quarter. However, along the way, BEA publishes two early estimates.

For example, the final GDP estimate for the fourth quarter of 2013 will not be known until the end of March in 2014. However, the first estimate, known as the *advance* estimate, is released at the end of January. Then the second estimate, known as the *preliminary* estimate, is released at the end of February.

How can you tell if the news is good or bad? The very best benchmark is the long run average rate. If you are looking at real GDP growth, you should always compare it to the historical average of about 3%. So the next time you read an article about U.S. GDP data, remember to compare the actual number to this benchmark of 3%.

BIG QUESTIONS

How is macroeconomics different from microeconomics?

Microeconomics is the study of individuals and firms but macroeconomics studies the whole economy. Many of the topics are the same; these include income, employment and output. But the macro perspective is much broader than the micro perspective.

What does GDP tell us about the economy?

GDP measures both output and income in a macroeconomy. It is a gauge of productivity and the overall level of wealth in an economy. We use GDP data to measure living standards, economic growth, and business cycle conditions.

How is GDP computed?

GDP is the total market value of all goods and services produced in an economy in a given year. We typically measure GDP by adding four types of expenditures in the economy: consumption (C), investment (I), government (G), and net exports (NX). For many applications, it is also necessary to compute real GDP, or adjust GDP for changes in prices.

What are some shortcomings of GDP data?

GDP does not include production of non-market goods, the underground economy, production effects on the environment, or the value placed on leisure time.

Conclusion

We began this chapter with the misconception that we have no good way to determine how well an economy is performing. But GDP works well. In the short run, it helps us recognize business cycles. When the economy is struggling through a recession, this shows up in the GDP data. When the economy is healthy and expanding, GDP data reinforces this too. GDP also serves as a good indicator for living standards around the globe and over time. As we'll see in Chapter 13, nations with better living conditions are also nations with higher GDP. Thus, even though there are some shortcomings in the GDP data, it is a sound indicator of the overall health of an economy.

In the next chapter, we look at a second macroeconomic indicator, the unemployment rate. The unemployment rate and other job indicators give us an additional dimension on which to consider the health of an economy.

Concepts You Should Know

Gross domestic product (GDP)
Per capita GDP
Inflation
Real GDP
Economic growth
Recessions
Business cycles
Expansion
Contraction
Services
Intermediate goods
Final goods
Consumption (C)
Investment (I)
Government spending (G)
Net exports (NX)
Nominal GDP
Price level
GDP deflator

Questions for Review

1. Explain the relationship between output and income for both an individual and an entire economy.

2. What is the single most important component (C, I, G, or NX) of GDP? Give an example of each component

3. A farmer sells cotton to a clothing company for $1,000 and the clothing company turns the cotton into t-shirts that it sells to a store for a total of $2,000. How much did GDP increase as a result of these transactions?

4. A friend of yours is reading a financial blog and comes to you for some advice about GDP. She wants to whether she should pay attention to nominal or real GDP. Which one do you recommend?

5. Is a larger GDP always better than a smaller GDP? Explain your answer with an example.

6. If Max receives an unemployment check would we include that transfer payment from the government in this year's GDP?

7. Phil owns an old set of golf clubs that he purchased for $1,000 seven years ago. He decides to Craigslist them and sells the clubs for $250. How does this sale affect GDP?

8. Real GDP for 2010 is less than nominal GDP for that year. But real GDP for 2000 is more than nominal GDP for that year. Why?

9. What are the five problems with using GDP as a measuring of well-being?

Study Problems

1. A friend who knows of your interest in economics comes up to you after reading the latest GDP data and excitedly exclaims, "Did you see that nominal GDP rose from $14.2B to $15.0B?" What should you tell your friend about this news?

2. In the following situations explain what is counted in GDP.
    a. You bought a new Wii at GameStop last year and resold it on eBay this year.
    b. You purchase an "Investing for Dummies" book at Barnes & Noble.
    c. You purchase a historic home using a Real Estate agent.

d. You detail your car so it is spotless inside and out.

e. Your purchase a new hard drive for your old laptop.

f. Your physical therapist receives $300 for physical therapy but reports only $100.

g. You receive $200 from concert tickets that you scalp.

h. Apple buys 1,000 motherboards for use in making new computers.

i. Toyota produced 10,000 new Camrys that remain unsold at the end of the year.

3. To which component of GDP expenditure (C, I, G or NX) does each of the following belong?

a. Swiss chocolates imported from Europe.

b. A driver's license you receive from the Department of Motor Vehicles.

c. A candle you buy at a local store.

d. A new home.

4. From the following information calculate GDP using the expenditure approach.

Item	Amount
Profits	$200 M
Government salaries	100 M
Imports	25 M
Exports	15 M
Government purchases	150 M
Interest	50 M
Consumption	500 M
Investment	100 M
Business taxes	75 M

1. A mechanic builds an engine and then sells it to a customized body shop for $7,000. The body shop inserts the engine into the car, and resells it to a dealer for $20,000. The dealer then sells the finished vehicle for $35,000. A consumer drives off with the car. How much does GDP increase? What is the value-added at each step of the production process? How does the total value-added compare with the amount that GDP increased?

2. Use the data in Table 7.4 to compute real GDP for the year 2000.

3. Many goods and services are illegally sold or legally sold but not reported to the government. How would increased efforts to count those goods and services affect our calculation of GDP?

4. Leisure time is not included in GDP, but what would happen if it was? Would high work countries like South Korea look better in international comparisons of well-being, or worse?

Solved problems

1. Fill in the missing data in the following table.

Year	Nominal GDP	Real GDP	GDP Deflator
2007	$100,000	_____	100.0
2008	_____	$110,000	108.0
2009	$130,000	$117,000	_____
2010	$150,000	_____	120.0
2011	_____	$136,000	125.0

Answer:

Year	Nominal GDP	Real GDP	GDP Deflator
2007	$100,000	$100,000	100.0
2008	$118,800	$110,000	108.0
2009	$130,000	$117,000	111.1
2010	$150,000	$125,000	120.0
2011	$170,000	$136,000	125.0

To solve for the missing data, use the following equation (and 2007 as the base year):

$$Real\ GDP_{year} = \frac{Nominal\ GDP_{year}}{Price\ Level_{year}} \times Base\ Year\ Price\ Level$$

- For 2007: Real GDP$_{2007}$ = ($100,000÷100.0) ×100.0 = $100,000
- For 2008: $110,000 = (Nominal GDP$_{2008}$÷108.0)×100.0.
  Nominal GDP$_{2008}$ = ($110,000÷100.0)×108.0 = $118,800
- For 2009: $117,000 = ($130,000÷GDP Deflator$_{2009}$)×100.0.
  GDP Deflator$_{2009}$ = ($130,000÷$117,000)×100.0
  GDP Deflator$_{2009}$ = 111.1
- For 2010: Real GDP$_{2010}$ = ($150,000÷120.0)×100.0
  Real GDP$_{2010}$ = $125,000
- For 2011: $136,000 = (Nominal GDP$_{2011}$÷125.0)×100.0
  Nominal GDP$_{2011}$ = ($136,000÷100.0)×125.0
  Nominal GDP$_{2011}$ = $170,000

2. Consider an economy that only produces two goods: strawberries and cream.

Year	Price of Strawberries	Quantity of Strawberries	Price of Cream	Quantity of Cream
2010	$3.00	100	$2.00	200
2011	$4.00	125	$2.50	400
2012	$5.00	150	$3.00	500

Use the table above to compute nominal GDP, real GDP, and the GDP deflator for each year. (2010 is the base year.)

Answer:

Year	Nominal GDP	Real GDP	GDP Deflator
2010	$700	$700	100.0
2011	$1,500	$1,175	127.7
2012	$2,250	$1,450	155.2

First, let's calculate nominal GDP for each of the three years by adding up the market values of the strawberries and cream produced in that year.

- Nominal GDP$_{2010}$ = $3.00*100 + $2.00×200 = $700
- Nominal GDP$_{2011}$ = $4.00*125 + $2.50×400 = $1,500
- Nominal GDP$_{2012}$ = $5.00*150 + $3.00×500 = $2,250

Now, let's calculate real GDP in 2010 dollars by multiplying the quantities produced in each year by the 2010 prices.

- Real GDP$_{2010}$ = $3.00×100 + $2.00×200 = $700
- Real GDP$_{2011}$ = $3.00×125 + $2.00×400 = $1,175
- Real GDP$_{2012}$ = $3.00×150 + $2.00×500 = $1,450

Finally, using the Nominal GDP and Real GDP numbers we calculated above, let's calculate the GDP Deflator by using the following formula:

$$Real\ GDP_{year} = \frac{Nominal\ GDP_{year}}{GDP\ Deflator_{year}} \times Base\ Year\ Price\ Level$$

$$GDP\ Deflator_{year} = \frac{Nominal\ GDP_{year}}{Real\ GDP_{year}} \times 100.0$$

- GDP Deflator$_{2010}$ = 100.0. Since 2010 is given as the base year, the GDP Deflator must be 100.0.
- GDP Deflator$_{2011}$ = ($1,500÷$1,175)×100 = 127.7
- GDP Deflator$_{2012}$ = ($2,250÷$1,450)×100 = 155.2

Chapter 8

Unemployment

Misconception: We should aim for zero unemployment.

It is commonly believed that even a small amount of unemployment is a sign of problems. This isn't true. On the one hand, it is never fun for any person to search unsuccessfully for work. On the other hand, some unemployment is caused by positive changes in the economy that make us all better off in the long run. For this reason, economists agree that we can never eliminate unemployment entirely, and attempts to eliminate all unemployment are misguided.

In this chapter we will take a closer look at the topic of unemployment. The unemployment rate is the second most important indicator of economic health, after GDP. We will examine the causes of unemployment and explain how it is measured. By looking at some historical data in context, we will begin to understand when unemployment is a matter of concern.

Big Questions

- **What are the major reasons for unemployment?**
- **What can we learn from the employment data?**

What are the major reasons for unemployment?

> **Unemployment** occurs when a worker who is not currently employed is searching for a job unsuccessfully.

Perhaps you know somebody who lost his or her job – a parent or a family friend. Losing a job is particularly difficult when a person is unable to easily transition to another one. After all, many of us depend on our jobs just to survive. There are few greater frustrations than this in a modern economy – being willing and able to work, but lacking an opportunity to do so. **Unemployment** occurs when a worker who is not currently employed is searching for a job without success. Unfortunately, the level of unemployment in the United States has been relatively high in recent years – during and after the Great Recession which began at the end of 2007.

People leave their jobs for many reasons. Some do so voluntarily: they may choose to have children, to return to school, or to take another job. Others lose a job they wish to keep. An employee might be let go for poor performance or because the company is downsizing. When macroeconomists consider unemployment, they explicitly look at workers who seek employment yet are unable to secure it. We use the *unemployment rate* to monitor the level of unemployment in the economy. The **unemployment rate (u)** is the portion of the labor force that is unemployed. Figure 20.1 plots the U.S. unemployment rate from 1960 to 2012. This picture is one way of quickly measuring national economic frustration. As the unemployment rate climbs, people are more likely to be disappointed in their pursuit of a job.

> **The unemployment rate (u)** is the percent of the labor force that is unemployed.

Figure 8.1:
United States Unemployment Rate, 1960-2012

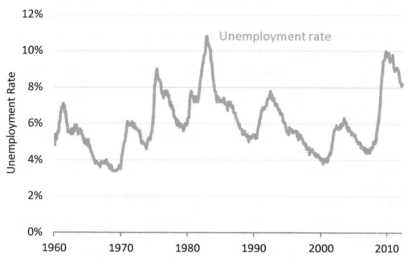

Source: Bureau of Labor Statistics.

> The unemployment rate is an important indicator of the economy's health. Since 1960, the average unemployment rate has been about 6%.

Economists distinguish three types of unemployment: *structural, frictional, and cyclical*. You can think of each type as deriving from a different source. As it turns out, structural and frictional unemployment occur even when the economy is healthy and growing. For this reason they are often called "natural unemployment." We consider them first.

Structural Unemployment

Unemployment is difficult on households, and it is a waste of resources when idle workers sit on the sidelines. However, a dynamic, growing economy is an economy that adapts and changes. Nobody would consider it an improvement if we returned to the economy of early America, where 90% of Americans toiled in manual farm work and were paid subsistence wages. The transformation to our modern economy brings new jobs but also requires completely different skills. Some jobs become obsolete, which leads inevitably to a certain amount of unemployment, even if just temporarily. Here is the dilemma. Dynamic, growing economies are also evolving economies. If we want an economy that adapts to changes in consumer demands and technology, we must accept some unemployment, at least temporarily, as a byproduct of the growth.

Consider that in the past we produced no computers, cell phones, or polio vaccines. Subsequent inventions of new products and technologies allow us to produce more and better output with fewer resources. But we also produce less of something else – like black & white televisions, cassette tapes, and typewriters. These kinds of structural changes leave some workers unemployed, even if just temporarily.

As new industries are created, some old ones are destroyed. Economist Joseph Schumpeter coined the term *creative destruction* to describe this process of economic evolution. **Creative destruction** occurs when the introduction of new products and technologies leads to the end of other industries and jobs, as some jobs become obsolete. This leads to **structural unemployment**, which is caused by changes in the industrial make-up (structure) of the economy. Although structural unemployment can create transitional problems, it is often a sign of a healthy, growing economy.

> **Structural Unemployment** is Unemployment caused by changes in the industrial make-up (structure) of the economy.

> **Creative destruction** occurs when the introduction of new products and technologies leads to the end of other industries and jobs.

The retail book market provides a good example. In the 1980s and 90s, Borders Bookstore rose from small Ann Arbor, Michigan bookseller to a national chain with 1,249 total locations. Borders success came from innovation; they were much larger than earlier bookstores, offered four to five times as many titles, comfortable reading areas and in-store cafes. These innovations led to the closure of many small independent booksellers, causing some temporary job shifts.

But innovations in the book market weren't over in the 1990s. The last decade saw greater competition from online booksellers like Amazon.com, and the introduction of e-readers like the Kindle, Nook, and iPad. These changes lead to the decline of Borders, which had 19,000 employees when it declared bankruptcy in 2011. Borders employees found themselves structurally unemployed; they lost their jobs as a result of market innovations.

The steel industry provides another example. Steel helped to revolutionize life in the late 19th and early 20th century. It is an essential component of automobiles, appliances, bridges, buildings, and even road construction. And while steel has been around for centuries, the number of workers needed to manufacture it has steadily dwindled. As recently as 1980, almost 500,000 people in the United States were employed making steel. That number fell to 225,000 in 2000 and declined again to about 150,000 in 2010. Where have all the jobs gone? Advanced engineering has made it possible for firms to replace workers with automated equipment. Steel production has become much safer and more efficient. The trade-off—jobs for safety and efficiency— is reflected in the employment numbers for the industry.

From this we can begin to understand why there is unemployment even in a healthy economy. For instance, in 2006—a typical year—real GDP in the United States grew by 2.7 percent, and 2 million new jobs were created. Yet there were approximately 5 million job separations, meaning people who either quit or were laid off, every month. In a dynamic economy, job turnover is normal.

In the long run, the evolving economy has led to drastic changes in the type of work Americans do. Figure 8.2 shows how jobs in the United States have evolved over the past two centuries. Two-hundred years ago, over ninety percent of Americans worked in agriculture, either as farmers or farm laborers. A century later, in 1900, only about half of U.S. workers were employed in farming. The rest were split between manufacturing jobs and service-related jobs. In 1900, a manufacturing job may have been in railroad or steel production, while service jobs would have included professions such as teaching and accounting. Today, five out of six American workers are employed in service-related jobs. Since 1979, manufacturing employment in the United States has fallen from almost 20 million jobs to just 11.5 million. Over the same period, employment in service industries has risen from 65 million to about 112 million. While we still have teachers and accountants, there are a multitude of new service jobs in fields such as engineering, finance, transportation, health, and government.

The trends presented in Figure 8.2 illustrate creative destruction: the structure of the economy evolves and this leads to different types of jobs. This long view presents the most positive angle on this. After all, most of us would prefer modern jobs to working with simple farm tools in a field all day. But along the way, as jobs shift, there is inevitably some temporary structural unemployment.

Figure 8.2:
The Evolution of Jobs in the United States

Source: Federal Reserve Bank of Dallas, *Annual Report*, 2003

Over the past two centuries, American jobs have evolved from agricultural to manufacturing and then to service.

While structural unemployment can't be eliminated, it can be reduced in a number of ways. Workers must often retrain, relocate, or change their expectations in some way before they can work elsewhere. Lumberjacks may need to become computer repair specialists, or workers may need to relocate from Detroit to Kentucky. While this is often painful for individuals, we all benefit in the long run. Government can also enact policies to alleviate the pain of structural unemployment, including job training programs and relocation subsidies.

Economics in the Real World:
Americans don't appear to want farm work

In 2010, Garance Burke of the Associated Press wrote an article about the frustration of U.S. farmers trying to find Americans to harvest fruit and vegetables. Even though the unemployment rate was very high, Americans did not apply for available farm jobs. Burke notes that the few Americans who do take such jobs usually don't stay in the fields for long. The AP analysis showed that from January to June, California farmers advertised 1,160 farm-worker jobs available to U.S. citizens and legal residents; only 36 were hired. One farmer named Steve Fortin noted problems with American workers: "A few years ago when domestic workers were referred here, we saw absentee problems, and we had people asking for time off after they had just started. Some were actually planting the plants upside down."

Comedian Stephen Colbert partnered with the United Farm Workers (UFW) union in a "Take Our Jobs" campaign, aimed at getting farm jobs filled with American workers. Colbert even spent a day picking beans in a field but concluded that farm work is "really, really hard."

Ironically, during the 2007-2009 recession many migrant farm jobs were available for unemployed Americans but they refused to apply for them. This contrasts with events during the Great Depression more than 80 years earlier, when displaced farmers from the plains states flooded California looking for work. So when people claim that immigrants are taking jobs away from American citizens, we can say that in the heart of the nation's biggest farming state, this is certainly not true. In addition, when we look at the long run trend in the U.S. jobs, which shows a movement away from agricultural work and into service-sector jobs, we probably shouldn't be too alarmed.

*source: http://www.usatoday.com/money/workplace/2010-09-27-farm-work_N.htm

Frictional Unemployment

> **Frictional unemployment** is unemployment caused by delays in matching available jobs and workers.

Even when jobs are available and qualified employees live nearby, it still takes time for workers and employers to find each other and agree to terms. **Frictional unemployment** is caused by time delays in matching available jobs and workers. Frictional unemployment is another type of natural unemployment – no matter how healthy the economy, there is always some frictional unemployment.

Consider how a successful new product launch at McDonald's affects Burger King. Suppose that McDonald's launches a new product called the *Quad-stack*, which is really just four Quarter Pounders stacked on top of each other. Also suppose that customers can't get enough of the new burger. Because of all the new business, McDonald's needs to hire more employees. At the same time, Burger King loses customers to McDonald's and decides to lay off some of its workers. Laid-off workers from Burger King will take some time to search for new jobs. McDonald's will take time to decide how many new workers it needs and which workers to hire some workers will be unemployed during this transition; this is frictional unemployment.

Frictional unemployment occurs even in the healthiest economy. Because we live in a world of imperfect information, there are incentives for employees to keep searching for the perfect job, or for employers to search longer for the best employee. Even if there was a perfect job available for every worker, it would still take time to match workers with the available jobs. For example, as you approach graduation, you will probably take some time to search for a job and to determine which offer to accept. You won't be interested in just any job. Similarly, employers rarely hire the first applicant they see, though it may be costly to leave a position vacant. Even if there is a perfect job available for every worker, it will still take time to match workers and jobs. These time lags create friction in the labor market, and the result is temporary, frictional unemployment.

Even though frictional unemployment is natural, the amount of frictional unemployment can still rise or fall over time. Let's look at two causes of changes in frictional unemployment levels: information availability and government policies.

Information Availability

Imagine looking for a job in the world without the Internet. You'd read a lot of newspaper ads, make dozens of phone calls, and probably make several in-person visits to firms where you think you might like to work. Yet after all that, you'd still have a great deal of uncertainty about the complete set of your job prospects.

Today, most job searches are done online. For example, let's say you graduate with a degree in accounting and pass your CPA exam. You decide to search for a job online at indeed.com. Even in 2012, with relatively high unemployment, a nationwide search yields over 31,000 potential matches. Narrowing this search to the state of Virginia nets 1,200 potential jobs. The point is that the vast new information available through the internet enables workers and companies to find each other more quickly and to make better matches with substantially lower costs. The result is lower frictional unemployment.

> **Unemployment insurance** is a government program that reduces the cost of being out-of-work by guaranteeing part of a worker's income while unemployed.

Government Policies

Anything that lengthens the job search process increases frictional unemployment. This includes government policies such as unemployment compensation and government regulations related to hiring and firing employees.

Unemployment insurance, also known as federal jobless benefits, is a government program that reduces the hardship of being out of work by guaranteeing that unemployed workers receive a percentage of their former income while they are unemployed. Governments provide unemployment insurance to workers for many reasons. It cushions the economic consequences of being laid off, and provides workers time to search for new employment. In addition, unemployment insurance can also help contain macroeconomic problems before they spread to other industries. Consider what happens if the auto industry is struggling and workers are laid off. These unemployed auto workers will not be able to pay for goods and services that they previously purchased. The reduction in overall spending will hurt other industries. For example, if unemployed workers can't pay their mortgages, lenders will suffer and the downturn will spread to the financial industry. Viewed this way, unemployment insurance serves to dampen the economic contraction.

However, unemployment insurance also creates unintended consequences. Unemployment benefits make it less attractive to search for and take a job. Workers spend more time unemployed when they have insurance; without unemployment insurance, workers are much more motivated to seek immediate employment, which reduces the time spent unemployed. For example, in late 2007, the U.S. economy entered into the Great Recession, which ended in mid-2009. But several years after GDP growth resumed and the recession was declared over, the level of unemployment remained high. One reason might have been frictional unemployment that occurred because of special policies put in place during the recession. In November 2009, the U.S. government extended unemployment insurance to 99 weeks, the highest level in history. While it certainly seems appropriate to help the jobless during recessions, this policy creates an incentive to search for a job longer, which, in turn, contributes to frictional unemployment.

Government regulations on hiring and firing also contribute to frictional unemployment. Regulations on hiring include restrictions on who can and must be interviewed, paperwork that must be completed for new hires, and additional tax documents that must be filed for employees. Regulations on firing include mandatory severance pay, written justification, and government fines. And while these labor market regulations may be instituted to help workers by giving them greater job security, they create unintended consequences. When it is difficult to hire employees, firms take longer to do so, which increases frictional unemployment. If it is difficult to fire employees, firms take greater care in hiring them. But this longer search time increases frictional unemployment.

The United States has relatively few labor market regulations. On the other hand, Germany and France have especially stringent labor market regulations. For instance, if a French employer wishes to fire a worker who has been employed for two years or more, the employer must give three months' notice, pay a fine to the government, and offer the worker up to three years of severance pay. Figure 8.3 provides evidence of the unintended consequences of government labor regulations from 2000-2012. First, consider the significantly higher unemployment rates of France and Germany over most of the years shown. Much of this can be attributed to frictional unemployment as the result of labor market regulations. At the end of the decade, the unemployment rate in the United States rose dramatically. However, this was not frictional unemployment; in the next section, we turn to the cause for that period of significant unemployment.

Figure 8.3:
Frictional Unemployment in France and Germany

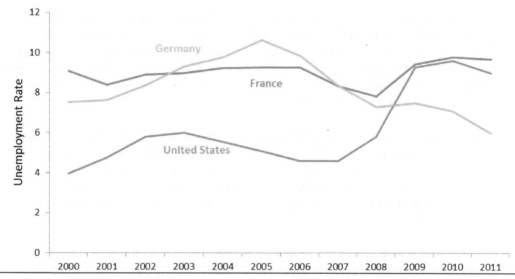

During normal economic times, unemployment in France and Germany tend to be higher than in the United States. This is largely caused by labor market regulations that lead to greater search time and frictional unemployment.

Economics in the Real World:
Employment, Italian Style

The intention of labor market restrictions may be to help workers, but too often, workers themselves bear the costs, as fewer jobs are created. Consider the labor market regulations in Italy, as reported in *The Wall Street Journal* on June 26, 2012. The key point of the article relates to the inability to draw the Italian economy out of stagnation. The authors point to hiring regulations as one big problem impeding employment.

The following comes directly from the article:

Imagine you're an ambitious Italian entrepreneur, trying to make a go of a new business. You know you will have to pay at least two-thirds of your employees' social security costs. You also know you're going to run into problems once you hire your 16th employee, since that will trigger provisions making it either impossible or very expensive to dismiss a staffer.

But there's so much more. Once you hire employee 11, you must submit an annual self-assessment to the national authorities outlining every possible health and safety hazard to which your employees might be subject. These include stress that is work-related or caused by age, gender and racial differences. You must also note all precautionary and individual measures to prevent risks, procedures to carry them out, the names of employees in charge of safety, as well as the physician whose presence is required for the assessment.

Now say you decide to scale up. Beware again: Once you hire your 16th employee, national unions can set up shop. As your company grows, so does the number of required employee representatives, each of whom is entitled to eight hours of paid leave monthly to fulfill union or works-council duties. Management must consult these worker reps on everything from gender equality to the introduction of new technology.

Hire No. 16 also means that your next recruit must qualify as disabled. By the time your firm hires its 51st worker, 7% of the payroll must be handicapped in some way, or else your company owes fees in-kind. During hard times, your company may apply for exemptions from these quotas—though as with everything in Italy, it's a toss-up whether it's worth it after the necessary paperwork.

Once you hire your 101st employee, you must submit a report every two years on the gender dynamics within the company. This must include a tabulation of the men and women employed in each production unit, their functions and level within the company, details of compensation and benefits, and dates and reasons for recruitments, promotions and transfers, as well as the estimated revenue impact.

From one view, these regulations can be seen as helpful to employees. After all, we all want greater job benefits. But these regulations clearly lessen incentives for hiring. The result is greater frictional unemployment.

Cyclical Unemployment

The third type of unemployment, **cyclical unemployment,** is caused by recessions or economic downturns. This is the type of unemployment that causes the greatest concern among economists and policy makers. It is the most serious type of unemployment because it means jobs are not available

> **Cyclical unemployment** is unemployment caused by economic downturns.

for many people who want to work. And while both structural and frictional unemployment are consistent with a growing, evolving economy, the root cause of cyclical unemployment is downturns in the business cycle. Cyclical unemployment is not considered a natural type of unemployment like structural unemployment and frictional unemployment.

Although all three types of unemployment are temporary and disappear when workers are matched with jobs, the duration of cyclical unemployment is open-ended. Nobody knows how long a general macroeconomic downturn might last. Fortunately, recent recessions in the United States have been fairly short. The 2008 recession, for example, lasted 19 months. This led to the more cyclical unemployment than any time in the previous 30 years.

The Natural Rate of Unemployment

We have seen that there are three types of unemployment: structural, frictional, and cyclical. Figure 8.4 illustrates the relationship among these types of unemployment and macroeconomic conditions. Structural and frictional unemployment are always present. However, during healthy economic periods, cyclical unemployment falls toward zero.

Figure 8.4:
Three Types of Unemployment

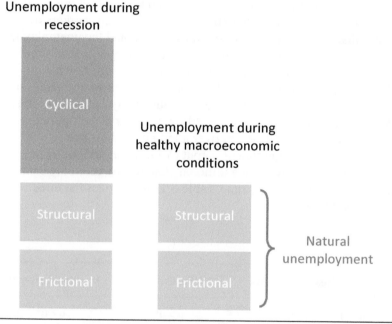

During normal, healthy economic conditions, both structural and frictional unemployment are present. During recessions, cyclical unemployment also appears.

We began this chapter with the misconception that we should aim for zero employment. However, we have seen that some unemployment remains even during periods of economic expansion. Zero unemployment is not attainable. Further, if policymakers consistently strive for zero unemployment, they may take actions that are harmful. For example, in the 1960s and 1970s, economic policy makers tried to push unemployment down past natural levels by putting more and more money into the economy. This led to other complications like *inflation*, but failed to reduce unemployment.

When we acknowledge a certain level of natural unemployment, we must also recognize a *natural rate of unemployment*. The **natural rate of unemployment (u*)** is the typical rate of unemployment when the economy is

> The natural rate of unemployment (u*) is the typical rate of unemployment when the economy is growing normally.

growing normally. This natural rate is a more appropriate goal for policy-makers. Zero unemployment is not possible – there is always some amount. We never know the exact numerical value of the natural rate, in part because it changes over time. Currently, most economists feel that the natural rate of unemployment is somewhere around 5 percent.

When the unemployment rate is equal to its natural rate—that is, no cyclical unemployment exists—the output level produced in the economy is called **full employment output (Y*)**. Recall that we measure economic output with real GDP, and our shorthand notation is: real GDP = Y. An unemployment rate that is above the natural rate indicates cyclical unemployment and we say that the economy is producing at less than full employment output levels (Y < Y*).

> **Full employment output (Y*)** is the output level produced in an economy when the unemployment rate is equal to its natural rate.

Sometimes the actual unemployment rate is less than the natural rate (u < u*). This can happen temporarily when the economy is expanding beyond its long-run capabilities. What conditions might bring this about? Demand for output might be so high that firms keep their factories open for an extra shift and pay their workers overtime. When output is at greater than full employment output (Y > Y*), and the unemployment rate is less than the natural rate (u < u*), resources are being employed at levels that are not sustainable in the long run. To visualize this situation, consider your own productivity as deadlines approach. Perhaps you have several exams in one week, so you decide to set aside most other activities and study for 15 hours a day. Studying for 15 hours a day may yield good results and you may be able to do it for a short period of time, but most of us cannot sustain such an effort over a long period of time.

Economists also refer to full employment output (Y*) as *potential output* or *potential GDP*. By this we mean that without additional changes the economy cannot sustain an output greater than Y* in the long run. Table 8.1 summarizes the three possible macroeconomic conditions.

Table 8.1:

	Healthy economy	Recession	Exceptional expansion
Where is the unemployment rate (u) relative to the natural rate of unemployment (u*)?	u = u*	u > u*	u < u*
Where is economic output (Y) relative to full-employment output (Y*)?	Y = Y*	Y < Y*	Y > Y*

Practice What You Know
Three types of unemployment

Which type is it?

Question:

In each of the following situations identify whether the unemployment that occurs is a result of cyclical, frictional, or structural changes.

(1) Workers in a high end restaurant are laid off when the establishment experiences a decline in demand during a recession.

Answer: *Cyclical changes*. Short-run fluctuations in the demand for workers are often the result of the ebb and flow of the business cycle. When the economy picks up the laid off workers can expect to be rehired.

(2) A group of automobile workers lose their jobs as a result of a permanent reduction in the demand for automobiles.

Answer: *Structural changes*. Since the changes described here are long-run in nature, these workers cannot expect their old jobs to return. Therefore they must engage in retraining in order to reenter the labor force. Since they will be unable to find work until the retraining process is complete this represent a fundamental shift in the demand for labor.

(3) A new college graduate takes three months to find his first job.

Answer: *Frictional changes*. The recent college graduate has skills that the economy values, but finding an employer still takes time. This short-run job search process is a perfectly natural part of finding a job.

What can we learn from the employment data?

Who exactly counts as "unemployed"? For example, many college students don't have jobs, but that doesn't mean they are officially unemployed. Before examining historical unemployment rates in detail, we need to understand how unemployment is measured. In this section we will also look at some challenges of measuring unemployment.

The Unemployment Rate

In this chapter, we defined the unemployment rate (u) as the portion of the labor force that is unemployed. We measure this as follows:

$$\text{Unemployment rate} = u = \frac{number\ unemployed}{labor\ force} \times 100 \qquad (8.1)$$

Let's look at this definition more cloesly. To be officially unemployed, a person has to be in the *labor force*. A member of the **labor force** is defined as someone already employed or actively seeking work. If a jobless person has not sought a job in four weeks, that person is not counted in the unemployment statistics. People not included in the official definition include retirees, stay-at-home parents, people in jail, military personnel, children under 16, and many full-time students.

> The **labor force** includes people who are employed or actively seeking work.

Figure 8.5 provides recent data for the different groups. Starting with the relevant U.S. population, we find that approximately two thirds of this population is in the labor force. Of the 154 million members of the labor force in April, 2012, 12 million were unemployed. Plugging these numbers in to equation 20.1 yields:

$$u = \frac{12}{154} = 0.081 = 8.1\%,$$

which is a relatively high unemployment rate.

Figure 8.5:
Unemployment in the United States, April 2012

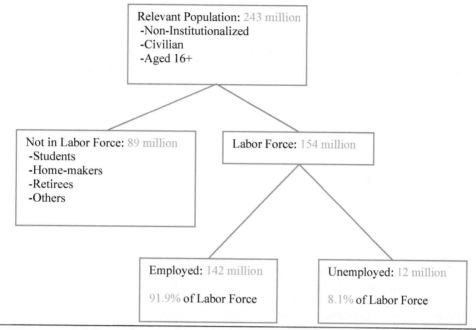

To compute the unemployment rate, separate the relevant adult population between those in the labor force and those who are not. To be in the labor force, a person must either have a job or be actively seeking work. The unemployment rate is the portion of the labor force that is unemployed.

Historical Unemployment Rates

We now turn to historical data. One of our goals is to give you a good sense of normal conditions. It's also helpful to examine periods when particularly high unemployment rates prevailed. In Chapter 14 we discuss possible reasons for these difficult periods. Figure 8.6 shows the U.S. unemployment rate from 1960 to 2011. The vertical shaded bars represent periods of recession.

Figure 8.6:
Unemployment Rate and Recessions, 1960-2012

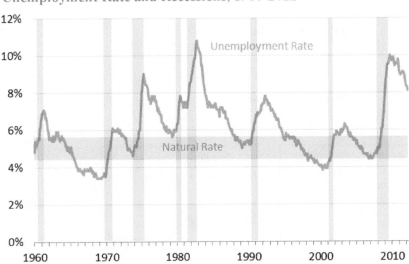

The United States unemployment rate consistently spikes up during recessions, which are indicated by the blue shading. During recessions, cyclical unemployment rises. During non-recessionary periods, the unemployment rate drops toward the natural rate of approximately 5%, and only structural and frictional unemployment remain.

The average unemployment rate in the United States since 1960 has been about 6%. On average, there is a small amount of cyclical unemployment, so this number is above the natural rate. But 6% is a good reference point for you to compare to unemployment rates across time and even nations. Rates above 6% are high by historical U.S. standards; rates under 6% are low.

Notice how the unemployment rate consistently spikes up during recessions. This vividly illustrates cyclical unemployment. Also note how long it takes for unemployment to return to the natural level of about 5% after a recession ends. As you can see, some unemployment always remains, no matter how significant or prolonged the economic expansion. This is because structural and frictional unemployment are always positive. For example, in early 2000, real GDP was expanding at a very significant 6.4%, and the unemployment rate was 3.8%. That's the lowest unemployment rate since 1970 – but still above zero.

Economics in the Media
Structural Unemployment

The Office

In the TV show *The Office*, Angela, Kevin, and Oscar are accountants at the Scranton branch office of Dunder-Mifflin, a paper company. In one episode from 2007, a representative from the corporate office (which oversees all branches) unveils a new accounting system that is being installed. B.J, from corporate, explains to Angela, Kevin, and Oscar that the new system automates most of the billing process, so that when a customer places an order, it gets emailed to the warehouse and a copy goes directly to the customer's inbox.

Angela then asks, "how do we bill them?" and B.J. responds, "You don't. The invoicing, account reconciliation, and all the follow up claims just go right to your Blackberry." At which point, Oscar says, "So what do the accountants do?" B.J. responds, "Well unless there is a real problem client, nothing."

Angela and Oscar immediately understand that their jobs are becoming obsolete right before their eyes. But Kevin still doesn't understand. So after B.J. has left the room he says, "This is the greatest thing that has ever happened to us." Angela responds, "No, it's not." Kevin still doesn't get it, jumping in with "Are you kidding me?" Oscar then delivers the bad news, "It was already a stretch that they needed three of us. Now they don't even need one."

In this story, you might think that technology is putting the accountants out of work. This is true in a short-run sense because less labor is needed to complete the billing process. However, this structural unemployment is a necessary by-product of a dynamic and growing economy. The workers who are no longer needed in accounting become available to perform other jobs in the economy where human capital is needed. However they may need retraining.

Shortcomings of the Unemployment Rate

The unemployment rate, released monthly, is a timely and consistent indicator of the health of the macroeconomy. However, it has two shortcomings as an economic indicator. Let's look at each in turn.

The first shortcoming of the unemployment rate is related to exclusions. People who are unemployed for a long time may just stop looking for work, not because they don't want a job, but because they are discouraged. When they stop looking for work, they fall out of the labor force and no longer count as unemployed. **Discouraged workers** are defined as those who are not working, have looked for a job in the past twelve months and are willing to work, but have not sought employment in the past four weeks.

> **Discouraged workers** are those who are not working, have looked for a job in the past twelve months and are willing to work, but have not sought employment in the past four weeks.

Another group not properly accounted for is the **underemployed**, defined as workers who have part-time jobs but would like to have full-time jobs. These

> **Underemployed** workers are part-time workers who would prefer to work full-time.

workers are not counted as unemployed. In fact, the official unemployment rate includes only workers who have no job and are actively seeking work. This definition excludes both discouraged and underemployed workers, groups that increase during economic downturns. Figure 8.7 shows the official unemployment rate versus an alternative measure that includes discouraged and underemployed workers. Not only is this alternative measure much higher than the unemployment rate, but the difference expands significantly during and after recessions, indicated by the shaded areas.

Figure 8.7:
A Broader Measure of Labor Market Problems

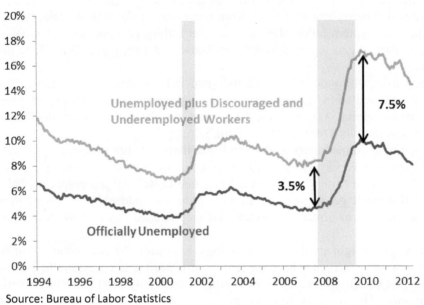

Source: Bureau of Labor Statistics

The orange line includes workers who are officially unemployed, discouraged workers who have given up the job search, and workers that are underemployed, or working part-time when they would rather work full-time. The gap between this broader measure and the official unemployment rate, shown by the blue line, grows when the economy enters recession. This is particularly evident beginning in 2008.

In addition to not counting discouraged workers and the underemployed, the official measurement does not answer another important set of questions about who is unemployed or how long they have been out of work. Are people unemployed for short spells, or is the duration of joblessness long-term? If most unemployment is short-term, we might not be as concerned with a higher unemployment rate, since this indicates that the unemployment is a temporary situation, rather than a long-term problem for people. To help fill in this part of the unemployment picture, the Bureau of Labor Statistics keeps an alternative measure of unemployment that tracks the length of time workers have been unemployed.

Table 8.2 shows the duration of unemployment in 2007 and 2011. The year 2007 was at the tail-end of a long expansionary period in the U.S. economy. At that time, more than two-thirds of total unemployment was short-term (14 weeks or less), and just 17.6% of those unemployed were out of work more than 27 weeks. On the other hand, consider 2011, after the United States economy experienced a significant recession. We see a big increase in the portion of those unemployed for the very long term—27 weeks or more—which was more than 43% of total unemployment in 2011.

Table 8.2:
Duration of Unemployment, 2007 and 2011

Duration	Percent of Total Unemployed	
	2007	2011
Short-term	67.4%	41.3%
Less than 5 weeks	35.9	19.5
5 to 14 weeks	31.5	21.8
Long-term	32.6	58.7
15 to 26 weeks	15.0	15.0
27 weeks and over	17.6	43.7

Other Labor Market Indicators

Macroeconomists use several other indicators to get a more complete picture of the labor market. These include the labor force participation rate, and the total number of full-time jobs.

Labor Force Participation

The size of the labor force is itself an important macroeconomic statistic. To see why, consider two hypothetical island economies that differ only in the size of their labor force. These two islands, called "2K" and "2K12," each have a population of one million people and are identical in every way except the size of their labor force. On the first island, called "2K," the labor force is 670,000. On the second island, called the "2K12," the labor force is just 630,000 workers. The island of 2K has 40,000 more workers to produce goods and services for the same sized population. This is why economists watch the *labor force participation rate*. The **labor force participation rate** is the portion of the population that is in the labor force:

> The **labor force participation rate** is the portion of the population that is in the labor force.

Labor force participation rate = (labor force ÷ population) x 100

On 2K, the labor force participation rate is 67%, but on 2K12, the labor force participation rate is just 63%.

By now, you may have guessed that these are the labor force participation rates for the U.S. economy in the years 2000 and 2012. Figure 20.8 shows the evolution of the labor force participation rate in the United States from 1990 to 2012. You can see that it peaks at 67.3% in 2000 but then falls to 63.6% in 2012. All else equal, this means fewer people working relative to the overall population in the United States.

Figure 8.8:
United States Labor Force Participation Rate, 1990-2012

Source: Bureau of Labor Statistics

The labor force participation rate in the United States peaked at 67.3% in 2000, but has since fallen below 64%.

The changing demographics of the United States population is likely to reduce the labor force participation rate even further over the coming decades. The "baby boom" refers to the period after the end of World War II when birth rates temporarily rose rather dramatically. The U.S. Census Bureau pegs this period at 1946-1964. So there is now a bubble in the U.S. population known as the "baby-boomers." Think of this group as "your moms and dads." But now, as the oldest baby boomers begin to retire, the labor force participation rate will fall. All else equal, fewer workers produce less GDP. And at the same time, federal expenses allocated toward retirees, for example Social Security and Medicare, will rise. As you can see in Figure 20.8, these demographic changes come at a time when the labor force participation rate in the United States is already declining.

Gender and Race Statistics

As you can see in Figure 8.9, the composition of the U.S. labor force today is markedly different from two generations ago. Not only are women working more—from 32 percent in 1948 to almost 60 percent today—but male labor force participation has fallen dramatically—from over 87 percent to 70 percent. Men remain more likely to participate in the labor force than women, but the participation gap has significantly narrowed. These changes are a function of shifting social attitudes.

Figure 8.9:
Trends in Labor Force Participation

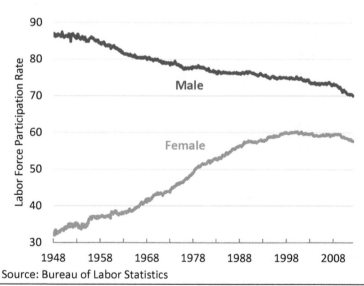

Source: Bureau of Labor Statistics

Over the past 65 years, the composition of the United States labor force has shifted drastically. While more women have entered the labor force, the portion of men in the labor force has dropped from almost 90% to just 70%.

How do we explain the fact that fewer males are working? There are a number of underlying reasons for the decline. Men are living longer, acquiring more education, and also spending more time helping to raise families. Since men who are retired, in school, or staying at home to take care of children are not counted as part of the labor force, these shifts have lowered the male labor-force participation rate.

Unemployment rates also vary widely across ages and races. Table 8.3 breaks down these statistics by age, race, and gender. Looking first at unemployment rates, in April 2012, the overall unemployment rate was 8.1%. But this ranges from a low of 6.8% for white adults (over 20 years old), to a high of 39.6% for black teenage males. Notice also that labor force participation rates are very low among teenagers, with white teenagers at about 37% but black teenagers at just 25%.

Table 8.3:
Unemployment and Labor Force Participation Rates by Gender and Race, April 2012

Group	Unemployment Rate	Labor Force Participation Rate
Overall	8.1%	63.7%
Adults (20+)		
Black males	13.6	67.3
Black females	10.8	62.8
White males	6.8	73.5
White females	6.8	58.8
Teenagers (16-19)		
Black males	39.6	25.7
Black females	36.8	24.5
White males	25.3	36.6
White females	20.3	36.7

Source: BLS

Case Study: Unemployment in the Great Recession

"By now, it's clear to everyone that we have inherited an economic crisis as deep and dire as any since the days of the Great Depression. Millions of jobs that Americans relied on just a year ago are gone; millions more of the nest eggs families worked so hard to build have vanished. People everywhere are worried about what tomorrow will bring."

-President Obama, February 5, 2009

The recession of 2008 has been dubbed the "Great Recession." The implication, of course, is that the depth of the contraction can only be compared to the Great Depression. As a college student, the Great Recession may be the only significant economic downturn you recall. Now that we've studied both real GDP growth and unemployment, it is a good time to put the 2008 recession into perspective. In the quote above, dated just two weeks after President Obama took office, he declares that the recession is as bad as any since the Great Depression. But while the Great Recession was certainly a rough patch for the U.S. economy, it wasn't nearly as severe as the Great Depression, which lasted for most of the 1930s. We'll look more carefully at the Great Depression when we get to Chapter 14.

There was also a relatively mild recession in 2001, and another in 1990. But it turns out that the contraction from July 1981 to November 1982 (let's call it the "1982 recession") is similar to the Great Recession, which officially lasted from December 2007 to June 2009. In this section, we compare the Great Recession to the recession that occurred from 1981-82. We find similarities and differences.

First, consider real GDP growth over the course of both recessions. Figure 8.10 compares quarterly GDP growth rates beginning near the official start of each recession. The two recessions were similar in duration: the 1982 recession lasted 16 months and the Great Recession lasted 18 months. They were also similar in depth: the worst quarter during the 1982 recession witnessed -6.4% growth, while the 2008 recession saw -6.8% growth in its worst quarter. If this quarterly rate had lasted an entire year, the U.S. economy would have produced almost 7% less GDP than the year before. However, the big difference between the two episodes is the economic recovery after the recessions officially ended. In 1982 and 1983, the economy rebounded with growth rates of almost 10%. But following the Great Recession, in 2010 and 2011, real GDP growth rates were 2-3%.

Figure 8.10:
Real GDP Growth Rates in Two Recessions

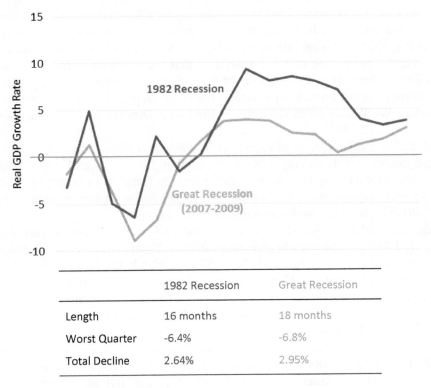

	1982 Recession	Great Recession
Length	16 months	18 months
Worst Quarter	-6.4%	-6.8%
Total Decline	2.64%	2.95%

Source: Bureau of Economic Analysis.

The quarterly changes in real GDP were very similar over the course of the 1982 recession and the Great Recession, of 2007-2009. However, real GDP rebounded to very high growth rates after the recession was over at the end of 1982. When the Great Recession ended in 2009, the growth rates were much lower and remained low for much longer.

Now let's compare unemployment rates for the two recessions, shown in Figure 20.11. The unemployment rate in the 1982 recession was consistently higher during the actual recession period, which lasted 16 months. But the real difference is the slow "recovery" following the Great Recession. In particular, excess unemployment, clearly above the natural rate, persisted for more than three years after the end of the official recession period.

Figure 8.11:
Unemployment Rates in Two Recessions

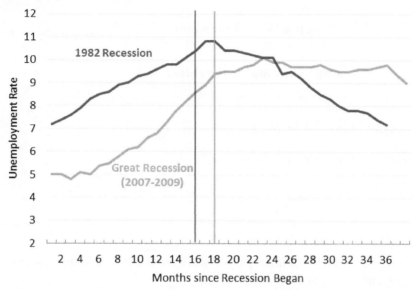

Source: Bureau of Labor Statistics

The 1982 recession and the Great Recession from 2007 to 2009 both led to unemployment rates above 10%. However, in each case the recovery, indicated by vertical lines, was very different. The most recent recession left lingering unemployment above 8% for several years.

The unemployment data is consistent with the GDP data. Both show two recessions similar in depth and duration. But the 1982 recession was followed by a swift recovery, while the effects of the more recent recession lingered for several years afterward. How do these compare to the Great Depression form the 1930s? Consider this: during the Great Depression, real GDP fell by 30% over three years and the unemployment rate, which actually topped 25% at one point, remained higher than 15% for an entire decade. Thankfully, we haven't seen conditions that bad at any time since.

Practice What You Know
Unemployment and labor force participation rates

Can you compute the rates?

The following data is from Germany in 2010:

Working-age population = 70,856,000
Labor force = 41,189,000
Employed = 38,209,000

Question:

Use the data to compute the number of unemployed workers, the unemployment rate and the labor force participation rate for Germany in 2010.

Answer:

The unemployment rate is the total number of unemployed as a portion of the labor force. First, we determine the number of unemployed as the total labor force minus the number employed:

Unemployed = labor force – employed = <u>2,980,000</u>

We use this to determine the unemployment rate, which is the number of unemployed divided by the labor force:

Unemployed ÷ labor force = 2,980,000 ÷ 41,189,000 = <u>7.2%</u>

Finally, the labor force participation rate is the labor force as a portion of the working-age population:

Labor force participation rate = labor force ÷ working-age population = 41,189,000 ÷ 70,856,000 = <u>58.1%</u>

You might notice that this rate is significantly below 63.6% which is the most recent labor force participation rate for the United States.

Economics for Life:

Finish your degree!

College students often fret over which major leads to the best chance of getting a job. Your major certainly matters for getting the job you want and it may also affect your income. But the figure below shows just how important it is to finish your degree, whatever your major.

The chart plots unemployment rates by educational attainment. This data is from April 2012, but you can find current data by visiting the Bureau of Labor Statistics (BLS) at www.bls.gov. Notice how the unemployment rate drops as educational attainment increases. This holds true across all majors. In particular, look at the big drop in the unemployment rate for those who complete the bachelor's degree. The unemployment rate is about half that of those who have some college but do not complete their bachelor's degree. It turns out the most important major is the one that guarantees you graduate.

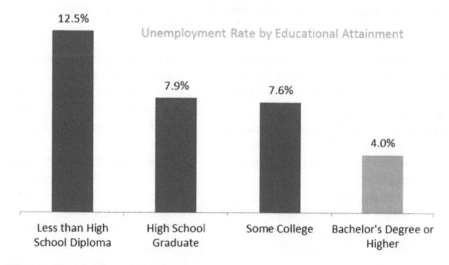

Notice the big drop in unemployment rate for those who complete the bachelor's degree. The unemployment rate is about half the unemployment rate for those who have some college but do not complete their bachelor's degree. One way to choose a major is to choose the one that guarantees you'll graduate!

Conclusion

We began this chapter with the misconception that we should aim for zero unemployment. However, during the course of the chapter we have learned that even a growing economy has some unemployment. We considered why policy makers shouldn't aim for zero unemployment – because some unemployment is natural. People pay attention to the unemployment rate because it can affect them personally. But we also monitor the unemployment rate as an important macroeconomic indicator. In addition to real GDP, we use the unemployment rate to assess the position of the economy relative to the business cycle. Because employment data is released more frequently than GDP, it gives us a timelier picture of current conditions. For this reason, the first Friday of every month, when the employment data is released, tends to be a nervous day, especially during turbulent economic times.

In the next chapter, we will look more closely at our third important macroeconomic indicator, inflation.

BIG QUESTIONS

What are the major reasons we see unemployment?

- Structural unemployment is caused by changes in the structure of the economy that make some jobs obsolete.
- Frictional unemployment is caused by imperfect information which leads to increased search time in the job market.
- Cyclical unemployment is caused by recessionary conditions that eliminate jobs during a downturn in the business cycle.

What can we learn from the employment data?

- The unemployment rate, one of our most reliable indicators of the economy's health, is the portion of the labor force that is not working and unsuccessfully searching for a job.
- The labor force participation rate tells us the portion of the population that is working or searching for work.
- Unemployment data allows us to examine social trends and reveals where the labor market conditions are particularly strong or weak.
- Unemployment data also helps us evaluate current conditions in a long run historical perspective. For example, the case study in this chapter helps us view the Great Recession in context of earlier economic downturns.

Concepts You Should Know

Unemployment	Unemployment insurance	Labor force
Unemployment rate	Cyclical employment	Discouraged workers
Creative destruction	Natural rate of unemployment	Underemployed workers
Structural unemployment	Full employment output	Labor force participation rate
Frictional unemployment		

Questions for Review

1. Until the late 1960's most economists assumed that less unemployment was always preferred to more. Define and explain the two types of unemployment that are consistent with a dynamic, growing economy.

2. Is there any unemployment when we have "full employment?" If so, what type(s)?

3. The news media almost always bemoans the current state of the U.S. economy. How does the most recent unemployment rate relate to the long-run average?

4. What type of unemployment is affected when online job search engines reduce the time necessary for job search? Does this affect the natural rate of unemployment? If so, how?

5. Who does the Bureau of Labor Statistics count in the labor force? Explain why the official unemployment rate tends to underestimate the true level of underemployment.

6. Does the duration of unemployment matter? Explain your answer.

Study problems

1. Indicate several factors that can cause the natural rate of unemployment to change. Given your answer to question 5a, do you think that the current unemployment rate is above or below the natural rate of unemployment? Defend your answer by discussing cyclical unemployment.

2. In each situation listed below, determine whether the duration of unemployment is likely to be short-term or long-term.

a. A telephone installer loses his job because of competition from voice-over-the-Internet companies.
b. A wood cutter loses his job when the local mill closes.

c. An automobile mechanic loses her job when another service center opens across the street.

d. An expert installer of pool liners, who never graduated from high school, loses his job when the company he works for starts selling pools that no longer need liners.

3. In *Allentown*, Billy Joel sings about the demise of the steel and coal industry in Pennsylvania. Why do you think the loss of manufacturing jobs was so difficult on the workers in areas like Allentown and other parts of the Midwest where manufacturing was once the largest employer? What type of unemployment is the song about?

4. In January 2008, the unemployment rate dropped to 4.9 percent. Oddly, employment also fell from the prior month. How is this possible?

5. A country with a civilian population of 90,000 (all over age 16) has 70,000 employed and 10,000 unemployed persons. Of the unemployed, 5,000 are frictionally unemployed and another 3,000 are structurally unemployed.

a. What is the size of the labor force?
b. What is the unemployment rate?
c. What is the natural rate of unemployment for this country?
d. Is this economy is in recession or expansion? Explain.

6. Visit www.bls.gov and search through the tables on unemployment to answer the following questions:

a. What is the current national unemployment rate?
b. What is the current unemployment rate among people most like you? (Consider your age, sex, and race)

7. Consider a country with 300 M residents, a labor force of 150 M, and 10 M unemployed. Answer the following questions:
a. What is the labor force participation rate?
b. What is the unemployment rate?
c. If 5 M of the unemployed become discouraged and stop looking for work, what is the new unemployment rate?
d. Suppose that 30 M jobs are created and this attracts 20 M new people into the labor force. What would be the new rates for labor-force participation rate and unemployment?

Solved Problems

1. Consider the following hypothetical data from the peaceable nation of Adirolf, where there is no military, the entire population is over the age of 16, and no one is institutionalized for any reason.

Classification	Number of People
Total Population	200M
Employed	141
Full-Time Students	10
Homemakers	25
Retired Persons	15
Seeking work but without a job	9

a. What is the unemployment rate in Adirolf?

Answer:

6%.

To calculate the unemployment rate, use:

unemployment rate = u = (number unemployed/labor force) x 100

- The number of unemployed: 9M
- Labor force can be calculated two ways:
    - Employed plus unemployed: 141M + 9M = 150M
    - Total population minus those not in labor force (students, home-makers, retirees):
    200M – 10M – 25M – 15M = 150M

    Note: because the total population is only composed of non-institutionalized civilians over the age of 16, we can use this as the relevant population.

Unemployment rate = u = (number unemployed/labor force) x 100 = (9/150)x100 = 6%

b. What is the labor force participation rate in Adirolf?

Answer:

75%

To calculate the labor force participation rate use:

Labor force participation rate = (labor force/population) x 100

- Labor force (calculated above): 150M
- Population: 200M

Labor force participation rate = (labor force/population) x 100 = (150/200) x 100 = 75%

For questions c through f: Assume 15 million Adirolfidian homemakers begin seeking jobs and that10 million find jobs.

c. Now what is the rate of unemployment in Adrilof?

Answer:

8.5%

To calculate the new unemployment rate use the same equation above. However, the figures have changed with new entrants to the labor force:

- The new number of unemployed: 9M + 5M =14M
- The new number of employed: 141M + 10M = 151M
- The new labor force can be calculated three ways:
  - Previous labor force plus new entrants: 150M + 15M =165M
  - Employed plus unemployed: 151M + 14M = 165M
  - Total population minus not in labor force (students, home-makers, retirees):
    200M – 10M – 10M – 15M = 165M

Unemployment rate = u = (number unemployed/labor force) x 100 = (14/165) x 100 = 8.5%

Note: even though the number of employed increased, because the size of the labor force increased by more, the unemployment rate has increased.

d. How does this change affect cyclical unemployment in Adrilof?

Answer:

It does not affect cyclical unemployment which is generally associated with economic downturns. Instead, the entrance of new workers into the labor force represents a change in labor force participation rate. In general, the entry of new workers to the labor force is associated with good economic times. Because most of the housewives were able to find jobs, we can conclude that the economy is growing.

e. What will happen to per capita GDP?

Answer:

With an increase in the number of employed workers, total output in the economy has increased. However, the size of the population has not changed. Thus, the GDP per capita has increased as a result of this change.

f. Is the economy of Adirolf better-off after the homemakers enter the labor force?

Answer:

Adirolf has a stronger economy with more working housewives. Even though the unemployment rate has increased as a result of the entrance of many housewives into the labor force, this increase in unemployment is not a result of economic downturn, but is a sign of a growing economy. Adirolf has a stronger economy with higher GDP per capita and greater labor force participation rate as a result of this change.

2. In each of the following situations determine whether or not the person would be considered unemployed.

a. A 15-year-old offers to pet-sit but no one hires her.

Answer:

No. The relevant population used to measure unemployment and the labor force is individuals 16 years or older. This 15-year-old is not part of the relevant population, so she is not considered unemployed.

b. A college graduate spends the summer after graduation touring Europe before starting a job search.

Answer:

No. To be counted in the unemployment statistics, an individual must have made efforts to get a job in the past four weeks. This college graduate is not actively seeking work during the summer, so he is not counted as an unemployed individual.

c. A part-time teacher is only able to work two days a week, even though he would like a full-time job.

Answer:

No. This part-time teacher is underemployed since he would prefer a full-time position, but under the unemployment rate measurements, the teacher is employed.

d. A worker is temporarily laid off from a construction job but expects to be recalled soon.

Answer:

Yes. This construction worker is part of the labor force and is actively seeking employment. Thus, he is a member of the labor force and is currently unemployed.

e. An automobile worker becomes discouraged about the prospects for future employment and decides to quit looking for work.

Answer:
No. The automobile worker is a discouraged worker if he has searched for work in the past year, but has stopped looking for work over four weeks ago. However, since he is not actively looking for work now, he is no longer part of the labor force.

Chapter 9

The Price Level and Inflation

Misconception: Inflation is no big deal.

For the last thirty years, inflation has been under control in the United States. As a college student, you have probably never experienced significant inflation. You may notice that many prices rise from year to year, but these are slow, steady, often predictable price increases. However, as recently as the 1980s, the annual inflation rate in the United States was close to 15% — about five times the average inflation rate over the last two decades. And 15% is actually low by international standards. So it may appear that inflation is not a significant problem. But it certainly has been in the past and there is no guarantee that we are safe from it in the future. Moreover, in looking at the global economy, inflation is an important macroeconomic issue for many countries. High inflation causes the destruction of wealth across an entire economy. Equally important, unpredictable inflation can wreak havoc in an economy, as we will see in the pages ahead.

Big Questions

- **How is inflation measured?**
- **What problems does inflation bring?**

How is inflation measured?

You might notice inflation on a routine shopping trip or especially when you see a reference to prices in an old book or movie. In the 1960 movie *Psycho*, a hotel room for one night was priced at just $10. In Chapter 7, we defined inflation as the percent change in the overall level of prices in the economy – so inflation occurs when prices rise throughout the economy. When overall prices rise, this affects our budget; it limits how much we can buy with our income. When overall prices fall, our income goes farther and we can buy more goods.

Imagine annual inflation of 100%. At this rate, prices double every year. How would this affect your life? Would it change what you buy? Would it change your savings plans? Would it change the salary you negotiate with your employer? Yes, it would change the way you live your life on a daily basis. Now imagine that prices double *every day*. This was the situation in Zimbabwe in 2008 when inflation reached almost 80 billion percent per month! This is an example of what we call *hyperinflation*, an extremely high rate of inflation, and it completely stymies economic activity. In Zimbabwe, for example, average citizens could barely afford necessities like bread and eggs.

Figure 9.1 shows inflation in the United States from 1960 to 2012. The average over this long-run period was 4%, a good benchmark for evaluating current inflation rates. In the 1970s and early 1980s, there were periods of very high inflation. At one point in 1980 inflation was almost 15%. But since the early 1980s, inflation seems well-controlled in the United States. In fact, with respect to inflation, this modern period has been termed the "Great Moderation". Looking again at Figure 9.1, you might also notice a brief spell of *deflation*, in 2009. **Deflation** occurs when overall prices fall; it is negative inflation. Note, too that periods of recessions—the shaded areas in Figure 9.1—often coincide with falling inflation rates. While this is not always true, you can see it in both 1982 and in 2009.

> **Deflation** occurs when overall prices fall.

Figure 9.1
Inflation in the United States, 1960-2012

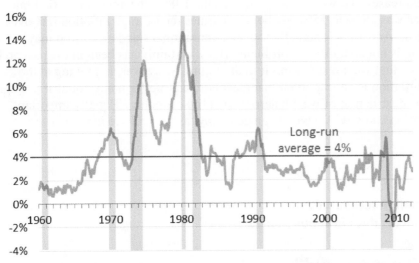

Source: Bureau of Labor Statistics.

> From 1960 to 2012 inflation rates in the United States averaged 4%. This number is high because of excessive inflation in the 1970s. Inflation peaked at over 14% in 1980. More recently, inflation rates have averaged between 2-3%.

Gauging price inflation across the overall economy is a straightforward goal. But actually measuring inflation requires great care. First, prices don't all move together; some prices fall even when most others rise. Second, some prices affect us more than others; a 10% increase in the cost of housing is significantly more painful than a 10% increase in the cost of hotdogs. Before we arrive at a useful measure of inflation, we have to agree on what prices to monitor and how much weight we'll give to each price. In the United States, the Bureau of Labor Statistics (BLS) measures and reports inflation data. In this section, we describe how the BLS estimates the overall price level. Its goal is to determine the prices of all the goods and services a typical consumer buys, and to determine how much of a typical consumer's budget is spent on these particular items.

The Consumer Price Index (CPI)

We start by looking at the most common price level used to compute inflation. The **Consumer Price Index (CPI)** is the measure of the price level based on the consumption patterns of a typical consumer. When you read or hear about inflation in the media, the report almost certainly focuses on the CPI. The CPI is essentially the price of a typical "basket" of goods purchased by a representative consumer in the United States. What's in that basket? In addition to groceries, there is clothing, transportation, housing, medical care, education, and many other goods and services. The idea is to include everything a typical consumer buys. This gives us a realistic measure of a typical consumer's cost of living.

> The consumer price index is a measure of the price level based on the consumption patterns of a typical consumer.

Figure 9.2 displays how the CPI was allocated among major spending categories in March 2012. Note that there are prices for very specific goods inside these categories. For example, "Food and beverages" includes prices for everything from potato chips to oranges (both Valencia and Navel) to flour (white, all purpose, per lb.). These are goods in a basket that typical American consumers buy.

Figure 9.2
The Pieces of the Consumer Price Index, March 2012

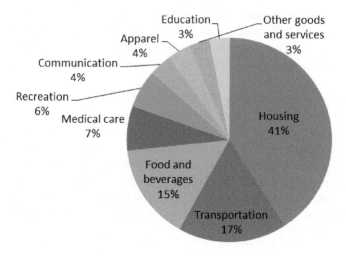

Source: Bureau of Labor Statistics.

> The weights given to the different categories of expenditures are based on the spending patterns of a typical American. For example, the 17% of a typical American's spending is on transportation, which includes car payments and fuel, among other expenses.

While the CPI is the predominant measure of the general price level, it is by no means the only one. For example, in Chapter 7 we saw that when adjusting nominal GDP data, the best choice is the GDP deflator, which includes prices from all the final goods and services that compose GDP. GDP includes consumer goods and services consumers never purchase, like large farm equipment and wind turbines. The GDP deflator is too broad for our purposes here, because we are focusing on the prices of goods and services purchased by typical American consumers.

Of course none of us is exactly typical in our spending. College students allocate significantly more than 6.4% of their spending on education, senior citizens spend a lot more than average on medical care, a fashionista spends more on clothing, and those with lengthy commutes spend more on transportation. The CPI reflects the overall rise in prices for consumers on average.

Computing the CPI

Each month the BLS conducts surveys by physically sending employees into stores to gather and input price information on over 8,000 goods and in 38 geographic locations. The BLS estimates prices on everything from apples in Chicago, IL, to electricity in Scranton, PA, to gasoline in San Diego, CA. In addition to inputting price information, the BLS estimates how each good and service affects a typical budget. To do this, they attach a weight to the price of each good once it is in the basket. For example, Figure 9.2 indicates the typical consumer spends 17% of his budget on transportation. Therefore, transportation prices are given 17% of the total weight in the typical consumer's basket of goods. Once the BLS has the prices and budget allocation weights, they can construct the CPI.

To illustrate how this works, let's build a price index using just three goods. Imagine that when you go to the movies you notice you are spending more for than you were last year. You decide to construct a price index to see exactly how these price increases affect your budget. You decide to name your index EPI (entertainment price index). For the sake of our example, assume a typical night at the movie theatre includes a movie ticket, two boxes of popcorn and two limeades. This is the basket of goods included in your EPI.

The first four columns of the table in Figure 9.3 show your EPI data for the first year, 2013. The second column shows the respective quantities of goods in your basket, and the third column displays the unit prices of these goods. The price of popcorn is $4 per box, the limeade is priced at $4 each, and the movie ticket is $8. The fourth column shows how much you pay in total for each good; this is just price multiplied by quantity. For example, in 2013, the price of popcorn was $4 per box, so you paid $8 for two boxes of popcorn. When we add these together, we get the total price for your basket of goods in 2013, which was $24. This is how much you spent for all the goods in your EPI in 2013.

Figure 9.3
Calculating a Simple Price Index

Good	Quantity	2013 Price	2013 Cost	2014 Price	2014 Cost
Popcorn	2	$4	$8	$6	$12
Limeade	2	$4	$8	$4	$8
Movie Ticket	1	$8	$8	$10	$10
Basket Price			$24		$30
Index (EPI)		$\frac{\$24}{\$24} \times 100 = 100$		$\frac{\$30}{\$24} \times 100 = 125$	

In calculating this entertainment price index (EPI), we use the same steps as those used when calculating the CPI. First, determine the typical basket of goods. Then, calculate the total price of the typical basket in a base year, which is 2013 in this example. After setting this base year at 100 (creating an index), subsequent years can be computed following the same steps. In 2014, you add up the new prices for the same basket of goods and then divide by the original price to see the new index number.

Let's now move to 2014. First, note that your consumption pattern hasn't changed; you still buy the same basket of goods. But some of the prices did change in 2014. Popcorn is now priced at $6 per box and the price of the movie ticket is $10. But note that not all prices changed. The cost of limeade remained the same.

To see how the new 2014 prices affect your spending, we compute the total cost required to consume the same goods at in the same quantities. The last column shows the costs of each component in your basket. The sum of these is now $30.

The last step is to create an index. We need an index because, in the real world, adding a lot of prices together yields a huge number that would be difficult to work with. So we create an index that is equal to 100 at a fixed point in time—our base year. In our example, we can let 2013 be our base year. To convert, we divide all years by the basket price value from the base year and multiply by 100:

$$\text{Price Index} = \frac{\text{Basket Price}}{\text{Basket Price in base year}} \times 100. \tag{21.1}$$

Using this formula, you can confirm that the EPI for 2013 is 100, and the EPI for 2014 is 125.

When the Bureau of labor statistics computes the CPI for the United States, it follows the same basic steps from this example:

1. Define the basket of goods and services and their appropriate weights.
2. Determine the prices of goods across time periods.
3. Convert to the index number for each time period.

Economics in the Real World:
Government shoppers track prices for the CPI

Tracking the prices in the CPI requires a great deal of effort and precision. In September 2007, Nancy Luna of the *Orange County Register* followed one of the 350 employees of the Bureau of Labor Statistics who is charged with finding current prices of the goods included in the CPI. The BLS employee, Frank Dubich, traveled 800 miles per month tracking prices.

And the items to be priced are very specific. For example, Dubich was asked to visit a grocery store to find the price of "an 18.5-ounce can of Progresso Rich & Hearty creamy chicken soup with wild rice," which turned out to be $1.98. Dubich also had to note that this was a sale price.

In another instance, Dubich was embarrassed to be seen pricing because prom dresses. He noticed several clerks staring at him as he hunted for the price tag, so he quickly got the price and left.

In macroeconomics, we generally see one single number that indicates how much prices have changed. But it helps to remember that there are thousands of prices tracked each month by government workers like Frank Dibuch.

(source: http://seattletimes.nwsource.com/html/businesstechnology/2003885392_cpishopper15.html)

Measuring Inflation

Once the CPI is computed, we use it to compute inflation rates. The inflation rate (i) is calculated as the percentage change in the price level (P). Using the CPI as the price level, the inflation rate from period 1 to period 2 is:

$$\text{inflation rate (i)} = \frac{CPI_2 - CPI_1}{CPI_1} \times 100 \qquad (21.2)$$

Note that this is a growth rate, computed just like the growth rate of GDP in Chapter 19. In our entertainment price index example above, the EPI rose from 100 to 125 in a year. So the inflation for that year was 25%, computed as:

$$\text{inflation rate (i)} = \frac{125 - 100}{100} \times 100 = 25\%.$$

    The BLS releases CPI estimates every month. Normally, inflation rates are
measured over the course of a year, showing how much the price level grows in twelve
months. Figure 21.3 shows the historical relationship between the United States inflation
rate and the CPI. Panel (a) plots the U.S. CPI from 1960 to 2012. The base period for
the CPI is set for 1982-1984, so it goes through 100 in mid-1983. The CPI was just 30 in
1961 and rose to 229 by 2011. This means the typical basket of consumer goods rose in
price more than seven-fold between 1960 and 2012.

Figure 9.3
The CPI and Inflation, 1960-2012

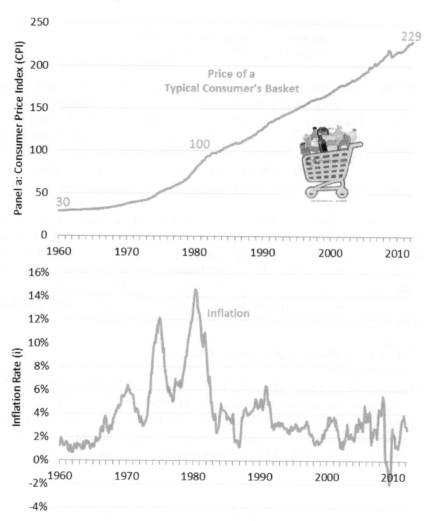

Source: Bureau of Labor Statistics.

Panel (a) shows the CPI since 1960. The index of prices for a typical consumer basket of goods was at
30 in 1961, but was up to 229 by 2012. Panel (b) is the inflation rate, computed as the growth rate of
the CPI. A rapidly rising CPI, like the CPI in the 1970s, is reflected in the inflation rate.

Panel (b) of Figure 9.3 plots inflation rates based on the CPI data in (a). The inflation graph reveals a number of historical observations that are important to our study of macroeconomics. For example, when you look at the graph, you might wonder what was going on in the 1970s. Before and after the 1970s, inflation was relatively stable and averaged less than 3%. But from 1970 to 1981, the inflation rate averaged 8%, including the year between April 1979 and March 1980 when inflation was over 14.5%. We'll explain the reasons for these historically high rates in Chapter 16. In comparing the two graphs in Figure 9.3, notice that the CPI increased more rapidly from 1979-1980 than any other period. Overall, the long-run average rate of inflation in the United States is about 4%.

Economics in the Real World:
Prices Don't all Move Together

While it's clear that prices generally rise, not all prices go up. When the CPI rises, it indicates that the price of the overall consumer basket rises. Some individual prices stay the same or even fall. For example, consumer electronic prices almost always fall. When flat-panel plasma TVs were introduced in the late 1990s, a 40 inch model cost more than $7,000. Fifteen years later, 50 inch flat panel TVs are available for less than $500. This is the result of technological advancements: as time passes, it often takes fewer resources to produce the same item or something better.

Computers are yet another example. In 1984, Apple introduced the Macintosh computer, at a price of $2,495. The CPU for the Macintosh ran at 7.83 MHz and the 9 inch monitor was black and white. Today, you can buy an Apple iMac for less than $2,000. This new Apple computer has a quad-core processor that runs at a total of 11,200 MHz, and the monitor is 27 inches (color, of course). The new computer is better by any measure, yet it costs less. These kinds of changes in quality make it difficult to measure the CPI over time.

Using the CPI to Equate Dollar Values over Time

Prices convey much information, but prices from different time periods can be quite confusing. For example, in 1924, ...but this 2011 iMac Price was just $1,999.

you could buy a fully constructed, 1600 square feet home through Sears at a price of just $1,969. But how does that price compare to today's prices? In addition to measuring inflation rates, we can also use the CPI to answer these types of questions.

To compare goods prices over time, we convert all prices to today's prices or "prices in today's dollars." Here is the formula:

$$\text{Price in today's dollars} = \text{price in earlier time} \times \frac{\text{price level today}}{\text{price level in earlier time}} \qquad (21.3)$$

Following this formula, we can compute the 2011 price of the 1924 Sears home. The CPI in 2011 was 220, and the CPI in 1924 was 17, so the computation is:

$$\text{Price in 2011} = \$1,969 \times \frac{220}{17} = \$25,481.$$

In fact, the 1924 Sears price would be pretty low even today.

Table 9.2 takes past prices from some of our iconic foods and converts them into today's dollars. For example, the price of a 12 oz. bottle of Coca-Cola was 5 cents in 1942, when the CPI was 16. The CPI in 2011 was 220. Dividing the price level today (220) by the price level in 1942 (16) yields a ratio of 13.75 so $0.05 times 13.75 equals the $0.69 listed under "today's dollars." The price in today's dollars corrects for the overall amount of inflation since 1942 and helps us make sense of historical prices and dispel the notion that everything was cheaper in the past. This is nominally true, but not especially interesting. Adjusting for inflation provides a real comparison, which is what good economists always look for.

Table 9.2
Converting Past Prices into Modern Dollar Values

Product	Year	Price	Conversion	Today's Dollars (2011)	Today's Actual Price
Coca-Cola (12 oz.)	1942	$0.05	$0.05 x (220/16)	$0.69	$0.63
Hershey's chocolate bar (1 oz.)	1921	0.05	$0.05 x (220/18)	0.61	0.69
McDonald's hamburger	1955	0.15	$0.15 x (220/27)	1.22	0.89
Nabisco's Oreo cookies (1 lb.)	1922	0.32	$0.32 x (220/17)	4.14	2.99

Economics in the Real World:
Which movies are most popular?

When a successful new movie comes out, the film industry totals up box office receipts and other revenue to see how well the movie has done. But since the receipt data are tied to the period in which the movie was released, they are nominal receipts, not adjusted for inflation.

For example, *Avatar* is now the highest-grossing film of all-time, meaning that it earned more revenue than any film from the past. *Titanic* held the top spot from 1998 to 2009 and *Star Wars* held the top spot from 1977-1997. The table below ranks the top 7 movies of all times first by total receipts. The list of movies may not surprise you—there are several modern movies there that you've probably seen. On the other hand, you may find it odd to think of Shrek 2 as the 7th most popular movie of all time.

Top Movies of all Time, Ranked by Total U.S. Receipts

Movie	Year	Receipts	Receipts adjusted for inflation	Adjusted Rank
1. Avatar	2009	$760,508,000	$770,262	14
2. Titanic	1997	658,547,000	1,074,258	5
3. The Dark Knight	2008	533,345,000	588,314	28
4. Star Wars Episode I – The Phantom Menace	1999	474,544,000	715,277	16
5. The Avengers	2012	472,240,000	472,240	58
6. Star Wars	1977	460,998,000	1,410,707	2
7. Shrek 2	2004	$441,226,000	562,723	31

Source: Box Office Mojo

The second-to-last column shows total receipts adjusted for inflation in 2012. After this adjustment, you can see that Avatar is no longer number 1 and in fact produced only about half the receipts of the original Star Wars movie, which was released in 1977. The last column shows the rank of these movies once inflation is accounted for. Notice that Avatar falls to number 14 and Shrek 2 falls to number 31. So what is the top movie of all time, based on total inflation-adjusted receipts? The answer is *Gone with the Wind*, released in 1939, with inflation adjusted receipts of over $1.6 billion.

Economics in the Media

Equating dollar values through time

Austin Powers: International Man of Mystery

The Austin Powers series is a hilarious spoof of the James Bond films. In *International Man of Mystery* we are introduced to British secret agent Austin Powers who was cryofrozen at the end of the 60s. Thirty years later Austin Powers is thawed to help capture his nemesis, Dr. Evil, who was also cryofrozen at the same time as Austin, and has stolen a nuclear weapon and holds the world hostage.

Being frozen for thirty years causes Dr. Evil to underestimate how much he should ask.

"Gentlemen, it's come to my attention that a breakaway Russian Republic called Kreplachistan will be transferring a nuclear warhead to the United Nations in a few days. Here's the plan. We get the warhead, and we hold the world ransom......FOR ONE MILLION DOLLARS!"

There is an uncomfortable pause.

Dr. Evil's Number Two speaks up. "Don't you think we should ask for more than a million dollars? A million dollars isn't that much money these days. Virtucon alone makes over nine billion dollars a year."

Dr. Evil responds (pleasantly surprised) "Oh, really? ONE-HUNDRED BILLION DOLLARS!"

International Man of Mystery takes place in 1997 and Dr. Evil was frozen in 1967. How much did the price level rise over those thirty years? The CPI was 33.4 in 1967 and 160.5 in 1997. Dividing 160.5 by 33.4 yields a factor of 4.8. So if Dr. Evil thought that one million dollars was a lot of money in 1967, an equivalent amount in 1997 would be $4.8 million. Dr. Evil does not let that stop him from asking for more!

The Accuracy of the CPI

We have seen that the CPI is not simple to compute. Yet in order to understand what is happening in the macroeconomy it is important that the CPI is accurate. For example, sometimes a rapid fall in inflation signals a recession, as it did in 1982 and 2008. Like real GDP and the unemployment rate, inflation is an indicator of national economic conditions.

But there is another reason the CPI needs to be accurate; when employers adjust wages for inflation, they generally use the CPI. For example, when the United Auto Workers union signs a wage agreement with General Motors, the agreement specifies wages for auto workers several years in advance. Since future inflation is unknown, and the UAW wants to protect its workers from excess inflation, the agreement stipulates that wages will be tied to the CPI. Therefore, when the CPI rises, wages rise; when the CPI falls, wages fall. So, if the CPI overstates inflation, it can cost companies millions of dollars. If the CPI understates inflation, this hurts workers, since their wages will not rise as much as they should.

How accurate is the CPI? If people always bought the same goods from the same suppliers it would be extremely accurate. We would be able to compare the changes in price from one year to the next very easily. But this is not realistic. We buy different goods, the quality of goods changes over time, and we buy goods from different stores at different locations. Because the typical basket keeps changing, it is difficult to measure its price. The most common concern is that the CPI overstates true inflation. There are three reasons for this concern: substitution of different goods and services, changes in quality, and the availability of new goods, services, and locations.

Substitution

When the price of a good rises, consumers instinctively look to substitute cheaper alternatives. This makes CPI calculations difficult because the typical consumer basket changes. When we calculated an entertainment price index we assumed that you always bought the same quantities of all goods, even when the price of popcorn rose and limeade remained the same. However, it is more realistic to assume that if the price of popcorn rises, then you will choose a less expensive snack. In other words, you will find a substitute for popcorn. But when consumers substitute cheaper goods, it changes the weights of all the goods in the typical consumption basket. Without acknowledging the substitution of less expensive items, the CPI would exaggerate the effects of the price increase, leading to upward bias. Since 1999, the BLS has used a formula that accounts for both the price increase and the shift in goods consumption.

Changes in Quality

Over time, the quality of goods generally increases. For example, the movie theatre you frequent may soon begin to offer all movies in 3D. Because this technology is more expensive, the price of a ticket might rise from $10 to $12. It looks like inflation, since movie-ticket prices will go up. On the other hand, you are getting "more" movie for your buck, since the quality has increased. If the CPI did not account for quality changes, it would have an upward bias. But the BLS also uses an adjustment method to account for quality changes

New Products and Locations

In a dynamic, growing economy, new goods are introduced and new buying options become available. For example, tablet computers, flash drives, and even cell phones weren't in the typical consumer's basket twenty years ago. In addition, Amazon.com and eBay weren't options for consumers to make purchases before the 1990s.

Traditionally, the BLS updated the CPI goods basket only after long time delays. This biased the CPI upward for two reasons. First, the prices of new products typically drop in the first few years after their introduction. If the CPI basket doesn't include the latest prices, this price drop is lost. Second, new retail outlets such as internet stores typically offer lower prices than traditional retail stores. If the BLS continued to check prices only at traditional retail stores, it would overstate the price consumers actually pay for goods and services.

> The **chained CPI** is a measure of the CPI in which the basket of goods considered is updated monthly.

In an effort to measure this upward bias, the BLS began computing a *chained CPI* in 2000. The **chained CPI** is a measure of the CPI in which the basket of goods considered is updated monthly. While it's more difficult to measure and takes longer to estimate, the chained CPI is a better indicator of inflation for the typical consumer. Figure 9.4 shows the two CPI measures together. The vertical distance between the two lines indicates the upward bias of the traditional CPI, which updates the basket of goods less often. Notice that the distance grows over time.

Figure 9.4
The Chained CPI versus the Traditional CPI

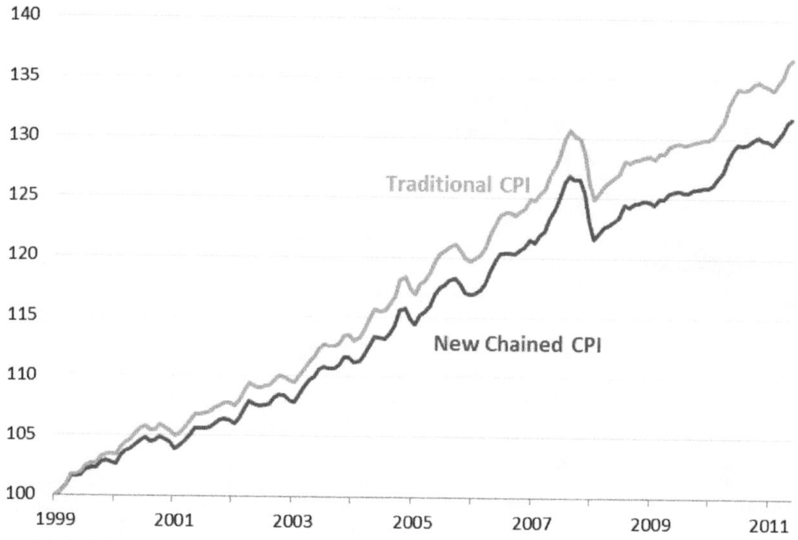

Source: Bureau of Labor Statistics.

The chained CPI reduces the upward bias of the traditional CPI by updating the consumer's basket of goods every month. This single correction accounts for price reductions that typically occur during the first few years after a new product has been introduced.

Economics in the Real World:
The Billion Prices Project

The Billion Prices Project (BPP) is an academic initiative at the Massachusetts Institute of Technology that monitors daily price fluctuations of approximately five million items sold by roughly 300 online retailers in more than 70 countries. Figure 9.5 shows the BPP (online) index along with the CPI. Obviously, they look very similar, but the BPP series estimates slightly more inflation than the CPI since 2009.

Figure 9.5
The Billion Prices Project

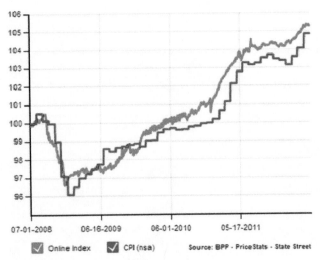

Source: http://bpp.mit.edu/usa/.

> The Billion Price Project is an independent index that tracks prices across the internet as an alternative to the CPI. As you can see from the data lines above, the BPP index looks very similar to the CPI yet is done without any government workers.

Why would researchers create an alternative measure to the CPI? The answer, in part, is because the internet makes the gathering of real time price data extremely easy. With time the researchers hope to be able to examine over a billion prices each day across every major economy. Since the BPP is based only on online sales there are limitations in generalizing the findings to the entire economy. However, the BPP data tracks the CPI quite closely. In relatively stable environments with low inflation the BPP and CPI are not likely to be very different. But that is not likely to be the case in high inflation environments, and certainly not when hyperinflation is present. When inflation is high (or highly variable) the BPP has the potential to be able to point out meaningful trends in prices long before the CPI data can capture those changes.

Practice What You Know
Using the CPI to equate prices over time

How cheap were the first Super Bowl tickets?

Ticket prices to America's premier sporting event, the Super Bowl, were much lower when it was first played in 1967. In fact, you could have bought a ticket for as little as $6. This seems very low by today's prices. In 2012, many seats sold for more than $2,500.

Question:

Use the CPI from 1967 (33) and convert the price of a $6 ticket in 1967 into 2012 dollars using the 230 for the CPI in 2012.

Answer:

For this question, we need to use equation 9.3:

$$\text{Price in today's dollars} = \text{price in earlier time} \times \frac{\text{price level today}}{\text{price level in earlier time}}.$$

The earlier price was $6, so we substitute this price and the two price levels from above to get:

Price in today's dollars = $6 x 230÷33 = $41.82

It turns out the old Super Bowl tickets were indeed cheap – you'd be lucky to get a hot dog and soda at a modern Super Bowl for $42.

What problems does inflation bring?

Many people believe that inflation is most harmful because it reduces the purchasing power of their income. For example, prices were much lower in the 1970s. Therefore, an annual salary of $10,000 could buy a lot more than it can today. Well, this is true, if all else were equal. But salaries are prices too, and inflation causes them to rise as well. Remember: inflation is a rise in prices all over the economy.

But this does not mean inflation is harmless - inflation does impose many costs on an economy. In this section, we cover these costs, which are *shoeleather costs, money illusion, menu costs*, future price level uncertainty, wealth redistribution and price confusion.

Shoeleather Costs

Inflation is costly for society when it causes people to do things they wouldn't choose to do in an environment of price stability. The higher the rate of inflation, the more likely you are to change your normal patterns of spending and money-holding. The reason is that inflation is essentially a tax on holding money. Prices of goods and services rise with inflation and this means the value of dollars in your wallet is falling. This problem is not currently severe in the United States because inflation rates are very low. But hyperinflation means that the value of dollars falls daily.

In order to avoid the tax on holding money, people hold less money and this means more trips to the bank to make withdrawals. This is where the term *shoeleather costs* comes from. **Shoeleather costs** are the resources wasted when people change their behavior to avoid holding money. In times past, these referred to actual shoes that might get worn out as a result of many trips to the bank. Today, these include fuel costs and the time and effort people expend when they make multiple trips to a bank or ATM.

> **Shoeleather costs** are the resources wasted when people change their behavior to avoid holding money.

Money Illusion

The second problem with inflation is among the least understood. Even when people know there has been inflation they do not always react rationally. So although wages and prices might rise because of inflation, people frequently respond as if the prices are higher in real terms. For example, if the price of a movie goes up ten percent, but our wages and all other prices go up by a similar amount, nothing has changed in real terms. But many people mistakenly conclude that movies have become more expensive. If they treat a price increase from inflation as a change in relative price, they may go see fewer movies, or make other decisions based on the new price. Economists call this a *money illusion*. A **money illusion** occurs when people interpret nominal changes in wages or prices as real changes.

> **Money illusion** occurs when people interpret nominal changes as real changes.

Money illusion may be irrational, but it is an easy trap to fall into. Let's see if we can trick you into it. Consider the cost of living data presented in Table 9.3. The index scores show relative living costs for an average inhabitant of various U.S. cities. The index is set so that 100 is the cost of living in an average U.S. city.

For this example, focus on two particular cities: Philadelphia, PA, and Charlotte, NC. The index score for Philadelphia is 124.1, for Charlotte, it is 90. These index scores imply that a salary of $90,000 for an average person living in Charlotte, NC is equivalent to a salary of $124,100 for an average person living in Philadelphia. The difference is more than $30,000.

Now imagine you are living in Charlotte and earning $90,000, but your firm offers to relocate you to Philadelphia at a pay rate of $120,000. Doesn't that seem like a pretty large raise? You might be excited to call your parents and tell them you are making "six figures." But in fact, it is a real pay-cut since you can buy less with $120,000 in Philadelphia than you can with $90,000 in Charlotte. The money illusion makes it feel like a raise.

Table 9.3
The Cost of Living in Selected U.S. Cities

City	Cost of Living Index Number
New York (Manhattan)	214.3
San Francisco, CA	169.5
Los Angeles, CA	145.4
Washington, DC	137.2
Boston, MA	135.4
Philadelphia, PA	124.1
Seattle, WA	121.5
Chicago, IL	110.8
Las Vegas, NV	110.3
Richmond, VA	106.9
Phoenix, AZ	101.0
Albuquerque, NM	98.7
Detroit, MI	98.6
Atlanta, GA	96.5
Dallas, TX	91.5
Charlotte, NC	90.0

The key distinction is between *real* wages and *nominal wages*. A worker's **nominal wage** is his wage expressed in current dollars. The nominal wage is similar to nominal GDP. It is the wage expressed in current dollars, like $60 an hour, or $120,000 per year. The **real wage** is the nominal wage adjusted for changes in the price level. The real wage is more informative, because it describes what the worker earns in terms of purchasing power. So while a salary of $120,000 a year may sound high, if the CPI doubles it will not go very far.

> The **nominal wage** is the wage expressed in current dollars.

> The **real wage is** the nominal wage adjusted for changes in the price level.

Significant macroeconomic problems arise if workers have a money illusion when they interpret the value of their wages. Money illusion causes workers to focus on their nominal wage instead of their real wage. For example, when prices fall, any given nominal wage is worth more in real terms. In Chapter 14 we'll see that macroeconomic adjustments can depend on whether workers are willing to let wages fall when other prices fall. The money illusion causes these adjustments to take longer than they should and this tends to lengthen economic downturns.

Menu Costs

The act of physically changing prices is also costly. **Menu costs** are the costs of changing prices. While some businesses can change prices easily—for example gas pumps and signs at gas stations are designed for this purpose—businesses such as restaurants can find it expensive to print new menus when their prices change.

> **Menu costs** are the costs of changing prices.

Other costs considered in this category are not directly related to menus. For example, changing prices can make regular customers angry. Think about your favorite lunch spot. Perhaps you regularly buy a bagel and an iced tea for $4 at Bodo's Bagels. What if the price for this combination suddenly increases to $5? You might be annoyed enough to go somewhere else next time.

Menu costs discourage firms from adjusting prices quickly. When some prices are slow to respond, the effects of macroeconomic disturbances are magnified. We'll talk about this more in Chapter 14.

Future Price Level Uncertainty

Imagine you decide to open a new coffee shop in your college town. You want to produce espressos, café mochas and cappuccinos. Of course, you hope to sell these for a profit. But before you can sell a single cup of coffee, you have to spend funds on your resources. You have to buy capital goods like an espresso bar, tables, chairs, and a cash register. You have to hire workers and promise to pay them. All firms, large and small, face this situation. Before any revenue arrives from the sales of output, firms have to spend on resources. This also applies to the overall macroeconomy: in order to increase GDP in the future, firms must invest today. The funds they need to make these investments are typically borrowed from others.

The timeline of production shown in Figure 9.6 illustrates how this process works. At the end, the firm sells their *output*. **Output** is the production the firm creates. The important point is that in a normal production process, funds must be spent today and then repaid in the future, after the output sells. But for this sequence of events to occur, businesses must make promises to deliver payments in the future; payments to workers and lenders. Thus, two types of long-term agreements form the foundation for production: wage and loan contracts. Both of these involve are agreements for dollars to be delivered in future periods.

> **Output** is the production the firm creates.

Figure 9.6
The Timeline of Production

The timeline of production illustrates the way output is typically produced. First, a firm invests by buying equipment and other resources to aid in production. All of this requires spending. The output and the revenue from output sales comes later. After all this, the firm can pay workers and repay loans. But if inflation makes these later payments riskier, it can slow down the entire production process.

Inflation affects the real value of future dollars. If inflation confuses workers and lenders, these essential long-term agreements are riskier and people are less likely to enter into them. Chapter 10 focuses on the market for loans in an economy and we cover this at a deeper level there. But inflation can cripple loan markets because people don't know what future price levels will be. When firms can't borrow or hire long-term workers, future production is limited.

Wealth Redistribution

Inflation can also redistribute wealth between borrowers and lenders. Returning to the coffee shop example above, imagine that you borrow $50,000 to help start your business. You borrow this from a bank with the promise of paying back $60,000 in five years. Now, if inflation unexpectedly rises during the course of the five years, then this inflation devalues your future payment the bank – you are better off, but the bank is off. Thus surprise inflation redistributes wealth from borrowers to lenders.

If the inflation is fully expected by you and the bank, they will require more in return for the loan, and so the inflation is not a problem. In the United States, inflation has been low and steady since the early 1980s. Therefore, surprises are rare. But nations with higher inflation rates are also nations with higher variability of inflation and this makes it difficult to predict the future. This is one more reason why high inflation increases the risk of making the loans that are an important source of funding for business ventures.

Price Confusion

Market prices are signals to consumers and firms—signals that help allocate resources in a market economy. For example, if demand increases, prices rise and firms have an incentive to increase the quantity they supply. All else equal, firms take rising prices as a signal to increase output and falling prices as a signal to produce less. But inflation also shows up as rising prices. If firms can't determine which price changes are due to inflation, resources may be misdirected in the economy.

Figure 9.7 illustrates the dilemma firms face. Initially it may appear that output prices are rising as a result of an increase in demand. But if the cause is inflation, prices throughout the economy will rise and the optimal output for the firm should remain the original output level. If firms always react to price changes by increasing output, they run the risk of over-building and this can be painful later.

Figure 9.7
The Signal Extraction Problem

Price changes send information to businesses. However, higher prices can be the result of an increase in demand or inflation. If upward pressure on prices is the result of demand, the profit-maximizing firm ought to increase output. But if the price increase is the result of general inflation, the firm should not change output.

The housing market in the United States provides a good example of price confusion. In 2005, house prices were high and rising. We can look back now and recognize a price bubble that did not reflect real long-run increases in demand. It appears now that rising housing prices reflected inflation. However, high prices spurred many builders to develop more properties. When housing prices later fell, many of these builders declared bankruptcy. The crash in housing prices was certainly one of the contributing factors to the Great Recession, which began at the end of 2007.

Tax Distortions

Even if inflation raises all prices uniformly, there are still distortionary effects from inflation. These arise because tax laws do not typically account for inflation. One area where this is particularly distortionary is in regard to *capital gains taxes*.

Capital gains taxes are taxes on the gains realized by selling an asset for more than its purchase price. For example, if your parents bought a house in 1980 for $80,000, and then sold it in 2012 for $230,000, they made a $150,000 capital gain on the sale of the house, and this capital gain is taxed. However, it turns out that the CPI rose by exactly the same amount between 1980 and 2012 – the CPI was 80 in 1980 and climbed to 230 by 2012. Therefore, the value of your parents' house just kept pace with inflation. In real terms, the value of their house did not climb. But they will still be required to pay a significant tax upon the sale of their home. As it turns out, the size of their tax was determined by inflation and not the tax laws – if there had been no inflation, they'd have owed no tax.

Capital gains are realized on more than just home sales. Capital gains also arise with sales of stocks, bonds and other financial securities. As we will discuss in Chapter 11, these securities are a crucial ingredient to a growing and expanding economy. But inflation combined with a capital gains tax means people will be less likely to make these purchases. One possible solution is to rewrite the tax laws to take account of inflation's effects. Another solution is to eliminate inflation.

Table 9.4 summarizes the costs of inflation.

Table 9.4
The Costs of Inflation

Cost of Inflation	Description
Shoeleather costs	Time and resources are spent to guard against the effects of inflation.
Money illusion	People misinterpret nominal changes as real changes.
Menu costs	Inflation means firms must incur extra costs to change output prices.
Future price level uncertainty	Long-term agreements may not be signed if lenders, firms, and workers are unsure about future price levels.
Wealth redistribution	Surprise inflation redistributes wealth between borrowers and lenders.
Price confusion	Inflation makes it difficult to read price signals and this can lead to a misallocation of resources.
Tax distortions	Inflation makes capital gains appear larger and thus increases tax burdens.

Practice What You Know
Problems with Inflation

How big is your raise in real terms?

Your boss calls you into his office and tells you he has good news. Because of your stellar performance and hard work, you have earned a 3% raise for next year. But when you think about your future pay, you should also know how much inflation has eroded your current pay. For example, if inflation is 3% per year, then you need a 3% raise just to keep pace with inflation. Note that you can see inflation rates for yourself by visiting the Bureau of Labor Statistics website (www.BLS.gov). Once there, look up inflation rates based on the CPI.

Question:

Describe a situation in which a 3 percent raise would signify a lower real wage?

Answer:

If inflation is greater than 3%, then a 3% raise is actually a decline in your real wage.

Question:

What inflation problem must you overcome to correctly see the value of your raise?

Answer:

Money illusion. You must evaluate the real, rather than nominal value of your pay.

Economics for Life

Inflation devalues dollars

Preparing your future for inflation

In this chapter, we talked about how inflation devalues money you currently hold and money you've been promised in the future. One problem you may encounter is how to prepare for retirement in the face of inflation. Perhaps you are not worried about this, since inflation in the United States over the past 50 years has averaged 4%, and , more recently, the average has been only 2%. But even these low rates mean that dollars will be worth significantly less forty years from now.

One way to think about the affect of inflation on future dollars is to ask what amount of future dollars it will take to match the real value of $1.00 today. The table below answers this question based on a retirement date of forty years in the future. The different inflation rates are specified at the top.

	Inflation rate				
	1%	2%	3%	4%	5%
Number of future dollars needed to match real value of today's $1.00	$1.49	$2.21	$3.26	$4.80	$7.04

Thus, if inflation averages 4% over the next four decades, you'll need $4.80 just to buy the same goods and services you can buy today for $1.00.

Let's see what this means for your overall retirement plans. Let's say you decide you could live on $50,000 per year if you retired today. If inflation is 4% between now and retirement, you would need enough savings to supply you with $240,000 per year, just to keep pace with inflation.

Conclusion

We began this chapter with a common misconception – that inflation really isn't a big problem. And while inflation rates have been low in the United States for several years now, they were very high in the 1970s. In addition, inflation rates in other nations remain high. Inflation and the problems it causes can be severe.

Inflation, along with the unemployment rate and changes in real GDP, is an important indicator of overall macroeconomic conditions. Now that we have covered these three, we move next to savings and the determination of interest rates.

BIG QUESTIONS

How is inflation measured?

- Economists use the CPI to determine the general level of prices in the economy.
- Inflation rates are calculated as the growth rate of the price level.
- Determining which prices to include in the CPI can be challenging for several reasons. Consumers change what they buy over time, the quality of goods changes, and new products and sales locations are introduced.

What problems does inflation bring?

- Inflation introduces uncertainty about future prices levels. This makes it difficult for consumers and producers to plan and therefore impedes economic progress.
- Inflation makes it difficult for producers to read price signals correctly.
- Inflation adds menu costs.
- Inflation can cause people make decisions based on nominal rather than real monetary values, a problem known as the money illusion.

Concepts You Should Know

Deflation	Money illusion	Output
Consumer price Index	Nominal wage	
Chained CPI	Real wage	Menu costs
	Shoeleather costs	

Questions for Review

1. The price of a typical laptop computer has fallen from $2,000 in 1985 to $800 today. At the same time the consumer price index has risen from 100 to 250. Adjusting for inflation, how much did the price of laptops change? Does this answer seem right to you, or it missing something?

2. What three issues are at the center of the debate regarding the accuracy of the CPI?

3. If the prices of homes go up by five percent and the prices of concert tickets rise by ten percent, which will have the larger impact on the CPI?

4. If a country is experiencing a relatively high rate of inflation, what impact will this have on the country's long-term rate of economic growth?

5. In a sentence or two, evaluate the accuracy of the following statement, including a clear precise statement of historical comparison:

"Inflation in the U.S. last year was zero percent. This is close to the historical level."

6. Wage agreements and loan contracts are two types of multi-period agreements that are important for economic growth.

Suppose you sign a 2-year job contract with Smith Barney which stipulates that you will be paid an annual salary of $93,500 each year plus an additional 2% over that in the second year to account for expected inflation.
      (a) If inflation turns out to be 3% rather than 2% who is hurt by this? Why?
      (b)If inflation turns out to be 1% rather than 2% who is hurt by this? Why?

Suppose that you also take out a $1000 loan at the Cavalier Credit Union. It stipulates that you pay it back with 4% interest in one year, and again, inflation is expected by all to be 2%.
      (c) If inflation turns out to be 3% rather than 2% who is hurt by this? Why?
      (d) If inflation turns out to be 3% rather than 2% who is helped by this? Why?

7. Briefly explain each of the seven problems caused by inflation.

Study Problems

1. In 1991 the Barenaked Ladies released, "If I had a Million Dollars I'd be Rich". How much money would you need in 2009 to have an equivalent amount of purchasing power in 2009? Note that the consumer price index in 1991 was 136.2 and in 2009 it was 214.5.

2. Visit www.bls.gov and access the data on the consumer price index. How much has the index increased over the last year? The last five years? Last ten years? Now examine the

individual categories includes in the CPI. Which categories of spending have increased the most? Which categories have increased the least?

3. Rooting through the attic you discover a bunch of old tax forms. You find that your grandmother made $75 working part time during December of 1964 when the CPI was 31.3. How much would you need to have earned in January of this year to have at least as much real income as your mother did?

Solved Problems

1.* The residents of Greenland play golf incessantly. Golf is the only thing that they spend their money on. They buy golf balls, clubs, and tees. In 2010 they bought 1,000 golf balls for $2 each, 100 clubs for $50 each, and 500 tees for 10 cents each. In 2011, they bought 1,100 golf balls for $2.50, 75 clubs for $75 each, and 1,000 tees for 12 cents each.

     a. Calculate the CPI for each year.

Answer:

Note: We'll use the quantities from the first year to designate the weights.

In order to build a price index we first need to choose which year we will use as our base year. Let 2010 be the base year. Next we will define our basket as the goods consumed in 2010, 1,000 golf balls, 100 clubs, and 500 tees. In 2010 this basket cost 1,000*$2 + 100*$50 + 500*$0.10 = $7050. In 2011 this basket costs 1,000*$2.50 + 100*$75 + 500*$0.12 = $10,060.

Dividing the cost of the basket in each by the cost of the basket in the base year and multiplying by 100 gives us the CPI for each year. For 2010 the CPI is 100, $7050/$7050*100 = 100. For 2012 the CPI is 142.7, $10,060/$7050*100 = 142.7.

b. What was the inflation rate in 2011?

Answer:

The inflation rate is defined as (CPI2 – CPI1) / CPI1 *100. Plugging the values from part (a) into the formula we get an inflation rate of 42.7%. (142.7 – 100)/100*100 = 42.7.

2.* If health care costs make up 10 percent of total expenditures and they rise by 15 percent while the other components in the index remain constant how much will the price index rise?

Answer:

1.5%. Suppose the CPI in the first year is 100. If health care costs are 10% of total expenditures then they account for 10 of the 100 points, with 90 of the other points falling in other categories. If health care prices rise by 15% in the second year then those 10 points become 11.5 points. Since the prices of the other categories have not changed the CPI now stands at 101.5, since $11.5 + 90 = 101.5$.

Using our formula for calculating the inflation rate, the rise in health care prices has raised the overall price level by 1.5%. $(101.5 - 100) / 100 * 100 = 1.5$.

Chapter 10

Savings, Interest Rates, and the Market for Loanable Funds

Misconception: The government sets interest rates

Almost all news related to interest rates gives the impression that the government raises and lowers interest rates. For sure, the government can influence many interest rates. But interest rates are determined privately, by the interaction of the market forces of supply and demand. In fact, you can understand why interest rates rise and fall by applying supply and demand analysis to the market for loans. That's what we will do in this chapter. Along the way, we also consider the many factors that influence savers and borrowers. In this chapter, we discuss many of the same topics you might study in a course on banking or financial institutions, but our emphasis is certainly different. We are interested in studying how financial institutions and markets affect the macroeconomy. When we are finished, you will understand why interest rates rise and fall, and also appreciate the necessity of loanable funds markets in the larger macroeconomy.

Big Questions:

- What is the loanable funds market?
- What factors shift the supply of loanable funds?
- What factors shift the demand for loanable funds?
- How do we apply the loanable funds market model?

What is the loanable funds market?

> The **loanable funds market** is the market where savers supply funds for loans to borrowers.

Financial markets are where firms and governments obtain funds, or *financing,* for their operations. These funds come primarily from household savings across the economy. In economics, we analyze financial markets in the context of a *loanable funds market*. The **loanable funds market** is the market where savers supply funds for loans to borrowers.

It is not a single physical location, but includes places like stock exchanges, investment banks, mutual fund firms and the commercial banks. In this section, we explain the particular characteristics of the loanable funds market and the significant role it plays in the overall economy.

Figure 10.1 illustrates the role of the loanable funds market. Savings flow in and become loans for borrowers. We could call it the market for savings, or even the market for loans. The term *loanable funds* captures the information in both.

Figure 10.1
The Role of the Loanable Funds Market

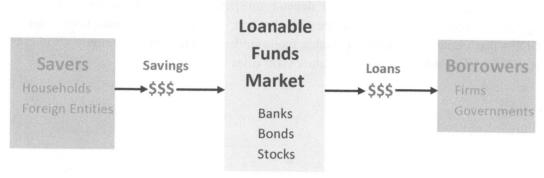

The market for loanable funds is where savers bring funds and make them available to borrowers. Households (private individuals and families) are the primary suppliers of loanable funds. Firms are the primary demanders of loanable funds. When this market is functioning well, firms can get the funds necessary for production and savers are paid for lending.

On the left side of the figure, the suppliers of funds—those who save—include households and foreign entities. Households are private individuals and families. Foreign entities include both foreign governments and private citizens that choose to save in the United States. For most of our applications, it helps us to focus on households as the primary suppliers of loanable funds.

If you have a checking or savings account at a bank, you are a supplier of loanable funds. You deposit funds into your bank account, but these funds don't just sit in a vault - banks loan out the majority of these funds. Household savings in retirement accounts, stocks, bonds, and mutual funds are other big sources of loanable funds.

The demanders of loanable funds include business firms and governments. In this chapter we focus on firms as the primary borrowers of loanable funds. We'll cover government borrowing in Chapter 15. To reinforce the significance of this market, think about why borrowing takes place. Firms borrow to invest. That is, firms, looking to produce output in the future, must borrow to pay expenses today.

Imagine you are an entrepreneur and you decide to start a company that will produce and sell college gear. If you succeed, you will contribute to national GDP. But you don't really think of it this way – you simply hope that you have discovered a great business opportunity. Now, before you ever sell your first shirt, hat, or sweatpants, you have to spend on the resources you'll use in the production process. For example, if you plan on silk-screening your college logo onto hooded sweatshirts, you have to buy sweatshirts, paint, and a screen printing press. Here is where we come to the loanable funds market: since you have no revenue yet, you need to borrow for these investments.

Figure 10.2 shows the production timeline first introduced in Chapter 9. At the end of the timeline is output, or GDP. When this output is sold, it produces revenue for the firms, and the revenue is used to pay bills. But future GDP depends on spending today for resources. This spending comes before any revenue from the sale of output. Therefore, firms must borrow for future GDP – that's how important the loanable funds market is to the entire economy. Without a well-functioning loanable funds market, future GDP dries up.

Figure 10.2
The Timeline of Production

The production timeline illustrates that GDP depends critically on the loanable funds market. At the end of the production timeline we see output, or GDP. But before a firm can produce output, it must purchase resources. Since these purchases come before the revenue, firms must borrow at the beginning of the timeline.

Borrowing fuels investment which creates future output. But *every dollar borrowed requires a dollar saved*. Without savings, we cannot sustain future production. If you want to borrow to fund the resources you need to produce college apparel, somebody else has to save. Working backwards, the chain of crucial relationships looks like this: output (GDP) requires investment; investment requires borrowing; borrowing requires savings. And all of this requires a loanable funds market that efficiently channels funds from savers to borrowers.

We will study this crucial market from the perspective of prices, quantities, supply and demand—like any other market. The good in this market is loanable funds. Demanders are borrowers; suppliers are savers. Figure 10.3 is a picture of supply and demand for loanable funds, and a summary of the distinctions of the loanable funds market.

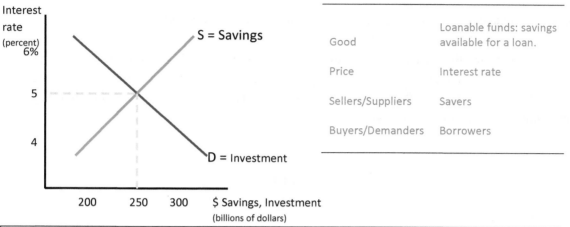

Figure 10.3
The Loanable Funds Market

Good	Loanable funds: savings available for a loan.
Price	Interest rate
Sellers/Suppliers	Savers
Buyers/Demanders	Borrowers

Savings is channeled into investment in the loanable funds market. In this market, loanable funds are the goods that are bought and sold. The price is an interest rate. This price, like any other market-determined price, is determined by the interaction of supply and demand.

One advantage of this demand and supply approach is that it clarifies the role of interest rates. An **interest rate** is the price of loanable funds. It is like the price of toothpaste, computers and hoodies; it is simply quoted differently – it is quoted as percent of the original loan amount. People who are thinking about retirement or a big purchase such as a house or car worry about interest rate fluctuations but do not necessarily understand why interest rates rise and fall. If we acknowledge that an interest rate is just the price of loanable funds, we can use supply and demand to reveal the factors that make interest rates rise and fall.

An **interest rate** is a price of loanable funds.

We now turn to the two different views of interest rates: the view of the saver and the view of the borrower.

Interest Rates as a Reward for Saving

If you are a saver, the interest rate is the return you get for supplying funds. For example, let's say your parents gave you some cash when you came to college this semester. After buying textbooks, groceries and other supplies, you have $1,000 left, which you consider saving. You go to a bank near campus and inquire about a new account. In this transaction, the bank is the buyer, and it offers a certain price for the use of your savings. When it does offer prices, it is not in dollars. The bank quotes a price in interest rates, or as a percentage of how much you save. But it communicates the same information. So if you are saving $1,000, the bank might tell you: "We'll give you 6% if you save that money for a year." Since 6% of $1,000 is $60, this is equivalent to saying "we'll give you $60 if you save that money for a year." If you save $1,000 for one year with an interest rate of 6%, this brings you $1,060 next year, which is computed as:

$1,000 + [6% of $1,000] = $500 + [0.06×$1,000] = $1,000 + $60 = $1,060.

For savers, the interest rate is a reward. Every dollar saved today returns more in the future. The higher the interest rate, the greater the returns in the future. Table 10.1 illustrates how interest rates affect $1,000 worth of savings. An interest rate of 4% yields $1,040 one year later, but an interest rate of 10% yields $1,100.

Table 10.1
Higher interest rates and greater future returns

Interest Rate	Value of $1,000 After 1 Year	
4%	$1,040	If you save $1,000 for one year at an interest rate of 6%, this yields $1,060 next year, computed as:
5%	1,050	$1,000 + (6% of $1,000)
6%	1,060	= $1,000 + (0.06 x $1,000)
10%	1,100	= $1,000 + $60
		= $1,060.

Savings is the supply of loanable funds. The higher the interest rate, the greater the incentive to save. This is the loanable funds version of the law of supply: the quantity of savings rises when the interest rate rises. This positive relationship between interest rates and savings is imbedded in the slope of the supply curve, illustrated in Figure 10.3. When the interest rate is 4%, the quantity of loans supplied is $200 billion dollars per year; at 5%, the quantity supplied increases to $250 billion and at 6%, it increases to $300 billion.

Incentives

Think of the interest rate as the opportunity cost of consumption. Consider the $500 savings in Table 10.2. With a 4% interest rate and a $500 purchase, you are giving up the $20 you would make by saving that $500. But at an interest rate of 10%, consumption today means giving up an additional $50 next year. Interest rates on savings accounts in the United States today are typically less than 2%. But imagine an interest rate of 10% for a savings account. This was actually the situation in the United States in the 1980s. With an interest rate that high, even college students find a way to save.

Interest Rates as a Cost of Borrowing

We now turn to the demand or borrowing side of the loanable funds market. For this, we shift to the firm's perspective and return to your plan to produce college apparel. Recall that you need to buy the sweatshirts, paint and screen-printing press to produce hoodies and other products. Assume you need $100,000 to start your business. If you borrow $100,000 for one year at an interest rate of 6%, you'll need to repay $106,000 in one year. It makes sense to do this only if you expect to earn more than 6%, or $6,000, on this investment.

For borrowers, the interest rate is the cost of borrowing. Firms borrow only if they expect the return on their investment to be greater than the costs of the loan. For example, at an interest rate of 6%, a firm would borrow only if it expected to make more than 6% return with their use of the funds. Let's state this as a rule. Profit maximizing firms borrow to fund an investment only if:

Expected return on the investment > Interest rate on the loan.

The lower the interest rate, the more likely a business will succeed in earning enough to exceed the interest it will owe at the end of the year. For example, if your firm can borrow at an interest rate of just 4%, you'll need to make a return greater than 4%. There are probably several investments available today that would pay more than a 6% return. But there's still more that would yield returns greater than 4% and more still that would pay greater than 2%. If we apply our rule from above, we'll get higher quantity of loans demanded as the interest rate drops. This gives us the inverse relationship between interest rate and quantity demanded of loans that is embedded in the slope of the demand curve for loanable funds.

The graph of the loanable funds market in Figure 10.3 illustrates the demand curve for loanable funds across the entire economy. At an interest rate of 6%, the quantity of loans demanded by all business firms in the economy is $200 billion. This indicates that firms believe only $200 billion worth of investment will pay returns greater than 6%. At an interest rate of 5%, firms estimate that another $50 billion worth of total loans will earn between 5% and 6%, and the quantity of loans demanded rises to $250 billion. Lower interest rates lead to a greater quantity of demand for loanable funds.

How Inflation affects Interest Rates

If you save $1,000 for a year at an interest rate of 6%, your reward for saving is $60. But inflation affects the real value of this reward. For example, imagine inflation is exactly 6% during the year you save. Next year, it will take $1,060 to buy the same quantity of goods and services you are able to buy this year for $1,000. In this case, your interest rate of 6% and the inflation rate of 6% cancel each other out. You break even and that's no reward.

> The **nominal interest rate** is the interest rate that is not corrected for inflation

When making decisions about saving and borrowing, people care about the *real interest rate*, not the *nominal interest rate*. The **real interest rate** is the interest rate that is corrected for inflation; it is the rate of return in terms of real purchasing power. The **nominal interest rate** is the interest rate before it is corrected for inflation; it is the stated interest rate. In our example, the interest rate of 6% is the nominal interest rate. But with 6% inflation, the real return on your savings disappears, and the real interest rate is zero. In general, we can approximate the real interest rate by subtracting the inflation rate from the nominal interest rate in an equation known as the **Fisher equation**:

> The **real interest rate** is the interest rate that is corrected for inflation

Real interest rate = nominal interest rate - inflation rate   (10.1)

For example, if inflation this year is 2%, a nominal interest rate of 6% on your savings yields a 4% real interest rate. The Fisher equation is named after economist Irving Fisher who formulated the relationship between inflation and interest rates.

Savers and borrowers care about the real rate of interest on a loan because this is the rate that describes how the real purchasing power of your funds changes over the course of the loan. Since interest rates are a result of supply and demand in the market for loanable funds, higher inflation rates lead to higher nominal interest rates to compensate lenders for the loss of purchasing power. We can rewrite the Fisher equation to see how inflation generally increases nominal interest rates:

Nominal interest rate = real interest rate + inflation rate   (10.2)

For a given real interest rate, the higher the rate of inflation, the higher the nominal interest rate. Table 10.2 shows how the nominal interest rate rises with inflation rates for a given level of real interest rates. If the real interest rate is 4% and there is no inflation, then the nominal interest rate is also 4%. But if inflation rises to 2%, the nominal interest rate increases to 6%. If the inflation rate rises further to 4%, then the nominal interest rate rises to 8%.

Table 10.2
How Inflation affects Nominal Interest Rates

Inflation		Real interest rate		Nominal interest rate
0%	+	4%	=	4%
2%	+	4%	=	6%
4%	+	4%	=	8%

We can picture the Fisher equation by looking at real and nominal interest rates over time. Figure 10.3 plots real and nominal interest rates in the United States from 1960 to 2012. The difference between them is the inflation rate. Notice that this gap was particularly high during the inflationary 1970s, but narrowed considerably as inflation rates fell in the 1980s. Since 2008, nominal interest rates in the United States have been less than one percent. Given that inflation rates have been around 2%, this implies to negative real interest rates.

Figure 10.3
Real and Nominal Interest Rates, 1960-2012

Sources: Federal Reserve Bank of St. Louis FRED database, BLS.

The difference between real and nominal interest rates is the rate of inflation. The experience of the 1970s illustrates that nominal interest rates are historically high when inflation is also high.

Unless otherwise stated, in this text we will use nominal interest rates. We do this for two reasons. First, nominal interest rates are the stated interest rates— the rates you read about and consider in actual financial transactions. Second, low and steady inflation means that the difference between real and nominal interest rates doesn't fluctuate much. That is, while we recognize that savers and borrowers care about the real interest rate, the current inflationary environment throughout much of the developed world leaves little to be gained by focusing on the real interest rate through the applications in this text.

In the next two sections, we consider the factors that cause shifts in the supply and demand for loanable funds.

Practice What You Know
interest rates and quantity supply and demand

U.S. interest rates have fallen

In 1981, many interest rates in the United States were 15%, but inflation rates were 10%. In 2012, many interest rates were less than 1%, with inflation rates of 2%.

Question:
Compute the real interest rate in both 1981 and 2012.

Answer:
Using equation (22.1), we compute the real interest rate as:

Real interest rate = nominal interest rate – inflation rate

For 1981, the real interest rate was: 15% - 10% = 5%.
For 2012, the real interest rate was: 1% - 2% = -1%.

Question:
All else equal, how does the drop in interest rates between 1981 and 2012 affect the quantity of loanable funds supplied?

Answer:
The quantity supplied decreases along the supply curve. Lower interest rates reduce the incentive to save.

Question:
All else equal, how does the drop in interest rates between 1981 and 2012 affect the quantity of loanable funds demanded?

Answer:
The quantity demanded increases along the demand curve. Firms can borrow for lower rates making many more investment opportunities profitable.

What factors shift the supply of loanable funds?

Recall that the supply of loanable funds comes from savings. If you have either a savings or checking account, you are a participant in this market. We turn now to three factors that determine the level of the supply curve for loanable funds: income and wealth, time preferences, and consumption smoothing. When these factors change, the supply curve shifts.

Income and Wealth

Imagine that a distant relative passes away and you inherit $20,000. What will you do with these unexpected funds? You might celebrate with a nice meal and a shopping spree. But most of us would also save some of this new-found wealth. All else equal, people prefer to have more savings. Thus, increases in income generally increase savings. If income declines, people save less. These changes shift the loanable funds supply curve.

The relationship between income and savings is true across the globe. As nations gain wealth, they save more. Over the past twenty years, the increase in foreign savings has often made its way into the U.S. loanable funds market. For example, a businessman in Mumbai, India may find himself with extra savings. He will probably put some into an Indian bank and some into Indian stocks and bonds. But there's a good chance he'll also channel some of his savings into the United States. Historically, U.S. financial markets have offered relatively greater returns than markets in other countries. In addition, the United States financial markets are often considered less risky than other global markets, because of the size and robustness of the U.S. economy. Therefore, as global economies have grown, there has been an increase in savings in the United States.

The increase in foreign savings came at a good time for the United States because domestic savings began falling in the 1980s. Without the influx of foreign funds, U.S. firms would have had difficulty funding investment. There is no guarantee that foreign savings will continue to flow into the United States at the same rates. But these foreign funds do offer new opportunities for domestic firms to borrow for investment.

Time Preferences

Imagine that your parents promised you a cash reward for a good grade in economics. Does it matter if they pay immediately or wait until you graduate? Yes, it matters – you want the money as soon as you earn it. This is not unusual. People always prefer funds sooner than later, and the same applies to goods and services; economists call this general tendency *time preferences*. **Time preferences** refer to the fact that people prefer goods and services sooner rather than later.

> **Time preferences** refer to the fact that people prefer goods and services sooner, rather than later.

Because people have time preferences, you must pay them to save. While time preferences are generally stable over time, if the rate of time preference in a society changes, the supply of loanable funds shifts.

While we all prefer sooner to later, some people have greater time preferences than others. Think of those with the strongest time preferences as being the least patient: they *strongly* prefer now to later. Someone with weaker time preferences has more patience. All else equal, people with stronger time preferences save less than people with weaker time preferences.

There are other ways that time preferences can be observed. For example, people with very strong time preferences may not even go to college, since the returns to college education are not typically realized until years later. Time spent in college is time that could have been spent earning income. The fact that you are a college student demonstrates that you are more patient than some others who choose instead to work for more income now.

You'll be happy to know that there is a definite payoff to college education. College graduates earn significantly more than high school graduates. Figure 10.4 shows median annual salary in the United States by educational attainment. Some college dropouts, for example Mark Zuckerberg, earn millions of dollars a year. But this data shows that the median worker with a basic college degree earns about $16,000 more a year than those who don't graduate from college. Patience pays off!

Figure 10.4

Median Salary and Educational Attainment

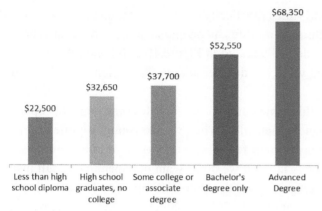

It takes patience, or relatively low time preferences, to stay in school. But annual earnings based on years of schooling shows that education pays off for most.

Source: BLS.

Economics in the Media:

Time preferences

Confessions of a Shopaholic

This movie follows a shopping junkie, Becky Bloomwood, who must come to terms with her exploding debt. Becky has very strong time preferences. She can't stop spending even though she owes almost $20,000 on her credit cards. When she finally realizes the mess she is in she attends a *Shopaholics Anonymous* meeting. This is where the fun really begins.

Becky, like many other first time visitors, is reluctant to tell her story. After listening to others speak of their trials during the past week, the leader turns to Becky and she begins to tell her story. The pure joy she experiences while shopping is immediately obvious to the others members of the support group. As they listen to her describe the feeling she gets from making new purchases, they long to feel the same way. Her story is not as much about repentance as it is about the need to shop more. This creates a euphoric response from the group. After talking for a short time, Becky has convinced herself, and most of the group, to go on a shopping spree. She bolts from the meeting and races home to her apartment where she keeps one last credit card in the freezer for emergencies. She takes the card and heads off to find something new to purchase.

This film conveys how easy it is to get into unmanageable debt and how hard it is to break the cycle. The desire for individuals to borrow, driven by a time preferences, reduces the supply of loanable funds.

Consumption Smoothing

Over the course of a typical lifetime, income varies drastically. Early in life, income levels are relatively low, but income generally rises through midlife. As people near retirement, income levels fall again. A typical economic lifecycle is illustrated in Figure 10.5 Income (the green line) is highest in the middle "prime earning years," and lower at both the beginning and end of life.

But nobody wants to consume with this same pattern over their lifetime – most people want to consume in a consistent way throughout their life. When we are young, we often borrow and spend more than we are earning. We may borrow for college education or to buy our first home. Also, when we retire, our income levels fall, but we don't want our spending to fall just as much. So we generally smooth our consumption over the course of our life. The blue line in Figure 10.5 represents a normal consumption pattern which is smoother than the income pattern. This consumption smoothing is accomplished with the help of the loanable funds market.

Figure 10.5
Savings over a Typical Lifecycle

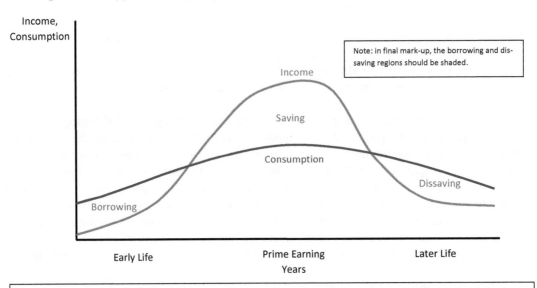

For most people, income is relatively low in early life, rises in their prime earning years, and falls in later life. But people generally prefer to smooth consumption over the course of their life. This means they borrow early in life for items like education and their first home. They save during the middle of their life when income is highest. Finally, they draw down savings when they retire.

Early in life we spend more than we earn. Therefore, we have to borrow. In Figure 10.5 borrowing is the vertical distance between income and consumption in early life. Midlife, or the prime earning years, is the time to repay loans and save for retirement. In this period of the lifecycle, the income line exceeds the consumption line. Later in life, when people retire and their income falls, they tend to live on savings. Economists call this *dissaving*.

We can use the concept of consumption smoothing to clarify a current situation affecting the United States economy. Savings are highest when people are in midlife. If we have a steady flow of people moving into each stage, the amount of savings in an economy is stable and there will be a steady supply in the market for loanable funds. But if a significant portion of the population leaves the prime earning years at the same time, overall savings will fall. As it turns out, this is the current situation in the United States because the baby-boomers are now retiring from the labor force. The oldest of this group reached retirement age in 2011. Over the next 10-15 years, U.S. workers will enter retirement in record numbers. This means an exit from the prime earning years and, consequentially, less savings. We'll come back to this in the last section of this chapter.

Figure 10.6 illustrates the effect on the supply of loanable funds when there are changes in income and wealth, time preferences or consumption smoothing. The initial supply of loanable funds is represented by S. The supply of loanable funds increases to S_1 if there is a change that leads to an increase in savings at all levels of interest rates. For example, an increase in foreign income and wealth would increase the supply of savings. Similarly, if people's time preferences fell—they become more patient)—the supply of loanable funds increases. Finally, if a relatively large group of the population moves into the middle of life, when savings is highest, this would also increase savings from S to S_1.

Figure 10.6
Shifts in the Supply of Loanable Funds

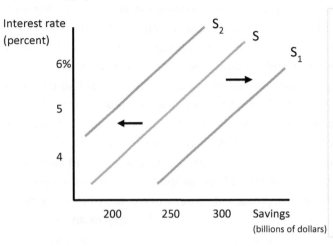

The supply of loanable funds shifts to the right when there are decreases in time preferences, increases in foreign income and wealth, and more people in midlife, when savings is highest. The supply of loanable funds shifts to the left when there are increases in time preferences, decreases in foreign income and wealth, and fewer people in midlife, when savings is highest.

The supply of loanable funds might also decrease. If income and wealth decline, people save less across all interest rates. This is illustrated as a shift from S to S_2 in Figure 10.6. Also, if time preferences increase, people become more impatient, and this reduces the supply of loanable funds. Finally, if a relatively large population group moves out of their prime-earning years and into retirement, the supply of loanable funds decreases. This last example describes what is happening in the United States right now.

Table 10.2
Factors that shift the supply of loanable funds

Factor	Direction of Effect	Explanation
Income and Wealth	*Increases* in income and wealth *increase* the supply of loanable funds. *Decreases* in income and wealth *decrease* the supply of loanable funds.	Savings is more affordable when people have greater income and wealth.
Time Preferences	*Increases* in time preferences *decrease* the supply of loanable funds. *Decreases* in time preferences *increase* the supply of loanable funds.	Lower time preferences indicate that people are more patient more likely to save for the future.
Consumption Smoothing	If *more* people are in midlife and their prime earning years, savings is *higher*. If *fewer* people are in midlife, savings is *lower*.	Income varies over the lifecycle, but people generally like to smooth consumption.

Economics in the Real World:
Why is the U.S. savings rate falling?

Are Americans becoming more and more short-sighted? Many people believe that American time preferences are indeed climbing. The cause of this belief is that savings rates have fallen significantly over the past few decades. Figure 10.7 shows the U.S. savings rate since 1960. The savings rate is personal saving as a portion of disposable (after tax) income. As you can see, the U.S. savings rate fell consistently for almost thirty years, beginning in the early 1980s. In 1982 the savings rate was almost 11 percent. The decline continued until about 2005 when the savings rate bottomed out at just 1.5 percent. We are now in a position to consider possible causes. In particular, is this change due to changes in income and wealth, time preferences, or consumption smoothing?

Figure 10.7
U.S. Savings Rate

Source: BEA.

In the United States, the savings rate (savings as a portion of disposable income) has fallen significantly over the past three decades. In 1982, the savings rate was 10.9%, but fell to just 1.5% in 2005.

We can out rule a decline in income and wealth as a cause of the savings decline. In fact, the decline began and continued throughout the 1980s and 1990s, which were both decades of significant income growth. In addition, the savings rate increased during the recession that began in late 2007. Second, we can also rule out the idea that the savings rate declined as consumption smoothing occurred. During the period of savings decline, the baby-boom population was a significant part of the labor force. Consumption smoothing would imply an increase in savings rates through the 1980s and 1990s, given that the baby boomers were working through this period.

Many people believe that savings dropped because time preferences have risen. Perhaps you have heard older Americans talking about the impatience of today's younger workers. If today's working Americans are more focused on instant gratification, they save less. Is this true? If so, why did it happen? Economists don't have consistent answers to these questions.

A closer look at the data indicates that there may be something else behind the decline in personal savings – it could just be a measurement issue. In reality, there are several alternative ways to *save* for the future, not all of which are counted in the official definition of "personal savings." For example, let's say you buy a house for $200,000 and the value of the house rises to $300,000 in just a few years. This means you now have gained $100,000 in personal wealth. The gain in the value of your house helps you prepare for the future just like increased saving. But gains of this nature are not counted as personal savings. In addition to real estate gains, the gains from purchases of stocks and bonds are also not counted in personal savings.

Here is an alternative view of the recent trends. From 1980 to 2007, real estate and stock market values rose significantly. Recognizing this as an alternative path to future wealth, many people shifted personal savings into these assets. The result is that personal savings rates, as officially measured, plummeted. Not convinced yet? Look what happened to personal savings rates in 2008 and 2009, as both real estate and stock prices tumbled: personal savings rates climbed to almost 6%.

Are today's Americans less patient than earlier generations? Perhaps. But the way personal savings rates are measured, it is difficult to determine a concrete answer to this question.

Practice What You Know
Time preferences
HIV in Developing Nations

In 2003 almost 40% of adults aged 15-49 in the nation of Botswana were living with HIV/AIDS, and life expectancy at birth fell below 35 years. There are many sad side effects from a situation like this. For now, let's focus on how a pandemic affects people's time preferences.

Question:
How does a drop in life expectancy affect time preferences and the supply of loanable funds?

Answer:
With life expectancy plummeting to under 35 years, people are certainly less likely to plan for the future. As time preferences increase, the supply of loanable funds goes down. Thus, when a nation is hit hard by an epidemic, one side effect is lower savings, which leads to lower output in the future. When it rains, it pours.

Source: http://www.indexmundi.com/g/g.aspx?v=32&c=bc&l=en

What factors shift the demand for loanable funds?

To look at the demand side, we shift perspectives to people who borrow in the loanable funds market. As we have seen, the demand for loanable funds derives from the desire to invest or purchase capital goods that aid in future production. We know the interest rate matters, and this relationship is embedded in the slope of the demand curve. We now turn to factors that cause shifts in the demand for loanable funds. We focus on two: the productivity of capital and investor confidence.

Productivity of Capital

Consider a firm that is trying to decide whether or not to borrow for an investment. Perhaps you're trying to decide whether to borrow to buy a new silk-screening machine, the SS-1000, for you college clothing business. This machine is capital and its purchase is counted as investment. To determine whether you should take a loan, recall our rule: a firm should borrow to fund an investment only if the expected return is greater than the interest rate on the loan. Therefore, if the interest rate on the loan is 6%, you will borrow to buy the SS-1000 only if you expect to earn more than a 6% return from it.

Let's say that, after crunching the numbers on expected costs and sales from the SS-1000, you estimate a return of just 4% from an investment in the SS-1000. You decide not to buy the new machine.

But then something changes. That something is the brand new SS-2000. The SS-2000 is a new and improved machine that prints t-shirts at double the rate of the SS-1000. Given this new machine, which is slightly more expensive, you calculate that your expected return is 7%, and so you decide to take the loan and buy the machine. Thus, your demand for loanable funds increased as a direct result of the new machine, which is twice as productive as the earlier machine.

What are the implications for the macroeconomy? Firms borrow to finance capital purchases. Therefore, the level of demand for loans depends on the productivity of capital. Changes in capital productivity shift the demand for loanable funds. If capital is more productive, the demand for loans increases; if capital is less productive, the demand for loans decreases.

Productivity can change for a number of reasons. Consider the impact of the Internet. A connection to the Internet provides quick access to data and networking capabilities people only dreamt about twenty years ago. The Internet increases the productivity of computers, a major capital expense. Over the past 20 years, an increase in expected returns associated with the Internet has made investment in computer equipment (capital) more attractive. This means that investment in capital yields greater returns, which in turn increases the demand for loans. When capital is more productive, firms are more likely to borrow to finance purchases of this capital.

Investor Confidence

The demand for loanable funds also depends on the beliefs or expectations of the investors at
business firms. If a firm believes its sales will increase in the future, it invests more
today to build for future sales. If instead, it believes its future sales will fall, it invests
less today. **Investor confidence** is a measure of what firms expect for future economic
activity. If firms feel the economy is poised to grow, that is, if it is confident, it is more
likely to borrow for investment at any interest rate. Economist John Maynard Keynes
referred to an investor's drive to action as "animal spirits," meaning that investment
demand may not even be based on rational or real factors in the economy.

> **Investor confidence** is a measure of what firms expect for future economic activity.

Figure 10.8 illustrates shifts in the demand for loanable funds. If capital productivity increases,
demand for investment increases from D to D_1. Similarly, if investor confidence rises, demand
for loanable funds increases from D to D_1. On the other hand, if capital productivity or investor
confidence falls, the demand for loanable funds falls from D to D_2.

Figure 10.8
Shifts in the Demand for Loanable Funds

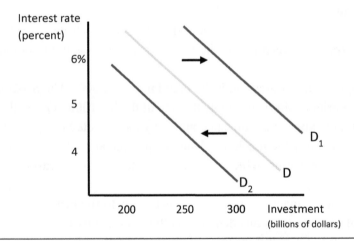

Increases in capital productivity and investor confidence lead to an increase in the demand for
loanable funds, shifting demand from D to D_1. Decreases in capital productivity and investor
confidence decrease the demand for loanable funds from D to D_2.

Practice What You Know
Demand for loanable funds

Sponge Bob and Loanable Funds

Determine if the following changes affect the demand for loanable funds and if so, how.

Question:
Business decision-makers become pessimistic about the future direction of the economy.

Answer:
Yes, the demand for loanable funds decreases as investor confidence falls. Business decision-makers are the investors because they decide whether or not to buy more capital.

Question
Research has shown that watching the cartoon *SpongeBob SquarePants* can shorten a choild's attention span. Now, assume that an entire generation of children grows up watching this cartoon and becomes less patient, or their time preference increase.

Answer:
No, this affects the supply of loanable funds. Less patience means time preferences increase and the supply of loanable funds declines.

Question
A technological advance leads to greater capital productivity.

Answer:
Yes, this increases the demand for loanable funds.

Question:
The interest rate falls.

Answer:
This change leads to a movement along the demand curve, rather than a shift in loanable funds. This can be caused by an increase in the supply of loanable funds.

How do we apply the loanable funds market model?

We are now ready to begin using the loanable funds market to study applications we see in the real world. First, we consider the implications of equilibrium in this market. After that, we will examine past and future views of the U.S. loanable funds market.

Equilibrium

Equilibrium in the loanable funds market is found at the interest rate where the plans of savers match the plans of borrowers. That is, where quantity supplied equals quantity demanded. In Figure 10.9, this occurs at an interest rate of 5%, where savers are willing to save $250 billion and borrowers desire $250 billion worth of loans. At interest rates above 5%, the quantity of loanable funds supplied exceeds the quantity demanded and this leads to downward pressure on the interest rate. At interest rates below 5%, the quantity demanded exceeds the quantity supplied and this leads to upward pressure on interest rates.

Figure 10.9
Equilibrium in the Market for Loanable Funds

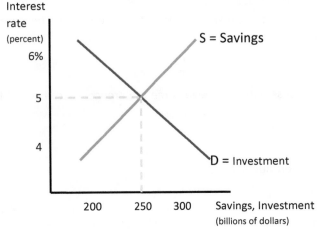

Equilibrium in the loanable funds market occurs where supply equals demand, at an interest rate of 5% and quantity of $250 billion dollars. Because investment is limited by savings, exactly $250 billion is saved and $250 billion is invested.

The loanable funds market, like other markets, naturally tends to move toward equilibrium where supply is equal to demand. This equilibrium condition reinforces a key relationship between savings and investment. Equilibrium occurs when

Savings = Investment.

In Figure 10.9 households and foreign entities have decided to save $250 billion worth at an interest rate of 5%. This $250 billion is borrowed by firms for investment. Dollars that are saved make their way into the loanable funds market and are then channeled to firms for investment purposes.

Equilibrium also helps to clarify an important principle we'll return to often in this text. Investment requires saving because:

Every dollar borrowed requires a dollar saved.

If an economy is to grow over time, somebody has to invest in capital that helps us produce more in the future. But investment requires savings. Without savings, we cannot grow.

Equilibrium is a helpful starting point for understanding how the loanable funds market functions. But in the real world, financial market conditions change frequently. We can account for these changes in our model by using shifts in the supply and demand curves. Let's consider two examples: a decline in investor confidence and a decrease in the supply of loanable funds.

A Decline in Investor Confidence

When the overall economy slows, firms often reduce investment since they expect reduced sales in future periods – this is a decline in investor confidence. This happened recently in the United States during the Great Recession that began at the end of 2007. Panel (a) of Figure 10.10 shows how a decline in investor confidence affects the loanable funds market. When investment demand declines, the loanable funds model predicts lower interest rates and a lower equilibrium level of investment. Panel (b) of Figure 10.10 shows that investment falling during both recessions between 2000 and 2012. During the Great Recession, real investment fell from $2.2 trillion to just $1.4 trillion – a 60% drop in less than two years.

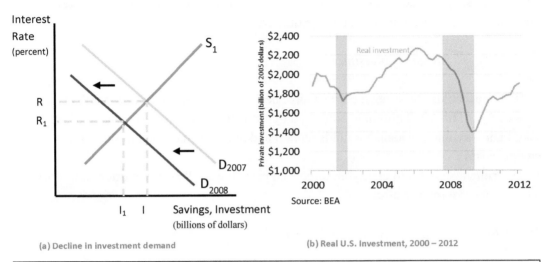

(a) When decision-makers at firms lose confidence in the future direction of the economy, investment demand declines and this leads to lower investment. (b) Real investment declined during both recessions that occurred between 2000 and 2012.

A Decrease in the Supply of Loanable Funds

Let's now return to the potential effects of the retirement of baby-boomers over the next ten to fifteen years. As we saw in the discussion of consumption smoothing, this will likely lead to a decrease in the supply of loanable funds in the United States. Figure 10.11 illustrates this kind of change. S_{2015} represents the supply of loanable funds in 2015. But as the baby-boomers retire, supply shifts back to S_{2025} one decade later.

Figure 10.11
The Future of the U.S. Loanable Funds Market?

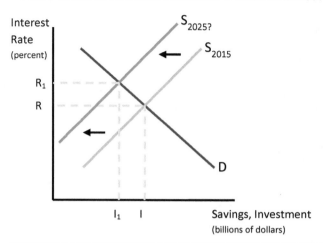

As baby-boomers retire and draw down their savings, supply shifts back. Without increases in savings from other sources, we will we see higher interest rates and lower investment.

All else equal, this means reduced investment and reduced GDP growth going forward. On the other hand, many other factors may change over the next few years to increase savings in the United States. For example, as other nations grow, foreigners may continue to increase savings in the United States. It is possible that this could offset the effects of the baby-boomer retirement and keep interest rates low for U.S. firms.

Practice What You Know
Working with the loanable funds model

Foreign Savings in the United States

Recently, China and India have begun to grow very rapidly. This increases the income and wealth of their citizens. In turn, these citizens increase their savings in their country and also in the United States.

Question:

When foreign savings comes into the U.S. loanable funds market, which curve is affected, supply or demand? How is this curve affected?

Answer:

The supply of loanable funds increases as savings increases.

Question:

Graph the U.S. loanable funds market both before and after the increase in foreign savings.

Answer:

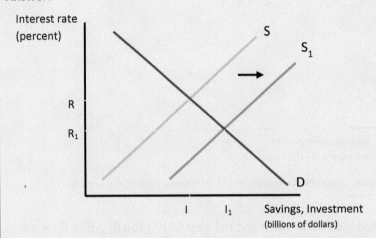

Before the increase in foreign savings, Supply is designated as S, and demand is D. These imply interest rate R and investment I. When new foreign savings comes into the market, supply increases to S_1, which decreases the interest rate to R_1 and increases investment to I_1.

Question:

How does the change in foreign savings affect both investment and future output in the United States?

Answer:

When the interest rate falls, the quantity of investment increases. Firms can afford to borrow more to build and expand their businesses. This increase in investment means future output, or GDP, will be higher in the United States.

Economics for Life
Compound Interest

When should you start saving for retirement?

When you graduate from college, get a job, and start earning a steady income, you'll have several choices to make. Should you buy or lease a car? Should you buy or rent a home? Should you donate money or time to charity? Whatever your decision, you should always make room in your budget for savings.

We know that everyone has positive time preferences, so all else equal, we'd rather consume now than later. But all else is not equal. That is, a little less consumption now leads to a lot more consumption later, even under very reasonable interest rate assumptions. The return to savings is like an exponential function. This means is that the longer you save, the greater your return to savings, even at a constant interest rate. The reason is based on compounding interest, which implies that the interest you earn becomes savings which also bears interest. Let's see how this works.

Consider two people who choose alternate paths. Dirk understands the power of compound interest and chooses to start saving $100 per month when he is 25 years old. Lee has stronger time preferences and decides to wait until age 45 to start saving $100 per month. If both Dirk and Lee work until they are 65 years old, Dirk saves for forty years and Lee saves for twenty.

You might guess that Dirk will end up with twice as much in his retirement account, since he saved twice as long. But you'd be wrong. It turns out that Lee's retirement savings will multiply to $53,988. That's not too bad, considering Lee saved just $100 per month over 20 years, or 240 months – the interest payments certainly helped. But what about Dirk? Dirk's retirement savings multiply to $281,767! That's more than five times the size of Lee's and Dirk only made twice as many payments.

What did we assume to get these returns? We assumed a 7% interest rate, which is the long run historical real rate of return on a diversified stock portfolio. But any interest rate illustrates the key point here: compound interest increases the value of your savings exponentially. So even with very strong time preferences, it makes sense to save early.

The graph illustrates the returns to saving $100 per month at an average annual return of 7% until retirement. The only difference is when you start saving. Notice that as you move along the horizontal axis, for each additional five years' worth of savings, the amount by which savings grows increases.

Dirk!

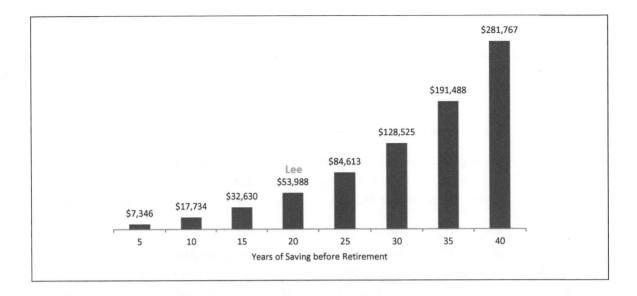

Conclusion

We began this chapter with the misconception that interest rates are set by the government. To be sure, the government influences interest rates, a topic we'll discuss further in Chapter 16. But interest rates are set in the market, through the interaction of supply and demand. Going forward, this chapter provides the foundation we need to discuss interest rates and financial market further.

In macroeconomics few topics are more important than investment. And investment is the result of equilibrium in the market for loanable funds. Savers supply the loans; borrowers are investors who demand the loans. Equilibrium determines the quantity of investment and the interest rate in an economy.

In the next chapter, we extend our analysis of the market for loanable funds by looking at other methods for borrowing and lending. These include stocks and bonds and other financial securities.

BIG QUESTIONS

What is the loanable funds market?

- The loanable funds market connects savers with borrowers.
- Savers are suppliers of loanable funds and they earn interest as a reward for saving.
- Borrowers are the buyers of loanable funds and they pay interest as the cost of borrowing.

What factors shift the supply of loanable funds?

- Changes in income and wealth shift the supply of loanable funds.
- Changes in time preferences also affect the supply of loanable funds.
- Consumption smoothing is the last factor that shifts loanable funds supply.

What factors shift the demand for loanable funds?

- Capital productivity is the main determinant of the demand for loanable funds.
- Investor confidence also affects the demand for loanable funds.

How do we apply the loanable funds market model?

- We can use the loanable funds market model to examine real world changes in both supply and demand for loanable funds.
- The loanable funds model also clarifies the important implication that every dollar borrowed requires a dollar saved.

Concepts You Should Know

Loanable funds market
Interest rate
Time preferences
Investor confidence

Questions for Review

1. Discuss the importance of the loanable funds market to basic GDP in a macroeconomy.

2. All else equal, what does a lower interest rate mean for firms? What does a lower interest rate mean for savers?

3. Consider two alternatives to prepare for retirement: (i) saving in a bank where you earn interest, and (ii) buying fine art that rises in value over time. Each grows your retirement account over time.

     a. If the rates of return on fine art purchases fall, how would you expect the allocation of retirement funds to change across the macroeconomy?

     b. If the national savings rate is based only on the first option (savings in banks), then what happens to the national savings rate when the allocation of retirement funds shifts as you describe in part (a)?

4. List the factors that affect the supply side of the loanable funds market. Which factor(s) determine the slope of the supply curve? Which factor(s) affect the level of the curve?

5. List the factors that affect the demand side of the loanable funds market. Which factor(s) determine the slope of the demand curve? Which factor(s) impact the level of the curve?

6. Explain why inflation has a positive effect on nominal interest rates.

Study Problems

1. Of the groups below, which do you think has the strongest time preferences? Be sure to give a brief explanation for each group.

(a) College student
(b) Empty nesters
(c) A toddler
(d) An inmate with five more years until parole.

2. Assume foreigners decide to increase savings in the United States by buying stocks and bonds.

       (a) What happens to the interest rate in the United States? What happens to the equilibrium level of investment in the United States? Explain your answers.
       (b) In the long run, how does increased foreign savings affect the levels of capital and income growth in the United States?

3. Many interest rates in the United States recently fell. Which of the following could have been the cause?

(a) Increase in demand for loanable funds.
(b) Decrease in demand for loanable funds.
(c) Increase in supply of loanable funds.
(d) Decrease in supply of loanable funds.

4. Use the Fisher equation to fill in the blanks in the following table:

Inflation Rate	Real Interest Rate	Nominal Interest Rate
_____	2%	7%
_____	0%	7%
2%	_____	6%
9%	_____	6%
2%	2%	_____
10%	2%	_____

Solved Problems

1. Consider two hypothetical nations: Nittany Island and Wahooland. Initially, these nations are identical in every way. In particular, they are the same with regard to population size and age, income and wealth, and time preferences. In addition, they have the same interest rates, saving, and investment.
       a. Suddenly, in the year 2015, the interest rate in Wahooland rises. After some investigating, economists determine that nothing has happened to supply of loanable funds. Therefore, what are the possible reasons for this rise in interest rates in Wahooland?

Answer: If supply does not change, this must be due to a change in demand. If rates went up, then demand must have increased. An increase in the demand for loanable funds occurs from one or both of the following:

- Increase in the productivity of capital.
- Increase in investor confidence.

b. Given your answer to part a what can you say about the level of investment in Wahooland relative to Nittany Island in 2015? What can you say about future income levels in Wahooland versus Nittany Island.

Answer: Investment will be higher in Wahooland than Nittany. Future GDP will be higher in Wahooland, and this means income will be higher.

c. Often, we think of lower interest rates as always preferable to higher interest rates. What has this question taught us about that idea?

Answer: Higher interest rates could be caused by very productive capital. Thus, an innovative nation that tends to have new productive ideas and then high capital productivity might also have higher interest rates. These interest rates can indicate very high returns to capital investment, and this is certainly not bad for an economy.

2. Some people have proposed an increase in retirement ages for Americans. Consider the effects of this and only this new policy.
    a. Show how this change would affect supply and demand in the market for loanable funds.

Answer: The key is to examine how this policy change affects savings through people's preferences for consumption smoothing. If Americans are working longer, then this delays the dissaving period in their life and increases savings. So supply increases (shifts outward). Demand does not change.

b. How does this change affect the equilibrium interest rate and investment?

Answer: The interest rate falls and investment increases.

c. In the long run, how will this affect real GDP in the United States?

Answer: Real GDP will be greater, all else equal, due to the increase in investment. Basically, the new savings becomes investment in capital. Thus, in the future, there are more tools for production in the United States and output will be higher.

Chapter 11

Financial Markets and Securities

Misconception: Borrowing from foreign countries is harmful.

Many people are concerned that foreign nations own significant amounts of U.S. national debt. China, in particular owns more U.S. debt than any other foreign nation. The worry is that since we owe them money, they can control us. But think of this in terms of loanable funds. From this perspective, the Chinese are lenders who are send their savings into the United States. Chinese savings keep our interest rates lower than they would otherwise be. This helps both our government and private firms in the United States.

      The financial institutions that we discuss in this chapter are necessary for economic growth and development. These include stocks, bonds, home mortgages and other financial instruments. Even though we are talking about finance topics, macroeconomics is the common thread that is woven through these topics – each of these helps you gain a more detailed understanding of the factors that impact the overall economy. Economic growth can happen only when financial markets function efficiently. When there are problems in financial markets, economic growth is impossible.

Big Questions:

- **How do financial markets help the economy?**
- **What are the key financial tools for the macroeconomy?**

How do financial markets help the economy?

In financial markets, borrowers and lenders come together. The buyers in financial markets are firms and governments in search of funds to undertake their daily operations. The sellers are savers looking for opportunities to earn a return on their savings. In Chapter 10, we introduced the loanable funds market as a way of thinking about financial markets through the lens of supply and demand. In this chapter, we present an *institutional* view of financial markets. That is, we consider what types of firms operate in the middle of financial markets, and what types of tools they use to facilitate the exchanges between savers and borrowers.

> **Financial intermediaries** are firms that help channel funds from savers to borrowers.

      The major players in the middle of financial markets are called *financial intermediaries*. **Financial intermediaries** are firms that help channel funds from savers to borrowers. *Banks* are one example of a financial intermediary. **Banks** are private firms that accept deposits and extend loans. Banks and other financial

> **Banks** are private firms that accept deposits and extend loans.

intermediaries are important for the macroeconomy because they are at the center of financial markets – they help connect borrowers with savers.

Direct and Indirect Financing

When firms seek funding to pay for resources for production, they go to the loanable funds market. There are two different paths through the loanable funds market: *indirect* and *direct finance*. **Indirect finance** occurs when savers lend funds to financial intermediaries that then loan funds to borrowers. Savers are indirectly financing the investments of firms.

Indirect finance occurs when savers deposit funds into banks that then loan these to borrowers

Direct finance occurs when borrowers go directly to savers for funds. If you want a loan to start or expand a small business, you might go to a bank. But large established firms can skip financial intermediaries and go directly to the lenders when they need funds.

Figure 11.1 shows the two alternate routes through the loanable funds market. The top half illustrates indirect finance, in which banks and other financial intermediaries act to facilitate the exchanges between lenders and borrowers. If you have a savings or checking account at a bank, you participate in the loanable funds market as a lender. Banks then package the savings of many people together to extend loans. The bottom half of Figure 11.1 illustrates direct finance, where borrowers bypass financial intermediaries and go directly to lenders for funds.

...but big businesses can use direct finance.

Direct finance occurs when borrowers go directly to savers for their funds.

Figure 11.1
Direct versus Indirect Finance

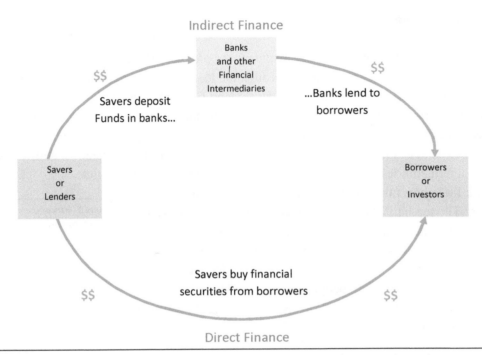

Funds make their way through the loanable funds market through two distinct paths. Indirect finance occurs when savers and borrowers utilize banks or other financial intermediaries. Alternatively, direct finance occurs when borrowers go directly to savers for their funds.

To undertake direct finance, firms need a contract that specifies the terms and conditions of the loan. These contracts usually take the form of a *security*. A **security** is a tradable contract that entitles its owner to certain rights. For example, a **bond** is a security that represents a debt to be paid. If you own a bond, it means that somebody owes you money—it is a formal IOU. Bonds are a tool of direct finance because they allow borrowers to go directly to savers for funds. If a firm sells a bond to an individual, it is borrowing funds that will be repaid at a later date. For example, in 2012, Target Corporation had $14.4 billion in bonds outstanding. This means the Target Corporation owed $14.4 billion to the owners of those bonds.

> A **security** is a tradable contract that entitles its owner to certain rights.

> A **bond** is a security that represents a debt to be paid.

The Importance of Financial Markets

Financial markets play a vital role in the macroeconomy. Macroeconomic growth is based on production of GDP across the economy. This production comes from individual firms like cupcake shops, department stores, computer producers and airplane manufacturers. Firms need funding to build and buy the resources they use to produce their goods and services. These funds come from financial markets. Sound financial markets are therefore a vital component of a growing economy.

Consider what happens when financial markets break down. In 2007, several U.S. financial institutions began faltering. In September of 2008, Lehman Brothers, a financial intermediary with over $600 billion in assets, actually went bankrupt. These financial difficulties foreshadowed the deep recession that lasted through July 2009.

Economics in the Real World:
Why bail out the big rich banks?

After the Lehman Brothers bankruptcy, it appeared there might be a domino effect that would lead to the collapse of many large banks. To avoid this fate, the U.S. government implemented the troubled asset relief program—which came to be known as TARP—in October 2008. The TARP program allocated $700 billion to help keep banks from failing. The money was used to aid banks that had made bad loans.

This program was very controversial from the beginning. On the one hand, the government was clearly bailing out big banks after these firms had made poor business decisions. It didn't seem right for the government to use taxpayer funds to help banks that seemed to contribute to the recession, especially since people were still struggling.

But we can also make an argument in favor of the TARP program. Think of financial intermediaries as the bridge to future GDP. When the bridge is strong and safe, savers can lend to borrowers and then firms can invest in future GDP. But if the bridge collapses, output grinds to a halt. If firms aren't producing, they certainly don't need workers. GDP falls and unemployment rises. That's how important the bridge is.

Economists are not in complete agreement about the need for the TARP program -- some still feel that it was misguided. But economists do agree on the necessity of healthy financial institutions.

Practice What You Know
Direct versus indirect finance

Which is it?

Your friend Krista wants to open a cupcake shop. She needs to buy many resources before she can sell cupcakes and earn revenue. She is uncertain as to whether she should use direct or indirect financing.

Question: For each of the following alternatives, determine whether the financing is considered direct or indirect.

A. Krista borrows money from a friend.
B. Krista takes a loan from her small local bank.
C. Krista arranges a loan from a large national bank.
D. Krista issues bonds and sells them to the people in her neighborhood.

Answers:

A. This is direct finance, as the borrower goes directly to the lender without the aid of a financial intermediary.
B. This is indirect finance; the bank makes the loan to Krista from the funds of various savers.
C. This is indirect finance; the size of the bank does not matter.
D. This is direct finance, as Krista goes directly to the lenders. It doesn't matter if the bonds are sold to people she happens to know.

What are the key financial tools for the macroeconomy?

In this section, we begin exploring the many tools used in financial markets to help fund investment. We focus on tools that matter for the macroeconomy, including bonds, stocks, Treasury securities, home mortgages, and private-sector securities created by the process of securitization. We start with bonds.

Bonds

Firms can issue several types of securities to raise funds, but we can view them all as variations of a basic corporate bond.

Let's say your friend Kara wants to open a new website design business. But first Kara needs a loan to buy computers and software. Maybe Kara goes to a bank for a loan, but it turns her away since her company is new and viewed as very risky. So Kara comes to you, and asks for a one-year loan. You know Kara well, so you agree to loan her some of your personal funds with the understanding that she will repay the funds plus interest exactly one year later.

To formalize your agreement, you decide to draw up an IOU contract like the one presented in Figure 11.2. This is the contract you sign with your friend, Kara Alexis. When you "buy" this contract from Kara, you are lending her funds with the promise that she'll pay you $10,000 in one year. This contract is essentially the same as a corporate or government bond, and it serves the same purpose. This is an example of direct finance, with the borrower going directly to the lender.

Figure11.2
A Basic Bond Security

I, <u>Kara Alexis</u>, owe you <u>$10,000.</u>

I will pay you on <u>February 20, 2014.</u>

Today's Date: February 20, 2013

Kara Alexis

A simple IOU contract between two friends is like a bond.

It specifies:

1. The name of the borrower - Kara Alexis.
2. The repayment date - February 20, 2014.
3. The amount due at repayment - $10,000.

Like any bond, your contract contains three important pieces of information: the name of the borrower, the repayment date, and the amount due at repayment. In this example, the name of the borrower is Kara Alexis; the repayment date is February 20, 2014. The date on which the loan repayment is due is known as the **maturity date**. Finally, every bond contract also specifies the *face value* or *par value* of the bond. The **face value (p_m),** or **par value** of the bond is the value of the bond at maturity—the amount due at repayment. For notation purposes, we'll call the face value p_m, since it is the price or value of the bond at maturity.

> **The maturity date** of a bond is the date the loan repayment is due..

> **Face value or par value** (p_m) of a bond is the value of the bond at maturity—the amount due at repayment

Perhaps you noticed that we gave the face value of the bond, but not the amount of the initial loan. In fact, you and Kara must come to an agreement about how much you will loan her. But with a bond agreement, the face value is typically set at a round number like $10,000. When you and Kara settle on the initial loan amount, you are agreeing to the dollar price of the bond (p). The price of the bond is the original dollar amount of the loan. For example, if you agree on a price of $8,000 for Kara's bond, that is the amount you loan her. From your perspective, you loan her $8,000 today for the promise that she'll pay you $10,000 in one year. From Kara's perspective, she now has $8,000 she can use to buy computers and software for her desktop publishing business, and she can begin producing GDP. But in one year she has to pay repay the $10,000.

That's how a basic bond security works. Many bonds also include *coupons* which specify periodic interest payments to the bond owner. That distinction is not important for our purposes, so we focus on bonds that entail a single payment when the bond matures.

We now build on this by discussing how interest rates relate to bond prices and how default risk affects the price of a bond.

The Bond Dollar Price and Interest Rate

In the discussion above, we described Kara's bond in dollar prices. But loan prices are generally quoted in interest rates. Therefore, we need to consider how the dollar price (p) is related to the interest rate (R) of a bond.   To determine the interest rate on this bond, we have to find the rate of return on the dollars that are loaned. For example, you buy Kara's bond for $8,000 and one year later, the bond is worth $10,000. In percentage terms the value of the bond increased by 25 percent. Thus, the rate of return, or interest rate, is computed as a growth rate, where the price of the bond is growing from its initial value (p$_0$) :

$$\text{interest rate} = R = \frac{\text{face value} - \text{initial price}}{\text{initial price}} = \frac{p_m - p_0}{p_0}. \quad (11.1)$$

If the price of the bond is $8,000, the interest rate is computed as:

$$R = \frac{p_m - p_0}{p_0} = \frac{\$10,000 - \$8,000}{\$8,000} = 25\%.$$

We used growth rates when we discussed GDP growth and inflation. Here, the interest rate is computed as a growth rate; it is the rate of growth of the original funds invested.

With bonds, the face value is fixed – it is printed on the front of the bond. Thus, *the dollar price of a bond determines the bond's interest rate.* If you know the dollar price of a given bond, you can determine the interest rate. Table 11.1 gives several alternative prices for the $10,000 bond.

Table 11.1
Dollar Price and interest rate for a $10,000 One-Year Bond

Dollar Price (p_0)	Interest Rate (R)
$9,000	11%
$8,000	25%
$7,500	33%
$5,000	100%

The face value (p_m) of a bond is fixed. Therefore, the price of the bond (p_0) determines the interest rate, since:

$$R = \frac{face\ value - price}{price} = \frac{p_m - p_0}{p_0}$$

Notice that the lower the price, the higher the interest rate, since it takes fewer dollars to earn $10,000 one year later.

Each price implies a different interest rate. For example, if Kara sells you the $10,000 bond for only $7,500, the interest rate rises to 33%. This is much better for you, since you buy the bond for $7,500 and are repaid that amount plus $2,500 in interest, only one year later. But this is worse for Kara because she is getting just $7,500 this year, with the same promise to repay $10,000 next year.

Notice that as the price of the bond lowers, the interest rate on the bond rises. If the bond price drops to $5,000, the interest rate climbs to 100%. This relationship holds by definition: *the dollar price and interest rate of a bond have an inverse relationship.*

In Chapter 10 we saw that the interest rate on a loan is the cost of borrowing and the reward for saving. Higher interest rates (lower dollar prices) hurt borrowers and help lenders. As a lender, you want to buy bonds for the lowest price possible because you want the highest possible interest rate on your savings. The borrower wants to sell her bonds for the highest price possible, so she can pay the lowest possible interest rate.

A primary factor in determining the interest rate on bonds is the default risk of the borrower, a topic to which we now turn.

Default Risk

Some financial transactions are very complex and potentially lead to many different outcomes. But bonds are not complex. If the bond owner holds the bond until maturity, there are only two possible outcomes: the borrower pays the maturity value of the bond, or the borrower defaults on the loan. These possibilities are illustrated in Figure 11.3. For the bond owner then, the risk of default is the primary concern. **Default risk** is the risk that the borrower will not pay the face value of the bond on the maturity date.

> **Default risk** is the risk that the borrower will not pay off the loan.

Figure 11.3
Two possible outcomes with a bond

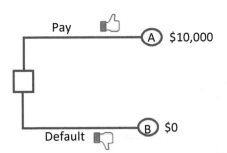

Pay   (A) $10,000

Default   (B) $0

> With a bond, both the maturity date and the face value are certain. Thus, there are only two possible outcomes if a bond owner holds the bond until maturity: either the borrower will pay the face value or she will default. Because there are only these two outcomes, default risk is the primary concern of a bond owner.

All else equal, the greater the default risk, the lower the price of a bond. Consider Kara's bond that she is selling to finance her startup website company. If you really trust Kara and believe her business will succeed, you might buy her $10,000 bond for $9,500. At this price she promises to pay you about 5.25% interest for the use of your funds for a year. On the other hand, if you are skeptical about either Kara's integrity or the prospects for her business success, you may be willing to pay only $8,000 for the bond. At this price she will pay 25% interest for the loan instead. This illustrates an important bond price principle: *bond interest rates rise with default risk.*

Consider bonds offered by the Target Corporation. Target is a big company with many capital investments. As we said previously, the Target Corporation had $14.4 billion of bonds outstanding in 2012. This means that there is a significant market for Target bonds. Let's imagine a hypothetical supply and demand for one-year $100,000 Target bonds, illustrated in Figure 11.4. Initially, with the demand curve at D and supply at S, the equilibrium price is $98,000.

Figure 11.4

How Increased Default Risk Affects the Market for $100,000 Target Bonds

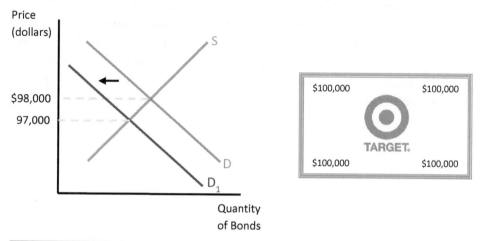

The initial price in the market for Target bonds is $98,000. But an increase in default risk reduces the demand for Target bonds, resulting in a lower price and higher interest rate. This drives up the borrowing costs for Target.

Now, let's assume something negative happens to the future prospects of Target business. Perhaps Wal-Mart continues to expand and attract customers away from Target. This news reduces the probability that Target will pay off its bonds as they mature; it increases Target's default risk. As such, the demand for Target bonds declines, from D to D_1. As demand declines, the market price of IBM bonds falls from $98,000 to $97,000, which means the interest rate rises. As a result, increases in default risk reduce the price firms can charge for their bonds and increases their interest rates.

Bond Ratings

Default risk is important to bond holders and it helps determine the price of the bond. But typical individuals have difficulty judging the default risk of any one company, let alone the thousands of firms that sell bonds in a developed economy. To contend with this problem, private rating agencies evaluate and then grade the default risk of borrowing entities. They give a grade that reflects the likelihood of default. Three ratings agencies are particularly prominent: Moody's, Standard and Poor's, and Fitch's. The ratings systems are similar for all three firms, so we'll choose Standard and Poor's (S & P) for explanatory purposes.

The most stable firms, those most likely to pay their debts, are given a rating of AAA. In the recent past, firms like Microsoft, Johnson and Johnson, and Bank of America have achieved AAA ratings. A high rating is desirable because it directly translates into higher prices and lower interest rates on the firm's bonds. The firm's operating costs are directly affected by its bond rating, since it is the cost of a key resource for its production. If Microsoft's bond rating falls from AAA to AA, this increases their cost in the same way that its costs would rise if its employees negotiated higher wages.

Table 11.2 shows selected bond ratings from 2011. As we move down the table, the grade falls and default risk increases. All grades below medium (BB and lower) are called *non-investment grade*. They are also known as *junk bonds.* Non-investment grade bonds have lower ratings, and these lower ratings mean higher interest rates for the borrowing firms, like General Motors and Delta Airlines. In an attempt to spin this positively, bond salesmen prefer to call these bonds *high yield securities*, because the higher interest rates mean higher yields to lenders when the firms do not default.

Table 11.2
Sample Bond Ratings

Moody's	S&P	Grade	Examples
Aaa	AAA	Prime	Microsoft, Johnson & Johnson, Bank of America, University of Virginia, Harvard University
Aa	AA	High	Berkshire Hathaway, Toyota, Wal-Mart, Intel, Virginia Tech, University of North Carolina, Duke University
A	A	Upper Medium	Coca Cola, AT&T, McDonalds, Target, Dell, Washington Post, Disney, Nike, Hewlett-Packard
Baa	BBB	Lower Medium	Home Depot, Anheuser-Busch, Time Warner, Nordstrom, Molson-Coors, Nissan
Ba	BB	Non Investment or Speculative	Sprint-Nextel, Best Buy, Republic of Turkey
B	B	Highly Speculative	Dillards, Delta Airlines, NY Times, General Motors, Ford, Goodyear
Caa	CCC	Extremely Speculative	Eastman Kodak, Jetblue, E-Trade
	D	In Default	

Stocks

Stock securities offer another option for firms that need funding to finance their production of output. **Stocks** are ownership shares in a firm. From the firm's point of view, stocks offer a new financing avenue, but they also involve ceding ownership of the firm. In this important sense, stocks are very different from bank loans or bonds: owners of stock securities are actual owners of the firm. When a firm sells bonds, it does not cede direct control of the firm to new owners.

Stocks are ownership shares in a firm.

Why would a firm sell stocks instead of bonds? Bond financing leaves the firm with a lot of bills that must be paid. When IBM sells $10 million worth of ten year bonds, the company takes on the obligation to pay $10 million in ten years. If the firm cannot pay these bills, the owners may need to declare bankruptcy and lose the firm altogether. With stocks, the owners can sell shares of the firm to others and move forward without the burden of debt.

From the lender's perspective, stock ownership is also different from bond ownership. Since stock owners (share-holders) are owners of the firm, they have some influence in the operations of the firm. A shareholder who owns more than 50% of the shares of the firm is the majority share-holder and controls more than 50% of the ownership votes. A majority shareholder can determine the direction of the company, an influence not available to bond holders.

Secondary Markets

Most people who purchase stock and bonds use brokers who buy them in *secondary markets*. **Secondary markets** are markets in which securities are traded after their first sale. Secondary markets are like used car markets, but the "used" assets are securities. There's nothing wrong with a used security, it just means you are not buying the security directly from the firm whose

> **Secondary markets** are markets in which securities are traded after their first sale.

name is on it. You will probably recognize that names of some important secondary stock markets. They include the New York Stock Exchange (NYSE), and the NASDAQ (National Association of Securities Dealers Automated Quotations).

The existence of a secondary market for a given security will increase the demand for that security. Consider the difference between a Target Corp. bond and the hypothetical bond you bought from Kara Alexis to help fund her website publishing company. Whoever buys the Target bond can sell it with a quick call to a broker or the click of a mouse. The ease of resale is valuable and therefore worth a higher price. But when you buy Kara's bond you have to hold on to it until you can personally locate another buyer. This greatly limits demands for bonds that cannot be re-sold in secondary markets, which lowers the price (raises the interest rate).

Figure 11.5 illustrates the impact that secondary markets have on security prices. If a secondary market exists for a security, the demand for the security increases and this increases the price of the security, all else equal. For the firm, this is helpful as it lowers the interest rate they pay on their bonds and therefore, their cost of borrowing.

Figure 11.5
The Effect of Secondary Markets

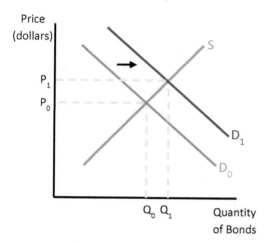

The existence of secondary markets increases the demand for securities. When demand increases, the price rises and interest rate falls. Secondary markets allow firms to borrow at lower interest rates

Secondary markets are a valuable institution of market economies because they lower the costs of borrowing. This is true for any asset. For example, let's say you are considering buying a particular home. Your real estate agent tells you the price is very reasonable, but there is one unusual stipulation: you can never sell the home once you buy it. Of course, this is not a realistic stipulation, but think about how that would affect your willingness to buy the home. The purchase would be more risky, and no buyer would pay as much for that home as for one that could be resold. Secondary markets, by offering future sale opportunities for securities, increase demand for them.

Economics in the Media:
Direct Finance

Boiler Room

This movie starts off as a potential success story for the main character, Seth Davis, who is played by Giovanni Ribisi. Davis is a college dropout who manages to land a job with an investment firm called J.T. Marlin. Davis's job at Marlin is to sell securities. Davis is right in the middle of direct finance. Firms come to Marlin so Davis can sell their securities to lenders.

Unfortunately, it turns out that Marlin is selling securities for firms that don't actually exist. Marlin is basically just stealing from lenders, rather than channeling the funds to actual firms. When Davis figures this out, the action in the movie really heats up.

Economics in the Real World:
Stock Market Indexes: Dow Jones versus S & P

Media reports about the stock market tend to focus on stock price indexes like the Dow Jones Industrial Average and the S & P 500. Just as the CPI tracks general consumer prices, these stock market indexes track overall stock prices. Recall that the CPI is a weighted average of all consumer prices, where the weights are determined by the portion of the typical consumer budget spent on the item. When the CPI rises, it indicates a corresponding rise in the general level of consumer prices. Similarly, when the stock indexes rise and fall, it indicates a corresponding rise and fall in the general level of stock prices.

The best known stock index is the Dow Jones Industrial Average (the Dow). When the Dow was first published in 1884 it tracked 12 companies. Today the Dow tracks 30 companies selected by the editors of *The Wall Street Journal*. The editors maintain the index so that it represents companies in all important sectors in the economy. To do this, the companies in the Dow must occasionally be changed. For example, when the technology sector came to the forefront in the late 90's, Intel and Microsoft were added.

One of the advantages of the Dow is that we have historical data all the way back to May 26, 1896. At that time, the calculation was very simple; an investor added the price of all 12 stocks and divided the sum by 12 to compute a simple average. Today, the Dow uses thirty stock prices in the average, but it is essentially computed in the same way. This means the Dow tracks only the price of the stock, not the overall value of a company or the relative values of the companies in the stock market.

The S&P 500 index weights the stock prices by the *market value* of the companies it tracks. The market value is the total number of stock shares multiplied by the price per share. Under a market value weighted index, the stock prices of large companies have a greater impact than smaller companies. For instance, Apple (with a market value of $542B in 2012) weighs much more heavily than Facebook (with a market value of $66B in 2012). There is another difference between the S&P 500 and the Dow Jones index: while the Dow tracks only 30 companies, the S & P 500 tracks 500 companies, a much broader representation of the stock market.

In many respects, the Dow is an artifact of simpler times, when computing a broad-based index was time-intensive. Today spreadsheets can crunch all the stock price data in milliseconds. Nevertheless, the Dow has been a very reliable measure of market performance and it also provides a continuous record of historical information that cannot be replaced by more recent indexes. In addition, people are accustomed to the Dow, and its simplicity makes is easy to understand and follow.

Treasury Securities

> **Treasury securities** are the bonds sold by the U.S. government to pay for the national debt.

We have considered firms as the major borrowing entity in an economy. But governments are significant borrowers too. For example, the U.S. federal government has about $16 trillion worth of debt – that's about $50,000 per citizen. All of this borrowing takes place through bond sales. The U.S. government bonds are called Treasury securities. **Treasury securities** are the bonds sold by the U.S. government to pay for the national debt.

Treasury securities are sold through auctions to large financial firms. The auction price determines the interest rate. After a Treasury security is sold the first time, anyone can buy it in the large and active secondary market for U.S. Treasury securities.

U.S. Treasury securities are generally considered less risky than any other bond, because nobody expects the U.S. government to default on its debts. There are times, in the midst of heated political debate, that politicians threaten actions that could lead to default. But this is generally considered just political rhetoric. In fact, global financial turmoil would certainly follow a debt default by the U.S. government.

Because Treasury bonds are safe, firms and governments from all over the world buy Treasury securities as a way to limit risk. In 2011, approximately $4.5 trillion (about 32%) of U.S. federal debt was held by foreigners. Figure 11.6 shows the breakdown of foreign ownership of U.S. Treasury securities.

Figure 11.6
Major Foreign holders of U.S. Treasury Securities, 2011, billions of dollars

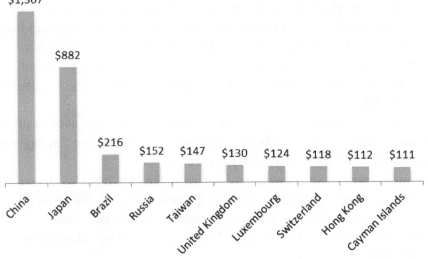

Source: U.S. Treasury.

Of the $16 trillion of U.S. government debt, approximately 32 percent is held by foreigners. China alone owns $1.3 billion of our national debt, but this represents less than 9% of the total outstanding.

As we noted in the opening misconception of this chapter, many people are concerned that nations like China will exert undue influence on the U.S. government if we owe them money. But this perspective misses a key point. Foreign savings keep interest rates lower in the United States than they would otherwise be. This means firms and governments can undertake their activities at lower costs. Lower interest rates mean more investment and greater future GDP. That is a clear benefit of foreign investment in the United States.

Treasury securities play many roles in the macroeconomy. They are used when the government alters the supply of money in the economy, which we discuss in Chapter 18. In addition, if the government decides to increase spending without raising taxes, the additional spending must paid for by borrowing, or selling bonds. We cover this role of Treasury securities in Chapter 16.

Home Mortgages

Another important borrowing tool in the United States is the home mortgage loan. Individuals use mortgage loans to pay for homes. The most common mortgage loan lasts thirty years from inception and is paid off with 360 monthly payments. These mortgages are really just variation on the basic bond security we have described in the chapter. A family wants to buy a home, and so they take a mortgage loan which is a contract that entails their willingness to repay the loan over several years, just like a firm signing a bond contract.

The macroeconomic significance of home mortgages has grown over time, as more and more people own homes. Figure 11.7 shows the growth in the U.S. mortgage market over the past thirty years. The graph plots the total size of the U.S. mortgage market, in real dollars. The home mortgage market in the United States expanded greatly leading up to the recession in 2008. In 1982, there was about $2.2 trillion dollars of home mortgages in the United States. By 2008, the market had expanded to over $11 trillion.

Figure 11.7

Total Size of U.S. Mortgage Market, 1980-2011, in billions of 2010 dollars

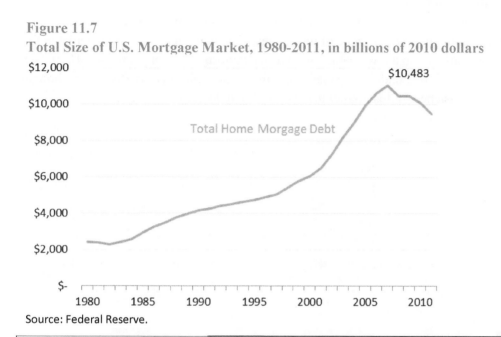

Source: Federal Reserve.

The home mortgage market in the United States expanded greatly leading up to the recession in 2008. In 1982, there was about $2.2 trillion dollars' worth of home mortgages in the United States. But by 2008, this expanded to over $11 trillion.

Securitization

Bonds, stocks, mortgages, and other financial securities channel funds from savers to borrowers. Opportunities for both firms and individuals expand when credit is available. In addition, lower borrowing costs certainly help borrowers. When interest rates are lower, investment opportunities expand for everything from factories to roads to homes to education. And, as we noted above, secondary markets reduce borrowing costs. For this reason, there are incentives to create new markets for all varieties of loan agreements. These new markets make it easier and cheaper for firms to borrow to fund investment. And the lower the investment costs, the more GDP we have in the future.

Take two common personal loans: home mortgages and student loans. The United States has secondary markets where home mortgages and student loans are bought and sold daily. This lowers interest rates on home and education loans which directly benefits homeowners and students. But these markets would not exist if the individual personal loans hadn't been *securitized*. **Securitization** is the creation of a new security as a combination of other securities.

> **Securitization** is the creation of a security as a combination of other securities.

Figure 11.8 illustrates how mortgage-backed securities are created. Each mortgage-backed security is a combination or bundle of mortgages. The new security is then available for resale in secondary markets. In a few years, you may use a mortgage to buy a home. There is a chance your mortgage will be bundled together with others into a big security that can be bought and sold. The mere existence of this market means you'll pay lower interest rates.

Figure 11.8
Securitization

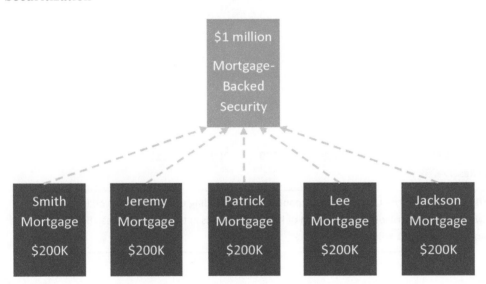

Securitization is the creation of a new security by combining otherwise separate loan agreements. For example, a $1 million mortgage-backed security is created by buying five separate $200,000 mortgages and then selling them together as a bundle.

Securitization lowers interest rates for borrowers. It also offers new opportunities for lenders. For example, people from all over the globe can now buy securities tied to the U.S. mortgage market. But this also means that lenders need to correctly evaluate the risk associated with these newly created securities. When the U.S. home mortgage market began collapsing in 2007, the negative reverberations were felt around the world. For example, because Icelandic banks owned a large number of securities tied to the U.S. home mortgage market, both the economy and government of Iceland collapsed in 2008 and 2009.

Practice What You Know
The Effects of Foreign Investment

What if we limit foreign ownership of our national debt?

Imagine that a new law significantly limits foreign ownership of U.S. Treasury bonds.

Question: Graph the market for Treasury bonds and show how the new law affects demand.

Answer: Demand declines since foreign demand is limited by the new law.

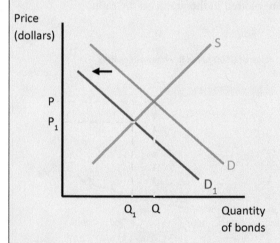

Question: What would happen to Treasury bond prices?

Answer: The price of Treasury bonds declines. When demand falls, the new equilibrium price is lower.

Question: What would happen to interest rates on Treasury bonds?

Answer: The interest rates on Treasury bonds would increase since dollar price and the interest rate move in opposite directions. A lower price means the government sells each bond for fewer dollars and so they are paying higher interest to the bond owner.

In the end, restrictions on foreign investment lead to higher domestic interest rates.

Economics for Life:

Long-run returns for stocks versus bonds

In this chapter, we focus on the importance of stocks and bonds for financing the activities of firms and governments. But you may be wondering which of these is the best use of your own personal savings.

Let's begin by looking at the historical returns for stocks versus bonds. The histogram below shows that, from 1960 to 2011, the average inflation-adjusted return for long-term Treasury bonds, was 3.18%. But over the same period, stocks yielded 6.67 percent. Thus, the return to stocks was more than twice the return to bonds.

But perhaps this doesn't seem like a huge difference to you. After all, 3% and 6% both seem small. Think of it this way: what if your grandparents had put $100 into both stocks and bonds in 1960. After adjusting for inflation, by 2011, your savings in bonds would have yielded $2,735.63, but the $100 in stocks would have return $10,027.78. These alternatives are plotted in the graph on the right.

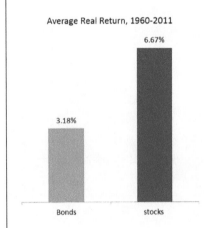

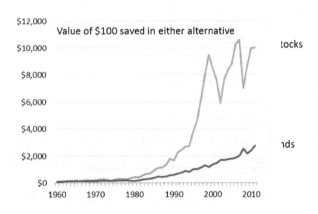

To be sure, stocks are riskier. Just look at how the value of your savings fluctuates over the years. With stocks, the value of your savings sometimes climbed or fell more than $1000 a year. With bonds, the fluctuations were much smaller. Therefore, if you are extremely averse to risk, you might choose bonds. But in the long run, your risk aversion will cost you dearly.

Conclusion

We began this chapter with a misconception that foreign ownership of the national debt is harmful to the macroeconomy. However, we have seen that this is not the case. Funds flowing into the U.S. loanable funds market help lead to economic expansion, no matter where they originate. One of the themes throughout this chapter is the importance of savings and lending to the macroeconomy. With indirect finance, banks and financial intermediaries help channel funds from savers to borrowers. With direct finance, firms sell securities like stocks and bonds directly to savers. These securities allow savers to earn returns on their savings while also giving firms access to funds for investment.

In the chapters that follow, we'll see that these financial institutions play a major role in the macroeconomy.

BIG QUESTIONS

How do financial markets help the economy?

- Financial markets help channel funds to investment opportunities throughout the economy.

What are the key financial tools for the macroeconomy?

- Bonds are a basic instrument of direct finance – they provide one tool for firms and governments to finance their activities.
- Stocks are an additional source of funds for firms, but one that allows the security-holder to take an ownership share in the firm.
- Secondary markets make securities more valuable and offer more avenues for funds to flow to investors.
- Treasury securities are the bonds sold by the government to finance the national debt. They play a prominent role in macroeconomic policy.
- Home mortgages are the contracts people sign to borrow for the purchase of a home. Because the mortgage market is so large, the entire macroeconomy is affected by its condition .

Concepts You Should Know

Financial intermediaries
Banks
Indirect finance
Direct finance
Security
Bond
Maturity date.
Face value (p_m)
par value
Default risk
Secondary markets
Treasury securities

Questions for Review

1. What is the difference between direct and indirect finance. Discuss the reasons why a firm (borrower) might choose each method. Discuss the reasons why a saver might choose each.

2. Explain securitization. Discuss how securitization benefits borrowers.

3. One principle we learned in this chapter is that the dollar price and interest rate on a bond move in opposite directions. Explain why this is always the case.

4. What is the primary use of U.S. Treasury securities? Why are the interest rates on Treasury securities so low? If people were worried about the U.S. defaulting on the national debt, what would you expect to happen to interest rates on U.S. Treasury securities? Why?

5. From a firm's perspective, why might you prefer to finance your investments with bonds rather than stocks? Alternatively, why might stocks be preferred to bonds?

Study Problems

1. Toyota bonds are currently rated AAA, and Ford bonds are rated CCC. Suppose the price of a $1000 one-year Toyota bond is $970.

   a. What is the rate of return on the one-year Toyota bond?
   b. The price of a $1000 one-year Ford Bond must be:

   i. Less than $970
   ii. Greater than $970
   iii. $970
   iv. Insufficient information to answer this question.

   c. The rate of return of a $1000 one-year Ford Bond must be:

   i. Less than the return on the Toyota bond.
   ii. Greater than the return on the Toyota bond.
   iii. The same as the return on the Toyota bond
   iv. Insufficient information to answer this question.

*2. In 2008, when the U.S. automobile industry was struggling, the price of Ford Motor Company bonds rose. In this question you need to calculate how the price rise also affects interest rate.
A. What is the interest rate on a one-year Ford bond with a face value of $5,000 and a price of $4,750?

Answer:

Using the formula:

$$R = \frac{p_m - p_0}{p_0},$$

We compute: R = ($5,000 - $4,750) ÷ $4,750 = $250 ÷ $4,750 = <u>5.26%</u>

B. What is the new interest rate on a one-year Ford bond with a face value of $1,000 and a price of $4,950?

Answer:

$$R = (\$5,000 - \$\$4,950) \div \$4,950 = \$50 \div \$4,950 = \underline{1.01\%}$$

Therefore, when the price of the bond rose $200, but this reduced the interest rate from 5.26% to just 1.01%.

*3. Let's say you own a firm that produces and sells ping pong tables. The name of your company is iPong because your tables have a plug –in jack for all Apple products. To finance a new factory, you decide to sell bonds and your bonds are rated BBB.

A. Use the axis below to draw supply and demand for your iPong bonds. Label the supply curve S_0, Demand D_0, equilibrium price P_0.

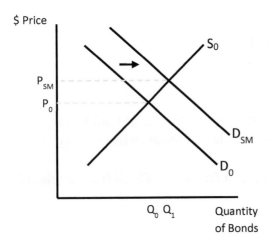

B. How is the demand for iPong bonds affected if a new secondary market agrees to buy and sell iPong bonds? Illustrate the new demand curve in the graph above and label it D_{SM}. How does this affect the price and interest rate on iPong bonds?

Answer:

If a secondary market is available to sell bonds, this increases the demand for the bonds since the bonds are more attractive to buyers. When a secondary market exists, you can always re-sell any bond you won. If there is no secondary market, you are stuck with it once you have it.

In the picture above, demand increases and price rises. This means lower interest rates for your iPong firm.

4. This question is also regarding the iPong firm from the question number 3.

A. How is demand affected if a ratings agency upgrades your bond rating to AA?
B. How does this affect the price of your bond?
C. How does this affect your cost of borrowing?

5. Use supply and demand curves to illustrate how default risk affects both the price and interest rate of a bond.

6. In this chapter, we used Target Corporation bonds to illustrate the effect of default risk on the price of a bond. In particular, when default risk rises, the demand for a bond falls and then the equilibrium price falls. In our example, the price of a $100,000 Target bond fell from $98,000 to $97,000.

A. What is the interest rate on a one year $100,000 bond that sells for $98,000?
B. What is the interest rate on a one year $100,000 bond that sells for $97,000?

Chapter 12: Economic Growth and the Wealth of Nations

Misconception: Natural resources are the key to economic prosperity.

Many people believe that natural resources like trees, oil, and farmland are the primary sources of economic growth. They believe that nations like the United States and Australia are prosperous because they have vast natural resources that can be used to produce goods and services. A variation on this idea emphasizes geography—nations with the best shipping locations and mildest climates have more prosperous economies. But what about the two Koreas? North and South Korea have the same natural resources and yet the two economies are as different as night and day. Over the course of the next two chapters, we explore what economics has to say about differences in economic growth across nations.

Striving for economic growth is not only about accumulating more wealth. Yes, economic growth brings iPads and jet-skis, but it's much more important than that. Economic growth means that more women and infants survive childbirth, more people have access to clean water and better sanitation, and people live healthier, longer, and more-educated lives.

In this chapter we begin by looking at the implications of economic growth for human welfare. We then consider the impact of an economy's resources and technology on economic growth. Finally, we discuss the key elements an economy needs to grow.

Big Questions

- Why does economic growth matter?
- How do resources and technology contribute to economic growth?
- What institutions foster economic growth?

Why does economic growth matter?

In 1900, life expectancy in the United States was 47 years. Income—adjusted for inflation—was less than $5,000 per person. About 140 of every 1,000 children died before their first birthday. Only about one third of American homes had running water. Most people lived less than a mile from their job, and almost nobody owned an automobile. Yes, this is a description of life in the United States in 1900, but this is also a description of life in many poor countries today. What happened in the United States since 1900? Economic growth.

In this section, we examine how economic growth impacts the lives of average people around the world. We also examine the historical data on economic growth and explain the mathematics of growth rates.

Some Ugly Facts

Before looking at data on growth, we need to recall how we measure economic growth. In Chapter 7, we defined economic growth as the change in real per capita GDP. We know that real per capita GDP measures the average level of income in a nation. But for most people, life is not all about the pursuit of more income. The fact remains that economic growth alleviates human misery and lengthens lives. Wealthier societies provide better living standards, which include better nutrition, educational opportunities, healthcare, freedom, and even sources of entertainment.

Let's look around the world and compare life in poor countries with life in rich countries. Table 12.1 presents human-welfare indicators for a selection of rich and poor countries. Among the poor nations are Bangladesh, Haiti, North Korea, Niger, Liberia, Tanzania, Nepal, Ethiopia and Zimbabwe. Wealthy nations include Australia, Denmark, Israel, Japan, Germany, South Korea, and the United States, among others.

Table 12.1:
Human Welfare in Poor versus Rich Nations

Life Indicators	Poor	Rich
GDP per capita, PPP (2005 international $)*	$1,095	$32,971
Infant mortality rate (per 1,000 live births)	76	5
Under-5 mortality rate (per 1,000)	118	6
Life Expectancy at Birth	57	80
Physicians (per 10,000 people)	1.8	29.3
Births attended by skilled health staff (%)	41	100
Access to improved water source (%)	64	100
Access to improved sanitation (%)	35	100
Personal computers (per 100)	1.7	70
Internet users (per 100)	2.7	74
Motor vehicles (per 1,000)	12	638
Mobile cellular subscriptions (per 100)	27	108
Literacy rate, adult male (%)	69	99
Literacy Rate, adult female (%)	55	99
Ratio of female to male secondary enrollment (%)	84	99
Ratio of female to male post-secondary enrollment (%)	64	121

Source: World Bank. Poor nations are 40 poorest; Rich nations are 31 high income OECD nations.
*GDP data is from 2010. Other indicators are from 2008 and 2009.

Consider the first group of indicators, which are related to mortality. In poor countries, 76 out of every 1000 babies die at birth or in the first year of their life, while in rich nations, the number is only 5 out of every 1000. This means infants are fifteen times more likely to die in poor nations. Those that survive one year in poor nations are about twenty times more likely to die before their fifth birthday, as indicated by the under-5 mortality rates. Overall, life expectancy in poor nations is 57 years, while in wealthy nations, it is 80 years. Just being born in a wealthy nation adds almost a quarter century to your life.

The second group of indicators in Table 12.1 helps to explain the mortality data. Rich nations have about 15 times as many doctors per person: 30 physicians per 10,000 people versus 2 per 10,000. Clean water and sanitation are available to only a fraction of people in poor nations, while these are generally available to all in rich nations. Children in poor nations die every year because they can't get water as clean as the water you get out of virtually any faucet in the United States. This leads to common ailments like tapeworm and diarrhea that, sadly, are life-threatening in poor nations. In fact, in 2010, The World Health Organization estimated that 3.6 million people die each year from water-borne diseases.

The third group of indicators lists a selection of nonessential conveniences we often take for granted. In wealthy nations, we have 70 personal computers for every 100 people; in poor nations, the number is only 1.7 per 100 people. Seventy-four people out of every 100 uses the internet in rich nations, but only 2.7 people per 100 are able to use the internet in poor nations. Rich nations have about 50 times more motor vehicles per 1,000 people, and four times as many cell phone subscriptions.

The last group of indicators in Table 12.1 tells the sad story about education. First, notice literacy rates in poor countries are significantly lower than literacy rates in wealthy countries. But there is also a significant difference in literacy rates between men and women in poor nations. Furthermore, women have less access to both secondary and post-secondary education than men in poor nations – equal access would imply an enrollment ratio of 100%. So while education opportunities are rarer for all in poor nations, women fare the worst.

The data in Table 12.1 support our contention that per capita GDP matters – not for the sake of more income per se, but because it correlates with better human conditions, which matter to everyone.

Learning from the Past

We can learn a lot about the roots of economic growth by looking at historical experiences. Until very recently, the common person's existence was devoted to subsistence, which is simply trying to find enough shelter, clothing, and nourishment to survive. As we saw in the previous section, even today many people still live on the margins of subsistence. What can history tell us about how rich nations achieved economic development? The answer to this helps clarify possible policy alternatives going forward.

We Were All Poor Once

When you look around the globe today, you see rich nations and poor nations. You can probably name many rich nations: the United States, Japan, Taiwan, and the Western European nations, among others. You might also know the very poor nations: almost all of Africa, much of Latin America, and significant parts of Asia. But the world was not always this way. If we consider the longer history of humankind, only recently did the incomes of common people rise above subsistence level. The Europe of 1750, for instance, was not noticeably richer than Europe at the time of the birth of Jesus of Nazareth.

Figure 12.1
Long-run World Per Capita Real GDP, 2010 U.S. dollars

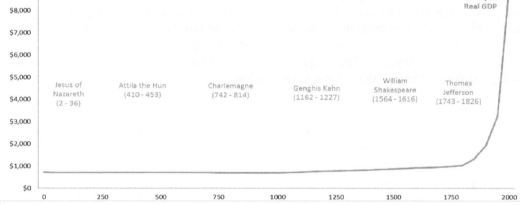

Historical accounts often focus on monarchs and other wealthy people. But for the average person, living standards across the globe didn't change considerably from the time of Jesus to the time of Thomas Jefferson. The data plotted here is per capita GDP in 2010 U.S. dollars, which is adjusted for prices across both time and place.

Consider the very long run. Angus Maddison, a noted economic historian, estimated GDP levels for many nations and for the whole world back to the year 1 A.D. Figure 12.1 plots Maddison's estimates of per capita GDP, in 2010 dollars. Clearly there was a historical break around 1800 that forever changed the path of average world living standards.

Maddison estimates that the average level of income in the world in 1350 was about $816. Given that is adjusted to 2010 prices, this would be comparable to you having an annual income of about $800. If you were given $816 to live on for an entire year, it's clear that your solitary focus would be on basic necessities like food, clothing, and shelter. Of course, there were certainly rich individuals over the course of history, but until relatively recently, the average person's life was essentially one of subsistence living. Consider Alice Toe, the Liberian girl profiled in the "Economics in the Real World" feature below. This type of life, where even meals are uncertain, was the basic experience for the average person *for nearly all of human history.*

There were global variations in income before 1700. For example, average income in Western Europe in 1600 was about $1,400, while in Latin America, it was less than $700. This means Western Europeans were twice as wealthy as Latin Americans in 1600. But average Europeans were still very poor!

The Industrial Revolution, which transformed many economies away from agriculture and toward manufacturing in the 1800s, is at the very center of the big break in world income growth. Beginning with the Industrial Revolution, the rate of technical progress became so rapid that it was able to outpace population growth. The foundation for the industrial revolution was laid in the preceding decades, and this included private-property protection and several technological innovations. We don't claim that the industrial revolution was idyllic for those who lived through it, but the legal and technological innovations of that era paved the way for the unprecedented gains in human welfare that we have experienced since.

This data doesn't imply that life is always easy and predictably comfortable for everyone in the modern world. But the opportunities afforded to the average person alive today are very different from the opportunities afforded to the average person in past centuries. Table 12.2 lists a sampling of some of the major innovations that have taken place in the past 150 years. Try to imagine life without any of these, and this gives you a picture of the gains since the industrial revolution.

Table 12.2
Important Inventions since the U.S. Civil War

Typewriter	1867	Electron Microscope	1939
Sheep Shears	1868	Electric Clothes Dryer	1940
Telephone	1876	Nuclear Reactor	1942
Phonograph	1877	Microwave Oven	1945
Milking Machine	1878	Cruise Control	1945
Two-Stroke Engine	1878	Computer	1946
Blow Torch	1880	Xerography	1946
Slide Rule	1881	Videotape Recorder	1952
Arc Welder	1886	Airbags	1952
Diesel Engine	1892	Satellites	1958
Electric Motor (AC)	1892	Laser	1960
X-Ray Machine	1895	Floppy Disk	1965
Electric Drill	1895	Microprocessor	1971
Radio	1906	Personal Computer	1975
Assembly Line	1908	Fiber-optic Cables	1977
Cash Register	1919	Fax Machine	1981
Dishwasher	1924	Camcorder	1982
Rocket	1926	Cell Phone	1983
Television	1926	Compact Disk	1983
Anti-Lock Breaks	1929	GPS	1989
Radar	1934	Lasik Eye Surgery	1989
Tape Recorder	1935	Internet	1991
Jet Engine	1939		

Source: Cox and Alm, *Myths of Rich and Poor, and misc. others.*

Some Got Rich, Others Stayed Poor

Although wealth has increased over the past two centuries, it is not evenly distributed around the globe. Figure 12.2 shows per capita GDP (in 2010 U.S. dollars) for various world regions. In 1800, the income of the average U.S. citizen was just less than $2,000 (in year 2010 dollars). Imagine trying to live on $3 per day in today's world – that is, $3 to buy all the food, clothing, shelter, education, transportation and anything else you might purchase. That was life in the United States in 1800 – and it's comparable to life in many nations today.

Figure 12.2:
Per Capita Real GDP over 200 Years

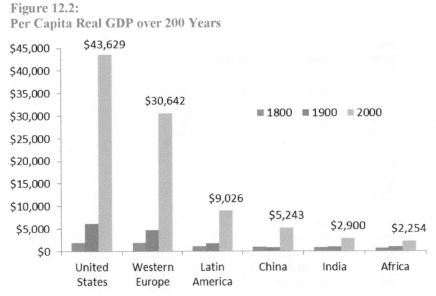

Source: Angus Maddison, *Statistics on World Population, GDP and Per Capita GDP, 1-2008 AD.*
All figures converted to 2010 U.S. dollars.

Two hundred years ago, all regions and nations were poor. The modern differences in wealth that we
see around the world began to emerge before 1900. But the twentieth century is when
unprecedented growth took hold in the United States and Western Europe. Sadly, some parts of the
globe today are no better off than the United States and Western Europe in 1800.

By 1900, some regions had broken the stranglehold of poverty. In 1900, per
capita GDP in Western Europe was $4,701; in the United States, it was $6,153. Prior to
1900, general income levels this high had never been experienced. But in China, India,
and Africa, the averages were still less than $1,000 in 1900. The twentieth century
proved to be even more prosperous for some, as the income gap widened between the
United States and Europe and the rest of the world. Sadly, per capita real income on the
African continent today is still less than that of the Unites States in 1850, which was
$2,768.

While many of the current disparities between nations began about 200 years ago,
some nations have moved from poor to rich as recently as the past few decades. In 1950,
for example, Taiwan, with per capita real GDP of just $1,404, was poorer than Liberia, at
$1,617. Today, Taiwan is one of the wealthiest countries in the world, with a per capita
income of more than $32,000 per person, while Liberia is near $1,200 in per capita
income.

Economics in the Real World:
One Child who needs Economic Progress

This is a true story about a girl named Alice Toe.   In the picture above, Alice is four years old. You can see from her eyes that Alice is mischievous and full of personality. When the photo was taken, she was digging for crabs for the sole purpose of frightening a visiting American economist.

Alice lives in Monrovia, Liberia, the capital of an impoverished country in West Africa about the size of the state of Virginia. She was three years old when she contracted tapeworms.   Unfortunately, her family could not afford to send her to a doctor. Her stomach became enlarged and her hair bleached—indicators of malnutrition caused by tapeworms. She was infected with the tapeworms from drinking contaminated water from a neighborhood well. Filtered water, which costs about $3.00 per gallon in Liberia, is too expensive and must be transported by foot.

Tapeworm infection is easily treated with a pill that costs less than twenty-five cents, and lasts for six months. But Alice and her grandfather could not afford even this inexpensive treatment – that's how poor they were. Fortunately, an American missionary happened to meet Alice and she received the treatment she needed. Without help, she probably would have died.

Alice's story is not unusual. Many thousands of children die each year from illnesses like tapeworm. Worldwide 122 of every 1,000 children born in the poorest nations do not reach the age of five, though many could be saved with treatments that literally cost pennies. The good news is that economics can help. We hope that economic growth and the improvements in quality of life it brings will take root in Liberia

Measuring Economic Growth

Overall, people today are much wealthier than they were 200 years ago. However, this prosperity did not come overnight. Rather, income grew a little bit each year. There is a striking mathematical truth about growth: small differences in growth rates lead to large differences in wealth levels over time. In this section, we explain how growth rates are computed and we consider the level of growth a nation needs for its population to experience significant improvements in living standards.

The Mathematics of Growth Rates

The big break out of poverty began during the 19th century. Table 12.3 shows data on world economic growth in different periods. From 1800-1900, average world GDP growth was only 0.64%. From 1900 to 1950, world economic growth increased to about 1%. The difference between zero and one percent might seem trivial; it certainly doesn't seem like much if your exam grade goes from 85 to 86. But when economic growth increases by one percent, it makes a big difference. In this section we show how growth is calculated.

Table 12.3:
World Economic Growth for Different Historical Eras

Years	Growth Rate
0-1800	0.02%
1800-1900	0.64%
1900-1950	1.04%
1950-2000	2.12%

Source: Angus Maddison.

We have seen that economic growth is the annual growth rate of per capita real GDP. It is our measure of how an average person's income changes over time, including an allowance for price changes. But the government reports overall GDP data in nominal terms. Therefore, to get an accurate growth rate, we need to account for both inflation and population growth. We can use the following equation to approximate economic growth:

Economic growth = %Δ in nominal GDP - %Δ Price level - %Δ population,   (12.1)

where %Δ indicates percent change in a variable.

Let's walk through the equation for economic growth using actual U.S. in Table 12.4. Starting with nominal GDP data for 2010 and 2011, we compute nominal GDP growth as 3.8 percent. But part of the increase in nominal GDP is due to inflation. In 2011, the price level, as measured by the GDP deflator, grew by 2.1%. We subtract this inflation from nominal GDP growth to get real GDP growth of 1.7%. This number applies to the entire nation, but population also increased by 1% in 2011. When we subtract population growth, we are left with 0.7 percent, the rate of economic growth for the United States in 2011. This growth rate was lower than normal: since 1950 average economic growth in the United States has been about 2.1%.

Table 12.4 Computing an Economic Growth Rate

U.S. GDP in 2010 (millions of $)		$14,456,500
U.S. GDP in 2011 (millions of $)		$15,087,700
	Nominal GDP Growth	3.8%
-	Price Growth (inflation)	2.1%
=	Real GDP Growth	1.7%
-	Population Growth	1.0%
=	Real Per Capita GDP Growth	0.7% = Economic Growth

Source: GDP Data , BEA; Population;, U.S. Census Bureau:
http://www.census.gov/popest/states/NST-ann-est.html

A word of caution about terminology is in order. There's a big difference between GDP growth, real GDP growth, and per capita real GDP growth. Looking at Table 12.3 you can see these terms highlighted in orange letters. But sloppy economic reporting sometimes confuses them. You may read something like: "the U.S. economy grew by 2.8% in 2011," which often refers to real GDP growth and this is not on a per capita basis. It would be an even bigger mistake to claim that U.S. economic growth in 2011 was 3.8%, which is not adjusted for either population growth or inflation. This is a common mistake in reports on international economic growth statistics.

Growth Rates and Income Levels

Before we consider policies that might aid economic growth, we need to look closer at how growth rates affect income levels.

First, consider how significant it is when income doubles, or increases by 100%. If your income doubled today—all else equal—you could afford twice as much of everything you are currently buying. Now imagine what would happen if income doubled for an entire country, or even all countries. In the United States, per capita real GDP more than doubled in the forty years between 1970 and 2010. This means the average person living in the United States in 2010 could afford twice as much food, clothing, transportation, education, and even government services as the average U.S. resident in 1970. That's quite a difference.

But increasing real income 100% in a single year is not realistic. Let's pick a number closer to reality, say 2% - a normal rate of economic growth for the United States. With a growth rate of 2%, how long would it take to double your income? For example, let's say you graduate and, given your expertise in economics, you get several job offers. One offer is for $50,000 per year with a guaranteed raise of 2% every year. How long before your salary is $100,000?

The first answer that pops into your head may be fifty years (based on the idea that 2% growth for 50 years adds up to 100% growth). But this answer is wrong because it ignores the fact that growth compounds over time. As your salary grows, 2% growth leads to larger and larger dollar increases. Because of this, it actually takes only about 35 years to double income at a 2% growth rate.

Table 12.5 illustrates how the process of compounding over time works by showing the increase from year to year. Income starts at $50,000 in year 1, and a two percent increase yields $1,000, so that one year of growth results in income of $51,000. Two percent growth in the second year yields $1,020 of new income (2% of $51,000), so after 2 years, income is $52,020. Two percent of this is $1,040.40. Each year, the dollar increase in income (the green column) gets larger, as two percent of a growing number continues to grow.

Table 12.5:
Compound Growth

	Income	Increase in Income	Income in Next Year
Year 1	$50,000.00	$1,000.00	$51,000.00
Year 2	$51,000.00	$1,020.00	$52,020.00
Year 3	$52,020.00	$1,040.40	$53,060.40
Year 4	$53,060.40	$1,061.21	$54,121.61
Year 5	$54,121.61	$1,082.43	$55,204.04
.			
.			
.			
Year 35	$100,000		

In fact, at a growth rate of 2% it takes only 35 years for income to double. This corresponds with the experience of the United States economy. Since 1970, per capita real GDP in the United States has more than doubled. Yet this jump was achieved while U.S. economic growth rates averaged "only" about 2%. Think about that - during your parents' lifetime average real income levels in the United States doubled.

Economics in the Real World:
How does 2% growth affect average people?

We have seen that economic growth in the United States has averaged 2 percent per year over the past 50 years. What does this mean for a typical person's everyday life? We've assembled some basic data on what the United States looked like to an average person in 1960. This may be about the time your grandparents were your age.

Today, average real income is four times the level of 1960. Americans live 10% longer, we have twice as many doctors, our houses are twice as big, we have more education, we own more and better cars and household appliances. We work 15% fewer hours and hold jobs that are less physically-taxing. In 1960 there were no cell phones and roughly three out of four homes had a single telephone. Today we have more telephones than people. In addition, many modern amenities were not available in 1960. Can you imagine life without a personal computer and the internet, DVDs, microwave ovens, and central air conditioning?

1960	2010
General:	**General:**
Per capita GDP (2010 dollars): $11,328	Per capita GDP (2010 dollars): $47,784
Life expectancy: 69.7	Life expectancy: 78.3
Physicians per 10,000: 14.8	Physicians per 10,000: 27
Median years of school completed: 10.5	Average years of school completed: 12
Income spent on food: 27%	Portion of income spent on food: 8%
Average weekly hours at work: 40.9	Averge weekly hours at work: 34
Workers in agriculture & manufacturring: 37%	Workers in agriculture & manufacturing: 19%
Home ownership: 61.9%	Home ownership: 67.4%
New Home:	**New Home:**
Size: 1,200 square feet	Size: 2,457 square feet
Bedrooms: 2	Bedrooms: 3
Bathrooms: 1	Bathrooms: 2.5
Central air conditioniong: No	Central air conditioniong: Yes
Best-selling car: Chevrolet Impala	**Best-Selling Car: Toyota Camry**
Price (2010 dollars): $19,753	Price (2010 dollars): $26,640
MPG: 13-16	MPG: 20-29
Horsepower: 135	Horsepower: 268
Air conditioning: optional	Air conditioning: standard
Automatic transmission: optional	Automatic transmission: standard
Airbags: No	Airbags: standard
Power locks and windows: not available	Power locks and windows: standard
Entertainment:	**Entertainment:**
TV: 23 inch Black and White	TV: 50 inch HD
Price (2010 dollars): $1,391	Price (2010 dollars): $700
No HD or remote control	

The Rule of 70

The **rule of 70** states that if the annual growth rate of a variable is *x* percent, the size of that variable doubles every 70 ÷ *x* years.

In the example above, we saw that when income grows at 2% per year it doubles in just thirty-five years. A simple rule known as *the rule of 70* determines the length of time necessary for a sum of money to double at a particular growth rate. According to the **rule of 70:**

If the annual growth rate of a variable is x percent, the size of that variable doubles every 70 ÷ x years.

The Rule of 70 is an approximation, but it works well with typical economic growth rates.

Table 12.6 illustrates the rule of 70 by showing how long it takes for each $1.00 of income to double in value, given different growth rates. At a growth rate of one percent, each dollar of income will double every 70 ÷ 1 years. If growth increases to two percent, then a dollar of income will double every 70 ÷ 2 = 35 years. Consider the impact of a four percent growth rate. If this can be sustained, income doubles every 72 ÷ 4 = 17.5 years. In 70 years, income doubles 4 times and is 16 times its starting value! China has been growing at about ten percent per year lately, and indeed its per capita income has been doubling about every seven years—a remarkable rate of growth.

Table 12.6: The Rule of 70 Applied to $1.00

Annual Growth Rate	Years to Double	Value after 70 Years
0%	Never	No change
1%	70	$2.00
2%	35	$4.00
3%	23.3	$8.00
4%	17.5	$16.00

The Rule of 70 shows us that small consistent growth rates, if sustained for a decade or two, can greatly improve living standards. Over the long course of history, growth rates were essentially zero and the general human condition was poverty. But over the past two centuries we have seen small, consistent growth rates and the standard of living for many has increased dramatically.

We can look at actual growth rates of various countries over a long period, to see the impact on income levels. Table 12.7 presents growth rates of several countries over fifty-eight years from 1950 to 2008. Start with Nicaragua and Turkey. In 1950, they had roughly the same income per person. But Turkey grew at over 2% annually and

Nicaragua didn't experience any net growth. As a result, the average income in Turkey is now four to five times the average income in Nicaragua.

Table 12.7:

Economic Growth, 1950-2008

Average Annual Growth Rate		Real PC GDP in 1950		Real PC GDP in 2008	
-1.4	Dem. Republic Congo	873		382	Growth near 0% means people in these nations are no better off than they were in 1950.
-0.7	Haïti	1,610		1,051	
0.1	Nicaragua	2,476		2,565	
0.2	Zimbabwe	1,074		1,194	
0.5	North Korea	1,309		1,719	
1.0	Tanzania	649		1,141	Growth near 1% means living standards nearly double over fifty-eight years.
1.1	Lebanon	3,722		6,824	
1.1	Rwanda	838		1,563	
1.2	El Salvador	2,282		4,507	
1.2	Nigeria	1,154		2,336	
2.1	United States	14,654		47,784	Growth near 2% means living standards almost quadruple in fifty-eight years.
2.1	Mexico	3,625		12,228	
2.1	Australia	11,359		38,777	
2.1	United Kingdom	10,635		36,388	
2.2	Chile	5,624		20,208	
2.7	India	949		4,559	Growth of 3% or more over fifty-eight years is enough to move some nations from the world's poorest to among the richest.
2.8	Turkey	2,487		12,363	
4.4	Japan	2,944		34,967	
4.5	Singapore	3,401		43,077	
4.8	China	687		10,307	
5.5	Taiwan	1,404		32,072	
5.6	South Korea	1,309		30,061	

Source: Angus Maddison data set, all figures converted to 2010 U.S. dollars.

Further down Table 12.7, you see other nations grew at rates faster even than Turkey. In 1950, Japan's per capita income was similar to Turkey's. Yet 4.4% growth led to income of $35,000 per person by 2008. Taiwan, with 5.5% growth over the entire period, moved from among the world's poorest to its richest.

Perhaps the biggest recent growth story is China. Only twenty years ago it was among the world's poorer nations. Over the past twenty years, China has grown at about

... and then in 2010.

9%. Even if China's astonishing growth slows considerably, it will still move into the group of the wealthiest nations in the coming decades.

Economic growth experiences have varied widely across time and place. But relatively small consistent growth rates are sufficient to move a nation out of poverty over the period of a few generations. And this movement out of poverty really matters for the people who live in these nations.

Practice What You Know
Computing Economic Growth

How much is Brazil Growing?

GDP in Brazil has grown rapidly in recent years. But historically Brazil is a country that has struggled with inflation rates. The table below gives 2010 statistics for Brazil.

Nominal GDP growth rate	GDP deflator growth rate	Population Growth rate
15.73%	8.23%	0.9%

Question: What was the rate of economic growth for Brazil in 2010?

Answer: First, recall equation 24.1:

$$\text{Economic growth} = \%\Delta Nominal\ GDP - \%\Delta Prices - \%\Delta Population$$

Now, for Brazil, we have:

$$\text{Economic growth} = 15.73 - 8.23 - 0.9 = 6.6\%.$$

Question: If Brazil continues to grow at 6.6% per year, how long will it take to double the level of per capita real GDP?

Answer: Using the rule of 70:

$$70 \div 6.6 = 10.6 \text{ years.}$$

Clearly, the growth of GDP in Brazil in 2010 was significant, even after accounting for both inflation and population growth.

Data Source: IMF, World Eocnomic Outlook, April 2012

How do resources and technology contribute to growth?

At this point, you may wonder what we can do to provide the best opportunity for economic growth. We see economic growth in many, though certainly not all, nations. But even in those that have grown in the past, future growth is not assured. So now we turn to the major sources of economic growth.

Economists continue to debate the relative importance of the factors that lead to economic growth. However, there is a general consensus on the significance of three factors for economic growth: *resources*, *technology*, and *institutions*. In this section we examine the first two; in the final section of the chapter, we will look at institutions.

Resources

All else equal, the more *resources* available to a nation, the more output that nation can produce. **Resources, also known as factors of production,** are the inputs used to produce goods and services. The discovery or cultivation of new resources is a source of economic growth. We divide resources into three major categories: natural resources, physical capital, and human capital.

> **Resources**, also known as **factors of production**, are the inputs used to produce goods and services.

Natural Resources

Natural resources includes physical land and the inputs naturally in or on the land. Coal, iron ore, diamonds, and lumber are examples of natural resources. Less obvious examples are mountains, beaches, temperate weather patterns and scenic views – resources that residents enjoy consuming and that sometimes lead to tourism as a major industry.

Natural resources are an important source of economic wealth for nations. The United States has fertile farmland, forests, coal, iron ore, and even oil; the United States supplies about 9% of the world's oil.

Geography, or the physical location of a nation, is also a natural resource that can contribute to economic growth. Geographic location facilitates trade and affects other important variables such as weather and disease control. The world map in Figure 12.3 shows GDP per square kilometer. Locations on coasts or along rivers have developed more rapidly than areas inland. These are the areas that were more naturally suited to trade in the days before railroads, trucks, and airplanes.

Figure 12.3
Global GDP Density

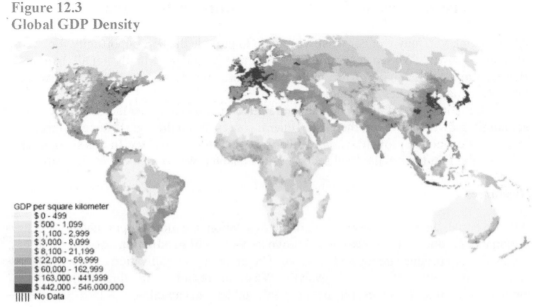

GDP per square kilometer
$ 0 - 499
$ 500 - 1,099
$ 1,100 - 2,999
$ 3,000 - 8,099
$ 8,100 - 21,199
$ 22,000 - 59,999
$ 60,000 - 162,999
$ 163,000 - 441,999
$ 442,000 - 546,000,000
||||| No Data

Source: Gallup, Sachs, and Mellinger, "Geogrpahy and Economic Development, *International Regional Science Review*, 1999

The world's wealthiest areas are often those areas that are located near natural shipping lanes and rivers where trade naturally flowed. This is evidence that geography matters in economic development.

Natural resources clearly help increase economic development, but they are not enough to make a nation wealthy. Many poor nations are rich in natural resources. Liberia has mahogany forests, iron-ore deposits, rubber-tree forests, diamonds, and a beautiful coastline along the Atlantic Ocean. Yet with all these natural resources, Liberia is still poor. On the other hand, consider Hong Kong, which is very small and densely populated with few natural resources. Yet the citizens of Hong Kong are among the wealthiest people in the world.

Physical Capital

The second category of resources is physical capital, or just capital. Recall that capital refers to the tools and equipment used in the production of goods and services. Examples of capital include factories, tractors, roads and bridges, computers, and shovels. The purpose of capital is to aid in the production of future output.

Consider the shipping container, a basic tool that has aided the movement of goods around the globe. The shipping container is a standard sized (20- or 40-foot long) box used to move goods around the world. In 1954 a typical cargo ship traveling from New York to Germany might have carried as many as 194,582 individual items. The transportation involved bags, barrels, cartons, and many other different means of packaging and storing goods. Loading and unloading the ship required armies of men, working long hours for days on end. Not surprisingly, shipping goods from one country to another was expensive.

The standardized shipping container was first used in 1956. Suddenly it was possible to move cargo around the globe without repacking every time the mode of transportation changes. Once the ship enters the port, cranes lift the containers 200 feet in the air, and unload about forty large boxes each hour. Dozens of ships can be unloaded at a time and most of the operation is run by computers. A container full of iPods can be loaded on the back of a truck in Shenzhen, China, transported to port and loaded onto a ship that carries 3,000 containers. The ship can bring the iPods to the United States where the containers are loaded onto a train and later a truck. This movement happens without anyone touching the contents. The shipping container is a tool that revolutionized world trade and improved our lives.

As the quantity of physical capital per worker rises, so does output per worker. Clearly, workers are more productive with more and better tools. Look around the world: the productive nations have impressive roads, bridges, buildings and factories. In poor nations, paved roads are nonexistent or in disrepair, vehicles are lower quality, and computers are a luxury. Even public electricity and sewage treatment facilities are rare in many developing nations.

Because of the obvious correlation between tools and wealth, many of the early contributions to growth theory focused on the role of physical capital goods. As a result, much international aid was used to build roads and factories, in the hope that prosperity would follow automatically. But today most people understand that capital alone is not sufficient to produce economic growth. Factories, dams, and other large capital projects bring wealth only when they mesh well with the rest of the economy. A steel factory is of little use in a region better suited for growing corn. Without a good rail network or proper roads, a steel factory cannot get the tools it needs and it cannot easily sell its products. Dams that are not maintained fall into disrepair within years. Water pipes are a wonderful modern invention, but if they are not kept in good shape, human waste from toilets infects the water supply. The point is, simply building new capital tools in a nation does not insure future sustained economic growth.

Human Capital

The output of a nation also depends on people to use its natural resources. **Human capital** is the resource represented by quantity, knowledge, and skills of the workers in an economy. Human capital expands by increasing the number of workers available, by educating the existing labor force, or both.

> **Human capital** is the resource represented by the quantity, knowledge, and skills of the workers in an economy.

We often think in terms of the sheer quantity of workers: all else equal, a nation with more workers produces more output. But more output does not necessarily mean more economic growth. Economic growth requires more output *per capita*. Adding more workers to an economy may increase total GDP without increasing per capita GDP. However, if more workers from a given population enter the labor force, GDP per capita can increase. For example, as we discussed in Chapter 20, women have entered the U.S. labor force in record numbers over the past fifty years. This certainly contributed to increases in measured GDP and per capita GDP. When the primary output of adult women in the United States was non-market output such as home-making services, it was not counted in the official GDP statistics. As more women join the official labor force, their output increases both GDP and GDP per capita.

There is another important dimension of human capital: the knowledge and skills of the workers themselves. Human capital also increases from education and training. Training includes everything from basic literacy to college education to software competencies to specific job training.

Not many would doubt that a more educated labor force is more productive. And certainly, to boost per capita output, educating the labor force is more helpful than merely increasing the quantity of workers. But education alone is not enough to insure economic progress. For many years, India struggled with economic growth, even while their workers were among the most educated in the world.

Technology

We all know that the world would be much poorer without computers, automobiles, electric light bulbs, and other productive ideas. **Technology** is the knowledge available for use in production. Though technology is often embodied in machines and productive techniques, it is really just knowledge. New technology allows us to produce more while using fewer of our limited resources. A **technological advancement** introduces new techniques or methods so that firms can produce more valuable outputs per unit of input. We can either produce more with the same resources, or use fewer resources to produce the same quantity. "More for less," is the basic idea.

> **Technology** is the knowledge available for use in production.

> A **technological advancement** introduces new techniques or methods so that firms can produce more valuable outputs per unit of input.

For example, the assembly line was an important technological advance. Henry Ford adopted and improved the assembly line method in 1913, at the Ford Motor Company. In this new approach to the factory, workers focused on well-defined jobs, such as screwing on individual parts. The conveyor belt moved these parts around the factory to worker stations. Workers, by staying put rather than roaming around, experienced a lower rate of accidents and mishaps.

Agriculture is a sector where technological advances are easy to spot. For example, we know land resources are necessary to produce corn. But technological advances mean that over time we grow and harvest more corn per acre of land. In fact, in the United States, corn yield per acre is now six times what it was in 1930. In 1930, we produced about 25 bushels of corn per acre but now the yield is consistently over 150 bushels per acre. How is this possible? The answer is technology that has produced hybrid seeds, herbicides, fertilizers, and irrigation.

Figure 12.6 presents another agricultural example of technological advancement. We now have significantly fewer milk cows in the United States than at any time since 1920. But total milk output is at historical highs because we now get about four times as much milk out of each cow. Technological advancements allow us to produce more while using fewer resources.

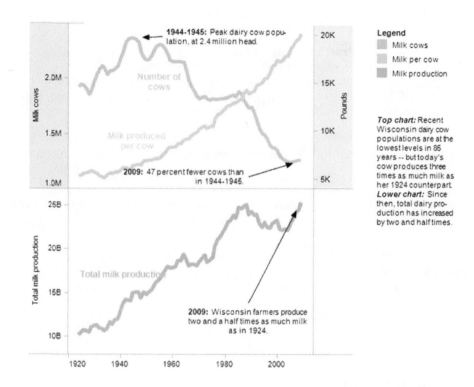

Top chart: Recent Wisconsin dairy cow populations are at the lowest levels in 85 years -- but today's cow produces three times as much milk as her 1924 counterpart. Lower chart: Since then, total dairy production has increased by two and half times.

Like capital, technology produces value only when combined with other inputs. For example, simply carrying plans for a shoe factory to Haiti would not create much economic value. The mere knowledge of how to produce shoes, while important, is only one piece of the growth puzzle. An economy must have the physical capital to produce shoes, it must have the human capital to man the factory and assembly line, and it must create favorable conditions and incentives for potential investors. Economic growth occurs when all these conditions come together. That is one reason why we should not identify technological innovations as the sole cause of differences in wealth across nations.

Technological innovations do not occur randomly across the globe. Some places produce large clusters of such innovations. Information technology comes from MIT and Silicon Valley, movie and television ideas come from Hollywood, and new fashion designs come from Paris, Milan, Tokyo, and New York. Technological innovations tend to breed more innovations. This leads us to reword an earlier question: Why do some regions innovate (and grow) more than others? A large part of the answer lies in our next subject, institutions.

Practice What You Know
Resources

Growth Policy

Many policies have been advocated to help nations escape poverty. Many are focused on the importance of resources.

Question: For each policy listed below, determine which resource is the primary focus of the policy.

a. International loans for inftrastructure like roads, bridges, and dams.
b. Mandated primary education.
c. Restrictions on the development of forested land.
d. Population controls.
e. International aid for construction of a shoe factory.

Answers:

a. Infrastructure is physical capital.
b. Education increases human capital.
c. These are focused on maintaining a certain level of natural resources.
d. Population controls are often due to a short-sighted focus on physical capital per capita. The fewer people you have, the more tools you have per person.
e. The focus here is on physical capital.

What institutions foster economic growth?

In 1950, residents in the African nation of Liberia were wealthier than those on the Southeast Asian island of Taiwan. Today, per capita GDP in Taiwan is more than twenty times that of Liberia. Yes much of this wealth gap stems from obvious current differences in physical capital, human capital, and technology. But we must ask how these differences came about. Without a doubt, the biggest difference between Taiwan and Liberia since 1950 is our final growth factor: *institutions*.

An **institution** is a significant practice, relationship, or organization in a society. Institutions are the official and unofficial conditions that shape the environment in which decisions are made. We often focus on institutions such as the laws and regulations in a nation. But other institutions such as social mores and work habits are also important.

An **institution** is a significant practice, relationship, or organization in a society.

Institutions are not always tangible physical items that we can look at or hold. There might be a physical representative of an institution, such as the U.S. Constitution, or the building where the Supreme Court meets, but the essence of an institution is comprised of expectations and habitual practices. The rules and the mindset within the Supreme Court are what is important, not the building or the chairs.

In this section we will consider the most significant institutions that affect production and income in a nation. These include *private property* rights, political stability and the rule of law, open and competitive markets, stable money and prices, and efficient taxes. Many of these are covered in detail elsewhere in this book, so we cover them only briefly here.

Private Property Rights

The single greatest incentive for voluntary production is ownership of what you produce. The existence of the right to hold **private property** means individuals can own property—including houses, land, and other resources—and when they use their property in production, they own the resulting output. Consider also the differences in private property rights between Liberia and Taiwan. In Liberia, the system of ownership titles is not dependable. Liberians who wish to purchase land often must buy the land multiple times from different "owners", because there is no dependable record of true ownership. Taiwan has a well-defined system of law and property rights protection. Without such a system, people have very little incentive to improve the value of their assets.

> **Private property** is the right of individuals to own property and use their property in production.

In the past two decades the government of China has relaxed its laws against private property ownership. This has led to unprecedented growth. These market reforms stem from a risky experiment in the rural community of Xiaogang. In 1978, the heads of 21 families in Xiaogang signed an agreement that became the genesis of private property rights in China.

The agreement stipulated that each family would continue to produce the government quota for their agricultural output. But they would begin keeping anything they produced above this quota. They also agreed to stop taking food or money from the government. This agreement was dangerous in 1978 – so dangerous that one part of the agreement stipulated that they would raise one another's children if any of the signees were put in jail.

The Xiogang agreement led to an agricultural boom that was copied in other communities. Seeing the success of this property rights experiment, Deng Xiaoping and other Chinese leaders then instituted market reforms in agriculture in the 1980s, and then in manufacturing in the 1990s. China's economy is growing rapidly today not because they found new resources or updated their technology. They are wealthier because they now recognize private property rights in many different industries.

Political Stability and the Rule of Law

To understand the importance of political stability and the rule of law, consider two separate places: Liberia and Taiwan. Before 2006, Liberia endured 35 years of political unrest. Government officials assumed office using violence and national leaders consistently used their power to eradicate their opponents. On the other hand, Taiwan's political climate has been relatively stable since 1949. If you were an entrepreneur and were deciding where to build your factory, would you want to invest millions of dollars in a country with constant violent unrest, or would you chose a peaceful country? You predict which nation is more likely to see new factories and technological innovation.

Political instability is a disincentive for investment. Investment only makes sense if there is a fairly certain payoff at the end. In an environment of political instability, there is no incentive to invest in either human or physical capital, because there is no predictable future payoff.

Consistent and trustworthy enforcement of a nation's laws is crucial for

Which location seems best for starting a business – a street littered with bullet casings...

economic growth. Corruption is one of the most common and dangerous impediments to economic growth. When government officials steal, elicit bribes, or hand out favors to friends, this reduces incentives for private investment. If individuals cannot count on consistent returns to investment in human or physical capital, investment declines and this reduces future growth.

The World Justice Project has collected data on the rule of law across the world. Figure 12.7 shows the nations broken down into five groups, based upon consistent enforcement of the rule of law. It is no surprise that nations that scored in the top group on this index are also the nations with the highest levels of per capita GDP. The most corrupt nations are also those with the lowest levels of income.

Figure 12.7
Rule of Law and Per Capita Income

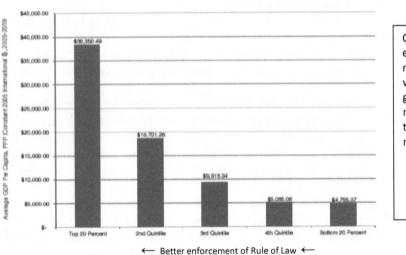

← Better enforcement of Rule of Law ←

> Consistent and fair enforcement of a nation's laws pays off with economic growth. Nations with more corruption are the world's poorest nations.

Source: World Justice Project, 2011 Report.
http://www.worldjusticeproject.org/sites/default/files/WJP%20Rule%20of%20Law%20Index%202010_2_0.pdf

Economics in the Real World:
What can parking violations teach us about international institutions?

Until 2002, diplomatic immunity protected UN diplomats in New York City from fines or arrest because of parking violations. This gave economists Raymond Fisman and Edward Miguel a unique natural experiment; it allowed them to study how officials responded to the lack of legal consequences for violating the law. Parking violations under these conditions are an example of corruption because they represent the abuse of power for private gain. Therefore, by comparing the level of parking violations of diplomats from different societies, the economists created a way to compare corruption norms among different cultures.

Fisman and Miguel compared unpaid parking violations with existing survey-based indices on levels of corruption across nations. They found that diplomats from high-corruption nations accumulated significantly more unpaid parking violations. Among the worst offenders were diplomats from Kuwait, Egypt, Chad, Sudan, and Bulgaria. Among those with zero unpaid parking violations were Australia, Canada, Denmark, Japan, and Norway.

This finding suggests that cultural or social norms related to corruption are quite persistent: even when stationed thousands of miles away, diplomats behave as if they are at home. Norms related to corruption are apparently deeply ingrained.

In 2002, enforcement authorities acquired the right to confiscate diplomatic license plates of violators. Unpaid violations dropped by almost 98%. This illustrates the power of incentives in influencing human behavior.

Competitive and Open Markets

In this section, we take a quick look at three institutions essential for economic growth: competitive markets, international trade, and flow of funds across boarders. These market characteristics are covered in detail elsewhere in this book.

Competitive Markets

In Chapter 3 we explored how competitive markets insure that consumers can buy goods at the lowest possible prices. When markets aren't competitive, people who want to participate face barriers to entry. This inhibits competition and innovation. Yet many nations monopolize key industries by preventing competition or through government ownership of industries. This limits macroeconomic growth.

International Trade

Recall from Chapter 2 that trade creates value. International trade is very much like trade between individuals in the same country. In some cases, trade allows nations to consume goods and services they would not produce on their own. Specialization and trade makes all nations better off because each can produce goods for which they enjoy a comparative advantage. Output increases when nations produce the goods and services for which they have the lowest opportunity cost and trade for the other goods and services they might wish to consume.

International trade barriers reduce the benefits available from specialization and trade. Chapter 19 is devoted to the study of international trade.

Flow of Funds across Borders

In Chapter 11 we talked about the importance of savings for economic growth. For example, the inflow of foreign savings has helped keep interest rates low in the United States even as domestic savings rates have fallen. If firms and individuals are to invest in physical or human capital, somebody has to save. Opportunities for investment expand if you also have access to savings from around the globe. That is, if foreigners can funnel their savings into your economy, your firms can use these funds to expand. However, many developing nations have restrictions on foreign ownership of land and physical plant within their borders. Restrictions on the flow of capital across borders handcuff domestic firms because they are forced to seek funds solely from domestic savers.

Efficient Taxes

On the one hand, taxes must be high enough to support effective government. Political stability, the rule of law, and private property rights protection all require strong and consistent government. Taxes provide the revenue to pay for government services. On the other hand, if we tax activities that are fundamental to economic growth, we will see less of these activities. In market economies, output and income are strictly intertwined. If we tax income, we are taxing output, and that is GDP. So although taxes are necessary, they can also reduce incentives for production.

Before the federal government instituted an income tax, government services were largely funded by taxes on imports. But international trade is also an essential institution for economic growth. So taxes on imports also impede growth.

Efficient taxes are taxes sufficient to fund the activities of government while impeding production and consumption decisions a little as possible. It is not easy to determine the efficient level of taxes or even to determine what activities should be taxed. We discuss this further in Chapter 16, when we discuss fiscal policy.

Stable Money and Prices

High and variable inflation is a sure way to reduce incentives for investment and production. In Chapter 10, we saw that inflation increases future price level uncertainty. When people are unsure about future price levels, they are certainly more reluctant to sign contracts which deliver dollar payoffs in the future. Because of this, unpredictable inflation diminishes future growth possibilities. In the United States, the Federal Reserve (Fed) is charged with administering monetary policy. The Fed is designed to reduce incentives for politically-motivated monetary policy which typically leads to highly variable inflation rates. We cover the Fed in greater detail in Chapter 17.

Practice What You Know
Institutions

Can You Guess this Country?

The following is a list of characteristics for a particular country:

(1) This country has almost no natural resources.
(2) No agriculture of its own.
(3) It imports water.
(4) It is located in the tropics.
(5) It has four official languages.
(6) It occupies 710 square kilometers.
(7) It has one of the world's lowest unemployment rates.
(7) A literacy rate of 96%.
(8) A per capita GDP of $35,500 in 2009.
(10) It has one of the densest populations per square mile on the planet.

Question: Can you name the country?

Answer: Congratulations if you thought of Singapore! At first blush it seems almost impossible that one of the most successful countries on the planet could have so little going for it.

Question: How could a country with so few natural resources survive, let alone flourish? How can you grow without any agriculture or enough fresh water?

Answer: What Singapore lacks in some areas it more than makes up for in others. Singapore has a lot of human capital from a highly educated and industrious labor force. It has been able to attract plenty of foreign financial funds by creating a stable and secure financial system that protects property rights and encourages free trade. Singapore also has a strategically-situated deep-water port in Southeast Asia that benefits from proximity to the emerging economies of China and India.

Economics for Life
Economic Growth Statistics

Deciphering Data Reports

Economics is all around us and the topics of economics are constantly reported in the media. In addition to monthly reports on unemployment and inflation, there are also monthly releases and revisions of GDP data for the United States and other nations. These often get a lot of attention. Unfortunately, media reports are not as careful with their economics terminology as we would like. Because they are not careful, the reports can be misleading.

After learning about historical experiences with economic growth, you might find new interest in the economic growth reports that appear almost every month in the mainstream media. However, you must carefully evaluate the data they present. Now that you have perspective on growth statistics, you can determine for yourself whether economic news is positive or negative. For example a *New York Times* article from April 2009 offers the following on economic growth in China for the previous quarter:

> China's economic output was 6.1 percent higher in the first quarter than a year earlier... China's annual growth rate appeared slow in the first quarter after the 6.8 percent rate in the fourth quarter of 2008, partly because it was being compared with the economy's formidable output in the first quarter of last year.

China's economy grew at over 6% and yet this rate is taken as "slow." By now you know that 6% is an incredibly fast rate of growth.

Good economists are very careful with language and certain terms have very specific meanings. For example, we know that "economic growth" always refers to changes in *per capita* real GDP, not simply GDP or real GDP. But economic reports in mainstream media outlets often blur this distinction. That is exactly the case with this report in this *New York Times* article.

Even though the author uses the term "annual growth rate," additional research reveals he is talking about real GDP growth, but not adjusting the data for population changes. This is common in everyday language so you should watch out for this when you read economic growth reports. It turns out that the population growth rate in China was about 0.6% in 2009. This means the growth rate of per capita real GDP in China was actually about 5.5%, which is still very impressive.

Source: http://www.nytimes.com/2009/04/16/business/global/16yuan.html

Conclusion

We began this chapter with the misconception that natural resources are the primary source of economic growth. While it doesn't hurt to have more resources, they are certainly not sufficient for economic growth. Modern economics points instead to the institutions that frame the environment within which business and personal decisions are made.

This chapter helps set a framework for thinking about growth policies. Many of the issues we touch on will see deeper treatment in later chapters. In particular, Chapter 13 presents the theory of economic growth. Hopefully, the current chapter serves as a catalyst to deepen your understanding of the theories behind these ideas.

BIG QUESTIONS

(1) Why does economic growth matter?

- Economic growth affects human welfare in meaningful ways.
- Historical data shows that sustained economic growth is a relatively modern phenomenon.
- Relatively small but consistent growth rates are the best path out of poverty.

(2) How do resources and technology contribute to economic growth?

- Natural resources, physical capital and human capital all contribute to economic growth.
- Technological change, which leads to production of more valuable output per unit of input, also sustains economic growth.

(3) What Institutions foster economic growth?

- Political stability and the rule of law.
- Private property rights.
- Competitive and open markets.
- Efficient taxes.
- Stable money and prices.

Concepts You Should Know

Institution
Effective labor   Resources
Factors of production   Technology
Growth rate   Technological advancement
Human capital   Rule of 70
Private property

Questions for Review

1. What are the three factors that influence economic growth?

2. What is human capital and how is it different from the just the quantity of workers available for work? Name three ways to increase a nation's human capital. Is an increase in the size of the labor force also an increase in the human capital? Explain your answer.

3. How is economic growth measured?

4. Describe the pattern of world economic growth over the past two thousand years. Approximately when did economic growth really take off?

5. List five human welfare conditions that are positively affected by economic growth.

6. Some history books claim the United States grew rich because of the abundance of natural resources.

    a.   What is missing from this argument?

    b.   Name five poor nations that have significant natural resources.

7. The flow of funds across borders is a source of growth for economies. Use what you learned about loanable funds in Chapter 11 to describe how foreign funds might expand output in a nation.

8. In 2011, when the U.S. unemployment rate was over 9%, President Barack Obama said:

> "There are some structural issues with our economy where a lot of businesses have learned to become much more efficient with a lot fewer workers. You see it when you go to a bank and you use an ATM, you don't go to a bank teller, or you go to the airport and you're using a kiosk instead of checking in at the gate."

Discuss the President's quote in terms of both short-run unemployment and long-run growth.

9. The difference between 1% growth and 2% growth seems insignificant. Explain why it really matters.

10. What do economists mean by the term "institutions?" Name five different laws that that are institutions that affect production incentives. Name three social practices that affect production in a society.

Study Problems

*1. Real per capita GDP in China in 1959 was about $350, but doubled to about $700 by 1978, when Deng Xiao Ping started market reforms.

A. What was the average annual economic growth rate in China over twenty years from 1959 to 1978?
Answer: *The rule of 70 tells us that we can divide 70 by the rate of growth to get the number of years before a variable doubles. Therefore, is we know the number of years that a variable actually did take to double, we can re-arrange the rule of 70 to determine the average growth rate. Using the rule of 70, we can determine the growth rate as:*

70 ÷ 20 = 3.5.

Therefore, China grew an average of 3.5% over the twenty year period from 1959-1978.

B. Chinese per capita real GDP doubled again in only seven years, reaching $1400 by 1986. What was the average annual economic growth rate between 1979 and 1986?

Answer: *Now, with real per capital GDP doubling in just 7 years, the rule of 70 implies:*

70 ÷ 7 = 10.

Therefore, China grew an average of 10% over the seven year period from 1979-1986.

*2. The table below presents long run macroeconomic data for two hypothetical nations.

Nation	Nominal GDP Growth	Inflation	Nominal Interest Rate	Unemployment Rate	Population Growth
A	12%	10%	4%	12%	1.5%
B	5%	2%	4%	5%	1%

Assume both nations start with real GDP of $1,000 per citizen. Fill in the blanks in the table below assuming the data above applies for every year considered.

Nation	Economic Growth Rate	Years Required for Real Per Capita GDP to Double	Real Per Capita GDP 140 years later
A	_____	_____	_____
B	_____	_____	_____

Answer: *To determine economic growth rate, we use the approximations formula:*

Nominal GDP growth rate – Inflation – Population growth rate = Economic growth rate.

For nation A: 12% – 10% – 1.5% = 0.5%.

For nation B: 5% - 2% - 1% = 2%.

To determine the years required for real per capita GDP to double, we use the rule of 70:

For nation A: 70 ÷ 0.5 = 140.

For nation A: 70 ÷ 2 = 35.

To determine Real per capita GDP 140 years later:

For nation A, their level doubles in exactly 140 years, so it will be <u>2 times the original level</u>.

For Nation B, their level doubles after 35 years, then doubles again after 35 more. SO after 70 years, their level of real per capita GDP is four times the original level. It doubles again in 35 years so after 105 years, it is eight times the original level. Then it doubles again in 35 more years, so after 140 years, their real per capita GDP is <u>16 times the original level.</u>

3. The data in Table 12.2 shows the following world economic growth rates for specific historical eras:

Years	Growth Rate
0-1800	0.02%
1800-1900	0.64%
1900-1950	1.04%
1950-2000	2.12%

How many years will it take for average per capita real GDP to double at each of those growth rates?

4. Use the data in the table below to compute economic growth rates for the United States for 2008, 2009, and 2010. Note that all data is from the end of the year specified.

Date	Nominal GDP (billions of current $)	GDP Deflator	Population Growth
2007	14,061.8	106.30	1.01%
2008	14,369.1	108.62	0.93%
2009	14,119.0	109.61	0.87%
2010	14,660.4	110.66	0.90%

5. The rule of 70 applies in any growth rate application. Let's say you have $1,000 in savings and you have three alternatives for these funds:

- A savings account earning 1% interest.
- A U.S. Treasury bond mutual fund earning 3% interest.
- A stock market mutual fund earning 8% interest.

How long will it take to double your saving in each of the three accounts?

6. Assume you are retiring in 40 years and you are evaluating the three different accounts in the question above. How much will your $1,000 be worth in 40 years under the three alternatives?

Chapter 13: Growth Theory

Misconception: Economic growth depends on physical capital such as factories, infrastructure, and other tools.

Looking around the world, you see many rich nations and many poor nations. Rich developed nations have impressive capital including highways, factories and office buildings. Poor under-developed nations have more dirt roads and fewer modern factories and buildings. Many people see that capital and wealth seem to go hand-in-hand and conclude that capital is the source of wealth. From this view, if poor nations can just acquire bigger and better tools, they too can be wealthy. But correlation does not prove causation. Modern economic growth theory indicates that capital is the result of growth, rather than the cause of it, and that the key to economic growth is institutions.

In the last chapter we saw that economic growth can transform lives. Consistent economic growth, even at relatively small rates, is the pathway out of poverty. In this chapter, we shed light on the causes of economic growth by examining growth theory. We also present policies that foster growth.

As the chapter title implies, much of the content of this chapter is theoretical. Yet because of the relationship between economic growth and human welfare, the theory is never far from real world. We begin the chapter with a brief description of how economic theories develop. After that, we consider the evolution of growth theory starting with the Solow growth model. After covering the theory and implications of the Solow model, we'll consider modern growth theory and the implied policy prescriptions.

Big Questions

- How do macroeconomic theories evolve?
- What is the Solow growth model?
- How does technology affect growth?
- What is modern growth theory?

How do macroeconomic theories evolve?

This chapter marks our first major step into macroeconomic theory, or modeling. In Chapter 2, we discussed how economic models are built: good models are simple, flexible, and able to make powerful predictions. In this chapter, we present a model of economic growth that simplifies from the real world, yet also helps us make powerful predictions about economic growth. The stakes are high because growth theory and policy have significant impacts on human lives. Therefore, it's important to consistently re-evaluate growth theory in light of real-world results.

Today economists agree that economic growth is determined by resources, technology, and institutions. But this consensus is the result of an evolution in growth theory that started almost sixty years ago, with the contributions of economist Robert Solow. Although the theory has changed significantly over the past two decades, Solow's growth model still forms the nucleus of modern growth theory.

The evolution of growth theory is driven by the interplay between theory and human experience. In many academic disciplines, new theories are fodder for intellectual debates, with no direct impact on human lives. But in economics, theories are put to the test in the real world, often very soon after they are first articulated. Figure 13.1 illustrates the relationship between economic ideas and real world events. At the top of the circle, we begin with observations of the real world, which inform a theory as it develops. Once an economic theory is developed, it can influence the policies used to pursue certain economic goals. These policies affect the welfare of people around the globe. Finally, as economists observe the effects of policy in the real world, they continue to revise economic theory.

Figure 13.1:
The Interplay between the Real World and Economic Theory

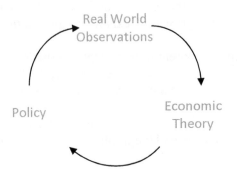

Observations of the real world shape economic theory. Economic theory then informs policy decisions that are designed to meet certain economic goals. Once these policies are implemented, they affect the real world. Further real-world observations contribute to additional advances in economic theory, and the cycle continues.

Economic growth models affect the welfare of billions of people around the world. This can be beneficial. However, if growth theory is wrong or incomplete, it can lead to faulty policy prescriptions which can result in sustained poverty for millions of real people. We will revisit this point toward the end of the chapter.

The evolution of growth theory

In 1776, Adam Smith published his renowned book: *An Inquiry into the Nature and Causes of the Wealth of Nations*. This book was the first real Economics textbook. As the title indicates, it focused on what makes a nation wealthy. The central question, paraphrased from the title is: why do some nations prosper while others do not? More than two centuries later, macroeconomists still grapple with the nature and causes of the wealth of nations.

Economists are not alone in their pursuit of answers to this question. Perhaps you or someone you know has visited a developing country. As travel becomes easier and the world economy becomes more integrated, people are more exposed to poverty around the globe. Many college students today ask the same questions as economists: why are so many people poor, and what can we do about it?

This link between economic theory and human welfare is what drives many to study the theory of economic growth. As Nobel Prize-winning macroeconomist Robert Lucas said:

> "Is there some action a government of India could take that would lead the Indian Economy to grow like Indonesia's or Egypt's? If so, what exactly? If not, what is it about the "nature of India" that makes it so? The consequences for human welfare involved in questions like these are simply staggering: *Once one starts to think about them it is hard to think of anything else.*"

Economic growth has not always been the primary focus of macroeconomics. After the Great Depression in the 1930's, macroeconomics shifted to the study of business cycles or short-run expansions and contractions. Over the past quarter century, the primary focus returned to long-run economic growth.

Growth theory began with the Solow Model, which was developed in the 1950s and still serves as the foundation for growth theory, both in method and policy. Therefore, while growth theory has evolved, it is helpful to consider the Solow model as both a starting point and as the nucleus of current theory.

What is the Solow growth model?

If you travel around the globe and visit nations with different levels of income, you will notice significant differences in the physical tools available for use in production. Wealthy nations have more factories, better roads, more and better computers—they have more capital. Simply viewing the difference in capital, it is easy to conclude that capital yields economic growth.

This was the basic premise of early growth theory: there are rich nations and there are poor nations, and the rich nations are those that have capital.   Throughout this chapter, we will often refer to capital as *physical capital* to distinguish it from human capital. Natural resources and human capital are also important in the Solow growth model, but it focuses primary on physical capital, or just capital. We begin by looking at a nation's production function, which describes how changes in capital affect real output.

A Nation's Production Function

The Solow model starts with a *production function* for the entire economy. In microeconomic theory, a firm's **production function** describes the relationship between the inputs a firm uses and the output it creates. For example, at a single McDonald's restaurant, the daily output depends on the number of employees, anything needed to make the final product such as hamburger patties, French fries, etc., and the capital tools that employees have to work with, including things such as space for cooking, cash registers, and drink dispensers. In equation form, the production function for a single firm is:

A **production function** for a firm describes the relationship between inputs a firm uses and the output it creates.

$$q = f(\text{human capital, physical capital}), \qquad (13.1)$$

where q is the output of the firm. Equation 13.1 says that output *is a function of* the quantities of human and physical capital that the firm uses. For McDonalds, the output is the number of meals produced.

In macroeconomics, we extend the production function to an entire nation or macroeconomy. The **aggregate production function** describes the relationship between all the inputs used in the macroeconomy and the total output of that economy, where GDP is output. In its simplest form, the aggregate production function tells us that GDP is a function of three broad types of resources or factors of production, which are the inputs used in producing goods and services. These inputs are physical capital, human capital, and natural resources. We can state it in equation form as:

$$Y = F(\ physical\ capital,\ human\ capital,\ natural\ resources)\quad (13.2)$$

> The **aggregate production function** describes the relationship between all the inputs used in the macroeconomy and the total output (GDP) of that economy.

where Y is real output or GDP. The equation tells us that GDP in any country depends on the three types of resources available for production.

We can think about the relationship between input and output in a very simple economy. Consider a situation in which there is only one person in the macroeconomy, for example Chuck Noland from the movie *Castaway*. Chuck's individual, or microeconomic decisions are also macroeconomic decisions, because he is the only person in the economy. The GDP of Chuck's island includes only what he produces with his resources. Let's say that Chuck spends his days harvesting fruit on the island. In this case, GDP is equal to whatever fruit Chuck harvests. Table 13.1 shows Chuck's production function and some of the resources he has available.

Table 13.1 Chuck Noland's Production Function

$$GDP = F(\ natural\ resources,\ human\ capital,\ physical\ capital)$$

GDP	Resources	Example
Fruit	Natural resources Human capital Physical capital	Fruit trees and bamboo Chuck's time and knowledge Bamboo ladder

Chuck's output is fruit he harvests from around his island. His resources include his human capital, a bamboo ladder, and the island's natural resources such as bamboo and fruit trees. All else equal, the more Chuck has of any of these resources, the more GDP he can produce. Economic growth occurs if Chuck figures out a way to produce more fruit per week.

The production function for a large developed macroeconomy like the United States is the same as Chuck Noland's in many ways. Output depends on the resources available for production. The United States has significant natural resources like oil, iron ore, coal, timber, and farmland. In terms of human capital, the United States has a large labor force composed of over 155 million workers. Of those aged 25 and over, more than 90% have graduated from high school. Finally, the United States has built up a very large stock of physical capital. All of these resources enable us to produce annual GDP of more than $15 trillion.

The Focus on Capital Resources

The early Solow models focused on the availability of capital goods. As we noted in the chapter opener, the early growth theorists saw that capital resources in wealthy nations far exceed those available in developing nations. There are more factories, highways, bridges and dams in wealthy nations. It seemed logical to conclude that capital is the key to growth.

In addition, periods of investment growth in developed economies are also periods of economic expansion.  plots quarterly U.S. economic growth rates with investment growth rates. The data shows a clear positive correlation between real GDP growth and the rate of investment growth. This is another reason to believe that investment and capital are the primary sources of economic growth.

Figure 13.2:
U.S. Investment and GDP Growth, 1960 - 2011

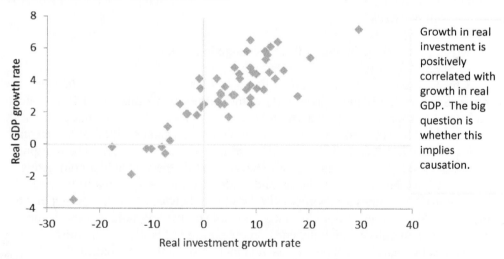

Growth in real investment is positively correlated with growth in real GDP. The big question is whether this implies causation.

Source: BEA
Note that in the final markup, these should be dates in place of markers.

Earlier we noted the interplay of theory and real world observations. This is one example. Capital *appears* to cause economic growth because there is such a strong correlation between wealth and output. And certainly, nobody would dispute that workers are more productive when they have more tools. For now we will continue our focus on capital, like the early growth theorists. Later, we will explore some of the missing pieces that contemporary growth theory has contributed.

Marginal Product

Chuck Noland would be happy if he found a new grove of mangoes on his island – more resources help produce more GDP. Resources also help actual large macroeconomies. For example, the discoveries of natural gas in the United States have increased dramatically over the past two decades. This new energy resource allows the United States to produce more with cheaper resources, because natural gas is less expensive than crude oil. To quantify how helpful a resource may be, economists employ the concept of *marginal product*. The **marginal product** of an input is the change in output divided by the change in input. More resources increase output, so we say the marginal product of each resource is positive.

> The **marginal product** of an input is the change in output divided by the change in input.

Let's take a closer look at Chuck Noland's production function. Initially, Chuck produces GDP by climbing trees and picking fruit. With this method, he is able to gather one bushel of fruit in a week. He produces this weekly GDP without the aid of any physical capital. Then Chuck decides to build a bamboo ladder. Building the ladder is a costly investment because it takes him away from producing fruit for a whole week. But then, after he has the ladder as physical capital, his weekly output grows to 4 bushels. Using the language we defined above, we say that the marginal product of his ladder is 3 bushels of fruit per week:

$$MP_{Capital} = \text{Change in output from a change in capital} = 3.$$

Chuck is so happy with his ladder that he builds a second ladder so he can leave one on each side of the island. His weekly output climbs to six bushels of fruit. Because he produces 4 bushels with 1 ladder and 6 bushels with two ladders, the marginal product of the second ladder is 2 bushels. Note that, while the marginal product of the second ladder is positive, it is less than the marginal product of the first ladder. The marginal product of the second ladder is not as large because while the first ladder completely altered how Chuck harvests fruit, the second ladder just makes his job a little easier.

Figure 13.3 shows a hypothetical relationship between Chuck's output and the number of ladders he uses. Looking first at the table on the left, note that the second column shows total output which depends on the number of ladders. The third column shows the marginal product of each ladder. Notice that the marginal product of ladders declines as more and more ladders are added. This reflects the principle of **diminishing marginal product**, which states that the marginal product of an input falls as the quantity of the input rises. Diminishing marginal product generally applies across all factors of production at both the microeconomic and macroeconomic level.

> **Diminishing marginal product** occurs when the marginal product of an input falls as the quantity of the input rises.

The right side of Figure 13.2 is a graph of Chuck's production function – it plots the points from the first two columns of the table on the left. With no ladders, the production function indicates one bushel of fruit, but then as ladders are added, output climbs along the curve. The slope of the curve flattens out because the marginal product of the added ladders diminishes.

This principle of diminishing marginal productivity is not special to our example of one man alone on an island. It is a phenomenon that holds for resources in a macroeconomy, and it is a cornerstone insight of the Solow growth model. Sometimes this principle is referred to as *diminishing returns*.

For example, in the United States, we have a system of interstate highways that was built by the federal government. This highway system is essentially a 50,000 mile capital good we use to help produce GDP. The network of highways connects the major cities of the United States. These highways increase GDP in the United States – they enhance our ability to transport goods and services across the nation. For example, a couch manufactured in High Point, North Carolina can be transported exclusively by interstate highway to Cleveland, Ohio in less than 8 hours. Before the construction of the interstate system, the same trip between High Point and Cleveland would have taken twice as long, required more gasoline due to inefficient speeds, and caused much more wear and tear on the vehicles used.

Our system of highways is a significant resource that contributes to our GDP. If the interstate highway system were somehow closed down completely, GDP would immediately fall. On the other hand, what would happen to GDP if we created a second interstate highway system, with 50,000 miles of new roads crisscrossing the United States? That is, what is the marginal product of an additional interstate highway system? The impact would be positive, but much smaller than the original network. This is because of diminishing returns: the marginal product of highways declines as we have more and more available. The production relationship is just like Chuck Noland's ladders.

Figure 13.4 is a picture of the aggregate production function; the production function for the entire economy. On the vertical axis, we have output or real GDP (Y). Economic growth is represented as movements up the vertical axis. On the horizontal axis, capital resources (K) increase from left to right. Notice that the slope of the function is positive, which indicates positive marginal product. But the marginal impact of capital also declines as more is added. For example, the difference in output from the increase in capital from K_1 to K_2 is larger than the change in output from a change in capital from K_3 to K_4. This is the declining marginal product of capital.

The aggregate production function forms the basis for most discussions in growth theory since 1956. Economic growth is represented by movements upward along the vertical axis. Indeed, if we focus *only* on this simple formulation, economic growth happens only with investment in capital.

Diminishing returns, or declining marginal productivity, is the key assumption of the Solow model. As we shall see, this single assumption leads to striking implications for the macroeconomy.

Implications of the Solow Model

We can use the basic framework of the production function with an emphasis on capital and diminishing returns to flesh out the two important implications of the Solow model: the conditions of a *steady state* and *convergence*.

The Steady State

How many ladders should Chuck Noland build? Each ladder takes a week to build, and each additional ladder adds less output than the one before. Therefore, at some point Chuck has no incentive to build additional ladders. Perhaps this happens after he builds two ladders. Looking back at Figure 13.3, you can see that a third ladder yields only one more bushel of fruit. Let's assume that Chuck decides it is not worth a week of work for one more bushel of fruit. Therefore, Chuck builds only two ladders. This means his output remains at 6 bushels a week. Economic growth for Chuck stops.

      The Solow model implies the same outcome for large macroeconomies. Because the marginal product of capital decreases, at some point, there is no reason to build more capital. Perhaps this occurs at K_3 in Figure 13.5. This means there is no incentive to build additional capital beyond the level of K_3 because the benefits in terms of additional output no longer exceed the cost of building capital. Since there is no incentive to build capital past K_3, and capital is the source of growth, the economy stops growing once it reaches K_3. This is called the economy's *steady state*. The **steady state** is the condition of a macroeconomy when there is no new net investment.

> The **steady state** is the condition of a macroeconomy when there is no new net investment.

      Once an economy reaches the steady state, there is no change in either capital or real income. The steady state is a direct implication of diminishing returns: when the marginal return to capital declines, at some point there is no incentive to build more capital. And this is not very encouraging. You can think of the steady state as the "stagnant state," because when the economy reaches its steady state, real GDP is done increasing and economic growth stops.

      It is important to distinguish between investment and net investment. Over time, capital wears out: roads get potholes, tractors break down, and factories become obsolete — this is known as capital *depreciation*. **Depreciation** is a fall in the value of a resource over time. Depreciation is natural with capital and it erodes the capital stock. Without new investment, capital declines over time and so some positive investment is needed to offset depreciation. But if investment is exactly enough to replace depreciated items, the capital stock will not increase and this means no *net investment*. **Net investment** is investment minus depreciation. In order to increase the capital stock, net investment must be positive.

> **Depreciation** is a fall in the value of a resource over time.

> **Net investment** is investment minus depreciation.

This distinction between investment and net investment is important when we consider the steady state. In the steady state, there is no net investment. There may be positive investment, but this is investment to replace worn out machines and tools. So when an economy reaches its steady state, the capital stock stays constant. For example, if three ladders represent a steady state condition on Chuck Noland's island, he may repair his ladders periodically. Repairing the ladders to maintain a level of capital counts as investment, but not net investment.

Convergence

If nations with large stocks of capital stop growing, then nations with less capital can catch up if they are adding to their capital stock. This means that nations all over the globe could converge to the same level of wealth. **Convergence** is the idea that per capita GDP levels across nations will equalize as nations approach the steady state. Here is the logic of the Solow model: rich nations are rich because they have more capital. But as these nations approach their steady state, the returns to capital decline and growth slows. When a nation reaches a steady state, economic growth stops. But if a nation has not yet reached the steady state, adding capital still leads to growth in that nation. Therefore investment in developing nations should yield relatively greater returns, and this should lead to more capital in developing nations.

> **Convergence** is the idea that per capita GDP levels across nations will equalize, as nations approach the steady state.

Consider the United States and China. In 1980, the United States was wealthy, but China was poor. Figure 13.6 shows both nations as they might have appeared on a production function in 1980. Yet since 1980, growth rates in China have exceeded growth rates in the United States. This blast of growth in China has been accompanied by a rapid industrialization – the creation of new physical capital. According to the Solow model, the new capital in China yields greater returns because it started with less capital.

If this basic model were true to reality, new factories would typically yield higher returns in poorer nations than rich nations. Investors seeking to build new factories would turn to nations like Haiti, Nicaragua and North Korea, nations with relatively small capital stocks.

According to the Solow theory, developing nations should catch up because the older, developed economies have already made new discoveries and documented mistakes to avoid in the development process. Developing nations can jump right into the best equipment, tools, and practices. For example, if they are building cars, they don't have to start with a Model-T and a basic labor-intensive assembly line, they can jump right to a modern plant resembling those of Honda and Volkswagen.

But reality looks much different. We may see some cases of rapid growth in poor nations, but convergence is rare. Some poor nations have grown rapidly over the past few decades. In addition to China, South Korea, Singapore, India, Chile, and others have done well. But these are exceptions. Most of poor nations continue to stagnate. Moreover, growth in developed nations hasn't stopped. In addition, growth in wealthy nations has not gone away. Figure 13.7 shows U.S. Economic growth rates in twenty-year time windows since 1820. If anything, growth was accelerating even as Solow wrote his papers. There is no evidence of either slowing down or catching up.

Figure 13.7
U.S. Economic Growth Rates Since 1820

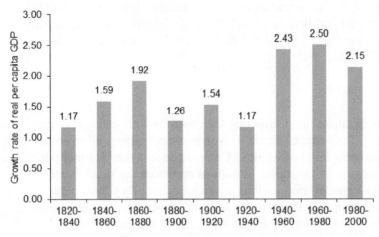

Source: BEA.

The Solow model implies that growth in the United States should slow down over time. However, there is little evidence of the United States reaching a steady state.

      Given that we have no evidence of either a steady state or of convergence, it is time to re-assess the model. In particular, we need to answer the question of why we see sustained growth in wealthy nations.   In the next section, we consider whether technology is the answer.

Practice What You Know
Changes in Resources

Natural Disaster

In 2011, a major earthquake and tsunami in Japan destroyed significant physical capital, including roads, homes, factories, and bridges.

QUESTION: Use an aggregate production function to illustrate how a major destruction of capital affects a macroeconomy in the short run.

ANSWER:

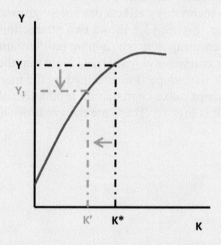

This is an unusual situation in which the level of capital in a nation actually falls. Since capital (K) is on the horizontal axis of the production function, the decline in capital moves Japan back along their production function. This means less GDP for Japan (Y falls) until they can get their capital rebuilt.

QUESTION: With no further changes, what happens to real GDP in the long run?

ANSWER: With no further changes, real GDP returns to the steady state output level in the long run. At the new level of capital (K') the marginal product of additional capital is relatively high, so there is a greater return to building new capital. But in the long run, since there was no shift in the production function, the level of capital returns to the steady state level (K*) which means output also returns to it's steady state level (Y*).

How does technology affect growth?

In this section we consider how technological innovations affect the Solow model and also address assumptions about the way they occur.

Technology and the Production Function

In 1994, Intel introduced a revolutionary computer chip for personal computers — the Pentium chip. The Pentium could perform 188 million instructions per second and was more than three times faster than its predecessor chip. But by 2011, just 19 years later, Intel's new chip, the Core i7 3960x could perform 178 billion instructions per second. The new chip costs less and uses less energy than the old chip, yet it is almost a thousand times faster!

These Intel chips give us a good picture of what technology does. A computer chip is physical capital—it is a tool that helps us produce. When we get faster chips, we can produce even more with the same amount of capital.

Now let's see how new technology affects the Solow growth model. First, consider the production function. Figure 13.8 shows two production functions: F is the initial production function, when computers are running on Pentium chips; F_1 is the production function after faster computer chips arrive. Note that the new production function is steeper than the old. The slope is determined by the marginal product of capital and the new computer chips make capital more productive at all levels. For any given level of capital, real GDP is higher. These are the kinds of changes that fuel sustained economic growth.

Figure 13.8
New Technology and the Production Function

$$Y = A \cdot F(natural\ resources,\ human\ capital,\ physical\ capital)$$

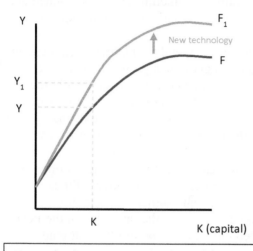

New technology increases the slope of the production function as the marginal product of capital increases. The old production function is shown as F, and the new production function is F_1. After the technological innovation, capital is more productive and this leads to new economic growth. If technology continues to advance, economic growth can be sustained.

We can also see how the production function is altered in equation form. The aggregate production function now includes an allowance for technological advancement:

$$Y = A \cdot F(natural\ resources,\ human\ capital,\ physical\ capital) \qquad (13.2)$$

Where the letter A accounts for technological change. This small addition to the basic model helps to explain continued economic growth. Without new technology, the economy eventually reaches a steady state and growth stops. But new technology means output is higher for any given level of capital, because the capital, which embeds the new technology, is more productive. The new technology shifts real output, and therefore income, up to new levels.

Before looking at policy implications that derive from the Solow model, we need to look more closely at how technological change occurs in the model.

Exogenous Technical Change

Why do people innovate? What drives people to create new and better ways of producing? If technology is the source of sustained growth, the answer to this question is critical.

In the Solow model, there is no real answer to the question of what causes technological innovation. The model assumes technical change occurs *exogenously*. Recall from Chapter 2 that exogenous factors are the variables not accounted for in a model. For our purposes here, this means that technological innovations just happen – they are not based on economics. In this sense, technological innovations occur randomly. If technology is exogenous, it is like rainfall – sometimes you get a bunch and sometimes you don't get any. If some nations get more technological innovations than others, then that is just their good fortune.

But if technology is the source of sustained growth, and technology is exogenous, then economic growth is also exogenous. **Exogenous growth** is growth that is independent of any factors in the economy. When we see innovation occurring in the same places over and over, the Solow model just chalks this up to luck. The innovations are not due to any inherent characteristics of the economies that experience them. Similarly, poor nations are poor simply because the random technology innovations happened elsewhere.

Exogenous growth is growth that is independent of any factors in the economy.

If you question the assumption that technological advance is a matter of pure luck, you are right. But why did the Solow growth model make this assumption? First, technological progress is tied to scientific advancements and sometimes scientific discoveries seem to happen by chance. One classic example is the invention of the Post-It notes. Researchers at 3M accidentally stumbled onto a formula for glue that made Post-It notes possible.

Second, most economic models are developed mathematically. The assumption of exogenous technical change made the theoretical growth models simpler to solve because it rules out a very complicated factor. But in the 1980s, economists developed models to help incorporate technical change into the heart of the model.

Economics in the Media:
Technological Change

Modern Marvels

"Modern Marvels" is a television series on the History Channel. It often showcases technological innovations that have revolutionized the way goods and services are produced. In Season, 13, an episode titled Harvesters 2 included a look at cranberry harvesting around the globe.

Cranberries are grown on short vines. In the past, cranberry harvesting involved many workers carefully hand-harvesting the cranberries off the bushes. But cranberries also have air-pockets inside them and these pockets allow farmers to employ a wet harvest. The big innovation in harvesting occurred in when farmers began flooding the fields and then knocking the cranberries off the bushes with water-reel harvesters called beaters. This innovation means just a few workers can harvest ten acres of cranberries in a single day, saving hundreds of hours of labor.

The beaters make the harvest go quickly, but they also tend to damage some of the berries. Recently, Habelman Brothers, a cranberry farm in Tomah, Wisconsin, began using a gentler method than the water –reel so they don't damage the cranberries. Their harvesters use water-wheels use wooden panels to knock the berries off the vines, damaging fewer berries in the process.

These two innovations – water-harvesting and the new gentler water wheel – are both examples of innovations caused by incentives. The first innovation cut harvesting costs significantly, and the second increased the return from the harvest. The innovators are the farmers – those who have the most to gain. Technology is not random; it is a result of individuals responding to incentives.

Policy Implications of the Solow Model

At the beginning of the chapter, we noted that macroeconomic theory has strong implications for policy; it translates into policy recommendations. What policy prescriptions follow from the Solow growth model?

If you believe the Solow model and its conclusions, the policy implications are straightforward. Wealth comes from capital and modern technology. Therefore, developing nations need the latest technology embedded in capital goods. Therefore, wealthy nations and individuals around the globe who wish to help poor nations should funnel aid to the poor countries for use in purchase of the latest capital.

Two specific types of aid developed during the 1950s and 1960s to implement this approach. First, actual capital goods were built with aid from developed nations. For example, in 1964, with funding from America, Great Britain, and the World Bank, the

Akosombo Dam was built in the West African nation of Ghana. The hydroelectric dam was intended to produce several benefits. It formed a lake that could be used for water transportation and a fishing industry. The dam could also generate electricity. But even a gift of this magnitude failed to jumpstart the Ghanaian economy. Forty-three years after the Dam was completed, average income levels in Ghana have risen just $300 per person.

Second, billions of dollars of international aid was given to developing nations to help them fund investment in infrastructure such as highways, bridges, and modern ports, as well as other types of capital. These aid payments were intended to help poor nations build capital infrastructure that would pave the way to economic growth.

However, even after billions of dollars in aid, nations such as Zimbabwe, Liberia, Nicaragua, and Haiti are just as poor today at they were in 1960. On the other hand, Taiwan, Chile, China, and India received almost no international aid and yet they have grown rapidly.

The application of the Solow model via growth policy was not always successful. In fact, most of the twentieth century witnessed faulty policy. This policy was based on incomplete growth theory and applied by well-meaning people. It resulted in very few success stories and a series of failures. Consider the continent of Africa, where policies based on Solow growth models were applied consistently. Solow's growth model was developed in 1956. Thirty-seven African nations achieved independence from 1956 to 1977, so these newly independent and poverty-stricken nations offered a unique opportunity to apply the Solow model. Yet now, half a century later, it is clear that these policies failed across the continent. Many African nations are no better off than they were fifty years ago, even while much of the rest of the globe experienced significant economic gains. These real world observations led to a re-examination of growth theory in the late twentieth century.

Practice What You Know
Technological Innovations

How is the production function affected?

When new technology is introduced, it makes capital more productive. For example, new modern tractors are faster and more powerful than tractors of old.

Question: Explain how this type of change affects the production function.

Answer: The production function gets steeper at each point. For example, when the level of capital is K, the slope of production function F_1 is steeper than the slope of F. The reason is that capital is now more productive at every level. The first unit of capital adds more to output than before, and the 500th unit of capital adds more to output than before. The marginal product of capital, which is embedded in the slope of the production function, is now higher at all levels.

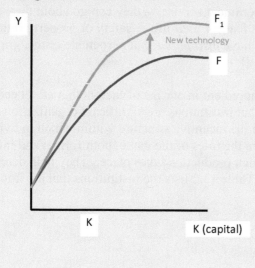

What is modern growth theory?

Over the past twenty years, a resurgence in growth theory has been spurred by the belief that *some economies grow faster for reasons particular to those economies*. In some nations, and even pockets within nations, technological advances arrive more rapidly. Growth is sustained through technological innovation, but these innovations do not occur randomly. Rather, economic growth is *endogenous*. **Endogenous growth** is growth driven by factors inside the economy. There must be some reason that assembly lines, sewing machines, air conditioning, personal computers and the internet were all developed in the United States. These advances spurred economic growth and improved people's lives. Why did they all occur here? Modern growth theory seeks to understand why such innovations occur in one place and not another.

> **Endogenous growth** is growth driven by factors inside the economy.

Nowadays, many economists stress the importance of institutions. We introduced institutions in Chapter 12. In this section, we develop a framework for thinking about which institutions best foster growth.

Institutions

Consider the city of Nogales which straddles the border of the United States in Arizona and Mexico. Average income in the northern half is of the city three times that in the southern half. The education level on the northern side is much higher, the roads are much better, and infant mortality much lower. The two halves of the city have the same geography, ethnicity and weather. Why are the two sides so different? According to economist Daron Acemoglu:

> The key difference is that those on the north side of the border enjoy law and order and dependable government services – they can go about their daily activities and jobs without fear for their life or safety or property rights. On the other side, the inhabitants have *institutions* that perpetuate crime, graft, and insecurity [emphasis added]

Institutions are the final ingredient in our list of factors that affect economic growth. Recall from Chapter 12 that institutions are significant organizations, laws, and social mores in society that frame the incentive structure within which individuals and business firms act. Institutions are the rules of the game, both formal and informal. They frame the environment within which production takes place. They help determine the costs and benefits of production. Table 13.2 lists the institutions that are important for growth.

Table 13.2
Institutions that Foster Economic Growth

1. Political stability and the rule of law	5. Flow of funds across borders
2. Private property rights	6. Efficient taxes
3. Competitive markets	7. Stable money and prices
4. International trade	

If we include institutions in the aggregate production function, we have:

$$Y = A \cdot F(\text{naural resources}, \text{human capital}, \text{physical capital}, \text{institutions}) \quad (25.3)$$

Certain institutions lay the groundwork for natural endogenous growth. With these institutions in place, there are incentives for new technology to emerge and drive growth.

<u>Figure 13.9</u> shows how institutions affect the production function. Consider the shift toward private property rights that occurred in China since the 1980s. As we talked about in Chapter 24, the shift toward private property rights changed incentives for producers who now get to keep much of their output. This change is behind the exploding growth we now see in China.

Figure 13.9
Efficient Institutions and the Production Function

$$Y = A \cdot F(natural\ resources, human\ capital, physical\ capital, institutions)$$

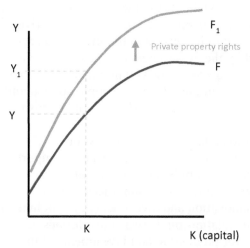

Private property rights

Adopting efficient institutions shifts a nation's production function upward. Efficient institutions make it possible for nations to produce more for any given level of resources, and they increase incentives for technological innovation.

Modern growth theory builds on the Solow model. The aggregate production function is still the core of all growth theory. Resources and technology are also considered important contributors to economic growth. But the fundamental characteristic of modern growth theory is the focus on institutions.

Institutions Determine Incentives

GDP is production. To determine what leads to endogenous economic growth, we need to consider how institutions affect production decisions. Let's focus on the decision to produce for an individual firm. Imagine you are considering whether to open a new website design business. You decide that you will only open such a business if you expect to at least break even – your payoff must cover your costs. This is not unusual. We can state this condition as follows: voluntary investment and production occurs only if:

Expected payoff ≥ *costs.*

The payoffs come later than the costs and are uncertain, which is why we call them *expected payoffs*.

No matter what your output – website designs, college gear, cupcakes or tractors — the payoffs come after production and after sales. The exact time lag depends on the type of output, but payoffs from all output come some time after expenditures on resources. Because of the delay and the resources required, people need to believe that the sacrifice, patience, and effort will offer a real payoff in the future.

Consider your decision to invest in your human capital by attending college. Why are you and your family voluntarily spending so much of your resources on human capital? The answer has to be that you expect the return to be greater than the cost. That is, you expect to gain more from your college education than you pay for it. And you probably will, even if it takes a few years to realize the greatest monetary returns.

Investment and production occur naturally if future payoffs are significant and predictable – if the incentives for them are strong enough. These incentives are determined by a nation's institutions. For example, if people are allowed to own private property and use it for personal gain, they have strong incentives to use their resources wisely. On the other hand, if property is owned by the government or a group, there is less incentive care for the property. For example, consider how you might care for your dorm room compared to a room in a house you or your parents own. People are generally less careful with rental property than their own property. This is why security deposits are standard policy for rentals.

Institutions that foster growth are institutions that create incentives for endogenous or natural growth. In Chapter 24, we covered the institutions most important for growth including private property rights, political stability and the rule of law, competitive and open markets, efficient taxes, and stable money and prices. These institutions create incentives for technological innovation and investments in both human and physical capital. Figure 13.10 illustrates this relationship between institutions and economic growth. Institutions create incentives for production and investment. If the right incentives are in place, production and investment occur naturally and the result is more human capital, more physical capital, and technological advancement—all of which lead to economic growth.

Figure 13.10
Institutions, Incentives, and Endogenous Growth

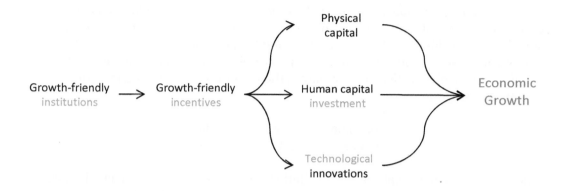

The goal is economic growth, but it all starts with institutions. Institutions provide the incentives that motivate choices by people in an economy. The right institutions provide incentives for people to invent new technology and to invest in human and physical capital. These lead to economic growth.

Some institutions also act to reduce expected payoffs. Among these are corruption, political instability, high and variable inflation, and high tax rates. One of the keys to sustained growth is to eliminate these barriers to natural growth. Figure 13.11 illustrates how inefficient institutions can impede growth. Since payoffs from productive actions come in the future, anything that reduces the likelihood of these payoffs reduces the incentive for investment today.

Figure 13.11:
Institutions that Inhibit Endogenous Growth

People must work and invest today in order to get payoffs from output in the future. Inefficient institutions reduce the expected future payoffs and thus reduce incentives for production. Growth-fostering institutions are those that maximize expected future payoffs for producers.

We can now understand why we don't see convergence across all economies: different institutions lead to different rates of growth. Resources and technology are not enough. Nations grow faster when they have more efficient institutions. Others grow slowly because they don't. Unless institutions are the same across nations, we should not expect to see convergence.

Modern growth theory acknowledges the core truths of the Solow model: resources and technology are sources of economic growth. But it also recognizes the importance of institutions. This emphasis on institutions matters for policy. For example, international aid, even aid that is directed for capital goods, cannot lead to growth if the recipient nation does not have efficient institutions. Institutions are the key ingredient to long run growth.

Economics in the Real World:
Chile: a Modern Growth Miracle

Chile is an excellent example of how institutions affect economic growth and, in turn, human welfare. Several nations, after struggling for centuries with little economic growth, have recently begun to grow at impressive rates. The best known examples are China and India. But less known is the recent economic growth in Chile.

Since 1985, the growth of real per capita GDP in Chile has averaged 4.3 percent. The rule of 70 tells us it only takes about 16 years to double living standards at that rate. In fact, real GDP rose from $7,709 per person to over $20,000 per person in the 23 years from 1985 to 2008. You can see this in the per capital real GDP shown in Panel a of Figure 13.12. Notice also the change from Chile's past experience. Chile grew by less than 1% from 1900 to 1985.

Figure 13.12:
Economic Growth and Life Expectancy in Chile

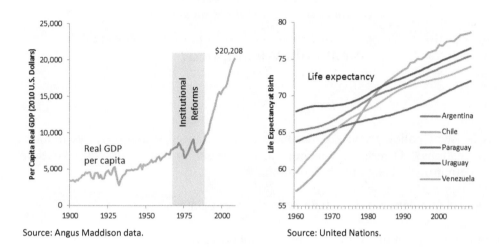

Source: Angus Maddison data.   Source: United Nations.

Institutional reforms in Chile have led to historic economic growth and this growth has helped the people of Chile in many ways. One clear improvement is the increase in life expectancy.

    As we have seen, economic growth means that most lives change for the better. One vivid indicator of these changes is life expectancy. Panel b of Figure 13.12 shows that life expectancy in Chile increased from 57 in 1960 to 78 years by 2009. This increase of 21 years in average lifespan moved Chile ahead of many Latin American neighbors.

    What is the cause of growth for Chile? In a word – institutions. In 1973, Chile began significant economic reforms. In addition to lowering trade barriers and instituting monetary and price stability (inflation was 665 percent in 1974), the government also privatized many state-owned businesses and removed controls on wages and prices. These institutional reforms paved the way for the historic economic growth happening now in Chile.

Data Sources: Angus Maddison data, Gapminder and author's calculations.

Practice What You Know
Solow Growth Theory versus Modern Growth Theory

What policy is implied?

Question:

Below is a list of policy proposals that have been advanced to help the economies of developing nations. Determine whether each proposal is consistent with the Solow model, modern growth theory, neither, or both.

A. Unrestricted international aid to help build a power plant

B. Aid for a power plant that is dependent on democratic reforms

C. Microfinance (very small short-term loans for small businesses)

D. Reductions in trade restrictions

Answers:

A. This is consistent with the Solow model: physical capital leads to growth.

B. This is consistent with both Solow and modern growth theory. The power plant is physical capital, but the aid is dependent on institutional reform.

C. Neither. This kind of program does not directly address the need for resources or the need for institutional reform.

D. Modern growth theory. Open trade is institutional reform that leads to greater competition and more options for citizens in developing nations.

Economics for Life:
Institutions of growth

Applying for a Patent

The late Apple CEO Steve Jobs is famous for having his name on 317 different patents. This means he is credited with participation in the 317 new inventions. Inventions are technological innovations and we've seen that these are a source of economic growth.

Patent laws are an institution that has helped pave the way for many new technological advancements. Patents create a twenty-year monopoly for the inventor or owner of the patent. This monopoly is an incentive that encourages innovation. Patent laws are thus an institution meant to encourage new inventions that shift up the economy's production function.

If you have an idea that you'd like to patent, you need to apply for your patent through the U.S. Patent office. In addition to a detailed description of your patent, you'll need to create a drawing that specifies exactly how your idea is new and different. Finally, it is a good idea to hire a patent attorney to edit your patent application so you can lessen the chances that somebody will copy your idea later.

Even if you don't have the resources to capitalize on your invention, you can always try to sell your patent to somebody who can.

You may not be as successful as Steve Jobs, but patents are a legal way to make monopoly profit.

Conclusion

We opened this chapter with the misconception that capital is the essential growth ingredient. We have seen that while capital is helpful, it is clear that physical tools are not enough to insure long-run growth. The same applies to other resources and technology. Without institutions that promote the incentive to produce, sustained endogenous growth does not take root.

Many people think that macroeconomics is all about business cycles and recessions. Our goal in this chapter was to present the ideas behind long-run growth theory, rather than short-run cycles. In Chapter 14, we present a model that we use to study short run business cycles.

BIG QUESTIONS

How do macroeconomic theories evolve?

- Macroeconomic theories evolve in relationship to observations in the real world. Policies often follow from theory. Policies produce results which, in turn, influence revisions of economic theory.

What is the Solow growth model?

- The Solow growth model is a model of economic growth based on a production function for the economy.
- The key feature of the production function is diminishing returns.
- The Solow growth model posits that diminishing returns lead economies toward a zero-growth steady state.
- The Solow growth model further posits that given steady states and, as a result, economies tend to converge over time.

How does technology affect growth?

- Technology is a source of sustained economic growth.
- In the Solow model, technology is exogenous.

What is modern growth theory?

- Modern growth theory emphasizes institutions as the key source of growth.
- Institutions determine incentives for production.
- Efficient institutions can lead to endogenous growth.

Concepts You Should Know

Aggregate production function	Endogenous growth	Net investment
		Production function
Convergence	Exogenous growth	
Depreciation	Marginal product	Steady state
Diminishing marginal product		

Questions for Review

1. Modern economic theory points to three sources of economic growth. Name these three sources and give an example of each.

2. About 50 years ago, Robert Solow contributed two significant papers to the literature on economic growth theory. What are the two key properties of the aggregate production function at the center of Solow's first contribution?

3. Explain why a nation cannot continue to grow forever by just adding more capital.

4. The Solow model assumes that technology changes are exogenous. What does this mean? Why does this matter for growth policy? What does this assumption imply about growth rates across nations over time?

5. Briefly explain the difference between modern growth theory and the Solow models.

6. China is a land of vast resources. In addition, technology is easily transportable across international borders. If we rule out these two sources of growth, to what can we attribute the economic growth in China since 1979?

7. The basic Solow growth models imply convergence. What is convergence? What key assumption about the marginal product of capital implies convergence?

8. Explain how an increase in educational opportunities can increase growth. Use a graph to illustrate how educational opportunities affect a nation's production function.

Study Problems

1. The Solow model focuses on how resources affect output. In this chapter, we focused on capital.

(a) Name the other two major categories of resources.

(b) Draw an aggregate production function with a typical shape; label this function F.

(c) Draw a second production function which indicates a technological advancement; label this new function F'.

2. Define human capital. Draw a graph that illustrates an increase in effective labor on a production function.

3. Suppose the people in the United States increase their savings rate. How will this affect the rate of economic growth in the United States?

Solved problem

1. Economic growth derives from many sources. Some of these cause a parallel shift in a nation's production function, while others change the slope of the production function. Below is a graph of three different production functions, F, F1, and F2. Assume that a nation begins with production function F. Production function F1 is a parallel shift up from F, and F2 is an increase in the slope from F.

For each of the following scenarios, determine which of the two new production functions, F1 or F2, best pictures how this affects their production function.

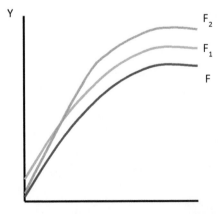

(a) Human capital rises through education

Answer: *The shift would be to F1, since it represents more output at all levels of capital.*

(b) Technological advancement occurs

Answer: *The shift would be to F2, since the marginal product of capital increases.*

(c) New natural gas reserves are found

Answer: *the shift would be to F1, since it represents more output at all levels of capital.*

Chapter 14

The Aggregate Demand-Aggregate Supply Model

Misconception: Recessions are inevitable and occur every few years.

Many people believe that every few years, the economy plunges into a recession and then, after a short period of slow growth, rises back up for a period of expansion. They consider this pattern to be inevitable, with recessions happening every 6-8 years. The term "business cycle" is a popular way to describe the recession-expansion phenomenon because so many are convinced that the recession-expansion pattern follows in a regular cycle.

But in fact, recessions are rarer today than at any other time in our history: while there have been 22 U.S. recessions since 1900, there have been just three since 1982. In addition, no two recessions are alike in either cause or effect.

If you came to macroeconomics with a desire to learn more about recessions and their causes, this is the chapter for you. In this chapter we focus on short-run fluctuations in the macroeconomy. We begin by building a model of the economy we can use to consider the causes of business cycle fluctuations. After that, we'll examine historical events in the context of the model. We finish this chapter with a look at some of the major debates in macroeconomics, which can be framed in terms of our model.

Big Questions:

- What is the aggregate demand-aggregate supply model?
- What is aggregate demand?
- What is aggregate supply?
- How does the aggregate demand-aggregate supply model help us understand the economy?
- What are the big debates in macroeconomics?

What is the aggregate demand-aggregate supply model?

In macroeconomics, there are two different paths of study. In one direction, you study long run growth and development. The second direction concerns short-run fluctuations or business cycles. The two paths are complimentary – both study GDP growth, employment, and the people, firms, and governments that impact the economy. But they are also different. Growth economics focuses on longer time horizons, say 5-10 years or more. Business cycle theory typically focuses on time horizons of 5 years or less.

In Chapter 19, we presented the idea of a basic business cycle, where real GDP increases for a while in the expansionary phase, and then decreases in the contractionary or recessionary phase. The business cycle appears most clearly in real GDP growth and unemployment rates. During recessions, real GDP growth slows and the unemployment rate rises. In expansions, real GDP growth expands and the unemployment rate falls.

Panel (a) of Figure 14.1 shows real GDP growth rates by quarter for the United States from 1985-2012. The three recessions during this period are shaded. During each recession, real GDP growth slowed and even turned negative. The fourth quarter of 2008 registered -8.9% growth, making it the worst quarter since 1958. Panel (b) plots the unemployment rate over the same period. The unemployment rate rises sharply during each of the recessions and then slowly falls afterwards. The highest unemployment rate in this period was 10% in October, 2009.

gure 14.1
U.S. Real GDP Growth, Unemployment Rates, and Recessions, 1985-2012

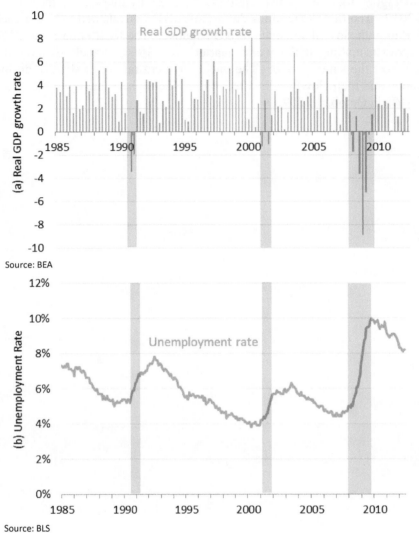

Source: BEA

Source: BLS

cycles are most readily observable in real GDP growth and unemployment rates. Panel (a) shows that quarterly real GDP growth declined during the shaded time periods, which indicate recessions. Real GDP growth also increased during the non-recessionary periods. Panel (b) shows that the unemployment rate spiked up during each of the three recessions, then gradually fell following the recessions.

The model we use to study business cycles is the *aggregate demand-aggregate supply* model. At the core of the model are the concepts of demand and supply, which are already familiar. In earlier chapters, we looked at the demand and supply of a single good, like savings. But now we look at the demand and supply of all final goods and services in the economy. **Aggregate demand** is the total demand for final goods and services in the economy. **Aggregate supply** is the total supply of final goods and services in the economy. The word *aggregate* means total.

We consider each side of the economy separately before bringing them together. The next section explains aggregate demand; after that, we will look at aggregate supply.

> **Aggregate supply** is the total supply of final goods and services in an economy.

> **Aggregate demand** is the total demand for final goods and services in an economy.

What is Aggregate Demand?

Here is an experiment you can try: ask five people the following question. "How can you personally help our economy?" Most responses will focus on buying something or spending money somewhere. In our model of the economy, this is demand. Aggregate demand is the spending side of the economy. When people spend on goods and services, aggregate demand increases. Most people believe that spending is what drives the economy. We'll see later that this is only partially true.

To determine aggregate demand, we sum up spending from different sources in the economy. These sources include private domestic consumers who buy cars, food, clothing, education and many other items. Business firms are another major group; they buy resources needed to produce output. The government is a large purchaser of labor and other resources used to produce government services. Finally, foreign consumers buy many goods and services produced in the United States. These four different major groups form the four pieces of aggregate demand: consumption (C), investment (I), government (G), and net exports (NX). The total of these four gives us aggregate demand (AD) in a given period:

$$AD = C + I + G + NX. \tag{14.1}$$

As we study aggregate demand, we'll consider factors that affect each of these sources. Figure 14.2 shows a graph of the aggregate demand curve. On the horizontal axis, we plot quantities of all final goods and services, which is real GDP (Y). On the vertical axis, we measure the overall price level (P) in the economy. This is not the price of any particular good or service, but a general level of prices for the whole economy. Since we are looking at all final goods and services, the correct price index to use is the GDP deflator. The GDP deflator is set at 100 in a particular period of time and then fluctuates from that level. A rise in P indicates inflation in the economy.

Figure 14.2
The Aggregate Demand Curve

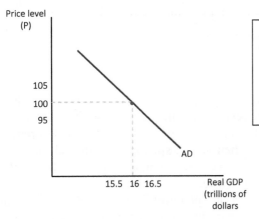

The aggregate demand curve shows the relationship between the quantity demanded of real GDP and the economy's price level (P). The inverse relationship between P and real GDP, embedded in the negative slope of the AD curve, is caused by the wealth effect, the interest rate effect, and the international trade effect.

On the graph, we have labeled a particular point where the price level is 100 and the quantity of aggregate demand is $16 trillion, which was the size of the U.S. economy in 2012. The negative slope of the aggregate demand curve means that increases in the price level lead to decreases in the quantity of aggregate demand. Similarly, when the price level falls, the quantity of aggregate demand rises. In the next section, we explain the reasons for the negative slope.

The Slope of the Aggregate-Demand Curve

All else equal, increases in the economy's price level leads to decreases in the quantity of aggregate demand. You might agree with this statement without closely evaluating it, because it sounds like the relationship between the quantity demanded of a single good and its price. But now we are evaluating the whole economy. The price level is the price of all final goods and services. Aggregate demand and aggregate supply don't just measure the quantity of pizzas demanded and supplied; they measure the production of all the firms in all of the markets that comprise the economy. Therefore, substitutions from one market to another have no effect on the total amount of output, or real GDP. Substituting out of pizza and into chicken nuggets doesn't change GDP.

There are three reasons for this inverse relationship between the quantity of aggregate demand and the price level: the *wealth effect*, the *interest rate effect*, and the *international trade effect*.

The Wealth Effect

If you wake up tomorrow morning and all prices have suddenly doubled, you'll be poorer, in real terms, than you are today. Your consumption will fall because your *wealth* has fallen. **Wealth** is the value of one's accumulated assets. Your wealth is

Wealth is the value of one's accumulated assets.

the total value of everything you own. The **wealth effect** is the change in the quantity of aggregate demand that results from wealth changes due to price level changes.

> The **wealth effect** is the change in the quantity of aggregate demand that results from wealth changes due to price level changes.

For example, if you and your friends have a $60 budget to buy pizza, you can afford to buy four $15 pizzas. But if inflation causes the price of pizzas to rise to $20, you can only afford three pizzas. Similarly, A rise in prices all over the economy reduces real wealth in the economy and then the quantity of aggregate demand falls. On the other hand, if prices fall, real wealth increases, and the quantity of aggregate demand increases.

The Interest Rate Effect

If the price level rises and real wealth falls, people also save less. Therefore, in addition to the wealth effect, an increase in the price level affects people's savings. Let's say that you are on a budget that allows you to buy groceries and save a little each month. If the price level rises, you'll probably cut back on each of these. When you spend less on groceries, that is the wealth effect. When you cut back on savings, it leads to the *interest rate effect*. The **interest-rate effect** occurs when a change in the price level leads to a change in interest rates, and therefore changes the quantity of aggregate demand. Remember that every dollar borrowed requires a dollar saved. Therefore, when savings declines, the quantity of investment must also decline, which affects aggregate demand.

> The **interest-rate effect** occurs when a change in the price level leads to a change in interest rates, and therefore changes the quantity of aggregate demand.

Figure 14.3 shows the loanable funds market before and after a decrease in savings. Initially, demand and supply of loanable funds is indicated by curves D and S and the equilibrium interest rate is 5%. If the economy's price level rises, people save less, which shifts supply to S_1. The reduction in supply leads to a higher interest rate of 6% and the quantity of investment falls from I to I_1. Because investment is one piece of aggregate demand, a decrease in investment decreases aggregate demand. Thus, a change in the price level initiates a cascade of events with the result that firms invest less at higher interest rates because individuals are saving less.

Figure 14.3
The Interest Rate Effect

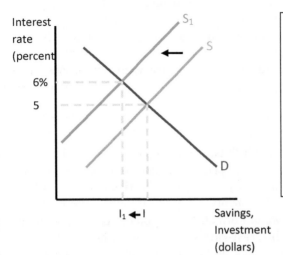

If the economy's price level rises, people save less than before. The decline in savings from S to S_1 leads to an increase in the interest rate from 5% to 6%. At this higher interest rate, firms invest less because investment is more costly: investment falls from I to I_1. Since investment is a component of aggregate demand, a fall in investment that occurs with a rise in price level causes the quantity of aggregate demand to fall.

The International Trade Effect

In our model, the price level and real GDP represent the domestic market. In the context of the world economy, we must also consider the prices of goods from the United States *relative to* the prices of goods from other countries. When the U.S. price level rises, ceteris paribus, U.S. goods are relatively more expensive than goods from other countries, and the quantity demanded of U.S. goods falls. The **international trade effect** occurs when a change in the price level leads to a change in the quantity of net exports demanded.

The **international trade effect** occurs when a change in the price level leads to a change in the quantity of net exports demanded

    Consider two similar sport-utility vehicles: a Jeep Wrangler and a Toyota FJ Cruiser. The Jeep is produced in the United States, in Toledo, Ohio. The Toyota is produced in a suburb of Tokyo, Japan. When prices of U.S. goods rise relative to Japanese goods, consumers are more likely to choose the Toyota, so U.S. exports fall and imports rise.

Toyota F.J. Cruiser: Produced near Tokyo, Japan.

    Figure 14.4 shows how the wealth effect, the interest rate effect, and the international trade effect work together to influence the quantity of aggregate demand. Each effect begins with a change in the economy's price level. When the price level rises from 100 to 110, consumption declines from the wealth effect, investment declines via the interest rate effect and net exports fall due to the international trade effect. In reality, The three effects do not influence aggregate demand equally. The international trade effect is relatively small because exports are a relatively small part of GDP. Since consumption is by far the largest component of GDP, the wealth effect is most significant.

Figure 14.4
The Slope of the Aggregate Demand Curve

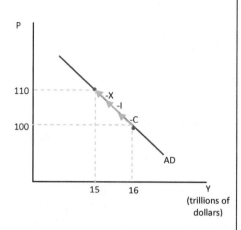

When the price level rises, the quantity of aggregate demand falls. This negative relationship is due to three different effects:

1.The wealth effect implies a lower quantity of consumption demand because real wealth falls at higher price levels.
2. The interest rate effect implies a lower quantity of investment demand due to higher interest rates.
3. The international trade effect implies a lower quantity of net export demand due to relatively higher domestic prices.

Each effect focuses on a different component of aggregate demand.

It is important to distinguish between *shifts in* versus *movements along* the aggregate demand curve. In this section, we discussed three effects related to movements along the aggregate demand curve. These three effects originate with a change in the economy's price level. Shifts in the demand curve occur when people demand more goods and services at a given price level. These shifts can come from any of the components of aggregate demand: consumption, investment, net exports, and government spending. In the next section we look at five factors that shift aggregate demand.

Shifts in Aggregate Demand

The price level is not the only factor that affects aggregate demand. When people demand more goods and services at all price levels, aggregate demand shifts in the positive direction.   In this section we consider five causes of aggregate demand shifts: changes in real wealth, expected income, expected future prices, foreign income and wealth, and the value of the dollar.

Real Wealth

One determinant of people's spending habits is their current wealth. If your great Aunt died and left you $1 million, you'd probably start spending more right away; you'd eat out tonight, upgrade your wardrobe, and maybe even shop for some bigger ticket items. This also applies to entire nations. When national wealth increases, aggregate demand increases. If wealth falls, aggregate demand declines.

For example, many people own stocks or mutual funds that are tied to the stock market. So when the stock market fluctuates, the wealth of a large portion of the population is affected. When overall stock values rise, wealth increases, which increases aggregate demand. On the other hand, if the stock market falls significantly, wealth falls, and aggregate demand decreases. Widespread changes in real estate values also affect wealth. For many, a house is a large portion of their wealth. When real estate values rise and fall, individual wealth follows, and this affects aggregate demand.

Economics in the Media:

Dumb and Dumber

Changes in wealth

In this movie, two likeable but incredibly simple-minded friends, Harry and Lloyd, try to return a suitcase to its owner. For most of the movie they have no idea that the suitcase that they are trying return is filled with a million dollars.

When they accidentally open the case while in route to Aspen, Colorado they discover the cash and decide to spend the money freely by writing "IOUs" and placing them in the suitcase to be repaid later. The newfound money creates a change in Harry and Lloyd's wealth. The two friends immediately enjoy their new found wealth by staying at a lavish hotel, providing $100 bills as tips for the staff, and even using money to wipe their noses when they cannot find ordinary tissues to do the job.

In one sense, Harry and Lloyd are much like the rest of us. If our wealth increases, it affects our demand for goods and services. But Harry and Lloyd are dumb and dumber in that their spending is completely based on somebody else's wealth.

Expected Income

In addition to people's wealth, expected future income also affects aggregate demand. If people expect higher income in the future, they spend more today. For example, graduating college seniors often start to spend more as soon as they secure a job offer, even though the job and the corresponding income don't arrive until months later. But expectations aren't always right. We consume today based on what we anticipate in the future, but the future is uncertain. Still, the entire economy can be affected by just a change in the general sentiment of consumers. Perhaps you've heard of the consumer confidence or consumer sentiment index. The consumer sentiment index uses surveys to estimate how consumers feel about the future direction of the economy. Confidence, or lack of confidence, in the future of economy changes consumer spending today. Consumer confidence might swing up and down with unpredictable events such as national elections or international turmoil. When these sentiments change, they shift aggregate demand.

Expected Prices

Expectations also matter when it comes to future prices. When people expect higher prices in the future, they are more likely to spend today, so current aggregate demand increases. Consider a nation with rampant inflation. When people get paid, they will spend their income quickly to take advantage of today's lower prices. If instead, people expect lower prices in the future, today's aggregate demand declines.

Foreign Income

When the income of people in foreign nations grows, their demand for U.S. goods increases, and this increases aggregate demand. On the other hand, if a foreign nation goes into recession, its demand for our goods and services falls. One recent positive example is the growth of large emerging economies and their demand for U.S. goods.

Economics in the Real World:
General Motors sales up in China, but down in Europe

General Motors, the world's largest car manufacturer now sells over 200,000 vehicles a month in China alone. According to China Daily, GM delivered 1.42 million cars and minivans in the first six months of 2012 alone. Sales to China are growing at more than ten percent per year thanks in part to the growing incomes of Chinese citizens. The GM product line Buick does particularly well in China. Buick now sells about four times as many cars in China as in the United States. In 2010, Buick sold 550,010 cars in China, and only 155,289 in the United States.

Increased sales in China has been offset by slowing sales in Europe, where many economies were in recession in 2012. In the second quarter of 2012, GM reported a loss of $361 million in their European division alone.

(source: http://www.chinadaily.com.cn/business/2012-07/06/content_15555232.htm)

Value of the Dollar

Exchange rates are another international factor that shift aggregate demand. We'll cover these fully in Chapter 20. For now, think in terms of the value of the dollar in world markets. When the value of the dollar rises relative to the currency of other nations, Americans find that imports are less expensive. At the same time it becomes more expensive for other nations to buy our exports. These two factors combine to reduce net exports, so a stronger dollar leads to a decline in net exports, which reduces aggregate demand.

Figure 14.5 summarizes the effects of the five factors that shift aggregate demand. Initially, aggregate demand is shown as AD. Aggregate demand shifts right to AD_1 with increases in real wealth, expected income, expected future prices, foreign income and wealth, or decreases in the value of the U.S. Dollar. On the other hand, Aggregate demand shifts left to AD_2 with decreases in real wealth, expected income, expected future prices, foreign income and wealth, or increases in the value of the U.S. Dollar.

Figure 14.5
Factors that shift the Aggregate-Demand Curve

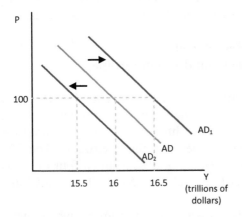

The aggregate demand curve shifts to the right with increases in real wealth, expected income, expected future prices, foreign income and wealth, or a decrease in the value of the dollar. The aggregate demand curve shifts to the left with decreases in real wealth, expected income, expected future prices, foreign income and wealth, or an increase in the value of the dollar.

Shift factor	Increase in factor leads to:	Decrease in factor leads to:
Real wealth	Increase to AD_2	Decrease to AD_1
Expected income	Increase to AD_2	Decrease to AD_1
Expected price level	Increase to AD_2	Decrease to AD_1
Foreign income	Increase to AD_2	Decrease to AD_1
Value of the Dollar	Decrease to AD_1	Increase to AD_2

Practice What You Know
Shifts in aggregate demand versus movements along the aggregate demand curve

Aggregate Demand

One of the difficult issues that arises in the application of the AD-AS model is the ability to distinguish shifts in aggregate demand from movements along the aggregate demand curve. Here we present four scenarios.

Question:
For each item below, indicate whether it causes a movement along the curve or a shift of the curve.

1. Consumers read positive economic news and then expect strong future economic growth.

Answer: This is an increase in expected future income, which increases aggregate demand, a positive shift in the curve.

2. Due to an increase in the price level in the United States, consumers substitute out of clothes made in the United States and into clothes made in Nicaragua.

Answer: This begins with a change in the price level so we know it will be a movement along the curve. Here, the price level rises, so it is a movement back along the curve, a decrease in the quantity of aggregate demand.

3. Several European economies go into recession.

Answer: Foreign recession leads to lower foreign income and wealth, and this decreases demand for goods and services made in the United States. Less demand for U.S. products causes a decrease in aggregate demand in the United States. This is a negative shift in the aggregate demand curve.

4. A decrease in the price level leads to greater real wealth and more savings, which reduces the interest rate and increases investment.

Answer:
Since this is caused by a change in the price level, it will lead to a movement along the aggregate demand curve. In this case, the lower prices lead to the interest rate effect and an increase in the quantity of aggregate demand.

What is Aggregate Supply?

Aggregate demand embodies the spending desires of an economy. It tells us how many goods and services people want at different price levels. But peoples' wants and desires alone do not determine GDP. We must also consider the supply side of the economy, which tells us about the willingness and ability of producers to supply GDP.

Most of us relate easily to the demand side because we are used to buying things on a daily basis. To understand the supply side of the economy, we need to think from the perspective of those who produce and sell goods and services. For example, imagine you own a coffee shop where you produce drinks like espressos, lattes, and iced coffee. Your inputs include workers, coffee beans, milk, water, and espresso machines. You buy inputs and combine them in a particular way to produce your output.

Figure 14.7 is an overview of the basic function of the firm. In the middle is the firm, where inputs are turned into output. The input prices, like wages and interest rates, help determine the costs of the firm. The output prices, like the cost of an espresso, determine the revenue.

In order to understand aggregate supply, we need to consider how changes in the overall price level (P) affect the supply decisions of the firm. But the influence of the price level on aggregate supply depends on the time frame we are considering. The **long run** exists when decision-makers have enough time to fully adjust. In the case of aggregate supply, the long run is a period of time sufficient for all prices to adjust. The long run doesn't arrive after a set period of time; it arrives when all prices have adjusted. However, in the *short run*, only some prices can change. The **short run** occurs when you can adjust, but only partially. In the case of aggregate supply and demand, the short run refers to the time in which prices have not fully adjusted. We begin with long-run aggregate supply.

Long-Run Aggregate Supply

As we've discussed several times in this text, the long-run output of an economy depends on resources, technology, and institutions. In the short run, there may be fluctuations in real GDP, but in the long run, the economy moves toward full employment output (Y*). The price level does not affect long-run aggregate supply. In the long run, the number of paper dollars we exchange for our goods and services does not impact our ability to produce.

Figure 14.8 plots the economy's long-run aggregate supply curve (LRAS). Notice that, since we plot this with the economy's price level (P) on the vertical axis and real GDP (Y) now on the horizontal axis, long-run aggregate supply is a vertical line at Y*, which is full-employment output. In Chapter 20, we defined full employment output as the output produced in the economy when unemployment is at the natural rate. This is the output level that is sustainable for the long run in the economy. Because prices don't affect full employment output, the LRAS curve is a vertical line at Y*. If the price level is 100, the quantity of aggregate supply is equal to Y*. If the price level rises to 110, or falls to 90, output in the long run is still Y*.

Figure 14.8
The Long-Run Aggregate Supply Curve

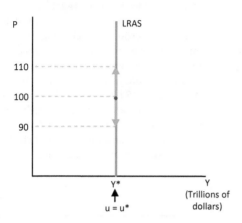

The LRAS curve is vertical at Y* because, in the long run, the price level does not affect the quantity of aggregate supply. Y* is full employment output, where the unemployment rate is equal to the natural rate.

Shifts in Long-run Aggregate Supply

The long-run aggregate supply curve shifts when there is a long-run change in a nation's ability to produce output, or a change in Y*. The factors that shift long-run aggregate supply are the same factors that determine economic growth: resources, technology, and institutions.

For example, new technology leads to increases in long-run aggregate supply. Consider what would happen if a firm develops a safe, effective and affordable hovercraft that allows people to travel more quickly and frees up congestion on our roads. This new technology leads to an increase in long-run aggregate supply, because it increases productivity in the economy: we can now produce more with our limited resources.

Figure 14.9 illustrates a shift in long-run aggregate supply. Initially, the LRAS curve is vertical at Y* which depends on resources technology and institutions. After the new hovercraft technology is introduced, LRAS shifts to LRAS₁ because now the full employment output in the economy is greater than before. Notice that both before and after the shift, the unemployment rate is at the natural rate, u*. The new technology does not reduce the unemployment rate, but workers in the economy are more productive. The new output rate, Y**, is designated with stars because it represents a new full employment output rate.

Figure 14.9
Shifts in Long-Run Aggregate Supply

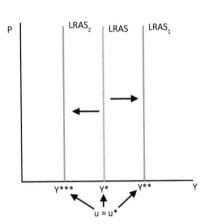

Shifts in the long-run aggregate supply curve occur when there is a change in an economy's resources, technology, or institutions. A technological advance moves an economy from LRAS to LRAS$_1$. This is a picture of economic growth. When the LRAS curve shifts this also indicates a change in the economy's full employment output level from Y* to Y**. The unemployment rate does not change, but workers are more productive.

We can illustrate economic growth using the long-run aggregate supply curve. As the economy grows over time, full employment output increases and the LRAS curve shifts to the right. But the LRAS curve can also shift back. This would occur with a permanent decline in the economy's resources or if inefficient institutions were adopted.

Short-Run Aggregate Supply

We just saw that the price level does not impact aggregate supply in the long run. However, in the short run there is a positive relationship between the price level and the quantity of aggregate supply. We point to three reasons for this relationship: inflexible input prices, menu costs, and money illusion.

First, consider input prices. At your coffee shop, your baristas are paid a particular wage, and this wage is set for a period of time. In addition, interest rates for your loans are normally fixed. Economists say these input prices are *sticky*, since they take time to change. On the other hand, output prices tend to be more flexible. Whereas input prices are typically set in a written contract, output prices are often more easily changed. For example, coffee shop prices are often written in chalk – that makes it pretty easy to change them from day to day.

The distinction between sticky input prices and flexible output prices is at the center of our discussion of aggregate supply because it affects how firms react when prices do move.

Think of this in terms of your coffee shop. You negotiate one-year contracts with your workers. Your coffee bean suppliers fix their prices for a certain period as well. If inflation begins to push up all prices in the macroeconomy, you pull out your chalkboard eraser and increase the price of lattes, espressos, and mochas. But your input prices are sticky—the coffee beans still cost the same and you are required to pay your employees the same amount—at least for a while. Therefore, your costs remain the same. And here is the link to aggregate supply: because your costs don't rise but your revenues do, it makes sense for you to increase output. When you and other firms raise output, GDP rises.

The dynamic between sticky input prices and flexible output prices explains the positive slope of the short-run aggregate supply curve. Figure 14.10 shows the short-run aggregate supply curve, labeled as SRAS. When the price level rises from 100 to 110, firms produce more in the short run because input prices are sticky, and real GDP rises from $16 trillion to $17 trillion. When the price level falls to 90, firms produce less in the short run because flexible output prices fall but sticky input prices stay relatively high. This leads to a decrease in real GDP to $15 trillion.

Figure 14.10
The Short-run Aggregate Supply Curve

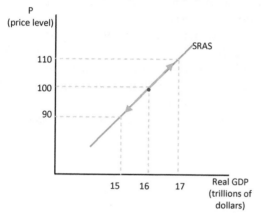

The positive slope of the short-run aggregate supply curve indicates that increases in the economy's price level lead to an increase in the quantity of aggregate supply in the short run. For example, if the price level rises from 100 to 110, the quantity of aggregate supply rises from $16 trillion to $17 trillion in the short run. The reason is that some prices are sticky in the short run.

There are other reasons why aggregate supply might be positively related to the price level in the short run. Menu costs, which we introduced in Chapter 10, are another factor that affects short-run aggregate supply. If the general price level is rising but a firm decides not to adjust its prices because of menu costs, customers will want more of its output. If firms decide to increase output rather than print new menus, the quantity of aggregate supply increases. So again, output is positively related to the price level in the short run..

We also talked about the problem of money illusion in Chapter 10. Recall that money illusion occurs when people interpret nominal values as real values. In terms of aggregate supply, if output prices are falling but workers are reluctant to accept nominal pay decreases, they reinforce the stickiness of input prices. As we said above, if input prices don't fall with output prices, firms reduce output in response to general price level changes.

Any type of price stickiness leads to a positively sloped aggregate supply curve in the short run. But keep in mind that since all prices can change in the long run, the long-run aggregate supply curve is vertical at the full employment output level.

Shifts in Short-run Aggregate Supply

When the long-run aggregate supply curve shifts, it is a permanent change that affects the long run and the short run. Therefore, all long-run aggregate supply curve shifts also move the short-run aggregate supply curve. In addition to the factors that shift long-run aggregate supply, we single out three factors that shift only short-run aggregate supply: temporary *supply shocks*, changes in expected future prices, and errors in past price expectations.

Supply Shocks

In December of 2010, frigid temperatures across most of Florida caused orange crops to freeze. The freeze reduced total orange output in the state by 450 million pounds for the season. As a result, the price of oranges in grocery stores rose over 10%. Surprise events that change a firm's production costs are called **supply shocks**. When supply shocks are temporary, they shift only the short-run aggregate supply curve. Supply shocks can be negative or positive. Negative supply shocks lead to higher costs of production; positive supply shocks reduce production costs.

> **A supply shock** is an event that changes firms' production costs.

A price change in an important factor of production is another supply shock. For example, in the year between July 2007 and July 2008, oil prices in the United States doubled from $70 a barrel to over $140 a barrel. You may recall this time period because gas prices rose from about $2 a gallon to more than $4 per gallon in the summer of 2008. Figure 14.11 plots the price of oil from 2005 to 2012. Oil is an important input to many productive processes, so when the price of oil doubles, it is felt as a macroeconomic supply shock.

Figure 14.10
Crude Oil Price, dollars per barrel Business

Source: Energy Information Administration.

The increase in crude oil prices is an example of a supply shock, since production costs for firms all over the economy rise drastically.

Expected Future Prices

If you are going to sign a long-term wage contract, you'll want to form some expectation about future prices. After all, the real value of your future income depends on prices in the future. All else equal, when workers and firms expect higher prices in the future, they negotiate higher wages. This leads to higher labor costs which reduces profitability, and makes firms less willing to produce at any price level. Therefore, higher expected future prices leads to a lower quantity of aggregate supply. The process works in reverse if workers and firms expect a lower price level. Subsequent negotiations produce a labor agreement with lower wages which reduces labor costs. When labor costs fall, additional production is more profitable at any price level and the short-run aggregate supply curve shifts to the right.

Corrections of Past Errors in Expectations

We have seen that workers and resource suppliers sign contracts on the basis of some expectation of future prices. But these expectations are not always correct. When the expectations turn out to be wrong, workers will want to re-negotiate or adjust their wages in later periods. This affects costs, which in turn, affects short-run aggregate supply. For example, let's say you sign a wage contract under the assumption that inflation will be about 2% this next year, but inflation turns out to be 5%. At the end of the year, you need to renegotiate with your employer. When workers re-negotiate their wages upward, this reduces short-run aggregate supply. If workers re-negotiate their wages downward, this increases short-run aggregate supply.

Figure 14.12 summarizes the three factors that shift short-run aggregate supply. The short-run aggregate supply curve increases or shifts to the right with the following changes: positive supply shocks, lower expectations of future prices and adjustments to lower price expectations. The short-run aggregate supply curve decreases or shifts to the left with the following changes: negative supply shocks, higher expectations of future prices and adjustments to higher price expectations.

Figure 14.12
Factors that Shift the Short-Run Aggregate Supply Curve

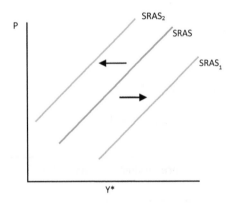

The short-run aggregate supply curve shifts right when there are positive supply shocks, decreases in expected price levels, and when anticipated price levels turn out to be too high. The curve shifts left because of negative supply shocks, increases in expected future prices, and when anticipated price levels turn out to be too low.

Shift factor	Positive change in factor leads to:	Negative change in factor leads to:
Supply shock	Increase to $SRAS_1$	Decrease to $SRAS_2$
Expected price level	Decrease to $SRAS_2$	Increase to $SRAS_1$
Corrections to past errors in expectations	Decrease to $SRAS_2$	Increase to $SRAS_1$

Practice What You Know
Long-run aggregate supply and short-run aggregate supply

Which curve shifts?

In the real world, change is typical. In our aggregate demand-aggregate supply model, change means that curves shift. Careful application of the model requires that you can determine which curve shifts, and in which direction, when real world events occur.

Question:

In the scenarios listed below, determine whether there is a shift in either the long-run aggregate supply curve, the short-run aggregate supply curve, both, or neither.

1. New shale gas deposits are found in North Dakota.

Answer: Increase in both long-run aggregate supply and short-run aggregate supply. The shale gas discovery represents new resources which shifts long-run aggregate supply to the right. In addition, every long-run aggregate supply curve shift also affects the short-run aggregate supply curve.

2. Hot weather leads to lower crop yields in the Midwest.

Answer: The lower crop yields are not permanent and so only the short-run aggregate supply curve shifts to the left. After the bad weather passes, the short-run aggregate supply curve shifts back to the right.

3. The Organization of Oil Exporting Countries (OPEC) meets and agrees to increase world oil output, leading to lower oil prices for 6 months.

Answer: This is a short-run aggregate supply curve shift, because it doesn't represent a permanent change in oil quantities.

4. U.S. consumers expect greater income in 2014.

Answer: Neither the short-run aggregate supply curve nor the long-run aggregate supply curve shift. A change in expected income shifts the aggregate demand curve.

How does the Aggregate Demand-Aggregate Supply model help us understand the economy?

In a market economy, output is determined by exchanges between buyers and sellers. As we shall see, this means the economy will tend to move to the point where aggregate demand is equal to aggregate supply. In this section, we bring aggregate demand and aggregate supply together and then consider how changes in the economy affect real GDP, unemployment, and the price level.

Equilibrium in the Aggregate Demand-Aggregate Supply Model

Figure 14.13 plots the aggregate demand and the aggregate supply curves in the same graph. The point where they intersect, A, is the equilibrium point where the opposing forces of supply and demand are balanced. At point A the price level is P* and the output level is Y*. Prices naturally adjust to move the economy toward this equilibrium point.

Figure 14.13
Equilibrium in the AD-AS Model

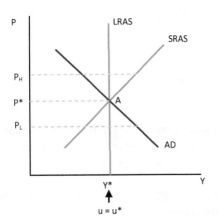

The forces in the economy naturally move it toward equilibrium at point A, where aggregate supply is equal to aggregate demand, P = P*, Y = Y*, and u = u*. At P_H, aggregate supply exceeds aggregate demand which puts downward pressure on prices, and moves the economy toward equilibrium at P*. At P_L, where aggregate demand exceeds aggregate supply, upward pressure on prices moves the economy toward equilibrium at P*.

To understand why the economy tends toward equilibrium at price level P*, consider other possible price levels. For example, if the price level is P_H, which is higher than P*, aggregate supply will be greater than aggregate demand. In this case, producers are producing more than consumers desire at current prices. Therefore, prices naturally begin to fall to eliminate a potential surplus of goods and services. As prices fall, the quantity of aggregate demand rises and the economy moves toward equilibrium at P*.

On the other hand, if the price level is P_L, which is lower than P*, aggregate demand will exceed aggregate supply. At those prices buyers desire more than producers are willing to supply. Because demand exceeds supply, prices rise and the price level moves toward P*. The only price level at which the plans of suppliers and demanders match is P*. Market forces automatically push the economy to the price level at which aggregate demand is equal to aggregate supply.

We can also describe this equilibrium in equation form. Therefore, in equilibrium, both long-run and short-run aggregate supply are equal to aggregate demand:

Long-run aggregate supply = Short-run aggregate supply = Aggregate demand.
     (14.2)

Aggregate supply is the real GDP produced, which we indicate as Y. Aggregate demand derives from four components: C, I, G, and NX. Therefore, we can rewrite equation 26.2 as:

$$Y = C + I + G + NX \qquad (14.3)$$

Now we know what equilibrium looks like in our model. This is our reference point for thinking about the economy at a particular point in time.

In the real world, things are always changing; everything from technology to weather to wealth and expectations can change. Now that we've built our model of the macroeconomy, we can use it to examine how changes in the real word affect the economy.

In what follows, both in this chapter and for the remainder of the book, we consider many real-world factors that lead to changes in the macroeconomy. When we consider a change, we follow a particular sequence of steps that help lead us to the new equilibrium. Once we determine the new equilibrium, we can assess the impact of the change on real GDP, unemployment, and the price level. The five steps are as follows:

1. Begin with the model in long run equilibrium.
2. Determine which curve(s) are affected by the change(s), and the direction(s) of the change(s).
3. Shift the curve(s) in the appropriate direction(s).
4. Determine the new short run and/or long run equilibrium points.
5. Compare the new equilibrium(s) with the starting point.

Next, we consider shifts in all three curves: long-run aggregate supply, short-run aggregate supply, and aggregate demand.

Adjustments to Shifts in Long-Run Aggregate Supply

We have seen that technological advances increase full employment output and shift long-run aggregate supply to the right. For example, the Internet is new important technology that was extended to the general public in the 1990s. The Internet makes millions of workers more productive. The effect on the macroeconomy is illustrated in Figure 14.14. We begin at long-run equilibrium point A, with the natural rate of output (Y*), and the price level 100. New technology means the long-run aggregate supply curve shifts from LRAS to $LRAS_1$. Recall that changes in long run-aggregate supply also affect the short run, so the short-run aggregate supply shifts from SRAS to $SRAS_1$.

Assuming this is the only change in the economy, we move to long-run equilibrium at B. Notice that at point B, the economy has a new natural output level at Y**.

Figure 14.14
How Long-Run Aggregate Supply Shifts Affect the Economy

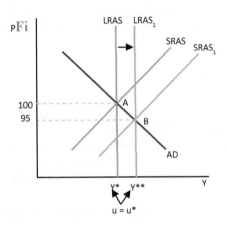

Beginning at long run equilibrium point A, the price level is at P_{100}, and output is at the natural rate (Y^*). New technology shifts long-run aggregate supply positively, from LRAS to $LRAS_1$ because the economy can now produce more at any price level. The new long-run equilibrium is at B and there is now a new, higher natural rate of output (Y^{**}). Note that the unemployment rate is equal to the natural rate both before and after the shift.

All else equal, technical change leads to more output and a lower price level. Before the Internet, the unemployment rate was at the natural rate (u^*). After the new technology, employment remains at the same level, but because we have better tools, workers are more productive. This analysis also applies to anything that increases the long run-aggregate supply curve, such as the discovery of new resources or the introduction of new institutions that are favorable for growth.

Adjustments to Shifts in Short-Run Aggregate Supply

Now let's examine the effects of a change in short-run aggregate supply. Consider what happens when there is a short-run supply disruption caused by an oil pipeline break – this is an example of a supply shock. Since oil is a resource used in many production processes, the disruption temporarily reduces the ability of the economy to produce goods. This is shown in Figure 14.15 by shifting the short-run aggregate supply curve to the left from SRAS to $SRAS_1$. The new equilibrium is at point b, with a higher price level, P_{105}, and lower level of output, Y'. This is a short run equilibrium, so we indicate this in the lower-case "b". The lower output means increased unemployment in the short run. Notice that nothing happened to long-run aggregate supply – in the long run, the pipeline will be fixed and we can produce at Y^* again.

Figure 14.15
How Short-Run Aggregate Supply Shifts Affect the Economy

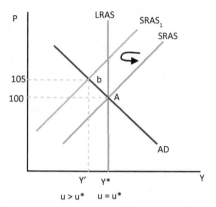

A temporary negative supply shock shifts short-run aggregate supply from SRAS to $SRAS_1$. In the short run, this moves the economy to equilibrium at point b. This equilibrium entails higher prices, lower real GDP and higher unemployment. In the long run, the economy returns to equilibrium at point A.

Since the disruption is temporary, eventually the short-run aggregate supply curve shifts to the right until it reaches SRAS. Short-run disruptions in aggregate supply do not alter the long-run equilibrium in the economy; eventually the price level, output, and the unemployment rate return to their long-run equilibrium levels at point A. But in the short run, this is an economic downturn, with higher unemployment and lower real GDP.

Economics in the Real World:
The Drought of 2012 Sends Prices Higher

According to the Associated Press (AP), the summer of 2012 was the hottest on record for the United States. High temperatures led to much lower yields in both corn and soybean crops – the USDA projected 123 bushels per acre of corn in 2012, down from 147 bushels in 2011.

According to the AP article, economist Rick Whitacre projected higher prices for many different consumer goods such as cereal, soda, cake mixes, candy bars, and even makeup. Since corn is an important feed source for cattle, Whitacre projected a 4 to 6 percent rise in beef and pork prices.

This is a classic supply shock and the result is exactly what the aggregate demand-aggregate supply model predicts: short-run aggregate supply shifts to the left and this leads to higher prices all over the economy.

(Source: http://www.washingtonpost.com/national/usda-estimates-of-corn-and-soybean-production-drop-as-drought-takes-its-toll-on-farmers/2012/08/10/0b11a126-e2ec-11e1-89f7-76e23a982d06_story.html)

Adjustments to Shifts in Aggregate Demand

Aggregate demand shifts for many reasons. Some shifts occur because of expectations rather than actual events – yet they still affect the macroeconomy. For example, let's say that consumer confidence rises unexpectedly: consumers wake up one morning with expectations of higher future income. This increases aggregate demand because consumers start spending more. Can this kind of change have real effects on the economy? That is, will a change in consumer confidence affect unemployment and real GDP? Let's look at the model.

Figure 14.16 illustrates the changes in the economy from the increased consumer confidence. We start at in long-run equilibrium at point A, where the price level is at 100, real GDP is at full employment output Y*, and unemployment equal to the natural rate. Then aggregate demand shifts to from AD to AD_1. This immediately moves us to short run equilibrium at b. The short run equilibrium is associated with higher prices (P = P_{105}), and higher real GDP (Y'). In addition, the unemployment rate drops to u', which is less than u*. Thus, changes in aggregate demand do affect the real economy, at least in the short run.

Figure 26.16
How Aggregate Demand Shifts Affect the Economy

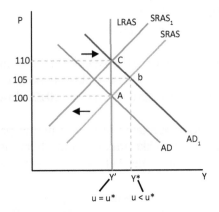

An increase in aggregate demand moves the economy from the initial equilibrium at point A to new short-run equilibrium at point b. The positive aggregate shift increases real GDP and decreases unemployment in the short run. In the short run, prices adjust, but only partially, since some prices are sticky. In the long run, when all prices adjust, the short-run aggregate supply curve shifts back to SRAS and the economy moves to long-run equilibrium where Y = Y* and u = u*.

Our example presents a positive result – after all, unemployment falls and real GDP rises. Now, let's complete this example by following through to long-run equilibrium. Recall the difference between the long run and the short run: in the long run all prices adjust. As all prices adjust, the short run aggregate supply curve shifts left from SRAS to $SRAS_1$. This moves us to long-run equilibrium at point C. Notice that at C, we are back to the original output level (Y*) and unemployment level (u*), but prices are higher. The model is telling us that demand changes have no real effects in the long run because only the price level, a nominal variable, is affected.

What are the consequences of this move to long-run equilibrium and how does it compare to the short-run equilibrium? At b, real GDP is up and unemployment is down. But not everybody is happy. For example, workers with sticky wages are now paying more for their final goods and services, but their wages did not adjust upward in the short run. In fact, any sellers with sticky prices are hurt in the short run when other prices rise.

Because everyone can adjust their prices eventually, there is a movement to C in the long run. In the long run, you can re-negotiate wages and all other long-term contracts. Thus if there is a 10% increase in prices throughout the economy, both input and output prices rise by 10%. The price of a \$4 latte rises to \$4.40, and the barista wage of \$10.00/hr rises to \$11.00/hr. When input prices rise to match output price changes, the short-run aggregate supply curve shifts to $SRAS_1$. In the long run, once all prices adjust, the price level does not affect the quantity of output supplied. This is why output returns to Y*, the full employment level.

Table 14.1 summarizes the economic effects of aggregate demand changes in both the short run and the long run. The last two columns summarize the effects of negative decreases in aggregate demand. These decreases in aggregate demand are a particular source of debate among macroeconomists. We will turn to these now with application to a particular incident: the recession of 2008.

Table 14.1:
Summary of Results from Aggregate Demand Shifts

	Increase in Aggregate Demand		Decrease in Aggregate Demand	
	Short Run	Long Run	Short Run	Long Run
Real GDP	Y rises	Y returns to original level	Y falls	Y returns to original level
Unemployment	u falls	u returns to original level	u rises	u returns to original level
Price Level	P rises	P rises even further	P falls	P falls even further

The Great Recession

In December 2007, the U.S. economy entered the recession we now call the Great Recession. Initially, most economists and policymakers assumed this was caused by a significant decline in aggregate demand. And while aggregate demand did fall, it is clear in hindsight that aggregate supply also fell. We can now look closer at this very difficult economic period in the context of the aggregate demand and aggregate supply model.

In 2007, it became clear that there was trouble brewing in U.S. financial markets. Much of the trouble stemmed from the declining values of U.S. real estate. Figure 14.21 plots an index of U.S. house purchase prices from 2001 to 2012, with the Great Recession time period shaded. You can see that home prices began to fell in the months before the Great Recession, with the decline accelerating through 2008.

Figure 14.21
U.S. House Purchase Price Index, 2001-2012

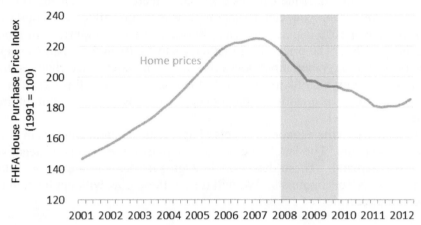

Source: Federal Housing Finance Authority.

U.S. housing prices began falling in mid-2007 and then fell consistently through the Great Recession time period.

You might recall, from Chapter 23, that home mortgages had become securitized into mortgage-backed securities and large quantities of these securities were held by most of the largest financial institutions in the United States. Thus, when real estate values fell, it led to systematic problem in U.S. financial markets. Due to the interdependence of the financial firms, this problem spread throughout the U.S. quickly, and then to the rest of the world. Financial crisis is a breakdown in the loanable funds market, which is a key institution of a market economy. When the loanable funds market is not functioning properly, firms cannot get funding to produce output. In terms of our aggregate supply and aggregate demand model, this is an institutional breakdown, and these affect long-run aggregate supply. Therefore, widespread financial market turmoil is indicated as a decline in long run aggregate supply.

But aggregate demand was negatively affected as well. At least two factors contributed to a large decline in aggregate demand. The first was a fall in wealth. People's homes are often the single largest piece of their overall wealth, so when real estate values fell, people's wealth dropped. In addition, the U.S. stocks lost a third of their value during the course of 2008. For millions of people, this meant their retirement savings dropped by a third. Both of these contributed to large declines in wealth, and so aggregate demand declined significantly.

Aggregate demand also fell due to a decline in expected income. Beginning in 2007 and then following, consumers realized that the economy was turning down. Figure 14.22 shows the consumer sentiment index, which also began falling ahead of the recession and then fell significantly during 2008. Together, these two factors led to a decline in aggregate demand.

Figure 14.22
U.S. House Purchase Price Index, 2001-2012

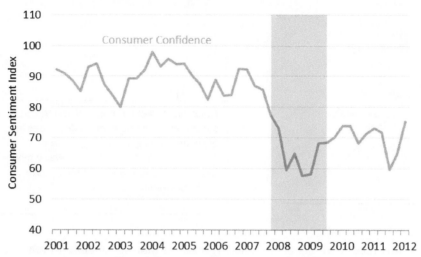

Source: St. Louis Federal Reserve FRED database.

The consumer sentiment index is a measure of consumer confidence. This index began falling in 2007 and then fell significantly during the Great Recession.

Let's now turn to the aggregate demand-aggregate supply model to see the implications of these shifts for the macroeconomy. Figure 14.23 shows a decline in both aggregate demand and aggregate supply from 2007 to 2008. Aggregate demand shifts from AD_{2007} to AD_{2008}, and long-run aggregate supply shifts from $LRAS_{2007}$ to $LRAS_{2008}$. In 2007, the economy was equilibrium at point A; the unemployment rate was below 5% and real GDP grew at a 3.6% rate in the second quarter of 2007. Then, housing prices fell leading to financial market turmoil, lower real wealth, and then lower consumer confidence. The declines in aggregate demand and long-run aggregate supply moved the economy to equilibrium at b. During this time, the unemployment rate climbed to 10% and by the last quarter of 2008 real GDP had shrunk by 8.9%.

Figure 14.23
The 2008 Decline in both Long-run Aggregate Supply and Aggregate Demand

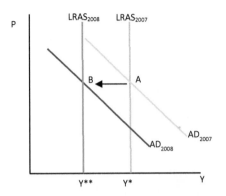

Financial market turmoil and lower consumer confidence led to decreases in both long-run aggregate supply and aggregate demand. The result was a new lower level of real GDP and higher rate of unemployment.

One reason this recession has been called "great," is that the decline in real GDP and the increase in the unemployment rate were large by historical standards. But another reason is that symptoms of the recession dragged on for several years after the recession was officially over. In 2012, real GDP was still expanding at less than 2% and the unemployment rate remained at 8%. The government employed many different tools to try to move the economy back to normal growth and low unemployment. We will discuss these tools over the next four chapters. But these tools were focused primarily on aggregate demand. World financial institutions remained in poor health for quite a while and this kept many economies from returning to normal growth rates.

Practice What You Know
Using the AD-AS Model

The Japanese Earthquake and Tsunami in 2011

In 2011, a record-breaking earthquake hit Japan and this was followed immediately by a Tsunami. This natural disaster led destroyed capital in Japan including roads, buildings and even nuclear-power plants.

Question: Use the aggregate demand-aggregate supply model to illustrate how this affected the Japanese Economy.

Answer: People often think that bad weather affects only short-run aggregate supply, because the effects are temporary. But if weather is so bad that it destroys resources, the long-run aggregate supply will also a decline.

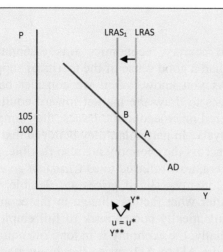

Notice that the unemployment rate is equal to the natural rate both before and after the shift. Jobs remain because there is plenty of work to do in the aftermath of a natural disaster. However, in the long run, Japan has fewer resources after the earthquake than it had before and this limits growth.

Question: How does this affect the U.S. economy?

Answer: Real foreign income falls in Japan, which leads to a decline in aggregate demand for U.S. goods and services.

What are the big disagreements in macroeconomics?

Most economists agree with the basic implications of the AD-AS model. However, economists do disagree about the role of government in the economy and whether the economy can correct itself. In this section, we try to clarify the disagreements in terms of the aggregate demand and supply model.

One of the most contentious issues among economists is the economy's adjustment to long-run equilibrium. Some economists believe it can and should occur naturally. We'll call this group *Classical Economists*. Others see it as an adjustment that occurs unpredictably and with much delay; this group typically calls for the government to speed the process back to full employment. We will call this group *Keynesian Economists*. While not every economist fits comfortably in either camp, these distinctions help clarify the debate.

Classical Economics

At the beginning of the twentieth century, economics was essentially focused on microeconomic issues. Economists had a good sense of the merits of supply and demand analysis for individual markets. As you know, when we consider basic supply and demand, the price of the good adjusts to draw the market toward equilibrium. To the extent that these economists considered macroeconomic issues, they simply extrapolated their ideas from microeconomic analysis. In particular, they believed that since prices for individual goods are flexible, prices across the economy are also flexible.

Economists from this earlier era, now referred to as *Classical economists*, assume prices are flexible throughout the economy. But if prices are flexible, the economy is essentially self-correcting — no matter what factors change in the economy, no matter what curves shift, the economy automatically comes back to full employment. Figure 14.18 shows the Classical view. Initially, the economy is in long run equilibrium at point A. If aggregate demand increases from AD to AD₁, price flexibility means the economy moves to B. At point B, real GDP is at full employment and the unemployment rate is at the natural rate. In short, the shift in aggregate demand was barely noticed in the economy because prices adjust.

Figure 14.18
The Classical View of the Macroeconomy

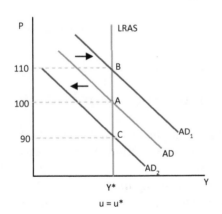

In the Classical view, prices adjust quickly in both directions. Therefore, shifts in aggregate demand do not lead to changes in output or employment because the output level stays at full employment. When prices are completely flexible, aggregate demand becomes less relevant and changes in long-run aggregate supply are primarily considered the source of economic prosperity.

The results are not much different when aggregate demand declines. If aggregate demand falls from AD to AD₂, price flexibility implies that the economy moves to long-run equilibrium at point C. This is very different from the results we got when we considered sticky prices, which you can see if you look back at Figure 26.16. When prices are flexible, the economy comes back to full employment output and the natural rate of unemployment relatively quickly. Classical economists probably slept well at night, without worries about long term economic contractions.

Because they believed the economy is self-correcting, Classical economists were essentially pro-market or laissez-faire in their policy recommendations. They had faith that market adjustments would take place quickly and therefore saw no significant role for a government macroeconomic policy that would focus on short-run fixes when the economy is under- or over-performing.

Today some economists are still in the Classical camp. They don't worry about aggregate demand shifts. After all, if prices are flexible, demand shifts merely lead to temporary fluctuations around the natural rate of output. Instead, they focus on economic policies designed to promote long-run growth. Since Classical economists are not worried about aggregate demand changes, their main focus is on shifting long-run aggregate supply. Given this, they see savings as a crucial positive factor in the economy, since savings is translated into investment and this increases capital and shifts long-run aggregate supply to the right.

The Great Depression

While the Classical economists dominated economics during the first part of the twentieth century, economic catastrophe challenged the predominant view. At the end of 1929, the United States entered the Great Depression, an economic event that affected the entire world economy for at least a decade and changed macroeconomics forever.

To give you a sense of the historic magnitude of the Great Depression, we have plotted long-run U.S. real GDP data in Figure 14.19 The data goes all the way back to 1870, but it is easy to see the Great Depression – the significant drop in real GDP beginning in 1930. There have been several contractions in the U.S. economy since 1870, but none as severe as the Great Depression. Real GDP fell from $977 billion in 1929 to $716 billion in 1933 (both equated to 2005 dollars). Imagine an economic contraction so severe that after four years, the economy is producing almost 30% less.

Figure 14.19
Real U.S. GDP, 1870- 2012

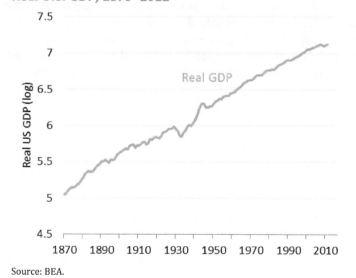

When we look at U.S. real GDP growth over the long run, the Great Depression is easy to spot, since it is the severe decline that occurred in the 1930s. To normalize across percentage changes, the plotted data is the log of real GDP.

Source: BEA.

The impact of the Great Depression on employment was equally severe. The unemployment rate reached 25% in 1933. One out of four workers was without a job. Particularly alarming was the long-term nature of the unemployment. The unemployment rate was above 15% for almost the entire decade of the 1930s.

The Great Depression fundamentally changed people's views of the economy and the role of government. It seemed that the economy was not correcting itself, so many assumed that something was missing from the Classical view.

Keynesian Economics

The Great Depression set the stage for a new approach to macroeconomics. John Maynard Keynes, a British economist, formulated this new approach. In 1936, Keynes published *The General Theory of Employment, Interest, and Money*. This book vaulted him into the forefront of macroeconomic debates, because it offered a theory about why cyclical unemployment might persist. Indeed the title of the book—*The General Theory*—implies that Keynes believed that an economy out of long run equilibrium is not unusual.

Keynes believed that wages did not adjust downward quickly enough during recessions because the presence of union contracts and money illusion. As a result, high real wages prevented the labor market from reaching equilibrium and restoring full employment. This led to prolonged recessions. Keynes believed that short-run economic circumstances could be improved through government intervention. He believed that the government should try to shift the aggregate demand curve back to its initial level. According to Keynes, it is foolish to wait for long run adjustments because "In the long run we are all dead."

Keynesian economists assume prices are sticky downward and they focus on the demand side of the economy as the source of instability. Figure 14.20 shows the macroeconomy after a significant decline in aggregate demand. Notice that aggregate demand shifts from AD_{1929} to AD_{1930ff}. According to Keynesian theory, individuals and firms both stopped spending as the stock market dropped in 1929 and firms became wary of future returns from capital – so consumption and investment both fell significantly.

Figure 14.20
Keynesian View of the Great Depression

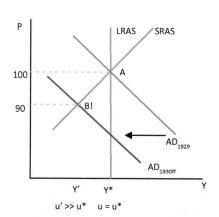

The Keynesian view of the Great Depression focuses on a significant decline in aggregate demand, shown here as a move from AD_{1929} to AD_{1930ff}. In addition, because some prices are inflexible downward, the economy has no tendency to move away from equilibrium at B!, where unemployment is very high and real GDP is well below its full employment level. Since some prices are very inflexible downward, B! is considered a long run equilibrium.

But if wages are sticky, there was no underlying tendency for the economy to return to full employment equilibrium. In essence, the equilibrium at B! is a long run equilibrium in the Keynesian model. What is the source of the extreme price stickiness? Keynesian economists have posited that resource prices like wages are very sticky downward, especially when they are negotiated through collective bargaining agreements by unions. Certainly, unions were very strong in the 1930s and this could have added to the wage rigidity. But money illusion may also play a role. Consider yourself an employee in the midst of the Great Depression, times are tough and now your employer is asking you to take a wage decrease. This would be a tough pill to swallow even if it is not a *real* wage decrease, so the employee refuses the wage decrease.

Keynes recommended that the British and U.S. governments take action to increase aggregate demand. If aggregate demand is too low because individuals and firms are reluctant to spend, the government might fill the void by increasing the government spending piece of aggregate demand. We will cover this topic in more detail in Chapter 30.

The Keynesian view of the economy offered an explanation for the Great Depression. After the nation emerged from the Great Depression, Keynesian theory became entrenched in economics. Table 14.2 summarizes the major differences between Classical and Keynesian economists. Today, the profession is mixed on whether this is the correct approach; economists debate the importance of sticky prices and the merits of government policy based on the Keynesian model.

Table 14.2:
Classical versus Keynesian Economics

	Classical	Keynesian
Key time period	Long run	Short run
Price flexibility	Prices flexible	Prices sticky
Savings	Crucial to growth	A drain on demand
Key side of market	supply	demand
Market tendency	Stability, full employment	Instability, cyclical unemployment
Government intervention	Not necessary	Essential

Practice What You Know
The Big Debates

Guess which view

Question:

Below, we give three statements. Determine which type of economist, Keynesian or Classical, would likely support the statement.

1. If you want to help the economy, you should increase your spending.

Answer: Keynesian. The Keynesian approach focuses on spending or aggregate demand as the fundamental factor in the economy.

2. If you want to help the economy, you should increase your savings.

Answer: Classical. The Classical approach focuses on long-run aggregate supply as the primary source of economic prosperity. Increases in savings are necessary for investment and this shifts out long run aggregate supply.

3. Government policy should focus on counteracting short run fluctuations in the economy.

Answer: Keynesian. The Keynesian approach emphasizes inherent instability in the macroeconomy and therefore the government is necessary to counteract the business cycle.

4. Government policy should not intervene in the business cycle since the economy can correct itself.

Answer: Classical. The Classical approach emphasizes price flexibility which means the economy can correct itself and naturally move back to full employment.

Economics in the Media
The Big Disagreements in Macroeconomics

Fear the Boom and the Bust

This highly original rap video imagines what two giants of economics, F.A. Hayek and John Maynard Keynes, would have to say to defend their ideas. F.A. Hayek is a representative of the Classical economists. Here is one of the best lines,

We've been going back and forth for a century
[Keynes] I want to steer markets,
[Hayek] I want them set free
There's a boom and bust cycle and good reason to fear it

F.A, Hayek was the 20th century's most significant defender of free markets. He wrote *The Road to Serfdom* in 1943. The book cautions against central planning. He characterizes markets as having the ability to organize spontaneously, to the benefit of an economy. *The Road to Serfdom* appeared in print just a few years after John Maynard Keynes wrote his *General Theory* in 1936. How could two giants of economics see the world so differently?

Hayek, who received the 1974 Nobel Prize in Economics, lived long enough to observe that economics had come full circle. His Nobel acceptance speech was titled, *The Pretense of Knowledge*. In the talk he criticized the economics profession for being too quick to adopt the ideas of Keynes. Keynes argued that the economy moves slowly to the long-run equilibrium. Hayek countered that efforts to stimulate demand presume that economists know what they are doing. Hayek argued that just because we can build fancy macroeconomic models does not mean that the model can anticipate every change in the economy. He pointed to the high inflation rates and high unemployment rates of the 1970s as evidence that the Keynesian model was incomplete. Accordingly, it would be best to put our faith in the one thing all economists generally agree on—that eventually,

452   The Aggregate Demand-Aggregate Supply Model

the economy will naturally return to full employment.

Fear the Boom and the Bust presents the views of Hayek and Keynes to make you think. While there are many references in the rap that you probably won't get just yet, watch it anyway (and tell your friends to watch it). This is an important, ongoing debate and one of the goals of your study of economics is to help equip you with the information you need to decide for yourself what approach is best for the economy.

Economics for Life

Recession-proof your job

Recessions are hard on almost everyone in an economy, but there are ways you can shield yourself from unemployment.

The first thing you need is your college degree. As we showed in Chapter 20, the unemployment rate in April 2012 was 8.1% for the entire labor force, but just 4% for college graduates.

One lesson we learned in this chapter is that unemployment persists in the macroeconomy when wages are inflexible downward. This applies to individuals too. If you do happen to lose your job, you may need to consider accepting a lower wage, or even a change of career so as to obtain a job. The more flexible your wage, the less likely you are to experience long-term unemployment.

Finally, if you lose your job, be sure to take advantage of all the modern job-search tools available today. There are millions of jobs available, even when unemployment rates are very high – you just need to know how to find them. For example, the website indeed.com turns up thousands of jobs vacancies for almost any job description. As of August 2012, searching for either "accountant," or "CPA," yields over 30,000 results; a search for "civil engineer" yielded 10,605 results, and "marketing" yielded 253,467 results.

BIG QUESTIONS

(1) What is the aggregate demand-aggregate supply model?

- The AD-AS model is the model we use to study short-run fluctuations in the economy.

(2) What is aggregate demand?

- Aggregate demand represents the spending side of the economy. It includes consumption, investment, net exports, and government spending.
- The slope of the aggregate demand curve is negative due to the wealth effect, the interest rate effect and the international trade effect.
- The aggregate demand curve shifts when there are changes in real wealth, expected income, expected future prices, foreign income and wealth, and the value of the dollar.

(3) What is aggregate supply?

- Aggregate supply represents the producing side of the economy.
- Long-run aggregate supply is relevant when all prices are flexible. This curve is vertical at full employment output and is not influenced by the price level.
- In the short run, when some prices are sticky, the short-run aggregate supply curve is relevant. This curve indicates a positive relationship between the price level and real output supplied.

(4) How does the aggregate demand-aggregate supply model help us understand the economy?

- We can use the AD-AS model to see how changes in either aggregate demand or aggregate supply affect real GDP, unemployment, and the price level.

(5) What are the big debates in macroeconomics?

- The big debates in macroeconomics focus on the flexibility of prices.
- If prices are assumed to be flexible, the implication is a generally stable macroeconomy without significant need for government help.
- If prices are assumed to be sticky, the implication is that the economy is inherently unstable and in need of government assistance.

Conclusion

We began this chapter with the misconception that business cycle fluctuations are a normal occurrence every few years. In fact, they are anything but normal. They occur with unpredictable frequency and are caused by many different factors. Business cycles are often caused by changes in aggregate demand, but the same symptoms can reflect short-run aggregate supply shifts.

This chapter introduced the aggregate demand-aggregate supply model of the economy, which helps us understand how changes in the real world affect the macroeconomy. It also gives us an important tool for analyzing government policy. Most economists believe the macroeconomy needs at least a little help from government. This help comes in the form of monetary policy, which adjusts the money supply, and fiscal policy, which adjusts government taxes and spending. Over the next four chapters, we will evaluate these policy alternatives and use the aggregate demand and supply model to understand how government policy affects the economy.

Concepts You Should Know

Aggregate demand	International trade effect	Short run
Aggregate supply	Keynesian economists	Supply shock
Classical economists	Long run	Wealth
Interest-rate effect		Wealth effect

Questions for Review

1. Explain the difference between Keynesian and Classical views on the economy.

2. Describe three reasons the aggregate demand curve slopes downward. Name at least three factors that cause the aggregate demand curve to shift.

3. Describe three reasons the short-run aggregate supply curve slopes upward. Name at least three factors that cause the short-run aggregate supply curve to shift.

4. How are the factors that shift the long-run aggregate supply curve different from those that shift the short-run aggregate supply curve?

5. Why is the long-run aggregate supply curve vertical?

6. How does strong economic growth in China affect aggregate demand in the United States?

Study Problems

1. Describe whether the following changes cause the short-run aggregate supply to increase, decrease, or neither.
    a. The price level increases.
    b. Input prices decrease.
    c. Firms and workers expect the price level to fall.
    d. The price level decreases.
    e. New policies increase the cost of meeting government regulations.
    f. The number of workers in the labor force increases.

2. Describe whether the following changes cause the long-run aggregate supply to increase, decrease or neither occurs.
    a. The price level increases.
    b. The stock of capital in the economy increases.
    c. Natural resources increase.
    d. The price level decreases.
    e. Firms and workers expect the price level to rise.
    f. The number of workers in the labor force increases.

3. In the following graph, illustrate the short-run and long-run effects of an increase in aggregate demand. Describe what happen to the price level, output, and employment.

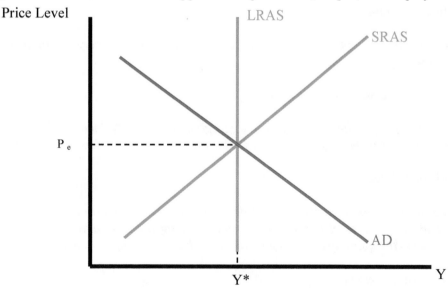

4. How does a lower price level in the United States affect the purchases of imported goods? Explain using aggregate demand.

5. Is it possible for the economy to operate beyond the natural rate of output in the short-run?

6. Suppose the economy is currently in a recession. If no policy action is taken what will happen to the price level, output and employment in the long-run?

7. Consider two economies, both in recession. In the first economy all workers have long-term contracts that guarantee high nominal wages for the next five years. In the second economy all workers have annual contracts that are indexed to changes in the price level. Which economy will return the natural rate of output the soonest?

8. Consider the following statement: "When the economy enters into a recession, the long-run aggregate supply curve shifts to the left" True or false? Explain your answer.

Solved Problems

1. Describe whether the following changes cause the aggregate demand curve to increase, decrease, or neither.

a. The price level increases.

Neither, a change in the price level (P) leads to a movement along the AD curve. When the price level rises, the quantity of aggregate demand declines along the curve.

b. Investment decreases.

Investment (I) is one component of aggregate demand so an decrease in investment decreases aggregate demand.

c. Imports decrease and exports increase.

Net exports (NX) is another component of aggregate demand. An increase in exports and a decrease in imports imply that net exports rise and so aggregate demand increases.

d. The price level decreases.

Aggregate demand neither increases nor decreases with a change in the price level (P). A change in the price level leads to a movement along the AD curve. When the price level decreases, the quantity of aggregate demand declines along the curve.

e. Consumption increases.

Consumption (C) is a component of aggregate demand so an increase in investment increase aggregate demand.

f. Government purchases decrease.

Government purchases (G) are a component of aggregate demand so an decrease in government purchases decreases aggregate demand.

2. Suppose that a sudden increase in aggregate demand moves the economy from its long-run equilibrium.

a Illustrate this change using the aggregate demand and supply model.

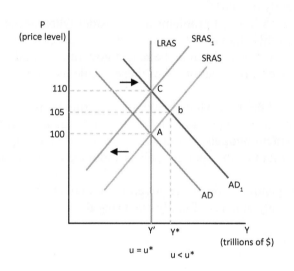

Aggregate demand increases from AD to AD₁.

In the short run, equilibrium will be at point b.

In the long run, equilibrium moves to point C.

b. What are the effects of this change in the short run and the long run?

In the short run, real GDP rises, the unemployment rate falls, and the price level rises. In the long run, real GDP goes back to the full employment level, the unemployment rate returns to the natural rate, and the price level rises further.

Chapter 15

Federal Budgets: The Tools of Fiscal Policy

Misconception: Governments never balance their budgets.

You don't have to look far to read about government budget problems. Does any government have enough money to pay its bills?! Debt problems seem to be mounting all over the globe, including various U.S. states and localities. Nationally, the U.S. budget has seen record shortfalls in recent years, with spending vastly greater than revenue. Given the current budget environment, one might assume that governments never balance their budgets. But in fact, the United States had a balanced budget as recently as 2001.

In this chapter, we examine the causes of budget problems and consider whether they can be avoided in the future. The primary goal of this chapter is to equip you with the knowledge you need to critically examine fiscal policy options. We will frame the recent government budget struggles in context, so you have a better sense of the magnitude of these problems both historically and globally.

Of all this chapters in this text, this and the following chapter on government policy responses to the business cycle are among the most important for your post-college life. Though most people do not actually work on government budgets, if you vote or otherwise participate in the political process, you'll need to decide what tax and spending plans endorsed by the various candidates make the most sense to you.

In this chapter we first consider the spending side of the government budget. We then move to the revenue side, where we look closely at taxes. Finally, we bring these together to examine budget deficits and government debt.

Big Questions

- How does the government spend?
- How does the government tax?
- What are budget deficits, and how bad are they?

How does the government spend?

Without question, we live in interesting macroeconomic times. Since the onset of the global financial crisis in 2007, federal budget crises have arisen in nations around the globe, including the United States, Japan, Greece, Italy, Peru and Argentina. Government budgets have moved into the spotlight, mainly because so many governments are deeply in debt. By "in debt" we mean that these governments are spending more money, sometimes much more, than they are acquiring through taxes. The United States federal government budget deficits are a constant topic of political and economic debate.

Perhaps you've created a personal budget for yourself. If so, you have laid out a plan for your funds – both incoming and outgoing. Similarly, a government budget is a *plan* for both spending and raising funds for the government. There are two sides to a budget: the sources of funds (income or revenue), and the uses of funds (spending or outlays). We start with the spending side. If we were looking at your personal budget, these categories might be items like tuition, books, food and housing.

We begin by looking at the spending side of government budgets.

Government Outlays

The U.S. government now spends over $3 trillion each year – that's nearly $10,000 for every citizen. Figure 15.1 shows real U.S. government outlays from 1960-2010. Notice how steep the line gets around the year 2000. Between 2000 and 2010, real outlays grew by more than fifty percent. There are many reasons for this rapid growth in government spending. Much of the increase is due to spending during and after the recession of 2007-2008, in an effort to keep the economy from sinking further. In addition, there have also been significant increases in government programs like Social Security and Medicare.

Figure 15.1
U.S. Government Outlays, 1960-2010
(billions of 2010 dollars)

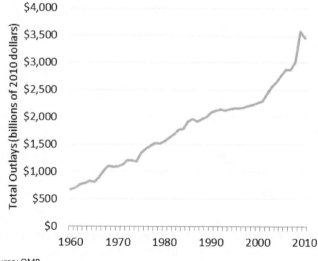

Total outlays represent the spending side of the government budget. This graphic shows real outlays (in billions of 2010 dollars) since 1960. Between 200 and 2010, real outlays grew by more than fifty percent. Total outlays are now over $3 trillion per year, or $10,000 per U.S. citizen.

Source: OMB.

When you think of U.S. government spending, your mind probably jumps to goods and services like roads, bridges, military equipment, and government employees. We considered these types of expenditures in Chapter 19, when we defined the government spending component in gross domestic product. But as we examine the total government budget, we must now also include *transfer payments*. **Transfer payments** are payments to groups or individuals when no good or service is received in return. With a transfer payment, the government transfers funds from one group in society to another. These include income assistance (welfare) and Social Security payments to retired or disabled persons. As we'll see later in this chapter, transfer payments encompass a large and growing share of U.S. federal outlays.

> Government spending includes purchases of military equipment.

> **Transfer payments** are payments to groups or individuals when no good or service is received in return.

When looking at government budgets, both spending and transfer payments are included in the broader category called government outlays. **Government outlays** are the side of the government budget that includes both spending and transfer payments.

> **Government outlays** are the side of the government budget that includes both spending and transfer payments.

Table 15.1 shows the major divisions in U.S. government outlays in 2010. We divide the outlays into three groups: *mandatory outlays*, *discretionary spending*, and interest payments. These divisions are important for critical budget analysis. We describe each of these now.

Table 15.1
2010 U.S. government outlays

Category	2010 outlays (billions of dollars)	Percent of total	
Social Security	$700.7	20.3%	Mandatory
Medicare	520.0	15.1%	
Income Assistance	710.5	20.6%	
Other Mandatory and receipts	-21.9	-0.6%	
Interest	196.9	5.7%	Interest
Defense	689.1	19.9%	Discretionary
Non-Defense Discretionary	660.1	19.1%	
Total	**3,455.8**		

Source: Congressional Budget Office.

By far the largest portion of the federal budget is dedicated to **mandatory outlays**, which refers to government spending determined by ongoing programs like Social Security and Medicare. These programs are mandatory because existing laws mandate government funding for them. In fact, mandatory outlays cannot be altered during the budget process; they require changes to existing laws, which take a long time to accomplish. Sometimes, these programs are known as *entitlement* programs, since citizens that meet certain requirements are then entitled to benefits under current laws. We talk more about these mandatory programs in the next section.

> **Mandatory outlays** refer to spending that is determined by ongoing long-term obligations.

Discretionary outlays are government spending that can be altered when the government is setting its annual budget. Examples of discretionary spending include bridges, roads, payments to government workers, and defense spending. When you think of examples of government spending, you may think of these discretionary items. But total discretionary spending accounts for less that 40% of the U.S. government budget.

> **Discretionary outlays** refer to spending that can be adjusted, even in the short run.

The final category we singled out in Table 15.1 is interest payments. Interest payments are paid to current owners of U.S. Treasury bonds. These payments are not easy to alter, given a certain level of debt, so they are also essentially mandatory payments.

> Dining out on steak might be important to you, but it is not actually a mandatory category in your budget.

To clarify these three categories, consider how your monthly budget might look after you graduate from college. On the spending side of your budget, you'll need to plan for groceries, gasoline, car payments, housing payments, utility bills, and perhaps some college debt payments. Some of these categories are discretionary – that is, you can alter them from month-to-month. These include groceries, gas, and utilities. Some categories are mandatory, so that their level is pre-determined each month. Mandatory categories include your monthly housing and car payments. Finally, your payments on your college debt are much like mandatory interest payments – your student loan has a specific interest rate that does not change.

We clarify this distinction between mandatory and discretionary spending because it's important to note that certain categories are pre-determined and not negotiable from year-to-year. The distinctions also help us understand the recent growth of governments spending in many nations. It turns out that much of the growth has been in mandatory spending. Returning to Table 15.1 we see that mandatory spending composed 55% of the U.S. budget in 2010. In fact, if we include interest payments as obligatory, that leaves less than 40% of the U.S. budget as discretionary. You might remember this the next time you read or hear about budgetary negotiations. While much of the debate focuses on discretionary spending items, like bridges or environmental subsidies or defense items, the majority of the budget goes to mandatory spending categories.

It wasn't always this way. Figure 15.2 plots U.S. federal budget categories as portions of total outlays for the years 1962 – 2010. The orange shaded categories are mandatory spending. Fifty years ago, mandatory spending was less than one third of the U.S. federal budget. The cause of this growth is largely political; more programs have been added to the government outlay budget. Miscellaneous mandatory spending programs include unemployment compensation, income assistance (welfare), and food stamps. Medicare was added in 1966, and then expanded in 2006. In 2010, Social Security and Medicare together accounted for more than one third of the U.S. federal budget, up from only 13% in 1962. Part of this increase is due to expanded benefits, such as Medicare coverage of prescription drug costs and increasing payments to retirees Social Security. In addition, as we shall see, the demographics of the U.S. population have contributed to the growth in mandatory spending.

Figure 15.2
Historical Federal Outlay Shares. 1962-2010

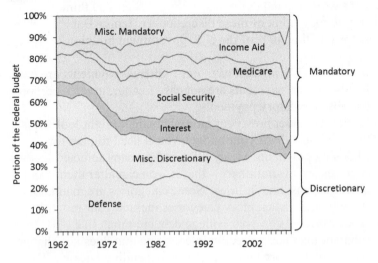

The portion of the budget allocated to mandatory spending programs has almost doubled since 1962. Conversely, discretionary spending is a shrinking part of the federal budget.

Source: Congressional Budget Office.

Social Security and Medicare

Because of the growing size of the Social Security and Medicare, it is important for you to understand what they are and why we devote so many resources to these programs in the United States.

Social Security

In 1935, as part of the New Deal and in the midst of the Great Depression, the U.S. Congress, and President Franklin Roosevelt created the Social Security program. **Social Security** is a government-administered retirement funding program. The program requires workers to contribute a portion of their earnings into the Social Security Trust Fund with the promise that they'll receive these back (including a modest growth rate) upon retirement. The goal of the program is to guarantee that no American worker retires without at least some retirement income.

FDR signed the Social Security Act in 1935.

Social Security is a government-run retirement funding program.

To understand our current budget situation, it helps to consider the Social Security program over time. In the beginning, there were no retirees receiving Social Security and many workers contributing to Social Security. This meant that payments into the trust fund began to pile up, even though at that time Social Security taxes were only 2% of wages. However, as time went on, more and more workers retired and became eligible for benefits. Thus, as workers retire and draw benefits from the program, the balance of the Trust Fund declines. In order to keep the Trust Fund from running out of funds, social-security tax rates have increased and now the tax is up to 12.4%.

Medicare

Medicare is a mandated federal program that funds health care for retired persons. This program was established in 1965 with the goal of providing medical insurance for all retired workers. Like Social Security, the law requires current workers to pay Medicare taxes with the promise of receiving insurance upon retirement. In 2003, Medicare was extended into reimbursements for prescription drugs for retirees as well.

> **Medicare** is the U.S. federal program that funds medical care for retirees

   Both Medicare and Social Security are concentrated on the elderly population and so are impacted greatly as population demographics shift. Given that they now comprise more than a third of all Federal outlays, we need to consider these demographic changes before we can completely understand the ongoing dynamics of the federal budget.

Demographics

Entitlement programs have come to dominate the federal budget, with Social Security and Medicare taking up ever-expanding shares. There are three major natural demographic reasons why. First, people are living longer today than ever before, which means they draw post-retirement benefits longer. In 1930, life expectancy after age 60 was less than 13.7 years. The amount of time that retirees would collect Social Security benefits was therefore limited. Today, Americans live an average of 22.6 years after age 60. This is a big change from assumptions on which the system was founded.

   Second, those who paid into the programs for many years are now retired and drawing benefits. To be eligible for Social Security and Medicare payments, workers have to pay taxes out of their earnings while they work. Thus, when Social Security and Medicare were first established, no workers were eligible for payouts but millions of workers were paying in. So both programs naturally generated substantial tax revenue with very few outlays for many years. But the honeymoon is over.

   Third, in addition to a normal flow of retirees, the baby-boomers, born from 1946 to 1964, are now retiring. Thus, over the next 15-10 years, workers will retire in record numbers and this requires record spending on these mandatory programs.

   Panel (a) of Figure 15.3 shows the U.S. population aged 65 and over by decade since 1900. Notice how each decade, a larger portion of the population is older than 65 – and eligible for mandatory benefits form Social Security and Medicare. This fraction will grow even larger over the next two decades as the baby-boomers retire. Going forward, the United States will have fewer and fewer workers paying into system, and more and more retirees drawing out. Panel (b) of Figure 15.3 shows the change in number of U.S. workers per Social Security beneficiary, beginning in 1960. In 1960, there were more than 5 workers per beneficiary in the Social Security system. With that number it wasn't very difficult to accumulate a large trust fund. But now, there are fewer than three workers per beneficiary, and as the baby-boomers retire, this is set to fall to just above two, as indicated by the projections for 2030 and 2050.

Figure 15.3
The Effects of an Aging Population on Social Security

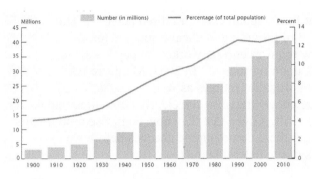

(a) U.S. population aged 65 and over.

Sources: U.S. Census Bureau and Social Security Administration

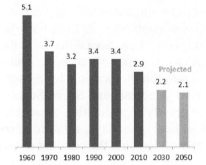

(b) U.S. workers per Social Security beneficiary

Panel (a) shows how the U.S. population is aging, with an increasing fraction aged 65 and older. With the baby-boomers now reaching this age, the fraction will increase even further in coming years. This also means that there are fewer and fewer workers per Social Security beneficiary, which is illustrated in panel (b).

Let's summarize the effects of these mandatory spending programs on the U.S. government budget. In 1962, mandatory spending made up less than one third of the U.S. budget. By 2010, mandatory spending grew to more than half of the U.S. budget. As we shall see, any discussion about the national debt and deficits must necessarily focus on these programs. If we are serious about reducing the national debt, we can't ignore them.

Economics in the Real World:
Are there simple fixes to Social Security and Medicare?

Either Social Security and Medicare programs must be re-vamped, or the U.S. government budget will be swamped by obligations to these programs in the future. But some people feel that a few relatively minor tweaks can solve the problems. Robert Powell writing for *MarketWatch* in 2011, explored potential solutions to the Social Security and Medicare funding problems. According to Powell, the budget problems can be largely alleviated with a few creative solutions. These solutions include:

1. Increasing the retirement age from 67 to 70.

People are living longer and healthier lives than when these retirement programs were implemented. When people work three years longer, this means three more years of saving for retirement and three fewer years of drawing benefits.

2. Adjusting the benefits computation to the consumer price index.

Benefit payments to retirees are adjusted for inflation using average wage levels when they retire. This policy is in place to insure that worker's benefits keep up with standard-of-living changes during their working years. Currently, these benefit payments are adjusted using an average wage index and this has historically increased faster than the CPI. If instead, the CPI were used to adjust benefits payments, the payments would not grow as fast and would still account for inflation.

3. Means-testing for Medicare and Social Security benefits.

As it stands now, retirees receive benefits from Medicare and Social Security regardless of whether they are able to pay on their own. Thus, one suggestion is to decrease the benefits paid wealthier recipients who can afford to pay for their own retirement and medical care.

While these three solutions may help shore up the federal budget, they each involve a change in existing law. Moving the retirement age to 70 years would completely alter the labor force going forward, but it would mean billions in savings for these federal programs. On the other hand, changing the benefits indexation from the average wages to the CPI would yield mixed effects – the CPI has actually increased faster than average wages in recent years. Finally, if means-testing is implemented, it completely changes the incentives going forward. Means-testing punishes retirees who have saved on their own and can therefore afford more in retirement. In addition, Medicare and Social Security are mandatory programs that all workers must pay into during their time in the labor force. Means-testing implies that some workers won't receive the benefits from a program they were required to pay into.

These three simple solutions might reduce the benefits paid out in the short run and, in so doing, will reduce pressure on the federal budget. But means-testing will likely lead to greater problems in the long run because of the incentive problem.

http://www.marketwatch.com/story/fix-social-security-by-hiking-retirement-age-2010-07-02

Spending and Current Fiscal Issues

Before turning our attention to the revenue side of the budget, we should take a look at the recent history with regard to U.S government outlays. Figure 15.4 shows real federal government outlays over the 25 years from 1986 to 2010. In the figure you can clearly see that federal government spending began growing quickly around 2001. And while there are many reasons for increased spending, we can identify three major factors:

1. Increased spending on Social Security and Medicare.

As we have seen, spending on these programs has grown significantly in recent years.

2. Defense spending in the wake of the terrorist attacks of September 11, 2001.

Prior to 2001, defense spending had consistently declined as a portion of the federal budget since the fall of the Soviet Union in 1991, to just 16.5% by 2001. But by 2010, defense spending comprised 19.1% of the federal budget.

3. Government responses to the Great Recession, beginning with fiscal policy in 2008.

We'll cover these policy responses (including their rationale) more fully in Chapter 30, but you should note that outlays increased from $2.87 trillion in 2007 to $3.58 trillion in 2009. That's a 25% increase in just two years.

.

Figure 15.4
U.S. government outlays, 1986-2010, trillions of 2010 dollars

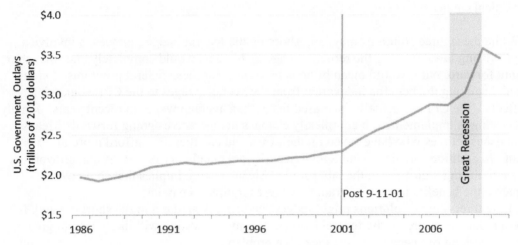

Source: OMB.

The rate of growth of U.S. government outlays has increased significantly in recent years. This graph shows a clear increase in spending after the terrorist attacks on September 11, 2001, and also large spending increases during and after the Great Recession.

Practice What You Know
Government Outlays

Mandatory versus Discretionary Spending

Question: Determine which of the following types of private spending are discretionary or mandatory components of a consumer budget:

1. Groceries

Answer: This is discretionary. Even though groveries are a necessity, you can increase or decrease your grocery spending.

2. Car payment

Answer: This is typically mandatory as you have a long-term agreement in place that entails monthly payments.

3. Cell phone monthly fee

Answer: This is mandatory if you have a longterm contract but discretionary if your phone plan is pay-as-you-go.

Question: Determine which of the following types of spending are discretionary or mandatory components of a government budget:

1. A new interstate highway

Answer: This is discretionary because the government can choose not to fund this item.

2. Medicare

Answer: this is mandatory since the government is obligated via previous-enacted laws to pay these expenses when recipients qualify.

3. International aid

Answer: This is discretionary. Each year, the government can choose how much to spend on aid to foreign governments.

How does the government tax?

Governments have several avenues to raise revenues. Fees assessed for government services, for example, admission fees to national parks, contribute small amounts of revenue. However, virtually all government revenue is raised through taxes.

Nobody enjoys paying taxes, but government activity must be funded. If we want the government to provide Social Security, Medicare, national defense, highways, and public education, then we have to pay taxes. In this section, we detail the principle means by which the federal government raises tax revenues.

Sources of tax revenue

Figure 15.5 shows the sources of tax revenue for the U.S. government in 2010. The two highest sources are individual income taxes and social insurance (Social Security and Medicare) taxes. Together, these two accounted for 81% of all federal tax revenue in the United States in 2010. Both of these taxes are deducted from workers' paychecks, so they are referred to as *payroll taxes*. The other major types of taxes together produce just 19% of the federal revenue. The largest of these is taxes on the income of corporations, which yielded $191.4 billion in 2010, or 9% of the total revenue. Estate and gift taxes are levied when property is gifted to others, particularly as an inheritance. Excise taxes are taxes on a particular good or commodity like cigarettes or gasoline. The federal tax on cigarettes is $1.01 per pack and the tax on gasoline is 18.4 cents per gallon. Altogether, excise taxes yielded $66.9 billion in tax revenue in 2010. Customs taxes are taxes on imports and these yielded just $25.3 billion in 2010. Because of the relative importance of payroll taxes to the financing of the U.S. government, we cover these in greater detail in the next section.

Figure 15.5
U.S. federal tax revenue sources, 2010

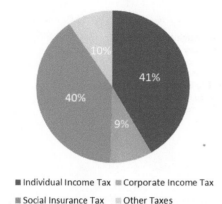

Type of tax	Revenue (billions)
Individual income	$898.5
Social insurance	864.8
Corporate Income	191.4
Other	
-Estate and gift	18.9
-excise	66.9
-customs	25.3
-misc	95.9
Total	**$2,161.7**

■ Individual Income Tax ■ Corporate Income Tax
■ Social Insurance Tax   ■ Other Taxes

Source: CBO, Historical Budget Data.

The major sources of tax revenue for the U.S. government begin with the two payroll taxes: individual income taxes and social insurance (Social Security and Medicare) taxes. Together, these two accounted for 81% of all tax revenue in 2010. Total tax revenue in 2010 was about $2.16 trillion.

Payroll taxes

When you graduate from college and get a full-time job, you'll probably receive bigger paychecks than any you have previously received. But that paycheck will probably be smaller than you expect. Remember, the government pays for activities with tax revenue predominantly raised from income. Payroll taxes include social insurance taxes and individual income taxes.

Social Insurance Taxes

Earlier in this chapter, we discussed Social Security and Medicare. You will recall that over one third of the U.S. Federal government outlays are for these two programs. And these programs are paid for with taxes on employee's pay – the benefits that a retiree receives depends on the taxes paid in during his or her time in the labor force. Currently, the tax for these two programs amounts to 15.3% of a worker's pay. This is typically split in half with 7.65% paid by employees and 7.65% paid by employers. People who are self-employed pay the full amount. This tax is applicable to the first $110,100 an individual earns. These dollars go into the trust funds that are to provide income and health care assistance to retirees.

Income Tax

U.S. federal income taxes are set according to a scale that increases with income levels. This is known as a *progressive tax system*. In a **progressive income tax system**, people with higher income pay a larger fraction of their income in taxes than people with lower income. Figure 15.6 shows 2012 U.S. federal tax rates for single individuals. Notice that the tax rate climbs with income levels.

A progressive income tax system is a system in which people with higher incomes pay a greater fraction of their income in taxes.

Figure 15.6
2012 U.S. federal tax rates

Taxable income	Tax rate
$0 - $8,700	10%
$8,700 - $35,350	15%
$35,350 - $85,650	25%
$85,650 - $178,650	28%
$178, 650 - $388,350	33%
Over $388,350	35%

These tax rates are marginal tax rates, which means they apply only to dollars within the specified income ranges. For example, all income earned between $35,350 and $85,650 is taxed at 25%, but if someone earns $86,651, that last dollar is taxed at the 28% rate.

Source: Tax Foundation (these are estimates and can be finalized before publication.)

The tax rates specified in Figure 15.6 are *marginal tax rates*. A **marginal tax rate** is the tax rate paid on an individual's next dollar of income. Let's say your first full-time job after college offers you a salary of $60,000. For simplicity, we'll also assume you have no tax deductions so that your entire salary is taxable income. In terms of the tax rates presented above, this income level puts you in the 25% tax bracket. This doesn't mean you pay 25% of all your income in taxes, it only means you pay 25% on every dollar of income above $35,350. You pay 10% on income up to $8,700, and 15% on the income between $8,700 and $35,350.

> **The marginal tax rate** is the tax rate paid on a person's next dollar of income.

When we consider fiscal policy in Chapter 17, it will be critical to understand the way income tax rates affect an individual's total tax bill. For this reason, we now go through a more extended example where we compute a person's tax bill based on the marginal tax rates in Figure 15.8. Let's use these rates to compute your tax bill based on taxable income of $60,000.

Before we go through the math, note that you'll pay three different tax rates: 10% on income up to $8,700; 15% on income between $8,700 and $35,350; and 25% on income above $35,650. Your total tax bill is determined as:

0.10 x $8,700	=	$870
+ 0.15 x ($35,350 - $8,700)	=	$3,997.5
+ 0.25 x (60,000 - $35,350)	=	$6,162.5
Total	=	$11,030

Therefore, your $60,000 income accrues a federal income tax bill of $11,030, which is about 18.4% of your income. This 18.4% is your *average tax rate*. An **average tax rate** is the total tax paid divided by taxable income. Notice that the average tax rate is below the marginal tax rate. This is generally the case in a progressive tax system, and is due to the fact that the marginal tax rate applies to the last few dollars taxed, but not all income.

> **Average tax rate** – total tax paid as a portion of taxable income.

Historical income tax rates

Though taxes may seem like a fact of life now, the income tax is only about 100 years old in the United States. Prior to 1913, there was no income tax in the United States; most tax revenues were generated by taxes on imports. But import taxes were set to decline and so the government looked to income taxes as another source of revenue. Figure 15.7 reproduces the actual Form 1040 from 1913—the form individuals submit to the IRS when they file their tax returns. In 1913, this form was essentially one page for all income-earners. The original income tax in the U.S. was similar to the current tax system, in that the rates were progressive. However, the highest marginal tax rate in 1913 was just six percent, which only applied to income greater than \$500,000—over \$11 million in today's dollars. Very few people were making this kind of income in 1913.

Figure 15.7
1913 individual income tax form

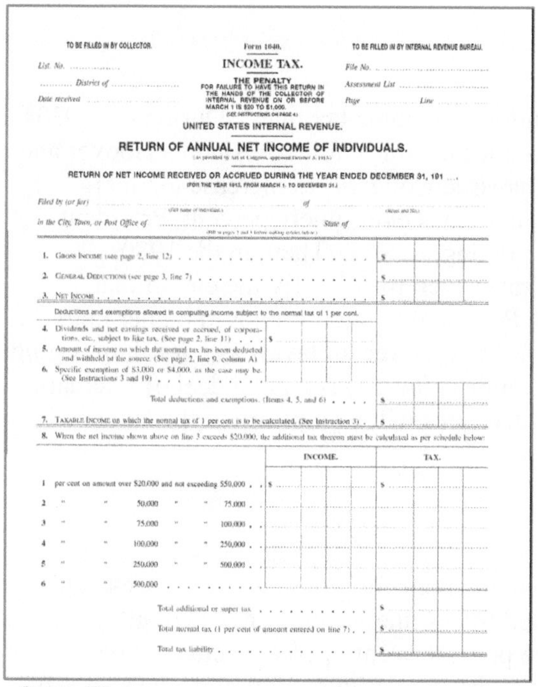

TO BE FILLED IN BY COLLECTOR.

Form 1040.

TO BE FILLED IN BY INTERNAL REVENUE BUREAU.

List No. ....

INCOME TAX.

File No. ....

.... District of ....

THE PENALTY FOR FAILURE TO HAVE THIS RETURN IN THE HANDS OF THE COLLECTOR OF INTERNAL REVENUE ON OR BEFORE MARCH 1 IS \$20 TO \$1,000. (SEE INSTRUCTIONS ON PAGE 4.)

Assessment List ....

Date received ....

Page .... Line ....

UNITED STATES INTERNAL REVENUE.

RETURN OF ANNUAL NET INCOME OF INDIVIDUALS.

RETURN OF NET INCOME RECEIVED OR ACCRUED DURING THE YEAR ENDED DECEMBER 31, 191 ....
(FOR THE YEAR 1913, FROM MARCH 1, TO DECEMBER 31.)

Filed by (or for) .... of ....

In the City, Town, or Post Office of .... State of ....

1. Gross Income (see page 2, line 12) . . . . . \$
2. General Deductions (see page 3, line 7) . . . . . \$
3. Net Income . . . . . \$

Deductions and exemptions allowed in computing income subject to the normal tax of 1 per cent.

4. Dividends and net earnings received or accrued, of corporations, etc., subject to like tax. (See page 2, line 11) . . . \$
5. Amount of income on which the normal tax has been deducted and withheld at the source. (See page 2, line 9, column A)
6. Specific exemption of \$3,000 or \$4,000, as the case may be. (See Instructions 3 and 19) . . . . .

Total deductions and exemptions. (Items 4, 5, and 6) . . . . \$

7. Taxable Income on which the normal tax of 1 per cent is to be calculated. (See Instruction 3) . \$
8. When the net income shown above on line 3 exceeds \$20,000, the additional tax thereon must be calculated as per schedule below:

	INCOME.	TAX.
1 per cent on amount over \$20,000 and not exceeding \$50,000 . .	\$	\$
2 " " 50,000 " " 75,000 . .		
3 " " 75,000 " " 100,000 . .		
4 " " 100,000 " " 250,000 . .		
5 " " 250,000 " " 500,000 . .		
6 " " 500,000		
Total additional or super tax		\$
Total normal tax (1 per cent of amount entered on line 7) . .		\$
Total tax liability		\$

Source: IRS.

This is the original Form 1040 – the form taxpayers submit to the IRS with their income taxes. Note that the form was just one page long. The six tax brackets are detailed towards the bottom of the form. As you can see they go from one to six percent. This means the highest marginal tax rate in 1913 was just six percent. This was on income greater than \$500,000 – which is more than \$11 million in current dollars!

Once the income tax was instituted, marginal tax rates rose quickly. In fact, by 1918, the top marginal rate rose to 77%. This applied only to income over \$2 million, but it means that every dollar earned yielded only 23 cents to the income-earner. Figure 15.8 plots the top marginal income tax rate in the U.S. from 1913 to 2012. Note that, while this figure shows only the top rate, it is a good indicator of the general level of rates over time.

Figure 15.8
Historical top U.S. marginal tax rates

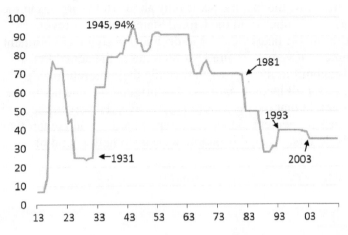

This graph plots the top marginal tax rate in the United States over time. Marginal rates are a good indicator of overall tax rates since 1913. There are several key historical dates. For example, in 1931, during the Great Depression, marginal tax rates increased significantly. Major downward revisions occurred in 1963 and 1981. In 1993, tax rates rose, but then fell in 2003.

Source: IRS

There are several important dates in the evolution of income tax rates. During the 1930s, in the throes of the Great Depression, income tax revenues naturally fell. Presidents Hoover and Roosevelt, in attempts to balance the federal budget, pressed Congress to increase top marginal rates to eighty percent. Later, in 1963, with top marginal rates over ninety percent, President JFK pushed for rate reductions that led to the top rate falling to 70%. Then, in the 1980s President Reagan led the push to lower marginal tax rates even further. By the end of that decade, the top marginal rate was just 28%. In 1993, President Clinton proposed higher rates and the top rate rose to 39%. Finally, in 2003, rates fell to their recent levels as a result of urging by President George W. Bush. Over the course of a century, there was a great deal of fluctuation in marginal tax rates. Going forward, it is not likely that rates will ever return to the levels witnessed prior to 1980.

Who pays for government?

In a progressive tax system, the wealthy pay more than the poor for government services. Of course, the very wealthy pay most of all. In the United States, the wealthiest 20% of all households paid 86% of all income taxes in 2007; the poorest twenty percent actually "pay" negative taxes, due to various tax credits and income assistance. Figure 15.9 plots the shares of income tax liability by U.S. household income levels from 1979 to 2007. Notice that the top one percent of all households alone paid almost 40 percent of all income taxes in 2007.

Figure 15.9
Portion of total federal taxes paid by various income groups, 2007

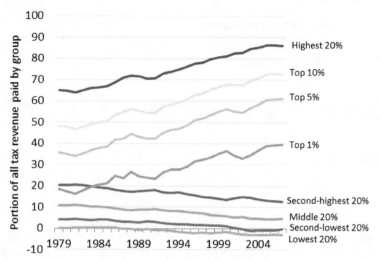

The share of tax liability by income group shows how much of the total taxes paid are contributed from each income group. For example, the middle income group in the U.S. now pays less than 10% of all income taxes paid. The wealthiest twenty percent (the top line.) of income earners paid 86% of all income taxes in 2007. Digging deeper into this top 20%, we can see that the top 1% of all income earners paid nearly 40% of all income taxes paid in 2007.

Source: Tax Policy Center.

Practice What You Know
Government Revenue

Federal Taxes

Assume your taxeable income is $100,000. Use the 2012 marginal tax rates from Figure 29.6 to determine your taxes.

Question: Compute federal income tax.

Answer:

The relevent tax rates are displayed in Figure 15.6. Keep in mind, the different rates apply only to the income in the specified bands. For example, the first tax rate of ten percent applies only to income up to $8,700. Income between $8,700 and $35,350 is taxed at fifteen percent. Use this patternt to determine the tax paid on all income up to $100,000. Take these rates and multiply them by the income in the respective brackests and sum these to get the total income tax:

$$
\begin{aligned}
&0.10 \times \$8,700 &&= &&\$870.00 \\
+\ &0.15 \times (\$35,350 - \$8,700) &&= &&\$3,997.50 \\
+\ &0.25 \times (\$85,650 - \$35,350) &&= &&\$12,575.00 \\
+\ &0.28 \times (\$100,000 - \$85,650) &&= &&\underline{\$4,018.00} \\
&Total &&= &&\$21,460.5
\end{aligned}
$$

Question: Compute your Social Security and Medicare tax. The relevent tax rate is 7.65%. Using this, you compute your tax as:

$$\$100,000 \times 0.0765 = \$7,650.00$$

What are budget deficits and how bad are they?

We are now ready to bring both sides of the budget together. Doing this allows us to examine the differences between spending and revenue. In this section we define budget deficits and debt and also consider these in a long-run historical context.

A budget deficit occu when government out exceed revenue.

Deficits

A **budget deficit** exists when government outlays exceed revenue. Panel a of Figure 15.10 plots U.S. budget outlays and revenues since 1901, converted to billions of 2010 U.S. dollars. Outlays, displayed in orange, have grown rapidly, especially since 2001. Over the long run, revenue has grown, but it has declined since 2007. You can see that outlays have generally exceeded revenue for much of the recent past. For example, in 2010, total outlays were almost $3.5 trillion while revenue was about $2.2 trillion. The difference, $1.3 trillion, is the budget deficit for that year.

Figure 15.10
U.S. Federal budget data, billions of 2010 dollars

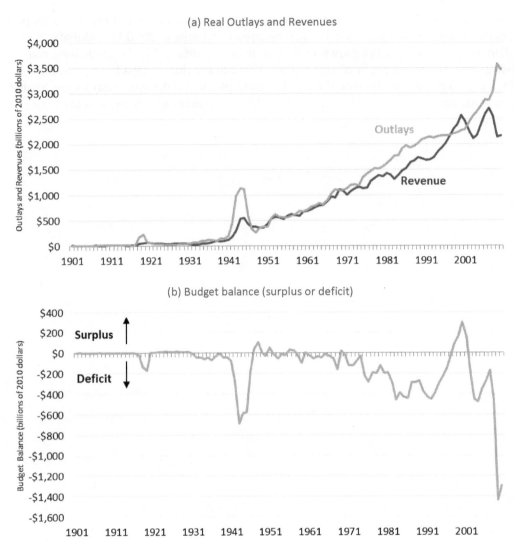

Source: OMB. Real figures generated using long CPI series from Minneapolis Fed.

(a) Real outlays are shown in orange and revenue is shown in blue for the U.S. federal government budget since 1901. When the outlays exceed revenue, the budget has a deficit for that year. (b) In the plot of the real budget balance, negative values indicate a deficit. The Great Recession and the government response to it helped to create the 2009 deficit of $1.4 trillion (in 2010 dollars), the largest in U.S. history.

It is also possible for the government to have a **budget surplus**, which occurs when revenue exceeds outlays. Panel b of Figure 15.10 shows budget surpluses and deficits in billions of 2010 U.S. dollars. The surplus is the vertical distance between the revenue and outlays, shown in Panel a. Note that at this distance, negative outlays exceed revenue.

A budget surplus occurs when government revenue exceeds

The Great Recession and government responses during the recession helped create the 2009 deficit of $1.4 trillion, the largest in U.S. history. Notice that this deficit is larger than the deficits generated during World War II. But dollar values for government budget figures are misleading over the long run, since the population and the size of the economy changes. To control for both population and economic growth, economists look at the deficit as a portion of GDP. When we divide budget data by GDP, we essentially scale it to the size of the economy. Figure 15.11 shows the U.S. federal outlays and revenue, both as a fraction of GDP, from 1960 to 2010. Over the entire period, outlays averaged 19.9 percent of GDP and revenues averaged 17.6 percent of GDP. These averages are shown as dashed lines in the figure. These long-run averages can be viewed as a target benchmark for future budgets.

      The shaded periods in Figure 15.11 are economic recessions. Since the onset of the Great Recession at the end of 2007, outlays, revenues, and deficits have all reached historic magnitudes. Both outlays and revenues currently lie well outside their long-run averages. Notice that deficits grow when outlays increase or revenues decrease.

Figure 15.11
U.S. Federal outlays and revenue as a portion of GDP, 1960-2010

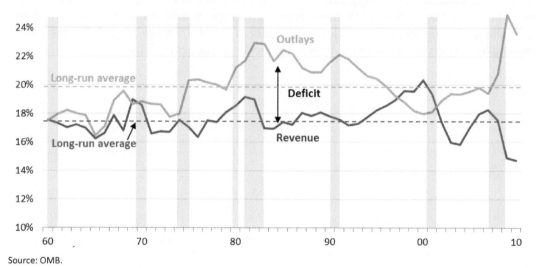

Source: OMB.

The deficit-to-GDP ratio is a more informative gauge of the magnitude of deficits over time, because it accounts for changes in population and economic growth. Here, we illustrate outlays (orange) and revenue (blue) as a portion of GDP. The deficit is the vertical distance between the lines. Long run averages are indicated by the dashed lines. These show us that recent spending has been above the long run average and recent revenue has been below the long run average. The shaded areas indicate recessionary periods. As you can see, deficits grow during recessions.

      When the budget is in deficit, government spending exceeds revenue. This means the government must borrow funds to pay for the deficit. In Chapter 10, we introduced U.S. Treasury bonds as important financial assets in the loanable funds market. In Chapter 14, we saw how these Treasury bonds are used in monetary policy. Now, we can understand how those bonds originate: when tax revenues fall short of outlays, the government sells Treasury bonds to cover the difference.

Deficits versus Debt

In your personal budget, it might happen that your spending (outlays) in a given month exceeds your income. In other words, you find that you have a deficit. You might rely on funds from parents or grandparents to make up the difference, but these count either as income (if it's a gift) or a loan (if you have to repay it). Often you will have to borrow, perhaps using a credit card. A loan, whether it is from a friend, relative, or credit card company, is a debt that must be paid.

National Debt – the sum total of accumulated budget deficits.

It's easy to confuse the terms "deficit" and "debt." A deficit is a shortfall in revenue for a particular year's budget. **A debt** is the total of all accumulated and unpaid deficits. Consider your tuition bill over the course of your time in college. If you borrow $5,000 to help pay for your first year of college, that is your first-year deficit. If you borrow another $5,000 for your second year, you have a $5,000 deficit for each year and your debt is now $10,000.

Figure 15.12 shows the U.S. national debt (in real terms) from 1990-2010. Notice that we distinguish between total debt and debt held by the public. The difference between these is debt owned internally by one of the many branches of the U.S. government. Sometimes a given federal agency will purchase Treasury bonds. For example, as part of its mandate to control the money supply, the Federal Reserve typically holds billions of dollars' worth of Treasury securities. Thus, it can be helpful to distinguish total government debt that is not also owned by the government itself, and this is the portion that is publicly held.   Figure 15.12 indicates that both measures have risen in recent years, caused by the large budget deficits.

Figure 15.12
U.S. national debt, billions of 2010 dollars

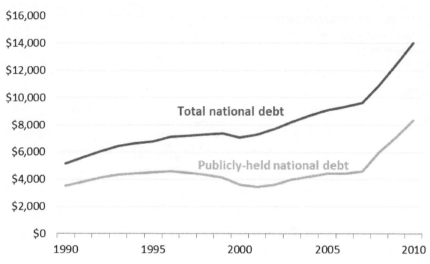

Source: *Treasury Bulletin*, U.S. Treasury.

The total amount of U.S. federal government debt (blue) has grown to over $14 trillion in recent years, even exceeding annual GDP in the United States. But much of this is owned by agencies of the government itself (the government owes money to itself), so many economists focus instead on the debt that is held publicly (by anyone besides the federal government). This amount (orange line above) is still less than $10 trillion, and about 60% of U.S. GDP. If you are curious about the current size of the U.S. national debt, you can visit the website: www.usdebtclock.org.

While the U.S. national debt is historically large, it is still smaller than many other nations, including many wealthy nations. Figure 29.13 shows publicly-held debt-to-GDP ratios for several nations in 2010. The United States comes in at about 61%, but Japan's ratio is over 180%. This means that if you added up all the publicly national held debt of the United States, it is came to 61% of GDP in 2010.

Figure 15.13
International Debt to GDP ratios, 2010 publicly held debt

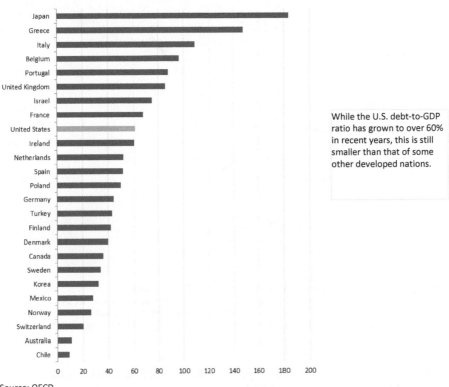

While the U.S. debt-to-GDP ratio has grown to over 60% in recent years, this is still smaller than that of some other developed nations.

Source: OECD.

National Debt is the sum total of accumulated budget deficits.

Economics in the Real World:
Several European nations are grappling with government debt problems

In the summer of 2011, Greece erupted in a series of demonstrations, some marked by violent encounters between the citizens of Greece and their national police. The issue at the heart of these protests was the national debt. The Greek national debt climbed to almost 150% of GDP in 2010. In order to avert a Greek debt default, other members of the European Union and the International Monetary Fund forged together aid packages of $146 billion in 2010 and $165 billion in 2011.

Austerity refers to strict budget regulations aimed at debt reduction.

But the aid from Europe was granted only with strict *austerity* requirements. In this context, **austerity** refers to strict budget regulations aimed at debt reduction. These austerity measures are what drove the Greek workers to protest. They included wage cuts and pension freezes for public workers, and they also included an increase on the sales tax to 23 percent. The Greek government had agreed to these measures in order to secure international aid and avert a default, but the Greek citizens rose up against their government after the agreements were signed.

Greece is not the only European nation with very high sovereign (national) debt. As of 2012, Italy and Spain, the 8th and 12th largest economies in the world, were both facing default and severe austerity measures. In September of 2012, Spanish rioters hurled gasoline bombs at police to protest the austerity measures their government agreed to. The fear of the other European nations is that there will be a "domino effect" since much of the sovereign debt is owned by other European governments and private banks. Therefore, if Greece defaults on its sovereign debt, then this is damaging to Spain. If Spain then defaults, then it may lead to others and so on.   All of this international unrest derives from excessive government debt.

Foreign ownership of U.S. federal debt

As we saw in Chapter 11, many people are concerned about foreign ownership of U.S. debt. The concern stems from a fear that foreigners who own U.S. debt will control the country. However, as of November 2011, about 70% of our national debt is held domestically, and just 30% is held internationally. The international breakdown shows that China, Japan, and the United Kingdom are the major foreign holders of U.S. debt.

Figure 15.3 shows foreign and domestic ownership of total U.S. debt from 1990 to 2010. Total national debt—indicated on the left-side vertical axis—grew from about $5 trillion to over $14 trillion. However, most of the new debt was purchased by domestic investors and U.S. government agencies. Still, the portion of U.S. government debt that is foreign-owned—measured on the right-side vertical axis—has doubled from about 15% to near 30% over that twenty-year period.

Figure 15.14
Foreign and Domestic ownership of U.S. government debt, billions of 2010 dollars

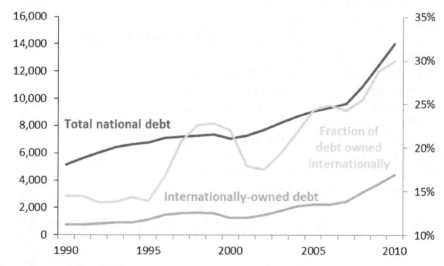

Source: *Treasury Bulletin*, U.S. Treasury.

Most U.S. government debt is owned by Americans or the U.S. government itself. This graph shows total debt and internationally-owned debt, both measured on the left-hand vertical axis. The fraction owned internationally has grown in recent years, but is still less than one-third (measured on the right-side vertical axis).

While this foreign ownership of U.S. government debt is troubling for many Americans, it is important to realize the importance of the foreign funds to the U.S. loanable funds market. As we discussed in Chapter 11, foreign lending increases the supply of loanable funds in the United States, which keeps interest rates low. Lower interest rates allow firms and governments of the United States can borrow at lower cost.

Economics in the Real World:
Does China own America?

In a July 2011 article in the *Global Post*, Tom Mucha addressed the fear of many people around the world. Namely, the question of who owns the U.S. government debt. The United States now has more than $15 trillion in debt. Many people fear that the owners of the bonds will have disproportionate influence on the activities of the U.S. government.

According to Mucha: "Many people — politicians and pundits alike — prattle on that China and, to a lesser extent Japan, own most of America's $14.3 trillion in government debt. But there's one little problem with that conventional wisdom: it's just not true. While the Chinese, Japanese and plenty of other foreigners own substantial amounts, it's really Americans who hold most of America's debt."

Here's a quick breakdown by total amount held and percentage of total U.S. debt, according to *Business Insider*:

- Mutual funds: $300.5 billion (2 percent)
- Commercial banks: $301.8 billion (2.1 percent)
- State, local and federal retirement funds: $320.9 billion (2.2 percent)
- Money market mutual funds: $337.7 billion (2.4 percent)
- United Kingdom: $346.5 billion (2.4 percent)
- Private pension funds: $504.7 billion (3.5 percent)
- State and local governments: $506.1 billion (3.5 percent)
- Japan: $912.4 billion (6.4 percent)
- U.S. households: $959.4 billion (6.6 percent)
- China: $1.16 trillion (8 percent)
- The U.S. Treasury: $1.63 trillion (11.3 percent)
- Social Security trust fund: $2.67 trillion (19 percent)

So the United States owes foreigners about $4.5 trillion in debt. But the United States owes itself $9.8 trillion.

Source: http://globalpublicsquare.blogs.cnn.com/2011/07/21/who-owns-america-hint-its-not-china/

Practice What You Know
Federal Budgets

The Greek Debt Crisis

The U.S. national debt grew substantially in the first decade of this century. The table below shows the data on the national debt from both 2001 and 2010.

Year	Total Debt (billions of $)	Nominal GDP (billions of $)
2001	$5,807	$10,286
2010	$13,561	$14,499

Question: Use the data to compute the U.S. debt-to-GDP ratio in both 2001 and 2010.

Answer:

For the year 2001, we compute the debt-to-GDP ratio as:

$5,807 \div $10,286 = 0.56$

For the year 2010, we compute the debt-to-GDP ratio as:

$13,562 \div $14,499 = 0.94$

Question: What are the major reasons why the national debt increased so much between 2001 and 2010?

Answer:

First, on the outlay side, governemnt spending increased due to increased spending on Social Security and Medicare, increased defense spending in the wake of the terrorist attacks of September 11, 2001, and government responses to the Great Recession beginning with fiscal policy in 2008.

Second, on the revenue side, tax receipts declined sharply during and after the Great Recession.

Economics for Life

Budgeting for your Take-home Pay

Most college students have not yet held full-time jobs. So you are probably still planning for that day when you graduate and get your first big paycheck. We certainly don't want to discourage you, but we will offer a few words of caution for when you are budgeting your major expenses.

Let's say you graduate and obtain a good job in the city of your choice. You agree to a salary of $60,000 per year. This is a good starting salary (probably due to the economics courses you took), and so you start thinking about your budget for the future. Consider a few of the biggest questions. How much can you afford for your monthly housing payment? How large a car payment can you afford? How much can you spend on groceries or dining out? How much should you save each month?

You are wise to think about these ahead of time. But when you plan, be sure to recognize that your take-home pay will be far less than your $60,000. It is tempting to make a monthly budget based upon the $5,000 per month that your basic salary promises. In the table below, we estimate the actual size of your paycheck.

First, we subtract federal income taxes. Based on the 2012 tax rates, we determined the annual payment is $11,030. Next, we subtract 7.65% for Social Security and Medicare, After that, we subtract 5% each for state income taxes (this is about average), benefits (like health insurance, dental and optical, and retirement contibutions.

	Monthly	Yearly
Salary	+$5,000	+60,000
Federal Income Tax	$919.00	$11,030
Social Security/Medicare Tax	$382.50	$4,590
State Income Tax	$250.00	$1,200
Benefits	$250.00	$3,000
Retirement	$250.00	$3,000
Take-home Pay	$2,948.50	$35,380

After these deductions, you are left with less than $3,000 per month! Your take-home pay is about 40% less than your salary.

Therefore, when you are making major spending decisions, like housing and car payments, be sure to budget based on this much-smaller figure. If instead, you budget based on your salary, you won't be able to save and you may even become dependednt on credit cards.

Conclusion

We started this chapter with the misconception that governments never balance their budgets. Certainly given the current size of U.S. budget deficits and the sovereign debt problems around the world, it would be natural to assume that national budgets are never balanced. But in fact, as we have seen, the United States had a balanced federal budget as recently as 2001.

This chapter lays the groundwork for us to examine fiscal policy in Chapter 16. Much of the debt and deficits we've observe are a direct result of government budgetary maneuvers to affect the macroeconomy. Going forward, we now understand the institutions of fiscal policy. In Chapter 17, we'll learn about the economic theories that support fiscal policy.

BIG QUESTIONS

(1) How does the government spend?

Government spending has grown sharply since 2000, and is now about $3.5 trillion.

Mandatory spending programs now comprise the more than half of government spending at the U.S. national level. These mandatory programs include Social Security, Medicare, and welfare programs. Interest on the national debt is nearly ten percent of federal spending. Defense spending is almost twenty percent of federal spending. The remaining fifth of the budget goes to discretionary government spending like highways, bridges and the salaries of many government employees.

(2) How does the government tax?

The U.S. government raises over eighty percent of its revenues through payroll taxes: income taxes and taxes for Social Security and Medicare. The income tax yields about $1 trillion in revenue per year. It is a progressive tax and so wealthier Americans pay more in taxes than the poor.

(3) What are budget deficits and how bad are they?

If total government outlays exceed revenue in a given year, the budget is in deficit. Deficits add to the national debt, which is the accumulated deficit over time. Recently, the U.S. government has tallied deficits of more than $1 trillion per year. This amounts to almost 10% of GDP and cannot be sustained indefinitely.

Concepts You Should Know

Average tax rate   Marginal tax rate
Budget deficit   Medicare
Budget surplus   National debt
Discretionary outlays   Progressive income tax system
Government outlays   Social Security
Mandatory outlays   Transfer payments

Questions for Review

1. Since the 1960s, Social Security and Medicare have grown as portions of U.S. government spending.

A. What major categories have shrunk during this same period?

B. Has the U.S. budget become more or less flexible as a result of the growth in the mandatory programs? Explain.

2. Explain the difference between a budget deficit and the national debt.

3. Going back to 1960, there have been a few years in which the U.S. government budget was in surplus. What years were these? Why do you think those surpluses disappeared when they did? Figure 29.2 might be helpful in answering this question.

4. This question refers to Figure 29.2 which shows the U.S. outlays and spending as portions of GDP.

A. List three time periods when the U.S. budget deficit was relatively large.

B. What historical event were taking place in the United States during these three periods that may have led to these large deficits? Be specific.

5. List five reasons why mandatory outlays are predicted to grow (as a portion of the total budget) over the next decade.

6. Explain the difference between average tax rates and marginal tax rates. Is it possible for your average tax rate to equal your marginal tax rate? If so, how?

Study Problems

1. Use the marginal income tax rates in Table 29.2 to compute:

A. Tax due on taxable income of $100,000, 200,000, and $500,000.

B. Average tax rate on taxable income of $100,000, $200,000, and $500,000

4. Portugal, Ireland, Greece and Spain (the "PIGS") all went through national budget difficulties in recent years. Use the data below to answer questions regarding the sovereign debts of these nations (all data comes from the OECD and is in billions of current U.S. dollars).

	2000		2010	
	Debt	GDP	Debt	GDP
Greece	138	127	455	308
Ireland	34	98	124	206
Portugal	62	118	203	231
Spain	292	586	734	1,420

A. Compute the debt-to-GDP ratio for all three nations in both 2000 and 2010.

B. Compute the average yearly budget deficit for each of the nations over this period.

C. In your judgment, which of the four nations (including Greece) was in the worst fiscal shape in 2010? Use your computations from above to justify your answer.

2. There are three different ways to report budget deficit data: nominal deficits, real deficits, and deficit-to-GDP ratios. Which of the three is most informative? Why?

Solved Problems

*1. Greece is a nation that has been through significant national budget turmoil. In 2010, it was discovered that the government had been concealing the true size of the national debt for several years. The data in the table below reveals just how much their officially reported national debt grew between 2000 and 2010. Note that the data is in billions of U.S> dollars.

2000		2010	
Debt	GDP	Debt	GDP
$138	$127	$455	$308

A. What is the average annual increase in the Greek debt over the ten-year span?

The debt grew from $138 billion to $455 billion over ten years, which is an increase of $31 billion, or an average of $31.7 billion per year.

B. What is the average annual budget deficit for Greece over this period?

Given that the debt increased by $31.7 billion per year, this number is also the figure for the average annual deficit over this period.

*2 Use the data in the table above to compute the debt-to-GDP ratio for Greece in both 2000 and 2010

For 2000, 138 ÷ 127 = 1.09
For 2001, 455/308 = 1.48

Chapter 16
Fiscal Policy

Economic Misconception: Government spending is a simple tool for fighting recessions.

Many people believe that government can quickly and predictably offset economic downturns. They believe the government can increase spending and decrease taxes in order to safely evade recessions. This belief is held by the media and also makes its way into many historical accounts of past economic troubles. But if past experience has taught us anything, it is that government actions have uneven and unpredictable effects on the economy. While the government may be able to influence the macroeconomy, many government spending initiatives have failed to quickly revive an ailing economy.

In this chapter, we examine the case for fiscal policy, which includes both government spending and taxes. We begin by framing fiscal policy in the aggregate demand and aggregate supply model. We will look at both expansionary and contractionary policies. We will consider potential shortcomings of fiscal policy, and then finish with a look at fiscal policy from the supply-side perspective.

Big questions:

What is fiscal policy?
What are the shortcomings of fiscal policy?
What is the supply-side approach to fiscal policy?

What is fiscal policy?

Over the past two chapters, we examined the use of monetary policy to counteract the business cycle. But government can also use taxes and spending to influence the economy and this is known as **fiscal policy**. Fiscal policy uses the tools of the federal budget to affect the economy. In the United States, tax and spending changes are legislated and approved by both Congress and the President. Sometimes fiscal policy occurs through changes in government spending; other times they might adjust taxes in order to influence the economy.

Fiscal policy is the use of government spending and taxes to influence the economy.

In this section, we first describe how the government can use fiscal policy to try to stimulate the economy and then how fiscal policy might be used to slow down rapid growth. Along the way, we consider how this affects government budget deficits and debt. Finally, we examine the multiplier process which describes the way fiscal policy ripples through the economy.

Expansionary Fiscal Policy

> **Expansionary fiscal policy** occurs when the government increases spending or decreases taxes to stimulate the economy toward expansion.

In the fall of 2007, the U.S. economy was slipping into recession. This led to the expectation by many that the government SHOULD do something to keep the recession at bay. In particular, many people expected the government to step in with tax reductions or spending programs to help stimulate the economy. **Expansionary fiscal policy** occurs when the government increases spending or decreases taxes to stimulate the economy toward expansion. In this section, we use the aggregate demand and aggregate supply model to examine the effects of expansionary fiscal policy.

In Chapter 14, we introduced the aggregate demand and aggregate supply model. In that model, we showed that recession can occur as a result of a drop in aggregate demand. In theory, the economy can move itself back to full employment in the long run, when all prices adjust. Consider the example presented in Figure 16.1. Initially, the economy is in long run equilibrium at point A, with P = 100, Y = Y* (full employment), and u = u* (the natural rate). If aggregate demand declines to AD_1, the economy moves to short run equilibrium b, with output Y', which is less than full employment output and the unemployment rate of u', which is greater than the natural rate.

Figure 16.1
Expansionary Fiscal Policy

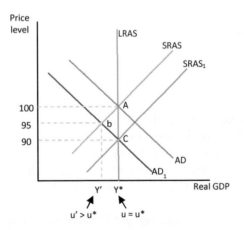

A decrease in aggregate demand moves the economy to from point A to equilibrium at b, with less than full employment output (Y'), and unemployment (u) greater than the natural rate. In the long run, all prices adjust, moving the economy back to full employment equilibrium at C. The goal of expansionary fiscal policy is to shift aggregate demand back to AD so that the economy returns to full employment without waiting for long-run adjustments.

At equilibrium b, government officials can wait for the economy to adjust back to full employment equilibrium at point C. This adjustment happens when all prices adjust downward and short-run aggregate supply shifts down. But prices can take a while to adjust. In addition, recessions are difficult times for many people in the economy and many expect the government to take action to ease their plight. Thus, government officials often choose to use fiscal and monetary policy to try to shift aggregate demand back to its original level. If this works, the economy resumes full employment equilibrium at point A.

Fiscal policy can use either government spending, taxes, or a combination of the two tools. First, government spending (G) is one component of aggregate demand. Therefore, increases in G directly increase aggregate demand. When private spending (consumption, investment, and net exports) is low, government can increase demand directly by increasing G. Fiscal policy can also focus on consumption (C) by decreasing taxes. Decreases in taxes can increase aggregate demand because people have more of their income to spend after they pay their taxes. If people to keep more of their paycheck, they can afford more consumption.

Recent history in the United States offers two clear examples of expansionary fiscal policy. The next section reviews these to clarify how both government spending and taxes are used in fiscal policy.

Fiscal Policy in the Great Recession

In the fall of 2007, the U.S. unemployment rate climbed from 4.6 to 5 percent. Thus, as it became clearer that economic conditions were worsening in the United States, the government took action. Political leaders decided that in addition to ongoing monetary policy, fiscal policy could also help. Figure 16.2 shows real GDP growth and the unemployment rate in the United States over the time period in of the Great Recession. The official dates of the recession are shaded blue. The top panel shows quarterly real GDP growth over the period, which fell to -1.8 percent at the beginning of 2008. The bottom panel shows the monthly unemployment rate which began climbing in late 2007 and remained at high levels through 2011, well after the recession officially ended.

Figure 16.2:
Major fiscal policy initiatives in the Great Recession period

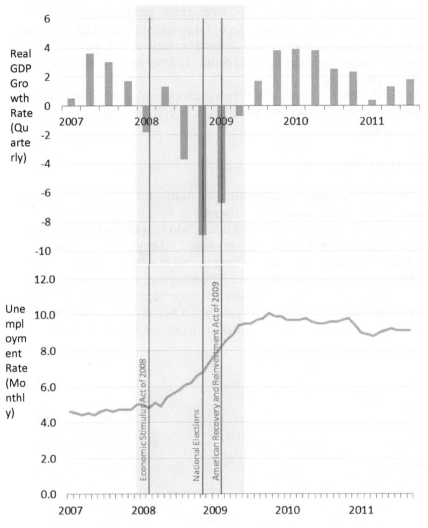

Source: GDP data is from the BEA; Unemployment rate is from BLS.

The Great Recession began in December 2007. In February 2008, President Bush signed the *Economic Stimulus Act of 2008* which focused on tax cuts to try to stimulate the economy and avoid recession. During 2008, the economy sunk deeper into recession. In February 2009, President Obama signed the *American Recovery and Reinvestment Act* which focused on government spending programs.

In this context, the government enacted two significant fiscal policy initiatives. The first, signed in February 2008 by President George W. Bush, was named the *Economic Stimulus Act of 2008*. The cornerstone of this act was a tax rebate for Americans. Americans had already paid their taxes for 2007, and the stimulus act included a partial rebate of these previously paid taxes. The government actually mailed checks to taxpayers. And these refunds were not insignificant; a typical four-person family received a rebate check for $1,800 ($600 per adult and $300 per child). This was not an unpleasant development for the authors of this book. The overall size of this bill was $168 billion; it refunded about one of every seven dollars paid in individual income taxes for 2007. The expectation was that people would spend rather than save most of this $168 billion, increasing aggregate demand and stimulating the economy.

However, after the first fiscal stimulus was passed, economic conditions worsened. In Figure 16.1, notice that real GDP growth plummeted and the unemployment rate rose significantly in 2008 after the first fiscal stimulus. National elections at the end of 2008 brought Barack Obama to the White House and changed the balance of power in Washington. In February 2009, less than one month after Obama took office, the new President signed the American Recovery and Reinvestment Act of 2009. The focus of this second act shifted to government spending. In addition, the size of this second fiscal stimulus—$787 billion—was much larger than the first.

These two major pieces of legislation illustrate the tools of fiscal policy: taxes and spending. The first focused on taxes, the second on government spending. The two acts may seem very different, but both sought to increase aggregate demand – they are based on the analysis we presented in Figure 16.2.

Fiscal policy generally focuses on aggregate demand. At the end of the chapter, we'll consider an alternative approach - an approach that uses government spending and taxes to affect aggregate supply in the long run.

Fiscal Policy and Budget Deficits

We have seen that the typical prescription for an ailing economy is to increase government spending, decrease taxes, or both. You may be wondering how the government pays for all the spending, or deals with the shortfall in tax revenue. The answer is through borrowing.

Let's start with a simplified example. Assume at the start that the government is currently balancing the national budget so that outlays equal tax revenue. Then, the economy slips into recession and the government decides to increase government spending by $100 billion. The government must pay for this by borrowing; it must sell $100 billion worth of Treasury bonds. As a result, federal budget is in deficit by $100 billion.

But that's only part of the story. In reality, the deficit will rise more than $100 billion because tax revenue will fall. Recall that more than eighty percent of U.S. tax revenue derives from payroll taxes. In a recession, in a recession, with income down and unemployment up, the amount of revenue that the government takes in from taxes falls, even if the tax rate stays the same.

It is easy to verify both of these phenomena by looking at recent U.S. recessions. Figure 16.3 shows U.S. federal outlays and tax revenue from 1985 to 2010, with recessionary eras shaded. First, look at the period of the Great Recession. Note how spending increased sharply in 2009, the year of the $787 billion fiscal stimulus. But falling income also led to less income tax revenue. Looking back over the three recessions shown in this graph, we see that spending increased but tax revenue fell in each.

Figure 16.3
Real U.S. outlays and revenue, 1985 - 2010

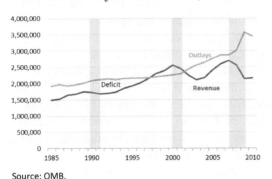

Using expansionary fiscal policy to counteract economic downturns leads to greater budget deficits. During recessionary periods, outlays increase and tax revenue falls. In 2001, these helped eliminate the budget surplus; in 1990 and 2008, these expanded the size of the deficit.

Source: OMB.

The bottom line is clear: expansionary fiscal policy inevitably leads to increases in budget deficits and the national debt during economic downturns. This policy prescription may seem odd. After all, if you personally fell on rough economic times, you might (reasonably) react differently. For example, if your employer cut you back to part-time employment, does it seem like a good idea to go on a spending binge? It might make you feel better while you are shopping, but it wouldn't help your financial situation much. One reason expansionary fiscal policy might work for the overall economy is that spending by one person becomes income to another, which can snowball into income increases throughout the economy. We discuss this aspect later in the chapter.

Contractionary Fiscal policy

We have seen that fiscal policy is often used to try to increase aggregate demand during economic downturns. But there are also times when fiscal policy is used to reduce aggregate demand.

There are two reasons a government may want to reduce aggregate demand. First, as we discussed above, expansionary fiscal policy creates deficits during recessions. An increase in taxes or a decrease in spending during economic expansion can work to eliminate the budget deficit and pay some of the government debt. For example, the U.S. government ran budget surpluses from 1998 to 2001, at the end of an extended economic expansion. These surpluses were not large enough to pay off the national debt, but they did shrink it somewhat.

Second, the government might also want to reduce aggregate demand if it believes that the economy is expanding beyond its long-run capabilities. Full employment output (Y^*) is considered the highest level of output sustainable in the long run. But if the unemployment rate falls below the natural rate (u^*), it indicates that output may be above Y^*. Some then worry that the economy may "overheat" from too much spending which can lead to inflation. Figure 16.4 illustrates this possibility. Beginning at point a, with aggregate demand equal to AD, notice that this level of aggregate demand leads to short run equilibrium where real GDP is higher than its full employment level ($Y' > Y^*$). In addition, at point a, the unemployment rate is below the natural rate ($u < u^*$) which is not sustainable in the long run.

Figure 16.4
Contractionary fiscal policy

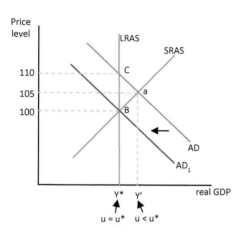

When policymakers believe the economy is producing beyond its long run capacity (Y′ > Y*), fiscal policy can be used to reduce aggregate demand. Contractionary fiscal policy moves the economy from equilibrium at point a to equilibrium at point B, thus avoiding inflationary outcomes at either b or C.

When aggregate demand is high enough to drive unemployment below the natural rate, there is upward pressure on the price level, which is at 105 at short-run equilibrium point a. Further, without a reduction in aggregate demand, the economy naturally moves toward equilibrium at point C in the long run, as prices fully adjust. But this equilibrium implies even more inflation. Thus, in order to avoid inflation, fiscal policy can be used to try to reduce aggregate demand from AD to AD_1. This moves the economy back to long run equilibrium with price stability at point B.

Together, contractionary and expansionary fiscal policy can be used to counteract the ups and downs of business cycles. We examine this combination more closely in the next section.

Countercyclical fiscal policy

All else equal, people generally prefer smoothness and predictability in their financial affairs. In Chapter 10, we talked about this characteristic in reference to consumption smoothing. In Chapter 11, we also considered how people are risk averse. Along these lines, an economy that grows at a consistent rate is preferable to an economy that grows in an erratic fashion. For these and other reasons, politicians generally employ fiscal policy to counter-act the business cycle.

The use of fiscal policy to counteract business cycle fluctuations is known as **countercyclical fiscal policy**. It consists of using expansionary policy in economic downturns and contractionary policy during economic expansion. Figure 16.5 illustrates the goals of countercyclical fiscal policy. The natural path of the economy includes business cycles where income and employment fluctuate. The hope is that countercyclical fiscal policy can dampen the fluctuations inherent in a business cycle.

> **Countercyclical fiscal policy** is fiscal policy used to counteract business cycle fluctuations.

Figure 16.5
Countercyclical Fiscal Policy and the Business

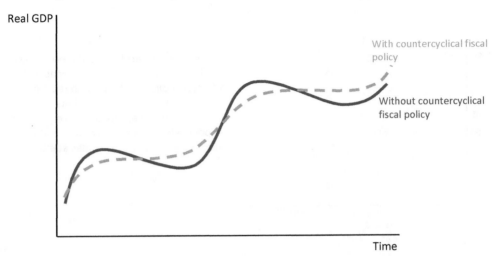

The goal of countercyclical fiscal policy is to smooth out the fluctuations in the business cycle.

You might recall from Chapter 14, that Keynesian economists focus on aggregate demand (total spending) in the economy. Keynesian economics provides the theoretical foundation for countercyclical fiscal policy. The ideas of Keynes provided a theoretical foundation for the New Deal government spending programs implemented in the United States in 1933 and 1935. But these Keynesian ideas are also behind the very recent fiscal policy initiatives in both 2008 and 2009.

Table 16.1 summarizes the tools of countercyclical fiscal policy, including the timing and effects of the policy and the effects on the government budget deficit.

Table 16.1:
Countercyclical fiscal policy tools

Fiscal Policy Action	Timing	Objective: How it affects aggregate demand (AD)	Byproduct: How it affects the budget deficit
Expansionary			
↑ government spending (G)	Economy contracting	G is one component of AD, so increases in G directly increase AD.	Increases budget deficit
↓ taxes (T)		Decreasing T leaves more funds in hands of consumers, who then spend more on consumption (C). When C rises, AD rises.	
Contractionary			
↓ government spending (G)	Economy expanding	Decreases in G directly decrease AD.	Decreases budget deficit
↑ taxes (T)		Increasing T leaves fewer funds in hands of consumers, who then spend less on consumption (C). When C falls, AD falls.	

Multipliers

The tools of fiscal policy are even more powerful than our initial discussion reveals. This is because the initial effects can snowball into further effects. When fiscal policy shifts aggregate demand, some effects are felt immediately. But a large share of the impact arrives later, as spending effects ripple through the economy. To see this clearly, we need to build on two concepts – one is review, the other is new.

First, the review concept. Recall from Chapter 7 that what one person spends becomes income to others. This is true for private spending and it is also true for government spending. For example, if the government uses fiscal policy to increase spending on new roads, the dollars spent on these roads become income to the suppliers of all the resources that go into the production of the roads. Now the new concept: increases in income generally lead to increases in consumption. When a person's income rises, they may save some of this new income, but they often spend part of it too. The **marginal propensity to consume (MPC)** is the portion of additional income that is spent on consumption:

> **The marginal propensity to consume (MPC)** is The portion of additional income spent on consumption..

$$MPC = \frac{change\ in\ consumption}{change\ in\ income} \qquad (16.1)$$

For example, say you earn $400 in income, and you decide to spend $300 and save $100. Your marginal propensity to consume is then $300 ÷ $400 = 0.75. In other words, you spent seventy-five percent of your new income. The MPC isn't constant across all people, but it is a fraction between zero and one:

$$0 \leq MPC \leq 1$$

Let's consider a simple example of how spending changes affect the economy. For this example, let's say the government decides to increase spending by $100 billion and spends all of the funds on salaries for government workers. This government spending becomes new income for government workers. Now, let's assume these workers spend about 75 cents of each dollar of their new income, or that their MPC is 0.75. In total, the government workers spend $75 billion and save $25 billion of their new income. The spending by the government workers becomes $75 billion worth of income to others in the economy. Thus, in sum, we now have $175 billion in new income.

It's clear that the initial $100 billion in government spending can create more than $100 billion in income, through this "multiplying" effect. The effect continues on, round after round, as new income earners turn around and spend a portion of their income.

This multiplying effect is significant when we focus on aggregate demand in the economy. Each time people earn new income, they spend part of it. After all the dust settles, the total impact is a multiple of the original spending created by the fiscal policy. Figure 16.6 illustrates this multiplier process for our current example. Panel a shows a table of how spending becomes income and then part of the new income is spent. The first round represents the government's initial spending of $100 billion. The following rounds represent the new income generated by consumption spending. Since the MPC is 0.75 in this example, each round generates 75% of the income produced in the round before.

Figure 16.6
The spending multiplier process

	Spending (MPC = 0.75)	Savings
Round 1	$100	
Round 2	(0.75) x 100 = $75	$25
Round 3	(0.75) x 75 = $56.25	$18.75
Round 4	(0.75) x 56.25 = $42.19	$14.06
	.	.
	.	.
	.	.
Sum	$400.00	$100

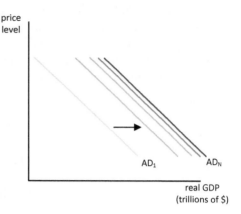

Assume that MPC = 0.75 and the government increases spending by $100 billion. In the table on the left, you can see how the spending multiplies through the economy; each round is 75% of the prior round. In the end, the total increase is 4 times the initial change in government spending. The right panel illustrates the shifting aggregate demand curve, as the spending multiplies through the economy.

On the right of Figure 16.6, we graph aggregate demand. Each time spending increases, aggregate increases (shifts outward). The initial aggregate demand is labeled AD_1. Each round of spending shifts aggregate demand to the right. Finally, aggregate demand settles at AD_N.

To determine the total impact on spending from any initial government expenditures, we need to use a formula known as the *spending multiplier*. **The spending multiplier (m^s)** tells us the total impact on spending from an initial change of a given amount. The multiplier depends on the marginal propensity to consume: the greater the marginal propensity to consume, the greater the spending multiplier. The formula for this spending multiplier is:

> **The spending multiplier (m^s)** is a formula to determine the total impact on spending from an initial change.

$$m^s = \frac{1}{(1-MPC)}$$ (16.2)

Since the MPC is a fraction between zero and one, the multiplier is generally larger than one. For example, if the marginal propensity to consume is 0.75, the multiplier is determined as:

$$m^s = \frac{1}{(1 - MPC)} = \frac{1}{1 - 0.75} = \frac{1}{0.25} = 4.$$

Sometimes this multiplier is called the *Keynesian* or *fiscal* multiplier.

Note that the multiplier concept applies to all spending, public or private. In addition, there is also a multiplier associated with tax changes. A reduction in the tax rate leaves more income for consumers to spend. This spending multiplies through the economy much as government spending multiplies.

The multiplier process also works in reverse. If the government reduces spending or increases taxes, people have less income to spend. In terms of the aggregate demand curve in Figure 16.6, the initial decline in government spending leads to subsequent declines as the effects reverberate through the economy.

The spending multiplier implies that the tools of fiscal policy are very powerful. Not only can the government change its spending and taxing, but then multiples of this spending ripple through the economy over several periods.

Economics in the Media

Pay it Forward

Spending Multiplier

In this movie, a young boy named Trevor (played by Haley Joel Osment), comes up with an idea that he thinks can change the world. Instead of paying people back for good deeds, Trevor suggests a new approach called "pay it forward." The idea is for him to help three people in some way. According to Trevor, "it has to be really big, something they can't do by themselves."

Then, each of those three people helps three more. You can see how this leads to a multiplication of people helping other people.

This is both similar to and different from the spending multiplier at the center of Keynesian fiscal policy. It is similar in that one person's spending leads to spending by others.

But the spending multiplier is a fraction, between zero and one, as people generally save part of any new income they earn. So the spending multiplication process slows down and eventually dies out.

However, the multiplier in Pay it Forward exceeds one because each person can help many people. In reality, the multiplier is three. So the good deeds can expand to more and more good deeds.

Practice What You Know
Expansionary Fiscal Policy

Shovel-Ready Projects

In early 2009, with the U.S. economy in deep recession, newly elected President Obama vowed to use fiscal stimulus spending on "shovel-ready" projects. The projects were deemed shovel-ready because they were already approved and just waiting for funding. Obama hoped this would create new jobs with minimal delays.

Question: Assume the economy is in short-run equilibrium with output less than full-employment output. Also assume, for this entire question, that the marginal propensity to consume (MPC) is equal to 0.50.

What is the value of the government spending multiplier in this case?

Answer: Equation 16.2 gives us the formula t=for the spending multiplier:

$$m^s = \frac{1}{(1-MPC)} = \frac{1}{(1-0.5)} = \frac{1}{0.5} = 2.$$

Question: Given the size of the multiplier, what is the implied change in income (GDP) from stimulus spending of $800 billion?

Answer: The total implied impact would be 2 x $800 billion = $1.6 trillion.

What are the shortcomings of fiscal policy?

At this point you may wonder why fiscal policy doesn't always work perfectly in the real world. If activist fiscal policy is as simple as tweaking G and T and letting the multiplier go to work, why do we still have recessions? Unfortunately, it's not so simple. Millions of people make individual decisions that affect the entire economy. How much fiscal policy is enough? How much will people save? We can't know the answers to these questions ahead of time.

But there are also more formal shortcomings of activist fiscal policy. In this section, we consider three issues that arise in the application of activist fiscal policy: time lags, crowding out, and savings adjustments.

Time lags

Both fiscal and monetary policies are intended to smooth out the economic variations that accompany a business cycle. So timing is important. But there are three lags that accompany policy decisions: recognition lag, implementation lag, and impact lag.

1. Recognition lag. In the real world, it is difficult to determine when the economy is turning up or down. GDP data is released quarterly, and the final estimate is not known until three months after the period in question. Unemployment rate data tends to lag even further behind. In addition, growth is not constant; one bad quarter does not always signal a recession and one good quarter is not always the beginning of an expansion. All of this together makes it very difficult to recognize when expansion or contraction starts.

2. Implementation lag. Fiscal policy takes time to implement. In most nations, tax and spending legislation must be approved by one or more governing bodies. In the United States, it must pass both houses of Congress and receive Presidential approval before becoming law. For this reason, fiscal policy takes much longer to implement than monetary policy. For example, as we discussed earlier in this chapter, the Economic Stimulus Act of 2008 entailed tax rebate checks to U.S. taxpayers. The Act passed in early February, yet most checks were not sent until about six months later. This delay occurred even though the recipients were known ahead of time – that's about as "shovel ready" as a project can get.

3. Impact lag. Finally, it takes time for the complete effects of fiscal or monetary policy to materialize. The multiplier makes fiscal policy powerful, but it takes time to ripple through the economy.

If lags cause the effects of fiscal policy to be delayed a year or eighteen months, there is a risk that the policy can actually magnify the business cycle. That is, if the effects of expansionary fiscal policy hit when the economy is already expanding, it may lead to excessive aggregate demand and inflation. Then, if contractionary fiscal policy is implemented with delays, the effects could lead to even deeper recessions.

Economics in the Real World:
Recognition lags in the real world

Hindsight is 20-20. But in reality, it is very difficult to determine instantaneously how the economy is performing. Looking back now, we know that the U.S. economy entered recession in December 2007. But this was far from clear at the time. In fact, as Edmund Andrews pointed out in a New York Times article from February 2008, the Bush administration was not convinced that the economy was in a recession. Reporting from Washington on February 12, Andres wrote:

> The White House predicted on Monday that the economy would escape a recession and that unemployment would remain low this year, though it acknowledged that growth had already slowed.   President Bush and Edward Lazear, chairman of the White House Council of Economic Advisers, said Monday that the economy should expand 2.7 percent this year. "I don't think we are in a recession right now, and we are not forecasting a recession," said Edward P. Lazear, chairman of the White House Council of Economic Advisers. …The administration's forecast calls for the economy to expand 2.7 percent this year and for unemployment to remain at 4.9 percent.

It's not inconceivable that this forecast was biased by political considerations, but, according to Andrews, even independent economists were predicting a 1.7% growth rate for 2008. In reality, real GDP fell by 3.5 percent and the unemployment rate rose to 7.3 percent by the end of 2008. Accurately recognizing current economic conditions is hard.

Automatic Stabilizers

One possibility for alleviating the lag problem is to put in place programs that automatically adjust government spending and taxes when economic conditions change. **Automatic stabilizers** are government programs that naturally implement countercyclical fiscal policy in response to economic conditions. Given that the prescription is to increase spending and decrease taxes during downturns and decrease spending and increase taxes during expansions, there are several government programs that accomplish this automatically. These include:

> **Automatic stabilizers** are government programs that naturally implement countercyclical fiscal policy in response to economic conditions.

- Progressive income tax rates guarantee that individual tax bills fall when incomes fall (during recession) and rise when incomes rise (in expansion).
- Corporate profit taxes lower total tax bills when profits are lower (during contraction) and raise tax bills when profits are higher (typically during expansion).
- Unemployment compensation increases government spending automatically when the number of unemployed rises and decreases government spending when fewer people are unemployed.
- Welfare programs also increase government spending during downturns and decrease government spending when the economy is doing better.

In short, automatic stabilizers can eliminate recognition lags and implementation lags, and thereby alleviate some concerns of destabilizing fiscal policy.

Crowding-out

The second shortcoming of activist fiscal policy addresses the actual impact of government spending and the multiplier effects. This critique is based on the idea that government spending may be a substitute for private spending. When this is the case, the impact on aggregate demand is smaller. Economists call this *crowding-out*. **Crowding-out** occurs when private spending falls in response to increases in government spending.

> **Crowding-out** occurs when private spending falls in response to increases in government spending.

  For example, say the government started a new program in which it buys a new car for every college student in America. Don't get too excited, this is just hypothetical. But if the government is buying cars for people, people won't buy as many cars for themselves. People may continue to spend on other items, but they will save too. When private spending falls in response to increases in government spending, we say that **Crowding-out** has occurred. In the example above, a government car-buying program leads to fewer private purchases of cars. When private spending falls in response to an increase in government spending, then aggregate demand does not increase and the fiscal policy will be ineffective.

  Let's look more closely at how crowding-out works. Assume that the government has a balanced budget. Then the government increases spending by $100 billion, but does not raise taxes. This means it has to borrow the $100 billion in the loanable funds market. But, as we know, every dollar borrowed requires a dollar saved. So when the government borrows $100 billion, the money has to come from $100 billion in savings.

  Figure 16.7 illustrates what happens when the government enters the loanable funds market to borrow $100 billion. Initially, the market is in equilibrium at A with demand for loans designated as D. The initial interest rate is 5%, and at this interest rate, there is $250 billion worth of savings. This savings funds $250 billion worth of private borrowing. The table on the right in Figure 15.7 summarizes these initial values.

  Now, when the government borrows, the demand for loans increases by $100 billion at all points. This is indicated as a shift from D to D_1. But this new demand for loans completely changes the equilibrium in the market. The increased demand for loans drives the interest rate up from 5% to 6%, and the new equilibrium quantity of loanable funds increases to $300 billion, shown as B on the graph. The interest rate rises because of the increase in demand for loans caused by government borrowing.

Figure 16.7
Crowding-out

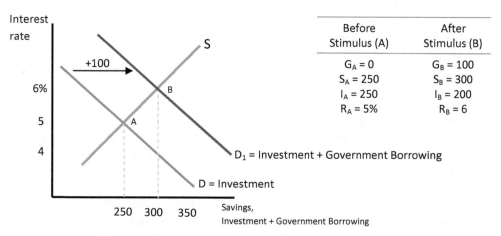

	Before Stimulus (A)	After Stimulus (B)
	$G_A = 0$	$G_B = 100$
	$S_A = 250$	$S_B = 300$
	$I_A = 250$	$I_B = 200$
	$R_A = 5\%$	$R_B = 6$

Initially, at point A, private savings of $100 billion all becomes private investment of $250 billion. But government borrowing shifts the demand for loans from D to D_1. The new demand for loans leads to equilibrium at B, with a higher interest rate. At the new equilibrium, there is $300 billion in private savings but $100 billion goes to government and $200 billion is left for private investment.

To see the overall effects of this new government borrowing, we compare the values of private savings and investment at the two equilibrium points. These are displayed in the table on the right of the graph in Figure 16.6. The new equilibrium quantity of loans is $300 billion, but $100 billion is borrowed by the government. This means borrowing for private investment spending (I) declines to $200 billion. Essentially, the higher interest rate discourages some private purchases and thus, the government purchases crowd out private spending.

Finally, note that that private savings increases from $250 billion to $300 billion— that is by $50 billion – because the higher interest rate has caused more individuals to devote more of their income to savings. But if savings rises by $50 billion, then consumption must fall by $50 billion. This is a direct relationship. The end result is that an increase of $100 billion in deficit-financed government spending leads to $100 billion less of private spending—$50 billion from investment and $50 billion from savings.

In this example, we have complete crowding out – every dollar of government spending crowds out a dollar of private spending. In reality, crowding out may be less than complete, but this example does illustrate an important caveat to the effects of fiscal policy.

Economics in the Real World:
Did government spending really surge in 2009?

Economist and New York Times editorial writer Paul Krugman is an ardent defender of
Keynesian counter-cyclical fiscal policy. During the course of the Great Recession,
Krugman used his column to consistently advocate for more and more government
spending.

Yet, after the historically large fiscal stimulus in 2009, many were baffled as to
why the economy struggled with high unemployment rates and slow real GDP growth
even through 2012. In a February 14, 2011 post on his blog, Krugman argued that the
increase in federal spending was offset by reductions on spending at the state government
level. According to Krugman: "Once you take state and local cutbacks into account,
there was no surge of government spending."

In a sense, even though he didn't identify it as such, Krugman is pointing out a
variation of crowding-out. Technically, crowding-out occurs when private individuals
substitute government (federal, state ,and local) spending in place of their private
spending. But Krugman's complaint is that the crowding out occurred in the government
sector. Federal government spending rose and then state and local government spending
fell. Most states were facing crises of their own, as a result of the recession. Thus, they
substituted federal spending for state spending. This helped them to balance their budgets
during the recession. But it also meant that total government spending did not rise as
much as the federal government intended. And this may help explain why the 2009 fiscal
stimulus failed to push the U.S. economy back to full employment.

The New Classical Critique

Imagine that you get a $1,000 check in the mail from the business office at your college.
You would probably wonder why you got the check, and whether you would have to pay
it back. But you might also get excited and begin thinking about goods and services you
could buy. How much would you spend and how much would you save?

Let's consider two different scenarios as to the source of these funds. First,
imagine that you are awarded a $1,000 scholarship after your bill is already paid. Thus,
this money is yours to keep.   In this case, you might spend much of the $1,000. But if
instead, the funds were sent to you in in error, meaning and you'll have to repay them. In
this second case, you probably wouldn't spend any of the $1,000 you got from the
college.

In some ways, government spending in the economy is
similar to this second scenario. New spending today has to be
paid for someday. This means taxes must rise sooner or later.
The **New Classical critique** of fiscal policy asserts that
increases in government spending and decreases in taxes are
largely offset by increases in savings, because people know
they'll have to pay higher taxes eventually. But if savings

> The **New Classical
> critique** of fiscal policy
> asserts that increases in
> government spending and
> decreases in taxes are
> largely offset by
> increases in savings.

increases, consumption falls and this mitigates the effects of the government spending.

Table 16.2 summarizes the three shortcomings of fiscal policy. Time lags can cause fiscal policy to magnify business cycles, crowding out can lead to lower private spending when the government spends, and the New Classical critique implies that savings rises when people anticipate higher future taxes. Each of these can diminish the effects of fiscal policy.

Table 16.2
Summary of fiscal policy shortcomings

Shortcoming	Summary	Result
Time Lags	The effects of fiscal policy may be delayed by recognition, implementation and effectiveness lags.	If lags are significant, fiscal policy can be destabilizing and magnify business cycles.
Crowding-out	Government spending can serve as a substitute for private spending.	Even partial crowding-out reduces the impact of fiscal stimulus.
New Classical Critique	In response to increases in government spending or lower taxes, people may increase current savings to help pay for inevitably higher future taxes.	If current savings increases by the entire amount of the federal stimulus, the effects of the stimulus are negated.

Practice What You Know

Crowding-Out

Does fiscal policy lead to more aggregate demand?

Imagine that the country is in recession and the government decides to increase spending. It commissions a very large statue for $50 million. To pay for the statue, the government borrows all of the $50 million.

After the government borrows $50 million, the interest rate rises from 3% to 4% and the equilibrium quantity of loanable funds increases from $500 million to $530 million.

Question:

Sketch a graph of the loanable funds market. Be sure to indicate all the changes that take place after the borrowing on this graph.

Answer:

Originally, the market is in equilibrium at point A with an interest rate of 3% and savings and investment equal at $500 million. The demand for loans increases by $50 million at all points when the government borrows $50 million. This moves the market to new equilibrium at point B.

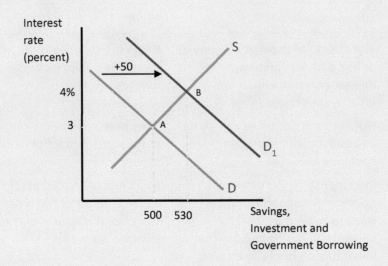

Question: Using the above information, and assuming complete crowding out, predict what happens to C, I, G, and total aggregate demand in response to the government's action.

Answer:

Government spending increases by $50 billion. Total savings increases to $530 billion, which means consumption falls by $30 billion. But since the government is borrowing $50 billion of the savings, private investment falls to $480 billion, a decrease of $20 billion. These changes are summarized in the table below.

Component	C	I	G	AD
Change	-30	-20	+50	-

What is supply-side fiscal policy?

We have considered typical fiscal policy, which focuses squarely on aggregate demand. It is also possible to implement fiscal policy with the intent of affecting the supply side of the economy. In this section, we begin by describing the supply-side perspective and some of the popular supply-side policy proposals. We then look more closely at marginal tax rates and consider how changes in tax rates can affect the economy.

The Supply-side Perspective

We can illustrate the supply-side perspective in the aggregate demand and aggregate supply model. For most of this chapter, we have focused on shifting the demand curve with fiscal policy. Now, we are exploring how taxes and government spending can affect long-run aggregate supply. **Supply-side fiscal policy** uses government spending and taxes to affect the supply or production side of the economy. In Figure 16.8, this is indicated as a shift from LRAS to $LRAS_1$.

> **Supply side fiscal policy** – The use of government spending and taxes to affect the production (supply) side of the economy.

Figure 16.8
Supply-side fiscal policy

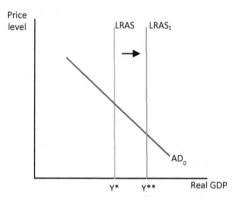

Typical (demand-side) fiscal policy uses government spending and taxes to shift aggregate demand.

Supply-side fiscal policy instead uses government spending and taxes to shift long run aggregate supply (from LRAS to $LRAS_1$).

Recall from Chapter 14 that shifts in long-run aggregate supply are caused by changes in resources, technology, and institutions. For example, we know that technological advances increase long-run aggregate supply. A technological advancement allows production of a greater quantity of output using the same or fewer resources. In the long run, much economic growth derives from technological advances. The government can implement fiscal policy and use the tax code to encourage technological advancement. For example, since 1981 in the United States, businesses have received tax credits for expenses related to research and development—firms that spend on research and development of new technology pay lower taxes than firms that don't. This is a significant incentive that encourages innovation and ultimately greater supply of output. Thus, the goal of this fiscal policy is to shift long run aggregate supply.

There are many fiscal policy initiatives that focus on the supply side of the economy. These include:

1. Research and Development (R &D) tax credits. Reduced taxes for firms that spend resources to develop new technology.

2. Policies that focus on education. Subsidies or tax breaks for education expenses create incentives to invest in education. One example is the Pell grant that helps pay for college expenses. Eventually, education and training increase effective labor resources and thus increase aggregate supply.

3. Lower corporate profit tax rates. Lower taxes increase the incentives for corporations to undertake activities that add more profit.

4. Lower marginal income tax rates. Lower income tax rates create incentives for individuals to work harder produce more, since they get to keep a larger share of their income. We will discuss this further below.

All of these initiatives share two characteristics. First, they increase the incentives for productive activities. Second, each takes time to affect aggregate supply. For example, education subsidies may encourage people to go to college and learn skills that help them in the workplace. But the full impact of that education won't be felt until after the education is completed. For this reason, supply-side proposals are generally emphasized as long-run solutions to growth problems.

Marginal income tax rates

We noted that lowering marginal income tax rates is one way fiscal policy can address the supply side. However, the relationship between tax rates and tax revenue is one of the most hotly debated in politics. Economists are not as divided over the issue as the public at large. But you don't often hear or read the entire explanation, because it doesn't consistently line up politically with either political side on the issue.

Some politicians consistently advocate for tax rate cuts, no matter how large the budget deficit. They claim that a tax rate cut always leads to an increase in tax revenues. How can this be? They argue that a tax rate cut can be creative; it can stimulate work effort and employment, income, and then lead to more income tax revenue to the government. Tax revenue rises because more people are employed and income levels are higher.

Consider the following quote:

The worst deficit comes from a recession. And if we can take the proper action in the proper time, this can be the most important step we can take to prevent another recession. That is the right time to make tax cuts, both for your family budget, and the national budget, resulting from a permanent basic reform and reduction in our rate structure. A creative tax cut, creating more jobs and income and, eventually, more revenue.

-35th President of the United States

You may be surprised to learn that the President quoted is John F. Kennedy. President Kennedy made this statement in in1962, when marginal tax rates were as high as 91 percent. Consider what a 91% marginal tax rate means: you get to keep nine cents from an additional dollar's worth of income. That certainly diminishes incentives for work effort and production. And that is the world in which JFK gave his speech. Most would agree that 91% marginal tax rates stifle economic growth. So although it may seem counterintuitive, it is possible to lower tax rates and increase overall tax revenue.

On the other hand, at low initial tax rates, an increase in the tax rate leads to an increase in tax revenue. For example, there was no income tax in the United States in 1912. As we saw in Chapter 15, the U.S. instituted the income tax in 1913, with a top marginal rate of just 6%. Of course, income tax revenue rose between 1912 when there was no income tax and 1913 when a modest tax was introduced! At low tax rates, increases lead to revenue increases.

Let's clarify the relationship between tax rates and tax revenue. Total income tax revenue depends on the level of income and the tax rate:

$$income\ tax\ revenue = tax\ rate\ \times income \qquad (16.3)$$

This equation straightforward. But with human beings reacting to incentives, it is not always easy to predict how tax revenue will change when tax rates change. The **Laffer Curve**, shown in Figure 16.9, illustrates the relationship between tax rates and tax revenue. Notice that we labeled two regions of the Laffer curve. Region I, in blue, reflects that increasing tax rates leads to increasing tax revenues:

The **Laffer curve** is an illustration of the relationship between tax rates and tax revenue.

$$\uparrow income\ tax\ revenue = \uparrow tax\ rate\ \times income$$

But at some point, tax rates are so high that they provide significant disincentives for earning income. This is the case in Region II, in orange, where decreases in the tax rate lead to more tax revenue. The United States was in region II in 1962, when some marginal tax rates were above 90 percent and President Kennedy gave his speech. At this point, an increase in the tax rate reduces income enough so that net tax revenue falls:

$$\downarrow income\ tax\ revenue = \uparrow tax\ rate\ \times \downarrow\downarrow income$$

In Region II of the Laffer curve, decreases in tax rates lead to increases in tax revenue. At the lower ate, people have greater incentives to work and earn more income. Thus, the lower tax rates stimulate the economy and lead to more tax revenue overall.

Figure 16.9
The Laffer curve

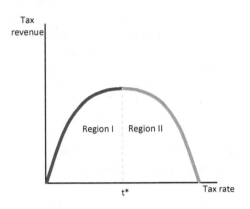

The Laffer curve is a mathematical relationship that helps us understand how tax rates affect tax revenue. In Region I, increases in tax rates lead to increases in tax revenue. This region applies at for all relatively low tax rates. In Region II, increases in tax rates decrease tax revenue. Region II applies to relatively high tax rates which create negative incentives for any activity that is taxed. Economists generally agree on the existence of a Laffer curve. The disagreements arise over the size of t*, the point at which tax rates are so high that further increases actually decrease tax revenue.

At some specific tax rate, tax revenue is maximized. In Figure 16.9, this is labeled t*. Economists don't know exactly what this amount is. But there is evidence from the United States that t* is below 70 percent. The evidence comes from the 1980s. Recall from Chapter 29 that in 1980 marginal tax rates on the wealthiest Americans were 70%. But in the 1980s, marginal rates fell across all income brackets. This was a very hotly debated political issue at the time. We now have the advantage of hindsight to determine what happened to tax revenue during the 1980s.

Considering all U.S. taxpayers, average tax revenue (adjusted for both inflation and the number of returns) went from $6,954 to $6,202 between 1980 and 1991. Many people point to these figures and designate them as proof that the Laffer curve doesn't exist, or even that supply-side economics is without merit.

But the Laffer curve has two distinct regions. A careful look at the data shows that the rate reductions led to less tax revenue both overall and for those who were paying relatively low taxes in 1980. But, for the wealthiest Americans, a rate reduction did lead to an increase in revenue. Table 16.3 shows data for U.S. taxpayers for both 1980 and 1991. Rate reductions led to greater revenue only for top taxpayers. Overall, revenues declined when we adjust for both inflation and population.

Table 16.3
U.S. income tax revenue for different income levels, 1980 and 1991

| | Income Tax Revenue Per Return (2009 dollars) | | |
	Top 1%	Bottom 50%	All Taxpayers
1980	$131,307	$1,005	$6,954
1991	$153,675	$692	$6,202

The point to be taken from Table 16.3 is that data from the 1980s confirms there really are two regions on the Laffer curve. Generally, conservative public figures tend to stress Region II, where tax rate reductions lead to increased revenue. Liberals emphasize Region I, where rate increases lead to more revenue. Both regions are important for economic policy.

Practice What You Know

Supply side versus demand side

The Bush Tax Cuts

In mid-2001, the Bush administration won congressional approval for lower income tax rates. One stipulation of this rate cut was that they were also applied retroactively to taxes from the year 2000.

Question:

Would you consider this fiscal policy to be demand-side focused, or supply-side focused?

Answer:

Both! Tax rate cuts are generally supply-side initiatives, since they frame incentives for production going forward. So the rate cuts applying to income taxes for 2001 and beyond were focused on the supply side.

But the Bush tax cuts also applied to taxes already paid. This meant refund checks were mailed to taxpayers, refunding part of the taxes they paid for the year 2000. This provision is clearly demand-focused, as the government hoped individuals would use the funds to increase spending, that is, aggregate demand.

Economics for Life

Planning for your future taxes

The U.S. national debt is over $16 trillion, or more than $50,000 per person. In 2007, the national debt per person was only $30,000. Thus, this increase is directly attributable to the Great Recession and the fiscal policy undertaken during that period.

What does this mean for you? It means your taxes are going to be higher in the future. All Americans will need to contribute to pay down this large national debt. So taxes in the future will be higher and you should plan for this.

In addition, economic growth will likely be lower until this debt is paid down. We know higher income taxes reduce incentives for production and so economic growth will be lower until this debt is paid off and taxes can come down again.

But you can also take actions to lower your tax bill. First off, you probably ought to budget for higher taxes. This may mean saving more now than you would have otherwise. In terms of your personal investments, you might consider buying securities that provide tax-free income. For example, the interest on municipal bonds (bonds issued by state and local governments) is not federally taxed.

Conclusion

We began the chapter with the misconception that government can consistently and predictably counteract business cycle fluctuations. It is certainly true that reductions in private demand accompany economic downturns. It is also true that government is able to use fiscal policy to increase expenditures or stimulate private spending through tax reductions. But the complete effects are difficult to predict. Recent experiences confirm this difficulty.

Looking ahead, we now turn our attention to monetary policy. In Chapter 16, we cover money and the Federal Reserve and Chapter 17 covers how monetary policy affects the economy.

BIG QUESTIONS

1. What is fiscal policy?

Fiscal policy generally focuses on aggregate demand. Countercyclical fiscal policy is designed to counteract business cycle fluctuations by increasing aggregate demand during downturns and decreasing aggregate demand during expansionary periods.

2. What are the shortcomings of fiscal policy?

Fiscal policy is subject to three significant lags: a recognition lag, an implementation lag, and an impact lag. In addition, crowding-out can diminish the effects of fiscal policy. Finally, according to the New Classical critique, savings adjustments by private individuals can further diminish the stimulating effects of fiscal policy.

3. What is supply-side fiscal policy?

The supply side approach to fiscal policy focuses on how government spending and tax policy influences peoples' incentives to work and produce. This is a long-run view that concentrates on institutional changes. A key proposal of supply-side fiscal policy is that lower marginal income tax rates can actually lead to greater tax revenue when tax rates are currently at a high level.

Concepts You Should Know

Activist fiscal policy
Automatic stabilizers
Contractionary fiscal policy
Countercyclical fiscal policy
Crowding out

Expansionary fiscal policy

Fiscal policy
Marginal propensity to consume (MPC)
Laffer curve
Spending multiplier
Supply-side fiscal policy

Questions for Review

1. How are government budget balances affected by countercyclical fiscal policy? Be sure to describe the effects of both expansionary and contractionary fiscal policy.

2. Using the aggregate demand and supply model, one might argue that the economy will adjust on its own when aggregate demand drops. How does this adjustment work? Why might this adjustment take some time (we discussed this in Chapter 12)?

3. Explain why the government budget deficit increases during a recession even without countercyclical fiscal policy.

4. Explain the difference between the three types of fiscal policy lags. What are automatic stabilizers? Which lags are affected by automatic stabilizers?

5. What are the circumstances in which contractionary fiscal policy would be recommended? How might you implement this type of policy? Why would you implement this policy – what are the reasons why it might make sense to slow the economy through government policy?

Study Problems

1. Explain the difference between typical demand-side fiscal policy and supply side fiscal policy. For each of the following fiscal policy proposals, determine whether the primary focus is on aggregate demand or aggregate supply:

   a) A $1,000 per person tax reduction.
   b) A 5% reduction in all tax rates.
   c) Pell Grants, which are government subsidies for college education.
   d) Government-sponsored prizes for new scientific discoveries.
   e) Increasing unemployment compensation.

2. To explore crowding-out, lets set up a simple loanable funds market in initial equilibrium.

A. Use the graph below and show initial equilibrium in the loanable funds market at $800 million and interest rate 4%. Label your initial supply and demand curves as S and D.

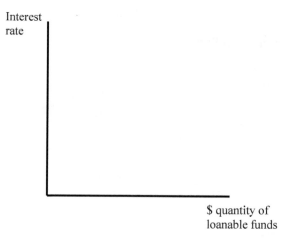

B. Now assume the government increases spending by $100 million and this is entirely deficit financed. Show the new equilibrium in the loanable funds market.

C. Write the new equilibrium interest rate and quantity of loanable funds in the blanks below:

New interest rate: _____
New quantity of loanable funds: _____

D. If we assume there was no government debt prior to the fiscal stimulus, determine the new quantities for the blanks below:

Savings: _____
Investment: _____
Government Spending: _____

E. How much did private consumption change as a result of the change in the quantity of savings?

3. The New Classical critique of activist fiscal policy is theoretically different from the crowding-out critique. Explain the difference using a graph of the loanable funds market.

Solved Problem

1. Fill in the blanks in the table below. Assume the MPC is constant over everyone in the economy.

MPC	Spending multiplier	Change in government spending	Change in income
_____	5	100	_____
_____	2.5	_____	-250
0.5	_____	200	_____
0.2	_____	_____	1,000

The table below contains the answers.

MPC	Spending multiplier	Change in government spending	Change in income
0.2	5	100	500
0.4	2.5	-100	-250
0.5	2	200	400
0.2	5	200	1,000

Chapter 17
Money and the Federal Reserve

Misconception: It's easy to control the amount of money in an economy.

Most people believe that controlling the amount of money in the economy is a simple task. After all, there is a fixed number of "green pieces of paper" floating around the economy and only the government has the authority to print more. But the job is very difficult. Banks and private individuals influence the money supply with their daily private decisions. That's right: even you can make the money supply rise or fall.

We begin this chapter by looking closely at what defines money. It turns out that money is more than just currency and coins. Because banks also play an integral role in the money supply process, we will discuss how they operate and how their decisions affect the amount of money in the economy. Finally, we look at the role of the Federal Reserve System, and examine how it oversees the amount of money in the economy. This provides essential preparation for the discussion of monetary policy in Chapter 15.

Big Questions:

What is money?
How do banks create money?
How does the Federal Reserve control the money supply?

What is money?

It probably seems strange to ask "what is money?" After all, we use money all the time. Even children know we use money to buy goods and services. But what is included in this? Certainly, the green pieces of paper we call *currency* are included. **Currency** is the paper bills and coins used to buy goods and services. But we also make many purchases without using currency.

> **Currency** is the paper bills and coins used to buy goods and services.

The quantity of money in an economy affects the ease with which individuals and firms can make purchases. It also affects the price level. For these reasons, we need to understand what constitutes money. In this section, we define the functions of money and then explain how the quantity of money is measured.

Three Functions of Money

Money has three functions: as a medium of exchange, a unit of account, and a store of value. Let's look at each in turn.

A Medium of Exchange

If you want to buy groceries, you offer money in exchange for them; if you work, you accept money as payment for your services. Money is our common **medium of exchange**, that is, it is what people trade for goods and services.

> **A medium of exchange** is what people trade for goods and services.

Modern economies generally have a government-provided medium of exchange. In the United States, our government provides our dollar currency. But even in economies without government provision, a preferred medium of exchange usually emerges. For example, in colonial Virginia, before any government mandate regarding money, tobacco became the accepted medium of exchange. Economist Milton Friedman wrote this about tobacco's use: "It was the money that the colonists used to buy food, clothing, to pay taxes – even to pay for a bride."

Invariably, some medium of exchange evolves in any economy; the primary reason is the inefficiency of money's alternative: *barter*. **Barter** requires individuals to trade some good or service they have for something they want – there is no commonly accepted medium of exchange. If you want food in a barter economy, you must find a grocer who also happens to want whatever you have to trade. Maybe you can only offer your labor services but the grocer wants a cash register. Then you have to try to find somebody who has a cash register and also wants to trade it for your labor. This takes more than a coincidence, it takes a double coincidence. Barter requires a **double coincidence of wants**, in which each party in an exchange transaction happens to have what the other party desires. A double coincidence is pretty unusual, and this is why a medium of exchange naturally evolves in any exchange environment.

> **Barter** is trade without a commonly accepted medium of exchange.

> **A double coincidence of wants** occurs when each party in an exchange transaction happens to have what the other party desires.

Historically, the first medium of exchange in an economy has been a commodity that is actually traded for goods and services. **Commodity money** is when an actual good is used for money. The good itself has value apart from its function as money. Examples include gold, silver, and the tobacco of colonial Virginia. But commodities are often difficult to carry around when you need to make purchases. Thus, due to transportation costs, money evolved into certificates that represented a fixed quantity of the commodity. These certificates became the medium of exchange, but were still tied to the commodity since they could be traded for the commodity if the holder demanded it. **Commodity-backed money** is money you can exchange for a commodity at a fixed rate. For example, until 1971, U.S. dollars were fixed in value to specific quantities of silver and gold. Figure 17.1 is a picture of a one Dollar U.S. silver certificate from 1957. It looks much like dollar bills in circulation today, but the print along the bottom of the note reads "one dollar in silver payable to the bearer on demand." Until 1964, we also had actual commodity coins in the United States. Figure 16.1 also shows quarters from 1964. These quarters look like the same quarters we use today but they are made of real silver.

> **Commodity money** is when an actual good is used for money.

> **Commodity-backed money** is money you can exchange for a commodity at a fixed rate.

While commodity money and commodity-backed money evolve privately in all economies, the type of money used in most modern economies depends on government. In particular, most modern economies make use of *fiat money* for their medium of exchange. **Fiat money** is money that has no value except as the medium of exchange; there is no inherent or intrinsic value to the currency. In the United States, our currency is physically just pieces of green paper. This paper has value because the government has mandated that we can use the currency to pay our debts. On U.S. dollar bills, you can read the statement: "This note is legal tender for all debts, public and private," which means that people are legally bound to accept dollars as a form of payment.

There are advantages and disadvantages to fiat and commodity monies. On the one hand, commodity-backed money ties the value of your money to something real. If the government is obligated to trade silver for every dollar in circulation, this certainly limits the number of dollars they can print, which probably limits inflation levels. Fiat money offers no such constraint on the expansion of money. Rapid monetary expansion and then inflation often occur without a commodity standard that ties the value of money to something real.

On the other hand, tying the value of your currency to a commodity is dangerous when the market value of the commodity fluctuates. Imagine how a new discovery of gold affects prices in a nation with gold-backed currency. An increased supply of gold reduces gold prices and therefore more gold is required in exchange for all other goods and services. This is inflation – the price of everything in terms of the money (gold) rises. This is exactly what occurred in Europe as Spanish conquistadors brought back tons of gold from Central and South America between the mid 15th to the mid 17th century. Because a change in the value of a medium of exchange affects prices of all goods and services in the macroeconomy, it can be risky to tie a currency to a commodity.

A Unit of Account

Money also serves as a *unit of account*. A **unit of account** is the measure in which prices are quoted. Money allows you and someone you don't know to speak a common language. When the cashier says your mangoes are 99 cents each, she is communicating the value of mangoes in a way you understand. Consider a world without an accepted unit of account. In that world, goods are priced in multiple ways. Theoretically, this means you might go shopping and find goods priced in terms of any possible currency or even other goods. Imagine how difficult it would be to shop. Using money as a unit of account is so helpful that a standard unit of account generally evolves, even in small economies.

> A unit of account is the measure in which prices are quoted.

Expressing the value of something in terms of dollars and cents also allows people to make accurate comparisons between items. Thus, money also serves as a measuring stick and recording device. Think of your checkbook for a moment. You don't write down that you bought a bagel and coffee in the ledger. You write down that you spent $4.00. You tally the debits and credits to keep track of your account and record transactions in a consistent manner.

Economics in the Real World:
The evolution of prison money

In the past, cigarettes were often the preferred unit of account and medium of exchange in prisons. This commodity money was useful as currency in addition to its manufactured purpose. But in 2004, the U.S. government outlawed smoking in federal prisons and this led to the development of a new medium of exchange.

In a 2008 *Wall Street Journal* article, Justin Scheck reported on one federal facility where cans of mackerel had taken over as the accepted money. According to one prisoner: "It's the coin of the realm." This "bartering" is not legal in federal prisons. Prisoners can lose privileges if they are caught exchanging goods or services for mackerel. However, mackerel remains the medium of exchange and the unit of account. For example, haircuts cost about 2 "macks". The cans of fish are also used as a reliable store of value. Some prisoners even rent lockers from others so they can store their mackerel money.

But while mackerel is popular, it is not the only commodity used as money in federal prisons. Some prisons use Power bars or cans of tuna. One reason why mackerel is preferred to other alternatives is because each can costs about one dollar – so it's a simple substitute for U.S. currency, which inmates are not allowed to carry.

(source: http://professional.wsj.com/article/SB122290720439096481.html?mg=reno64-wsj)

A Store of Value

Money's third function is as a *store of value*. A **store of value** is a means for holding wealth. Traditionally, money served as an important store of value. Think of bags of gold coins from the middle ages. In both fiction and non-fiction stories, forbidden treasures or pirate's treasures are generally represented by gold – this is how great values were stored. But in modern economies, this function is much less important. Today we have many other options for holding our wealth, many of which offer greater returns than keeping dollar bills in your sock drawer or stuffed under a mattress. We can easily put our dollars into bank accounts or investment accounts that earn interest. These options, money's have caused money's role as a store of value to decline.

> **A store of value** is a means for holding wealth.

Now that we have defined the three functions of money, we need to consider how money is actually measured.

Measuring the Quantity of Money

As we saw in Chapter 9, the quantity of money in an economy affects the overall price level. In particular, a nation's inflation rate is dependent on the rate of growth of their quantity of money. In addition, in Chapter 18 we'll see that the quantity of money can influence real GDP and unemployment rates. Therefore, since money has such profound macroeconomic influences, it is important to measure it accurately. But this is not quite as simple as just adding up all the green pieces of paper in an economy.

To think about the difficulties of measuring our money supply, think about all the different ways you make purchases. You might hold some currency for emergencies, to make a vending machine purchase, or do laundry. On top of this, you might write a check to pay for your rent, school bill, or utilities bills. After this, you probably carry a debit card that automatically withdraws from your savings or checking accounts. To measure the quantity of money in an economy, we must somehow find the total value of all these alternatives that people use to buy goods and services. Clearly, currency alone is not enough – you buy things all the time without using currency. Currency is money, but only a small part of the total money supply.

M1 and M2

As we broaden our definition of money beyond currency, we first acknowledge bank deposits for which checks can be written. **Checkable deposits** are bank deposits in accounts that allow depositors to make withdrawals by writing checks. These deposits represent purchasing power that is very similar to currency, since personal checks are accepted at many places. Adding checkable deposits to currency essentially gives us a money supply measure known as *M1*. **M1** is the money supply measure that is essentially composed of currency and checkable deposits. M1 also includes traveler's checks, but these account for a very small portion of M1.

> **Checkable deposits** are bank deposits in accounts that allow depositors to make withdrawals by writing checks.

> **M1** is the money supply measure that is essentially composed of currency and checkable deposits.

A broader measure of the money supply, **M2,** includes everything in M1 plus savings deposits. M2 also includes two other types of deposits: money market mutual funds and small denomination time deposits (certificates of deposit). The key point to remember is that the money supply in an economy includes both currency and bank deposits:

> **M2** is the money supply measure that includes everything in M1 plus savings deposits.

$$\text{Money Supply (M)} = \text{currency} + \text{deposits}. \qquad (17.1)$$

Equation 17.1 is an approximation of the general money supply. Actual data for both M1 and M2 is published by the Federal Reserve. Figure 17.2 shows the components of M1 and M2 as of July, 2012. Notice that currency in the United States is about $1 trillion. Adding checkable deposits of another $1 trillion yields M1 of about $2 trillion. But M2 was over $10 trillion in 2012, over $6 trillion of which was held in savings accounts. It is important to remember that the money supply includes both currency and bank deposits when we discuss monetary policy in the next chapter.

Figure 17.2
Measures of the U.S. Money Supply, 2012

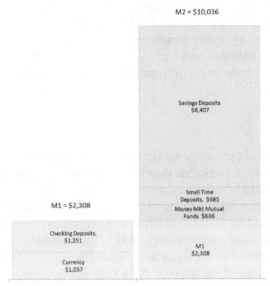

M2 = $10,036

Savings Deposits
$6,407

Small Time
Deposits, $685
Money Mkt Mutual
Funds $636

M1
$2,308

M1 = $2,308

Checking Deposits,
$1,251

Currency
$1,057

M1 and M2 are the most common measures of the money supply. M1 includes currency and checking deposits. M2 includes everything in M1 plus savings deposits, small time deposits, and money market mutual funds.

Source: Federal Reserve, Money Stock Measures.

Note that credit cards are not part of the money supply. Purchases made with credit cards involve a loan extended right at the cash register. When the loan is made, a third party is paying for the purchase, until the loan is repaid. Therefore, since credit card purchases use borrowed funds, credit cards are not included as part of the money supply.

M1 was the most closely monitored money supply measure until the 1970's because it was a reliable estimate of the medium of exchange. But the introduction of ATM machines basically rendered M1 obsolete as a reliable money supply measure. Prior to the ATM machine, holding balances in a checking account was very different from holding your funds in savings accounts. Funds held in checking accounts could be accessed easily by writing a check. However, funds in savings accounts required you to visit to the bank during business hours, wait in line, and fill out a withdrawal slip. Today, because of ATMs, depositors can make withdrawals at any time and at many locations. Since both checking and savings are now readily available for purchasing goods and services, M2—which includes both types of deposits—is now a better measure of our medium of exchange.

Practice What You Know!

The Definition of Money

People on the street sometimes use the word "money" in ways inconsistent with the definition given in this chapter.

Question: Determine whether each of the following statements is consistent with our definition of money.

A. "He had a lot of money in his wallet."

Answer: Yes, this is consistent since currency is part of the medium of exchange.

B. "She made a lot of money last year."

Answer: No, inconsistent. This is referring to income, not money.

C. "I use my visa card for money."

Answer: No, inconsistent. Payment with a credit card requires a loan and so is technically not counted in the money supply.

D. "She has most of her money in the bank."

Answer: Yes, this is consistent since bank deposits also count as money since they represent part of our medium of exchange.

How do banks create money?

We now have a working definition of money: money includes both currency and deposits at banks. And while private individuals and firms in the economy are not permitted to print currency, private actions absolutely influence the total supply of money in the economy, since individuals and banks affect deposits. In this section, we explain how banks create money simply as a byproduct of their daily business activity. Note that when we refer to 'banks," we are explicitly talking about commercial banks, which take in deposits and extend loans. We distinguish these from investment banks, which serve a different role.

We begin by looking closely at the daily activities at typical banks. After that, we can consider how they influence the money supply.

The Business of Banking

Banks serve two very important roles in our study of the macroeconomy. First, they are critical participants in the market for loanable funds. As we saw in Chapter 11, they provide a way for savers to supply their funds to borrowers without purchasing a financial security. In addition, they play a role in the money supply process.

To understand how banks create money, let's look at the functions of a bank, illustrated in Figure 17.3. Banks are middlemen in the market for loans. They are financial intermediaries; that is, they take in deposits and extend loans. Deposits are the primary source of funds and loans are the primary use of funds for banks. Banks can be profitable if they charge a higher interest rate on the loans they make than the interest rate they pay on deposits.

Figure 17.3
The Business of Banking: Financial Intermediation

The primary function of commercial banks is financial intermediation: they accept deposits and extend loans.

Banks are middlemen in the market for loans. They are financial intermediaries, that is, they take in deposits and extend loans. Deposits are the primary source of funds and loans are the primary use of funds for banks. Banks can be profitable if they charge a higher interest rate on the loans they make than the interest rate they pay on deposits. Figure 17.4 illustrates the gap between interest rates on bank deposits and bank loans for U.S. banks for the period 1985-2011. The two rates go up and down together, but the interest rate on deposits is consistently less than the interest rate the bank charges for loans. The difference between the two interest rates pays for a bank's operating costs and produces profits that can be channeled to firms in the loanable funds market.

Figure 17.4
Interest Rates on Bank Deposits versus Loans, 1985-2011

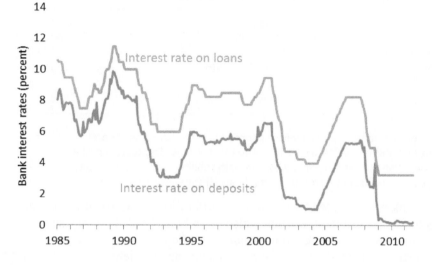

Banks charge more interest for loans than they pay for deposits. The difference helps pay expenses, and produces profits.

Source: FRED data, Federal Reserve Bank of St. Louis. The loan interest rate is the average prime interest rate across the U.S., while the deposit rate is the interest rate on 1 month certificates of deposit.

The Bank's Balance Sheet

The information about a bank's financial operations is presented in the bank's *balance sheet*. A firm's **balance sheet** is an accounting statement that summarizes the firm's key financial information. Figure 17.5 shows a hypothetical balance sheet for University Bank. The left side of the balance sheet details the bank's **assets**, which are the items the firm owns. Assets are how the banking firm uses the funds they've raised from various sources. The right side of the balance sheet details the bank's *liabilities* and *owner's equity*. **Liabilities** are obligations the firm owes to others. **Owner's equity** is the difference between the firm's assets and its liabilities. When a firm has more assets than liabilities, it has positive owner's equity. The right side of the balance sheet reveals the bank's sources of funds.

Assets are the items a firm owns.

A firm's **balance sheet** is an accounting statement that summarizes the firm's key financial information.

Figure 17.5
Balance Sheet for University Bank

Uses of funds →	Assets (in thousands)		Liabilities and owner's equity (in thousands)	Sources of funds ←
Loans		$400	Deposits	$500
Reserves		$60	Borrowings	$200
U.S. Treasury Securities		$140		
Other Assets		$200	Owner's equity	$100
Total Assets		$800	Total liabilities and net worth	$800

A bank's balance sheet summarizes its key financial information. The bank's assets are recorded on the left side; this is how the bank chooses to use its funds. The sources of the firms funds are recorded on the right side and these are both liabilities and owner's equity. The two sides of the balance sheet must match for the financial statement to be balanced.

University bank has extended $400 million worth of loans. Many of these loans are made to firms to fund investment, but some also go to households to purchase homes, cars, and other consumer items. A second important asset held by banks is *reserves*. **Reserves** are the portion of bank deposits that are set aside and not lent out. Reserves include both currency in the bank's vault and funds the bank holds in deposit at its own bank, the Federal Reserve. Banks also hold U.S. Treasury securities and other government securities as substantial assets in their portfolio. These securities earn interest and carry very low risk. Finally, banks hold other assets, such as physical buildings and furniture.

> **Reserves** are the portion of bank deposits that are set aside and not lent out.

Banks fund their activities primarily by taking in deposits. The deposits of typical households are the lifeblood of banks. But banks also borrow from other commercial banks and from the Federal Reserve. The third item on the right of the balance sheet is net worth or the owner's equity in the banking firm. Since the University Bank owns $800 million in total assets, but owes only $700 million in liabilities, the owners of the bank have $100 million in equity.

In the next section, we look more closely at bank reserves, which play an important role in money creation.

Bank Reserves

Our modern system of banking is called *fractional reserve banking*. **Fractional reserve banking** occurs when banks hold only a fraction of deposits on reserve. The alternative is 100-percent- reserve banking. Banks in a 100-percent-reserve system don't loan out deposits; they are essentially just a safe, keeping deposits on hand until depositors decide to make a withdrawal.

> **Fractional reserve banking** occurs when banks hold only a fraction of deposits on reserve.

Figure 17.6 illustrates the process of fractional reserve banking. Deposits come into the bank and banks send out a portion of these in loans. In recent years, U.S. banks have typically loaned out almost 90% of their deposits, keeping barely over 10% on reserve. Banks loan out most of their deposits because reserves earn very little interest; every dollar kept on reserve costs the bank potential income. In 2012 bank reserves paid just 0.25% interest.

Figure 17.6
Fractional Reserve Banking

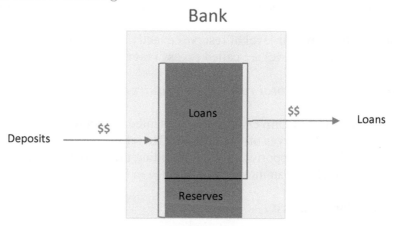

In a fractional reserve banking system, banks lend out only a fraction of the deposits they take in. The remainder is set aside as reserve.

Let's say a local business approaches a bank for a loan to expand its factory. Assume the bank has reserves available to be lent out and that the current interest rate on these commercial loans is 5%, which the firm is willing to pay. The alternative is to keep the funds on reserve, earning just 0.25 percent. If the bank rejects the firm's loan application and decides to keep the funds in its vault as reserve, the cost of this decision to the bank is the difference between these two interest rates: 5% − 0.25% = 4.75%.

Banks hold reserves for two reasons. First, they must accommodate withdrawals by their depositors. You'd be pretty unhappy if you tried to make a withdrawal from your bank and it didn't have enough on reserve to honor your request. If word spread that a bank might have difficulty meeting withdrawal requests of depositors, it would probably lead to a *bank run*. A **bank run** occurs when many depositors attempt to withdraw their funds at one time.

> A **bank run** occurs when many depositors attempt to withdraw their funds at one time.

Second, banks are legally bound to hold a fraction of their deposits on reserve. The **required reserve ratio (*rr*)** is the portion of deposits banks are required to keep on reserve. For a given bank, the dollar amount of reserves it is required to hold is determined by multiplying the required reserve ratio by its total amount of deposits:

> The **required reserve ratio (*rr*)** is the portion of deposits banks are required to keep on reserve.

$$required\ reserves = rr \times deposits \qquad (17.2)$$

Currently, the required reserve ratio is ten percent for almost all deposits ($rr = 0.10$). This means your bank can legally lend out up to ninety cents of every dollar you deposit.

Consider University Bank, whose balance sheet was presented in Figure 17.5. University currently has $500 million worth of deposits. University Bank pays some interest on the deposits and offers services, like checking, to the depositors. University bank can't afford to keep the $500 million sitting in the vault—the opportunity cost is too high. If University Bank is going to stay in business, it will need to loan out at least part of the $500 million. With a reserve requirement of ten percent of deposits, required reserves are $50 million and so University Bank can lend up to $450 million.

> **Excess reserves** are any reserves held in excess of those required.

Banks rarely keep their level of reserves exactly at the required level. Any reserves above the required level are called **excess reserves**:

$$excess\ reserves = total\ reserves - required\ reserves \qquad (17.3)$$

The balance sheet of University Bank, presented in Figure 17.5, indicates that they currently hold total reserves of $60 million. Therefore, they have $10 million in excess reserves. Given the opportunity cost of holding these excess reserves, University Bank will probably seek to loan most of this balance in the future.

The FDIC and Moral Hazard

Since a bank keeps only a fraction of deposits on reserve, if all depositors try to withdraw their deposits at the same time, the bank will not be able to meet its obligation. But in a typical day only a small fraction of deposits are withdrawn. However, if word spreads that a bank is unstable and may not be able to meet the demands of depositors—whether true or not—depositors will rush to withdraw their funds and that will lead to a bank run. No bank can survive a bank run.

During the era of the Great Depression, bank failures became common. From 1929 to 1933, over 9,000 banks failed in the United Sates alone—more than any other period in history. It is clear that many banks were extending loans beyond their ability to collect and pay depositors in a timely manner. Many depositors lost confidence in the banking system. If you became worried about your bank, and were not certain that your deposit could be withdrawn at some later point, you'd run to the bank to get your money out!

This is precisely what happened to many banks. The situation is perfectly captured in the Hollywood classic movie: *It's a Wonderful Life* (1946). In the movie, George Bailey is set to leave on his honeymoon, when the credit union he runs is subject to a run. When a depositor asks for his money back, George tells him "The, the money's not here. Well, your money's in Joe's house, that's right next to yours. And in the Kennedy House, and Mrs. Macklin's house, and, and a hundred others." This quote summarizes for us both the beauty and danger wrapped up in a fractional reserve banking system. Fractional reserve banking allows access to funds by many in an economy, but can also lead to instability when many depositors demand their funds simultaneously.

After the massive rate of bank failures from 1929 to 1933, the U.S. government instituted federal deposit insurance in 1933 through the Federal Deposit Insurance Corporation (FDIC). Deposit insurance guarantees depositors will get their deposits back (up to $250,000), even if their bank goes bankrupt. FDIC insurance greatly decreased the frequency of bank runs. But it also created a *moral hazard* situation. **Moral hazard** occurs when a party that is protected from risk behaves differently from how it would behave if it were fully exposed to the risk. FDIC insurance means that neither banks nor their depositors have an incentive to monitor risk; whatever happens, they are protected from the consequences of risky behavior.

> **Moral hazard** occurs when a party that is protected from risk behaves differently from how it would behave if it were fully exposed to the risk.

Consider two types of banks in this environment. Type A banks are conservative, take little risk and earn relatively low returns on their loans. Type A banks make only very safe loans with very little default risk and, consequently, relatively low rates of return. Type A banks rarely fail, but they earn relatively low profit and pay relatively low interest rates to their depositors. On the other hand, Type B banks take huge risks, hoping to make extremely large returns on their loans. Type B loans carry greater default risk but also pay higher returns. Type B banks often fail, but the lucky ones, the ones that survive earn very handsome profits and pay high interest rates on their deposits.

Moral hazard draws individual depositors and bankers to type B banking. There is tremendous upside and no significant downside, since depositors are protected against losses by FDIC insurance. This is the environment our modern banks operate in, and this is why many argue that reserve requirements and other regulations are necessary to help insure stability in the financial industry. The case is all the more important when we realize that recessions often start in the financial industry.

Economics in the Real World:
Twenty-first century bank run

For a modern example of a bank run, consider the example of England's Northern Rock Bank which experienced a bank run in 2007, the first British bank run in over a century. Northern Rock earns over $10 billion in revenue per year. But extensive losses stemming from investments in mortgage markets led it to near collapse in 2007. In September of that year, depositors began queuing outside Northern Rock locations because they feared they would not get their deposits back. Eventually, the British government offered deposit insurance of 100% to Northern Rock depositors. But not before much damage was done. In February 2008, Northern Rock was taken over by the British government because it was unable to repay debts or find a buyer. To make matters worse, there is some evidence that Northern Rock was solvent at the time of the bank run, meaning stronger deposit insurance could have saved the bank.

In the United States, over 300 banks failed between 2008 and 2011 without a bank run occurring. The difference is the level of deposit insurance offered in the two nations. In England, depositors are insured for 100% of their first $4,000 in deposits, and then only 90% of their next $70,000. So British depositors get a fraction of their deposits up to about $74,000. On the other hand, FDIC insurance in the United States offers 100% insurance on the first $250,000.

How Banks Create Money

We have seen that banks function as financial intermediaries. But as a byproduct of their everyday activity they also create new money. Modern U.S. banks don't mint currency, but they do create new deposits, and deposits are a part of the money supply. Money deposited in the banking system leads to more money. To see how, let's start with a hypothetical example that involves the Federal Reserve, which supplies the currency in the United States. Let's say the Federal Reserve decides to increase the money supply in the United States. They print a single $1,000 bill and drop it out of a helicopter. Perhaps you are the lucky person who finds this brand-new $1000 bill. If you keep the $1,000 in your wallet, then the money supply increases by only this amount. But, if you deposit the new money in a bank, then banks can use it to create even more.

Let's walk through how this works. Consider what happens if you deposit your $1,000 into a savings or checking account at University Bank. When you deposit $1,000, it is still part of the money supply, since both currency and bank deposits are in the money supply. You don't have the currency anymore, but in your wallet, you have a debit card and that allows you to access the $1,000 to make purchases. Therefore, the deposit still represents $1,000 worth of the medium of exchange.

But banks don't keep your $1,000 in reserve; they use part of your deposit to extend a new loan which earns interest income for the bank. You still have your $1,000 in your savings account (deposits), but somebody else receives money from the bank in the form of a loan. Thus, your bank creates new money by loaning out part of your deposits. What's more, you helped the bank in the money creation process because you put your funds into the bank.

This is just the first step in the money creation process. We'll now go through this in more detail, utilizing the balance sheet of your bank. For this example we need to make two assumptions to help us understand the general picture:

Assumption 1: All currency is deposited in a bank.

Assumption 2: Banks hold no excess reserves.

Neither of these assumptions is completely realistic. But let's work through example under these conditions and later we can consider the effect of each assumption.

Consider first how your deposit changes the assets and liabilities of your University Bank. The t-account below summarizes all initial changes to the balance sheet of University Bank when you deposit your new $1,000 (Assumption 1):

University Bank

Assets		Liabilities and Net Worth	
Reserves	+ $1,000	Deposits	+ $1,000

With a reserve requirement of ten percent ($rr = 0.10$), University Bank loans out $900 of your deposit (Assumption 2 implies that only ten percent of deposits are held on reserve). Perhaps they loan this to a student named Alexis, so she can pay her tuition bill. When University Bank extends the loan to Alexis, the money supply increases by $900. That is, you still have your $1,000 deposit and Alexis has $900.

Including your initial deposit and this $900 loan, the balance sheet changes at University Bank are summarized in this t-account:

University Bank

Assets		Liabilities and Net Worth	
Reserves	+$100	Deposits	+$1,000
Loans	+$900		

Alexis gives her college the $900 and the college then deposits this into their own bank, named Township Bank. But the money multiplication process does not end here. Township Bank also keeps no excess reserves, so they loan out 90% of the $900, which is $810. This creates $810 more in money supply, so that total new money is now $1,000 + $900 + $810 = $1,710. The balance sheet changes at Township Bank are then:

Township Bank

Assets		Liabilities and Net Worth	
Reserves	+$90	Deposits	+$900
Loans	+810		

You can now see that whenever banks make loans, they create new money. As long as dollars find their way back into the banking system, banks multiply them into more deposits – which means more money. Table 17.1 summarizes this money creation. The initial $1,000 bill leads to $10,000 worth of money. When monetary funds are deposited into banks, banks can multiply these deposits, and when they do, they create money.

Table 17.1
Money Creation

Assumption 1: **All currency deposited in banks.**

Assumption 2: **No excess reserves.**

Reserve requirement ratio (rrr) = 10%

Initial new money supply = $1,000

Round	Deposit	
1	$1,000	← Initial deposit
2	$900	
3	$810	
4	$729	
.	.	
.	.	
.	.	
Sum	$10,000	← Total Money

In the end, the impact on the money supply is a large multiple of the initial increase in money. The exact multiple depends on the reserve requirement ratio (*rr*). The rate at which banks multiply money when all currency is deposited into banks and they hold no excess reserves is called the **simple money multiplier.** The formula for the money multiplier is:

$$m^m = \frac{1}{rr} \qquad (17.4)$$

> **The simple money multiplier** is the rate at which banks multiply money when all currency is deposited into banks and they hold no excess reserves.

In our example above, $rr = 0.10$, so the multiplier is $\frac{1}{0.10}$, which is 10. When the money multiplier is 10, a new $1,000 bill produced by the Federal Reserve eventually leads to $10,000 in new money.

Of course in the real world, our two assumptions don't always hold. There is a more realistic money multiplier that relaxes the two assumptions. Consider how a more real world money multiplier would compare to the simple money multiplier. First, if people hold onto some currency (relaxing Assumption 1), banks cannot multiply that currency and so the more realistic multiplier is smaller than the simple money multiplier. Second, if banks hold excess reserves (relaxing Assumption 2), these dollars are not multiplied and, again, the real multiplier is smaller than the simple version. So in reality, money doesn't multiply at quite the rate represented by the simple money multiplier. The simple money multiplier represents the *maximum* size of the money multiplier.

Note that this money multiplier process also works in reverse. When funds are withdrawn from the banking system, these are funds that banks cannot multiply. When funds are withdrawn form the banking system, the money supply contracts. The maximum contraction is a multiple of the withdrawal, where the multiple is determined by the simple money multiplier.

Practice What You Know!
Fractional Reserve Banking

The B-Money Bank

Use this balance sheet of B-Money Bank to answer the questions below. Assume the reserve requirement ratio is 10%.

B-Money Bank

Assets		Liabilities and Net Worth	
Reserves	$50,000	Deposits	$200,000
Loans	$120,000		
Treasury Securities	$50,000	Net Worth	$20,000

Question: What are the required reserves of B-Money Bank?

Answer: B-Money is required to hold 10% of deposits, which is $20,000.

Question: What is the maximum new loan B-Money can extend?

Answer: B-Money has $30,000 in excess reserves, so it could extend a total of that amount in new loans.

Question: Re-write B-Money's balance sheet assuming this loan is made.

Answer: The only items that change are reserves, which declines by $30,000, and Loans, which increases by $30,000.

B-Money Bank

Assets		Liabilities and Net Worth	
Reserves	$20,000	Deposits	$200,000
Loans	$150,000		
Treasury Securities	$50,000	Net Worth	$20,000

Question: If the Federal Reserve bought all of B-Money's Treasury securities, how large a loan could B-Money now extend?

Answer: B-Money would now have $50,000 in excess reserves, so they could make a loan in this amount.

Question: What is the maximum impact on the money supply from this Fed action?

Answer: Using the simple money multiplier, we can see that the money supply could grow as much as $\underline{\$500,000}$ from this action alone:

$$\$50,000 \; x \; m^m = \$50,000 \; x \; \frac{1}{rr} = \$50,000 \; x \; 10 = \$500,000.$$

How does the Federal Reserve control the money supply?

There's a good chance you've heard of the U.S. Federal Reserve (Fed), even outside economics class. Ben Bernanke, the Chairman of the Fed's Board of Governors, is perhaps the most recognized economist in the world. And while we've referred to the Fed periodically throughout this text, it's time to examine it closely.

The Many Jobs of the Federal Reserve

The Fed was established in 1913 as the central bank of the United States. The Fed's primary responsibilities are threefold:

1. *Monetary Policy*: The Fed controls the U.S. money supply and is charged with regulating it to offset macroeconomic fluctuations.

2. *Central Banking*: The Fed serves as a bank for banks; holding bank deposits and extending loans to banks.

3. *Bank Regulation*: The Fed is one of the primary entities charged with ensuring the financial stability of banks, including the determination of reserve requirements.

In this section, we'll talk about the Fed's role as central bank and bank regulator. We'll then look at monetary policy for the remainder of the chapter and into Chapter 18.

The name *central bank* means the Fed is a "bank for banks." The Fed's role as central bank offers support and stability to the banking system. The first component of this is the deposits banks hold at the Fed. **Federal funds** are

> **Federal funds** are private bank deposits at the Federal Reserve.

deposits that private banks hold on reserve at the Fed. The word "federal" seems to denote that these are government funds, but they are private funds held on deposit at a *federal* agency— the Fed. These deposits are part of the reserves that banks set aside, along with physical currency in the vault at the bank.

   Banks keep reserves at the Fed in part because the Fed clears loans between them and other banks. When banks loan reserves to other banks, these are federal funds loans. These federal funds loans are typically very short-term (often overnight) and they allow banks to make quick adjustments to their balance sheet. For example, if University Bank somehow dips below its required reserve level, it can approach Township Bank for a short-term loan. If Township Bank happens to have excess reserves, a short-term loan allows it to earn interest. The interest rate on these interbank loans is known as the **federal funds rate.**

> **The Federal funds rate** is the interest rate in loans between private banks.

   Figure 17.6 illustrates how the relationship between the Federal Reserve and commercial banks is analogous to the relationship between these banks and households and firms. First, we hold deposits at banks, and banks hold deposits at the Fed – these are the federal funds. Second, we take loans from banks, and banks take loans from the Fed. The loans from the Fed to private banks are known as **discount loans**.

> **Discount loans** are loans from the Fed to private banks.

Figure 17.6
The Federal Reserve as a Central Bank

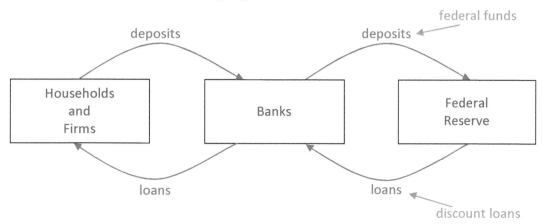

Central Banks operate as a bank for commercial banks. Commercial banks make deposits at the Federal Reserve. These deposits are called federal funds. The Federal Reserve also extends loans to commercial banks, and these loans are called discount loans.

   Discount loans are the vehicle by which the Fed performs its role "lender of last resort." Given the macroeconomic danger of bank failure, the Fed serves an important role as a backup lender to private banks that find difficulty borrowing elsewhere in the economy. The **discount rate** is the interest rate on discount loans. This interest rate is set directly by the Fed since it is a loan directly from a branch of the U.S. government to private financial institutions.

> **The discount rate** is the interest rate on discount loans.

Discount loans don't often figure prominently in macroeconomics, but in extremely turbulent times, they reassure financial market participants. For example, when banks were struggling in 2008, financial market participants were assured that troubled banks could rely on the Federal Reserve to fortify failing banks with discount loans. In fact, for the first time in history, other financial firms were allowed to borrow from the Fed. The Fed even extended an $85 billion loan to insurance company A.I.G. because it had written insurance policies for financial securities.

The Fed also serves as a regulator of individual banks. These responsibilities include the setting and monitoring of reserve requirements. The Fed monitors the balance sheets of banks with an eye toward limiting the riskiness of the assets banks hold. One might ask why banks are subject to this kind of regulation. After all, the government doesn't monitor the riskiness of assets owned by other private firms. However, as we have seen, the interconnectedness of bank assets means that banking problems often spread through the entire industry quickly. In addition, there the moral hazard problem we discussed earlier in this chapter – because of deposit insurance, both banks and their customers have reduced incentives to monitor the risk of bank assets.

Economics in the Media

Wall Street: Money Never Sleeps

Moral Hazard

This film is a sequel to the original Wall Street movie, from 1987. This film focuses on the historical events leading up to and during the financial crisis that began in 2007. One recurring theme in the movie is that some financial firms are "too big to fail." How can a firm be too big to fail? When one firm fails, or goes bankrupt, it can't repay all of its loans. But loans are what financial firms are all about.

If one bank fails, it won't be able to repay depositors and others creditors. This puts all the banks creditors into similar financial difficulty. If the failing bank is large enough, it can set off a domino effect in which bank after bank after bank fails and the entire financial system collapses. If regulators deem a bank too big to fail, they will use government aid to keep the bank afloat.

But this introduces a particularly strong case of moral hazard. Banks have incentives to take on risk so they can earn high profits. If we then eliminate the possibility of failure – there is almost no downside risk.

In this movie, Gordon Gecko, played by Michael Douglas, defines moral hazard during a public lecture. His definition is: "when they take your money and then are not responsible for what they do with it."

He's right – when a financial institution is not required to bear the costs of poor decisions, it is not responsible for mishandling their funds.

Monetary Policy Tools

When the Fed wants to alter the supply of money in the economy, it has several tools at its disposal. In this section we discuss these policy tools, but our emphasis will be on the single tool they use every day: *open market operations*.

Open Market Operations

If the Fed decided to increase the money supply, they could do this in a number of direct ways. Below, we list three possible means by which the Fed can directly increase the amount of money in the economy; you see if you can guess which of the three is correct:

A. Drop money out of a helicopter.

B. Hand students and others in the economy new backpacks full of money.

C. Use new money to buy something in the economy.

If you chose option C, you are correct. **Open market operations** are the purchase or sale of bonds by a central bank. When the Fed wants to increase the money supply, it buys securities; it sells securities when it wishes to decrease the money supply. In Chapter 11 we introduced the U.S. Treasury security as a special bond asset. These are the securities (bonds) the Fed typically buys and sells when implementing monetary policy.

> **Open market operations** are the purchase or sale of bands by a central bank.

Essentially, the Fed could realize its desired effects through buying other goods and services like real estate, fine art, or coffee and bagels. It is as if the Fed prints a whole batch of new currency and then goes shopping. When it is done shopping, it leaves behind all the new currency in the economy. Whatever it buys on its shopping spree becomes an asset on the Fed's balance sheet.

The Fed buys and sells Treasury securities for two reasons. First, the Fed's goal is to get the funds directly into the market for loanable funds. This way, financial institutions begin lending the new money and it quickly moves into the economy. Second, a typical day's worth of open market operations might entail as much as $20 billion worth of purchases from the Fed. If the Fed bought coffee and bagels, it would cause problems in that market. Imagine you are the manager of a bagel shop in Washington, DC and Ben Bernanke walked in with a request for $20 billion worth of bagels. But the market for U.S. Treasuries is big enough to accommodate these purchases seamlessly. The daily volume in the U.S. Treasury market is over $500 billion, so the Fed can buy and sell without difficulty.

Figure 17.7 summarizes how open market operations work. When the Fed purchases bonds, it creates new money and trades this money with financial institutions for their Treasury bonds. The result is more money in the economy. On the other side, when the Fed sells bonds to financial institutions, it exchanges bonds for existing money, taking the money out of the economy. The result is less money in the economy.

Figure 17.7
Open Market Operations

A: Open Market Purchase:
Fed buys bonds with new dollars.

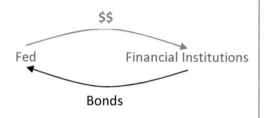

Result: **Money Supply Increase**

B: Open Market Sale:
Fed sells bonds back for dollars.

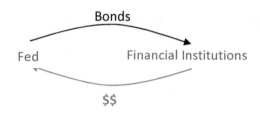

Result: **Money Supply Decrease.**

In open market purchases, the Fed buys bonds from financial institutions. This purchase injects new money directly into financial markets. In open market sales, the Fed sells bonds back to financial institutions and this action takes money out of financial markets.

The Fed undertakes open market operations every business day. Typically, it intends to keep market conditions exactly as they were the day before. But open market operations are also the primary tool used to expand or contract the money supply in order to affect the macroeconomy.

Quantitative Easing

The end of 2008 marked the single worst quarter for the U.S. economy in over a half a century. Real GDP declined 8.9% and the unemployment rate was ratcheting upward. In November 2008, hoping that more money would stimulate the economy, the Federal Reserve determined it should take additional measures to increase the money supply. The method they chose is a new variety of open market operations known as *quantitative easing*. **Quantitative easing** is a targeted use of open market operations in which the central bank buys securities specifically targeted in certain markets. Open market operations typically involve buying and selling short term Treasury securities—bonds that mature in less than one year. But with quantitative easing, the Fed expanded its purchases to include $300 billion of long term Treasury securities. It also purchased $1.25 trillion in mortgage-backed securities, specifically targeting the housing market. Together with an additional $175 billion in purchases of securities from government-sponsored enterprises, this amounted to almost $2 trillion worth of new funds injected into the economy.

> **Quantitative easing** is the targeted use of open market operations whereby the central bank buys securities specifically targeted in certain markets.

This move was bold and unprecedented both in size and scope. It amounted to the Fed printing trillions of new dollars and injecting them into targeted sectors of the economy. The first round of quantitative easing started in November of 2008 and continued into the first quarter of 2010. At that point, the Fed was convinced that

economic recovery was well underway. But conditions deteriorated over the second half
of 2010, as the unemployment rate stayed around 9 percent and real GDP growth stalled.

Because of the lackluster U.S. economic performance in November of 2010, the
Fed decided to engage in a second round of quantitative easing, dubbed "QE 2." This
round involved purchases of an additional $600 billion of long term Treasury securities.
Figure 17.8 illustrates the timeline for these quantitative easing programs along with the
quarterly growth rates of real GDP. The Fed implemented these two rounds of
quantitative easing when it was clear that traditional open market operations would not
return the economy to stable growth rates.

Figure 17.8
Quantitative Easing

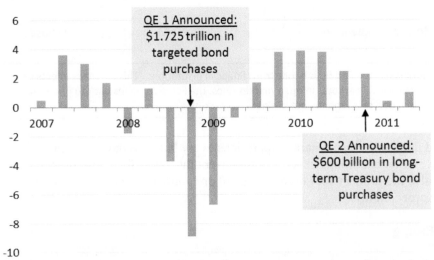

Source: GDP data is from the BEA; QE data from FOMC statements.

In September 2011, as the economy continued to struggle toward consistent
growth, Ben Bernanke announced yet another variation of quantitative easing. In
particular, the Fed would buy $400 billion worth of long term Treasury securities and
simultaneously sell $400 billion worth of short-term Treasury securities. This action
became known as a "twist," since it was not really adding money to the economy but
attempting to reduce long-term interest rates and thereby encourage business investment.
This twist operation did not seem to have a significant effect on the economy as
lackluster growth continued through 2012.

In summary, quantitative easing is a new variation of open market operations that
was introduced during the slow recovery from the Great Recession. However, this new
tool did not immediately return the United States economy to strong growth.

Reserve requirements and discount rates

In the past, the Fed featured two other tools in their administration of monetary policy: reserve requirements and the discount rate. Neither of these has been used recently for monetary policy, but they are available, and historically important.

Recall two earlier observations regarding reserve requirements:

1. The Fed sets the ratio of deposits that banks must hold on reserve. This ratio is the reserve requirement ratio.

2. The simple money multiplier (m^m) depends on the reserve requirement ratio (rr), since $m^m = \frac{1}{rr}$.

Taken together, these imply that the Fed can change the money multiplier by changing the reserve requirement ratio. If the Fed lowers the reserve requirement ratio, the money multiplier increases, and if it raises the reserve requirement ratio, the money multiplier falls.

For example, consider what would happen if the Fed lowered rr to 5% from its current level of 10%. The new simple money multiplier would be $1 \div 0.05 = 20$. This action alone would double the simple money multiplier. Lowering the reserve requirement means banks can loan out larger portions of their deposits. This enables them to create money by multiplying deposits to a greater extent than before.

If instead, the Fed raised rr to 20%, the simple money multiplier would fall to just $1 \div 0.20 = 5$. Table 17.2 shows different values of the simple money multiplier given different reserve requirements.

Table 17.2
Reserve requirements and the simple money multiplier

$$m^m = \frac{1}{rr}$$

rr	m^m	
0.05	20	$\uparrow rr \rightarrow \downarrow m^m$
0.10	10	
0.125	8	
0.20	5	$\downarrow rr \rightarrow \uparrow m^m$
0.25	4	

This tool is not as precise or predictable as open market operations. Since small changes in the money multiplier can lead to large swings in the money supply, changing the reserve requirement can cause the money supply to change too much. In addition, changing reserve requirements can have unpredictable outcomes because the overall effects depend on the actions of banks. It is possible that the Fed could lower the reserve requirement to 5% and banks would not change their reserves. For these reasons, the reserve requirement has not been used for monetary policy since 1992.

The Fed has also used the discount rate to administer monetary policy. Recall that the discount rate is the interest rate charged on loans to banks from the Fed in their role as lender of last resort. In the past, the Fed would increase the discount rate to discourage borrowing by banks and decrease the money supply, or decrease the discount rate to encourage borrowing by banks and increase the money supply. This tool was actively used by the Fed until the Great Depression era. Currently, the Fed discourages discount borrowing unless banks are struggling. Changing the discount rate to affect bank borrowing is no longer viewed as a helpful tool for changing the money supply.

Practice What You Know
Federal Reserve Terminology

Let's say the reserves at B-Money Bank fall below the required level and approaches University Bank for a loan. University Bank agrees to a short-term loan with B-Money bank.

Question: What is the name of the funds that private banks like University bank loan to other private banks (like B-Money)? What is the interest rate on these loans called?

Answer: The funds are called federal funds. "Federal," sounds as if it is a loan from the federal government. This wording has been adopted because the loan typically takes place through changes in the two banks' accounts at their bank, the Federal Reserve.

The interest rate is the Federal Funds rate.

Now assume B-Money has made some particularly troublesome loans, perhaps a lot of high risk mortgage loans and all private parties refuse to lend to B-Money. B-Money then approaches the Fed for a loan to keep its reserves at the appropriate level.

Question: What is the name of this type of loan? What is the name of the interest rate charged for this loan?

Answer: This is a discount loan and the interest rate is the discount rate.

Conclusion

We started this chapter with a common misconception about the supply of money in an economy. In general, people believe it is pretty simple to regulate the quantity of money in an economy. But while currency in modern economies is issued exclusively by the government, money also includes bank deposits. Banks expand the money supply when they extend loans, and cause the money supply to contract if they increase their level of reserves. In fact, even our influence is significant; individuals like you and me cause the money supply to rise and fall when we change how much currency we hold outside the banking system. Taken together, this means the Fed's job of monitoring the quantity of money is very difficult. It attempts to expand or contract the money supply, but its efforts may be offset by the actions of banks and individuals.

This material in this chapter sets the stage for a theoretical discussion of monetary policy and the way it affects the economy, which we will undertake in Chapter 18.

BIG QUESTIONS

1. What is money?

Money is primarily the medium of exchange on an economy; it's what people trade for goods and services. Money includes more than just physical currency; it also includes bank deposits since we often make purchases with checks or cards that withdraw from our bank accounts.

2. How do banks create money?

Banks create money whenever they extend a loan. A new loan represents new purchasing power while the deposit that backs the loan is also money.

3. How does the Federal Reserve control the money supply?

The primary tool of monetary policy is open market operations, which the Fed conducts through buying and selling bonds. It has several other tools, including reserve requirements and recently-created lending facilities that allow it to lend directly to specific economic sectors.

Concepts You Should Know

Bank run	Excess reserves	Moral hazard
Barter	Federal funds	Open market operations
Checkable deposits	Federal funds rate	Quantitative easing
Commodity-backed money	Fiat money	Required reserve ratio (rr)
Commodity money	Fractional reserve banking	Reserves
Currency	M1	Simple money multiplier
Discount loan	M2	Store of value
Discount rate	Medium of exchange	Unit of account
Double coincidence of wants		

Questions for Review

1. What is the difference between commodity money and fiat money?

2. What are the three functions of money? Which is the defining characteristic?

3. List the components of M1 and M2.

4. Suppose you withdraw $100 from your checking account. What impact does this have on (a) the money supply, (b) your bank's required reserves, and (c) your bank's excess reserves?

5. Why is the actual money multiplier usually less than what the simple money multiplier?

6. Why can't a bank lend out all of its reserves?

7. How does the Fed increase and decrease the money supply through open-market operations?

8. How is the discount rate different from the federal funds rate?

9. What is the current required reserve ratio? What would happen to the money supply if the Fed decreased the ratio?

10. Define quantitative easing. How is this different from standard open market operations?

Study Problems:

1. Create a balance sheet for the Kramer's Savings & Loan with the following financial items: Checking deposits of $3,000, Excess Reserves of $0, Treasury Securities of $1,000, and Loans of $2,700.

2. From the previous problem, show the initial changes to the balance sheet if George deposits $500 into his checking account at Kramer's. Then show the final balance sheet amounts assuming Kramer's lends all excess reserves to Elaine.

4. Suppose you take $150 in currency out of your pocket and deposit it in your checking account. Assuming a required reserve ratio of 10%, what is the largest amount by which the money supply can increase?

5. Consider balance sheet for the Bank of Quahog is presented below.

BANK OF QUAHOG BALANCE SHEET

Assets		Liabilities and Net Worth	
Government Securities	$1600		
Required Reserves	400	Liabilities	
Excess Reserves	0	Checking deposits	$4000
Loans	3000		
		Net Worth	$1000
Total Assets	$5000		

Using a required reserve ratio of 10% and assuming the bank keeps no excess reserves, write the changes to the balance sheet for each of the following scenarios:
(a) Quagmire withdraws $200 from his checking account.
(b) Stewie deposits $500 into his checking account.
(c) The Fed buys $1,000 of government securities from the bank.
(d) The Fed sells $1,500 of government securities to the bank.

6. Assuming a required reserve ratio of 10% and banks keep no excess reserves, which of the following scenarios produces a larger increase in the money supply? Why?
(a) Someone takes $1,000 from under their mattress and deposits it into their checking account.
(b) The Fed purchases $1,000 worth of government securities from a commercial bank.

7. Assuming a required reserve ratio of 10% and banks keep no excess reserves, what is the value of government securities the Fed must purchase if it wants to increase the money supply by $2 million?

8. Assuming a required reserve ratio of 10% and banks keep no excess reserves, $300 is deposited into a checking account. By how much more does the money supply increase if the Fed lowers the reserve ratio to 7%?

9. Determine if the following changes affect M1 and/or M2?
    (a) An increase in savings deposits.
    (b) A decrease in credit card balances
    (c) A decrease in the amount of currency in circulation
    (d) The conversion of a savings account into a checking account.

10. Determine whether each of the following is considered standard open market operations or quantitative easing:

(a) The Fed buys $100 billion worth of student-loan backed securities.
(b) The Fed sells $400 billion worth of short term treasury securities.
(c) The Fed buys $500 billion worth of thirty-year (long-term) Treasury Securities.

Solved Problems

1. What is the simple money multiplier if the required reserve ratio is 15%? What is it at 12.5%?

Answer:

$$m^m = \frac{1}{rr} = \frac{1}{0.15} = 6.67$$

$$m^m = \frac{1}{rr} = \frac{1}{0.125} = 8$$

2. Suppose the Fed sells $1 million worth of Treasury securities to a commercial bank. What effect will this have on the bank's reserves and the money supply? Assume a reserve requirement ratio of ten percent, that banks hold no excess reserves, and that all currency is deposited into the banking system.

Answer:

The immediate result will be that the commercial bank will $1,000,000 in excess reserves, since its deposits did not change. The commercial bank will loan out these excess reserves and the money multiplier process begins. Under the assumptions of this question, the simple money multiplier applies. Therefore, in the end, $10 million of additional deposits will be created.

Chapter 18

Monetary Policy

Misconception: Central banks can steer economies out of every recession.

From 1982 to 2008 – 26 years! – the U.S. economy hummed along with unprecedented success. There were two recessions, but they were neither severe nor lengthy. Economists and many other observers actually believed that the business cycle had been tamed once and for all. Much of the credit for this "great moderation" was given to Alan Greenspan, the Chairman of the Board of Governors of the Federal Reserve Board. It was believed that his savvy handling of interest rates and money supply had been the key to the sustained economic growth, and that enlightened supervision of central banks was the path to future economic growth throughout the world in the 21st century. Sadly, the Great Recession that started in 2008, which plunged the world into the worst economic downturn since the Great Depression, popped the bubble of this misconception. Moreover, since 2008, the extraordinary efforts by the Fed to help the US economy to return to robust economic growth have shown just how little power a central bank has when things get really bad

In this chapter we consider how changes in the money supply work their way through the economy. In doing this, we build on earlier material, drawing heavily on the discussions of monetary policy, the loanable funds market, and the aggregate demand-aggregate supply model. We begin by looking at the short run, when monetary policy is most effective. We then consider why monetary policy can't always turn an economy around. We conclude the chapter by examining the relationship between inflation and unemployment.

Big Questions
- What is the effect of monetary policy in the short run?
- Why doesn't monetary policy always work?
- What is the Phillips Curve?

What is the effect of monetary policy in the short run?

When economic growth stagnates and unemployment rises, many people look to central banks to help the economy. Central banks can use monetary policy to reduce interest rates and make it easier for people and businesses to borrow; this generates new economic activity to get the economy moving again. In the last chapter, we saw that the Federal Reserve generally uses open market operations to implement monetary policy. In this chapter, we look closely at how the effects of open market operations ripple through the economy.

We begin by considering the immediate or short-run effects. Recall the difference between the short run and the long run in macroeconomics. The long run is a period of time long enough for all prices to adjust. But in the short run, some prices, often the prices of resources, such as wages for workers and interest rates for loans, are inflexible.

Expansionary Monetary Policy

To gain some intuition about macroeconomic results of money supply changes, let's return to an earlier example—your college apparel business. Suppose you already have one retail location where you sell apparel, and you are now considering opening a second. Before you can open a new store, you need to invest in several resources: a physical location, additional inventory, and some labor. Of course, you plan to earn the revenue needed to pay for these resources eventually. But you need a loan to expand the business now, so you go to the bank. The bank offers a loan but the interest rate is higher than your expected return on the investment. So you regretfully decide not to open a new location.

Your college apparel sales are going well. Should you open a second location?

But then, the central bank decides to expand the money supply. It buys Treasury securities from banks, which increases the level of reserves in the banking system. As a result, interest rates fall at your local bank. You take a loan, open the second apparel shop, and hire a few employees.

In this example, as a direct result of the monetary policy, your actions affect the macroeconomy, even if the effects of only your actions are very small. First, investment increases because you spend on equipment, inventory, and a physical location. Second, aggregate demand increases because your investment demand is part of aggregate demand. Finally, as a result of the increase in aggregate demand, real GDP increases and unemployment falls as your output rises and you hire workers.

This is what new money can do in the short run – it expands the amount of credit available and paves the way for economic expansion.

Now, let's trace the impact of this kind of monetary policy on the entire macroeconomy. In doing this, we draw heavily on what we have presented in preceding chapters. Below is a short list of principles we have developed and that you will now need. If you are unclear on any of these, you might review them in the chapters indicated.

1. The Fed uses open market operations to implement monetary policy. Open market operations are the purchase or sale of bonds and normally these are short-term Treasury securities.
2. Treasury securities are one important part of the loanable funds market, where lenders buy securities and borrowers sell securities.
3. The price in the loanable funds market is the interest rate. Lower interest rates increase the quantity of investment demand, just as lower prices increase the quantity demanded in any product market.
4. Investment is one component of aggregate demand, so changes in investment demand indicate corresponding changes in aggregate demand (Chapter 26).
5. In the short run, increases in aggregate demand increase output and lower the unemployment rate .

Each point above is important in understanding the effects of monetary policy. We have studied each separately; now it is time to put them together.

Expansionary monetary policy – when a central bank acts to increase the money supply.

We start with *expansionary monetary policy*. **Expansionary monetary policy** occurs when a central bank acts to increase the money supply in an effort to stimulate the economy. Hypothetically, the Fed could do this by dropping currency out of a helicopter. But it typically expands the money supply through open market purchases: it buys bonds.

When the Fed buys bonds from financial institutions, new money moves directly into the loanable funds market. This action increases the funds banks can use for new loans. Figure 18.1 illustrates the effects of expansionary monetary policy in the loanable funds market and also on aggregate demand. First, notice that open market operations means the new funds enter directly into the loanable funds market, which is pictured on the left side of the figure. The supply of funds increases from S to S_1. This new supply reduces the interest rate from 5% to 3%. At the lower interest rate, firms take more loans for investment and the quantity demanded of loanable funds increases from $200 billion to $210 billion.

Figure 18.1
Expansionary monetary policy in the short run

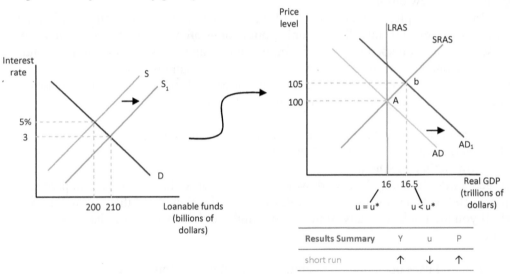

The central bank buys bonds which injects new funds directly into the loanable funds market. This increases the supply of loanable funds and decreases the interest rate from 5% to 3%. The lower interest rate leads to an increase in the quantity of investment demand, from 200 to 210, which increases aggregate demand. The increase in aggregate demand increases real GDP from $16 trillion to $16.5 trillion, and reduces unemployment in the short run. The general price level also rises to 105, but does not fully adjust in the short run.

Now, since investment is a component of aggregate demand, the increase in the quantity of investment demand also increases aggregate demand, which is pictured on the right side of Figure 18.1. Aggregate demand derives from four sources: C, I, G, and X. When investment (I) increases, aggregate demand increases from AD to AD_1.

In the short run, increases in aggregate demand lead to increases in real GDP. In Figure 18.1, the economy moves from an initial long-run equilibrium at point A, to a short-run equilibrium at point b. Real GDP increases from $16 trillion to $16.5 trillion. The increase in GDP leads to more jobs through the increase in aggregate demand, and therefore, lower unemployment. Finally, the general price level rises from 100 to 105.

This price level increase is only partial; in the short run, output prices are more flexible than input prices, which are sticky and do not adjust.

In summary, in the short run, expansionary monetary policy reduces unemployment and increases real GDP. In addition, the overall price level rises somewhat as flexible prices increase in the short run. These results are summarized at the bottom of Figure 16.1.

Before moving on, let's step back and consider the result of the expansion. They seem positive, right? After all, unemployment goes down and real GDP goes up. This macroeconomic result is consistent with how monetary policy affected your college apparel firm. Real employment and real output expand as a result of increasing the quantity of money in the economy. Later in the chapter, we shall see that not everybody is happy with this outcome.

Economics in the Real World:
Monetary policy responses to the Great Recession

In the fall of 2007, it was clear that the U.S. economy was slowing. The unemployment rate rose from 4.4% to 5% between May and June of 2007, and real GDP grew by just 1.7% in the fourth quarter. The U.S. economy officially entered recession in December 2007. We now know the U.S. economy was entering several years of low growth and high unemployment. Many economists believe that a decline in aggregate demand was a major cause of the recession. Certainly, the Federal Reserve's response attempted to increase aggregate demand.

Panel (a) of Figure 18.2 illustrates a decline in aggregate demand, from AD_{2007} to AD_{2008}. In this environment, what is the proper response of the central bank? We are now in a position to consider the possibility of using open market purchases to expand the money supply with the goal of increasing increase aggregate demand and restoring real GDP and employment.

Figure 18.2
Monetary Policy in the Great Recession

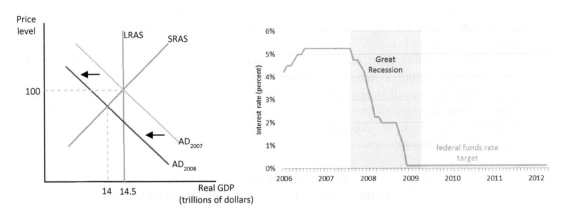

When the Great Recession began at the end of 2007, the Fed responded with expansionary monetary policy that led to lower interest rates. With growth low and unemployment high through 2012, the Fed continued to keep interest rates low.

We have seen that open market purchases drive down interest rates. This is exactly how the Federal Reserve responded, beginning in 2007. Panel (b) of Figure 18.2 shows the Federal Funds rate, which you should recall from Chapter 16 is the interest rate on short term loans between banks. Traditional open market operations involve buying short term Treasury securities, which decreases the short-term interest rate, or selling Treasury securities, which increases the short-term interest rate. As you can see in panel (b), the Fed actively worked to keep the Federal Funds rate at nearly zero for several years. This is a direct application of the monetary policy prescriptions that we have talked about in this section – expansionary monetary policy aimed at lower interest rates so as to increase real GDP and reduce unemployment.

Figure 18.2 shows that the Fed actions were consistent with basic macroeconomics: when the economy went into recession, they expanded the money supply to lower interest rates. But maybe you are now curious as to why the economy did not quickly return to full employment conditions. We return to this question later in this chapter.

Real versus Nominal Effects

We have seen that changes in the quantity of money lead to real changes in the economy. You may be wondering if it is really that simple. That is, if a central bank can create jobs and real GDP by simply printing money, why would it ever stop? After all, fiat money is just paper! Well, this is true – there is a short run incentive to increase the money supply, but these effects wear off in the long run as prices adjust and then drive down the value of money.

Think of it this way: let's say the Fed's preferred method of increasing the money supply is by handing you backpacks full of thousand dollar bills. Not a bad idea, right? But let's focus on the macroeconomic effects. Eventually, the new money will devalue the entire money supply, since prices will rise. But since you get the money first, you get it before any prices have adjusted. So these new funds represent real purchasing power for you. This is why monetary policy can have immediate real short run effects: because initially no prices have adjusted. But as prices adjust in the long run, the effects of the new money wear off.

Injecting new money into the economy eventually causes inflation, but inflation doesn't happen right away and prices do not rise uniformly. During the time that prices are increasing, the value of money is constantly moving downward. Figure 18.3 illustrates the real purchasing power of money as time goes by. The top panel shows adjustments to the price level. When new money enters the economy, the price level begins to rise in the short run and then reaches its new level in the long run. The bottom panel shows the value of money relative to these price level adjustments. When the new money comes into the economy, it has its highest value, as prices have not yet adjusted. In the short run, as prices rise, the real purchasing power of all money in the economy falls. In the long run all prices adjust, and then the real value of money reaches its lower level. At this point, the real impacts of the monetary policy dissipate completely. In the next section, we look at this adjustment to long run equilibrium in the aggregate demand and aggregate supply model.

Figure 18.3
The real value of money as prices adjust

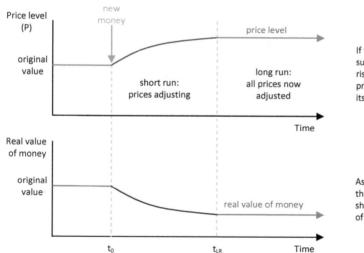

If the central bank increases the money supply at time t_0, the price level begins rising in the short run. In the long run, all prices adjust and the price level reaches its new higher level.

As the price level increases, this reduces the real value of money throughout the short run. In the long run, the real value of money has fallen to a new lower level.

Surprise Inflation Hurts some People

Let's now consider expansionary monetary policy affects different people across the economy. The basic macroeconomic results, summarized in Figure 18.1, seem very positive: real GDP goes up, the unemployment rate falls, and there is some inflation. Consider that you are living in an economy where these conditions exist. Everywhere you look, the news seems positive, as the media, politicians, and firms focus on the expanding economy. But not everybody is happy.

For example, consider the worker who signs a two-year contract just before inflation hits the economy. This worker now pays more for goods and services like groceries, gasoline, education and healthcare – yet their wages were set before the inflation. In real terms, this is a pay cut. Monetary policy derives its potency from sticky prices, but if your price is stuck, inflation hurts you.

In general, resource suppliers that have sticky prices are harmed by inflation. In addition to workers, lenders, the suppliers of funds used for expansion, are another prominent group that is harmed when inflation is greater than anticipated. Imagine that you extend a loan with an interest rate of 3%, but inflation turns out to be 5%. The Fisher effect implies that your real interest rate is actually -2%.

Later in this chapter, we talk about the incentives for these resource suppliers to correctly anticipate inflation. For now, we just note that surprise inflation, while potentially helpful to the overall economy, is also harmful to those whose prices take time to adjust.

Contractionary Monetary Policy

Expansionary policy is used to stimulate the economy and contractionary policy is used to slow the economy down. **Contractionary monetary policy** occurs when a central bank takes action that reduces the money supply in the economy. A central bank often undertakes contractionary monetary policy when the economy is expanding rapidly and it fears inflation.

> **Contractionary monetary policy** occurs when a central bank acts to decrease the money supply.

To trace the effects of contractionary policy, we again begin in the loanable funds market. The central bank reduces the money supply via open market operations; it sells bonds in the loanable funds market. Selling the bonds takes funds out of the loanable funds market because the banks buy the bonds from the central bank with money they might otherwise lend out. Financial institutions are not forced to buy the bonds, but the central bank enters the market and sells bonds alongside other sellers. The loanable funds market pictured on the left side of Figure 18.4 shows this reduction in supply from S to S_1. The interest rate rises and equilibrium investment falls from $200 billion to $190 billion.

When investment falls, aggregate demand falls. On the right side of Figure 18.3, this is illustrated as a fall in aggregate demand from AD to AD_1. In the short run, this causes a reduction in real GDP from $15 trillion to $14.5 trillion, an increase in the unemployment rate, and a decrease in the price level.

These short run results are again the result of fixed resource prices for the firm. A lower money supply leads to downward pressure on prices, but sticky resource prices mean that firms can't adjust the wages of their workers or the terms of their loans in the short run. Therefore, they reduce output and lay off some workers. This is why we see real GDP falling and the unemployment rate rising.

Figure 18.4
Contractionary monetary policy in the short run

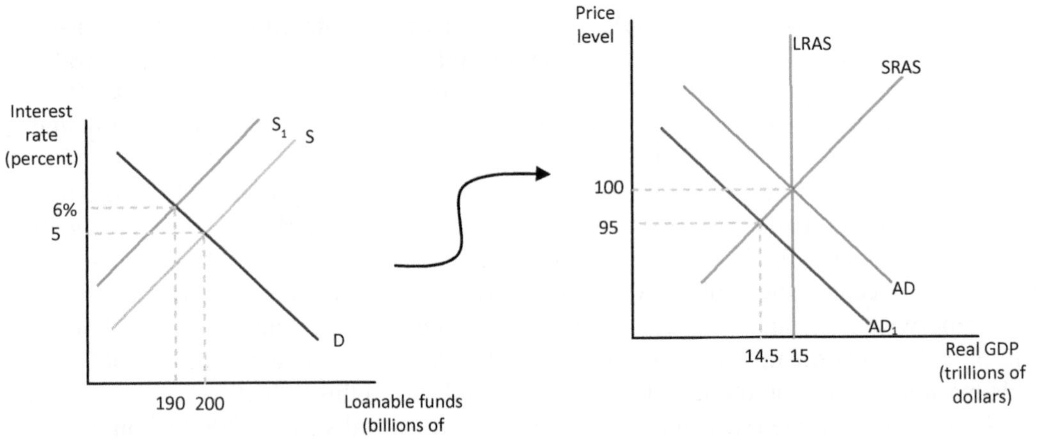

Results Summary	Y	u	P
short run	↓	↑	↓

The central bank sells bonds which pulls funds out of the loanable funds market. This decreases the supply of loanable funds and increases the interest rate from 5% to 6%. The lower interest rate leads to a decrease in the quantity of investment demand from 200 to 190, and this decreases aggregate demand. The decrease in aggregate demand decreases real GDP from $15 trillion to $14.5 trillion, and induces unemployment in the short run. The general price level also falls to 95 but does not fully adjust in the short run.

Economics in the Real World:
Monetary Policy's Contribution to the Great Depression

As if monetary policy is not hard enough, consider that the money supply is not completely controlled by a central bank. In Chapter 17, we explained how the actions of private individuals and banks can increase or decrease the money supply via the money multiplier. Banks increase the money supply when they lend out reserves and decrease the money supply when they hold more reserves. In addition, individuals like you and me increase the money supply when we deposit funds into bank accounts and the banks multiply the money by making loans. When we withdraw our funds and hold onto more currency, we decrease the money supply since banks cannot multiply these funds.

Now, imagine a scenario with massive bank failures and very little deposit insurance. As more and more banks fail, people withdraw their funds all over the economy. While it makes sense that individuals would want to withdraw their money, as people all over the country continue to remove money from banks, the money supply declines significantly. The reduction in the money supply then leads to economic contraction, similar to the scenario we saw in Figure 18.4.

This type of monetary contraction is exactly what happened at the beginning of the Great Depression. From 1929 to 1933, prior to federal deposit insurance, over 9,000 banks failed in the United States. Because of these bank failures, people began holding their money outside the banking system. This contributed to a significant contraction in the money supply. Figure 18.5 shows the money supply prior to and during the Depression. This drastic decline was one of the major causes of the Great Depression.

Figure 18.5
U.S. money supply before and during the Great Depression

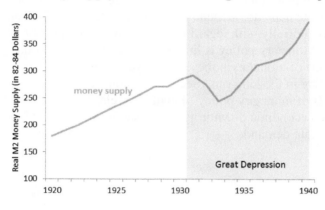

The huge decline in the money supply was a major contributor to the Great Depression.

Source: Historical Statistics of the United States, Colonial Times to 1970

Practice What You Know
Expansionary versus Contractionary Monetary Policy

Monetary policy in the Short Run

Question: In the short run, how does expansionary monetary policy affect real GDP, unemployment, and the price level in the economy?

Answer: Real GDP increases, the unemployment rate falls, and the price level rises as all flexible prices adjust.

Question: In the short run, how does contractionary monetary policy affect real GDP, unemployment, and the price level in the economy?

Answer: Real GDP decreases, the unemployment rate rises, and the price level falls as all flexible prices adjust.

Question: What real world circumstances might lead to contractionary monetary policy?

Answer: If the Federal Open Market Committee at the Federal Reserve believed that inflation was an immenent danger, they might implement contractionary monetary polciy.

Why doesn't monetary policy always work?

Thus far in this chapter, we have seen that monetary policy can have real effects on the macroeconomy. By shifting aggregate demand, monetary policy can affect real GDP and unemployment. But, as we discussed briefly with regard to the opening misconception to this chapter, recessions still occur. Monetary policy is limited in what it can do. In this section, we consider three limitations of monetary policy. First, we consider the diminished effects of monetary policy in the long run. Second, we consider how expectations can dampen the effects of monetary policy. Finally, we clarify the limitations of monetary policy when economic downturns are caused by shifts in aggregate supply, rather than aggregate demand.

Long-run Adjustments

We have noted that some prices take longer to adjust than others and that the long run is a period of time long enough for *all* prices to adjust. Output prices can adjust relatively quickly. Think about the output prices at a coffee shop which are often displayed in chalk behind the cash register; they are easy to change in the short run. On the other hand, resource prices, like worker's wages, are often the slowest prices to adjust. These prices are often set by lengthy contracts and money illusion also can make resource suppliers reluctant to lower their price. But the long run is a period of time sufficient for all prices to change, even worker's contracts, which eventually expire.

Both of these types of prices affect the decisions made at firms across the economy, and therefore affect output and unemployment. For example, consider your small business where you produce and sell college apparel. You secured a loan to open a new retail location because the Fed increased the money supply, which increased the supply of loans. When you initially received your loan, costs for resources such workers, equipment, inventory, and a physical plant were relatively cheap because prices for these things are sticky and had not yet adjusted. But in the long run, these resource prices adjust. If everything works out well for you, the monetary expansion leads to new demand for your product and you'll be able to keep your new store open. But it is also possible that when the prices of resources rise—in the long run—you may not be doing well enough afford them. At this point, with your costs rising, you may have to reduce your output, lay off some workers, or perhaps even close your new retail location. In the long run, as prices adjust throughout the macroeconomy, the stimulating effects of expansionary monetary policy wear off.

Let's see how this process works for the entire economy. Figure 18.6 illustrates long-run macroeconomic adjustments to expansionary monetary policy. Expansionary monetary policy shifts aggregate demand from AD to AD_1. This moves the economy from long-run equilibrium at point A to short run equilibrium at point b. In the long run, as resource prices rise, the short-run aggregate supply shifts upward from SRAS to $SRAS_1$, and the economy moves to a long-run equilibrium at point C. When we compare the new long-run equilibrium to the situation prior to monetary policy, we see that there is no change in real GDP or unemployment, but an increase in the price level from 100 to 110.

Figure 18.6
Expansionary monetary policy in the long run

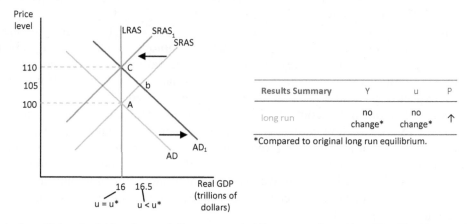

Beginning in equilibrium at point A, an increase in the money supply shifts aggregate demand from AD to AD_1; this moves the economy to a new short-run equilibrium at point b. Equilibrium at point b is only relevant in the short run, as all prices have not yet adjusted. In the long run, resource prices adjust. This shifts short-run aggregate supply from SRAS to $SRAS_1$, and the economy moves to a new long run equilibrium at point C.

One important implication of these long run results is the lack of real economic effects from monetary policy in the long run, because the long run is time enough for all prices to adjust. The idea that the money supply does not affect real economic variables is known as **monetary neutrality**. In the long run, monetary policy does not affect real GDP or unemployment. The only predictable result of more money in the economy over the long run is inflation.

> **Monetary neutrality** is the idea that the money supply does not affect real economic variables.

From one perspective, our long-run results may seem strange; central banks can't do much in the long run to affect the real economy. On the other hand, it might also seem logical since we can increase the money supply by just printing more paper. But printing more paper doesn't affect our long run productivity or our ability to produce – these are determined by resources, technology, and institutions.

Given that money is neutral in the long run, you might question the value of short-run monetary policy. In fact, many of the substantive debates in macroeconomics focus on the relative importance of the short run versus the long run. Some economists believe it is best to focus on short-run effects, which are very real. After all, during recessions, people often lose their jobs and this can be very painful. By expanding the money supply, firms can get loans more cheaply and then hire more workers. From this view, central banks ought to take a very active role in the macroeconomy: increase the money supply in economic downturns and contract the money supply during economic expansions. This activist policy can then potentially smooth out the business cycle.

Other economists discount the short run expansionary effects of monetary policy and instead focus on the problems inflation brings. In Chapter 9, we covered the negative effects of inflation. These included price confusion, wealth redistribution, and future price level uncertainty. These byproducts of inflation can stifle economic growth.

Expectations Adjustments

In addition to these problems from inflation, as we covered earlier in this chapter, surprise inflation harms workers and other resource suppliers who have fixed prices in the short run. Therefore, to avoid this fate, workers have an incentive to expect a certain level of inflation and negotiate their contracts accordingly. For instance, many contracts have cost-of-living adjustment clauses that force their employer to increase wages by the same percentage as inflation. The key incentive for anticipating the correct rate of inflation is straightforward: people are harmed when inflation is a surprise. But when inflation is expected, the real effects on the economy are limited.

Let's look at this in the context of the aggregate demand and aggregate supply model. Figure 18.7 shows how monetary expansion affects aggregate demand and aggregate supply when it is expected. Expansionary monetary policy shifts aggregate demand from AD to AD$_1$. But if this is expected, short run aggregate supply shifts left from SRAS to SRAS$_1$. In Chapter 26, we discussed how short-run aggregate supply shifts back when workers and resource suppliers expect higher future prices, since they do not want their real prices to fall.

Figure 18.7
Completely Expected Monetary Policy

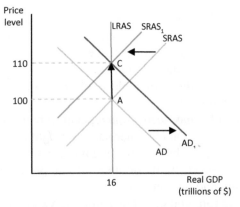

If expansionary monetary policy is expected, short run aggregate supply shifts along with the shift in aggregate demand and the economy moves directly from A to C. In this case, there are no real effects from the monetary policy, even in the short run.

If short run aggregate supply shifts along with the shift in aggregate demand, the economy goes immediately to equilibrium at point C. Therefore, monetary policy has no real effect on the economy – real GDP and unemployment do not change. Monetary policy only has real effects when some prices are sticky. But if inflation is expected, prices are not sticky— they adjust because people plan on the inflation. To the extent that all prices rise, the effect of monetary policy will be limited, even in the short run.

Aggregate Supply Shifts

We have seen that monetary policy affects the economy by shifting aggregate demand. Thus, if recession comes as a result of deficient aggregate demand, monetary policy has a chance to stabilize the economy and return it to higher levels of real GDP and lower unemployment. But not all downturns are a result of aggregate demand shifts. Declines in aggregate supply can also lead to recession. And when the cause of the downturn is due to supply shifts, monetary policy is much more limited in its ability to restore the economy to pre-recession conditions.

　　Let's consider a recession that is caused by declines in long-run aggregate supply and aggregate demand. For example, the Great Recession that began in 2007 seems to have included both types of shifts. In Chapter 26, we argued that the widespread problems in financial markets negatively affected key institutions in the macroeconomy. In addition, the financial regulations put in place then restricted the ability of banks to lend at levels prior 2008. The result was a shift back in long-run aggregate supply. In addition, as people's real wealth expected future income levels declined, aggregate demand shifted back as well.

　　Figure 18.8 shows how the decline in both aggregate demand and aggregate supply might affect the economy. Initially, the economy is in equilibrium at point A, with the supply and demand curves from 2007. Then, aggregate demand and aggregate supply shift back to their 2008 levels. When this happens, real GDP declines form $14.5 trillion to $14 trillion and the unemployment rate rises from 5% to 8%, levels similar to the actual experience during this period.

Figure 18.8
Aggregate Supply Induced Recession

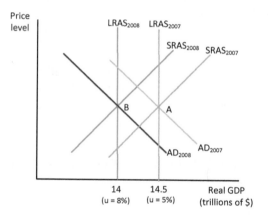

Initially, the economy is in equilibrium at point A. Then, the long-run and short-run aggregate supply curves shift back to LRAS2008 and SRAS2008. In addition, aggregate demand shifts back to AD2008. This combination of shifts takes the economy to new equilibrium at point B. At B, monetary policy is limited in its ability to move the economy back to its original level of real GDP because monetary policy affects the economy through aggregate demand.

　　The dilemma is that, at point B, monetary policy is limited in its ability to permanently move output back to its prior level. Even if monetary policy shifts aggregate demand back to AD_{2007}, this is not enough to eliminate the recession. Furthermore, as we have stressed throughout this chapter, the effects of monetary policy wear off in the long run.

　　Thus, in the wake of the Great Recession, the U.S. economy continued to struggle with slow growth and high unemployment, even with significant monetary policy interventions. The bottom line is that monetary policy does not allow us to avoid every economic downturn.

What is the Phillips Curve?

We have seen that monetary policy can stimulate the economy in the short run. Increasing the money supply increases aggregate demand and this lead can lead to higher real GDP, lower unemployment, and a higher price level (inflation). The relationship between inflation and unemployment is of particular interest to economists and non-economists alike - it is at the heart of the debate regarding the power of monetary policy to affect the economy. In this section, we examine this relationship by looking at the *Phillips curve*.

The Traditional Short-run Phillips Curve

In 1958, British economist A.W. Phillips noted an inverse relationship between wage inflation and unemployment rates in the United Kingdom. Soon after, American economists Paul Samuelson and Robert Solow extended the analysis to inflation and unemployment rates in the United States. This inverse relationship between inflation and unemployment rates became known as the **Phillips curve**. Before looking at the data behind the Phillips curve, we consider the theory behind the Phillips curve in the context of the aggregate demand and supply model.

> The **Phillips curve** indicates a short run inverse relationship between inflation and unemployment rates.

Panel (a) of Figure 18.9 shows how expansionary monetary policy affects the economy in the short run. Initially, with aggregate demand at AD and the price level at 100, the economy is in long run equilibrium at point A with real GDP at 16 and the unemployment rate equal to 5%. For this example, we assume that the natural rate of unemployment is exactly 5%.

Then, expansionary monetary policy shifts aggregate demand to AD_1, and this shift leads to a new short-run equilibrium at point b. Let's focus on the changes to prices and the unemployment rate. The monetary expansion leads to 5% inflation, as the price level rises to 105. The unemployment rate drops to 3%, as real GDP expands from 16 to 16.5. The end result includes both inflation and lower unemployment.

Figure 18.9
Aggregate Demand, Aggregate Supply and the Phillips Curve

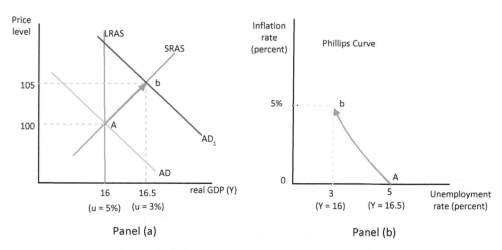

Panel (a)   Panel (b)

(a) This graph shows the effect of unexpected monetary expansion in the short run. Initially, the economy is in equilibrium at point A, with price level 100, real GDP of 16, and an unemployment rate of 5%. Aggregate demand shifts form AD to AD_1, which moves the economy to equilibrium at point b. The move to b is brought about by inflation of 5% (the price level rises from 100 to 105), but a lower unemployment rate of just 3%. (b) This graph shows the two equilibrium points in a new graph that plots inflation and unemployment rates. This graph, known as a Phillips curve, clarifies that higher inflation can lead to lower levels of unemployment in the short run.

This is the theory behind the Phillips curve relationship: inflation stimulates the economy and this reduces the unemployment rate. Alternatively, lower inflation is associated with higher unemployment rates. This inverse relationship between inflation and unemployment is captured in panel (b) of Figure 18.9, which graphs a Phillips Curve. Initially, at point A, the inflation rate is zero and the unemployment rate is 5 percent. But when inflation rises to 5%, the unemployment rate drops to 3%.

This inverse relationship between inflation and unemployment rates is consistent with Phillips observations and also what economists Samuelson and Solow saw when they plotted historical data. Figure 18.10 plots U.S. inflation and unemployment rates from 1948 to 1969, which includes the time period just before and just after the work of Samuelson and Solow.

It is not hard to visualize a Phillips curve relationship in the data – years with high inflation rates were also years with low unemployment rates, while years with low inflation rates are also years with high unemployment rates.

Figure 18.10
U.S. Inflation and Unemployment Rates, 1948-1969

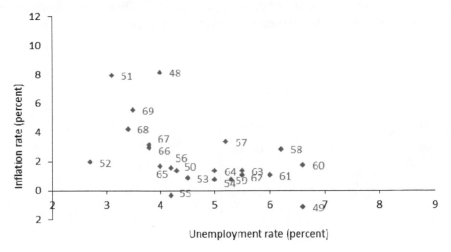

Data from 1948 to 1969 was very consistent with standard Phillips curve predictions – lower unemployment rates were consistently correlated with higher inflation rates.

The Phillips curve implies a powerful role for monetary policy. It implies that a central bank can choose higher and lower unemployment rates, simply by adjusting the rate of inflation in an economy. If this is realistic, then a central bank can always steer an economy out of recession, simply through creating inflation.

But one of the primary lessons of this chapter is that monetary policy does not always have real effects on the economy. In this section, we consider the long-run, when the real effects of monetary policy wear off. After that, we look at how expectations also mitigate the effects of monetary policy.

The Long-run Phillips Curve

When all prices adjust, there are no real effects from monetary policy. That is, there are no effects on real GDP or unemployment. Therefore, the long-run Phillips curve looks different from the standard, short-run Phillips curve. Figure 18.11 shows both short-run and long-run Phillips curves. Initially, at point A, there is no inflation in the economy and the unemployment rate is 5%. Then, monetary expansion increases inflation to 5% and the unemployment rate falls to 3% in the short run. This short-run equilibrium is indicated as point b. But when prices adjust, in the long run, the unemployment rate returns to five percent. When this happens, the economy moves to point C. Inflation is the only result of monetary expansion in the long run.

Figure 18.11
The Long-run Phillips Curve

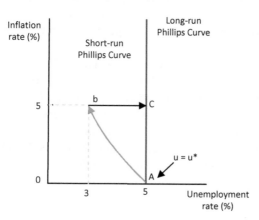

In the short run, inflation can lead to lower unemployment, moving the economy from point A to point b. But in the long run, the effects of monetary policy wear off and the unemployment rate returns to 5% at point C. Under normal economic conditions, without inflationary surprises, the economy naturally gravitates back to the natural rate of unemployment. Here, the natural rate is 5%. Therefore, in the long run, the economy comes back to 5% unemployment, no matter what the inflation rate. This implies a vertical Phillips curve in the long run.

In Figure 18.11, the unemployment rate is equal to the natural rate (5%) before inflation, and in the long run it returns to the natural rate. Thus, under normal economic conditions, including the situation in which there is no surprise inflation, we expect the unemployment rate to equal the natural rate. Monetary policy can push the unemployment rate down, but only in the short run.

But in this chapter we have also learned that the effects of inflation are dampened or eliminated when the inflation is fully expected. We saw this earlier in the context of our aggregate demand and aggregate supply model. Now, we look closer at inflation expectations and how they affect the Phillips curve relationship.

Expectations and the Phillips Curve

We have seen that expected inflation has no real effects on the macroeconomy, even in the short run. This happens because, when inflation is expected, all prices adjust. To think about this further, we consider alternative theories of how people form expectations. This may seem like a topic for microeconomics, or perhaps even psychology. But it is particularly relevant to monetary policy because the effects of expected inflation are completely different from the effects of unexpected inflation.

Adaptive Expectations

However, in the late 1960s, economists Milton Friedman and Edmund Phelps hypothesized that people would adapt their inflation expectations to something consistent with prior experience. For example, if actual inflation is consistently 2% year after year, people don't expect zero inflation, they expect 2%. The contributions of Friedman and Phelps came to be known as *adaptive expectations*. **Adaptive expectations** is the theory that people's expectations of future inflation are based on their most recent experience. If inflation is 5% in 2013, adaptive expectations theory implies that people expect 5% in 2014.

Adaptive expectations is the theory that people's expectations for the future are based on their recent experience.

Consider the hypothetical inflation pattern presented in Table 18.1. The second column shows actual inflation over the course of six years. Inflation starts at zero, but then goes up to 2% for two years, then increases to 4% for two years, and then falls to 2% in the last year. If expectations are adaptive, actual inflation in the current period becomes expected inflation for the future. For example, 2% actual inflation in 2014 means people will expect 2% inflation in the future. So when actual inflation is 2% in 2015, this is not a surprise. Adaptive expectations predicts that people do not always underestimate inflation.

Table 18.1:
Adaptive Expectations

Year	Actual Inflation	Expected Inflation	Error
2013	0	0	0
2014	2	0	-2
2015	2	2	0
2016	4	2	-2
2017	4	4	0
2018	2	4	+2

When the inflation rate *accelerates*, people do underestimate inflation. For example, since people experience 2% inflation in 2015, they also expect this level for 2016, but in our example, inflation increases to 4% in 2016. Note that it is also possible to overestimate inflation under adaptive expectations. This happens when inflation rates fall. For example, in 2018, people might anticipate 4% inflation since they experienced that level in 2017. But if instead, inflation is 2%, they will have overestimated the true value.

The idea behind adaptive expectations is not overly complex, but it revolutionized the way economists thought about monetary policy. If expectations adapt, then monetary policy may not have real effects, even in the short run. Expansionary monetary policy can stimulate the economy and reduce unemployment – but only if it is unexpected.

This was the insight of Friedman and Phelps. Their basic reasoning was that people are not quite as simple-minded as the basic Phillips curve implies. Given that surprise inflation harms people, they have an incentive to anticipate inflation and, at the very least, learn from past experience. On the other hand, the data from the 1960s (recall Figure 18.10) was certainly consistent with the traditional Phillips curve interpretation. But Friedman and Phelps challenge the accepted wisdom in 1968 and predicted that the Phillips curve relationship would not last. In particular, they predicted that high inflation could not always deliver low unemployment.

And they were right. Figure 18.12 shows U.S. unemployment and inflation rates for the period 1948 to 1979, with the 1970s data colored in orange. Clearly, the 1970s were a difficult decade for the macroeconomy. The prior Phillips curve relationship fell apart. Inflation was high, but so was unemployment. These macroeconomic conditions have come to be known as **stagflation**, which is the combination of high unemployment rates and high inflation. The stagflation of the 1970s baffled many economists who had come to believe in the Phillips curve

Stagflation is the combination of high unemployment rates and high inflation.

Figure 18.12
U.S. Inflation and Unemployment Rates, 1948-1979

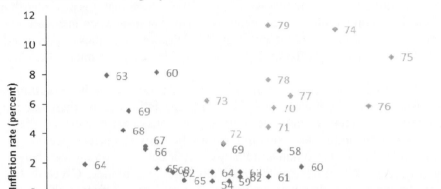

The 1970s showed that it is possible to have both high inflation and high unemployment. This decade proved there is no long run exploitable Phillips curve.

Rational Expectations

Expectations theory evolved yet again in the 1970s and 1980s, in part because of disenchantment with some particular implications of adaptive expectations. For example, according to adaptive expectations, market participants consistently underestimate inflation when it is accelerating and overestimate inflation when it is decelerating. Expectations are seemingly always a step behind. And these errors are predictable.

> **Rational expectations** is the theory that people form expectations based on all available information.

Rational expectations is the theory that people form expectations based on all available information. If people form expectations rationally, they use more than just today's current level of inflation to predict next year's. Rational expectations are different from adaptive expectations in that they are forward-looking, while adaptive expectations only consider past experience.

For example, imagine that inflation is trending upward. Perhaps the actual inflation rate for three periods is 0%, then 2%, and then 4%. Expectations formed rationally recognize the trend and, looking to the future, predict 6%. This is different from adaptive expectations, which would instead imply an expectation of 4% in the fourth period, since that is consistent with the most recent experience.

Rational expectations do not imply that people always predict inflation correctly. Nobody knows exactly what inflation will be next year. Prediction errors are inevitable. But people are unlikely to under-predict consistently, even when inflation is accelerating. Rational expectations theory identifies prediction errors as random, like the flip of a coin – sometimes positive, and sometimes negative.

Economics in the Media
(Expectations)

The Invention of Lying

Imagine a world where nobody lied. Ever. In the movie *The Invention of Lying*, this is the world that Ricky Gervais lives in. Then one day, Gervais accidentally lies. He misstates his bank account balance. After the bank adjusts his balance (upward!), Gervais realizes that nobody expects him to lie, and so they believe everything he says, no matter how outlandish. No matter how many lies Gervais tells, and no matter how unbelievable his statements, nobody ever changes their expectations regarding the truth of his statements – they always believe him. Eventually, he claims to be God. People are stunned. But they completely believe him.

The insanity and irrationality of the behavior of people in this movie illustrates exactly how silly it is to continually believe lies coming from the same source. The reason the movie is so funny is because nobody in the real world would ever be as gullible or stupid as the people in this movie. In the real world, people would come to expect lies from Gervais. In economics lingo: expectations adjust.

Similarly, in the real world, people come to anticipate inflation when they experience inflation period after period. It makes no sense to expect zero inflation if actual inflation has not been zero for quite some time. In the real world, expectations adjust.

A Modern View of the Phillips Curve

The short-run Phillips curve is built on the implicit assumption that inflation expectations never adjust. But economists today recognize that since inflation harms people in the economy, there is an incentive to predict inflation in the future. Therefore, not all inflation is surprise inflation. But when inflation is not a surprise, it does not affect the unemployment rate. So we need to reconsider how different expectations affect the Phillips curve relationship.

Consider a hypothetical economy in which policy makers have never used inflation to try to stimulate the economy. Let's say inflation is zero percent and market participants expect zero percent inflation going forward. Figure 18.13 shows this initial situation as point A. Now, at point A, if the central bank undertakes policy that raises inflation to 5%, the unemployment rate drops to 3% in the short run. This increase in inflation moves the economy up along the short-run Phillips curve that is labeled $SRPC_0$, to indicate that expected inflation is zero. The 5% inflation moves the economy to point b on $SRPC_0$.

Figure 18.13
The Phillips with Adjusting Expectations

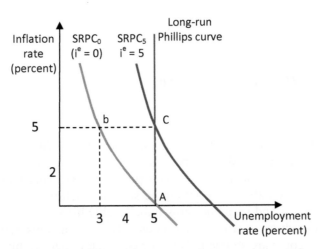

Initially, at point A, inflation is zero and people expect zero inflation. This means any positive inflation reduces the unemployment rate. If inflation is 5%, the unemployment rate falls to 3% , indicated by movement to point b.

But, if actual inflation is 5% and expected inflation is also 5%, the unemployment rate moves to the natural rate at point C.

There is a different short-run Phillips curve for each level of inflation expectations.

Now consider what happens if people come to expect 5% inflation. If workers and employers expect 5% inflation, they imbed this inflation into all long-term contracts. Therefore, when the 5% inflation arrives it does not stimulate the economy or reduce unemployment. The economy moves to point C, which is on $SRPC_5$, and this indicates that the expected rate of inflation is now 5%. When actual and expected inflation are both 5%, inflation does not reduce the unemployment rate. In summary, there may be a downward-sloping Phillips curve relationship between inflation and unemployment, but this relationship only holds in the short run. In the long run, when expectations adjust, the unemployment rate cannot be reduced by additional inflation.

Figure 18.14 shows unemployment and inflation data from 1948 through 2011. In looking at this complete data set, it is clear that there is no long-run stable relationship between inflation and unemployment. Economists today believe there are many factors that influence the unemployment rate in the economy, and the inflation rate is just one factor.

Figure 18.14
U.S. Inflation and Unemployment Rates, 1948-2011

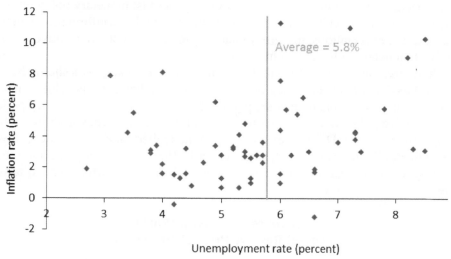

Data over the long-run presents a picture of inflation and unemployment rates that looks random. Clearly, the unemployment rate is influenced by factors other than inflation rates.

Implications for Monetary Policy

We can now use what we've learned about expectations theory and the Phillips curve to evaluate monetary policy recommendations. **Active monetary policy** is the strategic use of monetary policy to counteract macroeconomic expansions and contractions. In the 1960s, before expectations theory, monetary policy prescriptions were strictly activist: inflate during economic downturns and reduce inflation when the economy is booming. This policy assumed that the Phillips curve relationship between inflation and unemployment would hold up in the long run.

> **Active monetary policy** is the strategic use of monetary policy to counteract macroeconomic expansions and contractions

Modern expectations theory prescribes greater caution. If people anticipate the strategies of the central bank, the power of the monetary policy erodes. If expectations adjust, the optimal monetary policy is transparency and stability. This conclusion holds if expectations are formed either adaptively or rationally. Let's consider each of these in turn.

Consider a scenario in which policy-makers use inflation to decrease the unemployment rate. Say the unemployment rate is clearly above the natural rate, and real GDP is not growing. If expectations are adaptive, inflation will reduce the unemployment rate in the short run. Eventually, expectations adjust and then the central bank has to increase inflation again just to stay ahead of the adjusting expectations. For monetary policy to succeed in keeping the unemployment rate low, inflation has to accelerate and stay a step ahead of expectations. Essentially, this leads to more and more inflation. Worse yet, if the central bank tries to reduce inflation levels, expected inflation will exceed actual inflation, which will lead to increases in unemployment rates in the short run. Thus, if expectations are adaptive, activist monetary policy leads only to temporary short run gains in employment. In the long run it leads to high inflation or unemployment or both, as it did in the 1970s.

If instead, expectations are formed rationally, activist monetary policy may yield no gains whatsoever. Since market participants use all available information when forming inflation expectations, the central bank is unlikely to get any positive results from activist monetary policy, even in the short run.

Therefore, many economists feel that monetary policy surprises should be minimized. **Passive monetary policy** occurs when central banks purposefully choose to do no more than stabilize the money supply and price levels through monetary policy. In particular, passive policy does not seek to use inflation to affect real variables, including unemployment and real GDP, in the economy. In the United States, the Federal Reserve has moved markedly in this direction since the early 1980s. Ben Bernanke and other Federal Reserve Board chairmen have consistently taken actions which lead to fewer surprises in monetary policy.

> **Passive monetary policy** occurs when central banks purposefully choose to only stabilize money and price levels through monetary policy.

Economics in the Real World:
Federal Reserve Press Conferences

On April 27, 2011, Ben Bernanke held the first press conference by a Fed Chairman specifically to talk about the actions of the Fed's policy-making committee. This was an unprecedented leap toward transparency. In the past, the Fed consistently released carefully-worded official statements that often used cryptic language to describe the Fed's outlook for the future.

In the spring of 2011 the economy was struggling to truly emerge from the 2008 recession; unemployment was still over 9%. Yet, in the midst of this, the Fed still decided to lay all their cards on the table. Many saw this as risky. Jacob Goldstein, writing for NPR's *Planet Money*, explained why it mattered:

> Because everything the head of the Federal Reserve says is a big deal. One off-hand comment can send global markets soaring or plunging. And because Fed chairmen, as a general rule, don't give press conferences. They release official statements that are very, very carefully worded. And they appear before Congress. Since the financial crisis, though, the Fed has come under increased scrutiny. The carefully worded statements and congressional appearances weren't carrying the day. So the leaders of the Fed have decided to send the chairman out for press conferences every few months ("to further enhance the clarity and timeliness of the Federal Reserve's monetary policy communication," in Fedspeak). Source: http://www.npr.org/blogs/money/2011/04/27/135711990/why-bernankes-press-conference-matters

Bernanke's moves toward greater Fed openness reflect his belief that central bankers ought to be transparent. The move toward transparency reflects the modern view that expectations matter in macroeconomics – whether they be adaptive or rational.

Practice What You Know
Monetary Policy

Expectations

Recently, unemploymnent rates in Europe have been relatively high and infaltion has been low. Consider the European an economy in which all market participants expect 2% inflation and the unemploment rate is 9%. Now, assume the European Central Bank (ECB) begins increasing the money supply enough to lead to 4% inflation for a few years.

Question: If expectations are zero-inflation, what happens to the unemployment rate in the short run?

Answer: The unemployment rate falls below 9% since the new inflation is surprise infaltion and it can therefore stimulate the economy.

Question: If expectations are formed adaptively, what happens to the unemployment rate in both the short run and the long run?

Answer: The unemployemnt rate falls below 9% in the short run, since the new inflation is different from past experience. In the long run, expectations adapt to the 4% inflation and, all else equal, the unemployment rate returns to 9%.

Question: If expectations are formed rationally, what happens to the unemployment rate in the short run?

Answer: If expectaions are formed rationally, people understand the incentives of the central bank and therefore may anticipate the expansionary monetary policy. In this case, the unemployment rate does not fall.

Economics for Life

How to protect yourself from Inflation

In this chapter we have talked about how inflation harms some people. We have also talked about how inflation doesn't harm people if they know it is coming - if it expected.

If you are worried about inflation harming you, you can protect yourself from inflation. Now, in the recent history in the United States, inflation has been low and steady. When this is the case, it doesn't really harm anybody because it is easy to predict. But if you live in a country like Argentina where inflation has often been a problem, or perhaps you are worried about future inflation in the United States, then these tips are for you.

The two types of people most often harmed by inflation are workers with fixed wages and lenders with fixed interest rates. Let's look at how to avoid inflation trouble in both of these instances.

First off, let's say you are worker who is worried about inflation. One way to protect yourself is to avoid committing to long-term wage deals. If you must sign a contract, keep it short in duration. Better yet, include a clause in your contract that stipulates cost of living adjustments (COLAs) that are tied to a price index like the CPI. This way you are hedged against future inflation in your wages.

Second, perhaps you are more worried about inflation's effect on your savings or retirement funds. This is where you are a lender and thus susceptible to fixed interest rates. One way to avoid negative returns is to purchase securities or assets that tend to rise in value along with inflation. Stock prices generally go up with inflation, so you may want to allot more of your retirement funds into stocks, rather than bonds. Gold is another asset that tends to appreciate in inflationary times because its value is tied to something real.

But, stocks are too risky and the long-term returns on gold are historically very low. Thus, you might consider buying Treasury Inflation Protected Securities (TIPS). These are low risk U.S. Treasury bonds that are actually indexed to inflation rates. Therefore, if inflation goes up, you get a higher rate of return. These bonds guarantee a particular real rate of return, no matter what the rate of inflation.

Conclusion

We started this chapter with the misconception that central banks can always steer economies out of recession. If this were true, the U.S. economy certainly would not have experienced the sustained downturn that began at the end of 2007. So what can a central bank do? In the short run, if monetary policy is a surprise, central banks can actually stimulate the economy and perhaps lessen the effects of recession. But these results are mitigated when people come to anticipate monetary policy actions.

In the next two chapters we will consider the second major area of macroeconomic policy: fiscal policy. In Chapter 17, we set the groundwork by discussing federal budgeting. We'll cover topics such as deficits, debts, taxes, and government spending. In Chapter 19 we will tackle fiscal policy.

BIG QUESTIONS

(1) What is the effect of monetary policy in the short run?

In the short run, monetary can both speed up and slow down the economy. Some prices are sticky in the short run. When some prices fail to adjust, changes in the money supply are essentially a change in real financial resources. If the monetary policy is expansionary, this can stimulate the economy, increasing real GDP and reducing the unemployment rate. If the monetary policy is contractionary, this can slow the economy which may help to reduce inflation.

(2) Why doesn't monetary policy always work?

Monetary policy fails to produce real effects under three different circumstances. First, monetary policy has no real effect in the long run, since all prices can adjust. Second, if monetary policy is fully anticipated, then again, prices adjust. Finally, if the economy is experiencing shifts in aggregate supply, monetary policy may be unable to restore normal growth, since it works primarily through aggregate demand.

(3) What is the Phillips curve?

The Phillips curve is a theoretical inverse relationship between inflation and unemployment rates. The modern consensus is that the Phillips curve is a short-run phenomena but that it cannot be exploited in the long run.

Concepts You Should Know

Active monetary policy	Monetary neutrality
Adaptive expectations	Passive monetary policy
Contractionary monetary policy	Phillips curve
Expansionary monetary policy	Rational expectations
	Stagflation

Questions for Review

1. Explain why it is possible to change real economic factors in the short run simply by printing and distributing more money.

2. Many people focus on the effect of monetary policy on interest rates in the economy.

    a. Use the loanable funds market to explain how contractionary monetary policy affects interest rates in the short run.

    b. Now explain how these changes in the loanable funds market affect aggregate demand and supply.

3. During the economic slowdown that began at the end of 2007, the Federal Reserve used monetary policy to reduce interest rates in the economy. Use what we learned in this chapter to give a possible explanation as to why the monetary policy failed to restore the economy to long-run equilibrium.

4. Explain why stable 5% inflation can be preferred to inflation that averages 4% but varies between 1% and 7% regularly.

5. Who is harmed when inflation is less than anticipated? In what way are they harmed? Who is harmed when inflation is greater than anticipated? In what way are they harmed?

6. Explain the difference between active and passive monetary policy.

Problems

1. Use the aggregate supply-aggregate demand model to illustrate the principle relationship behind the short run Phillips curve: a little inflation can accompany economic expansion.

2. Suppose the economy is in long-run equilibrium, with real GDP = $16 trillion and the unemployment rate at 5%. Now, assume the central bank *decreases* the money supply by 6%.

   a. Illustrate the short-run effects on the macroeconomy using the aggregate supply-aggregate demand model. Be sure to indicate the direction of change in real GDP, the price level and the unemployment rate.

   b. Illustrate the long-run effects on the macroeconomy using the aggregate supply-aggregate demand model. Again, be sure to indicate the direction of change in real GDP, the price level and the unemployment rate.

   c. Now assume this monetary expansion was completely expected. Illustrate both short-run and long-run effects on the macroeconomy using the aggregate supply-aggregate demand model. Be sure to indicate the direction of change in real GDP, the price level and the unemployment rate.

3. Suppose the economy is in long-run equilibrium, with real GDP = $16 trillion and the unemployment rate at 5%. Now, assume the central bank *increases* the money supply by 6%.

   a. Illustrate the short run effects on the macroeconomy using the aggregate supply-aggregate demand model. Be sure to indicate the direction of change in real GDP, the price level and the unemployment rate.

   b. Illustrate the long run effects on the macroeconomy using the aggregate supply-aggregate demand model. Again, be sure to indicate the direction of change in real GDP, the price level and the unemployment rate.

   c. Now assume this monetary expansion was completely expected. Illustrate both short run and long run effects on the macroeconomy using the aggregate supply-aggregate demand model. Be sure to indicate the direction of change in real GDP, the price level and the unemployment rate.

Solved problems

*1. In the past, some people believed that the Federal Reserve routinely expanded the money supply during presidential election years in order to stimulate the economy and help the incumbent president. For this question, assume the Fed increases inflation by 3% in every election year.

  a. Describe the effect on the economy during election years if market participants expect zero inflation.

      If people expect zero inflation, any positive inflation will stimulate the economy and lower the unemployment rate.

  b. Describe the effect on the economy during election years if expectations are formed adaptively.

      If people form their inflation expectations adaptively, they will not anticipate inflation in an election year because it is a break from their recent experience. Therefore, inflation in election years will consistently lower the rate of unemployment.

  c. Describe the effect on the economy during election years if expectations are formed rationally.

      If expectations are formed rationally, then people consider the incentives of policy-makers during election years. Therefore, they will anticipate higher inflation in those years and the inflation will have no effect on the unemployment rate.

2. In each of the scenarios listed below, estimate the unemployment rate in comparison to the natural rate (u).

  a. Inflation is steady at 2% for two years, but then increases to 5% for a year.

      The increase in inflation is likely a surprise, which means stimulates the economy and reduce the unemployment rate to a level below the natural rate.

  b. Inflation is steady at 10% for two years, but then decreases to 5% for a year.

      The decrease in inflation is likely a surprise, which means slows the economy and increases the unemployment rate to a level above the natural rate.

  c. Inflation is steady at 8% for several years.

Here, there are no inflationary surprises and so the inflation does not influence the unemployment rate. Therefore, all else equal, we should expect the unemployment rate to be near the natural rate.

d. Inflation is steady at 2% for three years and then the Fed announces that inflation will be 3% one year later.

Even though the inflation rate increases, it is not a surprise, so all prices have time to adjust. Therefore, all else equal, we should expect the unemployment rate to be near the natural rate.

Chapter 19 – International Trade

Economic Misconception: International trade is a competition.

When we read or hear about international trade from our national leaders or from the news media, the conversation is often framed in terms of "winners" and "losers." The assumption is that, if one nation gains through trade, there must be some compensating loss on the other side. Many interactions or relationships in life are actually competitions and so it is easy to natural to default to this mindset. But not all relationships are this way. In this chapter, we examine international trade relationships and critically question who loses in these relationships.

Over the past few decades, global trade has risen dramatically. We begin this chapter with a look at global trade data to get a real sense of the extent of international trade. We then move to the theoretical discussion of how international trade affects an economy. Finally, we examine trade barriers and the reasons for their existence.

The Big Questions:

1. Is globalization for real?
2. Does international trade help the economy?
3. Why do we see trade barriers?

Is globalization for real?

International trade is exploding right before our eyes. Since the middle of the last century, nations the world over all over have increased imports and exports. What this means for you and me is that we now buy fresh Peruvian strawberries (in February!), roses from Kenya, cars made in Mexico (like the Ford Fusion), and electronics produced in South Korea.

Consider a single popular item: the iPhone. Inside the iPhone are parts from Germany, Japan, Korea and the United States. The phone is famously "designed by Apple in California," but assembled in China. This one (admittedly complex and technologically advanced) item relies on thousands of miles of global shipping before anyone ever receives a call on it.

Part of the modern trade explosion is because of a decline in shipping costs, part is due to a reduction in trade barriers, and part is due to increased specialization in world economies. The bottom line is that total world exports of goods and services are about one fourth the size of world GDP. Let's look at the data more closely.

Trends in world trade

In this section, we examine the facts of world trade. We present real data that confirms the general sense that the world economy is becoming more integrated all the time. The various economies of the world are more interdependent today than ever before.

We start with a look at total world exports over time. Figure 19.1 shows total world trade in merchandise (goods) since 1970. Panel A shows this trade in billions of 2005 U.S. dollars. Since 1970, world trade in goods has grown from $1.3 trillion to over $13 trillion. That's a ten-fold increase in just 40 years. Panel B shows merchandise trade as a portion of GDP. This too has expanded dramatically, more than doubling over the course of 40 years. The implication is that, even though global GDP is rising, the portion of GDP due to trade has more than doubled. These two graphs paint a picture of globalization for us.

Figure 19.1:
World merchandise trade

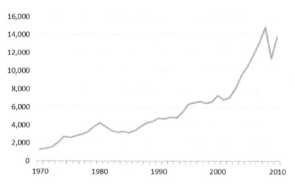
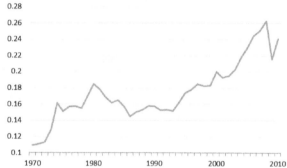

Panel A: Total world merchandise exports in 2005 U.S. dollars.

In forty years, world trade increased ten-fold in real terms, from $1.3 trillion in 1970 to over $13 trillion in 2010.

Panel B: Total world merchandise as a fraction of world GDP.

Even as a fraction of World GDP, trade has grown significantly. It more than doubled from 11% in 1970 to over 24% by 2010.

Source: WTO; World Bank.

Trends in U.S. trade

The United States is the world's biggest economy, with a huge amount of trade taking place between the individual states that make up the US. Residents of Michigan buy oranges from Florida, and Floridians buy cars from Michigan. Still, even with the ability to produce and trade so much within U.S. borders, international trade rose drastically in recent years. Figure 19.2 shows U.S. imports and exports (as a portion of GDP) from 1960 to 2010.

As you look at the data presented in Figure 19.2, note three clear features. First, both imports and exports have increased significantly over the course of fifty years. In the fifty years from 1960 to 2010, U.S. exports have grown from less than five percent to over twelve percent of GDP. Over the same period, imports have risen from less than five percent to over sixteen percent of GDP. Note also that these changes occurred even as GDP grew by over three percent a year. This is another clear glimpse at the modern trend toward globalization – the world's largest economy is becoming ever more intertwined with those of other nations.

Figure 19.2:
U.S. exports and imports (percent of GDP)

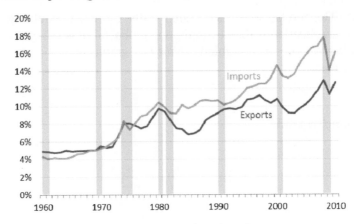

Panel A: Total goods and services

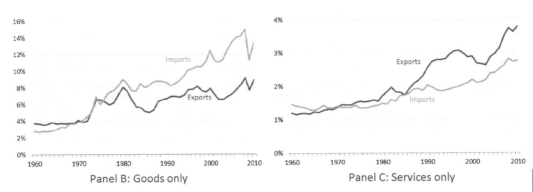

Panel B: Goods only   Panel C: Services only

Source: BEA, *U.S. International Transactions.*

> **Trade surplus** – When exports exceed imports.

> **Trade balance** – The difference between total exports and total imports.

> **Trade deficit** – When imports exceed exports.

Second, note that, since 1975, U.S. imports have exceeded U.S. exports. In Chapter 7, we defined net exports as total exports of goods and services minus total imports of goods and services. This is also called a nation's **trade balance**. If a nation exports more than they import, it has a positive trade balance, and this is called a **trade surplus**. On the other hand, if a nation imports more than they export, the trade balance is negative, and this is called a **trade deficit**. The U.S. has had a trade deficit since 1975. In 2010 alone, the U.S. exported $1.83 trillion in goods and services but imported $2.83 trillion, leading to a trade deficit of $1 trillion, no small sum. This is not the place for us to cover the causes of this significant trade deficit; that topic comes in Chapter 20.

The bottom two panels of Figure 19.2 reveal a little known fact about U.S. trade. While the merchandise (goods) trade deficit of the U.S. is large and growing, the U.S. actually has a service trade surplus. Popular service exports of the United States include financial, travel, and education services. To put a face on service exports, think about students in your classes that are not U.S. citizens (perhaps this is you!). In 2010, the U.S. exported over $21 billion worth of education services.

Finally, notice how the business cycle affects international trade. During each recessionary period (these are shaded above), imports drop. In addition, while exports often drop in recessions, the trade deficit tends to shrink during downturns. Part of this is due to the way imports and exports are calculated (more on this in Chapter 20), but this also shows us an important relationship between trade and economic activity: trade expands during economic expansions and contracts during recessions.

Major trading partners of the United States

In 2011, the United States imported goods and services from 238 nations. Sixty percent of these came from just seven nations. Figure 19.4 shows the imports from and exports to these top seven trading partners of the U.S. Total imports from China alone are now are now $400 billion. But this is a new phenomenon: Twelve years ago imports from China were just $105 billion (adjusted for inflation). Popular Chinese imports include electronics and toys. In fact, we challenge you to visit the toy department on a local store and find an item NOT made in China.

Is there anything in this picture NOT produced in China?

Traditionally, Canada and Mexico have been the chief trading partners of the U.S. Of course, this is not random but due to their locations. Transportation costs have always been important trade determinants, although this is decreasing. From Canada we get motor vehicles, oil, natural gas and many other goods and services. From Mexico, we get coffee, computers, household appliances, and gold.

Figure 19.4:
Major trading partners of United States in 2011, billions of dollars

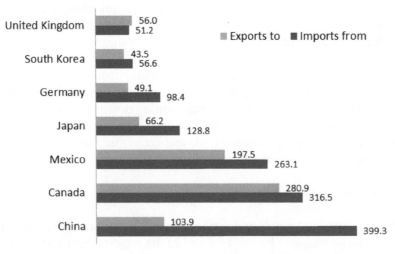

Source: BEA.

Canada and Mexico are the two nations that buy the most U.S. exports. To Canada, we export cars, car parts, computers, and agricultural products. To Mexico, we export cars, car parts, computers and meat among many other items. As we saw above, the U.S. has a service export surplus. Financial and travel services are major U.S. exports to all of our major trading partners.

Practice What You Know!
International Trade

The North American Free Trade Agreement (NAFTA)

In December 1992, the governments Canada, Mexico, and the United States signed the North American Free Trade Agreement (NAFTA). NAFTA, which went into effect on January 1, 1994, significantly freed up trade between the three nations. The Table below shows U.S. data on imports from and exports to both Canada and Mexico for two different years: 1993 and 2011.

United States trade, in millions of 2010 dollars

	Canada		Mexico	
	Exports to	Imports from	Exports to	Imports from
1993	182,693	180,469	79,967	76,348
2010	350,074	331,511	200,849	260,079

Source: BEA (http://www.bea.gov/iTable/index_ita.cfm).

A. How much have exports to Canada grown? To Mexico?

Answer:

Exports to Canada increased by $167.4 billion. Exports to Mexico increased by $120.9 billion.

A. How much have imports grown from Canada? From Mexico?

Answer:

Imports from Canada increased by $151 billion and imports from Mexico increased by $183.8 billion.

C. Use the data to compute the trade balance between the U.S. and the other two nations both before and after NAFTA.

Before NAFTA, the trade balance with Canada was a surplus of $2.224 billion, after NAFTA, it is a surplus of $18.563 billion.

Before NAFTA, the trade balance with Mexico was a surplus of $3.619 billion, after NAFTA, it is a deficit of $59.23 billion.

Does international trade help the economy?

In this section we explain how comparative advantage and specialization allow for gains from trade among nations. To keep the analysis simple we will assume that our two trading partners – the United States and Mexico – only produce two items, clothes and food. This will allow us to demonstrate that trade creates value in the absence of any restrictions.

Gains from Trade

The idea that trade creates value stems from the law of comparative advantage (which we learned about in Chapter 2). Gains arise when a nation specializes in production and exchanges its output with a trading partner. For this to work, each nation must produce goods for which they are a low opportunity cost producer and then trade the goods that they have produced in exchange for goods for which they are a high opportunity cost producer. In other words, each nation should produce what they are good at and trade it to other nations who are good at something else. When this happens, it leads to lower costs of production and maximizes the combined output of both countries.

When thinking about trade across countries, different nations have certain advantages. For instance, the United States has a more skilled workforce and much more land suitable for farming than Mexico. Mexico has a less skilled workforce and tends to produce products that do not rely as much on capital-intensive production processes. This means that Mexico has a comparative advantage in producing labor-intensive goods such as clothing while the United States has a comparative advantage in producing capital-intensive foods such as food.

In Figure 19.4 we see the production possibilities curve of each country when it does not specialize and trade. In panel (a) Mexico can produce at any point along its PPF. This means that it could produce 900M articles of clothing if it does not make any food, or 300M units of food, if it does not make any clothing. Neither of these combinations is especially desirable since it would mean that Mexico would have to do without either clothing or food. As a result, Mexico will choose to operate somewhere in between. In panel (a) we show Mexico operating along its production possibilities curve at 450M articles of clothing and 150 units of food. In panel (b) the United States could produce 400M articles of clothing if it does not make any food, or 800M units of food, if it does not make any clothing. Like Mexico, the United States will choose will choose to operate somewhere in between. In panel (b) we show the United States operating along its production possibilities curve at 300M articles of clothing and 200M units of food.

Figure 19.4: The Production Possibilities Frontier for Mexico and the United States without Specialization and Trade

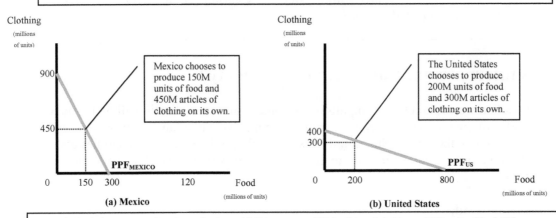

(a) Mexico

(b) United States

In panel (a) Mexico operates along its production possibilities curve at 450M articles of clothing and 150 units of food. This means that each unit of food incurs an opportunity cost of 3 articles of clothing, a ratio of 1:3. In panel (b) the United States operates along its production possibilities curve at 300M articles of clothing and 200M units of food. This means that each unit of food incurs an opportunity cost of 1/2 an article of clothing, a ratio of 2:1.

In this example Mexico and the United States do not specialize and trade does not exist. To see whether gains from trade are able to make both countries better off we must first examine the opportunity cost each countries faces when making these two goods. In Mexico the production of 150M units of food requires that 450M units of clothing be given up. This means that each unit of food incurs an opportunity cost of 3 articles of clothing, a ratio of 1:3. In the United States the production of 200M units of food requires that 100M units of clothing be given up. This means that each unit of food incurs an opportunity cost of 1/2 an article of clothing, a ratio of 2:1. Table 31.1 shows the initial production choices and the opportunity costs for both nations.

Table 19.1:
Output and opportunity costs for Mexico and the United States

	Output		Opportunity Cost	
	Food	Clothing	Food	Clothing
Mexico	300	900	3 C	1/3 F
United States	800	400	1/2 C	2 F

As long the opportunity cost of the production of the two goods differs between the two countries, as it does here, trade has the potential to benefit both countries. The key to making trade mutually beneficial is finding a trading ratio between 1:3 and 2:1. For instance, if Mexico and the United States establish a 1:1 trading ratio (or exchange rate), it would allow the Mexico to acquire food at a lower cost from the United States than making it themselves while simultaneously allowing the United States to acquire clothing from Mexico cheaper than producing itself.

Figure 19.5 shows the effects of a 1:1 trade agreement on the joint production possibilities of each country. This allows each country to specialize in its comparative advantage. This means that the U.S. produces food and Mexico produces clothing.

Notice that specialization and trade benefits both countries. Let's begin with Mexico in panel (a). Mexico specializes in the production of clothing, producing 900M units. It then exports 400M units of clothing to the United States and imports 400M units of food from the United States in return – this is the 1:1 trade ratio we identified previously. Therefore, Mexico ends up at M_2 with 500M units of clothing and 400M units of food. Notice that Mexico's production without trade was 450M units of clothing and 150 units of food. Therefore Mexico is better off by 50M units of clothing and 250M units of food once it specializes and trades. Now let's look at the United States in panel (b) which specializes in the production of food, producing 800M units. It exports 400M units of food to Mexico and imports 400M units of clothing from the Mexico in return. Therefore, the United States ends up at US_2 with 400M units of clothing and 400M units of food. Notice that the United States' production without trade was 300M units of clothing and 200 units of food. Therefore the United States is better off by 100M units of clothing and 200M units of food once it specializes and trades.

Figure 19.5: The Joint Production Possibilities Frontier for Mexico and the United States with Specialization and Trade

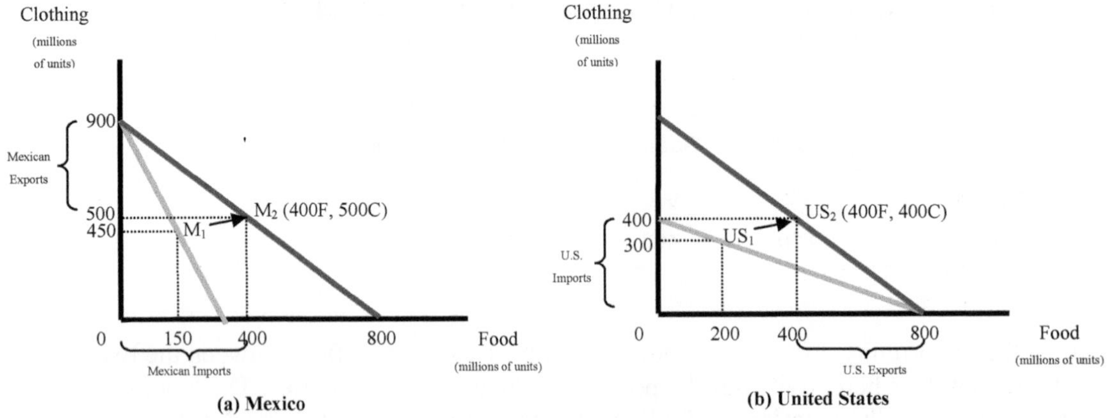

In panel (a) Mexico specializes in the production of clothing, producing 900M units. It then exports 400M units of clothing to the United States and imports 400M units of food from the United States in return. Mexico ends up at M_2 with 500M units of clothing and 400M units of food. Therefore Mexico is better off by 50M units of clothing and 250M units of food once it specializes and trades.

In panel (b) the United States specializes in the production of food, producing 800M units. It exports 400M units of food to Mexico and imports 400M units of clothing from the Mexico in return. The United States ends up at US_2 with 400M units of clothing and 400M units of food. Therefore the United States is better off by 100M units of clothing and 200M units of food once it specializes and trades.

The combined benefits that Mexico and the United States enjoy are even more amazing. When Mexico produced on its own is made 450M units of clothing and 150M units of food. The United States production is 300M units of clothing and 200M units of food when it does not specialize. The combined output without specialization was 750M units of clothing and 350M units of food. The joint output with specialization is 900M units of clothing and 800M units of food. Trade, as we have just described it, truly is a win-win proposition because each country is able to concentrate on the production of goods where it is a low opportunity cost producer and trade for goods which it is a high opportunity cost producer.

Other Advantages of Trade

Although comparative advantage is the biggest reason why many people favor liberal trade policies, there are other reasons as well. Economies of scale, competition, and the need to adopt sound institutions all contribute to making trade such a vital part of economic activity.

Free trade blocks exist when countries enter into a trade agreement which eliminates tariffs, import quotas, and other preferences on most goods and services that are traded between them. If people are also free to move between the countries, this allows individual nations to specialize and serve not only their domestic population but also to export to other nations. With increased export activity, comes economies of scale. This is especially important for smaller nations that do not have enough population to be able to support domestic production of large-scale manufacturing like automobiles, television sets, steel and aluminum. However, once a smaller nation has free access to larger markets, it can effectively specialize in what it does best and generate low per unit costs through exports.

Another largely unseen benefit from trade is increased competition. Added competition from foreign suppliers forces domestic firms to be more innovative and compete on price and quality. Competition also gives consumers more options to choose from. This allows consumers to purchase a broader array of products that better match their needs.

Finally, nations need sound institutional policy to facilitate trade. International trade can be difficult to navigate since laws vary across countries. Learning, abiding by and producing products that meet multiple standards is an added challenge for firms that wish to export. Meeting each of these standards increases the costs of doing business in a foreign country. Firms also need to know that the rule of law will be followed. As a result, nations that do not adequately enforce and defend the rights of private firms find that foreign companies are less willing to enter their markets. This is especially problematic in countries where corruption is rampant. Another complicating factor is price stability, or a lack thereof. Large fluctuations in a nation's currency exchange rate make trading more difficult. Therefore nations that adopt and adhere to sound monetary policies are often more desirable trading partners than countries which have too much inflation.

Reality Check

Trade agreements are not as straightforward as we just described, but our simplification cuts both ways. First let's examine why the benefits of trade might be larger than we've already established. In Figures 19.4 and 19.5 the production possibilities frontier is shown as a straight line. This makes the computation of the ratios simpler and holds the opportunity cost constant but that's not the way specialization works in the real world. Access to new markets can create economies of scale and therefore lower per unit costs as production expands. Increased production allows companies the opportunity to economize on distribution costs, marketing and to utilize assembly lines and other forms of automation.

Consider how a small textile company based in Mexico fares under this arrangement. With international trade, the company can now expand its sales into the United States – a much larger market. This creates additional demand and that translates into added sales. Those sales allow the textile firm to lower per unit costs by buying fabrics in bulk, expanding its distribution network, and volume advertising. All of these things make the textile firm's production process more efficient.

However, this is not always the case. Transportation costs may limit the gains from trade. When transportation costs are steep the potential gains from trade may disappear entirely. This is especially true when the good being produced is relatively heavy and it has a small profit margin. When this happens, large geographic distances mean that local producers maintain a cost advantage over low-cost foreign suppliers and international trade does not work as well as expected. In addition, countries may impose *tariffs* and *quotas* to protect domestic firms from foreign competition. We will consider how these limitations on international trade work in the next section.

Practice What You Know
Gains from trade

Comparative versus Absolute Advantage

Question: Your friend is convinced that comparative advantage does not apply when a nation has an absolute advantage. What could you tell them to convince them otherwise?

Answer: Many people mistakenly believe that comparative advantage only applies when one country is good at one thing, but not another. But that is not true. Comparative advantage, specialization and trade also make sense even when one country has all the resources and the other has none. Let's consider the United States and Bermuda. What could Bermuda possibly offer the United States in trade? The answer is warm weather, sandy beaches and great snorkeling. The United States is a manufacturing, military, technology and education superpower. Bermuda has none of these things. This has to end badly for Bermuda, right? Not so fast. Bermuda has learned to specialize in "tropical vacations" so well that many Northeasterners prefer to go to Bermuda over Florida and Hawaii. This not only benefits vacationers but it also benefits Bermuda, which uses the influx of U.S. dollars to buy many of the things that they could not easily produce on the island by themselves (like cars, televisions, airplanes and the like) from the United States.

Why do we see trade barriers?

Despite what we just learned about the benefits of free trade, significant barriers between potential trading partners often exist. In this section we explore two of the most common types of trade barriers, *tariffs* and *quotas*. Once we understand how these barriers work, we will look more closely at the economic and political justifications that are used to manage international trade.

Tariffs

Tariffs are taxes levied on foreign goods and services. A tariff is paid by the distributor of the imported good when it arrives in a foreign country. Figure 19.6 illustrates the impact of a tariff on foreign shoes. In order to assess how a tariff affects the market price of shoes in the United States we observe the relationship between domestic demand and domestic supply.

A Tariff is a tax levied on foreign goods and services.

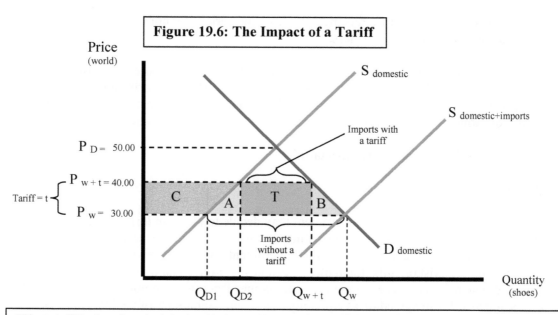

Figure 19.6: The Impact of a Tariff

Without a tariff the domestic market is dominated by imports. However, when a tariffs is imposed the price rises and domestic production expands to Q_{D2}. At the same time, imports fall to $Q_{w+t} - Q_{D2}$. Tariffs also create the deadweight loss, areas A + B; revenue for the government, area T; and increased producer surplus for domestic firms, area C.

We begin by noting that domestic supply and demand would be in equilibrium at $50 per pair of shoes. However, this is not the market price if free trade prevails. Notice that the world price, P_w, of shoes is $30. Since imports are free to enter the domestic market, supply increases and this reduces the domestic price to $30. At $30, imports supply $Q_W - Q_{D1}$. The remaining supply is met by domestic producers who produce Q_{D1}. Since domestic producers are able to exert political pressure and foreign producers cannot, the government may establish a tariff on imports to increase domestic production. The tariff, t, is added to the world price for any firm wishing to import shoes into the United States. This pushes the domestic price up from $30 to $40. Foreign producers must pay the tariff but domestic producers do not. One consequence of this is that the amount imported drops to $(Q_{W+t}) - Q_{D2}$. At the same time the amount supplied by domestic producers rises along the supply curve from Q_{D1} to Q_{D2}. Since domestic suppliers are now able to charge $40 and also sell more they are better off.

We can see this visually, by noting that suppliers gain producer surplus equal to the quadrilateral C. The government also benefits from the tariff revenue, shown as the rectangle T. The tariff is a pure transfer from foreign suppliers to the government. In addition, there are two areas of deadweight loss, A and B, which consumers lose because the price is higher and some people are forced to switch from foreign brands to domestic shoes. A and B are the efficiency loss associated with the tariff – or the unrealized gains from trade.

Consider for a moment just how damaging this is. Foreign producers are the lowest cost producer of shoes but they are limited in how much they can sell. This makes little sense, from an import/export standpoint. If foreign shoe manufacturers cannot sell as many shoes in the United States they will acquire fewer dollars to use in purchasing

U.S. exports. So not only does this mean higher shoes prices for consumers, but it also means fewer sales for U.S. exporters.

The tariff has the same effect as if you somehow moved your country further away from other nations, increasing transportation costs. Both the tariff and transportation costs add to the total cost of selling shoes in the domestic market. With a tariff, you isolate your nation from others around the globe, on purpose.

Now let's consider an alternative to a tariff.

Quotas

Instead of enacting a tariff, the government may decide to place an **import quota**, or a limit on the amount that can be imported into a country. In many respects, quotas work like tariffs with one crucial exception, the government does not receive any tax revenue. Quotas exist on milk, tuna, olives, peanuts, cotton, sugar and many more products. The most famous example of quotas comes from the automobile industry of the 1980s and 90s. Japan agreed to a "voluntary" quota on the number of vehicles it would import into the United States. Why would any group of firms agree to supply less than it could? The answer involves politics and economics. By limiting supply foreign producers avoid having a tariff slapped on their goods. Also since the supply is somewhat smaller than it would otherwise be this allows foreign suppliers to charge higher prices. The net result is that a "voluntary" quota makes financial sense if it helps avoid a tariff. Figure 19.7 shows how a quota placed on shoes would work. Figure 19.7 looks quite similar to Figure 19.6 – this is not an accident. If we set the quota amount on shoes equal to the imports after the tariff in Figure 19.6, the result is exactly the same with one notable exception, the green tariff rectangle in Figure 19.6, has been replaced with a tan rectangle, F.

> **Import quota** - a limit on the quantity that can be imported into a country.

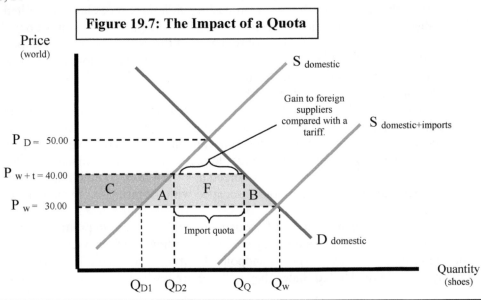

Figure 19.7: The Impact of a Quota

Without a quota the domestic market is dominated by imports. However, when a quota is imposed the price rises and domestic production expands to Q_{D2}. At the same time, imports fall to $Q_Q - Q_{D2}$. Quotas create deadweight loss, areas $A + B$; a gain for foreign suppliers, area F; and increased producer surplus for domestic firms, area C.

Since domestic producers are able to exert political pressure and foreign producers cannot, the government may establish a quota on imports to increase domestic production. The quota is a strict limit on the number of shoes that may be imported into the United States. This pushes the domestic price up from $30 to $40. Foreign producers must abide by the quota. One consequence of this is that the amount imported drops to $Q_Q - Q_{D2}$. The smaller amount of imports causes the supplied by domestic producers to rise along the supply curve from Q_{D1} to Q_{D2}. Since domestic suppliers are now able to charge $40 and also sell more so they are better off. We can see this visually, by noting that suppliers gain producer surplus equal to the quadrilateral C – like we observed in Figure 19.6. As a result, domestic suppliers are indifferent between a tariff and quota of equal magnitudes. So, like before, there are two areas of deadweight loss, A and B, which consumers lose because the price is higher and some people are forced to switch from foreign brands to domestic shoes. A quota, suffers the same efficiency loss as a tariff as seen in the deadweight loss in A and B. Even though domestic suppliers are indifferent between a tariff and a quota system, foreign producers are not. They are able to keep the revenue generated in the tan rectangle, F, under a quota. Under a tariff the equivalent rectangle shown in Figure 19.6 is taxed by the government.

Economics in the Real World:
Inexpensive Shoes Face the Highest Tariffs

Overall U.S. tariffs average less than 2%, but inexpensive shoes face a tariff twenty times that amount. What makes cheap imported shoes so dangerous? A history lesson is in order. Just forty years ago , shoe manufacturers in America employed 250,000 workers. Today the number of shoe workers is less than 15,000 – and none of those workers assemble cheap shoes. Most of the shoe jobs moved to China, and other low-cost labor countries, before 1980 but the shoe tariff, which was enacted to save domestic jobs, remains the same. Not a single sneaker costing less than $3 a pair is made in the United States, so the protection isn't saving any jobs. Shockingly, goods such as cashmere sweaters, snakeskin purses and silk shirts face low or no import tariffs. Other examples range from the 2.5 percent tariff on cars, to duty-free treatment for cell phones, and tariffs of 4 percent and 5 percent for TV sets.

Shoppers who buy their shoes at Wal-Mart and Payless shoe stores face a shoe tariffs that approach 50% for the cheapest shoes, tariffs average about 20% for a pair of name-brand running shoes, and about 9% for designer shoes from Gucci or Prada. This has the unintended consequence of focusing the tax burden on those who are least able to afford it, making the shoe tariff easily one of the most regressive taxes.

One could reasonably argue that the shoe tariff is America's worst tax. First, it failed to protect the U.S. shoe industry – the shoe jobs disappeared a long time ago. Second, the poor pay a disproportionate amount of the tax. Third, families with children pay even more because they have more feet that need shoes.

Economics in the Media
Free Trade

Star Wars I: The Phantom Menace

The Phantom Menace is a wonderful allegory about peace, prosperity, taxation and protectionism. As the movie opens we see the Republic slowly falling apart. At the heart of the galactic economy was planetary trade. Interplanetary trade could support a local economy, but, in many cases, the high levels of economic interaction and the massive scale of exchange required for an advanced society could only be funded by interplanetary exports. The central conflict in the movie is the Trade Federation's attempt to try to enforce its franchise by trying to intimidate a small peaceful planet, Naboo, which believes in free trade and peace. The leader of the Naboo, Queen Amidala, refuses to pursue any path that might start a war. Her country is subjected to an excessive tariff and blockade so she decides to appeal to the central government for help in ending the trade restrictions. However, she discovers that the Republic's Galactic Senate is ineffectual so Queen Amidala returns home and prepares to defend her country.

Meanwhile, two Jedi who work for the Republic are sent to broker a deal between Naboo and the Trade Federation, are stranded on Tatooine, a desert planet located in the Outer Rim. In the Outer Rim, three necessary ingredients: the rule of law, sound money, and honesty are missing for widespread trade to take place. As a consequence, when the Jedi try to purchase some new parts for their ship, they find out that no one accepts the credit-based money of the Republic for the necessary supplies. They are forced to barter, a process that requires that each trader has exactly what the other wants. This results in a complicated negotiation between one of the Jedi and a local parts dealer. The scenes on Tatooine show why institutions, economies of scale, and competition matter so much for trade.

We encourage you to watch The Phantom Menace again with a fresh set of eyes trained on the economics behind the special effects!

Practice What You Know
tariffs and quotas

The Politics of Trade Barriers

Your politically minded friend is convinced that tariffs are a great way to help close the federal government's budget deficit and trim the nation's national debt. They know enough about economics to know that a tariff creates tax revenues for the government and quotas do not.

Question: Is there anything you could tell your friend that might change her mind about the desirability of tariffs?

Answer: Just because the tax is paid by foreign firms does not mean that there are no effects in the United States. Tariffs and quotas each raise the price of domestic goods. Higher prices mean that consumers must dig a little deeper in other parts of their budget in order to be able to continue to buy the good. This results in deadweight loss, or a loss of consumer surplus from trade. Deadweight loss is the invisible reduction in economic activity associated with a tax increase. It is invisible because you can't track it the way we do tariff collections – which are highly visible. But that doesn't make it any less real. When consumers are forced to pay higher prices they have less money to spend on other goods and services. Social welfare declines. The logical fallacy here is that the tariff does not alter how the economy functions. The reality is that tariffs are a tax and taxes always distort economic activity. In economics, as in real life, you can't get something for nothing.

Reasons given for trade barriers

Given all that we have learned about the gains from trade and the inefficiencies associated with tariffs and quotas you might be surprised to learn that trade restrictions are surprisingly common. This is due in large part to the presence of special interests, rational ignorance and the belief that protecting certain industries has desirable short and long-term consequences.

Many people believe that certain industries, such as weapons, energy and transportation, are vital to our nation's defense. The argument is straightforward – without the ability to produce your own missiles, firearms, aircraft, and other strategically significant assets – a nation could find itself relying on its enemies to help fight a war. No country wants that to happen so military production is often a domestic endeavor even when comparative advantage, specialization and gains from trade argue otherwise. Here the need for security trumps the savings that can be gained from exchange.

Another argument for trade restrictions is that industries that are just starting sometimes need a helping hand to get going to fend off established foreign competitors. Once the fledgling industry gains traction and is able to support itself the trade restrictions are removed. It is that last sentence that gives economists pause. Why would an industry that benefits from trade restrictions want to lose them? Wouldn't they desire protection for as long as possible? It is this dilemma that makes protecting new industries so problematic. Establishing trade barriers is politically popular but finding ways to remove them politically difficult. There was a time when helping establish the steel, sugar, cotton, or peanut industries probably made sense. When each of those industries matured, removing the tariffs designed to help them get started, would have made economic sense, but the tariffs have remained, in one form or another, for over hundred years.

A third argument involves economic diversification. When a particular nation becomes too dependent on a single industry it sets itself up for contraction if that industry declines. Recall the example of Bermuda. What happens when tourism takes a dive? In Bermuda is a national emergency. In smaller countries that rely on a single industry, diversification is a big concern because of the instability that might arise. This is particularly true in a country like Kuwait, which relies on petroleum production for most of its wealth. When the oil stops flowing, will Kuwait be diversified enough to withstand the transition? However, in a country as naturally diverse and rich is resources as the United States, the diversification argument carries little weight.

> **Dumping** is the sale of a good by a foreign supplier at a price below what it is sold for in their home country.

Finally, nations sometimes erect trade barriers to protect their industries from dumping. **Dumping** is the sale of a good by a foreign supplier at a price below what it is sold for in their home country. As the name implies, dumping is often an effort on the part of a foreign supplier to place their product elsewhere. However, it could also be the result of foreign subsidies – and this is where the practice is problematic. Suppose that Canada decides it wants to sell more sweaters in the United States. Canada decides to subsidize the sweaters it makes in order to help its manufacturers. As a result, Canadian sweaters are now cheaper than those produced in the United States but the price difference is not associated with the cost of production, but instead a result of the subsidy. What should the United States do? In this case, the World trade Organization allows for special countervailing duties to offset the subsidies. In essence, the United States places a tariff on the imported sweaters to restore a level playing field. Or in other words, anytime a foreign entity decides to charge a lower price in order to penetrate market, whether this is from a firm or nation, the country that is dumped on is likely to respond by imposing a tariff or quota in order to protect its domestic industries from foreign takeover.

Economics for Life

The High Cost of International Travel

How much more will is cost you to fly from New York to London versus Los Angeles?

The flight time is not all that different but hidden fees certainly are. Domestic fares are subject to U.S. arrival and departure taxes. However, travel abroad can trigger additional airport, transportation, embarkation, security and passenger service taxes/surcharges of up to $250 apply depending on destination. For return travel from some countries, fares also do not include airport and/or departure taxes of up to $45, which may be collected by the foreign government when you reach the ticket counter. Many foreign carriers also follow different luggage rules in Europe than domestic airlines follow. Some charge for checked baggage by the pound so packing lightly can save money.

If you have never flown to Europe you will need a passport. An adult passport is valid for ten years and costs over $100.

When you land in Europe your cell phone may not work that way it would in Los Angeles. Without an international calling or texting plan, per minute phone rates can be as much as $4. Texting rates vary by the carrier but can be almost as expensive per text.

In Europe the Value Added Tax (VAT) is a common way to collect taxes on the purchases of good and services. VAT rates vary across the Continent but are typically near 20%. Since the VAT is not part of published hotel rates it pays to know this in advance. In the United States state and local tax sales taxes plus hotel taxes rarely exceed 10%.

Finally, any international traveler must consider how much cash to bring and how much to use credit. Carrying cash requires you to convert dollars into pounds. A transaction fee is imposed. Then, if you have any pounds left over at the end of your trip you pay to have them exchanged back into dollars. Obviously, don't convert more dollars than you reasonably think you need. When you use a credit card you're the company will charge you a convenience fee but this is less than the transaction cost you pay to carry cash.

The lesson here is simple. International travel is more expensive than domestic travel so you have to do more than compare the base fares on airlines – you have to keep in mind that hidden fees are will make your European getaway costlier than you might expect at first glance.

BIG QUESTIONS

1. Is globalization for real?

Since 1970, world exports have grown from 11 percent to about 25%. In the United States, imports and exports have both grown rapidly since World War II. There's no doubt that the world economy is becoming more integrated.

2. Does international trade help the economy?

Gains from trade arise when a nation specializes in production and exchanges its output with a trading partner. For this to work, each nation must produce goods for which they are a low opportunity cost producer and then trade they goods that they have produced in exchange for goods for which they are a high opportunity cost producer.

Economies of scale, competition, and sound institutions all contribute to making trade such a vital part of economic activity.

3. Why do we see trade barriers?

Trade restrictions are surprisingly common. This is due in large part to the presence of special interests, rational ignorance about economics works and the belief that protecting certain industries has desirable short and long-term consequences.

Proponents of trade restrictions often cite the need to protect defense-related industries, fledgling firms, provide for a diversified economy, and fend-off dumping.

Conclusion

International trade is expanding all over the world. The U.S. now imports more and exports more than in prior generations. Economic theory indicates that these changes are generally positive for all nations involved. Trade creates value. This foundational principle applies to trades that take place across borders too. We still see trade barriers around the globe for various reasons, but these barriers are eroding worldwide.

Going forward, in Chapter 20 we take a close look at exchange rates, which influence trade flows, and then at the balance of trade, a nation's balance between imports and exports.

Concepts You Should Know

Import quota	Trade balance	Trade surplus
Tariff	Trade deficit	

Problems:

1. Consider the following table for the neighboring nations of Quahog and Pawnee. Assume that the opportunity cost of produce each good is constant.

Product	Quahog	Pawnee
Meatballs (per hour)	4,000	2,000
Clams (per hour)	8,000	1,000

   a. What is the opportunity cost of producing meatballs in Quahog? What is the opportunity cost of producing clams in Quahog?

   b. What is the opportunity cost of producing meatballs in Pawnee? What is the opportunity cost of producing clams in Pawnee?

   c. Based on your answers in a and b, which nation has a comparative advantage in producing meatballs? Which nation has a comparative advantage in producing clams?

   d. Suppose that both nations decide to specialize in the production of goods in which they have a comparative advantage. They agree to exchange 1 meatball for 1 clam. At this exchange rate what is the maximum number of meatballs and clams that they could agree to trade?

2. What would happen to the standard of living in the United States if all foreign trade was eliminated?

3. How do a nation's endowment of natural resources, labor, and climate shape the nature of its comparative advantage?

4. How trade barriers that are designed to protect American workers accomplish that objective? Do these policies "protect" consumers from low prices?

5. Suppose that the Confederacy had "won" the Civil War and decided never to trade again with the North. How would the standard of living in these two separate countries compare with what we enjoy today?

6. Why might foreign producers voluntarily agree to a quota rather than face an imposed tariff?

7. Tariffs reduce the volume of imports. Do tariffs also reduce the volume of exports? Comment.

8. Why do most economist oppose trade restrictions?

9. Let's think about how imports affect official GDP statistics. Recall that GDP is computed as :

$$GDP = Y = C + I + G + NX$$

Assume U.S. GDP is $10 trillion but the economy is closed (no imports or exports). Now, Bataslava begins selling high quality automobiles (think Aston-Martin) in the U.S. but charging a very low price, say $5.00 each.

A. What happens to U.S. GDP going forward?

B. Is this a positive or negative development for the United States?

C. Give an argument (based upon the discussion at the end of this chapter) for erecting trade barriers on the Bataslavian cars.

10. Germany and Japan produce cars and beer. The table below lists production possibilities per worker in each country (i.e. one worker in Germany produces 8 cars or 10 beers).

	Labor Force	Cars	Beer
Germany	200	8	10
Japan	100	20	14

A. Which nation has an absolute advantage in car production? Which has an absolute advantage in beer production?

Japan has an absolute advantage in both b/c 20>8 and 14>10.

B. Which nation has a comparative advantage in car production? Which has a comparative advantage in beer production?

Japan has a comparative advantage in car production since opportunity cost is less (0.7 < 1.2). Germany hasa comparative advantage in beer production since the opportunity costc is less (0.8 < 10/7)

Now, assume Germany and Japan produce all their own cars and beer (no trade) and allocate half their labor force to production of each.

C. What quantities of cars and beer does Germany produce? What quantities does Japan produce?

Germany: (C,B) = (800,1000; Japan: (C,B) = (1000,700)

Now suppose Germany and Japan produce only the good for which they enjoy a comparative advantage in production. They also agree to trade half their output for half of what the other country produces.

D. What quantities of cars and beer does Germany produce? What quantities does Japan produce?

Germany: (C,B) = (0,2000; Japan: (C,B) = (2000, 0)

E. What quantities of cars and beer does Germany consume? What quantities does Japan consume?

Germany: (C,B) = (1000,1000; Japan: (C,B) = (1000,1000)

F. People often act as if international trade is a zero-sum game. State this books foundational principle that contradicts this idea.

Trade ceates value.

Chapter 20 – International Finance

Economic Misconception: Trade deficits signal problems for an economy.

Since 1975, the U.S. has had a trade deficit with the rest of the world – we import more than we export. Many people believe trade deficits are bad for an economy, and that they are an indicator of significant problems. The news media helps perpetuate these beliefs by often reporting trade deficit data in alarmist tones. After all, the word "deficit" never sounds good. But is this really the case?

The answer is no. Most economists are not bothered by trade deficits. By itself, a trade deficit does not indicate economic weakness. It may even indicate the opposite. A relatively wealthy economy is able to afford to buy goods and services from all over the world. By the time you are finished reading this chapter, you will see Trade Deficits in a new light.

2 Big Questions:

1. Why do exchange rates rise and fall?
2. What causes trade deficits?

Why do exchange rates rise and fall?

Have you ever tried to exchange currency? Perhaps you've seen exchange rates displayed on a sign at a bank or airport. You'll see national flags and a lot of seemingly random numbers. Each of these numbers is an *exchange rate*. An **exchange rate** is the price of foreign currency. This price tells you how much a unit of foreign currency costs you in terms of another currency. For example, the price of a single Mexican Peso in terms of U.S. Dollars is about $0.08, or eight cents. This is the exchange rate between the Peso and the Dollar.

> **Exchange rate** – the price of foreign currency.

A key message from Chapter 19 is that the world economy is becoming ever more integrated – globalization is real and increasing. And as more goods and services flow across borders, exchange rates become more important. In this chapter, one of our big jobs is to explain the reasons why exchange rates rise and fall.

Exchange rates matter to us because they impact the relative prices of goods and services. Any goods that cross borders have to pass through foreign exchange markets on their way to their sale. The price you pay in America for a Samsung television built in South Korea depends on the exchange rate between the U.S. dollar and the Won (the currency of South Korea). Zooming out to the macro view, this means exchange rates affect the prices of all imports and exports, and therefore GDP. The more integrated the world economy, the more closely we watch exchange rates since they affect both what we produce and what we consume.

Our approach to exchange rates is straightforward: *exchange rates are prices*. The exchange rate between the U.S. Dollar and the Won is the Dollar price of a Won, or the number of dollars required to buy a Won. In this way, it's just like the price of other goods we buy. Exchange rates are prices that are determined in world currency markets. Just as there are global markets where people buy and sell commodities like sugar, wheat and roses, there are also world markets where people buy and sell currencies. These markets, often called foreign exchange markets, are where people buy and sell international currencies.

Exchange rates are determined by the demand for and supply of currency in foreign exchange markets. Thus, if we want to explore the factors that make exchange rates rise and fall, we must consider the factors that affect demand for and supply of foreign currency.

Before we look directly at demand and supply, we need to examine some characteristics that are specific to foreign currency markets.

Characteristics of foreign currency markets

Whenever we talk about a specific market, we first must determine what is bought and sold in the market and also determine the price.

In foreign exchange markets, the good in question is foreign currency. Very likely, you've held foreign currency at some point in your life. Maybe you vacationed in a foreign country or studied abroad for a semester. But just traveling abroad doesn't require foreign currency. Your flight could land at the airport in Paris and immediately turn around and fly back to the United States, and if you stayed on board, you would not need to buy any Euros. But assuming that you actually plan to get off the plane and stay in Paris for a few days to see the sights, you'll probably want to purchase some Euros in order to get a hotel room and eat at the restaurants. The key is: you buy foreign currency so you can buy goods or services produced in foreign countries. Don't lose sight of this simple truth – it is at the core of this entire conversation about exchange rate determination.

The demand for foreign currency is a *derived demand*. **Derived demand** is demand that derives from demand for a separate good or service. For example, you buy Euros if you travel to Europe and desire to buy goods and services while you are there. If you go to Belgium, you should buy some of their chocolates. But first, it helps to buy Euros, since the Euro is the currency of Belgium. As such, the demand for Euros in world markets is derived from the demand for goods, services and financial assets produced in Europe. Figure 20.1 illustrates this relationship.

> **Derived demand** – demand for a good or service that derives from the demand for a separate good or service.

Nowadays, it is easier to travel abroad because you can often just use your credit or debit card to make foreign purchases – you don't have to physically buy foreign currency. This works because your bank or card company is willing to buy the foreign currency for you. To you, it feels like you are paying in U.S. Dollars, since you use the same card all over the world and you see deductions from your bank account in Dollars. But your bank takes Dollars from your bank account and then exchanges them for foreign currency so they can pay foreign companies in their currency. Your bank charges you a fee for this service, but it is certainly simpler for you.

Exchange rates – the price of foreign currency

In this section we consider two issues specific to the concept of the exchange rate being a special kind of price. First, we clarify how the prices are quoted; then we consider how appreciation and depreciation affects exchange rates. Table 20.1 shows some actual exchange rates from April, 2012.

Table 20.1:
Exchange Rates between the U.S. Dollar and other Currencies, April, 2012

	Units of foreign currency you can buy with one U.S. Dollar	Number of U.S. Dollars required to buy one unit of foreign currency
Indian Rupee	52.570	0.019
Turkish Lira	1.767	0.566
Chinese Yuan	6.299	0.159
Japanese Yen	80.815	0.012
Euro	0.757	1.321
U.K. Pound	0.618	1.618

Source: Yahoo Finance.

One challenge in studying exchange rate is the fact that they viewed from either side of the exchange. For example, the exchange rate between the U.S. Dollar and the Euro is viewed as either of the following:

1. The number of Euros you can buy with one U.S. Dollar (€ per $).
2. The number of U.S. Dollars required to buy one unit of foreign currency ($ per €).

While these communicate the same information, they are not the same price, and in fact they are reciprocals. Going forward, for consistency, we exclusively use the second option (represented in the last column in Table 20.1). We choose this option because it is the way we quote all other prices. If you walk into Starbucks and look at the prices posted on the wall, they are the number of dollars it takes to buy different coffee drinks. So when we refer to exchange rates, we're always talking about the number of dollars required to buy one unit of foreign currency.

Unfortunately, there is no single convention in exchange rate reporting by most financial news media. In fact, if you decide to look up exchange rates on the internet, any single table probably quotes both variations.

If a currency becomes more valuable in world markets, its price rises, and this is called an *appreciation*. **Currency appreciation** occurs when a currency increases in value relative to other currencies. On the other hand, **currency depreciation** occurs when a currency decreases in value relative to other currencies. If the Euro depreciates, this means it is less valuable in world markets.

> **Currency appreciation** – when a currency becomes more valuable versus other currencies.

> **Currency depreciation** – when a currency becomes less valuable versus other currencies.

Figure 20.2
Exchange Rates and Currency Appreciations and Depreciations

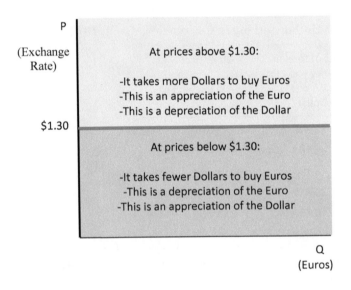

Figure 20.2 illustrate appreciation and depreciation with the exchange rate between the U.S. Dollar and the Euro. The exchange rate starts at $1.30. If the exchange rate rises above $1.30, this means it takes more Dollars to buy a Euro and this is an appreciation of the Euro, but a depreciation of the Dollar. If instead, the price falls below $1.30, this means it takes fewer Dollars for each Euro and this is a depreciation of the Euro but an appreciation of the Dollar.

Economics in the Media
Exchange rates

Eurotrip

In this 2004 movie, four American high school graduates travel to Europe and end up in a city in an impoverished country (Bratislava, which is the capital of Slovakia). They are particularly concerned when they pool their money together and find they have just $1.83. But then it turns out that the U.S. dollar is shockingly valuable in Bratislava. Using this small amount of money, they are able to have an amazing night on the town. At one point, they tipped a busboy just five cents but this was so valuable, the man promptly retired from his job to enjoy his wealth.

The point is that an appreciating and strong U.S. dollar is not bad news to people who are paid in U.S. dollars. The stronger your home currency, the more you can buy around the globe.

Some Historical Perspective

When exchange rates rise, foreign currencies are more expensive relative to the dollar. This means imports are more expensive. But it also means that US exports are less expensive and so foreigners around the globe can afford to buy more goods and services from the United States. These are the reasons why exchange rates are important macroeconomic indicators to watch.

The recent past offers a mixed picture of the world value of the dollar. Figure 20.3 plots exchange rates for the currencies of two different trading partners of the United States. The vertical axis measures the dollar price of one unit of the relevant foreign currency. Panel A shows the exchange rate with the Euro. The Euro exchange rate fluctuated wildly over the five years pictured, rising from $1.30 to almost $1.60 during the recession year of 2008. This rise indicates a sharp decline in the value of the dollar. But then, over the next three years, the exchange rate came back down to the $1.30 range.

On the other hand, the exchange rate with the Japanese Yen climbed steadily from 2007 to 2012. The rise in the price of the Yen means that Japanese goods are now more expensive in the U.S., and US goods are now cheaper in Japan.
We now turn to the factors that cause fluctuations in exchange rates. We begin by examining the demand for foreign currency. After that, we consider supply and then equilibrium.

Figure 20.3
Two foreign exchange rates

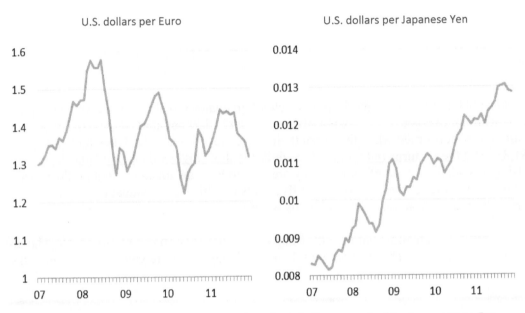

These exchange rates are reported as the number of U.S. Dollars per unit of foreign currency. For example, in looking at the exchange rate with the Euro from 2007 to 20011, the price of a Euro rose from $1.30 to over $1.50, but eventually back down to $1.30
The Japanese Yen became ever more expensive over the period shown above. This makes Japanese goods more expensive to Americans.
When the exchange rates rises, this indicates more dollars required for a unit of currency. Thus, a rise in the exchange rate is a depreciation of the U.S. Dollar (conversely, a decline of the exchange rate is an appreciation of the foreign currency).

Demand for foreign currency

In this section we go through the factors that affect the demand side of the market for foreign currency. We distinguish three primary factors: the price of the currency (the exchange rate), the demand for foreign goods and service, and the demand for foreign financial assets.

Price of foreign currency

When the price of the Euro falls, goods and services produced in Europe (like Belgian chocolates or German cars) are less expensive relative to other goods and services produced in the US. Therefore, if the price of Euros falls, the quantity demanded increases. If instead, price of a Euros rises, quantity demanded falls, since purchasing

European goods is more expensive. The law of demand holds in foreign currency markets.

We now turn to the factors that cause shifts in the demand for foreign currency.

Demand for foreign goods and services

Chances are you've purchased foreign currency. As we emphasized earlier, *you buy foreign currency so you can buy goods or services produced in foreign countries.* If you vacation in Cozumel, Mexico, you want to be sure to have plenty of Pesos in your pocket so you can make purchases easily while you are there.

Perhaps you are thinking, "wait, I buy goods from other countries quite often without purchasing foreign currency." It is true: you can buy imported TVs, cars, fruits, and clothing in your country without ever touching a foreign currency. But those goods were originally purchased with the foreign currency of the nation where they were produced.

For example, a Samsung television may be produced in South Korea, but you buy it a retail store here in the United States. The workers and factory owners in South Korea are all paid in Won (the currency of South Korea). This means that American companies that import products from overseas have to buy foreign currency (or pay the foreign company to do this) so they can pay for the imported goods. In summary, somebody has to buy the foreign currency to pay for the TV, even if it is not you. For this reason, the demand for a nation's currency depends on the demand for their exports.

When the demand for a nation's exports rises, the demand for their currency increases. If the U.S. demand for Volkswagen cars increases, the demand for Euros increases at all prices. Figure 20.4 illustrates changes in demand for Euros. An increase in demand for Volkswagens shifts the demand for Euros from D_1 to D_2. If the U.S. demand for Volkswagens decreases, then there are fewer reasons to buy Euros, and demand declines. This is illustrated as a move for D_1 to D_0 in Figure 20.4.

Figure 20.4
Demand for Foreign Currency

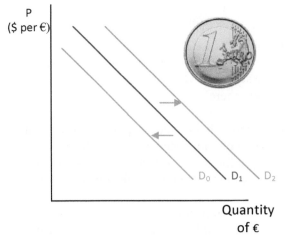

Increases in demand for foreign currency derive from:

- An increase in demand for foreign goods and services.
- An increase in demand for foreign financial assets.

Decreases in demand for foreign currency derive from:

- A decrease in demand for foreign goods and services.
- A decrease in demand for foreign financial assets.

Demand for foreign financial assets

Another reason to buy foreign currency is to buy financial assets in a foreign nation. To buy stocks or bonds in a foreign country, you have to convert to their local currency. Even to establish a foreign bank account, you first buy the currency of that country. If people from other nations want to buy U.S. stocks or bonds, they exchange their currency for U.S. dollars first.

Along these lines, one big factor in foreign exchange markets is interest rates across nations. If interest rates rise in one country (relative to the rest of the world), this increases the demand for their currency since there is a greater demand for the assets with higher returns. In Figure 20.4, this move is indicated as a shift from D_1 to D_2. When interest rates fall, this reduces demand for the nation's currency. In Figure 20.4 this is shown as a move from D_1 to D_0.

A primary reason why foreigners demand U.S. Dollars is to buy U.S. stocks, bonds, and real estate. Relative to the rest of the world, the U.S. is often seen as a stable, low risk economy. This has certainly changed since the financial turmoil during and around the Great Recession. But the long term productivity by U.S. firms still attracts foreign funds. For this reason, there is still a stable demand for U.S. dollars.

Supply of foreign currency

The supply of foreign currency is very straightforward. The government or entity that prints the money controls the supply. Remember currency is money. In Chapter 15, we talked about modern money, which is fiat currency. Fiat currency is printed and supplied by governments. As such, from a market standpoint, it is fixed in quantity at any one time. Governments increase and decrease the supply of currency very often, and when they do, this shifts the supply curve. We illustrate this in Figure 20.5. Initially, the supply of Euros is vertical at S_1. If the European Central Bank (ECB – the governing body of the European currency) increases the supply of Euros relative to the supply of dollars, the supply shifts out to S_2. If instead, the ECB reduces the supply of Euros relative to Dollars, the supply shifts back to S_0.

Figure 20.5
Shifts in the supply of foreign currency

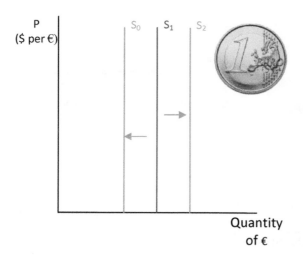

Since currency is generally fiat currency, the supply of foreign currency is determined by the government of the foreign nation.

For example. The European Central Bank (ECB) increases and decreases the quantity of Euros in world markets.

Applications

In this section we consider some real world applications of our model of exchange rates. In reality, exchange rates fluctuate daily, and these prices affect the prices of all imports and exports. These fluctuations are the result of shifts in demand, supply, or both. We start with changes in demand.

Changes in Demand

In most of the world, car-shoppers can choose between Japanese-produced Hondas to German-produced Volkswagens. In microeconomics, you might study the impact on these companies from a shift in consumer preferences away from Hondas and to Volkswagens. But these kinds of demand changes, which occur quite often, also affect the market for foreign currency. For example, if consumer preferences in the U.S. shift away from Hondas and toward Volkswagens, the demand for Japanese Yen declines, and demand for the Euro rises.

Figure 20.6 shows the results of this shift. Initially, market (for Euros) is in equilibrium with S_1 and D_1. The initial equilibrium exchange rate is $1.32. Then, after U.S. consumers demand more Volkswagens, the demand for Euros shifts to D_2. This causes the exchange rate to rise to $1.40.

Figure 20.6
How demand shifts affect the exchange rate

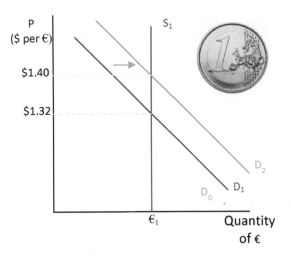

An increase in the demand for foreign currency leads to an increase in the exchange rate (from $1.30 to $1.40). This is a depreciation of the U.S. dollar relative to the Euro.

We get the same result if instead the cause of the shift were an increase in the demand for European financial assets. Thus, if interest rates in Europe rise, this sends a signal to investors around the globe to buy financial assets in Europe. This leads to an increase in demand for Euros and then an increase in the exchange rate. The higher exchange rate implies an appreciation of the Euro, and by comparison, a depreciation of the Dollar. Intuitively, people want more Euros, so their value versus the Dollar rises.

If instead, global demand for goods, services and financial assets moves away from Europe and toward the United States, the demand for Euros would fall (as people move toward dollars). In this case, the exchange rate falls, and the Euro depreciates, but the Dollar appreciates.

These shifts in demand occur naturally in a global economy where consumers across different nations choose among products produced in a wide variety of countries. Even just focusing on cars, we can choose to buy from the United States, Germany, Japan, South Korea, the United Kingdom, Canada, and Italy (think Fiat and Ferrari), just to name a few. But as international demanders change the products they demand, exchange rates are affected.

But there are also "unnatural" changes in exchange rates, caused by intentional actions of government monetary authorities all over the globe. For these, we look at shifts in currency supply.

Table 20.2
Shifts in demand for foreign currency

Condition	Cause	Exchange Rate Change
Increase	Increase in demand for foreign goods and services or financial assets	Exchange rate rises.
Decrease	Decrease in demand for foreign goods and services or financial assets	Exchange rate falls.

Changes in Supply

The supply side of the currency markets is determined solely by government changes to the supply of currency. Figure 20.7 illustrates a scenario in which the European Central Bank (ECB) increases the supply of Euros. This shifts supply from S_1 to S_2, and causes the exchange rate to fall from $1.30 to $1.20. The fall in the exchange rate means the Euro depreciates relative to the Dollar – a direct result of the increase in Euros. The ECB action means there are now more Euros per Dollar and so Euros are worth less in relative terms.

Figure 20.7
How supply shifts affect the exchange rate

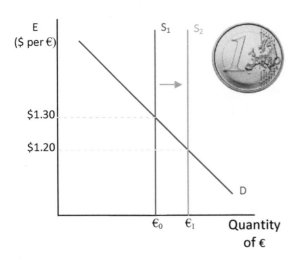

All else equal, an increase in the quantity of Euros shifts the supply of Euros outward.

This change decreases the exchange rate, depreciating the Euro and appreciating the Dollar.

This example pictured in Figure 20.7 is actually quite common in the real world. That is, government monetary authorities often intervene in markets to drive down their exchange rates. **Exchange rate manipulation** occurs when national governments intentionally adjust their money supply to affect their exchange rate.

It may seem odd to you that a government would take action to purposefully depreciate the value of their own currency. After all, don't we typically want the value of our assets to *appreciate*? If I told you that the value of your car depreciated drastically in the last year, do you take that as good news? What if the value of your parent's home depreciates; is that positive? No, these are both bad news.

Nations purposefully depreciate their own currency in order to make their exports more affordable to buyers around the world. If Euros fall in value, each Dollar buys more Euros and then Volkswagens become more affordable. All else equal, this leads to a greater quantity demanded of Volkswagens in the United States.

Therefore currency devaluation, through increasing the quantity of currency can certainly have a short run impact on aggregate demand. But to see how this affects the German economy, we need to consider it in the context of the aggregate supply and aggregate demand model. In Chapter 14, when we listed the factors that shift aggregate demand, we included the value of domestic currency. You may recall that a decrease in the value of domestic currency (depreciation) increases aggregate demand.

Let's now consider this in the context of our discussion in this chapter. If the Euro depreciates, aggregate demand for German goods and services increases. This is illustrated in Figure 20.8. In the short run, this leads to greater real GDP (Y') and lower unemployment. This happens because some prices are inflexible in the short run. But when all prices adjust, then output returns to its earlier level – leaving only inflation as the result of the increased quantity of Euros. In the end, Euros are cheaper, but it takes more Euros to buy German goods (due to inflation), so there are no real effects from the action in the long run.

Figure 20.8
Increase in German Aggregate Demand from Euro depreciation

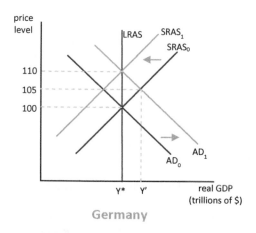

Germany

If the ECB acts to depreciate the Euro, this increases aggregate demand for European goods and services, including those produced in Germany. In the short run, this increases real GDP and decreases unemployment (not pictured here), due to some sticky prices. This is just another dimension of expansionary monetary policy. When a central bank increases their money supply, it reduces the exchange rate and increases AD in the short run. In the long run, when prices adjust fully, there are no real effects.

Pegging exchange rates

Panel A of Figure 20.8 plots the U.S. dollar exchange rate with the Chinese Yuan. Notice the eerily flat period between 2008 and 2010, then the gradual even-paced increases after that. This pattern is not due to natural market forces; it is because the Chinese government has chosen to maintain a pegged exchange rate with the Dollar. **Pegged exchange rates** are exchange rates that are fixed at a certain level through the actions of a government. The alternative to pegged or fixed exchange rates is flexible (or floating) exchange rates. **Flexible exchange rates** are exchange rates determined by market forces (supply and demand). Until now in this chapter, we've only considered flexible exchange rates.

Pegged exchange rates – exchange rates that are fixed at a certain level through the actions of government.

Flexible exchange rates – exchange rates that are determined by supply of and demand for currency.

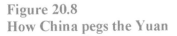

Figure 20.8
How China pegs the Yuan

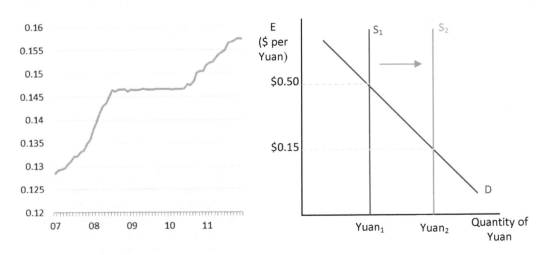

The Yuan is pegged to the dollar. This just means it's value is controlled by the Chinese government. For example, from mid-2008 until mid-2010, the peg was set at $0.147, after this, it was allowed to rise.

The exchange rate is pegged below market values with the goal of keeping Chinese exports inexpensive on world markets.

To keep the exchange rate below the natural market rate, the government has to buy U.S. dollars and other U.S. assets in world markets. They use Yuan to make these purchases so this is essentially increasing the supply of Yuan, shifting the supply curve to the right.

The Chinese Yuan has been consistently pegged at a value below the value that would prevail if the exchange rate were allowed to be flexible. The market-determined rate would be well above $0.16. For instance, the Yuan was pegged at $0.147 for two years (the flat region of the graphic). But you can't just pass a law that pegs the exchange rate – world markets are not subject to Chinese law. Instead, the Chinese government maintains the peg by adjusting the supply of Yuan in world markets.

The way they do this is by increasing the supply of Yuan relative to the supply of dollars. Panel B in the Figure 20.8 illustrates how an increase in supply drives down the price of the Yuan. In practice, the Chinese government buys U.S. dollars and U.S. Treasury securities in world markets. Notice the word "buy" in the last sentence. That's right, they have to buy these, and they buy them with newly minted Yuan. This is what shifts the supply curve outward. This action depreciates the Chinese currency. Essentially, they are conducting open market operations by buying U.S. Treasury securities. Ironically, this is exactly how the U.S. Federal Reserve enacts expansionary monetary policy.

The Chinese government devalues the Yuan so Chinese goods and services are less expensive on world markets. They want their exports to be very affordable because the Chinese government is trying diligently to build their economy through exports. They view this as a long-term strategy that will help their economy develop into an industrial economy.   Keeping the Yuan devalued on world markets incentivizes people around the globe to buy Chinese goods and services.   Since 2010, the Chinese government has been letting the Yuan slowly rise in, but, as the report cited below shows, they are having second thoughts.

Economics in the Real World:
Chinese export growth slows

An October 2011 Bloomberg news report (http://www.bloomberg.com/news/2011-10-13/china-trade-surplus-drops-to-lowest-in-four-months-as-export-growth-slows.html) noted that Chinese exports grew just 17% from a year earlier.   While this growth is substantial, it's relatively small compared to growth rates from earlier years.   The Bloomberg report goes on to say that the Chinese government might plan to stop letting the Yuan appreciate versus the dollar (recall the upward climb in Figure 20.8).

According to the report: "China may move to restrain the yuan, which has gained the most against the dollar among 25 emerging-market currencies in the past four years…"

The idea is that the appreciating Yuan makes it more expensive for Americans to buy Chinese goods.   Assuming that the Chinese government wants Americans to buy more Chinese goods, the government may move to slow the appreciation of their currency.

Now, let's think about how this peg affects the Chinese economy.   On the one hand, it is clear that the Chinese economy has been growing at historically large rates over the past two decades.   This seems to indicate that this devaluation strategy is helping their economy overall, not just the export sector.   Perhaps this is true, but be careful.   Many other changes have taken place in China over the past two decades.   Recall from Chapters 12 and 13, that institutional changes (the introduction of private property rights) have completely changed production incentives in China.   So it is incomplete to pin their success on currency devaluation alone.

In addition, the devaluation of their currency has other effects as well.   In particular, Chinese workers get paid in Yuan.   When the government devalues the currency, this effectively gives the workers a real pay cut.   Part of the reason why Chinese exports are so cheap is that labor costs are very low.   But this is not a positive situation for the actual laborers.

This brings us to the next major topic of this chapter.   In the next section we look closer at the balance of exports and imports.

Practice What You Know!
Exchange rates

The Bahamian Peg

While the Chinese government keeps the Dollar-Yuan exchange rate artificially low to encourage exports, other nations peg their currency to the dollar and to guarantee stability. In fact, as of 2011, there were 66 nations that pegged their currency to the U.S. dollar (http://www.economist.com/node/21525923).

Not all the exchange rates are held artificially low with their dollar peg.

Question: Assume the Bahamas wants to peg their currency to the U.S. at a one-to-one ration (one U.S. dollar = one Bahamian dollar). But the current exchange rate is at ninety cents (ten cents below the official peg), what must the Bahamian central bank do to return to the $1.00 exchange rate?

In this case, illustrated below, the supply and demand intersects at $0.90. Thus, the Bahamian central bank should reduce the supply of Bahamian dollars to increase the exchange rate back up to $1.00.

What causes trade deficits?

We began this chapter with a by considering the misconception that trade deficits are bad by definition. We are now ready to look at this issue more formally. It helps to state clearly the issue at both a macro and micro level.

A trade deficit just means that more goods and services coming in than are going out. On a micro level, individuals can have trade deficits with other individuals or business firms. Think about your favorite place to eat lunch near your campus. Perhaps you go there once a week. The fact is, you have a trade deficit with that restaurant (unless you also happen to work there). You buy more from them than they buy from you. Does this make you worse off or indicate weakness on your part? No. In fact, the wealthier you are, the more you may eat at your favorite restaurant – but then your trade deficit with them increases. If voluntary trade creates a trade deficit for you, it doesn't mean you are worse off. Remember: trade creates value.

Trade deficits are not always the result of greater wealth, but this is a possibility. Our point is to caution you against accepting the conclusion trade deficit indicate economic weakness – they may indicate something very positive. In fact, looking at historical data, the U.S. trade deficit often increases during periods of economic growth. Figure 20.9 shows the U.S. trade balance (exports – imports) with recession periods shaded. Notice that the trade deficit widens during periods of expansion and then shrinks during recessions (the shaded time periods). From this perspective, trade deficits seem to be a byproduct of positive economic time periods.

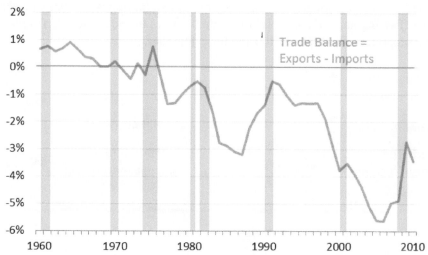

The US trade balance has grown ever more negative since 1975. A negative trade balance indicates a trade deficit. Notice that the deficit grows during economic expansions and shrinks during recessions.

Before we can explore the various causes of trade deficits, we need to learn more about the accounting of international trade and financial flows. For this, we turn to the balance of payments.

Balance of Payments

In this section, we introduce the terminology of international transactions accounts – the accounts used to track transactions that take place across borders. For a while, it may seem like we have left economics to study accounting. But we need to clarify how international transactions are recorded before we can understand the causes of trade deficits and surpluses.

Balance of payments – a record of all payments between one nation and the rest of the world.

A nation's **balance of payments** (BOP) is a record of all payments between that country and the rest of the world. The BOP is where nations track all funds that flow across borders - in both directions. If you buy a car made in Japan, the dollar amount of that transaction is recorded in the balance of payments; if someone from Canada buys shares of stock in a U.S. corporation, that payment is also tracked in the U.S. balance of payments (and Canada's too). These are just two of many possible examples. Any time a payment is made across borders, the payment is tracked in the BOP.

One key to understanding the balance of payments is to focus on the word "balance." Like a balance sheet for an individual or business firm, the balance of payments must actually balance. There are two main pieces to the balance of payments: the current account and the capital account. A change in one of these accounts is always offset by a change in the other so that together, they balance. Figure 20.10 illustrates the two major pieces of a nation's balance of payments. They are drawn on opposite sides of a scale to illustrate the offsetting and balancing relationship between the accounts. Let's examine each of these separately and then we'll bring them together.

Figure 20.10
The balance of payments

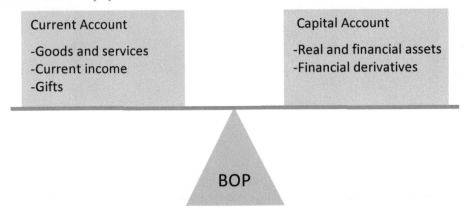

A nation's balance of payments tracks all payments across borders. The current account tracks all payments for goods and services, current income, and unilateral gifts. The capital account tracks payments for real and financial assets and financial derivatives.
While either account can be in deficit or surplus, together, they must balance. That is, a deficit in one account implies a surplus in the other of the same magnitude.

The current account and the capital account

The **current account** tracks payments for goods and services, gifts and current income from investments. Figure 20.10 lists these three categories on the current account side of the balance of payments. Table 20.5 shows actual values for the U.S. in 2010. Of the three categories, goods and service payments are by far the most important, as they comprise about 80% of total current account activity. Thus, in what follows, we focus primarily on goods and services when we discuss the current account.

> **Current account** – the BOP account that tracks all payments for goods and services, current income, and unilateral gifts.

From this perspective, when we evaluate the trade balance, we are really focusing on the current account. In fact, when you read about a "trade deficit," you are likely reading about a *current account deficit*. An **account deficit** exists when more payments are flowing out of an account than into the account. Generally, this means we are

> **Account deficit** - more payments flowing out of the account than in.

importing more goods and service than we are exporting. Table 20.3 shows the U.S. current account deficit in 2010 was $470,242,000,000 or almost $500 billion.

An **account surplus** exists when more payments are flowing in than out of an account. Since goods and services comprise most of the current account, a surplus of the current account would be driven by a trade surplus.

> **Account surplus -** more payments flowing into the account than out.

Table 20.3
2010 U.S. balance of payments, millions of dollars

Current Account		Capital Account	
Goods and Services		Real and Financial Assets	
Exports	$1,834,166	U.S.-owned assets abroad	-$1,024,723
Imports	-2,329,893	Foreign-owned assets in U.S.	1,244,831
Income			
Receipts	662,464	Net financial derivatives	15,143
Payments	-499,491		
Gifts	-137,489	Statistical discrepancy	234,992
Balance	-$470,242		$470,242
	deficit		surplus

The dollar amounts in this table represent changes in the various accounts during 2010. For example, on the current account side, the figures indicate that the U.S. exported about $1.8 billion worth of goods and services but imported about $2.3 billion. This trade deficit accounts for most of the current account deficit.
On the capital account side, U.S. individuals (and government) purchased about $1 billion worth of assets from abroad, but foreigners bought about $1.2 billion in U.S. assets in 2010.
In the short run, statistical discrepancies are common. We know that, in the long run the two accounts sum to zero by definition.

The **capital account** tracks payments for real and financial assets between nations. When residents of one nation buy financial securities like stocks and bonds from another nation, these payments are recorded in the capital account. Even if you trade for the currency of another nation, this transaction is recorded in the capital account. When the Chinese government buys U.S. Treasury securities, this transaction is recorded in the capital account. If an American deposits funds into a Swiss bank account, this transaction is recorded in the capital account.

> **Capital account –** the BOP account that tracks payments for real and financial assets and extensions of international loans.

Purchases of real assets also enter in the capital account. If you bought a vacation home in Cozumel, Mexico, this counts as an outgoing payment in the capital account. When the Abu Dhabi Investment Council purchased the Chrysler Building in New York City, this transaction was recorded in the capital account as an incoming payment.

id it hurt the
.S. when the
overnment of
he United Arab
mirates bought
he Chrysler
uilding in New
ork City?

Since much of the activity in this account is in financial securities, the capital account is sometimes called the financial account (the U.S. Bureau of Economic Analysis records capital account entries in the Financial Account).

We are almost ready to talk about the major causes of trade deficits. Before we do that, we need one more important link between the current and capital accounts. We call this the key identity of the balance of payments.

The key identity of balance of payments

If you buy a German-made automobile, you are trading your dollars for an imported car. That basic exchange is recorded twice in the balance of payments. First, it is recorded as an import in the current account. Second, it is recorded as the purchase of U.S. currency (a U.S. financial asset) in the capital account. These entries of equal magnitude and this is the principle behind the *balance* of payments.

Let's look at the transaction more carefully. Let's assume the following for this example:

- Before you buy your German car, the U.S. trade is completely balanced: imports = exports.
- Before you buy your car, the U.S. capital account is also balanced: U.S. ownership of foreign assets = foreign ownership of U.S. assets.
- The car costs $40,000

When you buy the car, U.S. imports exceed exports by $40,000, leading to a current account deficit of this amount. But you exchanged U.S. dollars (a U.S. financial asset) for the car and so the U.S. capital account now has a surplus of $40,000.

Now we arrive at an important principle with regard to the balance of payments. We'll call it the key identity of the balance of payments:

> *While it is possible for either account to be in deficit or surplus, together, they must balance.*

The German car example we constructed is not unusual and it illustrates the balance of payments identity. We can also write this in equation form:

current account balance = (-1) x capital account balance.

This identity is crucial to understanding the causes of trade deficits. Before moving on, let's consider two other scenarios within our German car example.

First, what happens if the new foreign owners of the $40,000 in U.S. currency decide to use it to buy Dell computers manufactured in the United States? This is $40,000 worth of U.S. exports and so the current account deficit disappears (along with the capital account surplus).

Finally, what happens if instead, the German owners of $40,000 in U.S. currency use the currency to purchase shares of stock in Dell computer company? In this case, the U.S. current account deficit stays at $40,000 and the capital account surplus stays at $40,000, as the Germans have simply shifted to a different U.S. financial asset. These three scenarios are summarized in Table 20.4. In all cases, the current account changes are offset by opposite capital account changes.

Table 20.4:
A balance of payments example

Example: U.S. citizen buys $40,000 German car.

Scenario I: The German company holds onto the $40,000.

        U.S. current account: -$40,000
        U.S. capital account: +$40,000
            Total   -0-

Scenario II: The German company buys $40,000 worth of U.S. produced Dell computers.

        U.S. current account: -$40,000 + $40,000 = -0-
        U.S. capital account: +$40,000 - $40,000 = -0-
                    Total   -0-

Scenario II: The German company buys $40,000 worth Dell Corporation stock.

        U.S. current account: -$40,000
        U.S. capital account: +$40,000
            Total   -0-

Figure 20.11 illustrates the identity with real historic data from the U.S. The orange line is the U.S. current account balance – clearly in deficit since 1975. This is the dollar value of the trade deficit we graphed earlier in Figure 20.9. Along with this, we plot the balance of the capital account which is clearly in surplus. The two lines are very close to mirror images, which they should be, based on what we just presented above.

Figure 20.11:
U.S. current and capital account balances since 1980

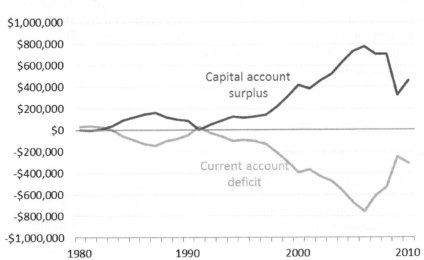

The graph above reflects our balance of payments identity since the current account and the
capital account are essentially mirror images of one another. If we say we have a current
account deficit, we are also saying we have a capital account surplus.

We're now just about ready to consider the cause of U.S. trade deficits. Since a trade
deficit essentially means a current account deficit, and since a current account deficit
means a capital account surplus, then:

1. Increases in the current account deficit increase the trade deficit.
2. Increases in the capital account surplus also increase the trade deficit.

Many people worry about the U.S. trade deficit and its implications for the U.S>
economy. We now turn to the three major causes of trade deficits.

Causes of trade deficits

As we said at the beginning of this section, people are often concerned about trade
deficits. The concern is one of fairness. After all, if our economy is buying goods from
around the globe, why are they not buying ours? This point of view is bolstered with the
method by which GDP is calculated. Recall that GDP is the sum of four components:

$Y = C + I + G + NX$.

The fourth piece is net exports. All else equal, net exports falls when a nation imports
more goods. In this sense, the greater current account deficit implies lower GDP. This
point alone seems sufficient to prove that nations are better off with fewer imports and/or
more exports. We caution you against jumping immediately to this conclusion.

Trade deficits are not always a sign of economic problems. There are several causes of current account deficits. For the U.S., even though we have consistently had a deficit since 1975, the reason varies by time period. We consider three primary causes of current account deficits.

Strong economic growth

One cause of current account deficits is strong domestic growth. A nation that is growing and increasing in wealth relative to the rest of the world is also a nation that can afford to import significant quantities of goods and services from around the globe.

Think of this first in terms of individuals. Imagine that you open a coffee shop and your business does very well. You earn significant profits and your personal wealth grows. This new wealth enables you to purchase many of goods and services you would not be able to afford if you were poorer. With your new wealth, you'll likely develop trade deficits with many stores and restaurants in your town. You might even establish trade deficits with ski resorts, golf courses and car dealerships. Bill Gates has personal trade deficits all over the world simply because he buys large quantities of goods and services.

This also applies to nations. During periods of rapid economic expansion in the United States, our current account deficit has grown. The prime example of this is the late 1990s. Look again at Figure 20.9. In the long (un-shaded) period during the late 1990s, the economy was growing and the current account deficit was growing as well. U.S. was increasing and this enabled us to afford more imports from around the globe. The reverse occurs during economic downturns. When U.S. wealth falls, we are less able to afford imports, and the current account deficit shrinks.

There are really two related but distinct effects causing the trade deficit to grow during economic expansion. The first is in the current account: wealthy domestic consumers can afford to import more goods and services.

But the second is in the capital account: growing economies offer higher investment returns, so funds from around the globe flow in to take advantage of high rates of return. When an economy is growing rapidly, relative to the rest of the world, the firms in that economy are willing to pay more for investment funds (the demand for loanable funds shifts out). This leads to higher interest rates in the growing economy and then international funds flow in to take advantage of these.

To clarify, let's return to the example where your coffee shop business is doing very well. One way to expand your business is to offer shares of stock in your business. And when people buy this stock, hoping to get in on the great new coffee shop business, this is a capital inflow or your business. This works exactly the same way for nations that are growing relatively quickly – funds from around the globe flow in to take advantage of the high returns.

Table 20.5 summarizes these two complimentary effects.

Table 20.5
Why strong growth leads to a balance of payments deficit

Primary account	Explanation	Result
Current Account	The growing economy leads to wealthier consumers who then import more goods and services from around the world.	Net exports fall and this leads to a greater BOP deficit.
Capital Account	The growing economy offers greater returns and this attracts international funds for investment.	This increases the capital account surplus which also reinforces the greater BOP deficit.

In recent years, even China has experienced a current account deficit, largely owing to their rapid economic growth. This result seems almost counter-intuitive, as the rapid Chinese growth has largely been in the area of manufacturing exports. Yet the income surge has also allowed their citizens to import goods and services from all over the globe. In addition, greater returns has brought an influx of global investment funds. These effects were so strong that by late 2010, China was recording current account deficits.

Lower personal saving

Let's return to the example where you own your own coffee shop and your business is doing well. Now you reach the point where you consider expansion. You decide you want to open another location for your coffee shop. If you have been frugal and saved a portion of your income, you can use your savings to expand your business. On the other hand, if you have spent your income, you'll need to rely on the savings of others to pay for your expansion. You'll have to borrow from a bank, or issue some bonds, or perhaps sell shares of stock in your coffee shop business. What this means is that others are buying financial assets in your firm. These are analogous to capital account purchases in the balance of payments.

This same principle holds true for a macroeconomy. If the individuals (and governments) in a nation save significant portions of their income, this savings can be used to fund investment. On the other hand, if savings falls, investment must be funded with outside sources. In the United States, personal savings rates dropped significantly since the early 1990s (recall Figure 22.*). So while the U.S economy was growing throughout the 1990s and into the first decade of this century, the necessary financing was coming from savers around the globe. This increases the capital account surplus. Of course any increase in the capital account surplus implies an increase in the current account deficit.

As we discussed in Chapter 10, the influx of funds from around the globe was instrumental in keeping interest rates low in the U.S. and allowing firms to fund expansion. These funds were critical as U.S. savings rates fell, but they did contribute to the widening current account deficit.

Fiscal policy

Large budget deficits also contribute to current account deficits. This is part of the reason for large U.S. current account deficits in the 1980s and then after 2000. Large government budget deficits devour both domestic and foreign funds. Remember this important principle from Chapter 10: *every dollar borrowed requires a dollar saved.* So when the U.S. government borrows trillions each year, this is similar to a further reduction in personal savings – the government is using funds that could have been used for private investment (in Chapter 17, we called this crowding out).

But not only are domestic savings necessary to fund the budget deficit, international funds also flow in for this purpose. The influx of international funds increases the capital account surplus and thus increases the trade deficit.

Table 20.6 summarizes these different causes of trade deficits. The bottom line is that many factors cause trade deficits, some that don't seem even seem related to goods and services. The past few decades of U.S. experience offer examples of all three. The 1980s were times of large budget deficits and the trade deficit widened. Beginning around 1990, personal savings rates fell and the economy grew rapidly so that the trade deficit widened even as the federal government balanced its budget. Finally, a recent return to historically large budget deficits has added to the pressure for capital inflows, reducing any prospects for elimination of the trade deficit anytime soon.

Table 20.6
Causes of current account deficits

Cause	Explanation
Rapid domestic growth	First, domestic buyers are able to afford imports given the increase in wealth and this widens the current account deficit. Second, foreign funds are attracted to higher rates of return in the growing economy and this increases the capital account surplus.
Declining domestic savings	Falling domestic savings leaves a finance gap for investment. The gap is filled with foreign funds and this increases the capital account surplus.
Government budget deficits	Increases in government borrowing means greater competition for investment funds. All else equal, more foreign funds are needed to lend to government and this widens the capital account surplus.

Practice What You Know!

Current versus capital account entries

Consider the following international transactions and determine whether they would be recorded in the United States' current account or capital account.

A. The purchase of a Canadian government bond by a resident of Pennsylvania.

This is recorded in the capital account, since it is the purchase of a financial asset.

B. The sale of a U.S. Treasury bond to a resident of Ontario, Canada.

This is recorded in the capital account, since it is the sale of a financial asset.

C. The purchase of a condominium in Cancun, Mexico by a U.S. resident.

This is recorded in the capital account, since it is the purchase of a real asset.

D. The purchase of a Samsung television by the Best Buy (a U.S. company).

This is recorded in the current account, since it is the purchase of a good.

E. The purchase of an American Airlines airplane ticket by a resident of Chengdu, China to come to the U.S. for college.

This is recorded in the current account, since it is the purchase of a service.

Conclusion

Exchange rates and trade deficits are important economic indicators but are both often misunderstood. This chapter clarifies that exchange rates are simply market prices and so depend on supply of and demand for foreign currency. But exchange rates can also be manipulated by governments. Depreciating your currency makes your exports cheaper and some nations have followed this strategy explicitly in recent years.

Trade deficits are easy to grasp but their causes are not straightforward. Goods and service flows are inter-related with real and financial asset flows. Given this, changes in personal savings rates and government budget deficits can even impact trade balances.

BIG QUESTIONS

1. Why do exchange rates rise and fall?

An increase in the exchange rate indicates a depreciation of the domestic currency. This occurs when there is an increase in demand for foreign goods, services and assets relative to the demand for domestic goods, services and assets. The exchange rate also increases is there is a decline in the supply of the foreign currency relative to the domestic currency.

A decrease in the exchange rate indicates an appreciation of the domestic currency. This occurs when there is a decrease in demand for foreign goods, services, and assets relative to domestic goods, services, and financial assets. The exchange rate also falls if there is an increase in the supply of foreign currency relative to the supply of domestic currency.

2. What causes trade deficits?

Trade deficits are essentially synonymous with current account deficits. As such, they increase when the current account deficit or the capital account surplus widens. Economic growth increases the current account deficit as wealthier residents demand more imports. It also works through the capital account, as higher rates of return attract foreign funds. A second cause is lower personal savings rates. The third cause is larger government budget deficits.

Concepts You Should Know

Account deficit	Current account	Exchange rate
Account surplus	Currency appreciation	Flexible exchange rates
Balance of payments	Currency depreciation	Pegged exchange rates
Capital account	Derived demand	Trade balance

Questions for Review

1. If interest rates in the India rise relative to interest rates around the world, how does this affect the world value of the Rupee (the currency of India)? Illustrate these effects in the market for Rupees.

*2. Explain why the supply curve for foreign currency is vertical. Let's say you return from a trip to Mexico with 1,000 pesos. If you decide to exchange these pesos for dollars, does this shift the supply of pesos?

The supply curve is vertical since the supply is completely controlled by the government and invariant to changes in price.

This does not shift the supply of Pesos, only the government can do that. Instead, it is a reduction in demand for Pesos.

3. From Chapter 9, we know that the primary cause of inflation is expansion of the money supply. In this chapter, we find an additional side effect of monetary expansion. What is this? Use demand and supply of foreign currency to illustrate your answer.

*4. For each of the following transactions determine whether i.) it will be recorded in the United States' current account or capital account, and ii.) whether the entry will be positive or negative.

   A. A resident of the U.S. buys an airplane ticket to England on Virgin Airways (a British company).

This is a purchase of a service so it enters the current account and it enters negatively since it is an import and thus funds are flowing out of the U.S. current account.

   B. The government of England buys U.S. Treasury securities.

This is a purchase of financial assets in the U.S. so it is entered in the U.S. capital account. The entry is positive since funds are lowing into the capital account.

   C. A U.S. citizen buys shares of stock in a Chinese corporation.

This is a purchase of financial assets abroad so it enters in the U.S. capital account. It enters negatively since funds are flowing out.

5. The U.S. economy currently has a current account deficit. Discuss how each of the following would affect this deficit, assuming no other changes.

   A. U.S. economic growth slows relative to the rest of the world.

   B. U.S. personal savings rates increase.

   C. U.S. federal budget deficits decline.

   D. Foreign rates of return (in financial assets) rise relative to the U.S.

6. Explain why current account balances are generally mirror images of capital account balances.

*7. Sometimes official government reserves are singled out in the balance of payments accounts. For example, when China buys U.S. financial assets (currency and Treasury securities), this is classified as "Official Government Reserves." On which side of the balance of payments should these purchases be reflected – the current account or the capital account? Explain your logic.

These should be reflected with the capital account as they are really just foreign purchases of domestic financial assets. It's not much different from a private foreign party making the same purchase.

8. Explain the numerical effects on both the current and capital accounts from each of these examples.

    A. Best Buy corporation (in the U.S.) buys $1 million worth of TVs from Samsung Corporation (a Korean firm), using U.S. dollars. In addition, Samsung keeps the U.S. dollars.

    B. Best Buy corporation (in the U.S.) buys $1 million worth of TVs from Samsung Corporation (a Korean firm), using U.S. dollars. Samsung then trades their dollars to a third party (in Korea) for won (Korean currency).

    C. Best Buy corporation trades $1 million for Korean Won and then uses the Won to buy TVs from Samsung.

9. Name three factors that might make a capital account surplus grow.

10. Is a trade deficit a sign of economic weakness? Why or why not?